The Corporate Economy:

Growth, Competition and Innovative Potential

HARVARD STUDIES IN TECHNOLOGY AND SOCIETY

The volumes in this series present the results of studies by the Harvard University Program on Technology and Society. The Program was established in 1964, by a grant from the International Business Machines Corporation to undertake an inquiry in depth into the effects of technological change on the economy, on public policies and on the character of the society, as well as into the reciprocal effects of social progress on the nature, dimensions, and directions of scientific and technological developments.

Other Volumes in the Series

Anthony G. Oettinger with Sema Marks, *Run, Computer, Run: The Mythology of Educational Innovation* (Cambridge, Mass., 1969).

Emmanuel G. Mesthene, *Technological Change: Its Impact on Man and Society* (Cambridge, Mass., 1970; paperback ed., New York, 1970).

Anne P. Carter, *Structural Change in the American Economy* (Cambridge, Mass., 1971).

Alan F. Westin (ed.), *Information Technology in a Democracy* (Cambridge, Mass., 1970).

The Corporate Economy

Growth, Competition and Innovative Potential

edited by

ROBIN MARRIS and ADRIAN WOOD

Harvard University Press
Cambridge, Massachusetts
1971

Contents

List of Tables

Prefatory Note

This book is the result of an investigation sponsored by the Harvard University Program on Technology and Society. In general, the investigation is concerned with the problems of the modern Western economic system in responding to the technical and social needs of the time. More particularly it is concerned with the large-scale corporate sector of the economy, on the one hand, and the public economic sector on the other, in relation to the strength or weakness of their respective and interdependent capacities to support the development of a 'good society'. In other words, the investigation is a response to a wide range of contemporary critical analysis implying that the present system fails to counter adverse effects of technology, fails to meet major social needs which are inadequately reflected in the feedback processes of the market economy, is far less competitive than is traditionally claimed, is biased against the development of demand and production in 'public' goods, is dominated by advertising, creates unnecessary wants and excessive product diversity, stimulates bellicosity and commits many other crimes. Our objectives are first to advance understanding of how the system actually works, and second, hopefully, to prescribe for improvement.

Much contemporary criticism focuses attention on the large-scale corporate sector, together with the government sector, with which it is believed to be closely linked in an amorphous 'technostructure', 'power elite' or 'bureaucratic establishment', according to taste in sociological epithet. It can well be argued, however, that many of the evils of special concern, especially those included under the general concept of 'pollution', are as much the result of the uncoordinated demands and activities of small units as of the large: the small firm facing a competitive market unable to afford not to pollute the river on which it is located; the householder who drives his car to work; and so on. The alternative view is that the environment in which the small unit works is so much controlled by the behaviour of large-scale government and business that the individual is left without choice. On this argument only the large units are transcendent, i.e. have power to influence their own and the total environment. Thus although according to some estimates as much as a half of the national product of the United States is still produced by relatively small units, it is believed that the large-scale corporate element sets the tone and pace of economic development in the 'private' sector, and, in association with government, in the economy as a whole. Certainly, the corporate sector is responsible for a large proportion of fixed investment and innovation.

It is well known that traditional economic theory has encountered considerable difficulties in analysing a system of competition and growth among giants. Theories of pure competition and pure monopoly are much more thoroughly established than theories of monopolistic competition, despite a considerable flowering of the latter in the 1930s. Consequently, the present climate of opinion has found the economic profession short of both facts and tools of analysis to perform the function of objective evaluation. This is precisely the situation in which objectivity is likely to be overwhelmed by prejudice.

It has frequently been suggested that the economist's traditional concentration of interest on the normative properties of competitive systems contains a strong political element, conscious or unconcious as the case may be. There is no doubt that the accusation has force. But it is also undeniable that the system of competition among giants who are constantly and deliberately striving to change the structures which economic theory has used as data – 'demand curves', 'production functions' and the market structure itself – is inherently difficult to analyse.

It was therefore decided to divide the project into two phases. In the first, a group of economists, variously qualified for the task, were invited to write an original paper intended to advance theoretical or empirical understanding of an important aspect of the corporate economy, with the hope that, after discussion and revision, the whole would add up to a significant improvement of our general understanding, as well as advancing knowledge on particular points. In the second phase, a more widely drawn group would attempt to draw out broader political, social, and organizational implications. Publication of the present book concludes the work of Phase I. Phase II is now in progress and should lead to a further publication in early 1972.

The work was organized in the following manner. The Harvard

Program on Technology and Society provided the required financial and administrative support. The project arose in fact from an original idea of the Program's Director, Dr Emmanuel Mesthene, to whom all concerned owe a very considerable debt indeed. General professional supervision, recruitment of contributors, direction setting, etc., were largely undertaken by the first-listed editor of the present volume, closely advised, however, by Robert Solow. The first drafts of the papers were circulated to all the contributors who then met in Conference for about three days, discussing not so much the individual papers in detail but the various major issues raised. A record of this Conference was taken by the second-listed editor of the present volume, who had also contributed an empirical paper which forms Appendix C below. In addition, the Conference was also presented with a commentary on the papers by the first editor as well as his own contribution and with the notes by Christopher Archibald mentioned below. Subsequently, the individual papers were revised in varying degree by the individual authors, the second editor wrote the survey which forms Chapter 2 of the present volume (it is based very much on his record of the Conference as well as on his reading of the papers) and the first editor wrote a new introduction (abandoning his previous attempt at a commentary) which concentrated on expounding the theory of the *growth* of the large corporation as it appeared to have emerged from the combined efforts of the contributors. He also wrote the preface which follows this note; it – unlike Chapter 1 (which was revised in the light of comments by Robert Solow) – has not been read before publication by any of the other contributors, and is thus entirely outside their responsibility.

We also feel that we must also acknowledge the debt to John Eatwell, whose distinguished Appendix A (on the empirical relationships between profitability, size and growth of firms) was contributed early in the proceedings but who was not able to attend the Conference; and to Christopher Archibald, who came in at a late stage, read the papers which had been circulated, wrote three original and stimulating notes of commentary (one of which is published below; the others have significantly influenced Chapter 2), and attended and played an important intellectual role at the Conference.

The reader should be reminded that although the project in hand has broad political and social objectives, the present volume is essentially a work of technical economics. Each author has used such mathematical and statistical methods as deemed required for his task, and in some cases, such as in the work of Arrow and Lintner, this has meant maths at quite a high level. In other cases, although the entire argument is in words, it is difficult to comprehend without some knowledge of the general theoretical background. The only overt attempt at pure exposition is found in Chapter 1, which is intended to be at about the level of an intermediate textbook.

From the foregoing description it will be seen that the book lies somewhere between a symposium and a completely integrated collective work. After careful consideration and some experiment it was decided that a general index would not be sufficiently helpful to most readers to justify the work of its construction, and we have instead provided a rather detailed table of contents listing each contributor's section headings. It was also decided, rightly or wrongly, to leave contributors' spelling, and methods of presenting notes and bibliographies, as the individuals originally intended.

Autumn 1970

R. L. M.
A. J. B. W.

Preface for Social Scientists

Robin Marris

Critics of J. K. Galbraith's *New Industrial State* said that the author's attack on professional economists for ignoring the most important phenomena in the modern corporate economy was exaggerated or misconceived. Others, such as myself,[1] conceded a higher truth in Galbraith's strictures but expressed doubts about the logical coherence of his own analysis. At the risk of flattering a friend and colleague, I could describe the present book as a professional response to both Galbraith and his critics. I am happy to agree at the outset that the pure theory of the large corporation has been neglected. Kenneth Arrow, introducing his own contribution below, points out that the business firm, large or small, played only a minor role in early classical economics. In the main stream of classical theory in the hundred years after *The Wealth of Nations*, the scale of individual firms was indeterminate, the main function of the entrepreneur being to equalize profits in different sectors and in so doing commit euthanasia. The actual foundations of modern theories of monopoly, oligopoly and competition were laid outside the main stream by the French mathematician Cournot, who turned away from economics after the disappointing reception of his book in the late 1830s and thus suffered a hundred years of oblivion for being ahead of his time. In the first half of the present century there was another phase in which theories much like those of Cournot were framed in terms of what Arrow calls a 'kind of orthodoxy' based on the crucial assumption that no individual firm could expand beyond a certain size without becoming increasingly inefficient. Total production in an industry or the economy, however, was not subject to organizational constraint because new firms could always form to enter the system as required – in other words the 'supply of entrepreneurship' was assumed perfectly elastic. Arrow's own paper is concerned with the general equilibrium properties of an economic system in which both assumptions are violated.

[1] See for example, *American Economic Review* (Mar 1968).

xvi   PREFACE

Nevertheless, although it is apparent that such systems present
considerable mathematical complexities, it remains extraordinary
that the role of the economic unit which is so central to the liberal
rationalization of the case for modern capitalism – the autonomous
business firm – should have been left in doubt for so long. The
situation would be less surprising, perhaps, if the relevant facts were
in dispute, but the empirical case against a general law of diminishing
returns to scale is now widely accepted except perhaps in the most
die-hard 'Liberal' quarters and is further supported by John Eatwell's survey of data relating size to profitability, in Appendix A
below.

Equally remarkable has been the relative neglect of the dynamic
innovatory role of the modern large corporation in mainstream
micro-economic theory, however widely this role may have been
accepted in other contexts, such as in Schumpeter's general descriptions of capitalism and his trade-cycle theory. Large corporations are
certainly the most prominent, even if not necessarily the most
important feature of Western capitalism, and their economic behaviour, perverse or benign as the case may be, must surely lie at the
heart of any analysis, defence, or criticism of our system. The liberal-
capitalist philosophy is based on the merits of decentralization and
devolution of economic power in order to avoid the real or imagined
dangers of power concentration or inefficiencies of central planning.
Surely, therefore, it is essential to try to understand better the
individual and aggregate behaviour of the institutions to which
decision-making has been devolved. And I would argue that the
proposition holds at least as strongly in a mixed or *dirigiste* economy
as in a more *laissez-faire* situation, because success in a mixed economy
depends on the government's understanding of the likely effects of
interventions.

One can of course still maintain that the role of the corporations is
basically passive and that the economic environment is mainly
determined either by the sovereign consumer or by other institutions,
such as those which plan highways, initiate wars and defence contracts or decide educational policy. At the other extreme are the views
of those who see the corporate sector as part of a unified establishment or power elite, embracing the directors and inside shareholders
of the corporations, the government, right-wing political organizations, international companies exploiting the underdeveloped peoples,
racialists and many other enemies. Most social scientists would

probably accept that the truth is more complex than either view. This book, I hope, is addressed to the majority.

What are the main problems the corporate economy presents to the economic theorist? What are the essential features on which a theory should be founded? Each of the following is, to me, of major significance although not every one is necessarily essential to a basic definition of the system. The actual existence of large firms with constant or increasing returns to scale appears essential. This also implies that there is nothing particular to prevent an individual firm from growing continuously and indefinitely (which is not the same thing as saying that all the firms will always in fact be growing). Large size and continuous growth are closely associated with diversification (see Adrian Wood's Appendix C below) and this power to diversify implies a power to mould the environment by activities which I have called 'development expenditure', Siro Lombardini calls 'commercial activities' and Robert Solow calls 'sales promotion'. These are all activities designed to shift the demand curve for the corporation's products and some also shift the production function. Many (such as advertising) create barriers to entry. The act of diversification, however, may also represent entering a new market, i.e. attacking already existing barriers. The effects on the competitive structure are therefore mixed. (One of the most important general barriers to entering the corporate sector is the large size of the existing members, because from gambling theory we know that in a war of economic survival, *ceteris paribus*, the firm with the largest total cash resources, rather than with the largest cash ratio, has the greatest inherent chance of winning. Consequently existing giants are the most effective rivals to other existing giants, except where small firms have a special advantage.)

Firms which are at present small or medium-sized do not in general tend to display either higher or lower growth rates than firms which are already large (see Eatwell). We cannot therefore find clear evidence of a natural life cycle in which, for example, a firm tends to grow rapidly up to a certain size and then slow down or stop growing altogether. The data also show, however, considerable variation in the growth rates of individual firms from one five-year period to the next and there is no systematic pattern in this variation except to the extent that there is sometimes a small significant positive correlation between the individual rates in successive periods. The regression coefficient of this relationship, in the cases where it is significant, is usually less than one, so that, statistically speaking, the individual members of the population do appear to tend to regress towards the mean.[1] But as a result of the operation of chance, there remains considerable variation in growth rates averaged over periods as long as fifteen years (see Appendix B) because many firms have long runs of good or bad 'luck'. If we observe that a firm has become large and want to know why, perhaps the most we can honestly say is that it has grown persistently for a long period or rapidly for a shorter period. The individual firms can influence their own growth rates by 'commercial activities', but since these activities require real resources the process is not unrestrained. The character and severity of the restraints depend on the pliability of the economy at large – on conditions in what I have termed the 'super-environment'. The chance effects which cause so much variation in the actual outcomes are disturbances in the super-environment or within the firm itself.

One of the first objectives of this book, therefore, has been to develop and consolidate theories for determining the growth rate of the individual firm. All the models in this area contributed by the various authors (mainly John Lintner, Robert Solow and myself) are of a type in which, once the management of the firm has chosen a policy as reflected in quantitative values of appropriate decision variables, the firm itself will continue to grow in size at a constant compound-interest rate, year after year, until either the policy, or the super-environment, changes, or both change. This methodology appears to conflict with the evidence of only weak persistence in actual growth rates cited above. We may, however, plausibly regard these theories as determining the *expected* (in the sense of most likely) long-run growth rate of the firm, knowing that the expectation is surrounded by a high degree of uncertainty. The policy of the firm can thus be said to determine a probability distribution of growth rates which in practice has a rather high variance. (Actual growth rates are fairly symmetrically distributed; John Lintner, below, makes fruitful use of the concept of a growth-rate probability distribution and includes among his implied super-environmental restraints a policy frontier giving maximum expected values of the growth rate for given variance, or minimum variance for given expected values.)

[1] This was my interpretation of the results on p. 119 in Singh and Whittington, op. cit. (App. A below), but for doubts see P. Hart, 'Concentration in the U.K.', in H. Arndt (ed.) *Konzentration in der Wirtschaft*, 2nd edn (Berlin, 1971).

The disturbances to the growth rates represent the slings and arrows of commercial fortune. It is well known that by virtue of the Central Limit Theorem a fixed population of firms subject to continuous and reasonably symmetrically distributed disturbances in the proportionate growth rates display increasing concentration over time. In our actual corporate economy, however, the effect, apparently, is often muted by the existence of a modest birth rate of new entrants into the giants' population.

The outstanding features of the corporate economy can therefore be explained by the laws of chance combined with the basic assumptions of increasing returns and potentially persistent individual growth. Concentration would be heavier still were it not for the small birth rate combined, in the United States perhaps, with some effect from anti-trust activity. To prevent *any* system of autonomous self-feeding organizational units from developing the same characteristics, it would be necessary to tax or otherwise restrain the further growth of already-large firms or to provide special advantages for small new entrants. As thing are, both the objective probability of death or of being confronted with opposition from a new firm born into one's own size group is negatively, rather than positively, correlated with size (Eatwell).

In pursuing the objective of explaining growth rates, we face additional problems which I have not so far discussed. Both the regime of monopolistic or oligopolistic competition and the regime of long-run rivalry in the environment leave individual firms with considerable discretion over their policy choices. Although there may be disadvantages in falling behind (which show up not in the statistics of profitability but in the statistics of survival), they are not over-riding and neither is any firm compelled to determine its shorter-run price and output policies strictly to equalize marginal revenue and marginal cost, or to play the oligopolistic game according to particular bargaining principles. The variation in the behaviour and experience of individual firms (including a great variation in their Stock Exchange performance) is such that it is quite impossible to support a case that only particular narrowly defined policies will survive. At this point, therefore, the theory of the corporate economy seems headed for indeterminacy, and has indeed been so regarded by many observers in the past. Galbraith, in his preface to the second edition of my *Managerial Capitalism*, suggested that theoretical economists were prone to strain unnecessarily after determinacy.

But the desire for determinacy here, at least at the level of pure theory, is not merely a product of the professional style; it also arises from the knowledge that indeterminate theories cannot easily be subjected to qualitative analysis, a failing which may be of great political importance if we desire to prescribe for improvement. A determinate theory is therefore particularly needed by those who wish to evaluate and prescribe as against those whose aim is merely to describe. It may well be the case that we cannot develop a theory which is both determinate and, in the present state of knowledge, fully testable. We may have to accept that, for this and for more inherent reasons (see below), the system's detailed behaviour is in some respects unpredictable. But until we attempt a logical and potentially determinate framework, we cannot even specify the nature and degree of our ignorance: we can say nothing.

Given the existence of considerable managerial discretion, to reduce the range of indeterminacy we must explore the consequences of specific hypotheses concerning managerial motivation and behaviour. More precisely, we must explore the implications of specific criteria for determining price policies, diversification and growth rates. Unfortunately this is not only a question of choosing optimands for maximization. It has been forcefully argued that, given the indeterminacy and uncertainty of the entire situation, maximizing behaviour is impossible or meaningless. Instead, so the Behavioural School have argued (their position is lucidly discussed and investigated by Baumol and Stewart below), firms operate by rules of thumb, which may be subjected to dynamic adjustment processes leading to solutions that are no more than good enough in relation to aspirations or for survival. I have never, myself, really come to grips with the implications of these rather convincing propositions. What do they imply for the working of the price mechanism, the macro-economic structure of the economy, welfare economics, and so on? Instead I have argued that in this particular field we do not yet have an established and well-articulated maximizing theory, and I am sufficiently conventional to believe that until one has thoroughly considered the boundaries of the maximizing problem, one cannot really say much about the possible implications of sub-optimal decisions (including 'optimally sub-optimal' decisions), since one cannot know whether the results of this or that type of satisficing behaviour fall within the attainable set of the problem.

The plausibility of any maximizing hypothesis, however, relating to any collective organization such as a large joint-stock company, must depend on its relation to the nature of the institution itself. This, of course, is where the controversy concerning the effects of separation of ownership from management enters the picture. The hypothesis, for example, that the directors of the company will attempt to maximize the economic welfare of the company's existing equity shareholders arises from the idea that shareholding is a form of collective ownership and that the shareholders are the residuary claimants on its income and assets. Whether, in face of the actual character of the Stock Exchange and of stockholders, or of the frequently changing stock-lists of every large firm, directors and other executives either must or will try to maximize shareholder welfare, is a controversial matter on which I will not dwell at length here; I have said my say in the past. The fact that directors, rather than share-holders' committees, determine executive salaries and other re-muneration, and the general imperfections of the stock Market, have led some to argue that the stockholder welfare maximization hypo-thesis was absurd. Oliver Williamson, in his earlier writing, explored the hypothesis that, subject to a minimum profit constraint, executives would aim to maximize a utility function in which major elements were their own salaries and emoluments and their 'expense' (employ-ment of subordinates, office amenities, sales budgets, etc.); this was an elegant static theory assuming a given environment. In the same period I adopted the hypothesis that enjoyment of salaries and expense was closely associated with the size and growth of the firm, and so built my 'managerial' model on a utility function with the long-run growth rate as the major argument. From the point of view of shareholders, a managerially motivated firm on the original Oliver Williamson model would pay too high salaries and use too much expense; on the Marris model it would grow too fast. Opponents of both types of hypothesis, arguing in support of a more 'classical' approach, point to the influence of stock-option schemes, of institu-tional investors and of take-over raiders as significant countervailing forces on the contemporary scene. It is certainly true that stock-option schemes grew rapidly during the bull-market of the late 1950s and early 1960s (in the previous period, corporate officers in the United States tended to be net sellers of their companies' stocks), and must now be accepted as a powerful force, but in my opinion it is likely that many schemes will be dissolved or fall into disuse in the stock-market conditions which prevail at the time of writing. Be that as it may, whatever position one holds in the debate, two points remain of crucial importance. In the first place, if for any reason one is concerned to predict the optimum growth rate of a firm, one must adopt an appropriate criterion of some kind: only by adopting a behavioural model, in which, presumably, the growth rate of the firm would be a thing that just happened (as a result of the environment and the rules of thumb), can the issue be evaded. In the second place, it is clear that so long as one is interested in joint-stock companies with many shareholders and readily marketable shares, the 'profit-maximizing' elements in the supposed utility function are most conveniently and appropriately framed in terms of stock-market values. The market in shares, after all, is the basic link between 'separated' owners and managers; although relatively unimportant as a source of new capital, it is the market for votes and titles. From a 'classical' viewpoint, 'correct' behaviour by managers in general should be aimed at maximizing at all times the aggregate value of all equity shares (the criterion adopted below by Solow). On a 'managerial' criterion, the share price is the objective indicator of the basic constraints, such as fear of take-over. Consequently, it is inevitable that a good deal of this book (and most especially the contribution of John Lintner) should be concerned with long-run theories of share valuation, an area which has previously been rather neglected. Until challenged by the managerial theories, no classical model, such as Lintner's or Solow's below, had been expressly formulated.

Thus, to the features of constant returns, monopolistic competition, corporate diversification and growth, we must now add the uncertainty concerning high-level motivation and the essential link with the share market. The resulting problems of analysis can be seen in two parts: the problem of finding an appropriate conceptual framework, of defining the relevant economic boxes, as it were; and then the problem of model-building and actual mathematical analysis of an inherently complex and potentially indeterminate structure. Various attempts at theoretical analysis are presented in this book and each author has thus implicitly contributed elements for a common conceptual or descriptive framework. I should like to conclude this Preface with an attempt at a personal synopsis of the framework.

We begin with the corporate economy at a point in time and will discuss later the kind of process by which it reaches an initial state. At this point in time it consists of a number (one or two hundred) of

stockholder corporations whose total capital and managerial resources for the moment are taken as given. As a result of the development of consumer tastes and technology in the past, in which the
corporations themselves have played a major role, they face a
structure of *markets* for individual final and intermediate products
and services. A market is a statement of a demand function for a
product defined in terms of all prices and short-run advertising
expenditures. The product set is discrete and no two products have
cross-elasticities of demand approaching infinity. The *firms* are also
characterized in terms of products; the firms differ essentially by
virtue of managerial specialization in the knowledge of how to administer the production and marketing of particular products. A
firm may be characterized by specialization in more than one product,
but no two firms may be characterized by the same product; there are
constant or increasing returns to scale in the firms and in the production of each product, so no two firms can survive marketing the
same product. The characterization of a firm will include a specification of its production costs for any vector of outputs of its characteristic products (which may include zero outputs of some or all of its
products; in the latter case the firm still 'exists' but is hardly in business). Because of the discreteness of the general product set, however,
it is not easy to define a sense in which one firm is generally more
efficient than another. Firms are groups of managers endowed with
assets, characterized by knowledge and ability. Products are characterized at a moment of time, by their general descriptions and by
their demand functions.

If we consider a period of time during which it is possible for a
firm to vary production of its individual products, subject to the
overall resource constraint, we may analyse the way in which, in
general equilibrium, they will determine prices and/or production of
their characteristic products. We may regard the household sector as
entirely passive (price-taking) in both product markets and the labour
market, or we may adopt some alternative assumption allowing for
the existence of labour unions (see Archibald). We may continue to
hold the characterization of firms by products constant, and go on
to analyse the same problem without any limitation on the total
productive resources of the individual firms. In a regime of monopolistic competition, in which each firm makes these decisions without
reference to possible retaliation, we can investigate the existence
and nature of the possible equilibrium; if all the firms successively

maximize their quasi-rents and the money wage rate is taken as given, it appears that there exists an attainable equilibrium which would yield a distribution of income between profits in general and wages in general with some analogies to Kalecki's original 'degree of monopoly' theory.[1]

If the general behaviour is more oligopolistic, with each firm taking account not only of possible reactions to its own price variations by other firms who are already producing positive outputs of products which happen to be close substitutes for their own, but also of the possibility that high prices and profits may induce another firm to produce a positive output of a fairly close substitute which happens to exist in its own characteristic set but which had previously appeared unprofitable to produce, we have oligopolistic competition with both entry and barriers to entry. This can be seen as a general game which I have attempted to investigate a little further in my main paper below. Under certain circumstances it may be possible to resolve the entire system, including the households, into a n-person game (limited by full employment of aggregate resources) in which the actual outcome and distribution of income will depend on the extent to which the active players (i.e. the firms) play competitively or co-operatively. This whole picture is very different from some of our traditional conceptions. With constant or increasing returns, there will be a wide range of situations in which an increase in the output of some products at the expense of reducing some others would be Pareto-optimal for consumers, but must shift profits

---

[1] These ideas are all derived from Arrow's paper. There is a passage in it of such importance that I quote: 'The notion of free entry . . . [has] no role here . . . the list of monopolies is assumed given. . . . [But] no doubt if there are several firms producing similar products which are close substitutes . . . it may well be that each is making little in the way of profit.' From this it appears that in a loose sense the general level of profits will depend on the discreteness of the chain of substitutes, and thus inversely on the average elasticity of demand which in Kalecki's earliest version of his theory (*Econometrica*, 1938) determined the degree of monopoly by determining the ratio of price to marginal cost when marginal cost equalled marginal revenue. One reaches a similar conclusion in a model of partly differentiated duopoly where two firms producing fairly close substitutes successively adjust price to maximize profits on the assumption that the competing price will remain unchanged; they reach a competitive equilibrium in which the ratio of price to marginal cost again depends specifically on the cross-elasticity. For a more precise statement, see p. 285 below. In his later versions, as published in *Economic Dynamics* (London, 1943), Kalecki's degree of monopoly was the general result of oligopolistic behaviour including entry. Arrow agrees that with oligopolistic behaviour, the role of entry may revive (p. 97 below).

between producers. Only with transferable utility and compensation procedures, it seems, could further Pareto-optimal improvements be made.

In any event, let us suppose that some kind of equilibrium is achieved (Herbert Scarf has suggested to me that the continual restructuring of the firms by merger and take-over observed in the real world may in fact be a response to a non-existing equilibrium). As a result, some firms make some profits and a dynamic process begins. These operating profits are any surplus over operating costs and wear-and-tear depreciation. Unlike in the conditions of equilibrium in pure competition, they can be positive and permanent. They thus present the firms with greatly enlarged strategic horizons, because they can be used in a number of different ways to alter the conditions in which the firm itself is operating.

In order to visualize the resulting situation, it is convenient to imagine that the firms are organized so that the units responsible for strategic decisions are entirely separate from, and superior to, the rest. (Oliver Williamson, below, contrasts this method with the 'unitary' form of organization, where operating and strategic responsibilities are mixed, and suggests that the former is gradually replacing the latter.) The strategic unit may be called 'headquarters' or 'staff' and the rest may be called operating divisions organized on product lines. In relation to economic theory, the operating divisions may be called 'quasi-firms', each responsible for a single product. Each may manage its own advertising and financial services and may be responsible for price and output decisions. In other words, these are the players of the game we have been discussing previously, and indeed, the greater part of previous economic theory in the field could well be described as 'the theory of the quasi-firm'. However, in the large corporation, the divisions depend entirely on headquarters for their supplies of finance capital, for their senior staff appointments and for general supervision and evaluation. Headquarters may instruct them to earn maximum profits in any way, or it may in fact lay down price-policy guidelines. The way the monopolistic or oligopolistic game is played, therefore, may not be entirely independent of the multi-divisional corporate structure which is superimposed, as it were, on the system as a whole (see Wood, p. 64).

Here, however, we are more concerned with other activities of headquarters. Having appropriated the operating surpluses of the divisions, headquarters may indulge in its own form of 'expense', which may include, perhaps, a strong preference for long-term growth (Oliver Williamson, below). Some dividends will be paid. The remaining funds, enhanced by any available external finance, may be used for long-term research or for immediate development of new products to marketability. Other companies or parts of companies may be bought. All this activity expands the firm's product set and leads to the establishment of new quasi-firms. Thus, in the aggregate, the whole game from which we originally began is itself changed – the set of firms, the characteristic products, the demand and production functions. In my view, this has to be seen as a learning process. Managers are learning new fields of specialization; consumers are learning new tastes.

It is a dynamic process, in which individual units may influence their own destinies but subject to restraint and considerable stochastic disturbance. The resulting behaviour is admittedly easier to describe than to predict; easier to value than to evaluate. The initial conditions are the rules or structures of a game whose pay-offs to the active players – the corporations – depend on that structure and the way they choose to play. But the pay-offs, in the form of operating profits, can be used in this other more far-reaching game which involves changing the structure of the original game, thus changing its pay-offs, subsequent developments and so on. Systems which, in responding to their own structure, change it, respond again and change it again, have been called 'self-organizing'.[1] The literature of cybernetics and systems analysis indicates that self-organizing systems prove to be analysable only by previously unfamiliar logical methods, and that although their behaviour is neither random nor indeterminate, there are senses in which it is unpredictable. This does not make a case for abandoning logical analysis of the corporate economy, but it does, in my view, suggest great caution in normative evaluation. This, perhaps, is why the values implied in my own writing on the subject are ambiguous: I have been told by students of the New Left that this work is capitalist apologetics, but I have not noticed great enthusiasm for it among leading capitalist apologists!

Cambridge, England
Summer 1970

    I repeat previous acknowledgements for the debt owed here to the ideas of Professor Gordon Pask of the Department of Cybernetics, Brunel University, Uxbridge, England.

1 An Introduction to Theories of Corporate Growth

Robin Marris

In recent years, economic analysis of advanced capitalist economies has paid increasing attention to the nature and determinants of the forces governing the size and growth of the corporations of which they are composed. Macro-economic models, describing the growth rate of the system as a whole, of course go back more than a quarter of a century (or much further if the contributions of the classical nineteenth-century writers are included), but most of these theories have left open the question of whether we should best see the growth of the system as a direct aggregation of the growth of the parts, or whether the parts mainly respond passively to underlying forces pervading the whole. More generally, 'macro-' and 'micro-' theory in this area have not been very well integrated, and the typical general model of the modern economy often appears almost indifferent to widely differing interpretations of the corporate function.

Yet it is clear that the twin phenomena of large-scale organization and persistent long-run corporate growth lie at the heart of our inquiry. Most of the contributors discuss these problems from one point of view or another, and three of the papers, those of Lintner and Solow and my own, will be found to contain explicit models for determining the long-run growth rate of a corporation from an arbitrary starting-point; while one, that of Solow, can also determine absolute size at all points of time without a starting point. These models display rather similar theoretical structures, which are also found in the work of other economists who have not been able to contribute to the project; indeed, at the time of writing, no substantially different type has been suggested (which is far from saying that no better could be conceived). Because the field was still generally unfamiliar, the author's original paper contained a good deal of basic exposition; at one point it seemed best to remove this to an appendix, but now, at the final editing, it has proved more convenient to present the material as a prologue. Apologies are due to readers for whom this resulting 'introduction' is too elementary. They may of course skip as much as they wish, although a special plea is entered for the Postcript, which contains some new points.

NATURE AND PURPOSES OF GROWTH MODELS OF THE FIRM

In the competitive model of capitalism, firms are neurons of the Invisible Hand. This function, though vital, should be passive: neurons are not supposed to grow large or directly influence behaviour. The fact that firms do grow, do become large, and the way the process occurs is thus one of the keys to explaining the difference between actual capitalism and the competitive ideal. Growth theory also helps explain a number of specific phenomena such as advertising, diversification and profit retention where 'traditional' theory has been less successful or less concerned. Growth theory may also, *en passant*, modify conclusions of traditional static theories of resource allocation and price formation.

I began work on *The Economic Theory of 'Managerial' Capitalism*[1] with the ambition of creating a theory appropriate to the system of functional specialization which we still describe as 'separation of ownership from control'. In reality, it appeared, a large proportion of industrial output occurred in firms controlled by no one, yet 'managed' by executives whose own motives had rarely been explicitly recognized in economic theory. I gave a number of reasons[2] for expecting managements to display a definite preference for growth, or size, as such, subject to competing desires to satisfy stockholders or to maintain their own security of employment. This line of inquiry led naturally to an inquiry into the factors determining the transformation relationships between the competing objectives, in other words into the field of growth models.[3] But by no means all such models

---

[1] See p. 4, n. below.   [2] Op. cit., chap. 2.

[3] We refer to growth models of a firm in a growing economy. If the economy was not growing, the average firm would not be growing unless concentration was increasing (which, of course, it often is). Even in a growing economy, a firm which persistently grew faster than the average would eventually swallow the economy, and, conversely, a growing economy could in principle be supported by an increasing number of firms rather than by increased average size of firms (in effect this latter was the classical assumption). In practice, although the birth rate into the population of new firms is significant, deaths by take-over are also frequent,

stem from the same initial approach. Their main common assumption is that constraints on the size of the firm, if any, are dynamic: otherwise, if we ignore the speed of adjustment, we all assume constant or increasing returns to scale. I then argued (forcefully, needless to say) that the organizational developments which made constant returns possible also devolved considerable power to managers, who could thus impose their own preferences on high-level decisions. No reader is compelled to accept this argument. A team of managers motivated solely and exclusively by a desire to maximize the economic welfare of stockholders can as well find an optimum growth rate according to that criterion as to any other. The rate they choose will not be the same as the rate chosen by a 'managerially' motivated corporation; it will generally be slower, but will by no means necessarily be zero. Other significant decisions of the two types of firm may also differ, but yet others of equal or (according to many) greater significance will be the same or similar.[1] Both types will probably display many of the distinctive qualitative features which have been attributed to the modern corporation in the affluent society.

Thus we can make growth models without any hint of 'managerialism' – we can also make 'managerial' models which are entirely static, and several distinguished writers (including two contributors to this project) have done so.[2] The former models belong to the subject of this Introduction; the latter for the time being do not.

Another feature common to the relevant class of models also deserves preliminary comment. Apart from the corporate growth rate and other variables, they all include as a major dependent variable the stock-market value of the firm's equity shares. Surprisingly, textbook 'theories of the firm' have largely ignored this link between the institution and its vicarious owners. Keynes argued[3] that a typical stock exchange behaved so capriciously that its role in resource allocation was either insignificant, harmful, or in contemporary epithet perhaps, 'irrelevant'. In the light of his own speculative

---

and the general picture varies at different times in history. Individual firms, even the giants, are in general sufficiently small, still, that they can grow at different rates for long periods, as if permanently, without dramatic increases in concentration.

[1] For example, see the last section of Solow's paper, pp. 335–41 below.

[2] See pt i of W. J. Baumol, *Business Behavior, Value and Growth* (New York, 1959) and O. E. Williamson, *The Economics of Discretionary Behavior* (Englewood Cliffs, N.J., 1964).   [3] *General Theory* (1936) p. 156.

successes, his view was influential and is still widely accepted. More recently, however, a modest literature has developed concerned with share prices in stable markets based on long-run values, and econometric studies have been not unsuccessful in explaining prices in terms of dividends, growth, etc.[1] But the subject has remained largely in the hands of specialists and the interest of general economists has been small by comparison with the enormous role of share ownership, transactions and speculation in the popular and more realistic picture of our institutions. For the present inquiry, the stock market must be seen as the essential interface between three equally important facets of the 'Anglo-Saxon' system of economic organization: the distribution of property between persons, the distribution of economic and administrative 'control', and the distribution of the means of production among the corporations themselves. Thus John Lintner, in an original article published in 1964 which led to his present contribution,[2] found that to determine an optimum growth rate for a firm under 'profit-maximizing' (i.e. owners' utility-maximizing) assumptions, he had to develop a theory of price formation in a rational but uncertain stock market because none suitable for his purpose had previously existed. I also found myself inexorably drawn to the conclusion that potential or actual transactions in votes (i.e. in shares) were the ultimate constraint on managerial autonomy and was so led into the same field,[3] although with notably less success. Solow, in his original contribution below, necessarily frames his several decision criteria in terms of effects on the firm's market value. The same conclusion has been reached by other writers.[4]

So, we are concerned with strictly economic theories[5] purporting

[1] For a critique of this work, see *Managerial Capitalism*, chap. 6. For later work see the bibliography in R. A. Brealey, *An Introduction to Risk and Returns from Common Stocks* (M.I.T. Press, 1969). I present some provisional previously unpublished results of my own in Appendix B of the present volume.

[2] *Quarterly Journal of Economics* (1964).

[3] *Managerial Capitalism*, chap. 1; the resulting share-price theory in chap. 6 was a bad one and should be ignored.

[4] See especially John H. Williamson. op. cit.

[5] A basic bibliography would consist of W. J. Baumol, 'A Note on the Expansion of the Firm,' *American Economic Review* (1962); J. Lintner, 'Optimal Dividends and Growth under Uncertainty', *Quarterly Journal of Economics* (1964), now partly replaced by Lintner's contribution to the present volume; R. Marris, 'A Model of the "Managerial" Enterprise', *QJE* (1964), now largely overtaken by my later work; R. Marris, *The Economic Theory of Managerial Capitalism* (London and New York, 1964); J. H. Williamson, 'Growth, Sales and Profits Maximization', *Economica* (Feb 1966); plus, of course, the present volume.

to determine the size and/or growth of the firm over time in association with major strategic variables such as advertising, diversification rates, price policy and especially stock market value. The theories we discuss all assume maximizing behaviour; we ignore (here only; see the contribution of Baumol and Stewart below) the important behaviourist or non-maximizing theories, and we do not deal directly with equally important related organizational and financial studies such as those of Edith Penrose and Athole Mackintosh.[1] Nor do we here discuss 'statistical' approaches to the problem of industrial concentration and corporate size-distribution, although these are highly relevant to other aspects of the project and are further discussed below in the writer's main paper.[2]

BASIC ELEMENTS IN THE MODELS

The theory of the growth of the firm begins with a consideration of the underlying *dynamic constraints*, or better, restraints, which either limit the maximum growth rate or permit faster growth only at the expense of other desiderata such as profits, dividends and stock-market values. The effects of these restraints are usually formulated in a *steady-state* system, in which the firm grows at a constant exponential rate over time with constant values of associated 'state' variables. A *utility function*, expressing the motives of management (shareholder-oriented, growth-oriented, etc., as the case may be) is then introduced to determine the choice between alternative possible steady-state paths and hence the optimum growth rate. In the following pages we discuss these elements in order and put them together in a 'basic model' intended to provide a general description of the whole model-class. We subject the basic model to some qualitative analysis and then return to discuss a subject of central importance to any theory of stock-market behaviour (it is the

[1] Edith Penrose, *The Theory of the Growth of the Firm* (Oxford, 1959); Athole Mackintosh, *The Development of Firms* (Cambridge, 1963). For the present writer's debt to Professor Penrose, see *Managerial Capitalism*, chap. 3, and his review of her book in *Economic Journal* (1961). For a critique of Mackintosh's findings, see also Marris, *EJ* (1965).

[2] For good surveys and analysis of this literature, see Gideon Rosenbluth, 'The Analysis of Business Size Distributions', *Econometrica* (1963) p. 745, and A. Singh and G. Whittington, *Growth, Profitability and Valuation* (Cambridge, 1968); the last-mentioned provides a considerable quantity of new data.

particular concern of John Lintner's paper), namely the effects of *uncertainty* concerning the actual outcomes and growth paths resulting from given policies. Finally, a Postcript responds to Robert Solow's paper and suggests how his propositions may be incorporated in, and analysed, by the basic model.

THE DYNAMIC RESTRAINTS

'Constant returns' mean that, given time, a single-product firm may expand output with a constant capital–output ratio and constant unit production costs assuming a given rate of capital utilization measured, e.g., in plant operating hours per annum. For the corresponding condition in the multi-product firm, we require that expansion of output for any or each product has a similar effect. In the long run, therefore, the size of the firm is unconstrained.

The rate of growth, however, is not. The various 'dynamic' restraints can conveniently be classified under the headings of 'supply' and 'demand'. On the supply side, for a variety of reasons discussed in the literature,[1] we expect that although unit costs under constant returns are independent of the level of output, they may be adversely affected by high rates of change of output. Beyond a certain point at least, the faster one tries to grow, it is believed, the lower becomes one's general efficiency. But even if this did not happen, there is a fundamental restraint arising from the fact that the growth of capacity must be financed, that the supply of finance is limited in time and that, in particular, finance is closely related to profits, and thus to dividend policy and to policy regarding new share issues and borrowing. For the firm growing mainly by internal finance, last year's profits and this year's retention ratio control next year's plough-back: profits and the growth rate therefore determine the dividend and influence the share price. For the firm employing external finance, new issues and borrowing affect both share prices and financial security. All aspects of the profits–growth–finance complex of relationships, therefore, react on important elements in the firm's objectives.

On the 'demand' side it is apparent that a firm cannot grow unless it can sell more goods: if productive capacity is increased without a

---

[1] See Penrose, op. cit., and *Managerial Capitalism*, chap. 3.

corresponding increase in sales, capacity utilization falls, and with this the average rate of return on assets and the ability to grow further. Increased sales as such, however, are not a sufficient condition for long-run, sustained growth. The process cannot be sustained, for example, if increased sales are bought at the expense of repeated reductions in prices and falling profitability. Sustainable growth requires a method for persistently increasing sales with at least constant profitability. It is achieved by the power of the modern corporation to shift its own demand curve and so *create* markets for its services.

The presumption of continuous creation is essential. Typically, the process is associated with diversification, but it may also occur in the single-product firm shifting demand by advertising. Joseph Schumpeter long ago emphasized the innovatory role of the large corporation, but his innovations came in waves and his monopoly capitalists, although vital agents in the transmission of change, did not include the rate of diversification specifically in their lists of decision variables.[1] Chamberlin[2] incorporated the effects of advertising and product variation in a static, continuously differentiable demand function for the firm, and could thus determine an optimum scale of output assuming profit maximization and given prices and marketing expenditures for competing products. The output and product structure of the 'industry' could also be determined given free entry and U-shaped cost curves.

A Chamberlin-type entrepreneur will shift his price–quantity demand curve by means of marketing expenditure until the marginal revenue from an additional dollar of expenditure equals marginal production cost plus one dollar. Clearly, if marginal production costs were constant there would be no solution to this problem (except zero or infinite advertising) unless advertising itself were subject to diminishing marginal effectiveness. But while one might expect diminishing effectiveness in the short period, the longer-run effects seem more likely to be cumulative, so that a constant expenditure per unit of sales could sustain a constant growth rate of sales with

[1] J. Schumpeter, *Capitalism, Socialism and Democracy* (1942). The above discussion was inspired by a stimulating contribution to the Long Island Conference by Professor G. C. Archibald, which is not included in the present papers and was distinct from his present contribution. My conclusions, however, are the opposite of Archibald's, as he argued that innovatory activity by firms was not, in fact, likely to be continuous.

[2] E. H. Chamberlin, *The Theory of Monopolistic Competition* (1933).

constant selling prices. Similarly, a firm expanding by diversification should be able to diversify continuously, at a steady rate over time, without necessarily adversely affecting profitability.[1]

To adapt static concepts of the theory of the firm to the phenomenon of diversification, it is necessary to transform the concept of the 'demand curve for the individual firm' (which was the demand curve for one differentiated product in a particular market, assuming all substitutes' prices given) into a 'demand curve for the corporation' relating to all its products. Since we cannot easily aggregate prices and outputs of a number of products, and since our models are particularly concerned with sustainable profits, it is convenient to transform the dimensions of the curve into a relation between *total capacity*, measured in replacement value of total corporate assets, and total *profits*, defined for the time being as the gross profits net only of depreciation as reported in a firm making no attempt to grow. Let us endow this firm with a fixed catalog of products it knows how to produce and sell, and let us not permit it to attempt to sell any quantity of any product not included in this catalog. It may, however, choose to produce a zero output of any or all of the products. Let us assume that productive capacity is flexible, i.e. that we are working within a 'medium' time period, too short for changes within it to qualify as 'growth' but long enough that a given volume of total capacity can be allocated between the catalogued products more or less at will. If we then postulate the existence of a production function over the whole catalog set (which is likely, of course, to include joint products) plus demand conditions – in the usual static sense of price–sales relationships for each product – plus wage rates and prices of factors other than capital, we can find an output combination, associated with techniques of production, utilization rates and a resource allocation, which will maximize profits as defined above for any given total volume of assets. We can do the same thing for alternative total asset volumes and thus, if we make a diagram with profits on the vertical axis and assets on the horizontal, we can define a frontier of maximum profits for indicated assets or minimum assets for indicated profits. This frontier is 'the demand curve of the corporation'.

An example of the generation of the profit–asset frontier may be seen by supposing that each product is sold under conditions of monopolistic competition; each has a determinate demand curve of

[1] See Solow in the present volume, and *Managerial Capitalism*, chap. 4.

less than infinite elasticity assuming that all other relevant prices are constant. Assume also a simple production function with fixed coefficients for all products over all outputs with no joint products. Then, to find points of maximum profits for given assets, we adjust outputs and asset allocation (subject to the overall asset constraint) until the excess of marginal revenue (multiplied by the relevant capital coefficient) over marginal cost (multiplied by the relevant coefficient of unit production costs to unit capital costs) is the same for all products. If we want to change the assumptions to perfect competition, we substitute price for marginal revenue.

If the markets are oligopolistic, the solution takes a different form but is none the less potentially determinate. In section III of my main paper below, I suggest a solution derived from the theory of games in which a group of oligopolists facing a given set of markets, each firm having given total assets, can find a 'co-operative' division of the markets and associated profits such that no firm can be made better off in terms of profits without another being made worse off, and which also reflects their relative bargaining strengths as represented by their total assets, comparative production advantages and so on. A firm with given assets, therefore, can expect to obtain no more than a maximum amount of total profit, after taking account of his rivals' powers to punish him by price retaliation if he does not accept the 'fair' division. With a larger volume of total assets, however, his own powers of threat are greater and he also has more to lose, so he may, up to a point, expect to obtain from this 'game' larger market shares generally. Beyond that point both the interests of other firms and the limited overall demand from consumers will begin to squeeze him, and further additions to the assumed level of total assets will yield diminishing returns in associated oligopoly profits.

If we assume there is a minimum size below which there are strong increasing returns to scale, and that a positive quantity of assets is required to produce any output at all, this 'demand curve of the corporation' will be a curve rising probably from a point below the origin (i.e. with assets near to zero, one would make negative profits from inability to produce a positive output),[1] with increasing slope at first, then gradually flattening to the horizontal when a size is reached beyond which it is impossible for this firm at that time to

[1] The significance of some of these assumptions (which I would have thought reasonable) becomes further apparent in the Postcript, pp. 26–36 below.

carve out any further additional profits from the economy and the competitors. The average return on capital employed at any point on the curve is a ray from the origin which on the assumptions stated will be at first negative but rising, reaching a positive maximum at a tangent on the 'shoulder' of the total profit curve. Thus the average rate of return can be represented as a function of size, as also can the marginal return, which is the slope of the demand curve. The traditional non-growing 'profit-maximizing' monopolist would move outward.

The 'creative' corporation, however, has the capacity to *shift* the demand curve, either by means of advertising or by research and development expenditure designed to expand its potential catalog. It has therefore two relevant choices, the choice of location *on* the curve, and the choice of intensity of effort to *move* the curve. To keep these choices distinct, we conceive that the first movement occurs 'quickly' (approximately instantaneously), while the second is long, slow and continuous, i.e. represents the growth process. Solow's paper is concerned with both choices, and we discuss some of the resulting implications in our Postscript. But in the meantime we are concerned with only one choice, the rate of growth. We assume that the corporation has already arrived at an arbitrary point in its demand curve, that it cannot move along the curve and that, subject to this constraint, we want a theory to determine the optimum subsequent steady-state growth rate. That is to say, given our starting-point on the curve, we want to find the optimum rate of progress along the ray through the origin which passed through the starting-point, so that profits and assets may grow through time at a common, constant, exponential rate.

The progressive shifting of the demand curve, however, incurs a definable and repeating cost in search, research, development and marketing expenditures. We generally assume that a constant value of these expenditures, *relative* to a measure of the current scale of output (a convenient normalizing variable is book-value of assets, a commonly used alternative is sales[1]) will be just sufficient to produce a constant growth rate; the higher, however, the constant normalized value of growth-creating expenditure, the higher the associated constant growth rate – an effect which is likely to be subject to diminishing effectiveness or 'dynamic diminishing returns'.

Demand-shifting expenditure – creating 'goodwill' – is not usually

[1] For an example, see Solow in the present volume.

accounted as tangible investment and in practice represents a reduction of reported profits. But the foregoing assumptions imply that the reported rate of return on assets is also constant with a constant growth rate, although lower, of course, than the rate which would be reported if no growth-creating expenditure were being incurred; the latter rate, for convenience, may therefore be called the 'operating profit rate'.[1] If development expenditure is normalized by assets, the reported profit rate is precisely defined as the operating profit rate less normalized development expenditure. Then, because higher growth rates require higher normalized development expenditure, we can say that the steady reported profit rate is a function of steady growth rate. For the present purposes we may assume that this function, which may be called the 'growth–profitability function', has negative first and probably negative second derivatives over the whole of its field (which is all growth rates from zero to infinity).[2]

GROWTH IN 'STEADY STATE'

Once it is accepted that demand may be continuously created, it is difficult to postulate any finite planning horizon. Firms are not infrequently liquidated or taken over, but the probability of liquidation among large firms does not appear to vary in a predictable way with the passage of time; age may lead to senility and inefficiency in some cases, but long establishment also creates security. The biological phenomenon of ageing is not inevitable, because the firm, conceived as a financial and administrative entity, has the capacity freely to renew its biological resources, i.e. to hire young humans to replace old humans. On the stock market, it may well be the case that investors attach an increasing subjective probability to liquidation in the more distant future, but as they must also discount the future on account of time preference, provided the rate of increase of subjective probability of liquidation is modest relative to the rate of time discount, the implications may be similar to those of a theory in which investors are assumed to believe with certainty that the firm

[1] For a further definition, see p. 282 below.
[2] In *Managerial Capitalism*, chap. 6, I argued that the first derivative would be positive for low growth-rates, implying, in effect, a positive relation between growth rate and operating profit rate. I still find my own arguments convincing, but the assumption is redundant to the present analysis.

will last for ever. We are thus again led towards a 'steady-state' type of analysis, and we require of our theory that the stock market can value shares as if they were perpetual bonds with a growing dividend.

'Steady state' is essentially a method of convenience. We do not believe that firms actually grow at steady rates for long periods, although it does appear from statistics that their longer-period behaviour is steadier than their shorter-period behaviour; and the longer the period that is taken, the more this seems to be so (see Appendix B below).

The actual path of development of a firm must obviously be affected by changing external conditions, changing quality of management, and factors other than these operating with chance effect. A steady-state model requires us to assume that if 'conditions' in some sense were 'constant', a steady growth path would be possible: clearly there are theoretical situations in which, even with 'conditions' constant over time, steady growth would be impossible, or be possible only in special circumstances; perhaps there may be only one value of the growth rate which could be steady.[1] The conceptual implications of the supposed 'steady state' therefore require further elucidation: we are accustomed to the concept of *ceteris paribus* in the exogenous conditions of static theory, but the extension of 'constancy' over long periods of time, during which the firm is supposed actively to attempt to *change* its own static environment – shift its demand curve – presents obvious difficulties. They are similar to, but perhaps sharper than, the difficulties involved at the corresponding point in macro-theory.

The concept of a steady-state environment is closely related to the

---

[1] For example, in the case of the firm creating demand growth by advertising, we may suppose that the position of the price–quantity demand curve depends on the accumulated stock of past advertising expenditures (subject probably to some depreciation or decay). If the relationship between quantity demanded, for given price, and the accumulated stock is unity, any constant normalized level of advertising produces a constant growth rate of the stock and an equal growth rate of demand, so quantity demanded, advertising and profits net of advertising grow together, and the common growth rate can be associated with a common profit rate. But if the elasticity is not unity, a changing normalized advertising level is required to keep demand growing at a constant rate, which would mean a non-constant profit rate.

The existence of an other-than-unity long-run advertising elasticity implies some kind of limitation in the capacity of the environment to absorb the particular product. Such a limitation is clearly more likely, however, than the corresponding limitation in the case of growth by diversification. This is probably the reason why continuous growth by diversification is common, while continuous growth of one corporation with only one product is relatively rare.

concept of a steady-state or long-run *policy* adopted by the firm. A policy is a choice of a set of values for a number of measurable instrumental variables, such as, for example, normalized research and development or normalized advertising expenditure, rate of investment in tangible plant, retention ratio and so on,[1] together with various less quantifiable decisions such as intensity of search-effort, price and marketing policy (types of super-strategies chosen for the oligopoly game), and so on. Some elements in these policy choices affect the firm's immediate environment, e.g. shift its price–quantity demand curve, and more generally they affect the rate at which the immediate environment is changing in the long run. Such effects, however, cannot be supposed to lack any dynamic restraints. We therefore conceive of a *super-environment*, a loose collection of general circumstances governing limits on the firm's environment-changing capacity.

The super-environment for the whole economy embodies the system's general responsiveness to growth and development effort. It may be thought of as like a large volume of jelly with constant physical properties: like jelly, it is malleable and given unlimited time can virtually be manipulated into almost any shape or spread; in the short run, however, its malleability is restrained by friction and inertia. At the macro-economic level, the total manipulative effect is the result of the total development effort of the corporations, plus that of the non-corporate sector; clearly, there will be some degree of cancelling.

We then go on to define the concepts of 'policy' and of 'super-environment' circularly, by saying that if the super-environment is constant, a constant policy will produce for the firm a steady state in which the main relevant quantifiable variables either grow at a common constant rate or, being variables defined as ratios between other variables, themselves remain constant. The steady state will be sustained until either the super-environment changes or the policy changes, or both. Analysis takes the form of comparative dynamics, that is, the comparing of alternative steady-state values. A steady-state growth model is therefore a closed system of relations between steady-state variables.

The main *steady-growth-rate* variables typically identified are

[1] A policy specification may also include a degree of uncertainty, e.g. measured by the variance of an appropriate probability distribution, associated with one or more of the variables; see Lintner's contribution, pp. 187 et seq. below.

sales, development expenditure (and/or advertising), dividends, assets debt and stock-market value. Typically steady ratios are profits/assets, sales/assets, dividends/profits (or typically, r, the retention ratio), debt/assets, market value/ assets (the so-called valuation ratio) and development expenditure/assets (or /sales).

Fig. 1.1 illustrates a steady-state path of a joint stock corporation growing at 5 per cent per annum, with an average reported profit

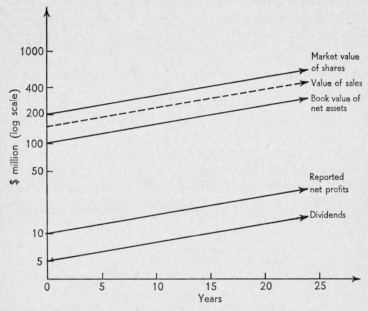

FIG. 1.1   Example of steady-state growth path of a large corporation

rate of 10 per cent, a retention ratio of 50 per cent and a valuation ratio of 2·0. The market value is growing at the common rate because the only source of capital appreciation (with a constant super-environment) is growth of dividends, which is also at 5 per cent, so the market value is growing at the same rate as assets, providing a constant valuation ratio. We could compare this path with another in which perhaps the growth rate was higher, the profit rate lower, the retention ratio higher and the valuation ratio lower. A *model* would be a system of equations for predicting the relations between these differences. For example, we have already discussed a relation between steady-state growth rate and profit rate, due to the cost of research and development. There is also a relationship on the 'supply' side between growth rate, profit rate and retention ratio, due to the need for investment finance to support the indicated growth of assets.

THE UTILITY FUNCTION

Growth models of the firm have been associated with, but are by no means tied to, the idea that strategic decisions are based on criteria derived from a managerial utility function which is not necessarily indentical with the collective utility function of the stock market. Before these models began to appear, however, there had not in fact existed any well-developed or widely used models for determining the optimum growth rate of a transcendent corporation on 'classical' or other criteria. One purpose of the models is to permit qualitative comparison of alternative criteria, as is done for example, in Solow's paper in the present volume and in my own and J. H. Williamson's work referred to above (see p. 4 n.).

For a variety of reasons discussed in the literature,[1] it is commonly believed that, while the welfare of stock-market investors is uniquely associated with discounted future dividends and capital gain, that of 'managers' may be associated with a variety of satisfactions, such as salary, bonus, power, prestige and role, which are in turn associated with measures of size (such as assets, sales or total profits) and/or with rate of change of size. O. E. Williamson associated managerial satisfaction directly with hierarchical expense (money, in effect, diverted from basic profits and spent on unprofitable expansion of subordinate staff, marketing expenditure, perquisites of office, etc.); in a static model, expense can vary relative to other measures of size, and Williamson's theory will therefore produce moderately different results from static theories based, e.g., on maximization of sales or assets.[2] In any model in which managerial utility is maximized over time, however, because the capacity to afford expense is necessarily dependent on capacity to earn profits in general, the difference

---

[1] For a survey, see *Managerial Capitalism*, chap. 2.

[2] See Baumol, *Business Behavior, Value and Growth*, for an example of the former, and J. K. Galbraith, *American Capitalism* (1952) for an example of the latter.

CE B 2

between O. E. Williamson's approach and the others will be less marked.[1]

If the analysis assumes that the 'initial' size of a firm is historically determined, and that steady-state growth begins from this point, and that no attempt would ever be made to move on to a higher or lower path, it is clear that we can be indifferent to the question of whether management satisfactions are derived directly from size as such or from the rate of change:[2] to maximize the growth rate subject to the constraints is also to maximize size at all points in time. Up to the appearance of Solow's paper, all the writers in the field had effectively adopted this approach, and it is again followed here, with the addition of a short postcript to indicate the elementary theoretical implications of Solow's contribution.

The general utility function will therefore contain two arguments, the market price of the equity shares and the steady-state growth rate of assets, sales, etc. In the 'classical' form, growth rate is removed, and only the stock-market value remains: the purpose of the growth model is simply to find the optimum growth rate for maximizing stock-market value. In the general 'managerial' form, there is a continuous trade-off between growth rate and market value; and in the convenient lexicographic managerial form, as used below, the first priority is to obtain a minimum valuation ratio, and the second priority is growth. Managers are assumed to attach some satisfaction to stock-market value, from traditional capitalist loyalties, from prestige associated with stock-market performance and/or from an association between stock-market value and the protection of managerial autonomy and job security. A low valuation ratio is seen as a threat to security by increasing the probability of involuntary take-over.

GROWTH BY INTERNAL FINANCE

Since stock-market value is a common element in all the utility functions, almost the first task of any growth model is to establish a

---

[1] See also Williamson's contribution to the present volume.

[2] In *Managerial Capitalism*, chap. 2, I argued that more prestige attached to the record of a manager who had made a medium-sized firm grow rapidly than to a man who headed a larger firm which grew more slowly. I still believe this, but the hypothesis is disposable.

relationship between the characteristics of the policy selected by management and the value which the stock market will place on the policy. At the highest level of abstraction, we have to assume that in pricing shares, the market correctly understand the management's policy and appreciates all its financial implications, *including* implications regarding present and future needs of finance. For example, if a firm is pursuing a policy of growing at a rate g, and can sustain this rate with a reported profit rate (net of development expenditure), p, and is known to favour a policy of financing all growth internally, then the required steady-state retention ratio, r, has to be g/p.[1] Given initial assets, the steady profit-rate and retention ratio, we have thus determined the whole path of dividends per share. This should enable a rational and well-informed market without destabilizing speculation to determine the share price. In this situation a choice of 'policy' is fully expressed either in terms of the retention ratio or in terms of the growth rate, and then uniquely determines the path of the dividend and share price, in other words provides values for both arguments in the utility function. A given utility function thus uniquely determines an optimum growth rate or retention ratio. This is the simplest statement of the basic structure behind all the growth models.[2] To express it in a system of equations, however, we need a more explicit statement of the stock-market valuation procedure.

A BASIC MODEL

For the time being (but see further discussions below), let us assume no more than that there is some positive number greater than 1, Y, which is a function $Y(g)$ of g – with Y' positive for all g – such that if the current dividend per share, d_0, is expected with certainty to

[1] $g = dK/K . dt = rP/K = rp$.

[2] Lintner defines a retention ratio which is the proportion of gross revenue not available for dividends; 'retentions' therefore include production costs, capital depreciation, tangible net investment required to support growth and development expenditure. The first two of these are determined, for any given output, from a production function, the third from the growth rate plus a choice of optimum technique with the given production function, and the last from the growth rate according to the same kind of considerations discussed above. These assumptions are sufficient to determine a unique retention ratio, and hence dividend path, for any growth rate and vice versa. Lintner presents this model with the retention ratio as the policy-defining decision variable.

grow at g, the value of one share on the open market is $d_0 . Y(g)$. $Y(g)$ is therefore 'the number of years' purchase' applied to a dividend growing at g, and is, of course, the reciprocal of the dividend yield. In other words we are saying no more than that the dividend-yield basis on which any share is valued is some declining function of the expected growth rate.[1] (In a special case, if the market for some reason ignores the growth element contained in any policy, and believes that the current dividend will continue for ever, $Y(g)$ is $Y' = 0$ for all g.) $Y(g)$ is called the *present-value function*. We can then set out our basic equations as follows:

$$p = p(g) \qquad \text{('growth-profitability function')} \qquad (1)$$

$$V = N . d_0 . Y(g) = p . K_0 (1 - r) . Y(g) \qquad (2)$$

$$r = g/p \qquad (3)$$

$$v = V/K = (p - rp) . Y(g) = (p[g] - g) . Y(g). \qquad (4)$$

Equation (1) states the 'demand' relation between growth and profitability (sometimes known as the *growth-profitability function*). Equation (2) states that the total stock-market value, V, is the value per share ($d_0 . Y[g]$), times the number of shares, N; then $d_0 N$, the total dividend, has to be the total profits ($p . K$, where K signifies the book-value of tangible assets) times the pay-out ratio ($1 - r$). Equation (3) repeats the finance–supply relationship between growth rate, retention ratio and profitability already described above (p. 17) and equation (4) combines the previous three equations.

It will be seen from equations (3) and (4) that if $p(g)$ and g converge, the retention ratio approaches 100 per cent and valuation ratio approaches zero. Since the valuation ratio cannot be negative, the value of g at which this convergence occurs represents an upper limit on the growth rate of the firm whatever utility function is applied: in no circumstances can the firm grow at a faster rate than its own reported profit rate. This is saying no more, at present, than that in a firm growing with internal financing only, assets can grow no faster than the rate at which all profits are reinvested; the retention ratio cannot exceed 100 per cent.

The expression ($p[g] - g$) is itself a declining function of g which we may express in a general dividend function, $D(g)$, (with $D'(g) = p'(g) - 1$

[1] See Appendix B, below for some statistical measurements.

for all g, remembering that $p'(g)$ is negative for all relevant g), and so the most general statement of the basic model becomes:

$$v = D(g) . Y(g) = v(g) \qquad \text{('growth-valuation function')} \qquad (5)$$

$$U = U(g, v) \qquad (6)$$

maximize U subject to (5).

Since D' is always negative and Y' always positive, $v(g)$, the *growth-valuation function*, may have a positive maximum with respect to g. If so, the 'classical' choice is to find this maximum. Alternatively, $v'(g)$ may be negative for all g, in which case the optimum classical growth rate is zero (or, if permissible, negative). The lexicographic managerial criterion (maximize U subject to $v = \bar{v}$) gives optimum growth rate where the constraint is effective, i.e. at the highest value where $v(g) = \bar{v}$. The managerial growth rate will always be higher than the classical, unless $\bar{v}$ is precisely equal to max (v) in (5).

QUALITATIVE ANALYSIS OF THE BASIC MODEL

By differentiating (5) for a maximum, we can obtain the optimum conditions on the *classical criterion*, namely:

$$- D'(g)/D(g) = Y'(g)/Y(g). \qquad (7)$$

The semi-elasticity of the dividend function, negatively defined, must equal the semi-elasticity of the present-value function, positively defined. (The proportionate decrease in the current dividend, caused by a one-point increase in the growth rate, must equal the corresponding proportionate increase in the number of years' purchase.) In partial equilibrium, the semi-elasticity of the present-value function, for given g, may itself be taken as given. Therefore a change in external conditions will change the classical optimum growth rate if, and only if, it changes the semi-elasticity of the dividend function. This semi-elasticity, evidently, is $(p'[g] - 1)/ (p[g] - g)$. Any change in the profit rate obtained from a given growth rate, even if it has the same proportionate effect on $p'(g)$ as on $p(g)$ (e.g. a change in corporation tax, basic costs of production or the cost of capital goods[1]), must in general change this semi-elasticity (because we have $-g$ in the denominator in place of -1 in the numerator), as must also, of course, any change in the relation between $p'(g)$ and $p(g)$. An example of the latter type of change would be a general increase in the effectiveness of develoment expenditure, leading to a general reduction in the negative value of $p'(g)$, without a change in the value of $p(g)$ when g is zero. Lower corporation taxes, lower basic costs and more effective development expenditure will all, therefore, increase the classical optimum growth rate.

A change which reduces numerator and denominator of the semi-elasticity formula in equal proportions, however, will *not* change the classical optimum growth rate unless it also has the same effect on the present-value semi-elasticity, but the latter eventuality is for the time being ruled out by our partial-equilibrium assumptions. An example of such a change would be found if company dividends were taxed at a higher rate than undistributed profits (as has been the case in the United Kingdom) and the differential factor were to change while leaving the average overall rate of profits tax unaffected.

With *managerial motivation*, where the optimum condition is that $v(g)$ equals a constant, *any* shift in the function must change the optimum growth rate. All the changes which affect the growth rate on the classical criterion will therefore have similar qualitative effects under the managerial criterion,[2] but unlike the classically motivated firm, the managerially motivated firm will also be affected by a dividend tax.

If we drop the partial-equilibrium assumptions, and assume that a change, e.g. a tax, affects all firms together, we have to take account of possible associated changes in the general forces governing the present-value function. If this function is ultimately based on a long-term monetary interest rate, and if the interest rate does not change net of tax, the present-value function applied to industrial equities might shift by enough to offset the effects of the tax, both on the classical and the managerial criteria. But an increase in a dividend tax, associated with an equal shift in the average rate of tax on bond interest, could perhaps have a predictable effect under the managerial criterion, with no significant effect under the classical criterion. It does seem to be the case, therefore, that the theory predicts that an

[1] See Solow, p. 335 below.
[2] See Solow, p. 339 below.

increase in company taxation in general will reduce the growth rates likely to be chosen by both 'classical' and 'managerial' firms, but if the increase discriminates in favour of undistributed profits (i.e. against dividends), the adverse effect on growth will be less marked for 'classical' firms than for 'managerial' firms.

SHARE VALUATION AND EXTERNAL FINANCE

I argued in *Managerial Capitalism* that external finance in the form of debt could not directly influence the long-run steady-state growth rate of a firm, because in steady state the growth rate of debt must equal the growth rate of assets; if that were not the case, the ratio of debt to assets would be continually changing, implying, *inter alia*, that the rate of profit net of interest itself must be changing. Steady state must imply a stable leverage ratio. The *level* of this ratio, however, will affect the steady-state reported profit rate in all circumstances except those where the steady-state reported profit rate before interest is precisely equal to the bond interest rate. Since the profit rate is a variable in the model, this would be a special case. I then assumed an upper limit on gearing based on considerations of financial security.

I have not altered my views on gearing, and they are confirmed by the result of cross-section study of several hundred large United States corporations, suggesting the prevalance of a policy of leverage stabilization (see Appendix B below). Attention should therefore be concentrated on external finance by means of new issues. It has been suggested by Modigliani[1] and others that rational behaviour in a stock market without 'frictions', etc., should imply that for a *given* growth rate the valuation ratio would be unaffected by the proportion of internal to new issue finance employed to support it. To investigate the point, we need a more detailed theory of stock-market values, i.e. we must reconsider the nature of the present-value function.

Under conditions of steady state and certainty, the expected rate of capital gain in a share must equal the expected growth rate of the dividend, because dividend growth is the only source of growth in capital value. Consequently, an investor will make the same return on his share purchase if he holds on to it indefinitely, and thus receives

[1] *Journal of Finance* (1961).

all his return in dividends, or if he sells at a finite date and receives his return partly in dividend and partly in capitalized value of expected future dividends, which latter, in turn, are the result of past growth and expected future growth. Consequently, unless there is differential taxation of dividends and 'capital gains', a valuation based exclusively on expected future dividends is equivalent to a valuation based partly on dividends and partly on capital gain.

A dividend d_0, to be declared tomorrow, expected with certainty to grow at a rate g_d, is an infinite series. If investors discount the future at a rate i, the present value of a member of the series t years hence is $d_0 . \exp[t(g_d - i)]$. If i is greater than g_d, each member of the series is smaller than its predecessor and the series converges to zero as t approaches infinity. The integral sum of the whole series is therefore finite, and is known to be approximately equal to $d_0/(i - g_d)$: with a zero growth rate, the value of a perpetual bond is the constant dividend divided by the interest rate; with positive growth the conclusion is modified with the growth rate acting like negative interest.[1] If i does not exceed g_d, the series does not converge and the present-value sum becomes infinite. For the time being we shall assume that the discount rate is given and exogenous, while the growth rate remains variable, but that policies in which the growth rate approaches or exceeds the discount rate are not permitted. Then the present-value function is $Y(g_d) = 1/(i - g_d)$. If new shares are issued at a rate g_n, the growth rate of the dividend, per share, g_d, is equal to the general growth rate, g (indicating the growth rate, *inter alia*, of the *total* dividend), less g_n. The appropriate modification of equation (4) therefore provides us with a growth-valuation function:

$$v = (p - rp)/(i - g + g_n). \qquad (8)$$

Equation (3) must also, however, be modified. The required retention ratio must be reduced to take account of the contribution of new issues. On the assumption that new shares are effectively issued at the same price as the ruling market price of old shares, the required modification is as follows:[2]

$$r = (g - g_n . v)/p. \qquad (9)$$

[1] For a more rigorous statement, see Lintner's paper, pp. 181–4 below.

[2] Equation (9) implies $rp = g - g_n . v$, which in turn equals

$$\frac{dK}{K} . \frac{1}{dt} - \frac{dN}{N} . \frac{1}{dt} . \frac{V}{K} = \frac{1}{dt} \left(\frac{dK - dN . V/N}{K} \right).$$

Since V/N is equivalent to the price of one share, the second part of the numerator of the final bracket represents the proceeds, per period, of new issues, and the

If we substitute $(g - g_n \cdot v)$ for rp in (8) we obtain:

$$v = (p - g + g_n \cdot v)/(i - g + g_n). \tag{10}$$

Cross-multiply by the numerator, and $g_n \cdot v$ appears on both sides. When it has been eliminated we can divide both sides by $(i - g)$ and obtain the general valuation formula:[1]

$$v = (p - g)/(i - g). \tag{11}$$

The surmise that under assumptions of certainty and full comprehension the value of a growth rate is independent of the method of finance is thus generally confirmed. Furthermore, the condition that g cannot exceed p (see p. 22 above) is retained. Remembering that p is a function of g, we can again obtain a well-behaved valuation curve provided that $p(g) = g$ at a lower value of g than $g = i$. But since this remains an arbitrary restriction, the 'growth-stock paradox' is still possible. To pursue the matter further, it is necessary to consider the effects of uncertainty.

THE EFFECTS OF UNCERTAINTY

It is natural to introduce uncertainty into the world of steady state by transforming the steady values associated with each policy into *expected* values, subject to probability distributions with specifiable characteristics. Clearly this transformation makes the steady-state approach more credible. It is one thing to say that one is sure that firms do not grow steadily; it is another to say that a particular form of 'unsteady' long-run growth path (e.g. an S-shaped growth curve) is more probable than a corresponding steady path. And it is one thing to say that there is only a weak serial correlation between the average growth rates of firms over successive five- or ten-year

---

whole bracket, therefore, the amount required from internal finance, as a proportion of K, namely rp. This proves (7).

[1] Due to R. F. Kahn, in an unpublished MS. The models of J. H. Williamson, op. cit., of Solow in this volume, as well as Lintner's certainty model, all carry the same implication, which can be proved by appropriate manipulation of the equations in each case. I did not obtain the result in *Managerial Capitalism* because I failed to assume consistent comprehension by the stock market: I assumed that the market fully comprehended the implications of retentions, but only partly comprehended the implications of new issues.

periods; it is another to say that the corresponding regression equation differs significantly from homogeneity – in other words, to
project the past growth rate into the future may yet remain the
estimate of maximum probability. (See Preface p. xviii n. above.)

The whole problem is comprehensively investigated by Lintner in
this volume. The central source of uncertainty is the level of the
growth function. Having chosen a policy characterized by a pair of
expected values of profit rate (p) and growth rate (g) as specified by
the growth function $p(g)$, we are uncertain as to the actual profit rate
we shall obtain from a given profit rate, or as to the actual growth
rate we shall obtain for a given growth rate. In this 1964 paper,
Lintner put the disturbance into the profit rate; in his present paper
it is in the growth rate or, more precisely, a policy is characterized
by a growth rate and a retention ratio, and the growth rate is uncertain, normally distributed with variance σ_g^2. In the 'quasi-linear'
model presented in my own paper, a normally disturbed 'operating
profit' which is exogenous to the model, generates a normally distributed succession of *chosen* growth rates.

If the normal variance of the probability distribution of growth
rates remains constant over time, the probability of the dividend
levels becomes log-normally distributed, and the variance of the
logarithms increases linearly with time; the logarithmic variance at
time t is, in fact, $t.\sigma_g^2$. Lintner makes assumptions concerning the
risk-aversion of investors, implying that the certainty equivalent of
an uncertain dividend at time t is equal to the expected value reduced
by a factor which is proportionate to the antilog of the logarithmic
variance. Since the latter is growing linearly with time, the reduction
factor grows at compound interest. So at the cost of some oversimplification, the 'risk effect' can be said to behave as if it were an
addition to the interest rate. Alternatively, we can say that the value
of a given growth rate in the present-value function is reduced by an
amount which is proportionate to the variance of that growth rate.
The amount of reduction, for given variance, depends on the general
degree of risk-aversion in the market. Either an increase in variance
or an increase in risk-aversion will, therefore, reduce the present-
value function for given growth rates, and so displace downwards
the whole valuation curve. Since these changes are equivalent to an
increase in the interest rate, and since this increase must reduce the
semi-elasticity of the present-value function in equation (7), the
change will also reduce the optimum growth rate in both the classical

and managerial utility functions. But there is again no guarantee that it would not be possible to find a growth rate whose expected value was less than the profit rate, while the certainty-equivalent value approached the interest rate; so the growth-stock paradox could remain.

In order to ensure that there is no growth rate capable of generating a series of certainty-equivalent dividends whose discounted present value fails to converge, we must have assumptions which ensure that the ratio of the certainty-equivalent value to the expected value declines at an accelerating rate over time, in other words the reduction factor must be growing at an increasing exponential rate. This would occur if, for example, the logarithmic variance of the dividend, instead of increasing linearly with time, increased quadratically with time. In this case, the path of the log of the certainty-equivalent of dividend, derived from any given constant-growth-rate path of the log of the expected dividend, has a constantly diminishing slope. However fast the expected value is growing for all time, the certainty equivalent must then at *some* future date begin to decline (except in the limit where the growth rate tends to infinity). Consequently, on this assumption, even with a zero riskless interest rate, the present-value function is always finite; with a positive interest rate, the *discounted* certainty-equivalent series converges earlier, and the present value is reduced. But any increase in the growth rate, with given interest rate, must increase the present value, because the point in time at which convergence begins is necessarily pushed forward. Hence $Y'(g)$ is always positive, but never infinite.

Lintner shows that the expectation of a simple type of random walk in the growth rate is sufficient to cause the variance of the growth rate itself to increase linearly with time (in the previously described 'stable' model, *this* variance was constant over time); from which it follows that the logarithmic variance of the dividend increases quadratically with time, in the manner above. The belief in a 'random walk' in the growth rate associated with a given profit rate implies conceiving that the expected value of the growth rate over a short period, t years ahead, is equal to whatever would have been the actual value in the immediately preceding short period, but is subject to a normally distributed disturbance term. (We do not have to believe that growth rates behave objectively in this particular stochastic fashion; we expect that when time t arrives, new information will have become available to enable us to assess the expected

value of the subsequent growth rate independently of the past
realized value; but in the meantime, in the absence of this information, we have less and less information about the more distant futures
and are therefore increasingly uncertain about them.) If the variance
of the disturbance term is constant, the variance of the growth rate
increases linearly with time at a rate equal to the disturbance term. A
constant disturbance term in this Markov chain is therefore sufficient
to generate an accelerating growth rate in the logarithmic variance
of the dividend, and so ensure the required convergence. Any other
form of increasing uncertainty providing the basically required
acceleration will do the job as effectively, if not as neatly. Lintner's
specific assumptions enable him to evaluate the relevant integral
quite precisely, in other words he provides a specific form for the
present-value function; the result is quite complicated but nevertheless specifically predicts the effects of changes in risk-aversion, riskless interest rate, degree of uncertainty, etc. The basic conclusion is
that on the assumption of effectively increasing uncertainty, one can
always obtain a well-behaved present-value function, free of the
possibility of infinite values, and that such assumptions conform well
with a reasonable interpretation of typical subjective views about the
future.

The implications of a model with increasing uncertainty, but
without the restriction to internal finance, have not been investigated.

A Postscript on Models which determine both Size and Growth. Note:
This section was written after the Long Island Conference in response to Robert Solow's paper. There would be a strong case, therefore, for placing it at the end of the volume, but it has been left here
partly for editorial convenience and partly because it attempts to
pursue the expository role of the Introduction and is based on the
same analytical framework. Many readers will obviously prefer,
however, to study Solow's original paper first. (The text of the
Postscript was seen by Solow before it went to press and a number of
alterations suggested by him were incorporated.)

There is a small but important change of *symbols*. Solow measures
size in physical units of capital, whose number is designated by K
and whose supply price is designated by m. Book-value of capital is
therefore mK. In growth models which do not determine initial size,
there is no need for a separate physical unit of capital, and I have
previously used K itself to designate book-value. In this Postscript

for consistency, I now follow Solow in the matter. *The meaning of K therefore changes as between the foregoing and what follows.*

THE CONCEPT OF INITIAL SIZE

The models discussed above all assume that the firm, at an arbitrary point in time, is found at an arbitrary size measured, e.g., by assets, and the models are concerned exclusively with the problem of determining an optimum steady-state path of growth from the arbitrary starting-point; they do not consider the possibility that it might be optimal to undertake a rapid, unsteady burst of growth before settling down to steady growth from a higher level, or alternatively, to undertake a corresponding descent to a lower level. Such an initial adjustment is called a choice of 'initial size'. It is analogous to the choice of optimum output in traditional monopoly theory or alternatively in William Baumol's original sales-maximization model.[1] Until Solow produced the model he describes in the present volume, however, no previous theory had effectively solved simultaneously the problem of optimum initial size and long-run optimum growth, i.e. the complete path of the firm over time.

Solow's lucid account and extremely effective use of his model are for the reader to follow. This Postscript is to relate his concepts to the Basic model described above and to discuss his argument that only a 'classical' criterion can solve the simultaneous problem of size and growth.

In the language suggested above, 'initial size' is a point on the demand curve of the corporation. Variations of initial size are movements along this curve, 'growth' is long-run steady-state movement *of* the curve. In Solow's account, the firm produces a single product and moves along the curve by price variation; it achieves growth, in contrast, by advertising. Growth occurs relatively slowly by expanding the stock of goodwill from accumulated advertising expenditure, but the effect of price variation is comparatively fast. Initial size in terms of assets is thus uniquely related to the initial volume of sales through a production function, and it must be assumed that when initial size is varied there exists some means of obtaining the required variations in productive resources, including capital, comparatively

[1] Baumol, *Business Behavior, Value and Growth*, (New York, 1959).

quickly also. How this might be done is discussed below.

There is no obvious difficulty in extending the concept of variable initial size to the multi-product firm: we have already introduced (p. 8 above) the concept of a profit-size frontier, which we have called the corporate 'demand curve', along which one moves by optimal adjustments of prices and outputs of the products one has already marketed. To move outward along this curve, in place of price reduction and sales increase, with appropriate capital injection, for a single product, we see an optimal set of price reductions, sales increases and aggregate capital injection. Other methods of variation could also be considered, but it is the essence of the concept of this kind of 'static' variation that it occurs sufficiently quickly to be treated as an approximately instantaneous adjustment for analytical purposes.

An optimum path for the firm thus consists of, on the one hand, an optimum point on the demand curve and, on the other, an optimum rate of movement *of* the curve, the two together tracing a path of the point over time. The curve, however, has been defined as a relation between total assets employed and total profits (cf. the single-product relation between price and quantity sold); consequently, given an appropriate property in the production function to provide the multi-product equivalent of a constant capital–output ratio, the path will permit both profits and assets to grow at the common exponential rate i.e. it will be a steady-state path.

A 'policy' now has two attributes – a choice of initial size, or point on the demand curve, and a choice of growth rate, or exponential steady-state movement of the curve. The choice of point determines the *level* of profits, the choice of growth rate determines the retention ratio and thus the current dividend rate for any profit level, so the policy determines the entire path of dividends and thus, in principle, stock-market value. Since a policy now determines profits for all sizes and growth rates, including zero growth rate, the rate of profit on capital is entirely endogenous.

INSTRUMENTAL VARIABLES FOR INITIAL SIZE

The instrumental variables for the growth rate are the intensity of development expenditure and the retention ratio. For initial size, the corresponding variable on the demand side is product price or product prices. What is to be the instrumental variable for the corresponding adjustment of assets? One possibility is that outward movements are financed by issuing bonds, inward movements by debt reduction. But rapid adjustments by means of leverage cannot easily be envisaged where the corporation is well established and already at or close to its maximum safe leverage ratio. An alternative, perhaps, would be a substantial 'unsteady' issue of new shares for the case of expansion, or a sale of tangible assets followed by repurchase of existing shares on the open market for the case of contraction. Open-market purchases of own shares, however, are rather unusual, and under the company law of a number of states and countries, such transactions are in fact illegal. A more realistic approach, therefore, is to suppose that adjustments are carried out by temporarily setting retention ratios at levels differing substantially from those appropriate to the growth rates expected on the intended long-run growth paths. If it is well understood that the 'unsteady' phase of the retention ratio is temporary, the market valuation of the firm should continue to be based mainly on the characteristics of the long-run path, thus reducing practical adjustment problems.[1]

'CLASSICAL' CRITERIA FOR SIZE AND GROWTH

The nearer we are to an optimum path, the less serious will be the adjustment problem. If we assume we are near enough to *any* path which might be optimal for adjustment problems to be ignored, we now have a policy set whose attributes are a set of paths, an associated set of instrumental variables consisting of prices and development expenditures, and a mapping of all into stock-market values. What criteria of choice correspond to the 'classical' and 'managerial' criteria previously applied? Solow shows, however, that with the additional dimension of choice, maximization of the stock-market value of the single firm no longer represents a general criterion for maximizing the welfare of the share-owning class.

---

[1] These remain, however, significant. The retention ratio is constrained between zero and 100 per cent, thus constraining the speed of adjustment. Time discount and risk increasing with futurity may well combine to give heavy weight to the results of the first few years, i.e. to the actual expected results during the adjustment process, compared with the results of the subsequent long-run path. If so, a good lot of fat is on the fire.

Imagine an economy with a number of listed corporations but only one share-owning investor, who wishes to maximize the value of his portfolio. Let all the firms choose the same, arbitrary, growth rate. They remain, however, free to vary initial size. If each decided to maximize aggregate stock-market value (V, not v), they would choose the points on their respective demand curves where aggregate profits were at a maximum. But unless all the demand curves were identical, the rates of return at these points (measured by the slopes of the rays from the origin) would differ, and the single investor would benefit if capital were moved from the firms with low returns to those with big returns. If managers cared nothing for size, the movement would be Pareto-optimal in the sense of making the stockholder better off and managers no worse off.

To understand better the implications, it is convenient to assume that the suggested adjustment of the relative initial sizes of the firms is achieved by issues and repurchases of shares according to the method described, and then dismissed, above. A firm whose size is to be reduced sells tangible assets and buys shares; an expanding firm issues shares and buys assets. If the first firm's reduction, measured in replacement value of assets, is $m.\,dK$ (where K measures capital and m is the price of capital goods), and this is also the corresponding increase in the second firm, the price at which the stock-market will agree to buy the new shares of the second firm must be such that the firm's total increase in market value, dV, is just equal to $m.\,dK$. This is clearly the intuitive criterion for ensuring that no movement of capital within the portfolio can increase the latter's aggregate value. Solow reaches the same result by the condition that incremental market value due to adding one *physical* unit of capital (K) to a firm shall be equal to the common supply price of physical capital goods, that is, m. We thus equalize the marginal physical profitability of capital, but not of course the value of the marginal physical product of capital, because we have a regime of monopoly rather than of competition.

'MANAGERIAL' CRITERIA FOR SIZE AND GROWTH

Does managerial satisfaction flow from size or from rate of change of size? In *Managerial Capitalism*[1] I argued for both, with the

[1] Chap. 2, esp. pp. 102–7.

balance of emphasis on the latter. With steady growth from an arbitrary starting-point, both criteria produce the same policy. But if in fact the starting-point is variable, and yet managers are concerned only with the rate of change, they appear to lack a criterion for the former; not caring about the problem, they would ignore it. Alternatively, if they care only for absolute size, how do they choose its rate of change?

We are concerned here only with the theoretical implications, rather than the plausibility, of the alternative interpretations of the underlying motivation. In my own view, there is a clear answer in both cases. In the first case, we note that any policy choice of size and growth, whether accidental or deliberate, implies a theoretical stock-market value. Any policy thus also implies a valuation ratio. The set of policies defined over size, growth rate and valuation ratio is convex. Consequently, if managers care only for the growth rate, and wish to maximize this subject to the customary minimum valuation, they should find a unique policy with the relevant property. Size is thus a determined but non-significant variable. The result is determin*ate* and will probably differ from the classical result: the firm will probably be larger and grow faster. (I am assuming an initial phase of increasing returns to scale, before constant returns set in – an L-shaped, but not U-shaped, cost curve – and it also makes sense, in fact, to assume that with zero assets profits would be negative. This gives me a profit-rate frontier with a positive maximum (see p. 10 above). But cf. Solow, p. 330 below.)

On the above assumptions the rule of adjustment is as follows. With an arbitrary initial size, vary the growth rate until the valuation ratio is at the minimum, and the growth rate at maximum subject to this constraint. Then vary the initial size with growth rate constant. If $dV/dK.m.\bar{v}$ (where $\bar{v}$ represents the constrained minimum valuation ratio) is greater than 1, add a little capital and so raise the valuation ratio. Then increase the growth rate until the valuation ratio is restored to the minimum. Repeat until $dV/dK.m.\bar{v}$ is unity. If at first $dV/dK.m.\bar{v}$ is less than unity, carry out the same process in the opposite direction.

In the second case, if management's sensations and benefits are based directly on size itself, rather than on the rate of change, managers must be endowed with some means for optimizing over time; they must be able to trade present size against future size. This is partly a matter of time discount, and partly a matter of uncertainty:

future size itself is uncertain, and so also personal benefits flowing from size (individuals may have resigned, been fired or died; the bonus rate may have changed; the firm may have been taken over). The degree of uncertainty is likely to increase with futurity for the same basic reasons as in the case of investors' uncertainty, namely that relevant information is expected to become available in the future which is not available now. There is no reason to suppose that the effects will be the same as in the case of managers and investors, but it can be supposed to take a similar form, and there is at least one important element – the uncertainty of the growth path itself – common to both cases. We can therefore make use of a concept similar to that of the present-value function. We propose to define managerial utility U_m associated with a firm of size K, growing at g, defined as $U_m = K . M(g)$, where $M(g)$ is a function of g with properties similar to, but not necessarily identical with, the present-value function. We shall want to retain, however, the assumption that management is also interested in the valuation ratio, especially in the form of a minimum constraint. The general managerial utility function is therefore

$$U = U(U_m, v).$$

In the lexicographic form of this, the first priority is to obtain a minimum value of v, namely $\bar{v}$, after which we maximize U_m. Such criteria can be applied to a suitably modified basic model, and should be sufficient to determine an optimum path.

A MODIFIED BASIC MODEL

The basic model, it will be remembered, consisted of a dividend function and the present-value function. In the dividend function, the current dividend payable by a firm making no growth effort would be governed by a rate of profit which we have previously regarded as an exogenous product of the general environment, competitive or oligopolistic as the case might be. We can now see initial size as a way of varying this profit rate (i.e. the profit rate of a firm with no growth effort and no development expenditure), and thus making it endogenous. So initial size becomes an additional argument in the dividend function, which will have negative first partial derivatives over the relevant range of adjustment.[1] The growth valuation function becomes

$$v(K_0, g) = D(K_0, g) . Y(g) \qquad (11)$$

or, as is needed when using the classical criterion,

$$V = m . K_0 . v = m . K_0 . D(K_0, g) . Y(g). \qquad (12)$$

For the *classical* criterion, following Solow, we set $\partial V/\partial K = m$ in (12) and $\partial v/\partial g = 0$ in (11). For the *managerial* criterion we either set g at a maximum subject to $v > \bar{v}$, or $K_0 . M(g)$ at a maximum subject to this same constraint in (11).

ECONOMIC IMPLICATIONS OF THE MODIFIED MODEL, WITH CLASSICAL MOTIVATION

Solow's single-product firm is a traditional profit-maximizing mono-polist simultaneously solving the problem of the optimum growth rate. The relation between the modified model and the familiar theorems of monopoly-profit maximization may conveniently be seen by putting the modified model in a special form, namely,

$$v = \frac{P(K_0)/m . K_0 - (1 + a)g}{i - g}. \qquad (14)$$

The numerator is a linear form of the dividend function (also discussed in section III in my main paper below). $P(K_0)$ indicates the profits which would be earned by the firm if it made no growth effort (the 'operating profits' defined in section I of my main paper, p. 282 below). They are a function of the initial size of the firm measured in physical capital units; this function is the 'demand curve of the corporation' defined above. $P(K_0)/m . K_0$ is the corresponding rate of return. The deduction $(1 + a)g$ represents the negative effects on the dividend of growth, due to the need to divert profits to research and development efforts (represented by the coefficient a whose constancy here represents a condition of 'dynamic constant returns') and to

[1] The demand curve is a relation between size and profits, and thus also a relationship between size and profits relative to size. The 'classical' adjustment, described earlier, will consist in driving down this rate of profit to the required general norm. The managerial adjustment will involve increasing size at the expense of profitability.

new plant investment (represented by the unit; see equation (10) above). The denominator represents the particular form of present-value function (inverted – it is actually $1/Y(g)$) used by Solow and explained in the text above on p. 23: it implies that the number of years' purchase applied to a dividend growing at g is the reciprocal of the interest rate, i (as would be the case for a perpetual bond with a constant dividend), less the growth rate (which acts like negative interest). (14) may be expressed in terms of total market value, V:

$$V = m . K_0 . v = \frac{P(K_0) - m . K_0(1 + a)g}{i - g}.$$ (15)

Solow's criterion for initial size, it will be remembered, requires $dV/dK_0 = m$. Partially differentiate (15) with respect to K_0, set equal to m, simplify, and obtain

$$\frac{\partial P}{m . \partial K_0} = i + a . g.$$ (16)

Now the partial derivative on the left-hand side is the *slope* of the demand curve of the corporation and will be positive in the relevant range. Assuming that we have, in fact, a single-product firm, the left-hand side is therefore equivalent to the excess of marginal revenue over marginal production cost divided by the marginal capital–output ratio. Multiply both sides of the equation by the last-named, carry marginal production cost to the right-hand side and the equation will read:

Marginal revenue = Marginal production cost + Marginal capital–
output ratio × $(i + a . g)$. (17)

This may be interpreted by assuming an arbitrary growth rate. Suppose it were zero, then the right-hand side would be marginal production cost plus rate of interest times marginal capital–output ratio, in other words marginal total cost if the rate of interest is regarded as the supply price of capital. If the growth rate is positive, the familiar equation of marginal revenue and marginal total cost is modified. In effect, marginal revenue must be equated with marginal cost *including* the cost of creating growth (measured by $a . g$); in Solow it is the cost of advertising the single product. But the (normalized) cost of advertising increases with whatever happens to be the steady-state growth rate; this is a necessary condition for the growth rate to be sustainable. In the presence of growth, 'marginal cost', traditionally defined, is enhanced by the cost of sustaining the growth.

Since the optimum growth rate is not arbitrary, but itself dependent on profitability, the simultaneity of the problems of growth and size is thus well illustrated. The simplifying assumptions are not significant, and it should be possible to extend the basic ideas to the multi-product corporation. Where the corporation is actually single-product, the result above can be given in terms of the elasticity of demand, for example in the explicit and ingenious manner suggested by Solow.

ECONOMIC IMPLICATIONS OF THE MODIFIED MODEL, WITH MANAGERIAL MOTIVATION

Equation (11) states that the valuation ratio is partly itself a function of initial size. For any *given* level of size, we can obtain a definite growth-valuation function by varying the growth rate with size constant. By repeating the procedure for alternative levels of size, we generate a family of these curves which, on our assumptions about the relationships (but not on Solow's; see p. 31 above and Solow p. 330) will contain a well-defined sub-family which does not intersect and within which all curves with high K_0-values will lie inside those with lower values. This sub-family forms the effective constraint on managerial action. When we define a minimum valuation ratio, a single point on each curve represents the maximum permissible growth rate for the indicated value of initial size; for any common minimum valuation ratio, we can therefore determine a frontier between initial size and maximum permitted growth rate. The modified managerial utility function described earlier defines, *inter alia*, a set of indifference curves between size and growth rate, so a tangential solution between these and the size–growth-rate frontier uniquely determines the optimum path.

Interestingly, but not surprisingly, analysis shows that if we set the minimum valuation ratio at a relatively high level, both size and growth are adversely affected: in other words, *ceteris paribus*, the optimum path of a 'managerial' corporation will be both steeper and higher than that of a 'classical' firm; the former will lie above the latter through all time. 'Managerial' motivation therefore appears to

lead not only to higher growth rates (and more consumption stimulation) but to less monopolistic restriction of output in the traditional
sense. The conclusion can be partly reversed, however, if classical
motivation is associated with greater intrinsic efficiency (e.g. due to
less 'slack' or less static Oliver Williamson-type hierarchical expense),
and would be represented in a 'superior' growth-valuation function
all along the line. There is some evidence that large corporations
which are in the stage where the distribution of their shares is still
highly concentrated (suggesting owner control, but with a managerial
bureaucracy installed to permit large-scale operations) do, in fact,
tend to display superior efficiency in this sense. An interesting study
on this point has been made by Mr H. Radice, at the time of writing
a graduate student at King's College, Cambridge, in an unpublished
paper originally written as an M.A. thesis when he was a graduate
student at Warwick University.

2 Economic Analysis of the Corporate Economy: A Survey and Critique[1]

Adrian Wood

This piece has two general purposes; it is intended mainly to provide a frame of reference within which the individual papers printed in this book may be read. It also incorporates as much as possible of the record of the conference held to discuss these papers: we decided not to include the discussion in the usual transcript form on grounds of readability, nor, in the present form, to attempt to allocate the points made among individuals.

I. INTRODUCTION: GENERALIZATION OF NEW MODELS OF THE FIRM

New models of the behaviour of the large corporation have recently been developed in which a variety of assumptions about business motivation have been inserted into traditional static frameworks, steady-state growth models of the firm, and non-maximizing 'behaviourist' analyses. In particular, the theoretical models of the growth of the firm which are discussed by Marris in the preceding paper are rapidly becoming rigorous, complete and accepted. Some of the papers in this volume make substantial contributions to both the general structure of these models and the effects of alternative motivations on their solutions.

But these are all models of the behaviour of the *single firm*; they

[1] I am extremely grateful to Robin Marris, George Eads, John Eatwell and Mervyn King, who have read and criticized an earlier draft of this paper, and with whom I have had fruitful discussions of its subject-matter at other times. I am responsible for the mistakes that remain.

are set in partial equilibrium and take the activities of all other firms as given. This is a very severe restriction on the scope of the questions, both analytical and practical, that they can attempt to answer. The most important subjects which economics seeks to investigate are ones which concern systems of many firms, or of all firms, which require consideration not only of how all firms, individually, behave, but also of how their individual activities interact and constrain each other, in markets, broad sectors and the whole economy. Examples of subjects of this kind are allocative efficiency, growth of per capita consumption and leisure, inflation, unemployment and the distribution of income: more specifically, models of the economy or parts of the economy can provide methods by which the consequences of proposed changes in government policy can be investigated.

Therefore, the object of this present paper is to view new models of the firm in a more general economic context, and especially to inquire into relationships that might be developed between these theories of the firm and existing and new models of markets and the economy. There are two main, though not independent, features of new models of the firm which might be generalized, and these will recur throughout the survey in different contexts. The first is the concept of the firm as a growing rather than a static organization, whose behaviour can be studied over time in a systematic way. Its actions at any moment of time cannot be understood without reference to the past and the future, although for some purposes the past and future need not explicitly be considered, and can be 'collapsed' into 'short-run' constraints on behaviour in the present period (provided by an inherited situation, and a set of expectations of the future. This is related to the concept of 'temporary' equilibrium which will be discussed below, in section V). The second is differences in motivation; or more explicitly, alternative business utility functions in situations which permit the exercise of 'discretionary power'. Some utility functions are related to particular model structures; for example, consideration of the total dynamic effects of 'growth maximization' can only occur in a growth model of the firm. But again, the consequences of *any* utility function may be studied in a short-run context by collapsing expected future behaviour into short-term decision rules.

The subject-matter of this paper could be divided up in a number of ways. The general purpose of the classification that I have chosen is to proceed from the discussion of the individual firm as a low-level unit of the economy to successively more 'general' levels – the market, many markets, and the total economy. This is not completely satisfactory, in that a diversified firm could convincingly be argued to be a higher-level economic unit than the market for a particular product. Moreover, the structure of the paper is modified to include discussions of certain econometric and normative questions. Thus section II considers developments of theories of the firm which make them more amenable to generalization, and section III discusses problems that arise in attempts to estimate econometrically models of the growing firm. Section IV deals with aspects of theories of market behaviour. Section V inquires into the possibilities of general equilibrium analysis of models of this type, and section VI into specifically macro-economic questions. Section VII considers some problems of normatively evaluating the corporate economy, and is followed by a short conclusion.

Thus the subject under discussion is the operation of a market economy dominated by large corporations. Although the individual papers in this volume bear upon this area, it remains enormous, difficult, and in places completely undeveloped. I have no pretensions to covering it adequately, and my aim is to raise questions more than to answer them. I shall deal principally with the corporate sector of the economy itself, and within this mainly with manufacturing.

II. THE STRUCTURE OF MODELS OF THE FIRM: SOME DEVELOPMENTS

Marris's 'Introduction to Theories of Corporate Growth' discusses some aspects of the contributions to models of the firm by the authors of this volume. Here, I shall draw attention to four further contributions of these papers and the conference to the analysis of the firm which are of importance in proceeding from partial equilibrium to more general analysis. They are the distinction between the corporation and the 'quasi-firm', some improvements in the exposition of steady-state growth models, alternatives to steady-state methodology, and further analysis of the effects of alternative motivations related to 'behavioural' and organizational factors.

Williamson's paper investigates the consequences of different organizational structures of diversified corporations. He draws a

CE C

distinction between the unitary (or U) form, and the multi-division (or M) form: the component units of the U-form are divisions which perform particular functions (sales, finance, production, etc.) for all the product lines of the firm. The M-form company, by contrast, is composed of 'operating divisions' or 'quasi-firms' which perform *all* these functions for each *single* product, and are responsible to a head office, which both supervises the operating decisions of the quasi-firms and allocates capital funds, research and development funds and possibly total advertising funds among them. Williamson then investigates some of the implications of this distinction for the efficiency of the firm. For our present purpose, the main implication of the two forms is that in the M-form firm there exists a concrete institutional realization of the analytical distinction made in studies of the firm between operating decisions and overall 'strategic' decisions. The relations between head office and the operating divisions provide a bridge between the analysis of the firm and the analysis of particular products and markets: economists must be concerned with the way in which the activities of each unit influence those of the others – both the influence which head office exercises on particular operating divisions (and vice versa), and the manner in which this links together the behaviour of all the quasi-firms of a particular corporation. The usefulness of this conceptual framework will become clearer at several points below; I shall tend to speak as if all diversified firms were M-form, which is not as yet true, although Williamson believes this to be a logically superior form. But even if the institutions do not conform, the analytical distinction between operating and strategic decisions remains valid and useful.

Lintner and Solow are concerned, *inter alia*, with more rigorous steady-state growth models of the corporation. Both make important individual innovations which are discussed by Marris above. But a feature common to both authors is much more detailed attention to the construction of the growth-profitability transformation function[1] from its constituent elements. For simplicity, both deal with the case in which the firm produces a single (or in Lintner's model, a 'composite') commodity (and hence avoid the significance of the distinction between firm and quasi-firm), for which the market structure is such that a normal demand function can be defined (which, although at first sight equivalent to assuming away oligopoly, may be consistent with oligopolistic markets in the manner suggested by Marris

[1] See Marris, p. 18 above.

on p. 9 above). Thus the relation between steady-state growth and recorded (as distinct from operating) profitability is assembled from a demand function, a current production function (or cost function) and factor prices, which together define the operating profit, and the 'cost-of-growth' function. This last specifies the rate of shift of the demand function over time as a function of the proportion of the firm's operating profit spent upon advertising, research and development, recruitment of new personnel, organizational adaptation and so forth. (Presumably it could be further divided into the costs of diversification and the costs of maintaining or expanding market share in current markets.) Plant and equipment expenditure is generated by the rate of expansion of demand, the form of the production function and the rate of depreciation.

This elaboration is of interest in the analysis of the individual firm. More importantly, the analysis of variables at a 'lower level' than growth and profitability is an essential stage in the development of more general analysis involving new models of the firm. One major reason why empirical 'industrial organization' economists have failed to relate their work to new thinking on the firm is that they have been concerned with market structure and performance as reflected in measurable variables such as advertising and research expenditures, cost functions and concentration, as well as growth and profitability.[1] Benefits from interchange of ideas may exist for both schools: for example, for theorists of the firm in estimating their models (see section III below). On the other hand, newer views of the firm may enable researchers in industrial organization to explain phenomena which are ill accounted for in terms of traditional static models of firms and markets. A necessary step towards achieving this interchange is the integration of models of the firm cast in terms of 'low-level' identifiable variables, on the one hand with the firm–quasi-firm distinction, which enables certain variables to be analysed in connection with particular products and others in connection with the whole firm, and, on the other hand with theories of markets,

---

[1] But even with reference to profitability alone, it should be pointed out that industrial organization studies, such as that of Comanor and Wilson, 'Advertising, Market Structure, and Performance', *Review of Economics and Statistics* (Nov 1967), have considered only 'reported' or 'measured' profitability, whereas new models of the firm attach great significance also to the operating profit rate, and to the extent of the difference between operating and reported profits. For example, *ceteris* (especially operating profits) *paribus*, higher advertising outlays should be associated with lower reported profitability, which is the reverse of the Comanor–Wilson finding. Other things are evidently not equal.

especially of oligopoly (since a considerable amount of industrial organization analysis examines differences between industries as well as those between firms).

At present a barrier to such an integration is the steady-state frame in which growth models of the firm are cast. The methodological advantages of steady-state solutions are their simplicity and their generality: the form of most of these models (as Arrow points out) is such that the conventional static determination of the equilibrium of the firm can be interpreted as a parable of its dynamic situation – although constant returns to scale mean that the static solution is indeterminate, diminishing returns in the cost-of-growth function produce dynamic determinacy. But although steady-state solutions are of inherent interest in that they reveal underlying aspects of the model, their full significance can only be understood by comparison with a range of other forms of solution. A variety of possible dynamic models exists, most of which have steady-state solutions as special cases (all of which may be collapsed into short-term temporary equilibrium form; see p. 38 above).

Lintner demonstrates how steady-state models behave in uncertain worlds in the case where management is making a once-and-for-all decision on strategy on the basis of expectations of the future common to them and to their stockholders. An alternative model would be one that took account of the possibility that, even having made a decision based on long-period expectations, the effect of non-realization of these expectations (as a result of random shocks or the incompatibility of the strategy with the actions of other firms) is to cause management to adjust both short- and long-run decision variables (although certain aspects of a chosen 'strategic posture' may be for all practical purposes irreversible). This requires 'behavioural' models of 'dynamic adjustment' (as discussed by Baumol) whose structure depends upon the nature of the possible adjustments and of the lags involved. In the case both of random shocks and of general systems of interaction between firms, specific enough assumptions will produce convergence of the dynamic adjustment process to a steady-state solution (reducing it to a type of stability condition).

Particular aspects of corporate growth have been observed to take place in an essentially discontinuous and non-steady manner. Examples of this are logistic curves of the saturation of markets, merger, expansion of market share and discontinuities in capacity expansion causing temporary excess capacity. Although appropriate assumptions about the regularity of repetition of such phenomena can integrate them into steady state (as Marris has demonstrated in the instance of logistic curves[1]), it may be of interest to construct 'lurching' models of the growth of the firm possibly with specific numerical solutions. These need not necessarily be permanent growth models: it is not difficult to envisage models covering adjustment to a set of initial conditions over a finite number of periods, possibly given a set of expectations about future periods up to an infinite horizon.

No new business motivations are suggested, but Solow and Williamson further the digestion of already proposed motives. The implications of Solow's study of response to exogenous changes in variables among differently motivated firms will be discussed below. Williamson investigates the effects of alternative corporate organizational structures on the efficiency of the firm and expense preference behaviour. He suggests that in the M-form or divisionally organized diversified firm, expense preference is confined to the operating divisions (or quasi-firms). This clarifies some of the links between expense motivation, 'behaviourist' analysis of the firm and maximizing steady-state models; most empirical behaviourist investigation has focused upon operating-level decisions, and might be thought of as subsumed into the cost and revenue functions of growth models. It now appears that in a possibly 'dominant' form of organization, expense preference, which is more difficult than other motivations to incorporate into steady-state models (although empirically more tractable), is also an operating-level characteristic, and can probably be integrated with other behaviourist phenomena. By contrast, the discretionary power of the head office (which is enhanced in Williamson's analysis by the superior profitability of an M-form firm) is exercised in the manipulation of 'enterprise-wide' variables, which of course include the growth-, sales- and valuation-maximizing motives analysed in the growth models of the firm.

III. THE ESTIMATION OF MODELS OF THE GROWING FIRM AND THE IDENTIFICATION OF MOTIVATION

Although there is considerable consensus on the general theoretical structure of growth models of the corporation, the existence and

[1] Marris, *Managerial Capitalism*, chap. 4.

significance of alternative motivations may be thought of as alternative locations of the corporation on its growth-valuation transformation function: the significance of the differences between them
depends upon the distance between the alternative locations relative
to the general order of magnitude of the variables under consideration. A major contribution of Solow's paper is to demonstrate that
at a theoretical level the effect of alternative motivations on the
response to changes in exogenous variables is to produce a response
differing in degree rather than in direction or kind. Thus without knowing the empirical form of the underlying functions it
is impossible to deduce motivation from a single observation on
a firm, much less assess its significance in the face of possible
alternatives.

Thus it would be necessary to estimate these models in order to
investigate the significance of differences in motivation; the problem
of identifying different motivations would remain, but there may be
alternative ways of identifying motivation other than estimating
complete models. In the following paragraphs, both the problems of
directly estimating these models and possible alternative methods of
achieving the same results will be discussed.

The models contain four principal relationships – the utility
function, the determinants of the operating profit rate, the cost-of-
growth function, and the stock-market discount function – the last
three of which combine to form the growth-valuation transformation
function. At least the utility function and the growth-valuation
function must be separately estimated to identify the model: reduced
forms such as regressions of recorded profit rate or stock-market
valuation on growth, or vice versa (as discussed and surveyed in
Appendices A and B of this volume), are insufficient. Possibly the
three components of the growth-valuation function must also be
separately estimated. If one can assume that the current sales and
costs and hence the position on the demand and production functions
can be taken as given, these 'exogenously' determine the operating
profit rate. (Situations under which this is a reasonable assumption
will be considered in the next section of the survey.) Attention may
then be focused upon estimating the two remaining elements of the
growth-valuation function: the cost-of-growth function and the
discount function. Estimating the first of these is dogged by an
accounting problem and a pooling problem.

The accounting problem is straightforward: one must be able to separate the expenditures of the firm into current costs, costs of growth and dividends (neglecting liquid assets, etc.). Within this framework it is convenient to distinguish more detailed elements, particularly of the costs of growth: research and development should be separated from expenditures on the promotion of future sales, the costs of recruitment and organizational change, and plant and equipment purchases. In practice, accounting conventions do not separate current from future costs except in the case of plant and equipment: thus neither the operating profit rate nor the costs of growth may be measured. It is arguable that the 'ideal' accounting convention for our purposes is impossible: certain cases can be identified (such as the Arrow–Nerlove stock of goodwill advertising model[1]) in which there is in principle no way to separate expenditures on current needs from those on future needs. But in general one supposes that not only are calculations of this sort possible but that they are made in practice as a necessary part of the running of a large corporation.

Even if this problem is soluble, the pooling problem remains: in order to estimate the cost-of-growth function we need more than one observation and preferably as many as possible, whether the function is estimated using the single variable 'costs of growth', or by breaking these costs down further. A single corporation in steady state can only provide one observation on this function, in that however many time periods are considered, all observations are identical. If the single corporation is out of steady state and thus generating a series of different values over time, one is faced with the further problem of telling apart movements along the function, movements of the function, and movements towards it, which requires additional theoretical and empirical information. Pooling of observations on corporations in steady state in cross-section is also illegitimate without additional restrictions, since the form and position of the function may differ among firms (if it did not, i.e. all firms were identically objectively situated and motivated, one would return to the problem of a set of identical observations). Although an obvious method of solving the cross-section pooling problem is to identify and insert as controls those factors which cause the form and position of the function to vary between firms (for example, the initial industry composition of output), if this is done perfectly

---

[1] K. J. Arrow and M. Nerlove, 'Optimal Advertising Policy under Dynamic Conditions', *Economica* (May 1962).

successfully, one will again be left with identical observations on the cost-of-growth function, unless motivation varies between firms. If the firms in cross-section are not in steady state (and this is clearly a reasonable if an inconvenient assumption), apart from the case in which the divergence from steady state is assumed to arise from a random disturbance with mean equal to zero, the problems are multiplied in the manner mentioned above.

Estimating the discount function is an aspect of the study of the empirical determinants of stock prices or rates of return upon which a considerable amount has been written that will not be discussed here.[1] But it may be noted in passing that in order that the steady-state approach should have empirical credibility, firms should be characterized by stable growth and profit rates over time (and the market should be aware of this). Previous econometric studies suggest that there is statistically significant serial correlation of these variables but that the proportion of variance explained by such a model is low, and declines with the length of the time interval separating the two periods in question.[2]

Finally, having estimated the form of the growth-valuation function, there remains the problem of deciding which motivations correspond with the observed differences of location of firms upon it. The most widely accepted motivational proxy variables are the extent of management stockholding in the corporation and the determinants of all forms of managerial remuneration. The latter pose problems in so far as estimation of the relations between salary, size and profitability is beset by the specification ambiguities that arise from multi-collinearity, and because patterns of managerial reward appear to alter quite rapidly over time.[3] Both also fail to cope adequately with the variation in risk-aversion that may produce a spread of observations along the growth-valuation function in a world in which take-over is a probabilistic rather than an absolute threat that

[1] See, for example, M. Nerlove, 'Factors Affecting Differences among Rates of Return on Investments in Individual Common Stocks', *Review of Economics and Statistics* (Aug 1968), and I. Friend and M. Puckett, 'Dividends and Stock Prices', *American Economic Review* (Sep 1964).

[2] See, for example, the material referred to on this subject by Eatwell in Appendix A of this volume, and especially the book by Singh and Whittington cited there.

[3] See D. R. Roberts, *Executive Compensation* (Glencoe, Ill., 1959), J. W. McGuire and others, 'Executive Income, Sales and Profits', *American Economic Review* (Sep 1962), and W. G. Lewellen, *Executive Compensation in Large Industrial Corporations* (New York, 1968).

varies with the size of the valuation ratio. Nor do they provide any criterion for distinguishing between, for example, growth and sales maximizers. But they are superior to managers' subjective assessments of their motivation, and, in terms of cost, also to individual case studies.

Some approaches to identifying motivation other than direct estimation of the model have been proposed and can be briefly listed:

1. Jorgenson and others have estimated investment functions for firms and industries upon the assumption of present-value maximization.[2] Alternative behavioural assumptions might yield different regression coefficients and/or fits; the work of Zanetti and Filippi in this volume is clearly relevant in this respect.

2. One form of economic regulation is that in which firms are constrained to make a given rate of reported profit ('fair return on fair value'). Since this holds constant one of the variables under analysis, it may be possible to investigate more clearly differences in other variables in view of possible differences of motivation. A major limitation of this approach is the restricted and distinctive range of industries to which this regulatory device has been applied.

3. It might be possible to investigate variations in business response to changes in tax differentials, both between dividends and retained earnings, and between personal income and capital gains.[2] However, the problem discussed by Solow remains, viz. that these changes affect corporations of all motivations in the same direction, and we lack any yardstick by which to tell them apart.

4. Reid and others have asserted that differences in the number of mergers undertaken by firms are associated with different motivations, high rates of merger being carried out by growth maximizers, while valuation maximizers merge less often.[3] Two types of empirical evidence have been offered to support this;

---

[1] See D. W. Jorgenson and J. A. Stephenson, 'Issues in the Development of the Neoclassical Theory of Investment Behaviour' (and references to seven other articles by Jorgenson in the bibliography of the article), *Review of Economics and Statistics* (Aug 1969).

[2] On this, see Solow, pp. 339–41.

[3] For a reference to Reid, and an exposition and discussion of his results, see my paper which appears as Appendix C of this volume.

both the higher growth rates and lower stock prices of frequently merging firms (implying either that stockholders dislike
excessive growth or that they dislike this *method* of growth), and
their lower earnings-per-share growth (supplying a reason for
the stockholders' dislike of mergers as a means of growth).
So far, deficiencies of data and analysis have prevented the
appearance of really clear results on these points.

IV. OLIGOPOLY AND MARKET STRUCTURE

Market structure defines the constraints on the behaviour of a set of
quasi-firms arising from their rivalry in selling a particular product
(or type of product in the case of 'near' substitutes). Market models
may be constructed for at least three possible purposes: first, for the
individual corporation, the structure of the markets in which it sells
is one determinant of the demand-side constraint, which is also
affected by the possibility of diversifying into existing markets
(possibly a function of their structure) and by the scope for developing and selling new products. Second, the structure of the market
determines the conditions of sale to consumers of the whole of an
individual product – its price, quality and quantity both at the present
and in subsequent periods. Third, studies of markets in the economy
as a whole have investigated the allocation of scarce resources among
competing demands. A model suitable for one purpose may be
unsuited for another and attempts to combine them may prove to be
unhappy compromises. The conference felt that future development should be directed towards the answering of particular
analytical questions rather than the development of 'complete'
theories.

Two analytical questions will be discussed here; the effects of
alternative business motivations on short-term price and output
behaviour in different market structures, and the possibilities of
longer-term analysis of non-competitive markets with particular
reference to the form of the firm's cost-of-growth function.

Care has to be exercised in making comparisons between the effects
of alternative motivations, because it is illegitimate to compare the
single-period decisions of a model in which the decision-maker
expects other periods to follow, with once-and-for-all decisions in the

face of currently defined constraints. Thus, short-run decisions in steady-state models of the firm cannot be compared with static solutions in 'conventional' market models.

Considering the case in which the firm produces in only one market (the firm is the quasi-firm), in the face of a defined demand function, John Williamson has asserted that growth and valuation maximizers produce at the same short-term output (and hence price), but that discounted sales maximizers have a higher output.[1] But Solow's analysis in this volume focuses more closely upon initial conditions, and concludes that growth and valuation maximizers will, in general, choose different initial sizes (and moreover that the growth-maximizing utility function will not determine both growth rate and size. Marris disputes this; see pp. 26–36 above.)

Continuing with the case of a defined demand function, comparison between static profit and sales maximizers is evidently interesting only in the case of monopolistic firms; the sales maximizers produce up to the point of average revenue equal to average cost, that is to say in general at a higher output and lower price than with profit maximization under 'pure' monopoly, and possibly at the same price and output as profit maximizers under monopolistic competition (assuming that the motive for entry becomes sales, not profits). Satisficing and 'optimally imperfect' decision-making in the face of uncertainty introduce a zone of indeterminacy around the objectively 'optimal' decision whatever the utility function of the firm. Expense preference raises the average cost function in some way; in the case of monopoly this results in a yet higher price and lower output. Under other market structures, expense might be squeezed by varying amounts of price competition.

Marris's principal contribution to the volume (pp. 270–327 below) is in part devoted to a static game-theoretic analysis of oligopoly, which breaks away from the assumption of a defined demand curve, and deals with the manner in which rivalry among a set of quasi-firms in a market determines, in the short term, the operating profit that is an element of growth models of the corporation. In his first model this is determined jointly by a 'rational' choice of pricing policy and by the structure of the market – its supply technology (economies of scale, discontinuities in cost functions) and its demand conditions (the scope and type of selling costs being primarily a

[1] J. H. Williamson, 'Profit, Growth and Sales Maximization', *Economica* (Jan 1966).

function of the nature of the product). The model assumes that the short-term decisions of the quasi-firm are independent of the longer-term decisions of the corporation of which it is a part; presumably this impinges in the form of the possibilities of earning an 'external' profit rate, when Marris deals with the question of entry.

Marris considers the possibility of expressing the pay-offs of his model in terms of variables other than the rate of return; he suggests hierarchic expense and sales volume, but other possibilities are the rate of growth of sales, market share, 'technical virtuosity', etc. These outcomes may either be expressed in terms of a vector of variables, or translated, as is done by Marris, into single-valued 'utilities'. The translation depends on the utility function of the firm which, as has been mentioned above, is a way of looking at its motivation.

Some effects of alternative motivations in the context of 'barriers-to-entry' models of oligopoly may be sketched: as they stand at present, the analyses of Bain and Sylos Labini[1] depend upon the assumption that all the firms involved, whether incumbents of or potential entrants into a market, have the same utility function. A successful genuine barrier to entry (as opposed to a bluff) depends upon the utility of the potential entrant after entry being less than the utility of remaining outside the market; in general it is also associated with the incumbents' utility being higher before than after entry. As long as utility is measured in the same way by all participants (total profit in the cases of Bain and Sylos Labini), no problems arise in determining the entry-deterrent price.

If one supposes that the utility functions of incumbent firms are at some moment of time different from those of potential entrants, matters become more complex. For instance, even with identical cost and demand conditions, rate-of-return maximizers within a market may be unable to deter the entry of discounted sales maximizers who are unworried by the fact that their entry will produce what is an unacceptably low rate of return to a rate-of-return maximizer. In this example, the incumbents are either driven out of the market, or forced to become sales maximizers and adopt an appropriate deterrent strategy; these examples could be proliferated, but in general it will be seen that the barriers theory in its present form survives only in those instances in which the same strategy deters all entrants, whatever their utility function, at the same time as raising the present

---

[1] J. Bain, *Barriers to New Competition* (Harvard U.P., 1956), and P. Sylos Labini *Oligopoly and Technical Progress*, 2nd ed. (Harvard U.P., 1969).

utility of the incumbents above that of the potential entrants. This raises the more general issue of which (if any) utility functions tend to 'dominate' others in the sense of making them non-feasible within particular market structures.

The implications for market behaviour of entry by merger and entry by internal development are very different, which is relevant in the contexts both of a choice of diversification strategy by the firm and of the performance of markets: in both cases, the important difference is that entry by merger leaves the structure of the market (number of and size of producers) initially unaffected. Hence, in assessing the subsequent effects of entry upon market structure and performance, a related question is the extent to which 'barriers' models of oligopoly depend upon the total commitment of the firm to the market in question. It is arguable that a diversified firm stands to lose less by upsetting oligopolistic apple-carts, for example if it regards increasing market share as an important source of growth; the reason is that the diversified firm's loss function enables it in particular markets to undertake more risky strategies for a given expected gain without jeopardizing its total existence in the same way as a single-product firm. This is relevant as long as either diversified firms are the exception rather than the rule, or diversified firms do not parallel each others' product structures, which might lead to the same type of tacit non-competitive behaviour that is observed to prevail in individual markets with single-product firms.

So far the effects of market structure and motivation have been considered with reference only to the short-term operating profit and sales volume of the quasi-firm. Market structure clearly also affects the corporation's cost-of-growth function which specifies expected sales volume and operating profitability over time as a function of the total amount of 'investment' in selling and development costs, given its optimal allocation among existing and potential new markets and optimal strategies for expansion into new markets. It is doubtful whether the relationships involved can be spelt out in any manner that is both detailed and general, but at present this is a neglected area.

Some aspects of Lombardini's paper are connected to this question in that it puts forward 'dynamic' rather than static market models, and raises the question of how these relate to dynamic models of the firm. In the Lintner–Solow analysis, the firm and the market are identical by definition; a dynamic model of the firm is a dynamic model of a market. An oligopolistic world poses more problems: one possible basis might be a function relating changes in market share to selling costs. But a steady-state solution is possible only with constant market shares in the long run, and such a function becomes only the method of reaching them. Since in some way the responses of firms to each others' behaviour must be incorporated in the analysis, it comes to resemble the adjustment process of reaction-curve models.

The relevant question is again what one wishes such a model to explain. Lombardini is concerned with the possibility that 'barriers' models of oligopoly are only valid in the short and medium run, and that over the longer term barriers may be eroded or raised by changes in demand and cost conditions that are partly exogenous and partly induced by business behaviour. But for both the theory of the firm and theories of general equilibrium of the economy, there may be sufficient mileage in the assumption that at any point in time there exists a historically determined 'stochastic' distribution of barriers and profit rates among industries (although the average profit rate requires additional explanation). The causes of the barriers and other structural aspects of any particular market require a detailed historical case study that may be irrelevant for the analysis of the firm or the total economy.

V. GENERAL EQUILIBRIUM OF PRODUCT AND CAPITAL MARKETS

In a world of diversified firms, the analysis of particular markets may be considered no more general than the analysis of particular firms. A truly general analysis would be one in which all firms and markets in the economy were studied. Under special assumptions, general systems of markets may be considered independently of the further relationships between the corporations of whose quasi-firms the markets are composed. Examples of such assumptions are a world of single-product firms, and a world in which all markets behave in the same manner regardless of whether the economic units competing within them are independent atomistic firms or quasi-firms linked in trans-market M-form federations. One has no reason to suppose that these assumptions are generally valid (see Marris, pp. 271–8 below), but without making them, matters become much more complex.

In various ways, the papers in this book by Arrow, Lintner, Lombardini, Marris and Solow are concerned with the analysis of all the firms or markets in the economy in a non-macro-economic fashion. Some attempt will be made here to relate particular aspects of their systems without attempting an exhaustive exposition of any of them.

General systems are ones in which the interdependent results of the decisions of many actors are analysed. General equilibrium systems are a subset of these in which the results of the decisions are mutually compatible, because the constraints on the choice sets and behaviour of decision-makers lead them to appropriate actions. (A special case of this is a model in which the choice set is reduced to a single point in which these points constitute a feasible solution.)

Part of Arrow's paper extends general equilibrium analysis of a static allocation model with profit and utility maximization assumptions. Most previous analyses have been able to demonstrate the existence of an equilibrium solution only when one of the constraints on the choice sets of individual producers was perfect competition, without increasing returns to scale, and with infinitely elastic demand functions and no super-normal profits in any firms. Arrow has provided an existence proof in the case of an economy in which a monopolistically competitive sector exists (in an otherwise perfectly competitive system) with increasing returns to scale and producers facing downward-sloping demand functions.

In the absence of defined demand functions, even the analysis of individual markets becomes more difficult, less rigorous, and particular models are less generally accepted. If 'barriers' and game-theoretic models are a good guide to the direction in which the analysis of oligopolistic markets is developing, it would seem likely that no market model complex and 'realistic' enough to answer all the questions posed from the point of view of the conditions of sale of the product as such could at present form the basis of a general equilibrium allocation analysis along the lines of Arrow's model. Marris does implicitly consider a general static system of oligopolies: in a world in which every oligopolistic market is characterized by a determinate solution in terms of rate of return (as described in the preceding section), corporations are faced with the 'higher-level' decision of which markets to enter. It is not clear under what conditions this system has an equilbrium solution: to know this, one would have to specify the constraints the corporations exercise on each other in terms of comparative advantage in particular markets, absolute size advantages and so forth, in order to determine the network of external profit rates of potential entrants which are given exogenously in the partial analysis of a single market. (An alternative method of incorporating oligopolistic markets into a general allocation system might be to assume that determinate allocative solutions exist in individual markets, and that each market *collectively* behaves like a single monopolistic firm and can therefore be directly incorporated into the Arrow model. Unfortunately, this would appear to require an oligopolistic solution with no super-normal profits.)

In principle there is no reason why general equilibrium systems should not be used to analyse the interrelationships of economic decisions over time. The simplest instance of this is one in which the same commodity in different periods is specified as a set of different commodities and the allocation process as such is unaffected. But it can be argued that this is not a true dynamic system, one in which the time dimension itself plays an important role. Arrow's paper suggests two approaches to 'dynamic general systems'.

In the context of a perfectly competitive allocation system, he considers a two-period case, in which the first-period allocation is a Hicksian 'temporary equilibrium' in which individual decisions are based upon both the 'objective' cost and demand constraints of the current period and expectations of these constraints in the second period. It is pointed out that expectations constrain decisions in a manner different from current market constraints; for example, expectations may be held with certainty and be wrong, or be incompatible with the expectations of other decision-makers. In order to demonstrate the existence of an equilibrium, the nature of the expectations that are held has to be closely bounded.

As suggested above (p. 38), 'temporary equilibrium' is a technique whose application is not restricted either to two periods (although more than two periods complicate the analysis) or to the particular type of allocation problem analysed by Arrow. In the context of systems of growing firms, the present allocation of research funds and selling costs, and the immediate directions of merger and diversification, might be analysed by collapsing future periods of time into a set of expectations.

There is yet another approach to dynamic general systems analysis in which the values of variables are determined over time rather than their values at a single moment being influenced by expectations of the future. To develop such an analysis beyond an intuitive stage is difficult. First one must consider the objective ways in which the actions of individual firms are interrelated: competition for sources of demand, and those 'factors of production' that are exogenously given, and an initial set of comparative and absolute size advantages in terms of product structure. Second, one must specify the mechanism that translates these interrelations into constraints on the decision sets of individual firms: in terms of current models of the corporation, one such constraint is the initial set of quasi-firm sales and operating profit rates. Another constraint, that operates over time, is the form of the cost-of-growth functions of all firms, which is determined by Marris's 'super-environment' which is itself in part the structure of objective interrelationships in the economy. (See p. 57 below for a further discussion of this point.) A different type of constraint is provided by the capital market, or more specifically, the stock market. Since Lintner's paper contains a general equilibrium model of the stock market, it can be discussed in terms of the role it might play in a general model of the economy. (The way in which the stock-market constraint is made to bind, that is to say by the threat of take-over, will be discussed in the next section.)

Lintner's model is general in that it considers all investors in the market, who have exogenously given and different risk and discount functions and initial stocks of wealth. It can also be regarded as a partial equilibrium model in the sense that the decisions of investors are analysed with respect to only one firm. The manner in which it generalizes to all firms depends upon whether or not the cost-of-growth function of each firm adequately reflects its interaction with all other firms. If it does, the investors may make decisions for each firm independent of all other firms, and the model not only generalizes to a temporary equilibrium, but also one in which a (steady-state) general equilibrium exists through time. By contrast, in a situation in which investors *erroneously* believe that they can make decisions on all firms independently, the model is one of temporary equilibrium, but it is not stable through time, because if investors are permitted to change their decisions at subsequent points they will do so, requiring the incorporation of a 'dynamic adjustment' process into the model. If investors believe that they understand the true interdependence structure among firms, and invest accordingly, the model will be one of permanent or temporary equilibrium depending upon whether or not their understanding is correct.

This will be altered in so far as Lintner's assumptions are unfulfilled, although some affect the character rather than the existence of the solution. One assumption whose relaxation may produce tricky problems is perfect competition among investors: although the phenomenon of large investors influencing the market by their decisions is not unknown, it now seems likely that in the near future the market will be dominated by a small number of large institutional investors,[1] which will precipitate the problems that have arisen in the analysis of oligopolistic product markets.

The preceding three paragraphs have suggested that there exists the possibility of a general analysis of a growing economy composed of growing firms and markets: the model might be one in which all economic units were growing at steady rates, or more ambitiously it might attempt the analysis of a less than infinite number of periods by a general system of dynamic adjustments to an initially defined situation. It is not, however, immediately clear what practical or analytical questions such a system would be directed towards answering, and there is a considerable risk that it would turn out to be an exercise in arid formalism.

VI. MACRO-ECONOMIC POSSIBILITIES

In the last thirty years, the analysis of systems of aggregate economic variables has been extensively developed with respect to both short-run income determination and secular economic growth. The relation of such models to the underlying micro-structure of firms, markets and other institutions has never been developed, except in so far as these are implicitly invoked to assist in the determination of exogenous variables and parameters. Not only does this limit understanding of the working of the economy, it also leaves open the question of whether or not existing macro- and micro-models are logically consistent.

This section will discuss three essentially macro-economic ques-

---

[1] This point is developed in an unpublished discussion note by G. C. Archibald, entitled 'Managerial Growth Models'.

tions, two of which have previously been raised by Marris:[1] the effects of corporate structure and motivation on the growth rate of the economy, the determination of the average profit rate, and the causes and effects of changes in the general level of stock prices.

It will be assumed that there exist no problems of measuring growth in real national income of the type associated with the appearance of new and improved products. Two initial simplifying assumptions that will be discussed below are that the economy is composed of one corporation, and that it can manipulate the proportion of national income devoted to 'growth-producing' expenditures. A further element is an 'aggregate cost-of-growth function' that relates increases in output to changes in 'growth-producing' expenditures. If one assumes a benevolent government maintaining full employment of productive capacity, growth-producing expenditures may increase effective supply in a number of ways: changes in output per man-hour or labour-augmenting technical progress may be a function of expenditures on research and development, or on-the-job training, or a higher rate of gross investment in physical capital (increased capital-intensity of production, and embodied technical progress); output per man-year may be additionally changed by the effects of advertising on the work–leisure decision. Hypothetically, one might derive a relation between total expenditures of this kind and increases in capacity. The form of such a function is an open question – it might be analogous to the well-behaved micro cost-of-growth function and exhibit diminishing returns in the growth rate relative to the proportion of income spent on costs of growing. Alternatively, the influences discussed might cause a once-and-for-all shift in the level of income rather than a rise in its permanent growth rate. In practice, a change in the level of income would be non-instantaneous, and probably take place over a long period of time, being observed as a 'temporary' increase in the rate of growth.

But to assume that the aggregate cost-of-growth function can be treated as the same analytical device as the cost-of-growth function of the individual firm is to assume away a very serious aggregation problem: the micro-function describes the rate of shift of the demand curve of the corporation over time as a function of development, selling and other costs. It is certain that part of this shift of demand for one firm can occur at the expense of demand for the products of

[1] *Managerial Capitalism*, chap. 8.

other firms. This could be so simply and directly by merger, or indirectly by reducing the market shares of 'passive' firms or relegating them to slower-growing markets. (The same might be true of whole managerial sectors such as manufacturing which might be growing at the expense of other sectors, including the public sector.) Thus the factor which determines the *form* of the micro cost-of growth function is the existence and behaviour of other firms: it exhibits diminishing returns because other firms are also competing for sources of demand,[1] and presumably the higher the proportion of 'transcendent' firms (those seeking to grow rapidly: see Marris, pp. 278–9) relative to 'immanent' (or passive) firms, the more sharply do returns diminish. In the limiting case in which all firms in the economy are equally 'transcendent' and none enjoys any comparative advantage over any other, the returns to expenditures to shift the demand curve drop to zero at the point at which the corporation is (and hence all corporations are) growing at the same rate as the economy.

Thus even if, for example, faster growth rates of 'managerially' motivated than other corporations could be empirically demonstrated, this might leave the growth rate of the economy unaffected, since the faster growth could be occurring at the expense of other firms. Somehow, in arriving at an aggregate cost-of-growth function, one has to 'net out' most of the influences that determine the micro-function for the individual firm. It is not implausible that some of the influences discussed above make the growth rate of the economy partly endogenously determined by the behaviour of firms. What is implausible is to suppose that individual firms take account directly of the aggregate function. In order to calculate the indirect effects of their individual growth decisions on the whole economy, one is obliged to consider only those expenditures that could possibly influence the aggregate net growth rate, and assess their influence. The problems of such an analysis in practice are obvious.

Leaving these problems for a moment, one may return to the case of the single-firm economy. In this case, a second critical initial assumption was that this firm was able to manipulate the proportion of national income devoted to 'investment' (very broadly defined). In

---

[1] In earlier versions of these growth models (see *Managerial Capitalism*), diminishing returns in this function manifested themselves also as a fall in operating profitability at higher rates of growth owing to 'Penrose effects'. These are essentially a fall in X-efficiency (see H. Leibenstein, 'Allocative Efficiency *vs.* "X-efficiency"', *American Economic Review* (June 1966) for an explanation of this concept).

practice this depends upon the extent of its operating profits, the proportion of them that it can retain, and the amounts it is able to borrow; this evidently leads to consideration of theories of the determination of the macro-economic profit rate, and the stock market as an aggregate constraint. It will be assumed below that we are dealing with .an economy composed solely of large quoted corporations.

It was asserted in a previous section that at any one time the variation of operating profit rates between different markets could be conveniently assumed to be historically or stochastically determined. Even if this is accepted, it leaves unanswered the question of what determines the (weighted) average rate of profit in the economy. One must make a clear distinction in answering this question between operating profits and recorded profits: at present in national income accounts (as in company accounts), fixed plant and equipment is the only cost considered to be 'investment'. Although I am aware of the accounting problems involved in generalizing this category to other types of future-oriented expenditure, I shall assume here that it is macro-economic operating profit that is under discussion. These questions of profit and investment determination may be neatly considered in the framework of the Keynesian or Kaldorian theory of distribution.[1] If one assumes a fixed 'retention ratio' (that is to say a fixed division of the operating profits between dividends and all types of investment) and fixed propensities to save out of earned incomes and distributed profits, the aggregate share of investment can be whatever the corporations wish it to be, because this desire for investment at the same time determines the share and rate of profit. Thus in an aggregate system the investment decisions of the corporations determine the profit rates earned by the quasi-firms. Although this is a long-term theory, short-run variations in corporate investment behaviour may also exert an influence on the 'average' rate of profit earned by quasi-firms through their effects on the level of business activity, unemployment and unplanned excess capacity.[2]

---

[1] See, for example, N. Kaldor, 'A Model of Economic Growth', *Economic Journal* (1957).

[2] In the context of this model, something may be said on the subject of the 'normal' rate of return in a non-competitive economy. One possible sense of 'normal' is 'average', and this problem is resolved by any model of aggregate profit determination. Another possible sense is 'that rate of return which causes neither entry into nor exit out of a market', in which case in equilibrium with

In the Kaldorian theory, because investment determines operating profits, the stock market cannot in any way constrain the aggregate amount of investment. However, if the aggregate rate of profit is determined in some other way (by the 'degree of monopoly' or the 'marginal product of capital') and the retention ratio and saving propensities are variables, then a more elaborate examination of the role of the stock market becomes necessary. At the micro-level, assuming the operating profit of the corporation to be exogenously determined, the operative constraint on the individual corporation with growth-maximizing motives is hypothesized to be the need to choose a growth rate that maintains a minimum stock price or valuation ratio to avoid or reduce the threat of takeover (see Marris, above). If the macro-economic operating profit is also exogenously determined (with respect to investment), the growth rate of the single-firm economy could be subject to a similar constraint, except that by definition there cannot exist the threat of takeover by another firm. Therefore, to avoid both this problem and the aggregation problem discussed above, I shall assume a many-firm economy in which the 'investment' of each firm is constrained by the fear of takeover, and I shall also assume that the relationship is known between all the individual 'investments' and net aggregate 'investment' and growth.

In addition I shall assume: (i) that the long-term weighted average discount rate of the stock market is exogenous with respect to investment (which could be relaxed to some extent without changing much); (ii) that one knows the probability of takeover for every firm in the economy, once one has been told its absolute stock price and the total frequency of takeovers in the stock market; (iii) that all relative stock prices are fixed. Hence the operation of the 'aggregate takeover constraint on growth' depends upon the absolute level of stock prices, the frequency of takeovers in the economy, and their interrelationship. These one can tentatively analyse.

Within the framework of Lintner's model, changes in the general level of stock prices may come about by alteration of the objective growth and profit opportunities facing firms (shifts in the cost-of-growth function or the exogenous operating profit rate) or by changes of investors' outlooks – expectations of growth and profit

---

barriers to entry *every* industry average profit rate is a normal rate: the difference from a competitive economy is that the profit rates of marginal firms in all industries are not necessarily equal.

opportunities, risk-aversion, discount rate and 'stock-price multiple' – or both, possibly not independently. As a consequence of my assumption about the long-term discount rate in the preceding paragraph, I shall assert that the secular level of stock prices is determined by 'objective' factors while short-term fluctuations are caused by changes in investors' outlooks plus speculative cumulative effects – the expectation of expectations.

Empirically there is a strong positive correlation between the level of stock prices and the aggregate amount of mergers and takeovers. On the face of it, causation may run in either or both directions or no causation may be involved, since both variables are independently influenced by some excluded variable such as the level of economic activity, or expectations of growth. A short-term positive effect of an increase in the number of mergers, especially by tender offer, on the level of stock prices is very plausible since it increases the probability that investors will be able to sell stock at above the market price (whatever that price may be).   At first sight, causation the other way is less plausible, since higher stock prices, *ceteris paribus*, should be associated with lower rather than higher merger rates.

But other things are evidently *not* equal; real underlying variables (the rate of growth, the level of economic activity) have independent effects on the level of stock prices and the motives for merger. They change investors' expectations of the growth and profitability of corporations and hence expected dividends and stock prices. They also increase businessmen's expectations of gain from mergers and at given stock prices would raise the number of mergers. These two effects evidently pull the number of mergers, and hence the height of the minimum stock-price constraint, in different directions. Empirically it would seem that the incentive to business is stronger, and hence the number of mergers changes positively rather than negatively with business conditions. This might be taken to imply the existence of a stabilizing mechanism constraining the economy to a particular rate of growth: above it, expectations are such that an increase in the number of mergers raises the minimum stock-price constraint, and vice versa for a lower growth rate. But this is a stabilizing mechanism that has been hypothesized to exist only in a world closely bounded by restrictive assumptions.

VII. NORMATIVE EVALUATION OF THE CORPORATE ECONOMY

(a) General

It is proposed to discuss briefly a few ways in which the performance of the corporate economy may be evaluated. Only economic causes of welfare will be considered, to the exclusion of the political and social influence of the large corporation. Although several dimensions of economic welfare can be distinguished – static allocative efficiency, intertemporal allocation, X-efficiency,[1] stability and distribution – this section will deal with only the first three of these. Static and intertemporal allocation are discussed below separately; some matters common to both receive immediate attention.

The two crucial ingredients of any evaluation of the economy are a yardstick of welfare, and a positive description of the operation of the economy that can be measured against the yardstick. These are not always independent in practice; for example, consumer sovereignty in a market economy is associated with both a yardstick and a positive theory. The choice among yardsticks of welfare lies broadly between following the tastes of individuals and imposing a Platonic social welfare function embodying 'higher' values. The conference devoted some time to discussing the problems that arise in the evaluation of corporate capitalist economies in terms of sovereign consumer welfare. The principal subjects of debate were the malleability of tastes, ignorance and externalities.

If changes in tastes are induced by changes in production – the emergence of new products or the advertising of old ones – changes in welfare can no longer be meaningfully assessed by observing changes in consumer behaviour.[2] But it can be argued that observed

[1] See Leibenstein, op. cit.

[2] But although consumer sovereignty as a criterion of welfare is damaged or destroyed, this does not necessarily make determinate analysis of consumption and production impossible. If supply and demand functions are not independent, the achievement of a determinate solution for price and output requires the introduction of additional functional relationships, for example a function specifying the costs of 'manipulating' demand by varying amounts. Decreasing returns in this may arise not only from residual elements of consumer non-malleability but also from the activities of other firms attempting to achieve the same ends. This is clearly a function similar to the 'cost-of-growth' function discussed above, in this case applied to the product or market rather than the firm. There are also analogies with Arrow's description of the 'parable-like' relation between static and dynamic models of the firm (see p. 58 above, and Arrow, p. 71 below).

'induced taste changes' are in fact quite different phenomena. The most sophisticated such explanation defines tastes in 'characteristic' rather than commodity space, and explains the observed consumption of new commodities as superior methods of satisfying (stable) tastes for characteristics.[1] The fixity of tastes then becomes an empirical issue; its investigation is complicated in practice and principle by other factors. First, even if all individuals have stable tastes (in either space), the proportions of individuals with different tastes may change as a result of alterations in sex and age structure and the relative sizes of social classes. Second, changes may take place in the tastes of individuals that are quite exogenous to the production process; consumer sovereignty survives, even if the evaluation of the extent of changes in welfare becomes impossible. Third, consumer ignorance and changes in its extent complicate the interpretation of changes in revealed preference: movements of or along the consumption possibility frontier have to be separated from movements within it. In this connection it is argued that both rapid product innovation and advertising generate ignorance, partly incidentally, partly intentionally.[2]

A more fundamental critique that is related to this last point rejects the idea of a defined set of tastes in any space, and regards consumption as a learning process characterized by irreversibilities which preclude comparison of the welfare of an individual at different points in time.[3] Alternative possible welfare criteria that emerge from this approach relate to the rate at which the learning process takes place, influenced both by movements towards the frontier and movements of the frontier itself.

On the subject of the external diseconomies alleged to be associated with economic growth,[4] it was suggested that pollution,

---

[1] This idea, first developed by K. J. Lancaster in 'A New Approach to Consumer Theory', *Journal of Political Economy* (1966) and 'Change and Innovation in the Technology of Consumption', *American Economic Review, Papers and Proceedings* (May 1966), was brought to the attention of the conference in an unpublished paper by G. C. Archibald, entitled 'Some Welfare Implications'. See also W. J. Baumol, 'Calculation of Optimal Product and Retailer Characterisics: The Abstract Product Approach', *Journal of Political Economy* (1967), and R. E. Quandt and Baumol, 'The Demand for Abstract Transport Modes: Theory and Measurement', *Journal of Regional Science* (1966).

[2] This case was strongly argued by Professor Carl Kaysen in the opening session of the preliminary conference for Phase II of this project: see the Prefatory Note above.

[3] See especially Marris, *Managerial Capitalism*, chap. 4.

[4] See E. J. Mishan, *The Costs of Economic Growth* (London, 1967).

congestion and so forth are in fact concomitants not of a high rate of growth as such but of high levels of income. The justification for restricting growth in order to alleviate them must rest on the premise that during the postponement of higher levels of income, more effective mechanisms of social control would be developed.

(b) Static allocative and X-efficiency

An initial simplifying assumption is to hold constant all market structures and the behaviour of quasi-firms and thus control two possible sources of misallocation. It may then be asked how the allocative and X-efficiency of a world of independent single-product firms compares with one in which they are the quasi-firms of conglomerate corporations.

Williamson argues that the achievement of allocative and X-efficiency is not cost-free, in that it requires elaborate evaluation and control procedures: not only do these exhibit economies of scale up to the point where 'control loss'[1] develops in very large firms, but the conglomerate firm's internal evaluation and allocation system allocates funds towards more profitable markets far more effectively than the imprecise, discontinuous and poorly informed control that the stock market exercises on single-product firms. A world of large conglomerate firms may therefore be more efficient than one of atomistic firms.

There are other influences that may lead to conglomeration, and it is less clear which, if any, of these impart social rather than private economies; certain types of risk may encourage diversification, as may tax and other institutional incentives, and 'economies of scale' in the capital markets, and in marketing and selling expenditures.

Retaining constant market structure, what effects do quasi-firms' motivations other than profit maximization have upon efficiency? Since the one-period 'temporary equilibrium' decision rules corresponding to various long-term strategies are not well developed (see pp. 38, and 42 above), in the static context only a limited range of alternative assumptions may be discussed. Sales maximization can only improve allocation by reducing or eliminating monopolistic restrictions of output. 'Behaviourist' motivation may have a number

[1] Control loss is the breakdown in accuracy of transmitting information through several layers of an organization: see Williamson, p. 345 below.

of effects; leisure preference and similar behaviour will produce a welfare loss through X-inefficiency; 'optimally imperfect' decisions, however, may be socially as well as privately optimal in an uncertain world; 'satisficing', if there is X-efficient production, may reduce monopolistic restriction of output. If expense preference raises average cost it further restricts output: it may or may not be regarded as X-efficient behaviour. If expense is regarded as an element of cost it is X-inefficient: if it is regarded as disguised profit, expense preference may be compatible with X-efficient minimization of other costs. In this context it must be noted that Williamson believes that the M-form firm spends less on expense than other forms of corporation.

So far the assumption of given market structures has been made, but the effects of conglomeration and different motivation on market structure are themselves important in making this type of evaluation. Nothing very conclusive can be said on the basis of existing theory, although Lombardini draws attention to some of the relationships involved.

(c) Inter-temporal allocative and X-efficiency

Evidently there exists a choice between increasing output by expending resources on improving static allocative efficiency, raising X-efficiency, and growth. As far as growth is concerned, it is necessary to distinguish the welfare of different growth rates from the most efficient or minimum-cost manner of achieving them.

It has been argued by Marris, Williamson, Galbraith[1] and others that the large diversified corporation is a more efficient vehicle of economic growth than small atomized firms. The underlying rationale is economies of scale in planning and forecasting, in deployment and control of resources to exploit opportunities, and in the crucial development phase of innovation that converts the invention of the individual or small firm into a widely diffused working product. It is also possible that where the social return to expenditures on research and development is higher than the private return, growth- and sales-maximizing firms may make more nearly socially optimal expenditures than valuation-maximizing firms, which will invest only up to the point at which marginal discounted expected profit is zero.

It is less clear how the aggregate rate of growth of a corporate

---

[1] J. K. Galbraith, *The New Industrial State* (Boston, 1967).

economy along the lines discussed in section VI of the survey should be evaluated (assuming that tastes are not malleable and thus that the commodity composition of growth is not 'distorted'). For a given super-environment, the growth rate of *valuation-maximizing* corporations is constrained by the weighted discount rates of investors, appropriately modified by their risk functions. Whether what is an optimal growth rate for investors is an optimal growth rate for 'society' is an open question,[1] since there are evidently the immense externalities of the effects of growth on non-investors (one such may be the results of induced changes in the work-leisure trade-off caused by advertising and so on, unless we assume that consumer sovereignty also includes non-malleable tastes for leisure). In the more general case in which corporations are not valuation-maximizing, and the discount functions of investors are not a binding constraint, the rate of growth depends upon the 'propensity to take over' of corporations themselves, and one is left without any immediate means of evaluation of the growth rate so achieved.

VIII. CONCLUSION

The general question which this paper set out to investigate was 'What is the impact of new theories of the firm upon economic analysis?' In an oblique way, by picking on a range of subjects scattered rather broadly through economics, I hope that I have provided some elements of an answer.

Although it would be foolish to reject the possibility of a sweeping revolution in economics in which a new theory of business behaviour played a crucial role, I believe that at this stage this is not the most fruitful light in which to regard these models of the firm. The most important development must be to extract the ideas which they contain from the sealed box labelled 'New Theories of the Firm', and try to use the ideas, piecemeal, in improving the answers to a wide range of specific analytical and practical questions. It would be absurd to attempt to build a 'complete new' model of the economy without inquiring into its purposes – as absurd, in fact, as attempting to list all the questions that economics should ask and designing a grand model to answer them.

[1] Possible divergences exist both between 'social' and 'private' riskless discount rates, and between social and private loss functions in the evaluation of risk.

As far as specific questions and answers are concerned, I have attempted to provide some examples in this paper of ways in which the new concepts available may be applied, in one form or another. Many of my examples are of rather general subjects, some conventional and familiar, others less so. I imagine that most applications would deal with much more specific subjects. But in no case have I done more than sketch possibilities in a rather superficial way; some of these might turn out to be blind alleys if one really looked thoroughly at them. Others might possibly reward more serious investigation.

3 The Firm in General Equilibrium Theory

Kenneth J. Arrow

I. INTRODUCTION

In classical theory, from Smith to Mill, fixed coefficients in production are assumed. In such a context, the individual firm plays little role in the general equilibrium of the economy. The scale of any one firm is indeterminate, but the demand conditions determine the scale of the industry and the demand by the industry for inputs. The firm's role is purely passive, and no meaningful boundaries between firms are established. No doubt the firm or the entrepreneur was much discussed and indeed given a central role in the informal parts of the discussion; the role was that of overcoming disequilibria. When profit rates were unequal, profit-hungry entrepreneurs moved quickly, with the end-result of eliminating their functions.

When Walras first gave explicit formulation to the grand vision of general equilibrium, he took over intact the fixed-coefficient assumptions and therewith the passive nature of the firm. In the last quarter of the nineteenth century, J. B. Clark, Wicksteed, Barone, and Walras himself recognized the possibility of alternative production activities in the form of the production function. However, so long as constant returns to scale were assumed, the size of the firm remained indeterminate. The firm did have now, even in equilibrium, a somewhat more active role than in earlier theory; it at least had the responsibility of minimizing costs at given output levels.

There were other economists, however, who were interested in the theory of the firm as such, the earliest being Cournot (1838). Anyone with an elementary knowledge of calculus and a theory that firms are maximizing profits under competitive conditions is led without thinking to the hypothesis of increasing marginal costs or diminishing returns to scale. As Cournot also knew, firms may be monopolists as well as competitors; and in those circumstances, profit maximization is compatible with increasing returns to scale.

As in other aspects of economics, both of these somewhat contradictory tendencies appear in Marshall's welter of imprecise insights. It would be tedious to follow the subsequent discussions of laws of return and their relation to competitive or other equilibrium, carried on intermittently by such authors as Wicksell, Pareto, Robertson, Sraffa, Shove, and Viner (with the famous assistance of Y. K. Wong). Among the literary economists in the Anglo-American tradition, a kind of orthodoxy has emerged, in the U-shaped cost curve for the firm plus free entry. In more modern language, the production possibility set of the typical firm displays an initial tendency toward increasing returns followed at higher scales by decreasing returns. The first phase is explained by indivisibilities, the second by the decreasing ability of the entrepreneur to control the firm. As one may put it, entrepreneurship should also be regarded as an input to the firm; then, after the initial phase at least, the firm would have constant returns to all inputs (including entrepreneurship), but, since by definition the firm has only one entrepreneur, there are diminishing returns to all other factors. (The indivisibility of the entrepreneur is sometimes invoked to explain the initial phase also, though of course there are typically also indivisibilities of a more definitely technological variety.) The assumption of free entry implies that the supply of entrepreneurship in the economy is infinite, or, more precisely that it is sufficiently large that its demand price will fall to zero at a point at which supply still exceeds demand.

The exact relation of this model of the firm to a full general equilibrium model has never been explored; in particular, the notion of an infinite supply of entrepreneurship is no more reasonable than that of an infinite supply of anything else.

The first mathematical model of general equilibrium was the work of Wald, summarized in Wald (1936), though some of the basic considerations in the model were suggested to him by K. Schlesinger (1933–4). In Wald's work, to the extent that production was involved at all, fixed coefficients were assumed. After the mathematical tools available had been greatly improved by von Neumann and others as part of the development of game theory, more general models were developed by McKenzie (1954) and Arrow and Debreu (1954). The best systematic account is that of Debreu (1959); detailed improvements are found in Debreu (1962) and a somewhat different viewpoint in McKenzie (1959).

The treatment of the firm in Arrow–Debreu is unchanged in

Debreu's later work. The set of firms is regarded as fixed. It should be noted, though, that a firm might find it most profitable to produce nothing; hence, what is ordinarily called entry here appears as a change from zero to positive outputs levels. The production possibility sets of the firms are assumed to be convex. This assumption excludes the possibility of an initial phase of increasing returns; it is compatible with either constant or diminishing returns to scale. The treatment of entrepreneurship in the model can then be interpreted in several ways. The most natural is to assume that entrepreneurship *per se* is not included in the list of commodities. Then where there are constant returns, entrepreneurship is not a factor of production, or, alternatively, it is not scarce. However, diminishing returns plus a finite fixed set of (potential) firms imply scarcity of entrepreneurship and positive pure profits. In this interpretation, too, we are not constrained to identify entrepreneurship as being supplied by any particular set of individuals; the diminishing returns can inhere in the operating properties of the organization.

Alternatively, we can assume that entrepreneurial resources are included among the list of commodities and are supplied by specific individuals. This is McKenzie's assumption (1959); he completes it naturally by assuming constant returns to scale in all commodities. Then firms are distinguished by their needs for specific entrepreneurial resources (it is not assumed that entrepreneurship for one firm is necessarily the same as for another) and are limited in scale by the limitations on these resources.

The two models differ in their implications for income distribution. The Arrow–Debreu model creates a category of pure profits which are distributed to the owners of the firm; it is not assumed that the owners are necessarily the entrepreneurs or managers. Since profit maximization is assumed, conflict of interest between the organization or its management, on the one hand, and the owners on the other, is assumed always to be resolved in favor of the owners. The model is sufficiently flexible, however, to permit the managers to be included among the owners.

In the McKenzie model, on the other hand, the firm makes no pure profits (since it operates at constant returns); the equivalent of profits appears in the form of payments for the use of entrepreneurial resources, but there is no residual category of owners who receive profits without rendering either capital or entrepreneurial services.

Several writers, especially Farrell (1959) and Rothenberg (1960), have argued that 'small' non-convexities, such as a limited initial phase of increasing returns, are compatible with an 'approximate' equilibrium, i.e. one in which discrepancies between supply and demand are small relative to the size of the market. Hence, the U-shaped cost curve is not basically incompatible with competitive general equilibrium theory, though so far there has been no rigorous development of the relations.

Substantial increasing returns to the firm, on the other hand, are obviously incompatible with the existence of a perfectly competitive equilibrium. It is of course in situations like this that monopolies arise. The theory of the profit-maximizing monopoly in a single market was developed in its essentials by Cournot and has been developed further only on secondary points, the most important of which has been the possibility of price disciimination. But, apart from some remarks in Pareto, the first serious discussions of monopoly in a general equilibrium context are those of J. Robinson (1933) and Chamberlin (1956, originally published 1933). The formulation of an explicit model of general equilibrium with monopolistic elements will be discussed in section III below.

In static theories of general equilibrium and in the absence of monopoly, then, the individual firm has been characterized by diminishing returns, a phenomenon associated with the vague concept of entrepreneurship. Kalecki (1939, chapter 4) suggested long ago that the reasons for limitation on the size of the firm might be found in dynamic rather than static considerations. Recent years have seen the beginning of dynamic analysis of the firm (especially Penrose (1959) and Marris (1964)). From the point of view of realism and of interpretation of observations, these are a major advance. But on the production side they still retain the basic structure of the static model, restated in dynamic terms. Specifically, while returns to scale are constant in the long run, there are diminishing returns to the rate of growth, which plays the same role as scale does in a static model. (This view of attaching costs to rates of change has also been urged by some of those close to operations research; see, *inter alios* Hoffman and Jacobs (1954); Holt, Modigliani, Muth and Simon (1960, pp. 52–3); Arrow, Karlin and Scarf (1958, p. 22).) Hence, the analysis of stationary states of the dynamic system has strong formal resemblance to purely static analysis; or, to put the matter the other way, static analysis remains useful provided it is interpreted parabolically rather than literally.

CE D

However, dynamic analysis may have deeper implications if we depart from the analysis of stationary states. The firm must now serve some additional roles. In the absence of futures markets, the firm must serve as a forecaster and as a bearer of uncertainty. Further, from a general equilibrium point of view, the forecasts of others become relevant to the evaluation of the firm's shares and therefore possibly of the firm's behavior. The general equilibrium to be analyzed is, in the first instance, the equilibrium of a moment, *temporary equilibrium* in the terminology of Hicks.

Some of these topics will be discussed below; for others, only open questions can be mentioned. The analysis will always concern itself with the existence of equilibrium under each of varying sets of assumptions. Existence of equilibrium is of interest in itself; certainly a minimal property a model purporting to describe an economic system ought to have is consistency. In practice, the development of conditions needed to insure the existence of equilibrium turns out in many cases to be very revealing; until one has to construct an existence proof, the relevance of many of these conditions is not obvious.

The proofs will not be presented in detail, but their general outlines will be indicated. In section II, a sketch will first be given of a proof of existence of competitive equilibrium under standard assumptions. In section III, a model of monopolistic competitive equilibrium will be presented and analyzed for existence; this will display the role of the firm as price-maker. In section IV, the existence of temporary equlilibrium and its preconditions are discussed. More detailed proofs of the results of these sections will be found in Arrow and Hahn (forthcoming, chap. vi, sections 4 and 3 respectively).

II. THE EXISTENCE OF GENERAL COMPETITIVE EQUILIBRIUM

Since proofs of existence of equilibrium in more extended contexts start from the methods used in the perfectly competitive case, it is indispensable to indicate the main lines of the proof in that case. Although it would doubtless be possible to use the proofs of Debreu or McKenzie (cited above) as starting-points, I have in fact used a new form of the proof which will appear in Arrow and Hahn (forthcoming, chaps. iii–v).

First, we list the assumptions made. Production is assumed

organized in firms; let Y_f be the production possibility set for firm f with typical element y_f.

(i) Y_f is a closed convex set, and 0 belongs to Y_f. The last clause means that a firm can go out of existence.

(ii) If $\sum_f y_f \geqq 0$ and y_f belongs to Y_f, all f, then $y_f = 0$, all f. (To assert that a vector is non-negative means that each element is non-negative.)

To see the meaning of (ii), note first that if $\sum_f y_f \geqq 0$ but not $\sum_f y_f = 0$ then the productive sector as a whole is supplying positive amounts of some goods with no inputs, a physical impossibility. If $\sum_f y_f = 0$ but not all y's are 0, then some firms are in effect undoing the productive activity of others. If we assume that there are some inputs such as labor that are not produced by any firm, then such cancellation is impossible.

In view of (ii), production is possible only if the economy has some initial supply of non-produced commodities; let $\bar{x}$ be this vector of initial endowments. We now assume that with the initial endowment it is possible to have a positive net output of all commodities, that is, we can use part but less than all of each initially available commodity to produce something of each produced commodity after netting out interindustry flows.

(iii) It is possible to choose $\bar{y}_f$ from Y_f for each f so that the net output vector, $\sum_f \bar{y}_f + \bar{x}$, has positive components for all commodities.

Among the three production assumptions, really only the convexity assumed in (i) can be regarded as dubious.

By a *production allocation* will be meant a specification of $y_f \in Y_f$ for each f. By a *feasible production allocation* will be meant a production allocation which does not require more net inputs than are available from the initial endowment:

$$\sum_f y_f + \bar{x} \geqq 0.$$

Then it is possible to demonstrate from (i) and (ii) that
the set of feasible production allocations is convex, closed, and bounded.

To discuss the assumptions about consumers, let X_h be the set of consumption vectors possible to household h. For present purposes, it can simply be regarded as the set of all non-negative vectors where leisure is taken as one good. (A somewhat more complicated description is required to take care of the possibility that an individual may be capable of offering more than one kind of labor.)

(iv) X_h is closed and convex and contains only non-negative vectors. Each household is assumed to possess some part of society's initial endowment, say $\bar{\mathbf{x}}_h$.

A somewhat technical assumption is needed to insure that in a certain sense households can make choices without any trade and even without using all of whatever initial endowment they possess.

(v) For each h, there exists $\bar{\bar{\mathbf{x}}}_h \, \epsilon \, X_h$, such that $0 \leqq \bar{\bar{\mathbf{x}}}_h \leqq \bar{\mathbf{x}}_h$; further, any positive component of $\bar{\mathbf{x}}_h$ is also a positive component of $\bar{\mathbf{x}}_h - \bar{\bar{\mathbf{x}}}_h$.

If we take X_h to be the set of non-negative vectors, then $\bar{\bar{\mathbf{x}}}_h$ can be taken equal to $\mathbf{0}$.

The final assumption about the consumer is the usual one about the continuity and convexity of consumer preferences.

(vi) The preferences of household h can be represented by a continuous utility function, $U_h\,(\mathbf{x}_h)$, with the following convexity property (referred to as *semi-strict quasi-concavity*): if $\mathbf{x}_h^1$ and $\mathbf{x}_h^2$ are consumption vectors such that $U_h(\mathbf{x}_h^1) > U_h(\mathbf{x}_h^2)$ and if α is a scalar, $0 < \alpha \leqq 1$, then $U_h[\alpha \mathbf{x}_h^1 + (1-\alpha)\mathbf{x}_h^2] > U_h(\mathbf{x}_h^2)$. Further, assume that there is no satiation in all commodities simultaneously, i.e. for every $x_h^1 \, \epsilon \, X_h$, there exists $\mathbf{x}_h^2 \, \epsilon \, X_h$ for which $U_h^2(\mathbf{x}_h) > U_h^1(\mathbf{x}_h)$.

The convexity condition implies that indifference surfaces are convex but not necessarily strictly so (thus, they may possess flat segments); however, there are no 'thick' bands in which all sufficiently close vectors are indifferent. Permitting flat segments on the indifference surfaces is necessary if one is to avoid assuming that all commodities enter directly into each household's utility function. The non-satiation condition is consistent with satiation in any specific commodity or group of commodities.

Assumption (vi) is restrictive, but the consequences of dropping it do not appear to be severe. If it is assumed that the endowment of no household is large relative to total endowment, then the discontinuities of individual household demand functions relative to the economy as a whole are small, and so the Farrell–Rothenberg argument shows that equilibrium is approximately attained; a fully rigorous version for the case of a pure exchange economy is to be found in Starr (1969).

Finally, we need an assumption about the relation between the initial endowment held by a household and the possibility of its improving someone's welfare. A given household, h', holds some commodities initially in positive amount and others in zero amount. Call that set of commodities the h'-*assets*. Now consider any allocation of resources to firms and households which is feasible for the given endowment vector. Such an allocation defines a *utility allocation*, a specification of the utility level of each household. Now suppose that some increase in society's endowment of h'-assets, all other components of the initial endowment remaining constant, permits a new resource allocation in which every household is at least as well off and household h'' better off. If this improvement is possible starting from any feasible allocation, then household h' is said to be *resource-related* to household h''.

A weaker relation between two households is the following: household h' is said to be *indirectly resource-related* to household h'' if there exists some chain of households, beginning with h' and ending with h'', such that each household in the chain is resource-related to its successor. We now assume:

(vii) Every household is indirectly resource-related to every other. (This definition is related to, but not identical with, that of irreducibility of the economy in McKenzie (1959) and (1961), and it generalizes assumptions introduced by Arrow and Debreu (1954, pp. 279–81, assumptions VI and VII).)

This assumption is very weak; each household is assumed to have something to offer the market which is valuable to someone, who in turn is similarly linked to someone else, and so forth till everyone is reached. Certainly in an advanced economy, it can easily be accepted.

The income of the household, available for its consumption, derives in general from two sources: the sale of its endowment and its share of the profits of firms. Since we are assuming convexity but not necessarily constant returns to scale, it is possible for firms to have positive profits even at equilibrium. It is therefore assumed that each household h has the right to a share, d_{hf}, in the profits of firm f. Necessarily,

$$d_{hf} \geqq 0, \quad \sum_h d_{hf} = 1 \text{ for all } f. \tag{1}$$

Then the income of the household is defined by

$$M_h = \mathbf{p}\,\bar{\mathbf{x}}_h + \sum_f d_{hf}\,(\mathbf{p}\,\mathbf{y}_f), \tag{2}$$

since the profits of firm f are defined by $\mathbf{p}\,\mathbf{y}_f$.

We now state formally the usual definition of competitive equilibrium:

D.1. A price vector $\mathbf{p}^*$ and an allocation $(\mathbf{x}_h^*, \mathbf{y}_f^*)$ constitute a competitive equilibrium if the following conditions are satisfied:

(a) $\mathbf{p}^* \geqq 0$ but $\mathbf{p}^* \neq 0$;

(b) $\sum_h \mathbf{x}_h^* \leqq \sum_h \bar{\mathbf{x}}_h + \sum_f \mathbf{y}^*$;

(c) $\mathbf{y}_f^*$ maximizes $\mathbf{p}^* \mathbf{y}_f$ subject to $\mathbf{y}_f \in Y_f$;

(d) $\mathbf{x}_h^*$ maximizes $U_h(\mathbf{x}_h)$ subject to $\mathbf{x}_h \in X_h$, $\mathbf{p}^* \, \mathbf{x}_h$
$$\leqq \mathbf{p}^* \bar{\mathbf{x}}_h + \sum_f d_{hf} (\mathbf{p}^* \, \mathbf{y}_f^*) = M_h^*.$$

It turns out that the demand functions of the consumer defined implicitly by (d) can be discontinuous if prices approach a limit at which $M_h^* = 0$. It is convenient first to introduce a slightly different and weaker definition of competitive equilibrium, prove its existence, and then show that under the assumptions made (particularly (vii)) it also satisfies the conditions of D.1. The new definition amounts to replacing the uncompensated demand functions of D.1 by compensated demand functions, i.e. the consumer's choice is that of minimizing the cost of achieving a given utility level. The relation between the two is the following: a demand vector which maximizes utility under a given budget constraint certainly minimizes the cost of achieving the resulting utility; but a demand vector which minimizes the cost of achieving some stated utility also maximizes utility without spending more if the amount spent is positive (but not in general if $M_h = 0$).

D.2. The price vector, $\mathbf{p}^*$, utility allocation (u_h^*) and allocation $(\mathbf{x}_h^*, \mathbf{y}_f^*)$ is a *compensated equilibrium* if:

(a) $\mathbf{p}^* \geqq 0$ but $\mathbf{p}^* \neq \mathbf{0}$;

(b) $\sum_h \mathbf{x}_h^* \leqq \sum_h \bar{\mathbf{x}}_h + \sum_f \mathbf{y}_f^*$;

(c) $\mathbf{y}_f^*$ maximizes $\mathbf{p}^* \, \mathbf{y}_f$ subject to $\mathbf{y}_f \in Y_f$;

(d) $\mathbf{x}_h^*$ minimizes $\mathbf{p}^* \, \mathbf{x}_h$ subject to $U_h (\mathbf{x}_h) \geqq u_h^*$;

(e) $\mathbf{p}^* \, \mathbf{x}_h^* = M_h^*$.

From the previous remarks, we can note:

Lemma 1. If $(\mathbf{p}^*, \mathbf{x}_h^*, \mathbf{y}_f^*)$ constitute a competitive equilibrium and $u_h^* = U_h (\mathbf{x}_h^*)$, all h, then $(\mathbf{p}^*, u_h^*, \mathbf{x}_h^*, \mathbf{y}_f^*)$ constitute a compensated equilibrium. If $(\mathbf{p}^*, u_h^*, \mathbf{x}_h^*, \mathbf{y}_h^*)$ constitute a compensated equilibrium and if $M_h^* > 0$, all h, then $(\mathbf{p}^*, u_h^*, \mathbf{x}_h^*, \mathbf{y}_f^*)$ constitute a competitive equilibrium.

Hence, to establish the existence of a competitive equilibrium, it suffices to establish the existence of a compensated equilibrium such that $M_h^* > 0$, all h. Two of the conditions stated above together are sufficient to insure this.

Lemma 2. If assumptions (iii) and (vii) hold, then $M_h^* > 0$, all h, at a compensated equilibrium, so that it is also a competitive equilibrium.

The argument runs roughly as follows: At a compensated equilibrium, firms are maximizing profits, by D.2(c). Since the firm can always shut down, by assumption (i), equilibrium profits must be non-negative, so that, from (2),

$$M_h^* \geqq 0, \text{ all } h. \tag{3}$$

Also, from profit maximization,

$$\mathbf{p}^* \, \mathbf{y}_f^* \geqq \mathbf{p}^* \, \bar{\mathbf{y}}_f,$$

where $\bar{\mathbf{y}}_f$ is the output–input vector for firm f referred to in assumption (iii). Sum over firms f and add $\mathbf{p}^* \, \bar{\mathbf{x}}$; from (2),

$$\sum_h M_h^* = \sum_h (\mathbf{p}^* \, \bar{\mathbf{x}}_h) + \sum_f \sum_h d_{hf} (\mathbf{p}^* \, \mathbf{y}_f^*)$$
$$= \mathbf{p}^* \, \bar{\mathbf{x}} + \sum_f (\mathbf{p}^* \mathbf{y}_f^*) \geqq \mathbf{p}^* (\bar{\mathbf{x}} + \sum_f \bar{\mathbf{y}}_f),$$

since $\sum_h d_{hf} = 1$, by (1). But from (iii), all the components of $\bar{\mathbf{x}} + \sum_f \bar{\mathbf{y}}^f$ are positive, while from D.2(a), all components of $\mathbf{p}^*$ are non-negative and at least one positive. Hence,

$$\sum_h M_h^* > 0,$$

which implies

$$M_h^* > 0 \text{ for some } h = h'', \text{ say.} \tag{4}$$

Suppose household h' is resource-related to household h''. Then the assets held by h' are valuable to h'', in the sense that its utility could be made to increase if the h'-assets increased; also h'' has an effective demand, since it has a positive income. It is then reasonable to assert and can be proved rigorously that at least one of the h'-assets must command a positive price. But this means, from (2), that $M_h^* > 0$ for $h = h'$. In turn that implies that $M_h^* > 0$ for any h

resource-related to h'. Continuing in this way leads to the conclusion that $M_h^* > 0$ for any h indirectly resource-related to h''; but by (vii), that includes every household, so that Lemma 2 holds.

We can therefore confine attention to the existence of a compensated equilibrium. One possible way of proceeding is to make use of the familiar relations between the competitive price system and Pareto efficiency. To simplify the discussion, we use some notation: an allocation (x_h, y_f) will be abbreviated to w. The set of all possible allocations will be denoted by W; the set of *feasible allocations* to be denoted by $\hat{W}$; are those for which

$$\sum_h x_h \leqq \bar{x} + \sum_f y_f.$$

Clearly, if $w = (x_h, y_f)$ is a feasible allocation, then (y_f) is a feasible production allocation, since $x_h \geqq 0$, all h. As noted earlier, the set of feasible production allocations is closed, bounded, and convex; from this, it is immediate that

$\hat{W}$, the set of feasible allocations, is closed, bounded
and convex.   (5)

Any feasible allocation $w = (x_h, y_f)$ determines a utility level, $u_h = U_h(x_h)$ for each household. The numbers (u_h) taken as a vector will be termed a *utility allocation*, denoted by u. We define a *Pareto-efficient utility allocation* in a slight variation of the usual manner:

D.3. The utility allocation u is Pareto-efficient if there is no other (feasible) utility allocation, u', such that $u_h' > u_h$ for all h.

By the basic theorem of welfare economics, there is associated with each Pareto-efficient utility allocation, u^0, a price vector, p^0 and a feasible allocation, $w^0 = (x_h^0, y_f^0)$, such that:

(a) $p^0 \geqq 0$, $p^0 \neq 0$;

(b) x_h^0 minimizes the cost, $p^0 x_h$, of achieving a utility level, $U_h(x_h)$, at least equal to u_h^0;

(c) y_f^0 maximizes profits, $p^0 y_f$, among production vectors in Y_f;

(d) aggregate expenditure equals aggregate income, i.e.
$$\sum_h p^0 x_h^0 = \sum_h p^0 \bar{x}_h + \sum_f p^0 y_f^0.$$

Actually, when there are constant returns to scale and/or production possibility sets formed from finitely many basic activities (the linear programming model), it is not difficult to see that the price vectors and allocations realizing an efficient utility allocation may not be unique. Thus we can state in formal language:

Lemma 3. For every Pareto-efficient utility allocation, $\mathbf{u}^0$, there is a set of prices, $P(\mathbf{u}^0)$, and a set of feasible allocations, $\hat{W}(\mathbf{u}^0)$, such that (a)–(d) above hold for every p^0 in $P(\mathbf{u}^0)$ and w in $\hat{W}(\mathbf{u}^0)$.

Notice that every price vector in $P(\mathbf{u}^0)$ supports every allocation in $\hat{W}(\mathbf{u}^0)$. It is not hard to observe from this that the sets $P(\mathbf{u}^0)$ and $\hat{W}(\mathbf{u}^0)$ are convex sets.

The lemma associates with each utility vector a set of prices (and similarly a set of allocations). This relation generalizes the usual concept of a function, which associates a number or vector with each vector. A relation which associates a set to each vector is sometimes termed a set-valued function, sometimes a *correspondence*; we follow Debreu (1959, sections 1.3, 1.8) in using the latter term here. The concept of continuity is important in dealing with ordinary functions; we will need a generalization of it here.

D.4. A correspondence, which associates the set $\Phi(\mathbf{x})$ to the vector $\mathbf{x}$, is said to be *upper semi-continuous* (*u.s.c.*) if, given a sequence $\{\mathbf{x}^v\}$ approaching $\mathbf{x}^0$ and a sequence $\{\mathbf{y}^v\}$ approaching $\mathbf{y}^0$, where for each v, $\mathbf{y}^v$ is an element of the set $\Phi(\mathbf{x}^v)$ associated with $\mathbf{x}^v$, then $\mathbf{x}^0$ belongs to $\Phi(\mathbf{x}^0)$.

In Fig. 3.1 is illustrated the graph of an upper semi-continuous correspondence where, in addition, $\Phi(\mathbf{x})$ is a convex set (possibly consisting of a single point) for each $\mathbf{x}$.

By straightforward if slightly tedious arguments, it can be shown that:

Lemma 4. The correspondences, $P(u)$ and $\hat{W}(\mathbf{u})$, defined in Lemma 3, are u.s.c. and convex for each u.

Let us go back for a minute to assumption (v); this guarantees the existence of a minimal consumption vector, $\bar{\mathbf{x}}_h$, available to household h at any set of prices whatever. In discussing competitive equilibrium, then, we can confine ourselves to consumption vectors which yield at least as much utility as $\bar{\mathbf{x}}_h$. We can assume, with no loss of generality, that

$$U_h(\bar{\mathbf{x}}_h) = 0, \tag{6}$$

and confine our attention to utility allocations which yield each household utility at least equal to 0. Let, therefore,

U be the set of non-negative Pareto-efficient utility allocations. (7)

CE D 2

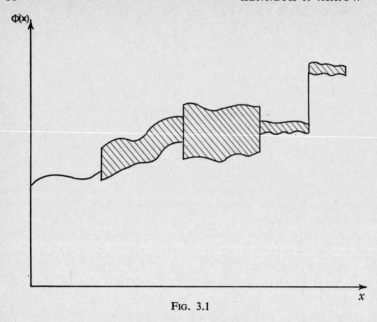

FIG. 3.1

For any feasible allocation, w in $\hat{W}$, and any price vector $\mathbf{p}$, the expenditures of each household, $\mathbf{p}\,\mathbf{x}_h$, and its income, M_h, as given by (2), are defined, and hence so is its *budget surplus*,

$$s_h(\mathbf{p}, w) = \mathbf{p}\,\mathbf{x}_h - M_h. \tag{8}$$

If we start with an arbitrary price vector and feasible allocation, we will 'correct' them by imposing a penalty for violating the budget constraint, i.e. for a negative value of s_h. This is done as follows: to each given price vector, $\mathbf{p}$, and feasible allocation, w, we associate the set of all non-negative utility allocations which yield 0 utility for those households with budget deficits. (The correspondence thus defined might be said to punish the improvident while being neutral with regard to others.) Formally, define,

$U(\mathbf{p}, w)$ is the set of all non-negative Pareto-efficient utility allocations, $\mathbf{u}$, such that $u_h = 0$ for all households, h, for which $s_h(\mathbf{p}, w) < 0$. $\qquad(9)$

To show the existence of a compensated equilibrium, we use the method of fixed points. That is, we start with a set of values for interesting economic magnitudes (in the present application, prices, utilities, and allocations). To each vector in the set we associate a vector in the set, or more generally, a set of vectors which is a subset of the original set. In the terminology we have introduced, we have a correspondence which maps the elements of some set into subsets of that set. Then under certain continuity hypotheses we find that there is at least one point of the set which belongs to the subset into which it is mapped by the correspondence. If the correspondence has been suitably constructed, then it can be shown that its fixed point is in fact the desired compensated equilibrium. The fixed-point theroem used here is that due to the mathematician Kakutani (1941). Kakutani's theorem is in turn derived from the fixed-point theorem of Brouwer. An excellent reasonably elementary exposition of the proof of Brouwer's theorem is to be found in Tompkins (1964); simple self-contained proofs of both theorems are given in Burger (1963, appendix).

Lemma 5. (Kakutani's Fixed-Point Theorem). Let S be a closed, bounded and convex set and $\Phi(\mathbf{x})$ a correspondence defined for $\mathbf{x}$ in S and u.s.c. such that, for each $\mathbf{x}, \Phi(\mathbf{x})$ is non-null, contained in S, and convex. Then there is some $\mathbf{x}^0$ such that $\mathbf{x}^0$ belongs to $\Phi(\mathbf{x}^0)$.

In our application, the elements of S will be triples $(\mathbf{p}, \mathbf{u}, w)$ consisting of price vectors, $\mathbf{p}$, non-negative Pareto-efficient utility allocations, $\mathbf{u}$ in U (see (7)), and feasible allocations, w in $\hat{W}$. The price vectors are assumed to be non-negative and have at least one positive component. Since multiplication of all prices by a positive constant has no economic significance, we can normalize the prices in some convenient way; we choose to make the sum of all prices equal to one. Then define the range of prices to be the set satisfying the conditions:

$$P \text{ is the set of price vectors } \mathbf{p}, \text{ with } \mathbf{p} \geqq 0, \text{ and } \sum_i p_i = 1. \qquad (10)$$

The domain S is then the set of all triples $(\mathbf{p}, \mathbf{u}, w)$ with $\mathbf{p}$ in P, $\mathbf{u}$ in U, and w in $\hat{W}$; each of the three components varies independently over its range. The set of all such triples is most conveniently denoted by

$$P \times U \times \mathbf{M},$$

and is referred to as the *Cartesian product* of the three sets. More generally, given m sets, $X_1, \ldots, X_m$, their Cartesian product,

$$X_1 \times X_2 \times \ldots \times X_m,$$

is the set of all m-tuples of vectors, $(\mathbf{x}_1, \ldots, \mathbf{x}_m)$, such that $\mathbf{x}_1$ belongs to X_1, $\mathbf{x}_2$ to X_2, \ldots, $\mathbf{x}_m$ to X_m.

To each point $(\mathbf{p}, \mathbf{u}, w)$ in $P \times U \times \hat{W}$, we associate a set which is the Cartesian product:

$$P(\mathbf{u}) \times U(\mathbf{p}, w) \times W(\mathbf{u}). \tag{11}$$

It is easy to see that P is a closed bounded set; since feasible allocations are bounded, by (5), it also follows that U is closed and bounded. Hence, the domain $P \times U \times \hat{W}$ is closed and bounded. The set P is convex, and the same is true of $\hat{W}$ by (5). It is not necessarily true that U is convex, however; it is after all simply the utility-possibility surface, and its shape is indeed dependent upon the choice of the utility indicator for each household, a choice which depends upon an arbitrary monotone transformation. For the moment, however, pretend that U is convex.

As asserted in Lemma 4, $P(\mathbf{u})$ and $M(\mathbf{u})$ are u.s.c. and convex for each; they are non-null by Lemma 3. It is easy to verify that $U(\mathbf{p}, w)$ is non-null for each $\mathbf{p}$, w, and that it is a u.s.c. correspondence. Pretend again that it is also convex. Then the Cartesian product, (11), can easily be verified to be u.s.c. in the variables, $\mathbf{p}$, $\mathbf{u}$, w, and to be non-null and convex for each set of values of the variables. Then Kakutani's theorem, Lemma 5, assures that there is a fixed point, i.e. a triple, $(\mathbf{p}^*, \mathbf{u}^*, w^*)$ such that

$$(\mathbf{p}^*, \mathbf{u}^*, w^*) \text{ belongs to } P(\mathbf{u}^*) \times U(\mathbf{p}^*, w^*) \times \hat{W}(\mathbf{u}^*).$$

By definition of a Cartesian product, this is equivalent to the three statements:

$$\mathbf{p}^* \text{ belongs to } P(\mathbf{u}^*), \tag{12}$$

$$\mathbf{u}^* \text{ belongs to } U(\mathbf{p}^*, w^*) \tag{13}$$

$$w^* \text{ belongs to } \hat{W}(\mathbf{u}^*). \tag{14}$$

From (12) and (14), we can apply Lemma 3. Statements (a)–(c) of Lemma 3 together with the definition of $\hat{W}(\mathbf{u}^*)$ as containing only feasible allocations yield immediately statements (a)–(d) of D.2. It remains only to verify D.2(e). In view of (8), this is equivalent to showing that

$$s_h(\mathbf{p}^*, w^*) = 0, \text{ all } h. \tag{15}$$

On the other hand, statement (d) of Lemma 3 is equivalent to

$$\sum_h s_h(\mathbf{p}^*, w^*) = 0;$$

hence, to prove (15) it suffices to show that

$$s_h(\mathbf{p}^*, \mathbf{w}^*) \geqq 0, \text{ all } h, \tag{16}$$

for, if a sum of non-negative quantities is zero, each must be zero. Suppose then that (16) is false:

$$s_h(\mathbf{p}^*, \mathbf{w}^*) < 0, \text{ some } h.$$

Then (13) and (9) together imply that $u_h^* = 0$ for any such h. But D.2(d) has already been demonstrated, i.e. at a compensated equilibrium each household is attaining its utility at minimum cost. By our convention (6), $u_h^* = 0$ can always be attained by choosing the consumption vector $\bar{\mathbf{x}}_h$, and this vector, by (v), can always be obtained without a budget deficit, so that (16) holds and therefore (15); condition (e) of D.2 is now verified and the demonstration of the existence of compensated equilibrium completed. From Lemma 2, then, the existence of a competitive equilibrium is now demonstrated.

We left one loose end; the application of Kakutani's theorem seems to require the convexity of U, the set of non-negative Pareto-efficient allocations, and of $U(\mathbf{p}, \mathbf{w})$, as defined in (9). We can relate U and $U(\mathbf{p}, \mathbf{w})$, however, to convex sets in a straightforward way; the process is illustrated in Fig. 3.2. Let V be the set of vectors $\mathbf{v}$, with as many components as households, such that

$$V \text{ is the set of vectors } \mathbf{v} \text{ for which } \mathbf{v} \geqq 0, \sum_h v_h = 1.$$

It is obvious that $\mathbf{0}$ is not a Pareto-efficient utility allocation. Hence, a line drawn from the origin to an element of U intersects V once and only once and can be used to associate a point of V to it. Therefore, selecting an element of U is equivalent to selecting an element of the convex set, V. Further, a member of U for which $u_h = 0$ is associated in this way with a point for which $v_h = 0$. By (9), $U(\mathbf{p}, \mathbf{w})$ consists precisely of points of U for which $u_h = 0$ for certain h; it is therefore associated with a set, $V(\mathbf{p}, \mathbf{w})$, which consists of those points of V for which $v_h = 0$ for the same h. (In Fig. 3.2, if $U(\mathbf{p}, \mathbf{w})$ is defined by the condition $u_1 = 0$, then it consists of the one point of U on the u_2-axis and is associated with the unique point of V for which $v_1 = 0$.) Then $V(\mathbf{p}, \mathbf{w})$ is a convex set.

If then we replace U and $U(\mathbf{p}, \mathbf{w})$ by V and $V(\mathbf{p}, \mathbf{w})$ in the above mapping, all the conditions of Kakutani's theorem are strictly fulfilled.

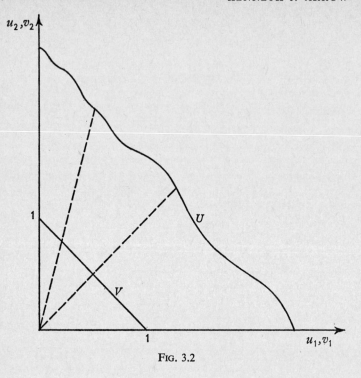

FIG. 3.2

III. THE FIRM AS PRICE-MAKER: EQUILIBRIUM UNDER MONOPOLISTIC COMPETITION

We now assume that there are some firms in the economy which are capable of exercising monopolistic or monopsonistic power over certain markets. We assume however, the absence of interaction among the monopolistic firms. Each firm takes the current prices of products not under its control as given and perceives a demand (or supply) function, which may or may not be correct. The perception is made on the basis of observed prices and allocation. It is assumed that, at least at equilibrium, the demand functions are correct at the observed point, though not necessarily elsewhere. That is, for the quantities actually produced, the firm correctly perceives the prices which will clear the markets. However, it is not necessarily assumed that the monopolistic firms correctly perceive the elasticities of demand at the equilibrium point.

A model with these properties was developed in a brilliant paper by Negishi (1960–1) and an existence theorem proved for it, the only previous work of this type known to me. The assumptions made here are much weaker than those of Negishi; comparisons between the present model and earlier models of monopolistic competition, including Negishi's are made at the end of this section.

The production possibility sets for monopolistic firms need not be convex; indeed, it is presumably the non-convexity (in particular, the increasing returns to scale) which is the reason for the existence of monopoly. However, it is assumed that the prices charged by monopolistic firms are continuous functions of other prices and other production and consumption decisions. If we assume in the usual way that monopolists are maximizing profits according to their perceived demand curves, then this assumption amounts to saying that the perceived marginal revenue curves fall more sharply than marginal cost curves.

Though we weaken the convexity assumptions on the production possibility sets of the monopolists, we will still need to make some hypotheses which will insure that the set of feasible production allocations satisfies some reasonable conditions, specifically that it is bounded if resources are bounded and that it is a set which does not break up into several parts or have holes in its middle. The second provision will be expressed more precisely by requiring that the set of those production possibility vectors for the monopolistic sector which are compatible with feasibility for the entire production sector can be expressed as the image of a closed bounded set under a continuous mapping.

The assumptions on the competitive sector will remain those made before.

There are then two kinds of firms, competitive and monopolistic. A *subscript C or M* will indicate a vector of *all* commodities which is possible for a competitive firm or for the competitive sector as a whole. Thus, Y_{Cf} is the production possibility set for competitive firm f, Y_{M_g} for monopolistic firm g. The production possibility set for the competitive sector as a whole is

$$Y_C = \sum_f Y_{Cf},$$

and similarly, $Y_M = \sum_g Y_{M_g}$. The elements of these sets are represented by lower-case bold-face **y** with the appropriate subscripts. A monopolized commodity will of course not be the output of any vector in

Y_C but it may be an input. Also, we use the term 'monopolized' to include 'monopsonized'.

(i) Assumption (i) of section II holds for the sets Y_{Cf}.

(ii) **0** belongs to Y_{Mg} and Y_{Mg} is closed, for each g.

It is possible to make assumptions parallel to (ii) of section II (impossibility of getting something for nothing) to include the monopolistic firms. To avoid complications, we will simply assume the implication we there drew from this assumption. By a *production allocation* $(\mathbf{y}_{Cf}, \mathbf{y}_{Mg})$ we mean a specification of the production vector for each firm, competitive or monopolistic. A production allocation is *feasible* if

$$\sum_f \mathbf{y}_{Cf} + \sum_g \mathbf{y}_{Mg} + \bar{\mathbf{x}} \geqq 0. \tag{1}$$

Then we assume:

(iii) The set of feasible production allocations is closed and bounded. (2)

An *allocation* is, as before, a consumption allocation and a production allocation, i.e. a complete specification $(\mathbf{x}_h, \mathbf{y}_{Cf}, \mathbf{y}_{Mg})$.

$\hat{W}$ is the set of feasible allocations, i.e. those for

$$\text{which } \sum_h \mathbf{x}_h \leqq \bar{\mathbf{x}} + \sum_f \mathbf{y}_{Cf} + \sum_g \mathbf{y}_{Mg}. \tag{3}$$

If we continue to assume, as we will, that consumption vectors, $\mathbf{x}_h$, are always non-negative, then from the definition (3) and assumption (iii) it follows immediately that

$\hat{W}$ is a closed bounded set. (4)

We introduce the concept of feasibility separately for the competitive sector (including households) and the monopolistic sector. An allocation in the competitive sector, $w_C = (\mathbf{x}_h, \mathbf{y}_{Cf})$ is *feasible* if there exists a monopolistic production allocation (not excluding **0**) such that the entire allocation $(\mathbf{x}_h, \mathbf{y}_{Cf}, \mathbf{y}_{Mg})$ is feasible. Similarly, a *monopolistic production allocation*, $y_M = (\mathbf{y}_{Mg})$, is feasible if there exists an allocation in the competitive sector, w_C, such that the entire allocation (w_C, y_M) is feasible. Let

$\hat{W}_C$ be the set of feasible allocations in the competitive sector, (5)

$\hat{Y}_M$ be the set of feasible monopolistic production allocations. (6)

Then (4) immediately implies:

$\hat{W}_C$ is closed and bounded. (7)

Y_M is closed and bounded. (8)

We now make a basic assumption on the structure of the monopolistic production possibility sets which amounts to saying that the extent of increasing returns there is not too great relative to the resources that the competitive sector would be capable of supplying. Let

$$z_C = \sum_h \mathbf{x}_h - \bar{\mathbf{x}} - \sum_f \mathbf{y}_{Cf}$$

be any possible excess demand vector of the competitive sector, and Z_C be the set of all such z_C. In effect, $-z_C$ is the vector of amounts made available to the monopolistic sector by the competitive sector. In general, z_C may have some positive components which denote net demands by the competitive sector. In particular, those positive components which represent monopolized goods measure demands by the competitive sector on the monopolistic sector. (If there are positive components of z_C which do not represent monopolized goods then the demands denoted cannot be met at all, and z_C certainly corresponds to an infeasible allocation.) For simplicity, suppose there is only one monopolistic firm and let Y_M be its production possibility set. Then from the definition of feasibility (3), $\mathbf{y}_M$ is feasible if and only if

$\mathbf{y}_M$ belongs to y_M, $\mathbf{y}_M \geqq z_C$ for some z_C in Z_C. (9)

For only one monopolistic firm, a monopolistic production allocation is simply the production vector for that firm, so that (9) characterizes the set of feasible monopolistic production allocations, Y_M.

For simplicity, assume that there is free disposal in both the monopolistic and the competitive sectors. Then (9) states that $\mathbf{y}_M$ is simply the intersection of the two sets, Y_M, the monopolist's production possibility set, and Z_C, the feasible excess demand vectors of the competitive sector. The set Z_C is convex by the assumptions made, but Y_M is not in general. The relation among these sets is illustrated in Fig. 3.3. If the competitive sector is large relative to the monopolistic, then the set Z_C will tend to be shifted to the left. The intersection, Y_M, will be 'fat'. It will then follow that if we inscribe a bounded closed convex set A, e.g. a sphere, as illustrated, every point of Y_M can be projected into some element of the sphere (including its

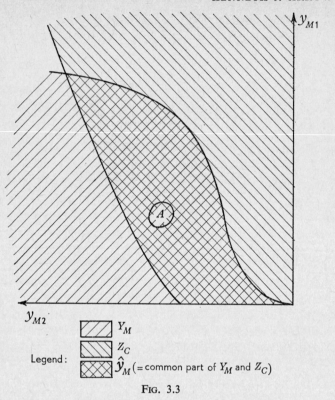

Legend:

Y_M

Z_C

$\hat{Y}_M$ (= common part of Y_M and Z_C)

FIG. 3.3

interior) in a continuous way and conversely every point in $\hat{Y}_M$ is the projection of some point in the sphere. We will make this an assumption, although it can be derived from more primitive assumptions.

(iv) There exists a continuous function, say $y_M(a)$, which maps a closed bounded convex set, A, into all points of $\hat{Y}_M$.

It is worth illustrating that if Z_C is not large relative to Y_M, then (iv) need not hold: see Fig. 3.4, which is the same as Fig. 3.3. except for the location of the boundary of Z_C. Now $\hat{Y}_M$ breaks up into two parts, and certainly cannot be the continuous image of any one convex set. It is now certainly conceivable that no equilibrium will exist (though no example has been constructed); from an initial allocation corresponding to one area, the monopolist might always be motivated to choose a price which moves demand into the other area. At the very least, the weak assumptions we will make on the monopolist's behavior will not suffice to exclude this possibility.

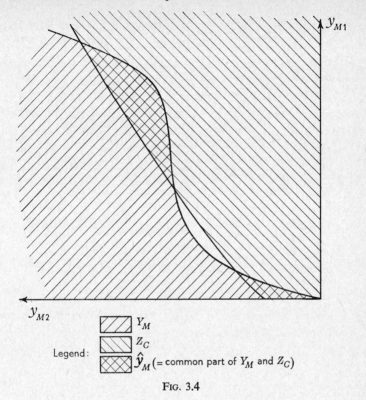

Legend:
Y_M
Z_C
$\hat{y}_M (= \text{common part of } Y_M \text{ and } Z_C)$

FIG. 3.4

We now turn to the behavior of the monopolist. As a matter of notation, we will use a *superscript M* to denote those commodities which are monopolized or monopsonized, the superscript C for the remaining commodities. Thus, $\mathbf{p}^M$ is the vector of prices for the monopolized commodities alone; similarly, if P is a set of prices, P^C is the set of prices for competitive goods which is obtained by deleting from each $\mathbf{p} \in P$ the components corresponding to monopolized goods.

At any given moment, the monopolists observe current prices and the current allocation and (individually) decide on their prices. We do not here make any hypothesis of profit – or utility – maximization, but take their behavior for granted. The only conditions we impose are those indicated at the beginning of this section: monopolists' behavior is a continuous function of their observations, and the monopolist will change prices if his markets are not clearing. The second provision is somewhat complicated to state precisely in a general equilibrium context. We take the following interpretation: suppose that the existing allocation is Pareto-efficient within the competitive sector (i.e. taking the supplies and demands of monopolists as given) and that the relative prices of competitive goods correspond to a set of all prices which would sustain this allocation. Then if the entire set of prices (for monopolistic as well as competitive goods) will not sustain this allocation, the monopolistic prices (or at least one of them) will change. (A price vector is said to *sustain* given allocation in the competitive sector if the production vector of each firm in the allocation is profit-maximizing at the given set of prices and the consumption vector of each household is utility-maximizing under the appropriate budget constraint at the given set of prices.)

Before stating the assumption, we need some further notation. For any fixed monopolistic production allocation, Y_M, there is a range of feasible allocations for the competitive sectors, provided $y_M \epsilon y_M$, namely those allocations, $w_C = (x, y_C)$, for which

$$\sum_h \mathbf{x}_h \leqq \sum_f \mathbf{y}_{Cf} + \bar{\mathbf{x}} + \sum_g \mathbf{y}_{Mg};$$

the productive activity of the monopolistic sector can be treated as a modification of the inital endowment from the viewpoint of the competitive sector.

We repeat the assumptions on consumer behavior in section II and add one mild condition:

(v) Assumptions (iv)–(vi) of section II hold.
(vi) No household is satiated in competitive goods alone, i.e. for every $\mathbf{x}_h = (\mathbf{x}_h^C, \mathbf{x}_h^M)$, there exists $\mathbf{x}_h^{C'}$, such that

$$U_h(\mathbf{x}_h^{C'}, \mathbf{x}_h^M) > U_h(\mathbf{x}_h) = U_h(\mathbf{x}_h^C, \mathbf{x}_h^M).$$

For fixed $\mathbf{y}_M$, then, we can use the arguments of section II to note that there is a range of non-negative Pareto-efficient utility allocations $U(\mathbf{y}_M)$, and, for each $\mathbf{u}$ in $U(\mathbf{y}_M)$, a set of Pareto-efficient competitive allocations, to be denoted by

$$\hat{W}_C(\mathbf{u}, \mathbf{y}_M),$$

and a set of price vectors which sustain these allocations,

$$P_C(\mathbf{u}, \mathbf{y}_M).$$

The 'Pareto efficiency' in question has to do only with allocation within the competitive sector for any given production behavior on the part of the monopolistic sector, and in no way implies the obviously false proposition that the allocation as a whole is Pareto-efficient. Similarly, the price vectors in $P_C(\mathbf{u}, \mathbf{y}_M)$ only sustain the given allocation as far as the behavior of the competitive sector is concerned.

In accordance with our conventions about superscripts, the set $P_C^C(\mathbf{u}, \mathbf{y}_M)$ is obtained by considering only those components of the price vectors in $P_C(\mathbf{u}, \mathbf{y}_M)$ which represent prices of competitive commodities. Then our assumption about the pricing behavior of the monopolistic sector reads:

(vii) The prices charged by the monopolistic sector form a continuous function, $\mathbf{p}^M(\mathbf{p}, w)$, of prices and allocation. If $\mathbf{p} = (\mathbf{p}^C, \mathbf{p}^M)$ and $w = (\mathbf{x}_h, \mathbf{y}_{Cf}, \mathbf{y}_{M_g})$ have the properties that, for some $\mathbf{u}$ in $U(\mathbf{y}_M)$,

$$\mathbf{p}^C = \lambda \mathbf{p}^{C'} \text{ for some } \lambda \geqq 0 \text{ and some } \mathbf{p}^{C'} \text{ in } P_C^C(\mathbf{u}, \mathbf{y}_M),$$

$$w_C = (\mathbf{x}_h, \mathbf{y}_{Cf}) \text{ belongs to } \hat{W}_C(\mathbf{u}, \mathbf{y}_M),$$

but

$$p \text{ does not belong to } P_C(\mathbf{u}, \mathbf{y}_M),$$

then

$$\mathbf{p}^M(\mathbf{p}, w) \neq \mathbf{p}^M.$$

It is further assumed that, if $\mathbf{p}^M(\mathbf{p}, w) = \mathbf{p}^M$, then $\mathbf{p} \, \mathbf{y}_{M_g} \geqq 0$, all g, and that the sum of prices charged by monopolists does not exceed 1.

The next-to-last clause means that if monopolists are satisfied with their existing prices, they are not operating at a loss; the last clause means that monopolists, even though they make their decisions independently, will not, in total, demand more than is compatible with the normalization of prices.

Note that, from assumption (vi) the prices of competitive commodities cannot all be zero if they sustain efficient allocation within the competitive sector.

For any $\mathbf{y}_M$ and any $\mathbf{u}$ in $U(\mathbf{y}_M)$, $\mathbf{p}^C \neq 0$ for any $\mathbf{p}$ in $P_C(\mathbf{u}, \mathbf{y}_M)$. \hfill (10)

Finally, we make an assumption corresponding to (iii) of section II, the ability of the economy to produce a positive amount of every good. We apply it, however, to the behavior of the competitive sector under the assumption that the monopolistic sector is not operating.

(viii) It is possible to choose $\bar{\mathbf{y}}_{Cf}$ from Y_{Cf} for each f so that $\sum_f \bar{\mathbf{y}}_{Cf} + \bar{\mathbf{x}}$ is strictly positive in every component representing a competitive commodity and zero in every component representing a monopolized commodity.

In defining equilibrium for monopolistic competition, we must provide for the distribution of monopolistic profits to households. Hence, the income of the household is now given by

$$M_h = \mathbf{p}\,\bar{\mathbf{x}}_h + \sum_g d_{hf}^C(\mathbf{p}\,\mathbf{y}_{Cf}) + \sum_f d_{hg}^M(\mathbf{p}\,\mathbf{y}_{Mg}), \tag{11}$$

where d_{hf}^C is the share of household h in the profits of competitive firm f and d_{hg}^M is the share of household h in the profits of monopolistic firm g, so that

$$d_{hf}^C \geqq 0,\ d_{hg}^M \geqq 0,\ \sum_h d_{hf}^C = 1,\ \sum_h d_{hg}^M = 1,$$

and therefore

$$\sum_h M_h = \mathbf{p}\,\bar{\mathbf{x}} + \mathbf{p}(\sum_g \mathbf{y}_{Cf}) + \mathbf{p}(\sum_f \mathbf{y}_{Mg}). \tag{12}$$

D.1. A price vector, $\mathbf{p}^*$, and an allocation, $w^* = (\mathbf{x}_h^*,\ \mathbf{y}_{Cf}^*,\ \mathbf{y}_{Mg}^*)$, constitute a *monopolistic competitive equilibrium* if:

(a) $\mathbf{p}^* \geqq 0$ and $\mathbf{p}^* \neq 0$;

(b) $\sum_h \mathbf{x}_h^* \leqq \sum_h \bar{\mathbf{x}}_h + \sum_f \mathbf{y}_{Cf}^* + \sum_g \mathbf{y}_{Mg}^*$;

(c) $\mathbf{y}_{Cf}^*$ maximizes $\mathbf{p}^*\,\mathbf{y}_{Cf}$ subject to $\mathbf{y}_{Cf}$ in Y_{Cf};

(d) $\mathbf{x}_h^*$ maximizes $U_h(\mathbf{x}_h)$ subject to $\mathbf{p}^*\,\mathbf{x}_h \leqq M_h^*$

$$= \mathbf{p}^*\,\bar{\mathbf{x}}_h + \sum_f d_{hf}^C(\mathbf{p}^*\,\mathbf{y}_{Cf}^*) + \sum_g d_{hg}^M(\mathbf{p}^*\,\mathbf{y}_{Mg}^*);$$

(e) $\mathbf{p}^{M*} = \mathbf{p}^M(\mathbf{p}^*, w^*)$.

As in section II, it is convenient to demonstrate first the existence of a closely related type of equilibrium.

D.2. A price vector, $\mathbf{p}^*$, utility allocation, $\mathbf{u}^*$, and an allocation $w^* = (\mathbf{x}_h^*, \mathbf{y}_{Cf}^*, \mathbf{y}_{Mg}^*)$ constitute a *compensated monopolistic equilibrium* if (a), (b), (c) and (e) of D.1 hold, and, in addition,

(d') $\mathbf{x}_h^*$ minimizes $\mathbf{p}^*\,\mathbf{x}_h^*$ subject to $U_h(\mathbf{x}_h^*) \geqq u_h^*$;

(f) $\mathbf{p}^*\,\mathbf{x}_h^* = M_h^*$.

We now construct the mapping used to prove the existence of compensated monopolistic equilibrium.

An allocation, w, specifies in particular a monopolistic production allocation, y_M. Start, then, with an allocation, w, a utility allocation **u** which is Pareto-efficient in the competitive sector for the given y_M, i.e. an element of $U(y_M)$, and a price vector, **p**. We form a set of price vectors associated with this triple as follows. The monopolistic components are assumed given by $\mathbf{p}^M(\mathbf{p}, w)$. For the given **u** and y_M, the set $P_C(\mathbf{u}, y_M)$ contains all vectors which would sustain that utility allocation in the competitive sector. For each **p** in $P_C(\mathbf{u}, y_M)$, consider the corresponding vector, $\mathbf{p}^C$, containing just those components which represent competitive goods. By (10), $\mathbf{p}^C \neq 0$. Hence, each such vector can be rescaled so that, with the given monopolistic components, the final price vector satisfies the normalization condition that the sum of all prices (monopolistic and competitive) equals one (the last clause of assumption (vii) is also needed here). Formally,

$\tilde{P}(\mathbf{u}, \mathbf{p}, w)$ is the set of all vectors **p** such that $\mathbf{p}^M = \mathbf{p}^M(\mathbf{p}, w)$, $\mathbf{p}^C = \lambda \mathbf{p}^{C'}$ for some $\lambda \geq 0$ and some $\mathbf{p}^{C'}$ in $P_C^C(\mathbf{u}, y_M)$, and $\sum_i p_i = 1$.

Here, y_M are the monopolistic production components of w, and **u** belongs to $U(y_M)$. (13)

Now define

$$s_h(\mathbf{p}, w) = \mathbf{p} \, \mathbf{x}_h - M_h(\mathbf{p}, w),$$ (14)

where M_h is defined by (11), and, as in section II, let

$U(\mathbf{p}, w)$ be the set of utility allocations in $U(y_M)$ such that $u_h = 0$ if $s_h(\mathbf{p}, w) < 0$. (15)

Define P as before (see (9) of section II). We start now with the quadruples $(\mathbf{p}, \mathbf{u}, w_C, \mathbf{a})$, where **p** belongs to P, **u** to $U(y_M)$, w_C to $\hat{W}_C$, and $\mathbf{a}$ to A. The set A has been introduced in assumption (iv). It will be recalled that w_C is an allocation in the competitive sector. From (iv) **a** defines a monopolistic production allocation, $y_M(\mathbf{a})$ in $\hat{Y}_M$, so that w_C and **a**, together, define an allocation, w. Then the quadruple $(\mathbf{p}, \mathbf{u}, w_C, \mathbf{a})$ is mapped into the Cartesian product

$$\tilde{P}(\mathbf{u}, \mathbf{p}, w) \times U(\mathbf{p}, w) \times \hat{W}_C(\mathbf{u}, y_M) \times \{\mathbf{a}\},$$

where $\{\mathbf{a}\}$ consists of the single point, **a**. Kakutani's theorem can then be applied to show the existence of a fixed point $(\mathbf{p}^*, \mathbf{u}^*, w_C^*, \mathbf{a}^*)$

Some difficult points in the proof are noted below. Let

$$y_M^* = y_M(\mathbf{a}^*), \quad w^* = (w_C, y_M^*). \tag{16}$$

By construction, $\mathbf{u}^*$ is Pareto-efficient in the competitive sector for the given y_M^*. By definition of a fixed point,

$$\mathbf{p}^* \text{ belongs to } \tilde{P}(\mathbf{u}^*, \mathbf{p}^*, w^*), \tag{17}$$

$$\mathbf{u}^* \text{ belongs to } U(\mathbf{p}^*, w^*), \tag{18}$$

$$w_C^* \text{ belongs to } \hat{W}_C(\mathbf{u}^*, y_M^*). \tag{19}$$

From the definition of $\tilde{P}(\mathbf{u}, \mathbf{p}, w)$ in (13), (17) states that
$$\mathbf{p}^{C*} = \lambda \mathbf{p}^{C'} \text{ for some } \lambda \geqq 0 \text{ and some } \mathbf{p}^{C'} \text{ in } P_C^C(\mathbf{u}^*, y_M^*),$$
and

$$\mathbf{p}^{M*} = \mathbf{p}^M(\mathbf{p}^*, w^*). \tag{20}$$

From assumption (vii), (19) and (20) could not both hold if $\mathbf{p}^*$ did not belong to $P_C(\mathbf{u}^*, y_M^*)$. Hence

$$\mathbf{p}^* \text{ belongs to } P_C(\mathbf{u}^*, y_M^*). \tag{21}$$

Now (21) and (19) together show that the fixed-point allocation and prices indeed define a Pareto-efficient allocation within the competitive sector. From Lemma 3 of section II, it follows, as in section II, that conditions (a), (b), (c) and (d') of D.2 hold, while (20) asserts that (e) holds.

From (14) and (18) it follows, just as in section II, that

$$s_h(p^*, w^*) = 0 \text{ for all } h,$$

so that D.2(f) also holds. Thus, (p^*, u^*, w^*) form a compensated monopolistic equilibrium.

The difficult points in applying Kakutani's theorem, referred to above, are the following:

(1) The range of the variable $\mathbf{u}$ now depends on y_M, since we assume $\mathbf{u}$ belongs to $U(y_M)$; also, as in section II, the range need not be a convex set. This can be met by extending the device used there; for each y_M, the set $U(y_M)$ can be mapped into a set V for which

$$v \geqq 0, \quad \sum_h v_h = 1.$$

Since $\mathbf{a}$ defines $y_M = y_M(a)$, a and $\mathbf{v}$ together define $\mathbf{u}$ in $U(y_M)$, the correspondence used above can be considered as defined on

$$P \times V \times \hat{W}_C \times A,$$

where P, V, and A are closed bounded convex sets. Similarly, any **u** in $U(\mathbf{p}, \mathbf{w})$ can be mapped into a member of V, with the property that $v_h = 0$ if and only if $u_h = 0$; it is not difficult to see that $V(\mathbf{p}, \mathbf{w})$, so defined, in convex.

(2) The set $\hat{W}_C$ is not necessarily convex; we recall that it is the set of allocations in the competitive sector which are feasible for *some* monopolistic production allocation; since the set of monopolistic production allocations is not in general convex, neither is $\hat{W}_C$ in general. However, the image set $\hat{W}_C(\mathbf{u}, \mathbf{y}_M)$ is always convex. Hence, all that is needed is to pick for the domain of definition a closed bounded convex set of competitive allocations containing $\hat{W}_C$.

From (10), (12), and assumption (viii) it follows, just as in section II, that

$$\sum_h M_h^* > 0.$$

We can define resource-relatedness and indirect resource-relatedness as in section II with respect to the competitive sector alone, for any given feasible monopolistic production allocation (which affects the competitive sector as if it were a change in initial endowment).

(ix) Every household is indirectly resource-related to every other for any given feasible monopolistic production allocation.

Then by the argument already given in section II, a compensated monopolistic equilibrium is a monopolistic competitive equilibrium.

Theorem. Under assumptions (i)–(ix), a monopolistic competitive equilibrium exists.

Remark 1. The model presented here is a formalization of Chamberlin's (1956, pp. 81–100; originally published in 1933) case of monopolistic competition with large numbers. As Triffin (1940) showed, the essential aspects of monopolistic competition appear as soon as one attempts to introduce some monopolies into a system of general competitive equilibrium. The only previous complete formalization is that of Negishi (1960–1). Negishi assumed that each monopolist produced only one commodity and maximized profits according to a perceived demand curve which was a function of all prices and the allocation but was in particular linear (or piecewise linear) in the price of the commodity. He saw the importance of a formulation of the type of (vii) here, that at equilibrium the monopolist's perceived demand curve should at least pass through the observed price–quantity point. In his formulation, which was originally suggested by Bushaw and Clower (1957, p. 181), the monopolist's price equalled the given one if at the given allocation, supply and demand were equal for that commodity. The assumption made here is considerably weaker, since it need only hold if the competitive sector is in equilibrium. Also Negishi restricted attention to the case where the monopolists have convex production possibility sets, a severe condition since under those circumstances the occurrence of monopoly is unlikely, as Negishi himself noted (p. 199, middle). He raised the possibility of more general assumptions, similar to (iv).

Remark 2. No explicit mention has been made of product differentiation, a central theme of monopolistic competition theory. But note that the model admits the possibility that any monopolistic firm can produce a variety of goods. Suppose that all conceivable goods are included in the list of commodities; even what are usually regarded as varieties of the same good must be distinguished in this list if they are not perfect substitutes in both production and consumption. A monopolist will, in general, find it profitable to produce a number of varieties. The definition of a monopoly implies that, for some reason or another, two different monopolists produce non-overlapping sets of goods, but of course the goods produced by one monopolist may be quite close substitutes for those produced by another. The usual idea in product differentiation that a firm produces just one commodity is not a convenient assumption for general equilibrium analysis, but it is equally certainly not a good description of the real world.

Remark 3. The notion of free entry and with it the famous double-tangency solution of Chamberlin and Robinson (1933, pp. 93–4) have no role here either. The list of monopolists is assumed given, so that in effect there is a scarcity of the appropriate type of entrepreneurship, and there is no reason for profits to be wiped out. No doubt if there are several firms producing products which are close substitutes in consumption and have very similar production possibility sets otherwise, they should behave about the same way, and, if there are enough of them, it may well be that each is making very little in the way of profit. But the question then is the one raised originally by Kaldor (1935): would not the elasticity of demand to the individual firm be essentially zero, so that the situation is essentially one of perfect competition? It cannot be said that this question has been fully answered, since a more specific model defining close substitutes and their production possibilities has not yet been explicitly formulated.[1]

Remark 4. An open and potentially important research area is the specification of conditions under which monopolistic behavior, as expressed in the function, $p^M(\mathbf{p}, \mathbf{w})$, is in fact continuous. The formulation is very general; it is certainly compatible with utility-maximizing behavior (e.g. preference for size or particular kinds of expenditures or products) as well as profit-maximizing behavior. However, the assumption of continuity may nevertheless be strong; in effect, it denies the role of increasing returns as a barrier to entry. As the demand shifts upward, the firm might pass from zero output (i.e. a purely potential existence) to a minimum positive output. A zero output must be interpreted as a price decision at a level corresponding to zero demand; but if the demand curve is downward-sloping, then entry at a positive level far removed from zero implies a discontinuous drop in price. The importance of this problem is not easy to assess. The situation can only arise if the (perceived) marginal revenue curve is, broadly speaking, flatter than the marginal cost curve, otherwise entry would be a continuous phenomenon; but then the demand curve must also be relatively flat and therefore the price discontinuity may be mild even if the output discontinuity is large. Also, if there were only a single monopolist who correctly perceived the excess demand correspondence of the competitive sector, he could choose his most preferred point, which would then be an equilibrium; the discontinuity of his behavior would be irrelevant. However, the problem may be important if his perceptions are accurate only at equilibrium or if there are several monopolists; the discontinuity in the behavior of any one affects the perceived demand functions for the others, though again, if the monopolists are relatively separated in markets and each relatively small on the scale of the economy, then the discontinuities involved may be unimportant.

Remark 5. It must always be remembered that monopolistic competition models of the type discussed here ignore the mutual recognition of power among firms, the oligopoly problem.

---

[1] As Robin Marris has pointed out to me, the above discussion presupposes the absence of oligopolistic interdependence, which may well be, in fact, the most likely outcome when there are extremely close substitutes. But the argument was directed against the likely validity of the double tangency solution, which has not hitherto been derived from an assumption of oligopoly.

IV. THE FIRM AS FORECASTER: THE EXISTENCE OF
TEMPORARY EQUILIBRIUM

Hicks (1939, pp. 130–3) introduced the analysis of temporary equilibrium; a more recent methodological discussion is to be found in Hicks (1965, chap. vi). To interpret general equilibrium theory in the context of time, the formally simplest procedure is to regard commodities at different points of time as different commodities. But then we immediately encounter the somewhat unpleasant fact that the markets for most of these commodities do not exist. Since production and consumption both have important dynamic elements, individual agents replace the non-existent prices for future commodities by expectations (certain or probabilistic). Given these expectations, equilibrium on current markets alone is arrived at (we here neglect the relatively few futures markets). There is, however, at least one current market in addition to those for the usual commodities, namely a market for bonds, to permit individuals to have planned expenditure patterns over time which differ from their income patterns.

We now understand that the components of the possible production and consumption vectors extend over several periods of time. For simplicity, we confine ourselves to two periods, present and future. We assume that the only commodities traded in currently are commodities of the current period plus bonds; a unit bond is a promise to pay one unit of the currency of account in the next period. Let the subscript, b, refer to bonds. We use here the notation $\mathbf{x}^1$ to refer to commodities of the current period, $\mathbf{x}^2$ to those of the future period, and $\mathbf{x}$ to be vector of commodities currently traded in by households; thus, $\mathbf{x} = (\mathbf{x}^1, x_b)$, *not* $\mathbf{x} = (\mathbf{x}^1, \mathbf{x}^2)$. Similarly, for firms, $\mathbf{y} = (\mathbf{y}^1, y_b)$, where y_b is the supply of bonds issued by firms, and $\mathbf{p} = (\mathbf{p}^1, p_b)$ is the vector of prices on current markets.

Before going into details, we discuss the main difficulties in applying the methods of section II and the strategy for overcoming them. The modifications to be made to the definition of and assumptions on the production sets are straightforward except for one particular. Consider some one firm. Its production plan for the future has consequences in current markets because it affects the current value of the firm and the amount it will now borrow. But since there is no current market for the resources of the subsequent period, the availability of resources then cannot be used to argue that production plans are bounded, This creates obvious difficulties, which, however, are partly academic, since one could argue that a firm is 'realistic enough' not to plan indefinitely large production. However, it is preferable to incorporate the argument from realism into our construction in a way more in the spirit of the perfectly competitive model. We do this by insisting that the price expectations of firms be 'sensible'. This is done in assumption (ii) (b) below.

As already noted, the plans for future production must have consequences in current markets. We shall in fact assume that each firm offers in the current bond market a quantity of bonds equal to its expected profit in the future. This means that there is a 'current' representation of the future plans, which in turn allows us to incorporate these in the framework of the model of section II. This is made precise in (1) and D.2.

When we come to consumers, a number of special problems arise. First, we must decide what we mean by the initial endowment of bonds held by a household. We simply take it to equal its anticipated receipts of the future period; i.e. it represents the maximum the household believes it could repay. Note that the household's anticipated receipts may differ from what any other agent would expect them to be, given the household's plans – that is, we allow for differences in price expectations.

The differences in expectations, however, also mean that different households will value any given firm differently. We assume that the actual current market value of any firm is equal to the highest value any agent places on it and suppose that the ownership of the firm will shift to the hands of that household or those households which value it most highly (D.5 and assumption (iv)). We therefore now treat d_{hf}, the share of household h in firm f, as a variable of the equilibrium. All this leads to modifications in the manner in which we must write the households' budget constraints (see (10) and (15)).

We must also insure that our assumptions about consumption possibility sets (iv) and (v) of section II) hold when reinterpreted in terms of the current market. This is fairly straightforward; see assumption (iii), (16), and D.6.

Lastly there is the following problem. We know that the household utility depends on its future plans, and in the existence proof of section II the utilities of the households play an important part. Our procedure of incorporating the expected future into arguments about the present is to use a 'derived utility function' (D.7). This will be the maximum utility of the household, given its first-period allocation, under an appropriate budget constraint. It will be obvious that this derived function can be treated as a function of current plans only, which is what we want.

We now proceed to detailed argument. Let us first consider the behavior of the firm. We take the viewpoint that the firm is an entity which, on its own, has expectations of future prices and maximizes profits in accordance with them. At the end of this section we will make some comments on this assumption.

We retain the assumptions on the production possibility sets of the individual firms with appropriate changes of notation, and add a hypothesis which embodies the possibility of abandoning a productive enterprise without loss.

D.1. The set of *possible two-period production vectors* for firm f is Y_f^{12}. An element is denoted by $\mathbf{y}_f^{12} = (\mathbf{y}_f^1, \mathbf{y}_f^2)$, where $\mathbf{y}_f^1$ are the components of $\mathbf{y}_f^{12}$ referring to the first period and $\mathbf{y}_f^2$ those referring to the second period. We also refer to $\mathbf{y}_f^1$ and $\mathbf{y}_f^2$ as *first-period* and *second-period* production vectors respectively.

(i) Assumption (i) of section II holds with $\mathbf{y}_f$ replaced by $\mathbf{y}_f^{12}$ and Y_f by Y_f^{12}. If $(\mathbf{y}_f^1, \mathbf{y}_f^2) \in Y_f^{12}$, then there exists $\mathbf{y}_f^{2\prime} \geqq 0$ such that $(\mathbf{y}_f^1\, \mathbf{y}_f^{2\prime}) \in Y_f^{12}$.

The firm observes current prices, $\mathbf{p} = (p^1, p_b)$, and is assumed to have subjectively certain expectations for prices in period 2, $\mathbf{p}_f^2$; since there are no futures markets, different firms may have different expectations. A production plan, $(\mathbf{y}_f^1, \mathbf{y}_f^2)$, yields net revenue $\mathbf{p}^1\, \mathbf{y}_f^1$ in period 1 and is expected to yield net revenue $\mathbf{p}_f^2\, \mathbf{y}_f^2$ in period 2. If bonds sell in period 1 at p_b, then a revenue of $\mathbf{p}_f^2\, \mathbf{y}_f^2$ in period 2 is equivalent on perfect markets to a first-period income of $p_b\,(\mathbf{p}_f^2\, \mathbf{y}_f^2)$. For simplicity, we will assume that the firm actually sells bonds to the extent of its anticipated second-period income, so that its offering of bonds is

$$y_{fb} = \mathbf{p}_f^2\, \mathbf{y}_f^2, \tag{1}$$

and its current receipts from a given production plan are

$$\mathbf{p}^1\, \mathbf{y}_f^1 + p_b(\mathbf{p}_f^2\, \mathbf{y}_f^2). \tag{2}$$

The firm chooses its production plan so as to maximize (2) among all production plans $\mathbf{y}_f^{12} \in Y_f^{12}$. Provisionally, we will assume that all price expectations are totally inelastic, i.e. that $\mathbf{p}_f^2$ is a datum for the firm independent of current prices. Then (1) maps the elements of

Y_f^{12}into a set Y_f of $(n+1)$-dimensional vectors; in effect, with fixed expectations, the firm's future possibilities amount to its ability to produce bonds for today's market.

D.2. The set of possible current production vectors, $\mathbf{y}_f$, for firm f is the set derived from Y_f^{12} by replacing the second-period components, $\mathbf{y}_f^2$, by the single element obtained from them by (1), i.e.

Y_f is the set of vectors $\mathbf{y}_f = (\mathbf{y}_f^1, y_{fb})$ such that $y_{fb} = \mathbf{p}_f^2 \, \mathbf{y}_f^2$ for some $(\mathbf{y}_f^1, \mathbf{y}_f^2)$ in Y_f^{12}.

It is easy to verify from assumption (i) that

> assumption (i) of section II holds for Y_f under D.2.   (3)

That is, $\mathbf{0}$ belongs to Y_f (derived from $\mathbf{y}_f^{12} = 0$); Y_f is closed, and Y_f is convex.

From D.2 and (2),

$$\text{the firm maximizes } \mathbf{p}\,\mathbf{y}_f. \qquad (4)$$

Suppose $p_b > 0$, and the firm has chosen a production plan, $\mathbf{y}_f^{12}$, for which there will be negative receipts in the future, $\mathbf{p}_f^2\,\mathbf{y}_f^2 < 0$. Then by the second half of (i) it is possible to choose another plan with higher profits.

> If $p_b > 0$, then $\mathbf{p}_f^2\,\mathbf{y}_f^2 = y_{fb} \geqq 0$ at any profit-maximizing plan.   (5)

We now make an assumption about the impossibility of production without inputs and about irreversibility which is somewhat stronger than that obtained by simply replacing $\mathbf{y}_f$ by $\mathbf{y}_f^{12}$ and Y_f by Y_f^{12} in assumption (ii) of section II. The reason the stronger assumption is needed is that future resource limitations do not directly restrain production, since there are no futures markets on which they appear. We do still have the constraints on first-period resources and in addition we will, in accordance with (5), restrict ourselves at certain stages in the argument to plans for which $\mathbf{p}_f^2\,\mathbf{y}_f^2 \geqq 0$, since only those will satisfy our equilibrium conditions.

(ii) (a) If $\sum_f y^1 \geqq 0$, then $y_f^1 = 0$, all f. (b) The future returns to any production plan requiring no first-period inputs are bounded for any firm, i.e. $\mathbf{p}_f^2\,\mathbf{y}_f^2$ is bounded as y_f^2 varies over all two-period production vectors $(0, y^2)$ in Y_f^{12} with no current inputs.

We will argue that this assumption is not unreasonable. First, it will have to be understood that any factor availabilities in period 1 as the result of earlier production (e.g. durable capital goods or maturing agricultural products) are to be included in the initial endowment of current flows, $\bar{\mathbf{x}}^1$. Hence, the absence of net inputs means the absence of capital, labor, and current raw materials; it is reasonable then to conclude that no production takes place in period 1, i.e. $\mathbf{y}_f^1 = 0$, all f. As far as (b) is concerned, if it were not true, then a firm could expect indefinitely large profits in the next period even if it were to shut down today. But then the firm would know that its price expectations are not consistent with any equilibrium and so it is reasonable to argue that it does not hold any such expectations. Thus (b) is really a weak requirement on the rationality of expectations.

It is convenient to define a two-period production allocation, $(\mathbf{y}_f^{12})$ to be *quasi-feasible* if it is first-period feasible and if the second-period components are not unprofitable to any firm (according to its own expectations), i.e. if it satisfies the conditions

$$\sum_f \mathbf{y}_f^1 + \bar{\mathbf{x}}^1 \geqq 0, \ \mathbf{p}_f^2 \, \mathbf{y}_f^2 \geqq 0, \ \text{each } f.$$

From assumption (ii), it is possible to prove, analogously to the corresponding discussion in section II, that

    the set of quasi-feasible two-period production allocations
    is closed, bounded, and convex. (6)

In the theory of consumer behavior, we apply again the assumptions made earlier to the intertemporal consumption vectors.

D.3. The set of *possible two-period consumption vectors* for household h is X_h^{12}, with elements, $\mathbf{x}_h^{12} = (\mathbf{x}_h^1, \mathbf{x}^2)$, the components being referred to as the *first-period* and *second-period* possible consumption vectors, respectively.

(iii) Assumptions (iv), (v), and (vi) of section II hold under D.3 with $\mathbf{x}_h, \bar{\mathbf{x}}_h, \bar{\bar{\mathbf{x}}}_h$, and X_h, replaced by $\mathbf{x}_h^{12}, \bar{\mathbf{x}}_h^{12}, \bar{\bar{\mathbf{x}}}_h^{12}$, and X^{12} respectively. We also assume that $U_h(\mathbf{x}_h^1, \mathbf{x}_h^2)$ is not satiated in $\mathbf{x}_h^2$ for any $\mathbf{x}_h^1$.

Like the firm, the household knows current prices, including that of bonds, and anticipates second-period prices, $\mathbf{p}_h^2$. It plans purchases and sales for both periods. In each period, there is a budget constraint. The two constraints are linked through the purchase of bonds, which constitute an expense in period 1 and a source of purchasing power in period 2 (or vice versa, if the household is a net borrower in period 1). The household can be considered to have an initial endowment of bonds, $\bar{x}_{hb}$, which is precisely its anticipated volume of receipts in period 2. The net purchase of bonds in period 1 is then denoted by $x_{hb} - \bar{x}_{hb}$. Total expenditures for goods and bonds in period 1 are $\mathbf{p}^1 \mathbf{x}_h^1 + p_b(x_{hb} - \bar{x}_{hb})$, while planned expenditures in period 2 are $\mathbf{p}_h^2 \mathbf{x}_h^2$.

The purchasing power available in period 1 is the sum of the sale of endowment, $\mathbf{p}^1 \bar{\mathbf{x}}_h^1$, and receipts from firms in that period. The planned receipts in period 2 equal the planned sale of endowment, $\mathbf{p}_h^2 \bar{\mathbf{x}}_h^2$, plus receipts from firms in period 2, and this sum equals $\bar{x}_{hb}$, as remarked. The purchasing power planned to be available in period 2 is the repayment to the houshold of its net purchase of bonds, x_{hb} minus $\bar{x}_{hb}$, plus planned receipts, and is therefore simply x_{hb}.

There is a feature in this model not present in the static model or its intertemporal analogue with all futures markets. Since different households hold different expectations of future prices, they have different expectations of the profitability of any particular firm. Hence, a market for shares in firms will arise; the initial stockholders may value the firm less highly than some others, and therefore the stock of the firm should change hands.

After the firm has chosen its production plan, $\mathbf{y}_f^{12}$, household h values the plan according to current prices and its expectations of future prices.

D.4. The *capital value of firm f according to household h* is

$$K_{hf}(\mathbf{p}, \mathbf{y}_f^{12}) = \mathbf{p}^1 \mathbf{y}_f^1 + p_b(\mathbf{p}_h^2 \mathbf{y}_f^2).$$

The value of the firm in the market is the highest value that any household gives to it.

D.5. The *market capital value of firm f* is

$$K_f(\mathbf{p}, \mathbf{y}_f^{12}) = \max_h K_{hf}(\mathbf{p}, \mathbf{y}_f^{12}).$$

We will assume that, for each production plan for each firm, there is at least one household that values the plan at least as highly as the firm itself does; one might rationalize this by noting that the firm's manager is presumably himself the head of a household.

(iv) The market capital value of a firm is at least equal to the maximum profits anticipated by the firm itself; in symbols,

$$K_f(\mathbf{p}, \mathbf{y}_f^{12}) \geqq \mathbf{p}\, \mathbf{y}_f, \text{ for all } \mathbf{p} \text{ and all } \mathbf{y}_f^{12} \in Y_f^{12}.$$

From D.4 and D.5,

$$K_f = \max_h [\mathbf{p}^1 \mathbf{y}_f^1 + p_b(\mathbf{p}_h^2 \mathbf{y}_f^2)] = \mathbf{p}^1 \mathbf{y}_f^1 + p_b \max_h (\mathbf{p}_h^2 \mathbf{y}_f^2),$$

CE E

since $\mathbf{p}^1 \, y_f^1$ and p_b are independent of h. Let

$$K_f^2(y_f^2) = \max_h \; (\mathbf{p}_h^2 \, y_f^2). \tag{7}$$

If we recall that $\mathbf{p} \, \mathbf{y}_f = \mathbf{p}^1 \, \mathbf{y}_f^1 + p_b(\mathbf{p}_f^2 \, y_f^2)$, then (iv) implies

$$K_f - p \, y_f = p_b(K_f^2 - \mathbf{p}_f^2 \, y_f^2) \geqq 0. \tag{8}$$

Let $\bar{d}_{hf}$ be the share of firm f held initially by household h; we assume that it sells its shares at the market price and buys others – only, however, in those firms which it values at least as highly as any other household. We assume the absence of short sales. Let d_{hf} be its share of firm f after the stock market has operated. Its net receipts from sale less purchase of stocks (possibly negative, of course) are given by

$$\sum_f (\bar{d}_{hf} - d_{hf}) K_f.$$

Also,

$$d_{hf} = 0 \text{ unless } K_{hf} = K_f. \tag{9}$$

It will be recalled that the current receipts of the firm are given by (2) or (4): it is assumed that they are all distributed among its new owners, so that household h receives

$$\sum_f d_{hf}(\mathbf{p} \, \mathbf{y}_f).$$

Hence, the budget constraint for period 1 reads:

$$\mathbf{p}^1 \, \mathbf{x}_h^1 + p_b(x_{hb} - \bar{x}_{hb}) \leqq \mathbf{p}^1 \, \bar{\mathbf{x}}^1 + \sum_f d_{hf}(\mathbf{p} \, \mathbf{y}_f) + \sum_f (\bar{d}_{hf} - d_{hf}) K_f. \tag{10}$$

In period 2, the household is responsible for its share of the bonds issued by firm f, which total $\mathbf{p}_f^2 \, y_f^2$. But according to its expectations, the firm will receive $\mathbf{p}_h^2 \, y_f^2$. From (9), the household only invests in firms whose production plans it values at least as highly as anyone else, so that from (7) any firm for which $d_{hf} > 0$ will be expected by household h to have second-period receipts K_f^2. Hence, the anticipated total receipts from firm in period 2 by household h will be

$$\sum_f d_{hf}(K_f^2 - \mathbf{p}_f^2 \, y_f^2).$$

From earlier remarks, then,

$$\bar{x}_{hb} = \mathbf{p}_h^2 \, \mathbf{x}_h^2 + \sum_f d_{hf}(K_f^2 - \mathbf{p}_f^2 \, y_f^2), \quad \bar{\mathbf{x}}_h = (\bar{\mathbf{x}}_h^1, \bar{x}_{hb}). \tag{11}$$

Then

$$\bar{x}_b = \sum_h \bar{x}_{hb} = \sum_h (\mathbf{p}_h^2 \, \bar{\mathbf{x}}_h^2) + \sum_f (K_f^2 - \mathbf{p}_f^2 \, y_f^2). \tag{12}$$

Note that $\bar{x}_b$ is a function of the y_f^2s, the second-period production allocation. Note also that, from (8), the summation terms in (11) and (12) are non-negative.

Define now

$$\bar{\bar{x}}_{hb} = \mathbf{p}_h^2 \, \bar{\bar{\mathbf{x}}}_h^2, \; \bar{\bar{\mathbf{x}}}_h = (\bar{\bar{\mathbf{x}}}_h^1, \, \bar{\bar{x}}_{hb}). \tag{13}$$

By a slightly tedious but elementary calculation, it can easily be seen that the vector $\bar{\bar{\mathbf{x}}}_h$, defined for current markets, in fact satisfies the conditions of assumption (v) of section II if assumption (iii) above holds.

$$\bar{\mathbf{x}}_h \geqq \bar{x}_h; \text{ if } \bar{\bar{\mathbf{x}}}_{hi} > 0, \text{ then } \bar{x}_{hi} > \bar{\bar{x}}_{hi}. \tag{14}$$

As already remarked, the budget constraint for period 2 is simply

$$\mathbf{p}_h^2 \, \mathbf{x}_h^2 \leqq x_{hb}. \tag{15}$$

We therefore define:

D.6. The set of *current consumption vectors*, X_h, consists of all vectors, $\mathbf{x}_h = (\mathbf{x}_h^1, \, x_{hb})$ such that $x_{hb} \geqq \mathbf{p}_h^2 \, \mathbf{x}_h^2$ for some $(\mathbf{x}_h^1, \, \mathbf{x}_h^2)$ in X_h^{12}.

In other words, X_h is the set of current market vectors which, at the price expectations of the household, permit a possible two-period consumption vector.

From (15) and assumption (iii), $x_{hb} \geqq 0$, also $\bar{\bar{\mathbf{x}}}_h$ belongs to X_h. Assumption (iii), (14), and D.6 then assure us that

assumptions (iv) and (v) of section II hold with the new interpretations of $\mathbf{x}_h$, $\bar{x}_h$, $\bar{\bar{\mathbf{x}}}_h$, X_h (see (11), (14), and D.6, respectively). (16),

The maximization of $U_h(\mathbf{x}_h^1, \mathbf{x}_h^2)$ subject to the budget constraints (10) and (15) can be thought of as occurring in two stages. For any given $\mathbf{x}_h = (\mathbf{x}_h^1, \, x_{hb})$, we can maximize with respect to $\mathbf{x}_h^2$ subject to (15); the maximum is now a function of $\mathbf{x}_h^1$ and of x_{hb}, i.e. of $\mathbf{x}_h$, with respect to which it can be maximized subject to (10).

D.7. *First-period derived utility* is

$$U_h^*(\mathbf{x}_h) = \max U_h(\mathbf{x}_h^1, \mathbf{x}_h^2) \text{ subject to } \mathbf{p}_h^2 \, \mathbf{x}_h^2 \leqq x_{hb}.$$

We do have to assume that the maximum in D.7 actually exists. The existence depends primarily on $\mathbf{p}_h^2$, the household's anticipations of future prices. It will be assumed that the household is sufficiently realistic for this purpose; this is not an unreasonable assumption since the household would know, from the fact that a maximum does not exist, that the prices could not be equilibrium prices.

(v) For given $\mathbf{x}_h^1$, the function $U_h(\mathbf{x}_h^1, \, \mathbf{x}_h^2)$ assumes a maximum subject to the constraint $\mathbf{p}_h^2 \mathbf{x}_h^2 \leqq x_{hb}$ for any x_{hb} permitting possible second-period consumption, i.e. for any $\mathbf{x}_h \in X_h$.

From (iii), it is easy to see that U_h^* is continuous. It is also true that it is semi-strictly quasi-concave and very easy to establish that U_h^* is locally non-satiated in $\mathbf{x}_h$. By a suitable choice or origin, we can insure $U_h^*(\bar{\mathbf{x}}_h) = 0$.

$U_h^*(\mathbf{x}_h)$ is continuous, semi-strictly quasi-concave, and

> admits no local satiation; $U_h^*(\bar{\mathbf{x}}_h) = 0$; U_h^* is strictly
> increasing in x_{hb} for any $\mathbf{x}_h^1$. $\qquad$ (17)

These properties, except for the last, are precisely those of U_h as assumed in (vi) of section II.

The aim of the household, then, is to maximize U_h^* subject to (10), which can be written

$$\mathbf{p}\,\mathbf{x}_h \leqq M_h, \qquad (18)$$

where

$$M_h = \mathbf{p}\,\bar{\mathbf{x}}_h + \sum_f d_{hf}(\mathbf{p}\,\mathbf{y}_f) + \sum_f (\bar{d}_{hf} - d_{hf}) K_f(\mathbf{p}, \mathbf{y}_f^1, \mathbf{y}_f^2). \qquad (19)$$

Another way of writing (19) will be useful. First, rewrite it slightly; then note that by our notation, $\mathbf{p}\,\bar{\mathbf{x}}_h = \mathbf{p}^1\,\bar{\mathbf{x}}_h^1 + p_b\,\bar{\mathbf{x}}_{hb}$; then substitute from (11):

$$M_h = \mathbf{p}\,\bar{\mathbf{x}}_h + \sum_f \bar{d}_{hf}(\mathbf{p}\,\mathbf{y}_f) + \sum_f (\bar{d}_{hf} - d_{hf})\,(K_f - \mathbf{p}\,\mathbf{y}_f)$$

$$= \mathbf{p}^1\,\bar{\mathbf{x}}_h^1 + \sum_f \bar{d}_{hf}(\mathbf{p}\,\mathbf{y}_f) + p_b\,[\mathbf{p}_h^2\,\bar{\mathbf{x}}_h^2 + \sum_f \bar{d}_{hf}(K_h^2 - \mathbf{p}_h^2\,\mathbf{y}_f^2)]. \qquad (20)$$

Recall that $K_f - \mathbf{p}\,y_f = (K_f^2 - \mathbf{p}_f^2\,\mathbf{y}_f^2)$ by (8). One important implication of (20) is that the actual final share allocation does not affect the household budget constraints and therefore does not affect the equilibrium. The reason is that, since shares in firms are assumed to be sold to those who value them most highly at a price equal to that value, each potential buyer is in fact indifferent between making the purchase and investing in bonds, and none of his other behavior is affected by the choice.

We now have all the threads of the model in hand. Since equilibrium occurs only on current markets, the only relevant prices are those for current commodities and bonds. Basically, the model is very similar to that of static competitive equilibrium; the aim of the firm is to maximize $\mathbf{p}\,\mathbf{y}_f$ subject to $y_f \in Y_f$, according to (4) and D.2, while the consumer aims to maximize a (first-period derived) utility function subject to a budget constraint (18). The feasibility conditions for the current markets have the same form as before; demand for first-period commodities and for bonds shall not exceed supply, including the initial endowment of bonds as defined. However, there are two complications: (i) the budget constraint, using the definition of M_h in (20), is somewhat different than that of section II and more especially contains variables, the y_f^2s, which are not in the standard system; (ii) by (12) one component of the social endowment vector, namely $\bar{x}_b$, also depends on the y_f^2s.

Let us formally define competitive and compensated temporary equilibrium.

D.8. Competitive and compensated temporary equilibrium are defined as in section II (see D.1 and D.2 there) with the notation introduced in this section, except that (i) the variables y_f^2 must be consistent with intertemporal profit maximization, (ii) the utility functions, U_h, are replaced by U_h^*, and (iii) the budget equations now take the form

$$\mathbf{p}^* \, \mathbf{x}_h^* = M_h^*$$

where M_h^* is given by (19) or (20) in terms of equilibrium magnitudes.

To prove the existence of compensated equilibrium, the previous mapping has to be only slightly modified; however, we here omit the details.

We have assumed to this point that all price expectations are totally inelastic; this assumption can easily be relaxed.

(vi) For each household and firm, anticipated second-period prices are a continuous function of current prices, i.e. $\mathbf{p}_h^2(p)$ and $\mathbf{p}_f^2(\mathbf{p})$ are continuous functions.

We now interpret those assumptions which referred to anticipated second-period prices, namely, (ii), (iv), and (v), to hold for all values of $\mathbf{p}_h^2$ and $\mathbf{p}^2$ in the ranges of the anticipation functions, $\mathbf{p}_h^2(\mathbf{p})$ and $\mathbf{p}_f^2(\mathbf{p})$. The various functions and correspondences now depend explicitly on $\mathbf{p}$, through $\mathbf{p}_f^2$ and $\mathbf{p}_h^2$; all the relevant continuity properties are easily seen to hold, and the existence of a compensated temporary equilibrium remains valid for elastic expectations.

Finally, to show that the compensated equilibrium is a competitive equilibrium, we need to redefine the concepts of resource-relatedness. We will say that household h' is *rescource-related* to household h'' for given $\bar{x}_b$ *and* $\mathbf{p}$ if the definition given in section II holds when Y_f is computed as of a fixed $\mathbf{p}_f^2$ determined by $\mathbf{p}$, U_h^* as of a fixed $\mathbf{p}_h^2$ determined by $\mathbf{p}$, and $\bar{x}_b$ is taken as given. Then household h' is said to be *resource-related* to household h'' without qualification if it is so resource-related for any given $\bar{x}_b$ and $\mathbf{p}$. As before, household h' is *indirectly resource-related* to household h'' if there exists some chain of households, beginning with h' and ending with h'', such that each household in the chain is resource-related to its successor.

(vii) Every household is indirectly resource-related to every other.

With (vii) and the earlier assumptions, a compensated temporary equilibrium is necessarily a competitive temporary equilibrium, so the existence of competitive temporary equilibrium is established.

Remark 1. The theory of the firm used here is somewhere between two currently popular views. It is 'managerial' in that only the expectations of managers enter into the firm's decisions; stockholders appear only as passive investors. However, in contradistinction to theories such as those of Marris (1964) and Williamson (1964), we do not ascribe to managers any motives other than profit maximization according to their expectations.

A more general model would introduce a utility function for managers which depends in some more complicated way on the firm's production vector and current and anticipated profits; we have not investigated such a model here.

An alternative theory has the firm maximizing the current market value of its stock. That is, it chooses $\mathbf{y}_f^{12}$ to maximize K_f. This could be included in the present model by identifying $\mathbf{p}_f^2$ with $\mathbf{p}_h^2$ for that household for which K_{hf} is a maximum, where, for each h, K_{hf} has itself been defined by maximizing over Y_f^{12} at given $\mathbf{p}$ and $\mathbf{p}_h^2$. The only difficulty with this theory in the present framework is that as current prices change, different households value the firm most highly, and so $\mathbf{p}_f^2$ might change discontinuously as $\mathbf{p}$ changed. This would be avoided if we assumed there is in fact a continuum of households, filling up a whole area in $\mathbf{p}_h^2$-space for any given p; then $\mathbf{p}_f^2$ as defined would vary continuously with $\mathbf{p}$. But such a theory requires advanced methods for analysis.

Remark 2. The model here has assumed that there are no debts in the initial period, though there will, in general, be debts at the beginning of the next period. If expectations are falsified, then it can happen that no equilibrium in the next period will exist without bankruptcy, because the distribution of debt which is the result of the present period's choices and therefore the initial distribution for the next period is inappropriate.

Remark 3. Of course, we are here neglecting uncertainty. This is a more serious problem than one might think; for in the presence of uncertainty it is unreasonable to assume that bonds of different firms and households are perfect substitutes. If we are not willing to assume that all individuals have the same probability distributions of prices, then it is reasonable to suppose that any firm or household has more information about matters that concern it most and therefore a household will have different subjective probability distributions for the bonds of different firms. If a given firm is then the only supplier of a commodity (its bonds) for which there are no perfect substitutes, then the capital markets cannot be assumed perfect.

Remark 4. The restriction to two periods prevents us from examining speculation in the market for shares based on other households' expectations, a matter to which Keynes (1936, pp. 154–9) has called attention in a dramatic passage. In a three-or-more-period model, a household may buy shares in a firm because he has expectations that in the second period others will have expectations which will make it profitable to sell the shares then.

References

Arrow, K. J., and Debreu, G. (1954) 'Existence of equilibrium for a competitive economy', *Econometrica*, XXII 265–90.

Arrow, K. J., Karlin, S., and Scarf, H. (1958) *Studies in the Mathematical Theory of Inventory and Production* (Stanford, Calif.: Stanford University Press).

Arrow, K. J., and Hahn, F. H. (forthcoming) *Competitive Equilibrium Analysis* (San Francisco: Holden-Day).

Burger, E. (1963) *Introduction to the Theory of Games* (Englewood Cliffs, N.J.: Prentice-Hall).

Bushaw, D. W., and Clower, R. W. (1957) *Introduction to Mathematical Economics* (Homewood, Ill.: Irwin).

Chamberlin, E. H. (1956) *The Theory of Monopolistic Competition*, 7th ed. (Cambridge, Mass.: Harvard University Press).

Debreu, G. (1959) *Theory of Value* (New York: Wiley).

Debreu, G. (1962) 'New concepts and techniques for equilibrium analysis', *International Economic Review*, III 257–73.

Farrell, M. J. (1959) 'The convexity assumption in the theory of competitive markets', *Journal of Political Economy*, LXVII 377–91.

Hicks, J. R. (1939) *Value and Capital* (Oxford: Clarendon Press).

Hicks, J. R. (1965) *Capital and Growth* (New York and Oxford: Oxford University Press).

Hoffman, A. J., and Jacobs, W. (1954) 'Smooth patterns of production', *Management Science*, I 86–91.

Holt, C. C., Modiglani, F., Muth, J. F., and Simon, H. A. (1960) *Planning Production, Inventories, and Work Force* (Englewood Cliffs, N.J.: Prentice-Hall).

Kakutani, S. (1941) 'A generalization of Brouwer's fixed-point theorem', *Duke Mathematical Journal*, VIII 451–9.

Kaldor, N. (1935) 'Market imperfection and excess capacity', *Economica*, n. s., II 33–50.

Kalecki, M. (1939) *Essays in the Theory of Economic Fluctuations* (New York: Farrar & Rinehart).

Keynes, J. M. (1936) *The General Theory of Employment Interest and Money* (New York: Harcourt Brace).

Marris, R. (1964) *The Economic Theory of 'Managerial' Capitalism* (Glencoe, Ill.: The Free Press of Glencoe).

McKenzie, L. (1954) 'On equilibrium in Graham's model of world trade and other competitive systems', *Econometrica*, XXII 147–61.

McKenzie, L. (1959) 'On the existence of general equilibrium for a competitive market', *Econometrica*, XXVII 54–71.

McKenzie, L. (1961) 'On the existence of general equilibrium: some corrections', *Econometrica*, XXIX 247–8.

Negishi, T. (1960–1) 'Monopolistic competition and general equilibrium', *Review of Economic Studies*, XXVIII 196–201.

Penrose, E. T. (1959) *The Theory of the Growth of the Firm* (New York and Oxford: Oxford University Press).

Robinson, J. (1933) *The Economics of Imperfect Competition* (London: Macmillan).

Rothenberg, J. (1960) 'Non-convexity, aggregation, and Pareto optimality,' *Journal of Political Economy*, LXVIII 435–68.

Schlesinger, K. (1933–4) 'Über die Produktionsgleichungen der ökonomischen Wertlehre', *Ergebnisse eines mathematischen Kolloquiums*, VI 10–11.

Starr, R. (1969) 'Quasi-equilibria in markets with nonconvex preferences', *Econometrica*, XXXVII 25–38.

Tompkins, C. B. (1964) 'Sperner's lemma and some extensions', chap. 15 in E. F. Beckenbach (ed.), *Applied Combinatorial Mathematics* (New York, London, and Sydney: Wiley).

Triffin, R. (1940) *Monopolistic Competition and General Equilibrium Theory* (Cambridge, Mass.: Harvard University Press).

Wald, A. (1936) 'Über einige Gleichungssysteme der mathematischen Ökonomie', *Zeitschrift für Nationalökonomie*, VIII 637–70. English translation (1951) 'On some systems of equations of mathematical economics', *Econometrica*, XIX 368–403.

Williamson, O. E. (1964) *The Economics of Discretionary Behavior* (Englewood Cliffs, N.J.: Prentice-Hall).

4 Comments on Arrow

G. C. Archibald

One who is anything but expert in modern general equilibrium theory may well hesitate to comment on Arrow's paper. The admirable 'mug's guide to the existence game' of Quirk and Saposnik,[1] however, both encourages the attempt, and ensures that some relevant ideas are common knowledge.

From the present point of view the most novel and important part of Arrow's paper is the proof of the existence of a solution in monopolistic competition *without* the requirement that the monopolists all experience diminishing returns. (There are novelties in the method of proof, too. It is shown that the existence of a 'compensated equilibrium', for a given utility level, implies the existence of an uncompensated equilibrium, and then the existence of the former is proved.) Arrow assumes the simultaneous existence of a competitive sector, which supplies goods (inputs) to the monopolistic sector and demands goods. The possibilities open to the monopolists obviously depend not only on their technology, but also on what they can sell to, and purchase from, the competitive sector. Thus the feasible set for the monopolists is the intersection of two sets, their production possibility set and the set of demands and supplies from the competitive sector. The former is allowed to be an awkward shape, but the latter, by the usual assumptions, is convex. It is then at least possible that the intersection will be sufficiently well behaved for existence to be proved in the usual way.

In the hope of bringing out the economic significance of this analysis, I am going to try to construct a very simple example. Arrow argues that, for the monopolists' feasible set to be well behaved, it is required that the competitive sector be 'large' relative to the monopolistic (p. 87). This is a little worrying: could we not prove existence in a world in which all firms were monopolists? In the hope of

---

[1] James Quirk and Rubin Saposnik, *Introduction to General Equilibrium Theory and Welfare Economics* (New York, 1968).

illuminating this question (and for simplicity) my example will have only one firm, a monopolist (obviously), who produces only one product, and the competitive sector will consist purely of households who supply labour and purchase the monopolists' product. In this very simple model (which we can analyse with a simple reinterpretation of Arrow's diagrams) we can investigate some relevant questions: given increasing returns to the monopolist, what restrictions do we require on household behaviour to ensure a solution? how much must the monopolist know? can we allow him not to maximize?

The assumption of a single monopolist is likely to induce a knee-jerk among some economists: he extracts all the consumers' income, i.e. his effective demand elasticity is unity, so he produces an infinitely small amount. This obviously will not do. The monopolist extracts all income, certainly, but the level of income depends on him (how much we allow him to perceive is obviously going to be important).

Consider Fig. 4.1, where the monopolist's product (say, wheat) is measured on the vertical axis and labour (an input) on the negative portion of the horizontal. There is some limit to possible supplies of labour, say at OL_0 (where everyone works twenty-four hours per day). The boundary of the monopolist's production function is OM. (We obviously assume that he is the sole proprietor of one indivisible fixed factor. Returns must diminish somewhere, but we may assume this to be to the left of L_0.) There are some technical reasons why it is convenient to endow the households with an initial stock of wheat, but this need not concern us here. We may also bound the consumption set by minimum physiological requirements, instead of by OL_0 and the vertical from L_0, but this need not concern us now either. Clearly, there is only one relative price in this economy, the relative price of wheat to labour. Thus when the monopolist sets a product price, he automatically sets a wage. By varying the price line, we may then trace out the household's offer curve, say OH. (We may make the standard assumptions about consumer preferences, including no bliss point.)

Consider two possible price lines, OP_1 and OP_2. OP_1 induces a labour supply OL_1, and a household demand for wheat of L_1Q_1. Production is L_1X_1 and rent ('surplus value'?) is Q_1X_1. Satisfaction of the budget constraint requires that the profit be spent on wheat, whether it is distributed among share-owning households, or retained

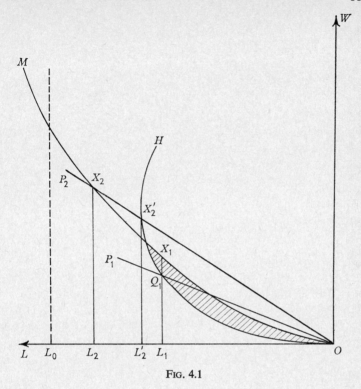

FIG. 4.1

by the single monopolist's household (which may also supply labour).
Hence a price ratio OP is feasible, and clears the market. It is, of
course, not necessarily the profit-maximizing price.

Price line OP_2 would generate output L_2X_2 if the labour were
forthcoming. Households, however, will only supply OL'_2 of labour
at this wage rate, and this would produce less output than they
demand. Obviously, then, X_2 is not feasible: the feasible set is
Arrow's intersection, the shaded area, and only price lines inter-
secting that set can clear the markets. The existence of a solution
(with non-zero output and positive prices) requires, then, that this
set be not empty. We shall investigate in a moment what might 'go
wrong'. First, let us return to the price line OP_2 and the monopolist's
behaviour. At OP_2 we have, it seems, an excess demand for labour,
and an excess demand for wheat if OL'_2 labour is actually at work.
We cannot have excess demand in both markets simultaneously!
But suppose we are actually at X'_2. Markets clear, but the monopolist

is making a loss. What we require is that he reacts by moving in the 'right' direction, i.e. increasing the price of wheat (it is obvious that we are dealing with the mechanics of disequilibrium rather than with the properties of equilibrium, but we are interested in how much the monopolist needs to know). Obviously, if he knows where the offer curve is, he moves in the right direction. But he need know less than this: he need only know that a smaller labour input would reduce output less than it would reduce demand. This is equivalent to knowing on which side of the intersection of marginal revenue and marginal cost one is.

The next question is whereabouts in the feasible set we may go. Any point, including the origin, provides non-negative profit. Profit maximization is achieved at the price line which maximizes the vertical distance between OM and OH. But the managers of the monopoly can maximize anything they please, provided they avoid losses! (Profit maximization is obviously sufficient for uniqueness. We should also have uniqueness if the feasible set contracted to a point. This would be a point of tangency between the offer curve and the production function. Any extraneous competitive rule that inhibited positive profit would do so by reducing the feasible set to a tangent point. A change in tastes, an increase in endowments, *or* alternative market opportunities could all move the household's offer curve to this monopolist in such a fashion as to reduce the size of the feasible area.)

Let us explore a little further the question of what pricing behaviour by the monopolist, and what knowledge on his part, ensures that we do get into the feasible set. Profit maximization does it, obviously, if the monopolist has sufficient knowledge. So, in the same trivial way, does maximization of something else (say, sales) subject to a profit constraint, as also maximization of a utility function containing profit as one argument. The required knowledge only seems to be awareness of the direction in which to move. The only pricing rule I can think of, off hand, that looks as though it might not work is a form of cost-plus pricing. It has sometimes been pointed out that this could lead to a price increase in response to a loss in the case in which output was to the left of the intersection of the marginal cost and marginal revenue curves. In fact, in Fig. 4.1, a price increase in response to a loss is required if the monopolist should be at, say, X_2, producing too much. It is only if the households have an initial endowment, so that the feasible non-negative-profit set excludes the origin, as in Fig. 4.2, that the monopolist can make a loss by producing too little. In this case it does seem that a sufficiently dumb cost-plus rule could send him in the wrong direction. But it is difficult to be formal about cost-plus rules in a world of only one relative price!

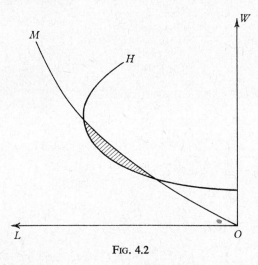

FIG. 4.2

Arrow's assumptions now seem sufficient to do the trick without the requirement that the competitive sector include a productive activity. What might go wrong? First, we notice that the origin is in the feasible set. This is simply disposed of by giving households an initial endowment of wheat, so that their offer curve starts from a positive intercept on OW. Secondly, then, the feasible set may be empty: OH and OM may not intersect at all. This simply says that the technology available to the monopolist is so poor that, with given tastes, no one finds it worth working for him at any price that yields a non-negative profit to him, so households live on their endowments. What happens if OH is backward-bending? It is drawn backward-bending in Fig. 4.1, but could be more so: consider Fig. 4.2, where households also have an initial endowment. This presents no problems. To obtain the disconnected set of Arrow's Fig. 3.4, one at least of OM, OH must have two points of inflection. In OM, this requires a region of increasing returns followed by one of decreasing returns; in OH, it seems impossible.

It seems, then, that in this simple example we have extended

Arrow's model by eliminating competitive firms. It also appears that the 'largeness' of the competitive sector relative to the mono-polistic is, perhaps, a not very well-defined concept. Can we make the model any 'more monopolistic'? Adding more monopolist producers adds nothing: it merely generalizes the problem to the one Arrow has already solved. Can we, then, make the household sector less competitive? If we reduce it to a single monopolist-monopsonist, we have bilateral monopoly, which is not the present game. Let us, therefore, keep the households competitive (price-takers) in the wheat market, but introduce a labour union. We walk right into a familiar problem: what does the union bargain for? There is only one relative price here, and it cannot be set by both parties. If the union sets the 'nominal wage', and the monopolist is then free to set the 'nominal' price of wheat, the latter sets the real price, and the situation is as before, so long as households still take price as a parameter in determining the quantities to be demanded and supplied. There appear to be two possibilities open to the union that are worth in-vestigating. The left-hand intersection of OM and OH in Fig. 4.1 gives the highest wage *and* the largest employment, therefore the largest labour income, within the feasible set. (Positive association of the equilibrium wage rate and employment and utility depend, given OM, only on where OH starts to bend back – see Fig. 4.2.) This intersection yields the maximum feasible household utility. If we assume that only the monopolist owns shares, this is the point for the union to aim for, either by demanding the appropriate level of employment, leaving the monopolist to set the price, or by setting the price, letting the monopolist determine employment. This re-quires, however, something like omniscience on the part of the union. Let us suppose, instead, that we start from an equilibrium within the shaded area (Figs 4.1 or 4.2). Such a situation yields rent, whether maximal or not. A union formed over the existing non-shareholding employees might well bargain for a share of that rent by, e.g., presenting the monopolist with all-or-none offers (see Archi-bald and North[1]). If the monopolist is a rent-maximizer, being forced to share the rent does not alter his optimal activity level: if he is not, it may. We obviously link up here with 'managerial models'.

Some elementary welfare implications may be mentioned. Given the derivation of the offer curves from indifference curves, and some

[1] G. C. Archibald and D. C. North, *On the Behavior of Labor Unions*, to be published.

standard assumptions, the 'best' attainable point is the north-west corner of the attainable set. This could be achieved by an omniscient union *or* by average cost pricing (if we exclude the origin). This may look odd, but the construction of the offer curves is such that, where a price line cuts, we have equality between the marginal rate of substitution of leisure for wheat, and the price ratio. The M.R.T. is given by the slope of OM. Given increasing returns, M.R.T. only equals the price ratio if we subsidise (i.e. give the price line an intercept on OL), as is familiar, and can be seen from the construction of Fig. 4.1. Without a subsidy, no point in the feasible set, including the 'best', gives equality of M.R.S. and M.R.T. We may also notice that, if the equilibrium involves rent, its distribution is irrelevant: if, for example, the monopolist sets the price OP_1 in Fig. 4.1, equilibrium allocation corresponds to X_1, which is non-optimal, whether the rent is shared out or not (provided that it is spent). This, too, is familiar.

We end with a conjecture that, given the usual assumptions of boundedness, etc., we only require competition on one side of the markets, i.e. enough to rule out bilateral monopoly (oligopoly). If this is correct, the required competitive sector may need only to consist of housewives.

5 On the Behavioral Theory of the Firm[1]

William J. Baumol and Maco Stewart

I. SUMMARY AND INTRODUCTION

The behavioral theorists have argued that in a world of uncertainty maximization models can offer very little help in explaining the behavior of firms and individuals since, when events are uncertain, apparently concrete maximands, such as the present value of the dis-discounted stream of profits, are no longer even well defined. In these circumstances the behaviorists have suggested that one must learn the firm's decision patterns from direct observation rather than *a priori* considerations.

In their first attempts to implement this view the behaviorists have undertaken several interesting empirical studies, largely confined to an examination of the working of rules of thumb governing fairly low-level business decisions.[2] Their studies have shown that at least in some enterprises rather simple-minded rules of thumb are adhered to with remarkable consistency. Moreover, a subsequent investigation by the present authors (reported in this paper) confirms that results are very similar to those obtained in a behaviorist study of department store pricing held several years later in another department store in a different city.[3]

Of course, the use of rule of thumb in areas of decision making

[1] The authors are grateful to the National Science Foundation for its help in the completion of this study.

[2] This is not meant to suggest that rules of thumb are used only in low-level decisions. While simple rules seem prevalent in the pricing of individual items in retail establishments, and used to be employed widely in inventory policy, they still seem to be employed rather frequently in such critical decisions as determination of the firm's overall advertising budget and in the choice of major investment projects.

[3] Despite a recent change in mark-ups in our own investigation, the pricing policies revealed by the two studies turned out to be surprisingly similar. The only major difference was that in our own sample special sales seemed to be much less significant than they were in the case examined in the earlier study.

which are particularly costly or where information is particularly poor is perfectly consistent with a maximization approach. One of the present authors has written elsewhere of a concept of 'optimally imperfect decisions' – decisions in which the process of information gathering and calculation has been carried to the point of zero marginal net yield. On this subject the recent history of inventory control procedures is illuminating. In the early 1920s some of the basic principles of inventory theory had already been discovered and reported in print. However, firms began to abandon simplistic rule-of-thumb inventory control techniques only when improved statistical methods and the availability of computers made it possible to provide the data needed for implementation of optimal inventory principles. In the case of mark-up pricing it may be argued that unavailability of marginal selling cost and demand elasticity data for individual items in a retail line makes recourse to rules of thumb unavoidable. If one argues that the effort involved in selling an item can be assumed roughly proportionate to the (wholesale?) price of the good, then mark-up pricing may even yield prices near proportionate to marginal costs.[1]

The behavioral analysis, then, seems to have been very successful in its attempts to predict simple business decisions on the basis of a careful study of rules of thumb. Moreover, the very simplicity of the rules leads us to suspect that the resulting decisions, while not 'irrational' by any means, may bear little relationship to the predictions that would be produced by some of the standard maximization models.

The behavioral analysis has, on the other hand, so far offered us few interesting analytical implications. It has, up to this point, provided no theory of the determination of the rules of thumb themselves. It has not suggested how these rules will vary with changes in the values of exogenous economic variables such as, say, the price level or interest rates.[2] As a result it has not been possible to account

---

[1] However, it is not plausible that this rule will generally yield near-profit-maximizing prices. It is well known that a fixed mark-up will maximize profits only if the demand curves for all of the seller's goods are equal in elasticity. For if we are maximizing profits, for any one item we must have $MC = MR = P(1 - 1/E)$. Thus, the profit-maximizing mark-up will be $(P - MC)/P = 1 - (MC/P) = 1/E$, which will be the same for all items only if the elasticity of demand, E, is also the same for all goods.

[2] However, at least in some cases the rules seem to be remarkably resistant to such outside influences. Cyert and March ([5], p. 138) cite reports that department store mark-ups have been stable for nearly half a century! Of course, they

for the rules that are in fact observed, or to draw many macro-economic inferences from the models. No doubt the influence which the behavioral analysis exerts over economics in the long run will depend critically on the degree of progress it can achieve in this area.

II. BEHAVIORAL MODELS

Cyert and March, and the writers who have followed their lead, then seek to provide a theory of the firm basing itself on observed behavior and utilizing analytic approaches derived from sociology and social psychology. As a result, their work does not always constitute very easy reading for those who, like ourselves, are trained primarily in standard economic theory. Because of the unfortunate gaps in our training in the other social sciences, we may not be at ease with concepts such as 'adaptive rationality' or 'quasi-resolution of conflict', and it is likely to take some of us some effort to become used to an explanation of decisions such as the following:

> Choice takes place in response to a problem, uses standard operating rules, and involves identifying an alternative that is acceptable from the point of view of evoked goals. Thus, the variables that affect choice are those that influence the definition of a problem within the organization, those that influence the standard decision rules and those that affect the order of consideration of alternatives. (Cyert and March [5], p. 116.)

Yet in dealing with the specifics of firm behavior they proceed from premises that are more clear-cut and narrow. They are willing to accept as a useful approximation the assumption that the firm is usually guided by no more than five important norms: a production norm which specifies an acceptable range of variation in that level, an inventory goal which sets up minimum levels below which stocks will not be allowed to fall, a sales goal, a target-market share, and a profit constraint.

They then argue that the time path of the firm's decisions is a learning process which can be described roughly as follows: suppose

---

vary considerably from one product line to another, and almost certainly from one class of department store to another – thus mark-ups in a store which caters to the luxury market seem to be relatively high, as one might expect.

some change in decision is under consideration. It is then subjected by management to two test calculations: (a) can the change be expected to meet the firm's satisficing requirements? and (b) is it likely to improve matters? If it meets both these tests the change is implemented. Moreover, if in retrospect it appears to have succeeded in doing so, further changes of this variety will be considered.[1] In this way price levels or advertising outlays or inventories may gradually adapt themselves over time. It may be observed that what has just been described may be viewed simply as an operational iterative solution to any standard maximization problem. By a process of trial and error, always seeking to move upward, one approaches a maximum step by step. There is a difference only because in reality the facts do not remain unchanged over time and so adaptation proceeds toward a moving target in a pattern which presumably is not described adequately by the maximizing models.

This all leads to a set of models of two general sorts: the learning models, in which the preceding outline is followed out explicitly, and the rule-of-thumb models, in which behavior is taken to follow some observed conventional patterns.

We will presently discuss in some detail an example of a rule-of-thumb model. A vastly oversimplified learning model is illustrated by the following two equations:

$$\pi_t = f(p_t)$$

and

$$p_{t+1} - p_t = k(\pi_t - \pi_{t-1})(p_t - p_{t-1})/|p_t - p_{t-1}|$$

where p_t is price in period t and π_t is the corresponding profit level. The second equation tells us in simple terms that the current price change will have the same sign as the preceding price change if profits rose in the preceding period, and that the current price change will reverse the direction of the preceding price change if profits have fallen. On such assumptions more complex duopoly models and other more sophisticated analyses have been constructed.[2]

There is one other characteristic step in the behavioral analysis: simulation and comparison with reality. Characteristically, the behavior of an actual firm or an actual decision-maker is chosen as a

---

[1] It is suggested, incidentally, that if neither the current state nor any proposed alternative meets the satisficing norms, the firm will revise its aspiration levels – management then just has to learn to live with more modest standards of acceptability.

[2] See, e.g., Cohen and Cyert ([3], pp. 339–50, 363–76).

standard of comparison and a model is used to try to predict his behavior. There has been an elaborate attempt to describe in this way the portfolio selected by a trust officer (see Clarkson [2]). Another study (see [3], pp. 339–50) has utilized the duopoly model described earlier to account for developments in the production of metal cans, and still another model has sought to describe pricing in a department store.

By and large these simulations seem to have been remarkably successful. For example, in the department stores pricing model, as we will see, Cyert and March were able to predict *to the penny* the prices of 384 items out of a sample of 414, a score well over 90 per cent. A somewhat comparable degree of success is reported by Clarkson. Thus the behavioral models would seem, at least at first glance, to accomplish what they had set out to do, to account for behavior.

III. IS IT A THEORY?

The behavioral models, then, do appear to pass their authors' tests with flying colors. Yet one is tempted to ask whether what they have produced is indeed a theory. We have no desire to argue semantics, and if one wishes to define a theory as a model which predicts behavior correctly we see no reason to quarrel with that use of terms.

But usually we have come to expect of a theory something more than the ability to deal with an individual case. At the very least we would ask of a model, before it is taken to constitute a theory, that it be shown to apply to a substantial number of cases under the postulated circumstances. We would want the pricing model to prove itself capable of accounting for prices in stores at other locations and at other points in time, at least so long as there were no changes in the underlying economic circumstances.

Perhaps we would be still more comfortable with the analysis if it were shown to hold even as circumstances varied, e.g. both in periods of inflation and deflation.

Best of all, presumably, we would like a model which calls for changes in behavior as circumstances vary but which predicts explicitly the relationship between the two. For then the model can serve analytic as well as predictive purposes. We can, for example, employ it to determine what response a change in the general price level elicits on the part of the typical firm. Indeed, this is one of the primary uses to which the more standard economic models are put.

So far, little seems to have been done to examine the performance of the behavioral models on any of these criteria. The next sections of this paper will report a modest first attempt in this direction. But first let us raise one additional issue.

While we have followed the standard discussion in contrasting the behavioral models with the more traditional maximization models, it does not follow that they are necessarily incompatible. One cannot assume in advance that they will inevitably yield conflicting predictions. Thus even if the empirical evidence turns out to favor strongly the behavioral models, we are not automatically forced to abandon our older tools even as instruments of description. It follows that it would be most useful to conduct a study investigating explicitly the extent of the conflict (if any) between the two types of analysis – a piece of work which apparently has not yet been undertaken. At the end of the paper we will return to this point, indicating some of the difficulties that are likely to be encountered in such a study.

IV. THE MARK-UP MODEL AND THE CYERT–MARCH RESULTS

In their investigation of pricing in a department store, Cyert and March develop three models designed to simulate the pricing decision in three general circumstances that apparently cover the bulk (and perhaps all) of the cases in the specific department that was examined. These are the normal pricing model (which will be referred to as the mark-up model), the sale-pricing model and the mark-down model. We turn now to a a re-examination of the first and third of these models with the aid of more recent data. Unfortunately, we did not obtain sufficient information to permit a restudy of the sale-pricing model.

The basic construct is the mark-up model, which represents the department's response to what the authors tell us is one of its two major objectives:[1] '. . . to realize a specified average mark-up on the goods sold' ([5], p. 129), though they do recognize that '. . . the

---

[1] The other is an annual sales volume objective.

mark-up goal adjusts to experience gradually' (p. 131).[1] The normal pricing model is composed of three very simple rules, respectively giving mark-up prices for 'standard items', 'exclusive items' (those not available to competitors) and 'import items'.

The first of these rules, which is the most relevant for our purposes, also represents the spirit of the other two rules. It asserts that the department in question calculates its normal price by adding a 40 per cent mark-up on an item's purchase price and then adjusting it so that the figure ends in $.95; i.e. the item sells for $5.95 or $6.95, etc. Thus the authors propose the following rule to describe normal price setting for standard items: 'Divide each cost by 0·6 . . . and move the result to the nearest $.95' (p. 138).[2]

The authors then proceeded to test the rule with the aid of a sample drawn from 197 invoices, comparing a price prediction formulated in accordance with the preceding rule with prices actually charged. Of the 197 predicted prices, 188 turned out to be correct to the penny.

V. MORE RECENT DATA AND THE MARK-UP MODEL

To test the stability of the Cyert–March mark-up rule over time and location, we attempted to replicate their results. For this purpose we utilized a department similar to the one that constituted the subject of their experiment. However, the department store selected was located in another city, it was unrelated to the store used in their study (the two are not parts of a common 'chain') and our data were, of course, collected several years later than theirs.

We discovered soon after we had begun to collect our data that mark-ups had only recently been increased and that, as a matter of

---

[1] The authors go on to state that '. . . mark-up is probably subject to long-run learning. For example, it varies in a general way from product group to product group according to the apparent risks involved, the costs of promotion or handling, the extent of competition, and the price elasticity. However, in any short run the normal mark-up is remarkably stable. The statement is frequently made in the industry that mark-ups have remained the same for the last 40 or 50 years' (p. 138).

[2] Notice that this involves a rather peculiar terminology: a 40 per cent mark-up is to be interpreted as a mark-up *that is 40 per cent of the final price*, not 40 per cent of the initial cost. Throughout the following discussion this Cyert–March terminological convention will be utilized.

fact, the management of the store was anxious to avoid publicizing this. At any rate, this gave some ground for the suspicion that some amendment in the Cyert–March mark-up rule would be required for it to fit our case.

In the store studied by us, the mark-up information seems to be available at only one spot in the corporate records, in a volume called the 'black book'. This book applies only to the current selling season, e.g. spring of 1968. Its primary purpose is to provide very current information to the buyer so that he will know how well each item is selling. The data in the book are classified by manufacturer, who is identified by a four-digit number, followed by another four-

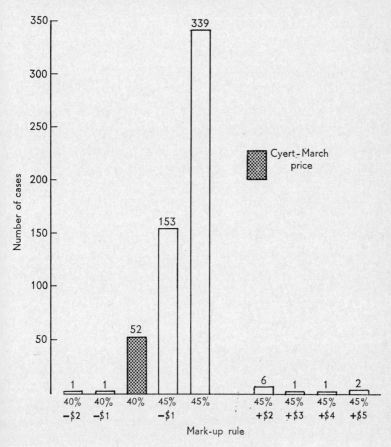

FIG. 5.1 Distribution of mark-up

digit number identifying the item. The black books for this department contained somewhat less than 600 items and so the complete
sample was examined, disregarding the relative sales volumes of the
different items. All observed combinations of purchase cost and
retail price were recorded in the form of a histogram indicating the
frequency with which any particular pair was encountered (Fig. 5.1).

In attempting to replicate the Cyert–March calculation, we found
one change on inspection. Instead of being rounded to the nearest
$.95 as in their data, the current figures were rounded to the nearest
dollar, with a few figures rounded to the nearest $.99.[1] After making
this adjustment, we found that less than 10 per cent of the items
(51 of a total of 555 cases)[2] exhibited the 40 per cent mark-up
predicted by the Cyert–March rule. This is shown in Table 5.1 and

Table 5.1

Distribution of Mark-ups: Retest of Cyert–March Model

	Level of mark-up	Number of cases	Percentage of cases
	40% – $2	1	0·2
	40% – $1	1	0·2
Cyert–March rule	40%	51	9·2
	45% – $1	153	27·6
Proposed empirical rule	45%	339	60·1
	45% + $1	0	0·0
	45% + $2	6	1·1
	45% + $3	1	0·2
	45% + $4	1	0·2
	45% + $5	2	0·4
Totals		555	100·0

[1] We are informed by Professor Cyert that even at the time he was engaged in
his study it was found that firms varied in the way they rounded off the endings
of their prices.

[2] The sample included all entries in the 'black books' for the period studied
with the following exceptions: 12 entries for imported items (for which Cyert and
March used special rules); 10 entries involving miscellaneous items at very low
prices; and 7 other entries involving very peculiar relationships. In one case,
because of rounding, the 40 and 45 per cent rules yielded the same results, and this
case was classed as a correct prediction for the Cyert–March (40 per cent) rule.

Fig. 5.1, which summarize our results. They indicate also that some 60 per cent of the cases follow an alternative empirical rule, formulated by us, which called for a 45 per cent mark-up. Of course, the fact that there has been a relatively small change in mark-up in the seven- or eight-year interval between their study and ours does not involve any basic conflict with their hypothesis.

In total, some 98 per cent of the cases involved a mark-up falling between 40 and 45 per cent. Thus, in our department store it is apparently not as easy to predict prices to the penny as it was in the Cyert–March sample. But this standard of forecasting performance, which they set for themselves, is clearly unusually stringent, though it is perhaps not totally inappropriate for a set of rule-of-thumb decisions. In any event, there seems to be little reason to doubt that the bulk of the prices did follow closely the dictates of the very simple rule of thumb of the general sort they described.

VI. THE MARK-DOWN MODEL AND THE CYERT–MARCH DATA

Cyert and March describe the mark-down as 'a contingent situation, produced by failure or anticipated failure with respect to organizational goals' (p. 137). Mark-downs are undertaken when sales or inventory of some items are unsatisfactory. According to Cyert and March, mark-downs are rarely instituted as a consequence of product defects or other such product characteristic limitations. Mark-downs in the department examined by them were determined by a set of standard rules. They tell us (p. 143):

> The general rule for first mark-downs is to reduce the retail price by $\frac{1}{3}$ and carry the result down to the nearest mark-down ending (i.e. to the nearest $.85). There are some exceptions. When the ending constraint forces too great a deviation from the $\frac{1}{3}$ rule (e.g. where the regular price is $5.00 or less) *ad hoc* procedures are occasionally adopted. On higher-priced items a 40 per cent mark-down is taken. . . .

In the more detailed description of the mark-down process in the author's flow charts, rounding to $.90 and 50 per cent mark-downs are also mentioned, and rules are given indicating when the less usual 40 and 50 per cent mark-downs apply.[1]

The mark-down model of Cyert and March was tested with the aid of data taken from 'mark-down slips', although these documents did not provide all the information needed to determine the mark-down category into which the item should fall, in accordance with the Cyert–March flow chart (see preceding footnote). They tell us: 'It was necessary, therefore, to use direct methods, such as the interrogation of the buyer and sales personnel, to get the information necessary to classify the items so that the model could be tested' (p. 147). (The data all referred to the preceding six-month period so that memories on the pricing decisions had some chance of being accurate.) In their test, for a sample of 159 items, 140 predicted prices turned out to be correct to the penny, thus yielding precisely correct results in 88 per cent of the cases.

VII. MARK-DOWNS IN THE MORE RECENT DATA

In gathering our more recent data we found that the 'black books' did not contain the information required to test the mark-down model. When it is decided to mark down the price of an item, the corresponding page is pulled from the black book and discarded. Instead, the buyer makes out a 'price change document' that describes the action taken on the particular line of merchandise. This is used for inventory control as well as for record-keeping. It still gives the vendor and style number and the original retail price. In addition, it contains a standard list of 17 possible reasons for a price change, and in each case the number corresponding to the reason for the mark-down is checked off. Of these reasons, many are technical matters involving such issues as breaking-up of sets, correction of errors, etc. Only four of the categories, 5 (unsalable at present price), 6 (past-season merchandise), and 7 and 8 (damaged), seem to correspond to the Cyert–March mark-down case. Finally, of course

---

[1] Thus the 40 per cent mark-down applies to items whose retail price is greater than or equal to $14.95. The 50 per cent mark-down applies to closing-out merchandise, where space needs are critical and more than 100 units of the item are in stock, where the item is no longer aesthetically appealing to customers (how determined?), and it is not subject to 'fair trade' pricing by the manufacturer.

the document records the marked-down price and the week of the selling season to which it applies. We had access to these documents for the first through the eleventh selling weeks of 1967, corresponding to the summer and fall selling seasons.

It was decided to select a sample of 25 items for each of the eleven weeks for which data were available to us, since the number of items marked down each week varied from about 50 to 250. On a first go-round we proceeded simply by enumerating each price change entry in a particular week (with no attempt to take into account differences in the number of items affected) and then selecting 25 cases with the aid of a table of random numbers.[1]

Table 5.2 reports the breakdown of our sample by the different classes of indicated reason for which the price reductions were undertaken. One interesting difference from the Cyert–March results is the relative frequency with which we encountered mark-downs that were instituted because the merchandise was returned by customers, or because it was soiled or damaged and sold as is (reason 7 and 8). Cyert and March reported that these were very minor components in their sample, whereas in our figures it constituted more than 23 per cent of the cases of reported price change.[2] Also notable is the very small number of cases (six in total) in which prices were reduced to meet a competitor's price or for a special sale (reasons 1 and 3).

Once again, when testing the Cyert–March rules we found that at least in one respect they require immediate modification. They tell us that prices are marked down to the nearest $.85 or $.90, whereas in our new sample they were rounded to the nearest $.99. From the

---

[1] We also undertook a second procedure in which the number of items selected for a given week was varied proportionately with the number of items marked down during that week. This was rather more time-consuming than the method involving a fixed sample size, and one had to know the week-to-week variation in number of mark-downs before selecting the sample size for each week. Hence, for future replications we hoped to obtain evidence that there is little to be gained by the refinement involved in the proportionate sample. In fact, the Kolmogorov–Smirnov test, when applied to the cumulative frequency of scores (number of prices predicted correctly), indicated that we were unable to reject either at the ·01 or ·05 per cent level of significance the the hypothesis that the observed differences were entirely random in nature.

[2] This disparity is, however, probably not as great as the numbers suggest, because our figures do not report the number of individual items affected. A decision to mark down last year's widget may reduce the price of all 300 of these items still in stock even though only one change in price is reported, while a single damaged widget returned by a customer will also be reported in a single price change entry.

Table 5.2

Distribution of Mark-down Sample by
Category of Reason for Mark-down

Category	Number of cases
Reasons	
1	2
3	4
5 and 6	118
7 and 8	64
13	2
15	1
Subsequent mark-downs ($.99 ending)	83
Total	274[a]

Definitions:

Reason 1 – meet competitor's price.
Reason 3 – special sale.
Reasons 5 and 6 – goods unsalable at
                current prices.
Reason 7 – soiled or torn merchandise.
Reason 8 – salvage.
Reason 13 – revise price up higher than
                original retail.
Reason 15 – making and breaking sets.

[a] This total resulted from the sampling of 25 items for each of 11 weeks with one case missing.

274 cases in our sample of mark-downs we included[1] only mark-downs on items that could not be sold at current prices (reasons 5 and 6 in the price change document). Moreover, we removed all cases in which the initial price ending was $.99 because this appeared to indicate that we were dealing with at least a second cut in the price of the same item (a 'subsequent' rather than an 'inital' mark-down) –

[1] We excluded reason 7 (soiled and torn) cases, and reason 8 (salvage) cases which constituted, respectively, 11·6 and 10·9 per cent or our sample. Among reason 7 and 8 cases, many items were simply written off completely.

price reductions to which there apply special rules about which more will be said presently. As a result, only 118 cases remained in our sample. A rather crude test of the Cyert–March mark-down rules (modified to take into account the $.99 rounding) was then conducted To each of the 188 cases the one third, 40 per cent and 50 per cent mark-down calculations were applied, and in each case, P_N, the nearest of the resulting figures to the actual price, P_a, was calculated. A successful prediction was then defined as a case in which P_a equalled P_N. That is, rather than attempting to predict for any particular item whether the one third, 40 per cent or 50 per cent mark-down applied, we undertook to see whether each particular change in turn could be explained by *any one* of the three.

Fig. 5.2 reports the results of our test of the mark-down rules. We see that in 86 cases, i.e. in 73 per cent of all possible cases, *one* of the three Cyert–March rules yielded a correct prediction. One of these

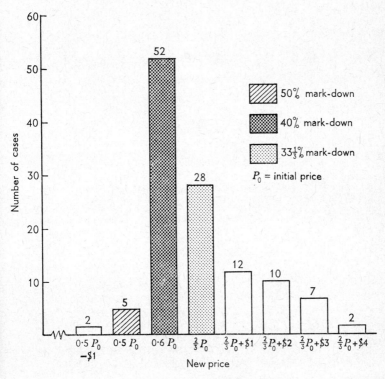

FIG. 5.2 Distribution of initial mark-downs

rules alone, the 40 per cent mark-down, predicted correctly in 44 per cent of the cases.

It seems significant that in 31 of the 38 cases in which none of the predictions was correct, the actual price exceeded the predicted price. (None of the misses involved prices between the highest and lowest prediction.) Moreover, of the three mark-down rules, the 0·5 rule, which yields the largest price reduction, now accounts for only a negligible proportion of the cases – some 4 per cent of the total. We conclude that in our sample not only are mark-ups typically higher than those observed by Cyert and March (Table 5.1.) but, in addition, the mark-downs have tended to decrease.

Sometimes an item is marked down a second time and even more than a second time, presumably because the effects of the previous mark-down are judged insufficient. Here, we are told, in the Cyert–March case the department did not appear to follow any explicit rule. However, the authors did, with obvious reservations,[1] derive such a rule from the data. The rule asserts: 'Insert the value of the initial mark-down price in the parabolic formula and carry the result *down* to the nearest \$.85 (\$.90)' (p. 143). Here the 'parabolic formula' refers to the (top half of the) parabolic curve $y^2 = 5(x - 2)$, where x is the initial (mark-down) price and y the suceeding mark-down price.

Let us turn, therefore, in our data to cases apparently involving a second or higher round of price reduction (the 83 items in our sample reduced either for reason 5 or 6 and for which the initial price ended in \$.99). In these cases the Cyert–March parabolic rule (section VI above) failed completely to explain observed prices. In every case it predicted a price reduction greater than that which was actually observed.

However, by a glance at Table 5.3, which reports the distribution of subsequent mark-down cases, we see that one simple rule of thumb accounts for 50 of the 83 observations. That rule instructs the decision-maker on a subsequent price reduction simply to cut the price by a flat \$2.[2]

---

[1] In presenting this rule, Cyert and March are careful to warn the reader that 'As a description of process, this rule is obviously deficient. However, in view of the limited number of cases involved and the inability of the department to articulate the rules, we have used this rough surrogate' ([5], p. 143).

[2] The performance of this rule can be improved slightly by setting up special rules for cases where initial prices were unusually low or unusually high. Accordingly, we formulated the following three-part rule: for an initial price of \$3.99 and below, reduced price by \$1. For an initial price of \$13.99 and above, reduce

Table 5.3

Distribution of Subsequent Mark-downs

Amount of reduction	$1	$2	$3	$4	More than $4	Total
Number of cases	8	50	11	11	3	83

VIII. EVALUATION: REPLICABILITY OF THE RESULTS OF THE MODEL

It is clear that a single attempt to duplicate the Cyert–March results is a most slender reed on which to rest an evaluation of the work of the behavioralists. Yet the results are suggestive in a number of respects even though they are more than a bit mixed.

First, our case study suggests strongly that the specifics of the rules of thumb do change with economic circumstances. The recent rise in mark-ups in the department studied seems quite clearly to have been a response to increasing costs. This implies that the behavioral models will have to be amended if they are to be applied in changed economic conditions. Unfortunately, at least the model in question gives us no clue as to the response in the values of its parameters to such exogenous changes in the economic data, and this clearly limits the analytic power of the construct. This point is not intended as a criticism of the approach. Rather it is meant to suggest that further work in behavioral theory should undertake to determine relationships between changes in observed rules and other economic variables. In fact, elsewhere in their book (chap. 8) the authors do address themselves to this issue.

More specifically, the predictive power of the original Cyert–March rules turns out to be rather less perfect than it was in their original case study. Even after *ad hoc* modification in its parameters it does not achieve nearly the degree of success which was attained by the original study. Yet the ability of the model, thus modified, to account *to the penny* for some 70 per cent of the prices remains

---

price by $4. In all other cases reduce price by $2. Since many of the cases in which the simple $2 price reduction rule failed lay in the tails of the distribution, the overall performance was somewhat improved, with 56 prices out of 83 now calculated correctly.

impressive. Moreover, the evidence does not rule out the possibility that more careful investigation would produce modified rules of thumb for the present case which would yield more successful predictions. On the other hand, the nature of our test does have one bias which favors the original model. We made no attempt to predict which of the three standard mark-downs should apply to a particular item. Our prediction took the form of the assertion 'one of the three mark-downs, one third or 40 per cent or 50 per cent (after rounding to $.99) will be observed for this item'. If we had done as Cyert and March undertook to do, and predicted which of the three figures applied to any specific item, we would undoubtedly have been wrong more often.

The upshot, it seems to us, is to confirm the notion that much of routine economic decision-making does follow fairly simple rules of thumb, as the behavioral approach predicts. As Cyert and March themselves were at pains to emphasize, the rules do change in slow response to economic pressures. Thus, mark-ups seem to have risen with time.

It is noteworthy, too, that the rules of thumb that emerge are simpler than one might infer from a hasty perusal of the rather complex diagrams which Cyert and March utilize to describe the decision process. The calculations utilized in arriving at pricing decisions or in checking them over are really minimal, in most cases involving no more than a single multiplication and adjustment to a conventional price ending.

IX. EVALUATION: RATIONALITY AND CONVENTIONAL MAXIMIZATION

Though we have sometimes heard the contrary implied by those who have not read the relevant writings with care, it must be re-emphasized that the behaviorists never even suggest that the pricing procedures which they describe are in any sense irrational. On the contrary, they maintain that these are part of a reasonable process of adaptation to the circumstances and, in particular, to the presence of uncertainty.

This position can easily be defended for the analysis in question. We have already noted that the very use of a simple rule of thumb may be taken to be a rational reaction to the costs of the decision process. Similarly, the use of a mark-up or a mark-down may be considered to represent adaptation to an inflationary environment. A fixed percentage mark-up offers the advantage of an automatic escalator since it means that the absolute amount of money which the retailer derives from a sale will rise proportionately with the wholesale price of the item in question. Thus, as the price level rises, the retailer's gross will tend to increase concomitantly.

In light of what has just been said, it may well be asked, if a fixed mark-up compensates for price inflation, why had our store recently found it appropriate to increase its mark-up? In part this may simply reflect demand conditions which might have permitted the retailer to collect more for his services. But an explanation which is perhaps more plausible can perhaps be found in the technology of the retailing process. Department stores may well be taken to constitute a service industry, and along with other such industries, it has found it very difficult to effect major innovations in its mode of operation. It can be classed in what one of the present authors has called the 'nonprogressive sector of the economy' because its workings still follow the handicraft operating patterns of earlier decades and it has not been able to achieve the cumulative increases in productivity per man-hour that characterize manufacturing. As a result, as wages rise in the economy as a whole, the costs of retailing tend to increase more rapidly than those of manufacturing because, in the latter, wage costs are offset by productivity increases, while in retailing they are not. It follows that growth in retailing costs will not be covered by rises in retailing margins which merely keep up with increases in the prices of the manufactured goods sold by the department stores. The rising relative cost of the retailing process will necessitate upward changes in margins from time to time.

There is at least another respect in which the mark-up/mark-down pricing procedure may be said to follow a clear pattern of rationality. The process whereby prices are first set at a relatively standard level and then decreased when sales of an item lag, may be interpreted as an approximation to market segregation, to something resembling discriminatory pricing. The good is made available only at high prices to those who are in a hurry to obtain it.[1] When this portion

[1] Presumably the upper bound is set by the prices charged by competitors. If everyone adheres to similar rules of thumb it becomes relatively simple to avoid overcharging in terms of the prices offered by the store's rivals. In this respect it is noteworthy that in our sample there were only two cases where records indicate that a price had been reduced to meet outside competition. Much more frequent were

of the market – the part made up of customers with inelastic demands – has been satisfied, prices can be lowered to get at the remaining body of purchasers. The range of mark-downs reported in Fig. 5.2 may then very well reflect the buyer's estimate of the demand elasticity of the second market, these estimates varying from item to item.

In sum, the pricing process described is not necessarily, on its face, irrational. Yet this does not settle what is perhaps the more interesting issue, the degree of its consistency with the standard maximization model.

One suspects in this case that the maximization analysis does not come off very well. It is hard to believe that demand elasticities and marginal costs are so similar for all the items in the product line that a maximizer's calculation would produce results all following so closely the simple rules of thumb that have been enunciated. One may perhaps try to retrieve the situation by repeating the argument about the high costs of the decision process and the optimally imperfect decisions which are consequently appropriate. But that line can at best produce a Pyhrric victory. For there is no evidence that the rules of thumb in question, while imperfect, are anywhere near optimal approximations. Moreover, if we claim no more for our maximization models than the prediction that management will grasp at any traditional rule of thumb because a study of the alternatives is costly, then we do not leave very much substance to that approach.

Of course, without a specific test we cannot be sure that the rules of thumb produce results sharply at variance with the requisites of maximization. Such a test is, however, very difficult to carry out. The basic difficulty is that, as Professor Machlup has pointed out so forcefully [8], the two types of model do not normally perform the same tasks and hence they are not easily compared in relevant terms.

To be more specific, the maximization models are rarely in a position to provide quantitative predictions about the behavior of individual firms as the behavioral models are designed to do. One simply does not know enough about their cost structures and the demands for their products, so that one cannot tell from observed pricing decisions whether or not they come close to maximizing

---

reductions whose reported reason was 'equalization', i.e. alignment with the price charged for the same item by a different department in the same store. Perhaps such differences also represent an attempt to treat different markets differently.

anything. On the other hand, because they do not relate the parameters of the decision process to the relevant variables exogenous to the firm, the behavioral models generally have had little power to help in the prediction of the more macroeconomic phenomena for which the maximization models have been most useful (cf. Professor Machlup's discussion of this point).

It follows that a direct confrontation of the two approaches in terms of their predictive power is not easy to arrange and does not seem imminent.[1]

X. BEHAVIORAL ANALYSIS AND THE DECISIONS OF THE FIRM

Of course, the fact that the behavioral and maximizational models have been used to deal with different issues may render them complementary rather than competitive. This is recognized clearly by Cohen and Cyert, who assert:

The behavioral theory is viewed as supplementing the conventional theory of the firm. The traditional theory is essentially one in which certain broad questions are asked. Specifically, the conventional theory of the firm is designed to explain the way in which the price system functions as a mechanism for allocating resources among markets; relatively little is said about resource allocation within the firm. For the purposes of the classical theory, the profit maximization assumption may be perfectly adequate. It is clear, however, that as one asks a different set of questions, specifically questions designed to uncover the way in which resources are allocated within the firm, the profit maximization assumption is neither necessary nor sufficient for answering these questions. Therefore the behavioral theory of the firm should be

[1] Cf. also the following comment by Professor Cyert: 'The use of behavioral rules has occasionally been rationalized by arguing that such rules lead to the same result as profit-maximizing behavior. This argument, however, ignores the basic reason for the firm having recourse to such rules. The use of these rules is the way that the firm deals with the problem of uncertainty. If maximizing behavior could be defined in such situations the firm would maximize. As we have shown earlier there is no unique meaning that can be given to profit maximizing under uncertainty. (Does one then maximize mean profit? median profit? or does one minimize variance? etc.).

viewed as focusing on a different set of questions, questions concerning the internal decision-making structure of the firm.

We may agree, then, that the usefulness of the more conventional models is simply not at issue. They have served well both in the analysis of market behavior, as Professor Machlup has reminded us, and also in the investigation of the problems of the individual business firm, where the maximization process remains the central tool of the operations researcher.

The behavioral model lays claim primarily to the territory between these two, taking on the task of describing and accounting for the individual actions of the individual decision-maker. We are not yet in a position to provide a categorical evaluation of its accomplishment in this limited area. Yet we can offer a number of observations that may be relevant.

First, it is not clear, even at this level, that marginalist considerations are totally irrelevant. It is not difficult to provide examples of major business decisions which can only be explained in marginal terms – substantial moves which were promising in terms of their incremental costs and incremental revenues, though they would not seem capable of passing a full-cost test. The long history of pricing policy by railroads readily confirms this view (see, e.g., Hadley [7]). Similarly, many a firm's decision to expand its product line would seem to be explained in terms of the incremental costs of the new items.

Second, because of the maximizing orientation of the operations researcher it is obvious that as his role in the business firm expands, the behavior of the firm will perhaps come to conform somewhat more closely to the predictions of the marginalist's models. We suspect, for example, that the past decade or two has witnessed a major change in industry's inventory behavior, with the more traditional rules of thumb replaced by procedures derived with the aid of inventory theory. If this is so, it represents some enhancement of the role of the maximization approach. Thus, the domain of applicability of the classcial model in the explanation of business behavior may well be expected to increase over time with the expanding use of the computer as a decision tool and increasing reliance on the advice of the operations analyst. It still remains to be seen how substantial this expansion will be in our world of uncertainty, which is so difficult for maximization models to handle.

On the other hand, it is impossible to deny some of the basic behaviorist tenets. First, a bit of observation does suggest that the decision process within the large and impersonal corporation cannot be described as a single-minded codification of rationalism. On the contrary, it is a sociological process, in which personalities, conflicting views and objectives and administrative structure play an important role. It is very illuminating to trace the history of an important decision in a major corporation. The length of the process (often a matter of years) and the complexity of its vicissitudes will very likely astonish those who think of the firm as a tightly run autocracy. Indeed, the power of the firm's higher officers to enforce a decision is severely restricted by middle management's ability to delay or to act only with limited drive and enthusiasm. The mayor of a large city once remarked at his shock on learning how things work when he first assumed office. 'On Friday I would announce that beginning Monday things will change in such and such a way and on Monday absolutely nothing happened.' This was said by the mayor to a gathering of top corporate officers, who expressed sympathy and commented that this was also the story of their own lives!

It must also be recognized that the behaviorists are right also in pointing out the wide range of business decisions in which each decision taken by itself is not terribly critical, and where, because of the absence of data or for other associated reasons, marginal analysis has not proved terribly helpful. The pricing decisions in the department store model are a prime example. An error in the setting of any one price is not likely to be very serious in its consequences and, in any event, the store simply does not have the demand elasticity and cross-elasticity data or the information on the incremental costs of the retailing process needed to implement a marginal calculation. As a matter of fact, a similar observation probably applies to decisions considerably more critical for the business firm. For example, the decision on the magnitude of the (frequently enormous) advertising budget is made, typically, with no quantitative evidence on the contribution to sales of an increment in advertising outlay. No wonder, then, that this decision process does not seem to bear any resemblance to calculations of maximization theory.

Thus, the behaviorists are undoubtedly right in reminding us that there is a wide area of decisions for which any of our received maximization models – whether the profit-maximization model, or any of the proposed alternatives – offer little help in accounting for observed behavior.

So far the behavioral theorists have offered us as a substitute in this area a variety of fairly general observations, many of them very illuminating; some extremely interesting learning models; and a number of simulation exercises that have added strong evidence that there are rules of thumb, some of them rather simple-minded, governing at least portions of business behavior. These pieces of analysis have been illuminating and stimulating but clearly they represent only a beginning along the path the behaviorists have set for themselves.

XI. MACROECONOMIC IMPLICATIONS OF BEHAVIORAL ANALYSIS

More recently the behavioral analysis has begun to strike out in a new direction. Recognizing that the behavior of the firm can have profound implications for the workings of the economy, the behavioral theorists have started to investigate the macroeconomic consequences of their hypotheses.

Several examples will make the relationship clearer. In a recent paper [4] Cyert discusses the policy of guidelines for wages and prices utilized under the Johnson Administration in an attempt to increase the level of employment consistent with any acceptable rate of inflation. He points out that such a policy grows out of the standard oligopoly analysis which assumes that fiscal measures designed to increase employment will only lead to price increases as demand curves shift rightward. Such oligopolistic behavior obviously increases the level of prices corresponding to any given level of output and employment.

But, argues Cyert, in reality things may proceed in quite another manner:

... Because of an expansionary macroeconomic policy the firm's demand curve increases. How can the firm recognize a shift in its demand curve, never having known where it was in the first place? Obviously it must look at the effect of feedback from the environment on its orders, inventory, and on its plant utilization. The firm begins to think in terms of price increases when inventories cannot be built to desired levels and orders are beginning to build to longer than desired backlogs. One response of the firm, of course, is to expand output within the given plant, assuming that it is not operating at full capacity already.

Cyert concludes:

Assume that the behavioral rule is of the simple capacity utilization type we have described. Then it is clear that a price guideline designed to keep the firm from changing price as the demand curve shifts is unnecessary to achieve the desired objectives and frustrates the working of the price system.

This discussion is offered by Cyert only as a 'rather speculative analysis', designed to show how a model of the firm encompassing empirically based decision rules may throw light on appropriate policy measures.

One of the noteworthy characterisics of the preceding illustration is the key role of uncertainty and imperfect information which leads to the employment of rules of thumb significant in their policy implications. It should be clear that not only macroeconomic policy is subject to this sort of influence. Another illustrative analysis should make this clear.

Recent work by Averch and Johnson [1] has used a static profit-maximization model to discuss the public utility whose profits are regulated with the aid of a ceiling on its rate of return on investment. Their analysis suggests that such a firm would tend to use an excessive proportion of capital among its inputs, in intuitive terms, because under such an arrangement capital brings with it a bonus in the form of an addition to the total amount of profit the firm is permitted to earn. However, in a recent paper [10], E. E. Zajac has argued that in a dynamic world in which the equilibrium point is always shifting and information is highly imperfect, the firm may never find the elusive profit-maximization point. If the firm knows little about its demand functions but is well informed by its engineers about its cost structure, it may always seek to operate, as a rule of thumb in the face of uncertainty, at the point of minimum cost for whatever output combination it happens to produce. This may, indeed, yield profits as high as or higher (over time) than a set of attempts, subject to wide margin of error, to find the Averch–Johnson maximum-profit point. But if the firm does minimize cost for any output level, clearly there can be no excessive use of capital. If corporate behavior were to follow the Zajac hypothesis, the policy problems raised by Averch and Johnson would tend to disappear.

It follows from all this that the sorts of consideration that have been called to our attention by the behavioral models may be of substantial importance for economic policy analysis at both the micro- and macroeconomic levels. The phenomena encompassed by the behavioral models are neither imaginary nor irrelevant, and it may be that as the analysis advances in sophistication it will give us a great deal to reconsider among the matters we now tend to take for granted.

At the present stage of the analysis, however, these arguments generally take the form of conjectures, which can do no more than prevent excessively ready acceptance of received notions. Before it can accomplish much more than this, behavioral economics will have to undertake a number of ambitious tasks: it will have to amass and investigate substantially more empirical evidence; from this it will have to distill relationships showing the connection between the parameters in the rules of thumb it ascribes to the business firms and the exogenous economic variables which constitute the company's environment. Having done this, it will perhaps be able to undertake some quantitative and qualitative analysis showing what responses on the part of the firm can be elicited by various specified changes in the behavior of the public sector and in the state of the economy generally. In this way the policy implications of the behavioral models will emerge directly and they may begin to offer much the same sorts of opportunities for analysis which are now provided by the maximization models.

This is clearly a tall order and I am certain that the behaviorists will be the first to admit that they have only just begun to work toward meeting it. How much of this program they will be able to effect remains to be seen, and it also remains to be seen whether, say, the resulting macroeconomic predictions are significantly different from those of the standard theory. But the points at issue are of sufficient importance for it to be worth the effort.

References

[1] Averch, Harvey, and Johnson, Leland L., 'Behavior of the Firm under Regulatory Constraint', *American Economic Review*, LII (Dec 1962) 1052–69.

[2] Clarkson, G. P. E., *Portfolio Selection*: *A Simulation of Trust Investment* (Prentice-Hall, Englewood Cliffs, N.J., 1962).

[3] Cohen, K. J., and Cyert, Richard, *Theory of the Firm*: *Resource Allocation in a Market Economy* (Prentice-Hall, Englewood Cliffs, N.J., 1965) chaps. 16–17.

[4] Cyert, Richard, 'Uncertainty, Behavioral Rules, and the Firm', *Economic Journal* (Mar 1969).

[5] Cyert, Richard, and March, J. G., *A Behavioral Theory of the Firm* (Prentice-Hall, Englewood Cliffs, N.J., 1963).

[6] Cyert, Richard, March, J. G., and Feigenbaum, E. A., *Behavioral Science*, IV 2 (Apr 1959) 81–95.

[7] Hadley, A. T., *Railroad Transportation* (New York and London 1886).

[8] Machlup, Fritz, 'Theories of the Firm: Marginalist, Behavioral, Managerial' *American Economic Review*, LVII (Mar 1967).

[9] Simon, H. A., 'New Developments in the Theory of the Firm', *American Economic Review*, LII (May 1962).

[10] Zajac, E. E., 'A Geometric Treatment of Averch–Johnson's Behavior of the Firm Model', *American Economic Review*, LX (Mar 1970).

6 Exogenous and Endogenous Factors in the Growth of Firms

Enrico Filippi and Giovanni Zanetti

This paper is a summary of certain results of the authors' research on the finance and development of large firms, sponsored by the Consiglio Nazionale delle Ricerche.[1]

It is based on an analysis of data for the 200 largest quoted Italian companies taken on the basis of the size of net sales in 1963. Taken together, these firms account for 38·68 per cent of the employees of Italian firms with more than fifty employees and for 64·10 per cent of the gross investment of all limited companies. Total sales vary from 866 billion lire for the largest firms in the group to 8·6 billion for the smallest.

The balance sheets for the period from 31 December 1957 to 31 December 1963, together with information gained from special questionnaires and other fiscal documents, have been examined and elaborated.

The homogeneity of the data has been improved by systematic adjustment, reclassification, etc., of the balance-sheet items. More especially, corrections were made for the undervaluation of tangible and financial assets on the one hand, and for the undervaluation of reserves and profits on the other. These operations were carried out separately for all the firms considered; in order to avoid systematic mistakes, average adjustment coefficients were not used.

These operations were essential because Italian firms' balance sheets do not conform to a standard pattern and various policies to conceal operating profits are usually adopted. For example, more than half of the companies examined 'conceal', on the average, more than 50 per cent of profits earned, while a sixth of them hide *all* their profits and only 12 per cent publish figures which are close to the real results. The firms that publish more or less exact figures are

---

[1] The results of this research work were published in G. Zanetti and E. Filippi, *Finanza e Sviluppo della Grande Industria in Italia* (F. Angeli, Milano, 1967).

usually those working at a loss and/or at an early stage of their development.

Analysis of the corrected figures permitted the formulation of a number of hypotheses to explain the expansion of Italian industrial firms, with particular reference to exogenous and endogenous factors. The term 'exogenous' refers to external factors acting outside the firm, such as, for instance, the trend of aggregate demand, the cost and supply of labour, and the financial policy of the monetary authorities. On the other hand, the term 'endogenous' relates to all those factors acting within the firm, such as, for example, managerial skills, investment policies, profitability and size.

I. EXOGENOUS FACTORS IN THE GROWTH OF THE FIRM:
Demand in the productive sector

Considering one of the more recurrent problems in the development of the firm, let us ask to what extent the economic development of a country can explain the growth of a single productive unit. It is well known that some theories assume an economic trend, or better, an expansion of total demand to explain the growth of the firm. Acknowledging this, it is nevertheless felt to be insufficient to explain the phenomenon completely.

Empirical research has been directed to ascertaining to what degree changes in demand have influenced the recent growth of the largest Italian firms.

The gross product of manufacturing industry increased by 78 per cent during the six years from 1958 to 1963 (Table 6.1), whereas the group of the 200 largest firms shows a rate of growth, in terms of sales, of more than 85 per cent.

The same increase, about 89 per cent, is shown by the rate of growth measured in terms of value-added (value of production less purchases from other firms). In other words, the rates of development for the leading Italian firms were, on the average, higher than those of all manufacturing industry.

This does not, however, mean that all the 200 largest firms increased their sales at a rate higher than the rate of growth of total demand. The average data are, in fact, a synthesis of very heterogenous components. This is shown by the level of the relative variability σ/M

Table 6.1

Rates of Growth of the Gross Production of Italian Manufacturing
Industries and of the Sales of the 200 Largest Industrial Companies
Classified by Different Sectors of Production for the Period 1958–63

Industrial group	National data	Figures of the 200 largest industrial companies		
	Rate of growth of gross production	Average rate M	Variability σ	$\dfrac{\sigma}{M} \times 100$
Food	36	63·55	50·83	79·98
Cotton	73	41·97	23·13	55·11
Synthetic fibres	*	122·63	17,732·98	14,460·56
Iron, steel and non-ferrous metals	55	56·35	44·03	78·14
Mechanical engineering	113	125·06	124·43	99·50
Electromechanical engineering	*	109·24	195·33	178·81
Vehicles and accessories	*	144·05	70·02	48·61
Shipyards	*	18·35	18·18	99·07
Building materials	75	59·40	69·90	117·68
Glass and pottery	*	168·52	61·59	36·55
Chemicals	79	101·38	554·45	546·90
Rubber and electrical materials	60	78·07	26·59	34·06
Petroleum refining	105	38·85	88·26	227·18
Paper	67	55·52	980·72	1,766·43
Various	*	89·08	95·76	107·50
All companies	78	85·45	3,560·50	4,166·76

* Figures not available.

calculated around the average value of the rate of growth of the
various sectors in which the 200 largest firms operate (Table 6.1).

Apart from the high values of certain rates (synthetic fibres, paper),
which are likely to be caused by abnormal circumstances, they never
fall below 34 per cent and they reach 546 per cent, showing a wide
dispersion around the central data. The growth of each firm must be
studied individually, as it is affected but not caused by the general

trend of the sector. Each firm does not wait for the expansion of total demand of the sector, nor does it just react to its changes. It shows an autonomous process of growth. This can be explained in the conquest of the market by increasing sales in a certain area at the expense of competitors: in this case there may be an increase in the production of the single firm without having an increase in the total sales of the sector. Alternatively, the expansion may be through the discovery of some previously latent needs and their satisfaction through the firm entering new branches of production or through the diversification of production. Such a process of expansion raises many external and internal problems which not all firms are able to overcome. The different behaviour of the firms is illustrated in Table 6.2, which considers the distribution of the firms according to the size of deviations in their individual rates of growth of sales from that of the whole sector, both for the period 1958 to 1963. It is worth pointing out, by the way, that having excluded some very heterogeneous categories, the number of firms considered was reduced from 200 to 133.

On the whole, only 11 per cent of the firms examined showed a deviation within 10 per cent from the average rate of growth for the respective sector. The maximum concentration is in the extreme categories, that is to say, in relation to deviations of more than 50 per cent of the average rate of growth. This means that a good 43 per cent of the firms had a rate of growth significantly different from that of the sector. This situation is emphasized at the level of the single productive categories, where in some cases (cotton, mechanical, electromechanical engineering and paper) the concentration in the extreme categories reached levels of 50, 46, 45, and even 80 per cent.

Thus it is possible to state that the trend of total demand is not a sufficient explanation for the growth of the firm.

The labour factor

Other theories tend to explain growth on the basis of the existence, or better, the availability of the different factors, the availability of labour being of particular interest.

The study of this aspect of the Italian industrial economy is summarized in Tables 6.3 and 6.4.

Table 6.2

200 Largest Industrial Companies Classified on the Basis of the Deviation in the Rate of Growth of their Production from the Average Rate of Growth of Total Production of Industry Group for the Period 1958-63

Percentage deviation	Cotton		Synthetic fibres		Iron, steel and non-ferrous metals		Mechanical		Electro-mechanical		Vehicles and accessories		Building materials		Chemicals		Rubber and electric materials		Paper		Total	
	No. of companies	%	No. of companies	%	No. of companies	%	No. of companies	%	No. of companies	%	No. of companies	%	No. of companies	%	No. of companies	%	No. of companies	%	No. of companies	%	No. of companies	%
Over −50	4	33	2	25	3	16	4	20	3	17	2	18	0		6	19	0		2	40	26	20
−25 to −50	0		2	25	5	26	2	11	2	11	0		1	20	8	26	1	20	0		21	16
−25 to −10	3	25	0		2	11	2	11	1	05	3	27	1	20	7	23	0		0		19	14
−10 to +10	0		2	25	0		3	16	4	22	1	10	1	20	2	07	2	40	0		15	11
10 to 25	2	17	1	12	3	16	0		3	17	0		0		1	03	0		1	20	11	08
25 to 50	1	08	0		1	05	3	16	0		3	27	1	20	1	03	1	20	0		11	08
Over 50	2	17	1	13	5	26	5	28	5	28	2	18	1	20	6	19	1	20	2	40	30	23
Total	12	100	8	100	19	100	19	100	18	100	11	100	5	100	31	100	5	100	5	100	133	100

Table 6.3

Trend of Employment, Hours Lost because of Strikes, and Labour Cost
during 1958–63

	1958	1959	1960	1961	1962	1963
mployed ('000)	6,961	7,394	7,787	7,948	8,105	8,361
Fixed based index	100	106	112	114	116	120
nemployed ('000)	480	467	332	251	191	161
Fixed based index	100	97	69	52	40	34
orking hours lost cause of strikes 000)	33,375	73,523	46,289	79,127	181,732	91,158
Fixed based index	100	220	139	237	545	273
abour costs (gross erage salary per ur in lire)	293·88	299·86	312·22	334·74	385·64	450·55
Fixed based index	100	102	106	113	131	153

Table 6.4

Annual Rates of Growth of Gross Fixed Assets, of Sales and of
Employment in the 200 Largest Industrial Companies
(percentage)

Rate of growth	1958	1959	1960	1961	1962	1963	*Whole period*
Gross fixed assets	11·17	9·79	11·09	14·95	18·52	15·83	90·86
Sales	*	8·81	15·64	13·19	13·61	14·61	85·45
Value-added	*	9·67	14·00	14·90	14·78	14·75	91·49
Workers	*	–0·29	4·61	5·13	6·80	3·15	20·81

* Figures not available.

The period under consideration, from 1958 to 1963, can be divided
into two distinct phases: from 1958 to 1960 and from 1961 to 1963.
The first phase is characterized by a considerable availability of manpower and its rather orderly absorption, whilst labour costs rose only

slightly and the hours of work lost through strikes, after an exceptional rise in 1959, returned to almost the 1958 level (Table 6.3). Output during this period expanded mainly through the better use of productive capacity which previously had not been fully used and through a limited amount of new investment of an extensive character. Instead, after 1960, the cost of labour experienced unexpected increases, above all due to strong trade union pressure reflected in the large number of hours lost through strikes. The firms faced this problem of increased incidence of labour costs in their cost structure by changing the product mix in such a way as to improve the labour – capital ratio in favour of the latter. Investment, in this period, was of a substituting character and, given its rigidity, it required that productive capacity was utilized to a greater degree.

This phenomenon was particularly evident in the 200 largest Italian industrial companies (Table 6.4). During the period 1958 to 1963 employment increased by 20·81 per cent while output and plant increased by 85·45 per cent and 90·86 per cent respectively. The increases in labour costs stimulated the larger firms to invest and modernize with the intention of increasing the productivity of the factors and reducing the incidence of labour costs. Italian experience during this period seems to be that the labour factor mainly acted as a stimulus for new investment, tending to increase the productivity of capital, and in this way promoting the process of growth in the firm.

At this particular moment of the Italian economy, characterized by a certain degree of technological backwardness in some sectors and by changes in the degree of competition due to the opening of new markets and the introduction of new producers, the dialectic contrast between firm and trade union therefore appears to be a factor which contributed to the substantial improvement in the organizational structure and, in the last analysis, to the evolution of the economy.

The financial incentives

In the study of the possible exogenous factors of growth, it is necessary to consider what was the importance and what was the influence of the credit policy of the monetary authorities of the country in which the firms were operating. The analysis of the 200 largest companies in response to changes in the liquidity of the Italian financial system during 1958 to 1963 leads us to conclude that the abundant supply of money at low cost was not of decisive influence in regard to investment and expansion. Italian firms profited from these periods of high liquidity more to consolidate or to improve their cash position than to embark on new investment projects. For example, 1959 was a year of abundant liquidity, and a study of the firms' financial position reveals an exceptional expansion of trade debts and credits and a notable increase in financial commitments compared to changes in investment in equipment. The abundance of capital at low cost certainly enters into the entrepreneurs' calculations but more as an obstacle than as an incentive. The authorities' attempts to stimulate investment were in vain because of the cautious behaviour of the entrepreneurs who decided to invest only, although not always, when there was a constant rhythm of growing demand. On the contrary, investment, once started, continues even in periods of scarce and expensive money. At the beginning of the crisis in 1963, the investment of the 200 largest companies continued to increase and in fact reached its highest absolute level. The necessity to complete vast investment programs which were already under way obliged firms to turn to external sources, especially short-term debt, and was a direct cause of the reduction or loss of autonomy in the individual firm in relation to financing organizations.[1]

Also in respect to the financial considerations, there was a difference between the general behaviour of the economy and the behaviour of the individual firms. The various measures may have had a certain influence when they were intended to slow down the economy, but they had very little effect when they were intended to act as a stimulus to investment and expansion.

Once again an external factor is shown to be insufficient to explain the growth of the firm.

This analysis of total demand, the availability of manpower and the financial policies of the monetary authorities shows that external factors are insufficient to explain the growth of the firm. In order to understand the phenomenon of the growth of the firm better, analyses were made of the behaviour of single firms to see what influence was exerted by such internal factors as profitability, size

[1] Fiscal data were made available by the Commissione Parlamentare d'Inchiesta sui Limiti Posti alla Concorrenza nel Campo Economico.

and managerial skill to introduce innovations in organizational and marketing techniques.

II. ENDOGENOUS FACTORS AND THE GROWTH OF THE FIRM

The 200 largest companies were examined separately and classified according to their rate of growth in sales.

The rate of growth of net sales was calculated for each company, relating the increase in turnover from 1958 to 1963 to the level of turnover in 1958.

On the basis of the results obtained, the companies studied were divided into five categories and show the following distribution:

Rate of growth of sales in the period 1958–63	No. of companies	%
Up to 25%	29	14·5
25–50%	31	15·5
50–100%	65	32·5
100–250%	60	30·0
Over 250%	15	7·5
Total	200	100·0

Initially the role played by investment in plant and by labour for the companies studied is examined.

Table 6.4 shows that for the companies taken as a group, the rates of increase of gross fixed assets is slightly higher than that for output; the former in fact shows an increase of 90·86 per cent compared to an increase of 85·45 per cent for the latter. The differences between the two for the separate years is more marked: the increase in turnover was continually more than the increase in gross plant until 1960, the year it reached its peak; while, instead, from 1961, the annual increases in gross plant were always greater than the increases in sales.

The changes for the whole group in these phenomena gave a substantially constant figure for the average coefficient of capital intensity (Table 6.5), that is to say, the ratio between the figures for gross plant and tools and those for sales.

In other words, for the period, the amount of plant necessary to obtain one lira of production was on average not changed. The fast rate of technological progress shown in the years considered, with the consequent changes in productive processes and the exceptional increases in sales, has not caused any appreciable movement in the value of the coefficient of capital intensity from around 90 per cent: after touching minimum levels in 1960 and in 1963 it returned to near the initial value. The fixed base index (1958 = 100) falls to 95 in 1961 and then rises again to 99 in 1963. As can be seen, these slight movements can be accounted for by the different degrees of utilization of productive capacity and the delay between the moment of investment and when such investment enters into production.

In relation to the large increase in the volume of investment in plant, there were very small variations in the labour factor (Table 6.4). This signifies that production of 100 lire was obtained in 1963 with an unchanged amount of capital stock compared to that necessary in 1958 but with appreciably less labour.

These observations could be partially modified by taking into consideration the changes in the degree of vertical integration which took place during the period.

In order to eliminate the influence of this phenomenon, the analyses were repeated by taking total added value instead of sales. This alternative method did not show any relevant differences, as is shown in the resulting data (Table 6.5). The figures examined up to now are a synthesis of the appreciably different behaviours which seem to be connected to the different rates of growth of the separate companies. The analysis of the different categories of growth in Table 6.5 in fact shows a number of particularly interesting trends. During the period under consideration there was an increase in the average coefficient of capital intensity for companies in the categories of slow growth, while for those firms which experienced a fast rate of growth the coefficient fell substantially: for the former, the fixed base index rose to 121 while it fell to 57 for the latter.

Further, in the slow-growth categories plant per worker increased at a faster rate than total sales per worker, while exactly the opposite occurred for those firms included in the fast-growth categories. These trends may in part have been caused by the delay which exists between the time when plant is bought and the moment it enters into production – delays caused both by technical factors and by the unavoidable period of learning in the initial period of production. Such factors, however, are not sufficient explanation for the differences recorded.

Table 6.5

Average Coefficients of Capital Intensity and Rates of Productivity for the 200 Largest Industrial Companies

Rate of growth		1958 Value ratio	Index	1959 Value ratio	Index	1960 Value ratio	Index	1961 Value ratio	Index	1962 Value ratio	Index	1963 Value ratio	Index
Up to 25%													
Gross fixed assets / Sales	×100	95·55	100	112·66	118	113·95	119	117·36	123	115·27	121	115·57	121
Gross fixed assets / Added value	×100	248·43	100	265·04	107	280·66	113	276·33	111	268·70	108	260·03	105
Gross fixed assets / Workers	('000)	5,543	100	6,205	112	6,659	120	7,237	131	7,919	143	8,736	158
Sales / Workers	('000)	5,573	100	5,350	96	5,783	104	6,043	108	6,576	118	7,267	130
25–50%													
Gross fixed assets / Sales	×100	90·16	100	93·66	104	92·76	103	90·52	100	90·59	100	87·70	97
Gross fixed assets / Added value	×100	266·64	100	270·41	101	270·78	101	262·55	98	262·63	98	251·74	94
Gross fixed assets / Workers	('000)	5,996	100	6,549	109	6,988	117	7,554	126	8,163	136	8,068	135
Sales / Workers	('000)	6,430	100	6,781	105	7,294	113	8,012	125	8,714	135	9,363	146
50–100%													
Gross fixed assets / Sales	×100	92·95	100	93·39	100	89·48	96	93·13	100	102·31	110	113·21	122

Ratio	Unit												
Sales / Workers	('000)	5,514	100	6,095	111	6,843	124	7,257	132	7,433	135	8,106	147
100–250%													
Gross fixed assets / Sales	×100	86·88	100	80·44	93	71·98	83	70·33	81	70·59	81	69·71	80
Gross fixed assets / Added value	×100	202·14	100	189·78	94	171·65	85	167·22	83	167·63	83	166·74	82
Gross fixed assets / Workers	('000)	5,565	100	5,814	104	5,884	106	6,187	111	6,567	118	7,312	131
Sales / Workers	('000)	6,117	100	6,988	114	7,680	126	8,117	133	8,521	139	9,683	158
Over 250%													
Gross fixed assets / Sales	×100	186·46	100	161·68	87	149·28	80	126·39	68	114·84	62	106·39	57
Gross fixed assets / Added value	×100	393·05	100	375·18	95	360·60	92	345·62	88	326·30	83	294·71	75
Gross fixed assets / Workers	('000)	17,832	100	16,170	91	15,784	89	16,362	92	18,725	105	18,038	101
Sales / Workers	('000)	7,579	100	8,805	116	9,679	128	11,778	155	14,673	194	15,615	206
All Companies													
Gross fixed assets / Sales	×100	92·69	100	93·52	101	88·71	96	88·03	95	89·92	97	91·33	99
Gross fixed assets / Added value	×100	231·32	100	231·55	100	222·81	96	217·80	94	220·22	95	223·34	96
Gross fixed assets / Workers	('000)	5,768	100	6,307	109	6,650	115	7,240	126	7,959	138	8,894	154
Sales / Workers	('000)	5,923	100	6,464	109	7,145	121	7,693	130	8,184	138	9,093	154

The results obtained seem to permit the conclusion that the faster rates of growth are to be found where innovation of a technical-organizational character has increased the productivity of both capital and labour.

While, at the beginning of the period considered, there were in fact no large differences between the ratios of gross plant to sales and sales to workers, with the exception of very fast-growth companies formed in and around the first year of the period considered, these ratios differ greatly during the whole period, however. The slow-growth companies increased their average coefficient of capital intensity while at the same time gross plant per capita showed a net increase over sales per worker.

The investment in these firms was therefore directed more to reduce the number of workers than to improve the efficiency of capital invested.

As the rate of growth increases, an inversion in the analyzed ratios appears: the coefficient of capital intensity tends to diminish (the fixed base index for the second category of growth falls from 100 to 97), while sales per worker increased more rapidly than gross plant per worker. Such a tendency is emphasized in passing to the categories of rapid growth, with the only exception in the growth category 50–100 which shows an irregular behaviour during the last three years under consideration which can be largely explained by the presence in this group of the company Italsider, the main Italian steel company, a subsidiary of I.R.I., which started to build a large new works in 1960.[1]

The companies which more than doubled their sales (the growth category 100–250) during the six years had the lowest coefficient of capital intensity in 1958 and reduced it further during the period. At the same time the level of sales per worker increased by 58 per cent compared to an increase of 31 per cent for gross plant per worker.

In the last growth category (over 250 per cent) the plant per capita remained almost stable (an increase of 1 per cent) while sales per worker more than doubled (the fixed base index = 206).

The fastest rate of growth was in those firms where investment in new plant/tools gave a substantial increase in the productivity of labour and capital.

An analogous conclusion is obtained by analyzing the marginal

[1] For further information, see Zanetti and Filippi, op. cit., II p. 134.

coefficient of capital intensity (that is the amount of new investment necessary to increase the volume of sales by one unit).

The regression equation for total sales (independent variable) and the total of existing gross plant was calculated for each class of growth, and the level of significance through the calculation of the square of the coefficient of regression was determined for each equation (see table below).

Categories of sales growth	Regression equation	r^2
Up to 25%	$y = -60,714 + 1 \cdot 29x$	0·58
25–50%	$y = 192,637 + 0 \cdot 72x$	0·90
50–100%	$y = -815,642 + 1 \cdot 64x$	0·94
100–250%	$y = 191,138 + 0 \cdot 67x$	0·98
Over 250%	$y = 103,113 + 0 \cdot 91x$	0·98

x = total sales (million lire).
y = total of gross fixed assets (million lire).

The level of significance of the line of regression is decidedly low for the slow-growth categories where the angular coefficient of the line is high; while the opposite is shown for the more rapid rates of growth. In other words, the variations in plant only partially explain the changes in production for the companies with slow growth, while such a relationship is evident for the fast-growth companies.

Profitability and growth of the firm

The pattern of figures examined suggests a deepening of the study of the interrelationship between growth and profitability. They both seem to have a direct relationship. Table 6.6 reveals that especially for the early years considered, the ratio between profit and net capital increases appreciably with the growth in the rate of expansion. It must be noted, however, that very frequently in the Italian experience the process of rapid expansion was accompanied by a reduction or even a cancellation of profit capacity. It was rare for the growth process to be very uneven and often the exceptional increase in investment was accompanied by large errors. These errors were particularly in respect to forecasts of the trend of demand, the possibility of employing at remunerative rates the products obtained, and the estimation of the trends of costs deriving from changes in

Table 6.6

Ratios of: Net Profit or Loss/Net Capital, Annual Depreciation/Gross Fixed Assets, in the 200 Largest Companies Classified According to the Growth of Sales and of Gross Total Assets
(percentage)

Rate of growth	No. of companies	1958 Net profit or loss / Net capital	1958 Annual depreciation / Gross fixed assets	1959 Net profit or loss / Net capital	1959 Annual depreciation / Gross fixed assets	1960 Net profit or loss / Net capital	1960 Annual depreciation / Gross fixed assets
Sales							
Up to 25%	29	5·37	4·79	7·56	4·62	5·40	4·75
25–50%	31	6·30	4·92	6·63	5·27	6·59	5·33
50–100%	65	9·11	5·19	9·82	5·08	9·57	5·46
100–250%	60	8·44	5·73	11·15	6·85	12·38	8·07
Over 250%	15	10·58	4·29	10·21	5·54	9·10	5·61
Gross total assets							
Up to 30%	13	1·58	4·76	6·04	4·46	6·04	4·97
30–60%	35	5·14	4·03	5·97	4·50	5·28	4·52
60–120%	63	8·43	5·56	9·84	6·47	10·30	7·41
120–300%	69	9·40	5·46	10·53	5·52	10·10	6·09
		13·07	6·67	15·96	5·73	16·99	5·17

Sales						
Up to 25%	29	5·98	4·31	4·25	4·38	4·12	4·01
25–50%	31	6·74	5·53	8·16	5·17	5·27	5·05
50–100%	65	8·87	5·52	7·35	4·57	5·45	4·76
100&–250%	60	11·62	7·84	9·12	7·42	6·75	8·22
Over 250%	15	7·63	5·62	6·77	6·48	4·24	8·37
Gross total assets						
Up to 30%	13	6·09	4·37	4·02	4·24	4·80	3·92
30–60%	35	5·43	4·80	4·53	4·37	3·95	4·39
60–120%	63	10·30	7·32	9·47	7·22	9·50	7·55
120–300%	69	9·27	5·98	7·72	5·28	5·22	5·68
Over 300%	20	11·90	5·14	7·67	4·59	−6·96	5·99
All companies	200	9·05	6·07	7·72	5·65	5·63	6·06

size. Such errors consequently caused serious imbalances and had a negative effect on profit levels. The variations shown in the rates of profit, particularly, for the later years, are explained by such factors.

Table 6.6 also show how, while at the beginning of the period there were no significant differences in the rates of depreciation between the various growth categories, later the tendency appeared for the more rapidly expanding companies to shorten the depreciation period. In fact in the fast-growth categories the rate rises from 4·29 per cent to 8·37 per cent, while in the slow-growth categories it falls from 4·79 per cent to 4·01 per cent.

In order to illustrate these points further, Tables 6.7 and 6.8 have been prepared showing the companies classified according to their rates of profitability and depreciation instead of their rates of growth.

The inverse relationship between levels of profitability (or depreciation) and the size of the average coefficient of capital intensity emerges very clearly in each of the years considered, not being invalidated by the values for the first category which includes exclusively companies which made a loss. It is deduced from these figures that profitability is above all the result of the productivity of factors. In particular, profitability more than the size of investment undertaken seems to be related to the efficient product mix which causes a lowering of the ratio between investment and quantity produced. Technical progress, and improvement in the organization of production and marketing policies tending to keep sales and productive capacity in line, have therefore exercised an important influence on profitability.

On the other hand the rate of increase in gross plant (Table 6.7 and 6.8) is directly related to the rates of profitability and to the rates of depreciation. In 1963 the companies with profitability greater than 20 per cent showed increases in gross plant equal to 129 per cent compared to increases of around 90 per cent for the companies with low rates of profitability.

New investment in plant gives, above all, different results in the various categories of profitability. In fact, noting the increase in plant necessary to raise sales by 100 units, expressed by the marginal co-efficient of capital intensity, it is possible to see how it is inversely proportional to profitability or to depreciation capacity. That is to say, the productivity of investment undertaken by the more profitable companies was clearly greater (as much as four times) than that being used by the companies with lower profitability.

Table 6.1

Rates of Growth of Sales and Gross Fixed Assets, Marginal and Average Coefficient of Capital Intensity for Groups of Firms Classified by the Level of Net Profitability at the Beginning and at the End of the Period

Net profit / Net capital companies	No. of companies	Rate of growth of sales %	Rate of growth of gross fixed assets %	Marginal coefficient of capital intensity %	Annual average coefficient of capital intensity					
1958 %					1958	1959	1960	1961	1962	1963
Up to 0	26	78·04	92·23	87·98	70·25	76·15	76·90	73·35	74·24	73·79
0–5	25	69·27	38·44	85·38	149·29	150·44	140·75	135·37	133·82	125·50
5–10	47	91·54	101·24	133·60	114·97	112·80	104·75	105·80	108·48	113·80
10–15	32	65·51	88·40	105·27	74·06	75·75	73·61	73·57	77·58	79·48
15–20	45	80·75	110·57	83·15	56·97	60·43	58·60	58·81	61·29	63·51
Over 20	25	137·99	172·03	47·22	35·34	35·16	34·98	36·96	38·16	38·36
	200									
1963 %										
Up to 0	26	62·94	87·35	100·89	68·64	76·43	77·56	76·82	73·55	76·49
0–5	44	70·05	89·04	157·91	118·03	116·68	114·70	112·80	125·22	126·71
5–10	50	102·36	91·66	108·27	116·00	113·28	101·92	101·64	101·84	104·22
10–15	43	77·21	84·76	68·27	58·40	61·87	58·57	58·03	57·54	58·45
15–20	29	110·68	121·85	49·94	43·03	41·65	41·05	43·51	44·89	43·00
Over 20	8	200·18	129·66	32·03	47·12	45·59	44·28	37·23	35·52	32·61
	200									

Table 6.8

Rates of Growth of Sales and Gross Fixed Assets, Marginal and Average Coefficient of Capital Intensity for Groups of Firms Classified by Depreciation Capacity at the Beginning and at the End of the Period

Annual depreciation fixed assets 1958 %	No. of companies	Rate of growth of sales %	Rate of growth of gross fixed assets %	Marginal coefficient of capital intensity %	Annual average coefficient of capital intensity					
					1958	1959	1960	1961	1962	1963
Gross fixed assets 1958 %										
Up to 2·5	13	85·19	83·27	144·35	136·30	159·69	150·05	155·83	139·81	138·35
2·5–5	84	79·55	81·42	121·69	113·72	112·62	105·97	105·32	106·86	110·01
5–7·5	43	94·01	115·95	82·48	63·28	63·79	62·20	61·88	65·78	66·80
7·5–10	44	85·00	118·03	77·08	52·67	55·63	54·21	55·08	57·54	58·69
Over 10	16	128·78	168·23	58·97	42·02	43·66	43·08	42·11	45·84	45·50
	200									
1963 %										
Up to 2·5	13	28·36	39·36	120·33	84·14	91·46	95·82	95·26	87·39	87·81
2·5–5	71	67·25	94·52	166·26	113·27	117·33	112·70	113·35	119·23	125·65
5–7·5	31	81·70	79·42	62·28	60·66	61·40	59·44	57·75	58·79	58·03
7·5–10	64	113·87	95·99	68·86	77·87	74·36	67·35	67·83	68·32	68·02
Over 10	21	173·42	119·27	66·76	84·00	84·85	82·98	74·30	73·50	68·39
	200									

We may conclude that technical progress quickly introduced into the company, together with an efficient organization, has, in the Italian experience of the period, contributed the most convincing explanation for the growth of the firm, of which profitability represents one of the more important results.

Profitability and size

Since the firms are largely heterogeneous in respect to their size, varying from the smallest with sales of 8 billion lire to the largest with sales of 900 billion lire, it is useful to consider what influence the difference in size had on the phenomena considered so far. The companies were classified according to size of sales and gross total assets at the beginning of the period, and for each category the rates of growth in sales were calculated.

The results obtained are reported in Table 6.9, where it can be

Table 6.9

Rates of Sales Growth of the 200 Largest Industrial
Companies Classified by Size in 1958

Size groups (million lire)	No. of companies	Rate of growth %
Sales, 1958		
Over 100,000	4	97·65
50,001–100,000	5	46·39
25,001–50,000	15	76·88
15,001–25,000	26	62·80
Up to 15,000	150	102·57
Total	200	85·45
Gross Total Assets, 1958		
Over 100,000	10	98·61
50,001–100,000	12	54·57
25,001–50,000	32	68·16
15,001–25,000	32	84·67
Up to 15,000	114	101·71
Total	200	85·45

seen that the highest average rates of growth in sales are found in the extreme categories both when size of sales or size of gross assets is considered.

The rates of growth for the three intermediate categories are decidedly smaller in size, and the existence of a critical zone in the process of the growth of the firm is revealed. After a phase of rapid and sometimes exceptional growth, during which many firms reach a critical size, they enter a period of crisis which only a few manage to overcome and continue their expansion process.

The range corresponding to this critical zone is rather wide and ranges from 15 to 100 billion lire. It must, however, be remembered that the 200 companies belong to fourteen different sectors and therefore this critical zone occurs at different levels according to the degree of technical progress in each sector. Considering the 200 companies together, acknowledging the compensatory phenomena which are certainly present, the range, which is rather wide, tends to extend between the minimum and maximum critical levels of the various sectors.

A deeper study of the inquiry permits hypotheses to be advanced explaining the existence of this intermediary phase.

The regression equation between the amount of gross fixed assets (dependent variable) and the amount of net sales (independent variable) was calculated for different groups of companies included

Table 6.10

Regression Lines between the Amount of Gross Fixed Assets and the Amount of Sales for the Period 1958–63 for the 200 Largest Industrial Companies Classified by the Size of Gross Total Assets

Size groups (million lire)	*Regression equation*	*r (regression coefficient)*	r^2
Gross Total Assets			
Over 100,000	$y = 22,249 + 1 \cdot 18\, x$	0.99	0.98
50,001–100,000	$y = -93,855 + 1 \cdot 18\, x$	0·99	0·98
25,001–50,000	$y = 163 + 0 \cdot 88\, x$	0·99	0·98
15,001–25,000	$y = -19,634 + 0 \cdot 67\, x$	0·99	0·98
Up to 15,000	$y = 18,270 + 0 \cdot 36\, x$	0·99	0·98

x = total sales (million lire).
y = total gross fixed assets (million lire).

in the five categories based on the size of gross assets in 1963. The angular coefficient of the various regression lines indicates the amounts by which investment in plant increased in order to increase the amount of sales by one unit. The results are shown in Table 6.10.

A direct relationship between the size of gross assets and the size of the angular coefficient of the line is shown. The larger firms (with

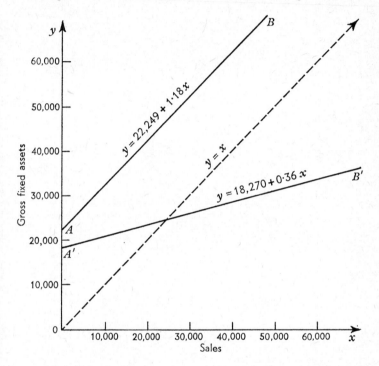

FIG. 6.1. Regression lines between the total of gross fixed assets and the total of sales for the period 1958-63 for the companies with gross total assets of more than 100 billion lire and for those with gross total assets less than 15 billion.

gross total assets of more than 50 billions) had to invest three times more than the smaller firms in order to increase their output by one unit (1·18 compared to 0·36). The larger the firm is, the more it has to increase the equipment necessary to extend its sales, that is to say the more it has to increase the marginal coefficient of capital intensity.

This is clearly shown from Fig. 6.1, where the line AB representing the regression equation for firms with gross total assets of more than 100 billions slopes more than the line bisecting the first quadrant (dashed line), while the line $A'B'$ representing firms with gross total assets of less than 15 billions is clearly less.

This signifies that the technical progress, on the one hand, enables the productivity of the factor mix to be increased, and on the other causes a movement inside the firm through which an ever larger increase of mechanization in the production processes must be adopted in order to continually improve the existing level of efficiency.

This challenge is a possible explanation of the critical zone described above. The larger a firm becomes, the more successive increases in production feel the incidence of fixed costs deriving from growing production capacity. This creates two types of problems.

The first is financial and is related to the supply of funds necessary to cover increasing needs of capital. The increase in the incidence of invested capital per unit produced in fact reduces the possibility of self-finance. Therefore firms must turn mainly to external sources which are not always sufficient or economic.

The second type of problem is a marketing one, and is related to the necessity of obtaining a stable and high level of utilization of productive capacity through the control of demand.

These factors create a number of obstacles to the growth process which are particularly important when the firm passes from the medium-small to the medium-large category.

During this phase of development, the average firm is faced with problems typical of the large firm but without the resources to overcome them.

Turning to an analysis of profitability according to the size of the firm, it is possible to show (Table 6.11) an inverse relationship between the levels of profitability and depreciation and the size of gross total assets.

This phenomenon, already evident in 1958, became greater during the period considered. In fact in 1963 the larger firms showed a depreciation rate of 5·71 per cent while the smaller firms reached 7·27 per cent. The rate of profit was no different and rose from 3·81 per cent for larger firms to 12·35 per cent for smaller firms. This very interesting result stimulates further comment.

A firm should derive benefits from economies of scale with the increase in size. Mass production can give lower unit costs. A large firm can be assured of and can control a wide market, it can finance research programs, turn to different sources of finance more easily, obtain top-level management and train its own personnel; in short,

Table 6.11

Ratios of: Net Profit or Loss/Net Capital, Annual Depreciation/Gross Fixed Assets, in the 200 Largest Companies Classified by the Size of Gross Total Assets
(percentage)

Size groups (million lire)	1958		1959		1960	
	Net profit or loss / Net capital	Annual depreciation / Gross fixed assets	Net profit or loss / Net capital	Annual depreciation / Gross fixed assets	Net profit or loss / Net capital	Annual depreciation / Gross fixed assets
Gross total assets						
Over 100,000	6·99	4·69	8·35	5·34	8·33	6·00
50,001–100,000	6·91	5·73	8·37	5·75	8·78	5·88
25,001–50,000	8·99	5·62	9·62	5·76	9·49	6·11
15,001–25,000	12·90	5·95	14·56	6·08	14·26	6·93
Up to 15,000	10·36	6·59	13·71	6·31	14·77	6·66

Size groups (million lire)	1961		1962		1963	
	Net profit or loss / Net capital	Annual depreciation / Gross fixed assets	Net profit or loss / Net capital	Annual depreciation / Gross fixed assets	Net profit or loss / Net capital	Annual depreciation / Gross fixed assets
Gross total assets						
Over 100,000	8·09	5·96	6·93	5·30	3·81	5·71
50,001–100,000	8·51	6·20	7·24	5·77	5·27	6·00
25,001–50,000	8·93	5·90	7·90	6·00	7·25	6·28
15,001–25,000	13·03	6·79	10·79	6·81	11·21	7·81
Up to 15,000	14·53	6·54	12·01	6·81	12·35	7·27

it can obtain the various factors of production more easily and can at the same time increase productivity.

On the other hand, increased size creates many and complex problems which Italian firms have probably not yet resolved. In some cases investment was increased beyond the organizational capacity of the firm, creating a situation which gave negative economies.

The lower profitability of the larger firms compared to the small-sized firms could therefore depend not on the size but on the rhythm of growth. The period from 1958 to 1963 is too short to be able to give a reply to this question; nevertheless the research figures help to clarify the problem of the coexistence and growth of small and large firms.

The profitability of small-sized firms is the essential condition for their survival and expansion. This, in fact, is both their strength and weakness, for in order to survive they must be more efficient than the larger-sized firms.

Where this higher efficiency is not reached (either for internal or external reasons), the small firm cannot continue alone and must either merge with a large firm or disappear.

The situation is completely different above a certain size (at least in the Italian structural situation) where even firms which were not competitive are permitted to continue to operate and remain on the market.

In other words, errors in forecasting and in expansion policies which lead to failure for the smaller firms are minimized or avoided in the macro-firm, a situation which is typical of developing countries where a large disequilibrium in the industrialization process persists, and where the number of large firms is still small.

The fall in net profitability compared to growth in size can be further explained in that the macro-firm tends to have objectives other than the maximization of profit, and is obliged to move within social constraints. The observed relationship naturally influences the behaviour of the firm in respect to the different sources of finance.

The figures available and the calculations carried out confirm the existence of an inverse relationship between self-finance and the size of the firm. Such a relationship is found for every year under consideration, though with some variation. Taking the whole period and passing from the firms with gross assets over 100 billions to the smaller firms, the percentage of financial needs covered by self-finance rose from 30·63 per cent to 47·45 per cent (Table 6.12).

Table 6.12

Annual Degree of Gross Self-financing of the 200 Largest Industrial Companies Classified by the Volume of Gross Total Assets
(percentage)

Gross saving		Gross total assets				
		over 100,000	50,001–100,000	25,001–50,000	15,001–25,000	up to 15,000
1958 as percentage of:	Investment in gross total assets	43·29	75·43	59·69	53·06	61·44
	Investment in gross fixed assets and stock	57·51	88·97	83·16	75·09	73·81
	Investment in gross fixed assets	61·98	89·75	84·83	90·26	106·43
1959 as percentage of:	Investment in gross total assets	48·74	52·25	51·52	45·26	54·09
	Investment in gross fixed assets and stock	85·13	101·61	93·03	71·10	105·36
	Investment in gross fixed assets	84·47	103·84	97·51	90·39	152·96
1960 as percentage of:	Investment in gross total assets	28·46	45·68	54·27	50·90	44·63
	Investment in gross fixed assets and stock	53·71	61·48	105·20	66·76	64·68
	Investment in gross fixed assets	88·97	87·58	110·70	107·36	135·31
1961 as percentage of:	Investment in gross total assets	39·44	40·16	40·73	47·13	52·27
	Investment in gross fixed assets and stock	53·76	59·24	63·46	67·89	77·56
	Investment in gross fixed assets	64·69	77·81	83·23	94·36	128·35
1962 as percentage of:	Investment in gross total assets	24·84	26·66	47·00	48·46	42·74
	Investment in gross fixed assets and stock	37·16	36·41	60·58	61·67	67·19
	Investment in gross fixed assets	44·79	48·26	81·84	75·90	99·87
1963 as percentage of:	Investment in gross total assets	23·02	28·00	36·95	42·53	42·75
	Investment in gross fixed assets and stock	31·75	42·23	51·81	59·32	61·74
	Investment in gross fixed assets	44·43	51·03	76·60	81·17	110·74
Whole period as percentage of:	Investment in gross total assets	30·63	37·11	45·96	46·98	47·45
	Investment in gross fixed assets and stock	46·06	53·83	69·22	65·13	71·13
	Investment in gross fixed assets	58·63	67·21	86·85	87·56	118·76

Considering only investment in plant and machinery, the two percentages become 58·63 and 118·76 respectively.

The latter figure indicates that the small-sized firms invest in plant and machinery less than the amount of internal finance available. The inverse relationship just described is partially explained by the fact that the larger firms have registered higher rates of growth during the period. That is to say, they had to finance a larger and constant need which could be only partially covered by internal finance even when profitability is high.

The inverse relationship may be further explained by other financial factors. The possibility of issuing share capital increases with the increase in size. Together with this ability to attract capital, the shareholders' fear of losing control of the company is reduced. Instead, the small firms, even when nominally quoted on the stock exchange, have great difficulty in borrowing from this source. Therefore they often had to limit their expansion to the availability of internal finance and thus in many cases self-finance offered the only way to increase capital. The possibility of issuing new shares diminishes with the size of the company and so the small companies had to find the means to expand their capital internally. Thus it can be concluded that the importance of self-finance as a limiting factor of growth increases as the size of the firm decreases. The figures available confirm this and highlight the close relationship between self-finance and issued capital. It can be seen that, independent of

Table 6.13

Rates of Self-financing and of Financing through Capital Issues during 1958–63 in the 200 Largest Industrial Companies classified by the Size of Gross Total Assets

Size groups (million lire)	Saving as percentage of investment in gross total assets *a*	New capital issues as percentage of investment in gross total assets *b*	Gross saving and new capital issues as percentage in gross total assets *(a + b)*
Gross Total Assets			
Over 100,000	30·63	20·06	50·69
50,001–100,000	37·11	11·83	48·94
25,001–50,000	45·96	16·07	62·03
15,001–25,000	46·98	12·52	59·50
Up to 15,000	47·45	9·23	56·68

size, the company's own means, self-finance plus capital issues, provided on average between 50 and 60 per cent of total needs (Table 6.13). Such results are, however, the results of the clearly separate and distinct behaviour of the different firms. As the size of the firm increases, so the incidence of issued capital grows while the incidence of self-finance diminishes.

We have thus an experimental confirmation of M. Kalecki's theory of growing risk. The amount of entrepreneurial capital in all cases appears to be a limiting factor to the process of growth.

Although the larger firms have the possibility, within fixed limits, of relying on the capital market for some funds, internal finance is for them also the principal way of increasing their capital and expanding investment.

III. CONCLUSIONS

The period under consideration, which was characterized by dramatic changes, is so short that it does not allow us to draw any final conclusions on the growth of the firm. However, the consideration of the available data has shown some basic aspects of the process of growth and has proved the inadequacy of those theoretical approaches which try to explain growth by the causal action of separately considered factors.

Substantially the Italian experience of the years 1958–63 has shown that the growth of the firm cannot be explained by the growth of aggregate demand or by the availability of the labour factor, or by financial incentives deriving from measures of economic policy.

Instead, the growth of the firm appears above all to be the result of managerial action devoted to introducing technical progress quickly and to creating conditions, both on an organizational and a marketing plane, for actually improving the efficiency of the product mix. This efficiency is the element that allows the firms to overcome marketing and financial obstacles, that is to say those elements that the study has helped to characterize more as limiting factors than as incentives to the process of growth.

7 Optimum or Maximum Corporate Growth under Uncertainty

John Lintner

I. INTRODUCTION

1. *The setting*

Consider a firm selling in a less than perfectly competitive market. It produces and markets a more or less closely related set of products to customers who have varying degrees of preference for its output in the face of competitors' offerings. It has an 'image', an established reputation, and a history. It has a vigorous, enterprising management who are charged with responsibility for the direction, allocation and use of the company's resources. Its resources include its plants and a wide-ranging collection of equipment; its employees of all ranks and skills; the 'goodwill' of its established market position; and very importantly, the organization of its human and physical resources into effective economic units. This organization produces relatively efficient flows of work through the firm's plants and distribution system; at the same time, it provides efficient flows of information to and from all operating and administrative levels for purposes of effective decision-making as well as control of operations and performance.

This representative firm of the modern capitalist world is not much interested in the quick kill or short-run coup that has no future. It plays for bigger, longer-run continuing stakes and results. It operates in a growing economy, and more specifically in a set of expanding markets concurrently served by other companies eager to push their wares, expand their market shares and grow profitably at its expense. In this economic environment, its management is well aware that failure to keep pace – and specifically a failure to grow – is a sure recipe for absolute decline, if not doom and oblivion. As a consequence, it plans for growth.

Efficiency is stressed, and a great deal of what an economist would recognize as 'short-run optimization' occurs; but the *optimization is optimization along the targeted trend-trajectory of a dynamic growth path* and specifically not just the one-period-only static optimization of the elementary economic course.[1] These firms may rather alertly take advantage of the unexpected chance short-run opportunity, but only if its longer-run stretegies and prospects are not compromised. Both the short- and longer-run opportunity costs of any diversion of its resources from plans are carefully weighed.

This typical firm not only plans for growth but it does so in an *inherently uncertain environment.* These uncertainties of course relate to all the numerous relevant aspects of business conditions and prospective changes in the underlying economy, as well as their conditional consequences for the company. The uncertainties also include the possible moves and counter-moves of its oligopolistic competitors and their consequences for the given firm. And conditional on all these environmental factors, management can at best give a probabilistic assessment of just what changes in sales, costs and profits will follow upon any of its own initiatives or counter-moves, whether they be new products, new investments or new efforts at sales promotion. But as if all these basic and interacting uncertainties were not enough, it is also clear that management acts upon the basic realization that neither it (nor its staff nor its most clairvoyant or prescient consultants) can possibly know as much about the more distant future as it knows about the shape of events less remote in time.

In this dynamic and uncertain environment, a company develops *policies and strategies for growth.* The individually distinguishable but coordinated policies include programs to enlarge the market for existing products and for the development, introduction and promotion of new products. They include policy standards for the acceptance of individual investment projects and programs in the company's capital budgets, and with respect to the use of alternative sources of funds to finance the planned continuing growth of the company. They also include plans for the staffing, coordination and administration of the growing and increasingly complex enterprise. Taken together, these basic policies determine the *strategic posture* of the firm. All these elements of the strategic posture of any company

[1] For an illustration that, in strictest theory, this alternative to short-run single-period maximization is optimal, see Appendix, A, p. 222, below.

are clearly subject to mutually interdependent decision and choice within some set of feasible alternatives.

Research has shown that firms tend to operate in terms of *expectations* or *targets* of *average* rates of growth out into the considerable future together with some assessment of the degree of shorter-run fluctuations to be expected from these longer-run averages.[1] These assessments of expected longer-run average growth prospects and the expected variability about such averages are of course in effect a composite summary of the assessment of the more detailed underlying environmental and competitive factors and the prospective success of the implementation of the company's policies and strategies for growth in such an evolving environment. Moreover, assessments of the company's average growth prospects are based on judgments of the expectations (in the statistical sense) of the results of *maintaining some specified strategic posture* in the dynamic but inherently stochastic environment within which the firm operates. And given the stochastic character of its environment, the assessed variability of its operating results and the prospective distribution of deviations from trends and target paths over time is also judged relative to the firm's maintaining its set of basic longer-run policies, its strategic posture, over the foreseeable (or assessable) future.

Within certain constraints, the firm is free to choose among alternative strategic postures. The evidence seems clear that these strategic choices are made in terms of the assessed desirability of their respective longer-run prospects and risks. In particular, *each feasible posture has associated with it both a time path of expected growth and also a measure of risk or pattern of random variability over time* (assessed about the expected growth trend), and these basic policy decisions can effectively be regarded as choices among *alternative pairs* of expected rate of growth and level of risk. These observations suggest that we may model this choice process in a manner analogous to the long-run comparative static equilibrium of the firm, with growth rates replacing levels of activity, and with risks introduced explicitly into its objective function.

This framework seems particularly appropriate as a basis for

[1] This is clearly set forth in the classic paper [6] written forty-five years ago by Donaldson Brown of Du Pont and General Motors which has been the seminal prototype for the rapidly expanding 'management', 'control' and growth-planning literature over the subsequent years. Its influence is clearly reflected in the more recent studies and in the business practices reflected in empirical observations of Dean [7], Downie [10], Penrose [28] and Marris [25].

analyzing companies' choices of strategic postures, since the evidence also seems clear that once a company has chosen a given strategic posture, it will continue to maintain it and live with it until such time as the accumulated objective evidence has shown rather clearly that the old set of policies is not working so that a basic reorientation of the company's strategic posture is required. Such basic reorientations of the interrelated set of long-run policies are not undertaken frequently or lightly because they are usually very costly and even traumatic. Also, in part, such basic reorientations are not needed frequently precisely because, given the stochastic character of the firm's environment, the set of policies is selected in terms of their stochastic characteristics and prospects within this environment. In particular, the set of long-run policies always includes *strategies* of adaptation to transient shorter-run stochastic developments.

These seminal properties of company planning and policy selection are clearly illustrated by the evidence on dividend and debt policies and standards for the selection of individual investment projects. In relation to expectations of average profitability and the variability of profits and investment requirements for growth, firms have evolved patterns of dividend distribution keyed to a *target payout ratio* which is relatively quite stable over substantial periods of time, and a somewhat more flexible pattern of adjustment to unforeseen stochastic displacements of profits [16, 5]. In much the same way, companies have evolved policies with respect to the use of outside financing (except for utilities, usually debt) which generally take the form of acceptable or target debt–equity ratios which are to be exceeded only for good cause and temporarily [9, 14]. It is quite clear that target dividend payout ratios, target or *ex ante* maximum debt–equity ratios and standards for investment selection are *interdependent decisions* made in terms of assessments of long-run average profitability and risk considered as a function of the policy choices made. In particular the selection of the target dividend payout is made in the light of the expected average profitability of investments over considerable periods of time (when the investments themselves are selected in terms of given policy standards) and the regression over time between the company's cash flow and the (funds required for the) volume of new investments which would satisfy a set of investment standards over the cycle. But the target dividend payout is associated with a (somewhat more flexible) speed of adjustment so that the actual dividend payment in a given year is only partially (but

CE G 2

progressively) adjusted to the target level.[1] Correspondingly, the investment policy includes the strategy of having the investment standards ('required returns') applicable to each future short-run period vary in line with the opportunity costs of funds for investment purposes in each successive short period.[2] The long-run dividend policy and the investment strategy are thus mutually determined in terms of expected long-run average outcomes whose assessment – like the long-run policies themselves – incorporates strategies or planned patterns of short-run adaptation to stochastic short-run developments.

2. *Specific assumptions used with respect to the firm*

The essential features of the preceding generalizations suggest the following structure for our model of a representative growing corporation in a modern capitalist, dynamic and stochastic environment:

1. Firms have non-negligible degrees of 'market power' on the product side, but all financial resources are obtained in purely competitive markets. For simplicity, we also assume that all other inputs are acquired without the exercise of any monopsony power.

2. For any firm, given its unique environment, there is a constrained, interdependent feasible set of long-run policies or

---

[1] In consequence, the *short-run* retention ratio is usually very much smaller than the long-run target ratio, and this characteristic is part of the dividend policy itself.

[2] This in part reflects the fact that the dividend policy itself is chosen with a recognition that the high 'information content' of changes in dividend payments requires that the dividend outflows in line with a dividend policy once established will be a claim of dominating priority on the firm's funds in each future short-run period, and the opportunity costs of funds for investment at given times will be assessed subject to this constraint. See Lintner [16] and [19].

This policy structure explains the observed facts that even though dividend and investment *policies* are interdependent, there is no demonstrable effect of investment requirements on annual dividend payments. See Lintner [16], Brittain [5] and Turnovsky [34]. The apparently contrary finding of Dhrymes [8] is to be seriously discounted because of his failure to include a lagged dividend variable. By leaving out the long-run dividend policy – and there is no doubt companies do have such long-run policies – he failed to construct an appropriate test of whether *within the context of the long-run policy* there is a short-run effect. The Turnovsky study did meet these requirements and confirmed my own earlier negative finding.

strategies available with respect to (a) new product development and product-market expansion costs, (b) cash outlays for plant and equipment to provide capacity to produce the anticipated growing volume of profitably saleable output, and (c) 'internal' expansion costs which are associated essentially with the rate of change of the size of the firm itself because of the unavoidable costs of acquiring new personnel of the appropriate skills, and molding them into the ongoing human organization and administrative structure.

3. The environment is a *dynamic and stochastic steady state*. Conditional on any feasible policy mix chosen in (2(a), (b), (c)), assessments regarding the environment exhibit the following characteristics: (a) the expected values of outlays for research and development, product-market stimulation, plant and equipment outlays, internal expansion costs, dollar sales, operating costs, profit rates, earnings, dividend payments, book values of assets, equity values and so on will all lie on exponential growth trends;[1] (b) as of any given point in time t_0, a firm's assessment of the current variance (i.e. variance as of t_{0+}) of profitability or any growth rate is a function of the policy mix chosen; and (c) its assessment of *future* variances (i.e. variances as of $t_0 + \tau$) depends upon futurity $\tau > 0$ as well as the assessment of the current variance. Note that the variances for different variables will generally differ (and be functionally related) for any given futurity τ, and the variance assessed for any jth variance will be greater with respect to a longer futurity than for a shorter futurity. (Indeed, the latter assumption is an important characteristic of our basic models.)

4. The policy mix of (2a), (b), (c)) is selected in the expectation that the chosen long-run or strategic posture will be maintained over substantial periods of future calendar time.[2]

5. The opportunity-sets within which policies (2(a), (b) and (c)) are chosen, together determine the feasible set of alternative expected growth paths for the firm. But these opportunity-sets

---

[1] We also assume that as of any current time τ, the current expected value of the expectations of growth rate of any variable which *would* be assessed in the future (conditional on the same policy mix) is the same as the expectation in the current assessment.

[2] The rationality of this policy is also buttressed by foreknowledge of the major costs involved in major *changes* in policy strategies in large firms noted above (p. 175).

also involve variances and patterns of variances over future time intervals. With greater generality, therefore these opportunity-sets within which policies (2(a), (b), (c)) are chosen, taken together, determine the feasible set of *combinations* of (a) expected growth rates of company variables of interest, and (b) their 'initial' variances (i.e. their variances assessed as of time t_{0+}), and (c) the time rate at which the assessed variance in the more distant future increases with the futurity τ.

6. The firm's choices among available policy mixes in this environment thus reduce essentially to *choices among triplets* of these summary statistics. In particular, for any given rate of increase in uncertainty with futurity, the firm's choices of policy mixes involve choices among available pairs of expected values of growth rates and their associated initial risk or variance.

3. *The criterion function*

To complete the model analytically, we must specify a *preference ordering* over these feasible combinations of expected growth rates, their initial variances, and the rate of increase in variance with futurity.[1] Most of the previous work in this field has offered models in which the objective is maximization of 'the' growth rate of the firm, subject perhaps to such constraints as acceptable levels of profits or ratios of debt to equity – or else it has followed neo-classical prescriptions and, with no attention to uncertainty, developed rules for the maximization of equity value under conditions of strict prescient certainty.

In this paper, we follow the neo-classical tradition and assume that the policy mix is chosen to maximize the current market value of the firm's equity. However (in contrast to other work), this market value is functionally dependent not only on the current dividend payment and its expected rate of growth overtime, but also upon the variance of this growth rate and its time pattern with futurity. For us, in short, the current market value of the equity does provide a true preference ordering over available combinations of expected growth rates, their initial 'risk' and the increasing uncertainty of assessments pertaining

[1] Even when the latter variable is exogenous and not subject to change or selection by the firm, it enters as an explicit parameter influencing the firm's policy choices of expected growth rates and initial risk levels. See section IV below.

to the more distant future. In particular, we assume that the objective is the maximization of the current equilibrium value of the equity in a purely competitive stock market in which all investors are risk-averse, and all stock-price assessments are lognormal and reflect the expectation that deviations of future prices from expected exponential trend values will be generated by a random walk. (Comparisons with the results obtained with other preference functions are given near the end of the paper.)

4. *Brief outline of the paper*

In section II we present a 'dry-run' of the analysis under dynamic steady states in which all uncertainties are absent. After explicitly deriving the simultaneously optimal time paths of prices, rates of investment, promotional outlays and costs of expansion using a demand-generating function and production function, we develop a 'reduced-form' model (with the same optimal properties) which provides a more convenient basis for the introduction of uncertainty in the rest of the paper.

In section III, uncertainty is introduced under the simplifying assumption that logarithmic variances are expected to be constant over time. After specifying an appropriate stock-price model, we derive the optimal growth rate to maximize the value of the stock under these simple stochastic conditions when the level of 'risk' is not subject to the firm's control. In this section we also examine the trade-offs between expected growth rates and risk and derive the optimal combination or mix of the two criteria under these simplified conditions of risk. In section IV, random walks are introduced into expectations of future stock prices and management similarly allows for the fact that its assessments of the more distant future involve greater uncertainty than its judgments of nearer-term prospects. After examining the implications of the more realistic assumptions for the firm's basic policy choices of expected growth rates and initial (near-term) risks when its objective is the maximization of the current market value of its equity, we conclude the paper by offering a comparison of these results reached on neo-neo-classical assumptions with those reached by other writers who have assumed or concluded (as the case may be) that corporations seek to maximize growth as such. Important conclusions at each stage of the analysis are italicized in the text.

Three final introductory comments. Since our primary objective in this paper is to develop, with explicit allowance for uncertainty, a model of the optimal choice of growth rates and level of risk under neo-classical criteria in an environment where expectationally steady-state growth is possible, we also concentrate all our analysis upon choices among such steady-state growth paths. Our focus is upon the vector of flow variables along the steady-dynamic state which is preferred to all alternative feasible expectationally steady-state paths, and for this purpose we simply assume that stock variables have previously been brought sufficiently close to the optimal levels given by the preferred steady-state growth path not to alter the latter choice significantly.[1]

For simplicity, we also assume throughout that the firm produces and sells a single 'composite' product, leaving the further issues involved in optimizing the product mix behind the scenes. For the same reason, in this paper we also simply assume that all growth must be internally financed, since an analysis confined to growth financed by retained earnings exhausts the possibilities of equity-financed growth under steady-state conditions.[2] Although, under appropriate additional assumptions, the use of debt financing will enlarge the firm's opportunities for growth and change the numerical size of the optimal growth rate, *none* of the qualitative conclusions and comparisons made in the present paper is affected.[3]

[1] Except for effects of uncertainty, the reader may think of our analysis as corresponding to the vertical of K^* in Solow's Fig. 10.1 in this volume [31]. Alternatively, he may regard our analysis as assuming that the primary choices of steady-state paths have been made sufficiently far in the past that the essentially transient effects of the then initial conditions on stock variables, and the problems which were involved in the selection of the optimal 'catenaries' for stock variables to approach their optimal 'turnpikes' of expectationally steady growth, are all in the past. In our assumed environment of purely competitive factors and financial markets, this additional assumption seems quite reasonable.

[2] I have elsewhere shown [17, 19] that in a frictionless economy the alternative of issuing new equity does not enlarge the set of alternative growth rates available to the firm. See also Williamson [35].

[3] The question of the optimal debt–equity mix is a complex one whose examination here would divert space and attention from the central issues of concern in this paper. The full analysis including debt financing will appear in my forthcoming book [21]. Readers who wish to include debt may simply read all of our results and conclusions as if we had added (in transparent ink) the phrase 'subject to the firm's maintaining an optimal debt–equity mix at all points in time'.

II. THE MODEL UNDER CERTAINTY

In this section, we invoke the simplification of assumed prescience in order to develop most clearly certain fundamental relationships between (a) the endogenous (policy-determined) and exogenous parameters of the demand-for-output functions which the firm will face over time, (b) its current and future production functions as related to technological change and the firm's cumulative outlays on productive capacity, (c) the administrative, managerial and 'non-productive' labor costs of *changing the scale* of the firm's operations within any time interval, (d) the (exogenously given) levels of input factor prices, and (e) the firm's decisions on current and future levels of outlays on product development and promoton, its outlays on productive capacity, and the levels and rates of growth in profits, dividends, capital stock, sales and market prices of stock. After optimal policies with respect to each discretionary variable which will maximize the market value of the equity are derived, we show that that set of these simultaneously optimal policies can rigorously be summarized by the solutions to a much simpler formulation in which optimal value of a retention ratio is determined subject to an appropriately specified efficient set of constraints.

1. *The objective function*

In perfect markets with no uncertainty, well-known theorems establish that all assets at all points in time will sell at prices such that the sum of current rate of return provided by cash receipts and the current relative rate of change in asset price must equal the current (short) rate of interest in the market. If we assume the rate of interest κ is constant over time, and identify the current rate of return with the ratio of current cash dividend receipts D_t to market value P_t, the general solution of $D_t/P_t + d \log P_t/d_t = \kappa$ establishes a price at each point in time equal to

$$P_t = \int_t^\infty D_\tau \exp(-\kappa\tau)d\tau. \tag{1}$$

An optimal dividend (and in our case, growth) policy requires that as of any decision point t_0, that *time path* of D_τ be selected which will maximize P_t in (1).

2. *Simultaneous policy optimization with explicit demand, promotion and production functions*

At each point in time, a company sells a quantity of output q_τ which depends upon its price p_τ, the state of the economy z_τ and its (cumulative) promotional efforts A_τ – i.e. upon its *demand function* $q_\tau = q_\tau(p_\tau, z_\tau, A_\tau)$. The output q_τ must be produced subject to a production function whose arguments are capital stock K_τ, labor L_τ and other inputs such as materials. Given the prices of all inputs and its production function, the firm has a *cost of production* which we write $C(q_\tau; K_\tau)$ to emphasize its dependence upon the capital stock available at τ. After adding back depreciation $\delta_K K_\tau$ on capital stock, the firm's 'operating profit' at any point in time[1] is thus

$$R_\tau = R[p_\tau, A_\tau, z_\tau, K_\tau] = p_\tau q_\tau - C(q_\tau; K_\tau) - \delta_K K_\tau. \qquad (2)$$

This operating profits function clearly incorporates all the constraints upon the firm's options at any time due to (exogenous) prices of inputs and its demand function and production function.

By the accounting identity of the 'sources and uses of funds' statement, we know that the dividends which can (and will) be paid at any time are simply the excess of operating profits R_τ over current outlays on product promotion $I_A(\tau)$ and upon productive capacity or capital stock $I_K(\tau)$:

$$D_\tau = R_\tau - I_A(\tau) - I_K(\tau). \qquad (3)$$

As of any point in time t_0, therefore, the optimal policy mix for the firm will be that set of time paths of product prices p, promotional outlays I_A and capital investment I_K (and hence by (3) of dividends D) which will maximize Pt_0 in (1) using the constraints summarized in (2) and (3). The resulting set of time paths represent optimal policies in the sense that neither shifts of funds between different uses at any one time nor shifts of funds for any given use between time periods will improve results.

Now, Arrow and others (e.g. [2, 24]) have shown that the sets of policies which will maximize (1) subject to (2) and (3) will in fact be those which maximize a 'net return' function

$$\Pi(p, A, z, K) = R(p, A, z, K) - (\kappa - \delta_A)A - (\kappa - \delta_K - \dot{p}_K)K \qquad (4)$$

---

[1] For simplicity we suppress the realistically important costs of expansion *per se*, for the time being.

at all points in time where δ_A represents the rate of evaporation of goodwill, and $\dot{p}_K$ the rate of change in capital-goods prices.[1] Consequently, the necessary conditions[2] upon the optimal policies are that they satisfy (5a), (5b), (5c) simultaneously and at all points in time, where

$$\partial\Pi/\partial p = \partial R/\partial p = 0 \tag{5a}$$
$$\partial\Pi/\partial K = \partial R/\partial K - (\kappa + \delta_K + \dot{p}_K) = 0 \tag{5b}$$
$$\partial\Pi/\partial A = \partial R/\partial A - (\kappa - \delta_A) = 0. \tag{5c}$$

These equations respectively require that (a) for optimal stocks of capital and goodwill, product prices be set to equate marginal revenue and marginal production costs; (b) current investment outlays (capital budgets) be set to equate the marginal return to an increase in capital stock to the sum of the rate of interest and evaporative depreciation and change in capital-goods prices; and (c) current outlays to expand sales be set to equate the marginal return to an increase in the stock of goodwill to the sum of interest and the rate of depreciation of goodwill.

In section A of the Appendix, we derive explicit solutions simultaneously satisfying these conditions at all points in time under the following set of simplifying assumptions: (a) the production function is Cobb–Douglas in terms of efficiency units; (b) the demand function is linear in the logarithm of price p, the cumulative (depreciated) stock of past promotional outlay or 'goodwill' A, and an exogenous economy-wide growth factor z; and (c) the growth rate of the exogenous factor g_z, the interest rate, all input prices, the evaporative depreciation rates on capital stock and goodwill, and all elasticities are constant over time. Under these conditions: (1) the optimal capital stock K^* at any time will be proportional to sales; (2) given optimal capital stock, product prices will be constant over time; and (3) the optimal stock of 'goodwill' A^* will also bear a constant ratio to sales. From these results, we then show that the optimal rate of (gross) investment is a constant fraction $f_K^*(\tau)$ of sales revenues over time; the optimal rate of outlay on demand promotion is also a constant fraction $f_A^*(\tau)$ of sales revenues over time; and all direct or marginal costs similarly absorb a constant fraction f_d^* of sales

[1] To insure convergence of the present-value integral it is necessary to assume that the limits of $\exp(-\kappa\tau)K_\tau$ and $\exp(-\kappa\tau)A_\tau$ are finite. This is insured by our assumption (until section IV) that all growth rates of dividends satisfy $g_d < K$.

[2] The sufficient conditions will also be satisfied by virtue of the appropriate convexity assumptions.

receipts. Since, under such stable growth conditions, it is also reasonable to assume that optimal levels of overheads including the internal costs of expansion *per se* will also absorb a constant fraction f_O^* of sales revenues,[1] the optimal dividends at all points in time will be given by

$$D_\tau^* = (1 - f_d^* - f_O^* - f_K^* - f_A^*)S_\tau^*, \tag{6}$$

after using (3), and recalling that operating profits $R = (1 - f_d - f_O)S$. Under these simple steady-state assumptions, the optimal growth rate of dividends g_D^* is the same as the optimal growth in sales. Finally, since all the above analysis has implemented the requirement that the firm's policy mix should be chosen to maximize (1) under the constraints of (2) and (3), it follows that the maximum attainable price of the firm's equity at $t_0 = 0$ is

$$\max P_{t_0} = \int_0^\infty D_0^* \exp - [(\kappa - g_D^*)\tau d_\tau] = \frac{(1 - r^*)S_0^*}{\kappa - g_D^*} \tag{7}$$

where we write $r = \Sigma_i f_i$ so that the entire parenthesis in (24) is $(1 - r^*)$ and let S_0^* be on the steady growth path picked by the optimizing policy.

This derivation illustrates the determination of the optimal time path for dividends as a residual using the accounting identity (3) when *all other* aspects of the firm's broad policy mix individually and simultaneously satisfy the normative profit-maximizing local conditions at all points in time. The particular assumptions concerning elasticities, input prices and so on were merely the simplest consistent with steady growth in the resulting dividend stream (and hence in the price of the stock). It is immediately apparent that a large array of more complex sets of assumptions – involving, for instance, regular time paths of change (rather than constancy) in input prices or various elasticities or the exogenous growth rate g_z – are also consistent with

---

[1] These 'internal' expansion costs (distinct from either advertising or plant investment) are associated essentially with the rate of change of the size of the firm itself to provide appropriate administrative, management and other personnel (usually termed 'nonproductive labor' in the economics literature) required to administer the larger organization effectively. It is reasonable to assume that these outlays are proportionate to the time-derivative of sales volume. With the relative rate of growth of sales constant under present assumptions, expansion costs are thus proportional to dollar sales S_t, and to avoid further notation they may be included along with 'other overheads' in the variable f_O^* above. (The perhaps more realistic assumption that such costs are a function of gS rather than S_τ, and even an increasing function of g_S, fits easily into the more general models outlined under the next heading.)

constancy in the rate of growth in dividends when the various other elements of the broad policy mix change in offsetting ways as they are simultaneously and continuously optimized over time. For some of these assumption-sets, the dividend payout ratio will also be constant over time when expressed as a fraction of sales receipts; under a larger number of sets of assumptions, it will be constant with respect to operating profits; and it will be constant with respect to economic profit still more generally.[1]

3. *Summary model under certainty*

This analysis suggests a convenient formulation which effectively summarizes the results of more detailed analysis of the simultaneous optimization of each separate policy component. Specifically, consider the full set of alternative *policy mixes* with respect to product prices, advertising, plant investment, the employment of labor and the incurrence of 'other overheads', *each mix* satisfying the condition that the growth rate in dividend payments be constant over time. (So long as *this* condition is met, the relative rates of spending on different parts of the overall policy mix may change over time as appropriate under changing conditions.) We classify each eligible policy mix in terms of its associated dividend growth rate and dividend payout ratio, suitably denominated. It is clear from our criterion (equation (1)) that, among mixes having the same dividend payout ratio, those offering the highest growth rate will be preferred to any of the others. Proceeding in this way for each dividend payout ratio, we determine the *efficient set* of policy mixes (or growth rates) and dividend payout ratios. Now suppose that these alternative efficient policy mixes are sufficiently numerous as to make it reasonable to treat the alternative growth rates and dividend payouts themselves as variables related by a continuous and differentiable function $g_D = f(r)$. It is clear from the structure of constraints that the dividend payout ratio is inversely related to attainable growth rates: faster growth requires greater retentions for their financing, and this necessarily reduces dividend payouts – i.e. $dg_D/dr > 0$ everywhere in the relevant range.

Now from our criterion function, equation (1), with r and g_D

---

[1] For a development based directly upon a constant dividend payout as a fraction of profits, see my earlier [18]. See also Appendix, subsection A.4.

constant over time we would have an equation like (7) without asterisks:[1]

$$P_0 = \int\limits_0^\infty D_0 \exp - [(K - g_D)\tau]dt = \frac{(1 - r)X_0}{k - g_D} \qquad (8)$$

which gives the market valuation of all the alternative efficient combinations of r and g_D available to the firm. Differentiation with respect to the retention ratio shows that

$$\frac{dP_0}{dr} = P_0 \left[-\frac{1}{1 - r} + \frac{dg/dr}{k - g_D} \right]. \qquad (9)$$

Consequently, $dP_0/dr > 0$, *and there is an improvement in the policy mix so long as the sum of the growth rate itself and the dividend payout of the marginal improvement of the growth rate exceeds the interest rate k* – i.e. so long as

$$(1 - r)dg/dr + g_D \geqslant k. \qquad (10)$$

When all the improvements in the policy mix through added retentions and greater growth have been exhausted (under our wealth-maximizing criterion), the derivative in (9) will have ceased to be positive: an equality will have replaced the inequality in (10) and the variables r and g_D will have taken on the values shown in (7) from the 'building-block' approach.

This alternative 'short-cut' formulation clearly identifies *precisely the same optimum* as the more detailed approach developed before *under any given set of assumptions* consistent with a constant rate of growth in dividend payments and with a constant (suitably denominated) dividend payout ratio over time. The present formulation of the model also brings out the critically important property of such models under certainty – equation (10) written with an equality – which is to be sure implicit in, but not made explicit by, the earlier formulation. With full rigor we can regard equation (8), and the equality in the limit on the condition for policy improvements given by (10), as effectively subsuming more detailed analysis of all policy mixes consistent with steady-state growth under certainty with constant dividend payouts. These equations are also uniquely

[1] I use X here instead of S as in (7), to cover in one notation the possibilities mentioned at the end of II.2 for the payout ratio to be denominated by operating profit or economic profit instead of sales.

convenient to use in our subsequent analysis in sections III and IV of optimal growth under conditions of uncertainty.

III. THE MODEL WITH 'STABLE' UNCERTAINTY

We now introduce a simple 'stable' form of uncertainty into our analysis. Management still plans for growth and seeks to maximize the value of the firm's equity as before. But it no longer assumes itself to have prescient foreknowledge of the precise consequences of all of its acts over all future time. Any policy mix it selects will be associated with some specified dividend payout ratio and an *expectation* of a growth rate – but the actual growth rate realized will be a random variable. Consequently, with a fixed payout ratio, future dividend payments and stock values are also uncertain.

The present section is intended to bring out in the simplest possible way some of the minimal consequences of the introduction of uncertainty into the standard analysis which ignores it entirely.[1] For this purpose we assume that assessments of growth rates for various short intervals in the future will have the same variance regardless of the time to which they apply. The growth–risk–dividend trade-off function under these stochastic assumptions is specified in III.1 below. We assume that growth rates over any time interval will be normally distributed, and consequently that future stock values – as well as prospective dividend payments and the dollar values of other firm variables such as assets, profits, sales and so on – will be lognormally distributed. The equilibrium market value of a company's stock in a purely competitive 'lognormal' securities market of risk-averse investors is set forth in III.2, and we assume that management will select policy mixes to maximize stock value in this market environment. In III.3, we determine the impact of an exogenously given level of 'risk' upon the optimal choices of dividend payouts and expected growth rates, and we also examine the optimal *combinations* of 'risk' with expected growth and dividend payouts where more

---

[1] With this material clearly in hand, we will then be in a position to develop in section IV the further consequences of the fact that assessments of the more distant future involve greater uncertainty than judgments of nearer-term prospects, and that consequently and in particular, stock prices over time meander in essentially a logarithmic Brownian motion or 'random walk'. But for this section to lay the foundations, we leave out these important additional features of the environment.

realistically the level of risk is also subject to (constrained) choice by the firm. This section concludes in III.4 with a reinterpretation of the impacts of uncertainty in terms of the Macaulay–Hick concept of the 'duration' of an income stream.

1. *The dividend–growth–'risk' trade-off function*

In section II.3 above, under assumptions of prescience, the basic constraint upon the policy mixes open to the firm could be summarized in an *efficient set* of dividend growth rates and retention (or dividend payout) rates of the form $g_D = f(r)$, and this function was assumed to be constant over future time. Associated with any retention ratio r which the firm might choose and maintain was a conditionally optimal policy mix which would maximize g_D for the given r. The unconditionally optimal policy mix was found by maximizing the criterion function (1) subject to the efficient set of constraints $g_D = f(r)$.

Under uncertainty, it is clear that the corresponding efficient set of constraints will have the form

$$\bar{g}_D = f(r, \sigma_g^2). \tag{12}$$

When growth rates are normally distributed under steady-state uncertainty, each feasible policy mix must be summarized in terms of three rather than two parameters: It involves a retention ratio r which will be held constant over time by assumption; but conditional on this retention ratio, it also involves an *expected* rather than certain growth rate, and a measure of the uncertainty or randomness associated with this combination of $\bar{g}$ and r. Because of the wealth-maximizing criterion function and the risk-aversion of investors, several properties of the efficient set (11) are clear:

  (a) of all feasible policy mixes having the same $\bar{g}$ and r, only the one with the *minimum* σ_g^2 enters the efficient set;
  (b) of all mixes with the same r and σ_g^2, only the one with the maximum $\bar{g}_D$ enters the efficient set;
  (c) of all policy mixes with the same $\bar{g}_D$ and σ_d^2 properties, only the one associated with *minimum* retention ratio r is admitted; and

(d) for the usual reasons, the efficient set is convex.[1]

For present purposes, we can ignore discreteness and discontinuities. The summary constraint function (11) is thus assumed to be continuous and twice differentiable with the following properties in keeping with (a)–(d):

$$\partial \bar{g}_D/\partial r > 0, \qquad \partial^2 \bar{g}_D/\partial r^2 < 0; \tag{11a}$$

$$\partial \bar{g}_D/\partial_g^2 > 0, \qquad \partial^2 \bar{g}_D/\partial(\sigma_g^2)^2 < 0. \tag{11b}$$

$$(\partial^2 \bar{g}_D/\partial^2 v_0)\,(\partial^2 \bar{g}_D/\partial r^2) > (\partial \bar{g}_D/\partial v_0 \partial r)^2. \tag{11c}$$

The geometry of this efficient set or constraint function is indicated in Fig. 7.1. The dots within the heavy lines represent the expected growth $\bar{g}_D$ and growth variance σ_g^2 associated with *all* the policy mixes associated with a *given r*, say r_1. Since linear mixes of policies are also policies, we will have a limiting envelope which is drawn in as the solid line on the figure.[2] For the same reason that increased

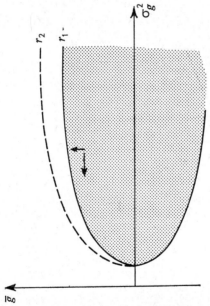

7.1. Illustration of constraints on policy-mixes

[1] Because of the lognormal distributions of dollar returns and the constant elasticity of utility functions used in this paper, the convexity is in terms of variances and means, rather than standard deviations and means, as in the usual Markowitz formulation.

[2] Because of risk-aversion, all points to the right of the envelope are dominated by those *on* the solid lines lying to their left with the same ordinate $\bar{g}_D$ (property (a) above). Similarly, because of wealth maximization, all points below the solid

retentions permit greater growth under certainty (when variances are zero) – if the firm chooses a larger $r > r_1$, it would operate upon a higher contour of the efficient set as indicated by the dashed line in Fig. 7.1.

Empirically there is evidence that larger retention undertaken to raise expected or average growth rates also leads to greater variability in the growth rates realized. We can readily allow for such a direct dependence between σ_g^2 and r within the general constraint function (11) by adding a subsidiary relation

$$\begin{cases} \sigma_{gD}^2 = \sigma_g^2(r) = v_0 + v(r) \\ v(0) = 0, \ v'(r) \geqq 0, \ v''(r) \leqq 0. \end{cases} \tag{11'}$$

After substituting (11') into (11), the effective constraint set upon the firm's choices of policy mix becomes

$$\bar{g}_D = f(r, \ v_0 + v(r)). \tag{12}$$

With this more general formulation of the effective constraints, the firm's basic policy choices involving growth are summarized in the selection of the *optimal pair of values* for the retention ratio r, and the 'basic' risk variable v_0. The analysis of the determination of the best pair of values r^* and v_0^* in this general form will also enable us as a by-product to note the optimal retention rate or dividend payout under two interesting sets of more restrictive assumptions regarding the risk choices available to the firm – namely, (a) the special case in which the risk level of the firm's growth is fully exogenous,[1] and (b) the intermediate case in which v_0 is not subject to decision by the firm, but $v'(r) > 0$ so that the firm's choice of optimal retention and expected growth rates will be affected by the dependence of total rise upon the retention ratio even though the firm cannot affect its 'basic risk'.

The choice of the best policy mix subject to (12) clearly depends essentially upon expectation of the future as well as upon current values. We specifically assume that if *any* efficient policy mix (and its

---

line are dominated by those *on* the solid line lying above them with the same abscissa σ^2 (property (b) above). In consequence, only the more heavily drawn (upper part) of the solid line – the part which is rising to the right – is included in the efficient set of (11) for the given r_1: i.e. maximization subject to the given r would involve choosing some point on this heavily shaded solid part of the curve whose shape is summarized in (11b) above.

[1] In this case, $v'(r) = 0$ and v_0 is completely determined by the characteristics of the business in which the firm is engaged and may not be changed or chosen by any policy action of the firm itself.

associated retention ratio r) has been selected, and is *maintained in the future*,

(e) The associated growth rate of the company's operations (and dividends) over *any* short future interval $\Delta\tau$ beginning at time τ is $\tilde{g}(\tau) = \bar{g}(\tau) + \epsilon(\tau)$ where $\tilde{g}(\tau)$ for all τ is a *normally distributed* random variable with mean $\bar{g}(\tau)$ and variance $\sigma_g^2(\tau) = \epsilon^2(\tau)$.

(f) The *expectation* of $g(\tau)$ is *the same* for all short intervals in $0 < \tau < \infty$, given the policy mix. In consequence, the expectation of the average of g over a time interval of any length is also the same number.

(g) The $\epsilon(\tau)$ in (c) are *independent* variables, with the *zero covariance* between all pairs of short time intervals in the future. They are independent drawings from the same distribution.

(h) In consequence, the variance of the *cumulated* growth over an interval of any length τ (beginning at any t and extending to $t+\tau$) will simply be $\tau\sigma_g^2$.

The effect of assumptions (e)–(h) can be summarized in the following statements: (1) As a result of (e), the distribution assessed at t_0 regarding the value of any company variable (such as sales, profits, or dividends) at a time $t_0 + \tau$ will be *lognormal*. (2) As a result of (f), the *expectation of the logarithm* of the size of any ith company variable at time $t_0 + \tau$ will be (log of initial value) plus $\bar{g}_i\tau$. For instance, using the rate of cash dividend payments we have with $t_0 = 0$:

$$E[\log D_\tau] = \log D_0 + \bar{g}_D\tau. \tag{13a}$$

(3) Finally, as a result of (g) and (h), the variances of the logarithm of a company variable will be equal to its variance in any short unit interval multiplied by the futurity τ.

$$\text{var}[\log D_\tau] = \sigma_{g_D}^2\tau. \tag{13b}$$

In III.3 and 4, we analyze the choices of an optimal policy mix in an uncertain world by a company subject to the constraints of equation (12) embodying assumptions (a)–(d) where the environment is the dynamic but stochastic steady state specified in assumptions (e)–(h). Since we assume that the relative desirability of any policy choice depends upon the market value of the stock, we now turn to the specification of stock prices in a lognormally uncertain world.

2. *The criterion under uncertainty*

I have elsewhere [18] derived the equilibrium vector of stock prices in a purely competitive frictionless market in which all investors choose portfolios to maximize the expected utility of their end-of-period[1] wealth $\tilde{W}_{1k}$, given their intial stock of investible assets W_{0k}, and their jointly lognormal assessments of the distribution of outcomes over available securities.[2] Each investor is a risk-averter whose utility function $U_k(W_{1k}) = -W_{1k}^{-\alpha_k}$ has a constant elasticity $\alpha_k > 0$; both α_k and W_{0k} differ among investors. Given his wealth constraint, assessments and value of W_{1k}, each investor's optimal vector of (dollar) investments in each security maximizes[3] $\theta_k = \bar{g}_{pk} - \alpha_k \sigma_{pk}^2/2$, the *certainty-equivalent* of his *portfolio's* logarithmic return (the expected return less a risk adjustment proportional to logarithmic portfolio variance). Conditional on *any possible* vector of market prices, the number of shares of each security in his optimal portfolio is determined.[4] Summation of these conditionally optimal holdings over all investors in the market and the imposition of market clearing conditions on all securities yields a set of equations which is solved to give the (unique) set of market prices which (a) simultaneously clears the markets for all securities and 'cash' when (b) *all* investors hold the (Pareto-optimal) portfolios they each prefer to all others available to them at these market prices. These equilibrium market prices P_0^* are shown to be the solutions of the set of equations

$$\alpha_m[n_i P_0 \sigma_{im}^2 + \sum_{j \neq i} n_j P_{0j} \sigma_{ijm}] = W_{0m}[\bar{g}_{im} - \omega_m];$$
$$1, \ldots, N \text{ securities} \qquad (14)$$

where α_m are weighted averages of the investor's α_k, and assessments

[1] In the absence of transaction costs and taxes, it has been shown (e.g. [11], [15] and [26]) that decisions made under a multiperiod constant elasticity preference function are 'myopic' and depend only upon the single-period assessments, so the 'one-period' restriction is no limitation on our results.

[2] We assume that the investor assesses the outcomes of different portfolios (as well as of individual stocks) to be lognormal. Although linear mixtures of lognormals are not strictly lognormal, the assumption made regarding investor behavior is reasonable. See [20].

[3] First note that $E[-W_{0k}\exp(\tilde{g}_p)]^{-\alpha_k} = -W_{0k}^{\alpha_k}E[\exp(-\alpha_k g_p)]$. But when $\tilde{g}_p$ has a normal distribution, the expectation on the right may be evaluated as the '$(-\alpha_k)$th' moment in the usual moment-generating function for the normal distribution, i.e. as $\exp(-\alpha_k \theta_k)$ where θ_k has the value given in the text. See [1], p. 8.

[4] The equations at this point are based on series expansions good to the *fourth* power of logarithmic returns with relatively small remainders. See Appendix, section B.

of *expected* logarithmic returns $\bar{g}_{im}$; σ_{im}^2 and σ_{ijm} are functions of weighted averages of investor's logarithmic variance and covariance assessments; ω_m is a weighted average of the shadow prices of the wealth constraints. W_{0m} is a simple sum of the investible wealth of the investors in the market, and n_i is simply the total number of shares of each security outstanding.

Now we observe that the aggregate equilibrium market value, $n_i P_0$, which satisfy (14) are the values which will maximize the market $\theta_m = \bar{g}_{pm} - \alpha_m \sigma_{pm}^2 / 2$ and thereby the *certainty equivalent of end-of-period wealth for the market as a whole*. But the latter is clearly also equivalent to a current-market-value-weighted average of the certainty-equivalents of the end-of-period values of the individual securities. And the shadow price ω_m of the market's wealth constraint over a one-period horizon has the effect of a one-period discounting at a riskless rate. We further observe that as of the end of the first period, the value of the stock will be based upon the certainty-equivalent of its value (including dividends received) at the end of the second period, and so on iteratively over time. With respect to any time interval, the *certainty-equivalent* of the ending outcome, measured by market value and dividend receipts together, is thus related to the initial market value as the pre-known outcome would be in the case of assumed certainty. With the 'constant elasticity' utility functions which we have assumed,[1] the effects of the 'disutility' of the uncertainties present are fully reflected in the reduction of *expected* relative returns to *certainty-equivalent* relative rates of return.

Under certainty, the fundamental requirement that the sum of the dividend yield D_τ / P_τ plus the relative gain in market value $d \log P_\tau / d\tau$ must equal the interest rate κ at all points (or short intervals) of time gave us our basic value equation (1). In the same way under uncertainty, the certainty equivalents of these anticipated relative rates of return at all points in time must equal the shadow price of the wealth constraint ω_m (which we assume to be constant over time).

---

[1] This statement is true over any period from $\tau < t$ to t regarded as a single time unit, and it is also true of any multiple unit interval of time when the stochastic process of receipts shows no autocorrelation. In addition, a theorem in an unpublished memorandum by John Pratt [29] establishes that when utility functions exhibit constant proportional risk-aversion, the valuation of any uncertain future receipt is independent of the time at which the uncertainty is 'resolved'. By inference, the valuation of any stochastic *stream* of receipts will be independent of its autocorrelation. Since the 'constant elasticity' utility posited here has constant proportional risk-aversion, we need not be concerned with autocorrelation in the text.

As shown in section B of the Appendix, with log-variances incrementally stable over time, the current value of any stock is equal to

$$P_0 = \int_0^\infty \hat{D}_\tau \exp(-\tau\omega_m)\,d\tau = D_0\int_0^\infty \exp[-(\omega_m - \hat{g}_D)\tau]d\tau \tag{15}$$

$$= D_0/(\omega_m - \hat{g}_0) \tag{15a}$$

provided the relevant *certainty-equivalent* of the growth in dividends $\hat{g}_0 < \omega_m$, the shadow price which serves as a discount factor. This derivation of (15) and the structure of (13) in turn require that the certainty-equivalent $\hat{g}_D$ be evaluated by

$$\hat{g}_D = \bar{g}_D - \alpha_m C\sigma_{g_D}^2 - \alpha_m f(\sigma_{ij}) \tag{16}$$

where $f(\sigma_{ij})$ is a function of the company's stock price-covariance with other stock prices, and the factor $C > 1$ reflects the fact that the uncertainties reflected in the current stock price reflect the (larger) uncertainties of future stock prices as well as uncertainties regarding the future dividend itself. For simplicity later, we will treat the summed covariances with other stock as a scalar parameter of the analysis; their *level* affects our results but we will not also examine the effects of *changes* in covariances at this time.[1]

It is immediately obvious that the net result of our restrictive assumptions about the character of the uncertainty admitted to the point has been merely to create a situation in which *certainty-equivalents* replace known or certain data in the value formula (8) obtained in section II, and the riskless shadow value of the market's wealth constraint over a unit period takes the place of the riskless interest rate under certainty. But this isomorphism in the value formula should not obscure the major differences in content. Firms and investors must respond to probability distributions of outcomes rather than certain data. The certainty-equivalents not only involve expectations and variances, but 'pricing' or 'discounting' of the variances depends on *market* phenomena – both the weight average elasticity of the investor's utility functions, and the variance of future prices (as well as of future dividends) which is subsumed in the parameter C. In addition, the firm's choices among different policy mixes can (and usually will) have differential effects on expectations and variances subject to a multivariate constraint like (11), which in turn must be transformed into the certainty-equivalents entering into the stock-price criterion.

In deriving what optimal policies would be under this richer

[1] On all the preceding points, see Appendix, section B.

(though still quite restricted) set of circumstances, we will continue to use sales receipts as the base for assessing the payout ratio, just as in the derivation under certainty in section II. We thus have $D_\tau = xS_\tau = (1 - r)S_\tau$, where x and r are to be held constant over time once the optimizing value has been selected.[1] Since an increase in the retention ratio r will reduce dividends at all points in time, it is appropriate in particular to set $D_0 = xS = (1 - r)S_0$ and regard S_0 as an exogenous variable.[2]

3. *Optimal steady-state growth policies when $\sigma^2_{g_D}$ does not increase with futurity*

Under these steady-state conditions, the firm's choices of all efficient policy mixes satisfying the constraint (12) may be summarized by choices of the two policy parameters r and v_0. The optimal policy mix to maximize equity value in equation (15) will consequently be given by the values r^* and v_0^* which simultaneously satisfy the equations[4]

$$\partial P_0/\partial v_0 = +P_0(\partial \hat{g}_D/\partial v_0)/(\omega_m - \hat{g}_D) = 0 \qquad (17a)$$
$$\text{i.e.} \quad \partial \hat{g}_D/\partial v_0 = 0 \qquad (17a')$$

and

$$\partial P_0/\partial r = P_0[-(1/1-r)+(\partial \hat{g}_D/\partial r)/(\omega_m - \hat{g}_D)] = 0 \qquad (17b)$$
$$\text{i.e.} \quad (1 - r)(\partial \hat{g}_D/\partial r) + \hat{g}_D = \omega_m. \qquad (17b')$$

Under stochastic conditions of expectationally steady-state growth, in which uncertainties regarding outcomes do not increase with futurity, firms optimizing equity values will consequently:

(i) *Select a risk level v_0 which will maximize the certainty equivalent of the prospective growth rate of dividends, conditional on any retention ratio*; and

[1] Quite obviously, the payout ratio could equally well be denominated in terms of cash flow, operating profit earnings, or book values so far as our steady-state analysis is concerned, so long as a consistent specification is carried through all equations including (11) and (12).

[2] As emphasized in the introduction, since the purpose of the present paper is to examine alternative *steady-state* growth paths, we will not be concerned with the problem of the optimal time path of the movement from a given initial condition *to* the optimal steady-state growth path.

[3] Note that $\hat{g}_D$ in (15) depends on $\bar{g}_D$ and $\sigma^2_{g_D}$ and the latter are both determined by r and v_0 using equations (11) or (12).

[4] These equations, of course, represent only the necessary conditions for a maximum, but sufficiency is insured by assumptions (11a–c) above.

(ii) *Select a retention (or dividend payout) ratio such that the dividend payout of the marginal certainty-equivalent of the growth rate, plus the certainty equivalent itself, must equal the unit-period shadow value of wealth ('riskless interest rate'), conditional on any risk level.*

With respect to (i), note that after using (16) and the constraints (11) and (11′), we have

$$\partial \hat{g}_D / \partial v_0 = \partial \bar{g}_D / \partial v_0 - \alpha_m C. \tag{18}$$

The conditional maximization of the certainty-equivalent of the growth rate consequently requires that the firm vary its 'basic risk' v_0 along any contour of Fig. 7.1 (i.e. in equation (11)) so that the *slope* is equal to the *product* of the market's wealth elasticity α_m and the ratio C of the logarithmic variance of stock values $(P_\tau + D_\tau)$ to the variance of company operating data and dividend payments. The optimal risk posture for a company maximizing equity values will thus be determined by its $\bar{g}_D - \sigma_{gD}^2$ 'production function' and the *market* risk parameters α_m and C. Moreover, since in practice we will always find the value of the product $\alpha_m C < \infty$, it follows as a corollary that *the optimal risk posture of the company will never be the minimum risk position attainable in the efficient set.*

To interpret requirement (ii) above, note that (16) and the constraints (11) imply

$$\partial \hat{g}_D / \partial r = \partial \bar{g}_D / \partial r - (\partial \bar{g}_D / \partial v_0 - \alpha_m C) v'(r). \tag{19}$$

The marginal certainty-equivalent growth rate thus reduces to the marginal *expectation* of the growth rate whenever (a) risk levels are *independent* of retention ratios (i.e. $v'(r) = 0$), or (b) *optimal* policies with respect to *basic risk* v_0 are being pursued (i.e. (18) is set to zero to satisfy (17a′)). In both cases,[1] therefore, the best retention (or

---

[1] Two other special cases of interest. First, suppose that $\bar{g}_D$ in equation (11) is a function of r but *not also* of σ_{gD}^2 (i.e. so that the contours in Fig. 7.1 are horizontal lines for each value of r). Using (11′) we then have

$$\partial \bar{g}_D / \partial \sigma_{gD}^2 = \partial \bar{g}_D / \partial v_0 = 0, \text{ and}$$
$$\partial \hat{g}_D / \partial r = d\bar{g}_D / dr - \alpha_m C v'(r), \tag{19a}$$

which was the case considered in [18], pp. 72–6. In this special case, the marginal certainty-equivalent of growth is necessarily *less* than the marginal expectation (if $v'(r) > 0$). The impact of uncertainty to reduce optimal retentions (and increase dividend payouts) noted in the later text is thereby reinforced.

The second special case arises when the level of risk is exogenous to all policy decisions other than retention rates (i.e. v_0 is fixed by circumstances or business dividend payout) ratio will be that for which the *dividend payout of the marginal expectation of the growth rate, plus the certainty equivalent of the growth rate, will equal the 'riskless interest rate'* ω_m. Formally the requirement is

$$\begin{cases} (1-r)\,(\partial\bar{g}_D/\partial r) + \hat{g}_D = \omega_m \\ \text{when } v'(r) = 0 \text{ or } \partial P_0/\partial v_0 = 0. \end{cases} \tag{17b''}$$

If we compare this requirement for optimal retentions and expected growth rates under uncertainty with the corresponding requirement under certainty (equation (10) in section II), we can readily identify the marginal impacts of retentions on (expected) growth $\partial\bar{g}_D/\partial r$ with dg_D/dr. But the certainty-equivalent growth $\hat{g}_D$ is necessarily *less* than expected growth $\bar{g}_D$ because of risk-aversion whenever variance or uncertainty is present, and this difference is larger as the level of risk being borne by the firm is greater. Consequently, the optimal dividend payout ratio x^* will be higher (and the best retention ratio r^* will be lower) than under certainty, and in general, *the best dividend payout x^* will vary inversely – and the best retention ratio will vary directly – with the level of the risks being borne by the firm. These statements are true whether the level of basic risk v_0 is exogenously fixed or is being simultaneously optimixed.*

4. *A reinterpretation of the effects of simple uncertainty in terms of the 'duration' of the dividend stream*

In his classic study of the structure of interest rates, Macauley [24] found some of his empirical observations could best be explained in terms of the weighted average futurity of the cash receipts, when the present values of the respective receipts were used as weights, and used the term 'duration' for this weighted average futurity of the stream. Within a year, Hicks in his *Value and Capital* [12] introduced

---

context, but $v'(r) > 0$). This limited dependence of risk on retentions again keeps the marginal certainty-equivalent from being equal to the marginal expectation of growth. Indeed, if the slope $\partial\bar{g}_D/\partial\sigma^2_{g_D}$ at the value of v_0 exogenously given is greater than the market term $\alpha_m C$, then the marginal certainty-equivalent will actually be greater than the marginal expectation of growth for increases in retentions. But the concavity of (11) in the $\bar{g}_D - r$ plane and the non-positive value of $v''(r)$ insure a true maximum of our price equation, and in the region of the optimum the further conclusions stated in the text clearly hold.

the same concept and referred to it as the average period of a capitalistic production process (or elasticity of income stream). Hicks also noted that this 'average period' was identically equal to the *relative differential change in the present value of the entire stream* with respect to changes in either the interest rate or growth rate of the stream and settled on the term 'crescendo' of the stream to describe this property. In his recent *Capital and Growth* [13], he again uses the concept and expresses a stronger preference for think-ing in terms of the 'tilting' or 'crescendo' of the stream instead of its 'average period'. But . . . a rose is a rose is a rose. The con-cepts are mathematically identical, and I shall use the terms 'duration', 'average futurity', 'crescendo' or 'relative tilting' inter-changeably.

By whatever name, the concept is useful to us because it provides another significant dimension to choice problems involving alternative growth rates over time which forms a very useful bridge between the certainty, the simple uncertainty of the present section, and the richer context taken up in the next section. It also at the moment provides a clear rationale for the important result just reached that, even when risk levels are subject to choice and chosen to maximize equity values, the optimal dividend payouts will be larger – and the optimal retention rates and expected growth rates will be lower – the greater the degree of (optimized) uncertainty.

To introduce the concept, consider first the situation under certainty. From equation (8) we have $P_0 = D_0 A_1$ if we write

$$A_1 = \int_0^\infty \exp(-Z_1\tau)d\tau, \tag{20}$$

where $Z_1 = k - g_D > 0$. Now let

$$B = \int_0^\infty \tau \exp(-Z_1\tau)d\tau = dA_1/d(-Z_1) = dA_1/dg_D = dA_1/d(-k). \tag{21}$$

The weighted average futurity or 'duration' is clearly

$$T_1 = B_1/A_1 = \int_0^\infty \tau \exp(-Z_1\tau)d\tau / \int_0^\infty \exp(-Z_1\tau)d\tau. \tag{22}$$
$$= d\log A_1/d(-Z_1) = d\log A_1/dg,$$

and the last equations clearly identify the concept also with the differential relative tilting or 'crescendo' of the stream. When we evaluate the integrals, we find that $A_1 = (Z_1)^{-1}$, $B_1 = (Z_1)^{-2}$, and

$T_1 = (Z^{-1})^{-1}(Z_1)^{-2} = (Z_1)^{-1}$. Consequently, under certainty, the price of the stock is equal to the product of the current dividend and the 'duration' of the dividend stream, where the 'duration' properly subsumes and incorporates the effects of both the interest rate and the growth rate of the dividend stream. Stated differently, under certainty, the current dividend yield is the reciprocal of the duration of the dividend stream. Moreover, the rule for the optimal retention or dividend payout under certainty (equation (8)) says that *the product of the optimal dividend payout ratio and the marginal growth rate is equal to the current dividend yield of the stock*. Alternatively, *under certainty the optimal dividend payout of the marginal growth rate over a period equal to the 'duration' of the dividend stream equals unity*.

Now consider the form of the corresponding propositions under the limited uncertainty introduced in the present section. If we let $Z_2 = \omega_m - \hat{g}_D > 0$ and redefine an A_2, B_2, and T_2 in terms of Z_2 according to equations (20) and (21), we find that $A_2 = (Z_2)^{-12}$ $B_2 = (Z_2)^{-2}$ and $T_2 = (Z_2)^{-1}$. Since, under this kind of uncertainty, equation (15) can now be written $P_0 = D_0 A_2$, it is clear that the preceding statements under certainty will apply to the simple case of uncertainty examined in this section if we merely speak of the 'duration' of the *certainty-equivalents* of the dividend stream. Specifically, the *price of the stock under uncertainty which is constant over time is equal to the product of the current dividend and the 'duration' of the certainty-equivalents of the future dividend stream*, $P_0 = D_0 T_2$ – or, in other words, the product of the current dividend yield and the 'duration of certainty-equivalents' is one. Moreover, when risk is fully exogenous ($v'(r) = 0$ and v_0 is given) *or* when retentions affect risk ($v'(r) > 0$) *and* basic risk levels are optimized, so that (17a') is satisfied, then equation (17b') can be written

$$x^*(\partial \bar{g}_D / \partial r)T_2 = 1, \tag{17c}$$

and also as

$$x^*(\partial \bar{g}_D / \partial r) = y_a = D_0 / P_0, \tag{17d}$$

when we write the optimal dividend payout ratio $x^* = (1 - r^*)$. Thus, uncertainty with stable variances over time leaves the statement of the optimal decision rules the same as under certainty (when basic risk v_0 is either exogenous or optimzed): the product of (a) the optimal dividend payout of (b) the marginal *expected* growth rate

CE H

over (c) a time period equal to the 'duration' of the *certainty-equivalents* of the uncertain dividend stream will equal unity,[1] and *the optimal dividend payout of the marginal expected growth rate will still equal the current dividend yield of the stock*. The *level* of the optimal retention ratio and growth rate are of course reduced by even this restricted uncertainty, as we now show.

Since certainty can be regarded as simply the limiting case of uncertainty when all dispersions approach zero, we can identify the shadow value of the wealth constraint ω_m under uncertainty with the riskless rate k under certainty, and the expected growth rate $\bar{g}_D$ under uncertainty with 'the' growth rate g_D under certainty. But the *certainty-equivalent growth rate $\hat{g}_D$ falls short of the expectation $\bar{g}_D$* by amounts which increase with α_m the elasticity of the market's 'as if' utility function, which represents the market's risk-aversion; with the level of the risk or variance in the growth rate of the company's own operations or dividend payment σ_{g_D}; and with the ratio C of the logarithmic variance of $(P_t + D_t)$ to that of D_t itself. Consequently, T, the *'duration' of the certainty-equivalents of the stream, will vary inversely with each of these elements*, other things equal. Since $P_0 = D_0 T_2$, current stock prices will be lowered by an increase in any of these elements. Most significantly for us, however, it also follows by (17b') that *the optimal retention ratio will be lowered (and the optimal dividend payout will be increased) by an increase in any of these elements*. Moreover, from the constraint in equation (11), expected growth rates vary directly with the retention ratio, so that *the optimal expected growth rate will also be lowered* by an increase in *any* of these elements of 'company risk', 'market risk', or 'market risk-aversion'. As we shall see, all these results are perfectly general in a *qualitative* sense and are found in even stronger form as we develop more general (and realistic) models in the next section, even though equation (17d) and the optimization of retentions by reference to current dividend yields will no longer hold.

[1] Under the conditions considered in n. 1, p. 196 above, the same statement holds for optimal dividend payouts except that 'marginal *certainty-equivalents* growth rate' replaces 'marginal *expected* growth rate' in element (b). But note that the *duration* is in terms of the certainty-equivalents of the stream in all subcases.

IV. THE MODEL WHEN UNCERTAINTIES INCREASE
WITH FUTURITY

1. *Introduction*

The present section will examine the choice of optimal policy mixes to maximize equity values when neither investors nor management has as 'tight' an assessment of the more distant future as it has of the nearer-term consequences of adapting and maintaining any given strategic posture or set of policies. The two assumptions (g) and (h) on p. 191 (which made the current assessment of the uncertainty (variance) of the growth rate in every future short interval of time (conditional of course on maintaining any currently chosen policy mix) *the same regardless of its futurity*) will be relaxed in the interest of greater realism, but all the other assumptions of section III will be maintained.

The need for a more general and richer model of uncertainty is indicated by the fact that our previous assumptions regarding variances meant that the certainty-equivalents of future dividend receipts $\hat{D}_t = D_0 \exp(\hat{g}_D{}^t)$ would *grow at the same rate without limit and for ever* (presumably into the hereafter!), *provided only that $\hat{g}_D > 0$ by any margin however small*.[1] They also imply that a stock whose certainty-equivalent growth over the next few years is larger than the riskless rate (by any margin however small) will sell in the market at an *infinite* price. (For this reason, we simply had to *assume* that $\omega_m > \hat{g}_D$ to avoid what is commonly known as 'the growth-stock paradox'.) Basically, both these implausible implications reflect the fact that to this point, we have allowed for uncertainty only to the extent of introducing probability distributions to take the place of 'point estimates' treated as certainties, and managers and investors alike have been assumed to act *as if* the probability distribution over results five, ten, fifty, or a hundred years in the future were *exactly the same distribution* (same mean or expectation and *same variance*)

---

[1] As an illustration, if the reader's favorite growth stock has an *expected* growth rate of 20 per cent a year, and this is regarded by the market as the equivalent of a 10 per cent *sure* growth over the next few years, the model in the previous section implies that the current price of the stock would be the same as if *each dollar* of current dividend were certain to become $12.18 in twenty-five years, $148.41 in the year 2019, $1,096.60 in 2169, and $1,202,531.56 in 2269, *and so on for ever* with compounding increases!

as the distribution relevant to the next year. We now need to allow for the unquestionable fact that the uncertainties of the outcomes in, say, the fifth, or the tenth, or any other year in the future will be the *compound resultant of the uncertainties in each of the intervening years.*

The reader can readily convince himself that he also believes uncertainties compound over the future by recognizing that he cannot make as good (as 'tight') an estimate of his probable salary (or the cost-of-living index, or the G.N.P., or the level of the stock market) for the year 1980 at the present time as he is sure he *will* be able to make for the same outcomes in, say, 1975. The reason he is sure he can make better estimates later is that a good many of the chance events which will affect the situation (and outcomes) in 1980 will already have occurred by 1975 and will be known by that time. An assessment regarding 1980 outcomes *which is made now* must allow for all of the uncertainties regarding the relevant random events which will occur between now and 1975 *as well as* the uncertainties regarding relevant random events which will occur between 1975 and 1980.

For precisely the same reason, company managements *cannot* make as good estimates now regarding the 1980 outcomes of policies adopted now and maintained till then as they will be able to make in, say, 1975 – *and they do not act 'as if' they could do so.* They do allow for the greater uncertainties necessarily involved in outcomes over the more distant future in their current assessments and judgments – and this allowance for greater uncertainty with greater futurity does affect their choices of best policy mixes even under expectationally 'steady-state' conditions.

The need for this generalization or enrichment of our model is further indicated by the fact that this allowance for increasing uncertainties over more distant futures will introduce 'random walks' into our model of stock prices. Whether or not one accepts the large body of empirical work on this subject as establishing that successive differences in the logarithms of stock prices are strictly independent over time, it is surely clear that such a model of the market over time gives an entirely adequate approximation for a wide range of purposes. Our model of stock prices in section III assumed that the current price reflects no more uncertainty in the minds of investors over the distribution of what stock prices will be in 1980 than they now have (early 1969) over what prices will be in 1970. But in fact the dispersion in estimates regarding values is very much greater and the model must be adjusted to allow for this fact. It turns out, however, that with constant elasticity utility functions, our basic log-normal stock-price model is entirely appropriate to the more complex situation after we allow for the greater variances in the more distant future in our specification of the certainty equivalent receipt $\hat{D}_\tau$. Moreover, when we allow in this way for uncertainties which cumulate over time, this same stock-price model becomes a 'random walk' model. We show below that this allowance for the cumulative randomness of future company data and stock prices significantly affects the *current* equilibrium price of the stock itself.

2. *Constraints and assumptions to allow for increasing variance with futurity*

In keeping with the focus of the present paper on the choice of best policy mixes for expectationally sustained growth in a dynamic but stochastic steady-state environment, we continue to assume that the *expected values* in the future for any variable of interest lie on *exponential growth trends* (assumptions (e) and (f) on p. 191 above),[1] and we will use the same specifications of the constraints within which the firm must choose among alternative sets of efficient policy mixes (assumptions (a)–(d) and equations (11) and (11′) on pp. 188–90 above). But the variance assumptions (g) and (h) on p. 191 above must clearly be changed in order to meet the objections outlined in the introduction to this section.[2] Instead of assuming (as in section III) that the deviations in each short period from the expectation of growth $\bar{g}_D$ are normal, mutually independent random variables, we now assume that as of any point in time the future growth rates which will result from the maintenance of any given policy mix will form a random walk. Specifically, we now assume that

(g′) The *changes* (first differences) in realized growth rates between all pairs of short time intervals in the future are mutually

[1] It will be noted that these embody characteristics (a) and (b) of the environment specified under heading (3) on p. 177 above in our introduction.

[2] These changes are also required to make our assumptions correspond to characteristics (c) and (d) of the environment specified under heading (3) on p. 171 above in the introduction to the whole paper. The model in section III based on assumptions (g) and (h) was simply an enlightening and convenient 'half-way house' for all our fuller models presented in this section.

independent, normally distributed random variables. Formally we now assume that $\tilde{g}(\tau+1) = g(\tau) + \tilde{u}(\tau)$, where $u(\tau) = 0$ for all τ, and $2\sigma_u^2(\tau)$ for all τ, and $\text{cov}[u(\tau), u(\tau+\tau')] = 0$ for all pairs of values τ and τ'.

(h') The variance of the growth rate currently assessed for any short interval τ periods in the future will be *larger than the current variance* of the growth rate σ_g^2 by the product $2\tau\sigma_u^2$, i.e. $\sigma_g^2(0+\tau) = \sigma_g^2 + 2\tau\sigma_u^2$. The variance of the *cumulated growth* between the current decision point and any time τ periods in the future will be the *integral* from 0 to τ of $(\sigma_g^2 + 2\tau\sigma_u^2)$, which is $(\sigma_g^2 + \tau\sigma_u^2)\tau$.

Our maintained assumption of constant elasticity utility functions for investors means that the current price equilibrium price of each stock is still equal to the present value of the *certainty-equivalents of the future cash dividends*[1] *discounted at the riskless wealth-constraint rate* ω_m (as in equation (15) before), but the closed-form solution of the present-value integral will now be more complicated because our richer variance assumption (h') makes

$$\text{var}[\log D_\tau] = (\sigma_{D_g}^2 + \tau\sigma_u^2)\tau. \tag{13b'}$$

The certainty equivalent of the current assessment of the cash dividents to be distributed τ periods in the future consequently becomes

$$\hat{D}_\tau = D_0 \exp[\hat{g}_D(\tau)] = D_0 \exp\{[g_D - \alpha_m C(\sigma_{gD} - \tau\sigma_u^2) - \alpha_m f(\sigma_{ij})]\tau\}, \tag{23}$$

which varies *quadratically* rather than linearly with time. It is convenient to separate the elements in the brackets into an *initial* or *short-run* certainty-equivalent growth rate $\hat{g}_D^0$

$$\hat{g}_D^0 = \bar{g}_D - \alpha_m C\sigma_{gD} - \alpha f(\sigma_{ij}), \tag{24}$$

whose elements are still invariant over time, and the term $\tau\sigma_u^2$ which increases over time. With this substitution, the certainty-equivalent future dividend receipt simplifies to

$$\hat{D}_\tau = D_0 \exp[\hat{g}_D(\tau)] = D_0 \exp[(\hat{g}_D^0 - \alpha_m C\tau\sigma_u^2)\tau]. \tag{23'}$$

Before proceeding further, we should emphasize what has been accomplished by our new and more realistic variance assumptions. From

$$g_D = \partial \log \hat{D}_\tau / \partial \tau = g_D^0 - \alpha_m C\tau\sigma_u^2 \tag{25}$$

---

[1] Constant elasticity utility functions justify discounting certainty-equivalents even if there is autocorrelation in the flows. See n. 1, p. 193 above.

we see that *the growth rates of the certainty-equivalents of future dividend receipts continuously decline over all future time* with $\sigma_u^2 > 0$ as we now assume. (In contrast, with $\sigma_u^2 = 0$ as in section III, the growth rate of the certainty-equivalent dividend was constant over all future time.) Moreover, for *any set* of positive values of $\bar{g}_D$, α_m, and C, regardless of how large or small, so long as $\sigma_u^2 > 0$, we see that *the certainty-equivalents of the future dividends will rise at ever diminishing rates to a true maximum,*[1] *and thereafter fall at ever increasing rates to a limiting value of zero* as $\tau \to \infty$. (In contrast, with $\sigma_u^2 = 0$ in section III, $\hat{D}_\tau$ increased *for ever* at the constant rate $\hat{g}_D$ with *no limiting value*.) Our assumption that $\sigma_u^2 > 0$ consequently also insures that *our stock-price integral converges regardless of the values of the expected growth rate $\bar{g}_D$ or any other variables*, whereas in section III with $\sigma_u^2 = 0$ the growth-stock paradox was an ever present possibility, which had to be ruled out by gratuitous assumption. Table 7.1 offers some illustrations of the behavior of $\hat{D}_\tau$ (per

Table 7.1

Illustrations of the Certainty-Equivalents of Future Dividends (per Dollar of Current Dividend) under Different Assumptions of Risk

Values of $\hat{D}_t/D_0$ at indicated time when:

Year	Certainty (section II) $g_D = \cdot2$	Constant risk (section III) $\bar{g}_D = \cdot2$ $\alpha_m C \sigma g^2 = \cdot1$ $\hat{g}_D = \cdot1$	Uncertainty increases with futurity (section IV) $\bar{g}_D = \cdot2$ $\alpha_m C \sigma^2 g_D = \cdot1$ $\hat{g}_D^0 = \cdot1$ $\sigma_u^2 = \cdot001$
0	$1.00	$1.00	$1.00
10	$7.39	$2.72	$2.46
25	$148.41	$12.18	$6.42
50	$1,096.62	$148.41	$12.18 (max)
100	$810,303.48	$1,096.62	$1.00
200	$5,987,413.44	$810,303.48	$.8(10)^{-5}$
∞	∞	∞	0

[1] The maximum occurs at $t = g^0/2\alpha_m C\sigma_u$ periods into the future.

dollar of *current* dividend D_0) under different sets of values of $\bar{g}_D$, $\sigma^2_{g_D}$, and σ^2_u.

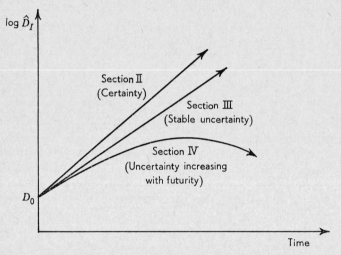

Fig. 7.2. Illustrative graph of growth of certainty-equivalents for future dividend receipts.

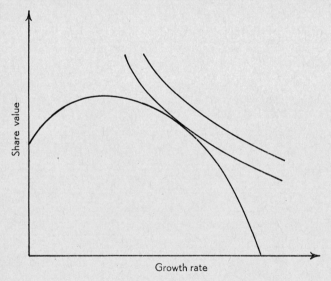

Fig. 7.3. Illustration of share value and managerial indifference curve (Marris)

3. Stock prices when variances increase with futurity

To determine the value of the stock with our more general variance assessment, we must substitute the value of $\hat{D}_\tau$ from equation (23) into our basic value equation (15). For convenience, we write the resulting price of the stock in the form

$$P_0 = D_0 A_3 \tag{26}$$

where

$$A_3 = \int_0^\infty \exp(-Z_3\tau)d\tau \tag{27}$$

and

$$Z_3 = \omega_m - \hat{g}_D^0 - \alpha_m C\tau\sigma_u^2, \tag{28}$$

using eq. (24).

If we now define two new variables

$$R = \sqrt{(2\alpha_m C\sigma_u^2)} \tag{29}$$

and

$$w = [\omega_m - \hat{g}_D^0]/R, \tag{30}$$

we find that[1]

$$A_3 = G(w)/f(w)R, \tag{27'}$$

so that

$$P_0 = D_0 G(w)/Rf(w) \tag{26'}$$

where $G(w)$ is simply the *area* in the right tail of the standardized normal distribution, and $f(w)$ is the ordinate of this distribution at the point w.

Although (26') has a considerably different appearance than the usual present-value formula, this merely reflects the fact that we have allowed for the progressive increase in uncertainty with longer futurities by using (28) rather than $Z_2 = \omega_m - \hat{g}_D^0$ in our present-value equation (15). The price equation (15a) in section III, and (8) in section II, are both limiting special cases of the present formulation.[1]

---

[1] Complete the square in $Z_3\tau$ using (29) and (30) to find

$$Z_3\tau = (R^2\tau^2 + 2wR\tau)/2 = (w + R\tau)^2/2 - w^2/2 = (z^2 - w^2)/2.$$

Substitution in (27) shows that

$$A_3 = \exp(w^2/2)\int_0^\infty \exp(-z^2/2)d\tau = \exp(w^2/2)R^{-1}\int_w^\infty \exp(-z^2/2)dz$$

where

$$z = w + R\tau, \quad f(w) = (2\pi)^{-1/2}\exp(-w^2/2), \quad \text{and} \quad G(w) = \int_w^\infty f(\S)d\S.$$

Now substitute the equations for the unit normal to get (27').

CE H 2

Moreover, in (26') the stock price is finite for all finite values of w and for all finite $\bar{g}_D$ regardless of the size of the other variables, and in particular regardless of the relative size of $\bar{g}_D$ and the riskless rate ω_m or the variance terms.[1] *This model is thus entirely free of any possibility of a 'growth-stock paradox'.*

The properties of this stock-price equation are also those which would be expected:[2] *Ceteris paribus*, the current price of any stock will vary *directly* with the *expected growth* rate of the dividend stream; but it varies *inversely* with (a) the shadow price of wealth which functions as a *riskless interest* rate ω_m, and (b) with α_m, the composite elasticity of the utility of wealth in the market, which varies with composite relative *risk-aversion*, and with (c) the level of the growth *covariance* with other stocks $f(\sigma_{if})$, and with (d) the basic own-*variance* of the company growth rate $\sigma_{g_D}^2$, and with (e) the *time rate of increase in variances with futurity* σ_u^2.

Important features of a company's optimal policies when variances increase with futurity involve the *duration* of the certainty-equivalents of the prospective cash flows to investors. The duration of these certainty-equivalents is now $T_3 = dA_3/d(-Z_3) = B_3/A_3$ with

$$B_3 = \int_0^\infty \tau \exp(-Z_3\tau)d\tau, \tag{31}$$

which, remarkably, turns out to equal

$$B_3 = L(w)/R^2 f(w) \tag{31'}$$

where $L(w)$ is the 'linear loss' function of the standardized normal cumulative density function.[3] Using (27'), the duration of the certainty-equivalents is thus

$$T_3 = B_3/A_3 = L(w)/RG(w). \tag{32}$$

---

[1] In the limit as $\sigma_u^2 \to 0$, using l'Hopital's rule, equation (26') reduces to (15a); the latter in turn reduces to (8) in the limit as $\sigma_{g_D}^2$ and the covariance term approach zero.

[2] See mathematical notes in Appendix, section C.

[3] To fill in intermediate steps, note that

$$\int_0^\infty \tau \exp(-Z_3\tau)d\tau = \int_0^\infty (z-w)R^{-1}\exp(-Z_3\tau)d\tau = R^2 \int_w^\infty (z-w)\exp(-Z_3\tau)dz$$

$$= \exp(w^2/2)(2\pi)R^{-2}\int_w^\infty (2\pi)^{-\frac{1}{2}}(z-w)\exp(-z^2/2)dz$$

$$= L(w)/R^2 f(w),$$

where

$$L(w)\int_w^\infty (\xi - w)f(\xi)d\xi = f(w) - wG(w) > 0 \text{ for all } w < \infty.$$

See [26], pp. 295, 356.

The signs of the partial variation of duration with respect to each parameter are the same as those given in the previous paragraph for stock prices themselves.[1]

4. Optimal growth policy when the increase in variances with futurity is exogenous

We will first consider the choice of optimal growth policies in this model when σ_u^2, the increase in variance with futurity, is independent of the firm's decisions with respect to its retention rate and basic variance v_0. Under our continuing assumption that the policies are chosen to maximize the current value of the equity, the optimal policy mix will be that which corresponds to the pair of values r^* and v^* which maximize P_0 in (26'), subject to the constraints of (11) and (11'). These values are those which simultaneously satisfy the equations,

$$\frac{\partial P_0}{\partial v_0} = P_0 \left[\frac{\partial A_3/\partial w}{A_3} \frac{\partial w}{\partial \hat{g}_D^0} \frac{\partial \hat{g}_D^0}{\partial v_0} \right] = 0. \tag{33a}$$

$$\frac{\partial P_0}{\partial r} = P_0 \left[\frac{-1}{x} + \frac{\partial A_3/\partial w}{A_3} \frac{\partial w}{\partial \hat{g}_D^0} \frac{\partial \hat{g}_D^0}{\partial r} \right] = 0. \tag{33b}$$

These equations in turn, using (24) and the constraints, reduce to

$$\partial \hat{g}_D^0/\partial v_0 = \partial \bar{g}_D/\partial v_0 - \alpha_m C = 0 \tag{34a}$$
$$x^* T_3 \partial \hat{g}_D^0/\partial r = 1, \tag{34b}$$

where

$$\partial \hat{g}_D^0/\partial r = \partial \bar{g}_D/\partial r + (\partial \bar{g}_D/\partial v_0 - \alpha_m C)v'(r). \tag{35}$$

A comparison of (34a) with (17a') and (18) shows that in this case *the firm's optimal level of basic current risk v_0 is not affected* by $\sigma_u^2 > 0$. This is to be expected because in this subsection we are *assuming* that the time rate of increase in variances with futurity is *independent* of the firm's choice of policy mix. Maximization of the initial or short-run certainty-equivalent growth $\hat{g}_D^0$ (with respect to v_0) will maximize the certainty-equivalent *at all points in time* over all future values of τ. (Since σ_u^2 is taken to be exogenous in (26), it behaves like a fixed cost.)

Also we see from (35) that – as in section III when σ_u^2 was zero – the marginal certainty-equivalent of the growth rate in (34b) reduces

---

[1] See Appendix, section C.

to the marginal *expectation* of the growth rate whenever (a) initial risk levels are independent[1] of the retention rate (i.e. $v'(r) = 0$), *or* (b) optimal policies with respect to the basic initial risk v_0 are being followed (i.e. $v_0 = v_0{}^*$ to satisfy (34a)). In either case,

$$x^* T_3 \partial \bar{g}_D / \partial r = 1, \tag{34b'}$$

and the optimal *expected* growth rate is the one associated in (11) with this optimal retention rate or payout ratio. Comparison of (34b') with (17c) shows that allowance for future variances which increase with futurity at a rate σ_u^2 which is independent of any action of the firm does not change the formal requirement that the optimal dividend payout of the *marginal expected growth* rate over a time period equal to the *duration* of the certainty-equivalents of the uncertain dividend stream must be unity. But even though this rule reads the same as that derived in section III – and even though by assumption it is not affected by any policy action the firm may take – *the optimal retention ratio and the optimal expected growth rate are lowered* by the presence of a $\sigma_u^2 > 0$, and they both vary inversely with the magnitude of σ_u^2. This is because the exogenous σ_u^2 makes the duration of the certainty-equivalents of the future stream $T_3 < T_2$, since T_3 varies inversely with the size of σ_u^2. The product $x^* \partial \bar{g}_D / \partial r = (1 - r^*) \partial \bar{g}_D / \partial r$ must be larger if σ_u^2 is larger; and by our basic constraint (30), this is possible only if r^* is reduced – and the optimal *expected* growth rate $\bar{g}_D^*$ varies directly with r^*.

Moreover, when variances increase with futurity (even though exogenously), the product of the optimal dividend payout and the marginal expected growth rate – indeed, *the optimal payout of the marginal certainty-equivalent of the growth rate – will be greater than the dividend yield* on the stock when optimal policies are pursued. These conclusions follow from (34b) because *any* tendency for variances to increase with futurity *necessarily*[2] makes the *duration of the certainty-equivalents of future receipts smaller than the price–dividend ratio* (the reciprocal of the current dividend yield) *of the stock*. Any equation corresponding to (17d) of section III would now have to be written with an *inequality*; the observed dividend yield can no longer substitute for a direct assessment of the duration of the

---

[1] The results in the two other special cases noted in n. 1, p. 196, are also unchanged by an $\sigma_u^2 > 0$ which is independent of the firm's choices of r.

[2] Using (26') and (32), $T_3 < P_0 / D_0$ if $G^2(w) > f(w) L(w)$ which is proved for all $w < \infty$, as Lemma 2 in Appendix, section C.

growing stream even at the optimum. *A fortiori*, these conclusions hold in the more general case to which we now turn.

5. *Optimal growth policy when the increase in variance with futurity σ_u^2 depends on the basic risk posture of the corporation*

To this point we have assumed that the rate at which variances increase with futurity is completely exogenous to any policy action the firm may take. But while this simplification has been convenient and instructive, we now need to allow for the fact that σ_u^2 itself will usually be affected by at least the firm's policy choices with respect to its current basic risk posture as summarized in the variable v_0 in our constraint equation (11'). Happily, allowance for this interaction requires no change in our price equation, but it does change the policies which are optimal to maximize this price.

The simplest way to introduce this interaction between v_0 and σ_u and to show its principal effects on policy is to let[1]

$$\sigma_u^2 = \sigma_{u0}^2 + \beta v_0; \ \beta > 0. \tag{36}$$

We will continue to assume that σ_u^2 is independent of $v(r)$ in equation (11'), and hence not directly affected by any change in the retention ratio chosen by the firm.

The consequences of making σ_u^2 depend at least partially upon the basic initial risk posture of the firm v_0 are threefold. First, *the firm will no longer choose its v_0 to maximize the initial certainty-equivalent of its growth rate $\hat{g}_D^0$*. In addition to its effect upon $\hat{g}_D^0$ in the numerator of w (which was its only effect before), any change in basic risk v_0 now directly affects the R term which appears both in the denominator of A_3 and in the denominator of w. Combining the latter impacts, we have

$$\frac{\partial P_0}{\partial v_0} = \left[\frac{P_0}{A_3} \frac{\partial A_0}{\partial R} \frac{\partial R}{\partial v_0} + \frac{\partial A_3}{\partial \hat{g}_D^0} \frac{\partial \hat{g}_D^0}{\partial v_0} \right] = 0. \tag{37}$$

But since the first term in the bracket is strictly negative[2] and $\partial A_3 / \partial \hat{g}_D^0 = L(w)/R^2 f(w) = B_3 > 0$, it follows that the basic risk position of the company v_0 is optimized when the marginal variation of the

---

[1] The effects of the constant term in the relation between σ_u^2 and v_0 are the same as those shown in the previous subsection.

[2] See Appendix notes.

certainty-equivalent growth rate is *strictly positive* (rather than set equal to zero, as heretofore); i.e. we now have

$$\frac{\partial \hat{g}_D^0}{\partial v_0} = +\frac{\partial \bar{g}_D}{\partial v_0} - \alpha_m C > 0; \text{ with } v_0 = v_0^*. \tag{37a}$$

Whenever an increase in basic risk position is also accompanied by greater increments in future variances, *this 'byproduct' effect on expectations of future risks inhibits the amount of risk the firm will find it desirable to take initially in determining its basic risk position.*

The second consequence of this interdependence of σ_u^2 on v_0 follows directly from the first. The fact that the firm concurrently optimizes its initial basic risk posture by setting $v_0 = v_0^*$ means that it is *no longer* possible for the firm to determine its optimal retention ratio and optimal *expected* growth path with reference to the *marginal expected* growth rate: *optimal retention and expected growth rates must now be evaluated in terms of the marginal initial certainty-equivalent of the growth rate.*[1]

Finally, although a dependence of σ_u^2 on v_0 necessarily reduces the optimal basic risk v_0 a firm will undertake, this dependence has partially offsetting effects on optimal retention ratios and rates of expected growth. The dependence of σ_u^2 on v_0 means that the firm operates with a greater rate of increase in variances with futurity, and we saw above that larger values of σ_u^2 reduce optimal retention and expected growth rates.[2] Also, this dependence of σ^2 on v_0 means that the parenthesis in (35) is now strictly positive when v_0 is optimized; and since $v'(r) > 0$, we have the marginal initial certainty-equivalent growth $\partial \hat{g}_D^0/\partial r > \partial \bar{g}_D^0/\partial r$, the marginal expectation which otherwise suffices in equations like (34b) for the determination of optimal retention policies. Since the $\partial \hat{g}_D^0/\partial r$ is increased for any given retention, the optimal retention will tend to be lowered for this reason also. As at least a partial offset, however, the fact that v^* is reduced by its effect upon σ_u^2 means that the firm's optimal position involves less 'early-on' risk which induces a 'substitution effect' in favor of increased retentions and reduced dividend payouts.[3] It

[1] Partial differentiation of P_0 with respect to r still gives the same optimizing condition written out in (34b) before, and (35) is still valid since σ^2 is not involved in any term. But (37a) shows that setting $v_0 = v^*$ now leaves the parenthesis in (35) *strictly positive*; the marginal certainty-equivalent consequently must be retained in determining the optimum $r = r^*$.

[2] From equation (36), with $\beta > 0$ *any* $v_0 > 0$ will raise σ^2 for any given σ^2_0.

[3] *Ceteris paribus*, the optimal retention (and hence *expected* growth rate), conditional on any level of basic risk v_0, varies *inversely* with the assigned level of v_0.

appears probable that for most reasonable values of the relevant parameters, the influences *reducing* optimal retentions and expected growth rates will dominate. But in the risk domain, a counterpart of the well-known indeterminacies of offsetting income and substitution effects intrudes when the model is pushed to this level of complexity – or, as I would hold, realism.

V. CONCLUDING OBSERVATIONS

We have developed a model of corporate decisions regarding policies to implement growths under expectationally steady-state conditions in which the outcome of any policy is uncertain. We have assumed that decisions are made to maximize the current market value of the equity of the corporation. The results should be of considerable interest in their own right, since this objective is the modern counterpart, under uncertainty in a dynamic context, of traditional profit maximization in the static theory of the firm. Our purpose has been to explore the consequence of this objective under a richer and more realistic set of assumptions, and very importantly, to provide a basis for comparison with behavior if firms follow other objectives. In an essentially theoretical paper, we have not sought to argue that equity maximization is the sole objective of management decisions in practice.

Section II established that the conclusions concerning desirable levels of steady-state growth which are indicated by share-price maximization under a simple constraint relating attainable growth to retention ratios are *identical* to those reached by detailed and separate optimization of fixed investment, advertising budgets and 'expansion costs' in accordance with modern dynamic investment theory under certainty (when steady-state conditions are assumed). Under this simple constraint, firms could buy greater growth with greater retentions, and the optimal scale of added current investment (reduced current dividends) depended upon the riskless interest rate, the amount of growth associated with each retention level, and the degree to which 'diminishing returns' inhibited further expansion.

Firms maximizing equity values never maximize their rate of growth. Firms maximizing growth under certainty would increase retentions until the *marginal* growth rate was pushed down to zero. Firms maximizing market value stop at the point where the dividend payout of the marginal growth rate plus the growth rate itself no

longer exceeds unity. Growth maximizers would act *as if* there were
no costs to growth. (To be consistent in a price–quantity problem,
they should find optimal quantity where $MR = 0$, *not* where $MR = MC$!) Equity maximizers stop short their growth at the point
where marginal gain no longer exceeds the marginal (opportunity)
cost as determined by the riskless rate in the market.

Sections III and IV derived optimal growth policies for firms
which maximize equity values in lognormal security markets of risk-
averse investors with constant elasticity utility functions in circumstances where the outcomes associated with any policy involve
uncertainty. Under the constraints on company policies, corporations may 'buy' more expected growth by undertaking policy mixes
involving more risk (even when retention ratios are held constant),
and may also 'buy' more expected growth by increasing their
retention ratio (even if the risk level of the strategic posture is held
constant). Both options are of course subject to diminishing returns.

In section III, we examined the simplified situation in which the
uncertainties associated with any policy are considered to be constant
over time (along with expected growth rates). Under these assumptions, maximizing equity value involves adjusting *risk levels* to
maximize the certainty-equivalent of the growth rate, conditional on
any retention ratio – and it also involves choosing a *retention* (or
dividend payout) *ratio* which will provide investors with a marginal
expected return that just equals the riskless rate in the market
adjusted upwards by the market's risk-averse valuation of the
(optimal) level of risk involved in the company's future dividend
payments and stock price.

Several observations are appropriate. First, although the choice of
risk levels to maximize certainty-equivalents of growth rates *sounds*
like what a 'growth-maximizer' who was risk-averse would do, the
level of risk chosen will be different. A growth-oriented but risk-
averse management, responsible to no one else and owning no stock
in the company, would presumably determine the maximum growth
rate by consulting *its own* utility function ordering different attainable combinations of expected growth and risks of growth. But it
would be sheer coincidence if *its* trade-offs between $\bar{g}$ and σ_g^2 were
the same as that relevant to equity-value maximizers. The risk-
aversion relevant to the latter managements is equal to the market-
composite elasticity of the *investors* in the market (rather than a
job-oriented or internal 'empire-building' management itself); in

addition, the optimal marginal condition for equity-value maximizers also involves the ratio of market-price variance to 'company-variance' (the term C in our mathematics) which is presumably ignored in a utility function for management *per se*.

Moreover, while equity-maximizers choose *risk levels* to maximize conditionally certainty-equivalents of growth (using market parameters for the trade-offs), they *never* choose retention ratios or *expected* growth rates which will maximize the certainty-equivalent growth rate. Neither will they ever choose *retention ratios* to maximize the expected growth rate, nor even the 'duration' of the certainty-equivalents of the stream of returns to investors. The differences between maximum and optimum in each respect always increase with the level of the company's operating uncertainty (even when the latter is optimized) and with the degree of risk-aversion in the *market, and* with the 'C-ratio' of security-market risk to company operating risk.

When we allowed in section IV for the fact that less is known of the more distant future, so that variance assessments increase with futurity and future data (including stock prices) have characteristics of 'random walks', we found that all the above general conclusions continue to hold true – and in stronger form. Indeed, we found that if there is any tendency for the rate of increase of variance with futurity σ_u^2 to increase with greater current on short-run risk levels v_0, equity-maximizers will no longer choose basic risk levels which will maximize even the conditional certainty-equivalents of their 'early-on' growth rates. Under this very reasonable set of assumptions, *equity-maximizers do not maximize certainty-equivalent growth rates with respect to any decision variable under their control.* The contrast with the presumptive behavior of an internal management group feathering its own nest in terms of its own utility function over $\bar{g}$ and σ_g^2 could hardly be sharper. Nor only are market measures of risk-aversion substituted for managements', but market risks are added. Also, even the certainty-equivalents of growth rates are not maximized if equity values are made as large as possible.

Extensions and comparisons with other models

The similarities and differences between the models in this paper and those developed by Marris [25] and other authors should be noted. Most other authors (such as Downie, Penrose, Baumol and Williamson) who have proposed 'growth models' have worked with certainty, or have simply argued that firms maximize growth without introducing uncertainty explicitly. In the previous comments, I have filled in this gap by supposing that what has been meant by those who argue that management seek maximum growth is that managements seek to maximize the certainty-equivalent of growth in terms of their own utility function. In effect, I have imputed to them a richer model in which uncertainty is recognized and evaluated by management in terms of a preference function $U^m = U(\tilde{g}, \sigma_g^2)$. Max U^m is then equivalent to max $\hat{g}$ using management's risk-aversion, or its marginal rates of substitution between expected gains and risks, subject of course to the prevailing constraints on its opportunities.

But Marris' position is different and more sophisticated than the others. He urges that management is interested in both growth and security. Management insecurity is identified primarily with fear of a takeover raid rather than directly with uncertainty concerning the growth rate itself, and the insecurity from possible takeover is related to the discrepancy between the maximum attainable equity value and that lower value actually realized because of the premium put on growth itself. Marris thus urges that managements seek to maximize growth *per se* subject to a minimum acceptable ratio of stock price to book value (in order to thwart takeovers) – or, in his more general version, that management optimizes a utility function which increases (at diminishing rates) with both the 'valuation ratio' (market value of the equity) and the growth rate itself as separate variables. He posits $U^M = U^M(P/B, g)$ with positive first (and negative second) derivatives, where B is the (given) current book value, and regards management as maximizing U^M subject to a valuation constraint in the form $P/B = f(g)$ where $f'(g) > 0$ and $f''(g) < 0$. The optimum is of course given by a tangency condition between the valuation constraint and the slope of management's indifferences curve as indicated on Fig. 7.3 (p. 206 above). Because of the premium attached to growth as such, market value will be maximized only if it is so low that fear of takeover completely dominates management's preferences. Similarly (as in our model but in contrast to others) growth itself will not be maximized, because (for Marris) of increasing insecurity to management as market value falls below its attainable maximum.

In comparing our models with Marris's, we should emphasize that *all* the models in this paper produce the same *shape* of the relation between market value and the attainable growth rate as that suggested by Marris – because of the constraints on attainable policy mixes to implement growth, the price function rises at diminishing rates to a maximum and then falls at ever increasing rates. But the *content* of our value function differs in important respects from his. In particular, Marris introduces uncertainty concerning the growth rate itself only as a factor increasing the interest rate at which the future stream is discounted. As shown in section III, this turns out to be a valid short cut when variances of the growth rate are treated as constant over time, but when variance assessments increase with futurity (as in section IV), there is *no* risk-adjusted or 'as if' discount rate which can be used in discounting either the certainty-equivalents or the expected values of future returns. Our models also allow for the effects on current stock prices of randomness (and, in particular, the prospects of 'random walks') in *future* stock prices. They also recognize the choices managements have concerning the riskiness of their operations – whether to 'buy' greater expected growth rates with no added financing by pursuing riskier policy mixes. Nevertheless, the analysis in this paper shows that the *qualitative* conclusions Marris reached hold up under these more general conditions, in so far as these conclusions depend on the general form of his value function.

It is natural and reasonable to generalize an 'equity-maximizing' model such as developed in this paper by adding 'the' growth rate as as added argument of a more general utility function in the spirit of positive economics to describe actual behavior. In the same spirit, it may well prove appropriate to add still other dimensions, such a community prestige secured through support of the arts and education, or through leadership in absorbing hard-core unemployment. But even when only growth *per se* is added, it would be useful to have at least the expectation and variance of the growth rate added separately as in $U^M = U^M(P/B, \bar{g}, \sigma_g^2)$, since the relative weights on the latter variables in management's utility will differ from those (determined by investors in the market) which are subsumed in the value term – and in general, management's own marginal rates of substitution between $\bar{g}$ and σ_g^2 will also depend at least partially upon the current and prospective market prices of the company's stock. Recent evidence [22, 23] showing the large fraction of management's total compensation which derives from bonus arrangements geared to profits and from their holding of the equity of 'their' companies also clearly suggests that share price enters management's own utility functions as a direct and important 'good' in its own right, and not merely as a protection against possible takeovers.

These last few comments open up interesting and possibly fruitful avenues of further theory-building within the framework of 'managerially motivated' models such as Marris's. But at this stage, it is probably a reasonable judgment to conclude that the more important advances in our knowledge will come from better evidence on the relative weights to be given to 'equity-value increasing' objectives and to other elements in the utility function of business as they affect and determine actual decisions in different situations. These 'other elements' would include but not be confined to those which are management-motivated in Marris's sense.

The evidence to date is clear that not all corporations maximize equity value (relative to a general market index) at all times. Other elements do affect policy in many firms. We need much more evidence on these matters and how they affect performance. In particular, we need to be able to make a much better assessment of the *extent* to which these other matters modify the implications of equity maximization as such, and this requires a clear benchmark from which to measure departure. The present paper has undertaken to contribute to this effort by clarifying the context and implications of the classical presumption and prescription of value-maximizing behavior in an uncertain world.

Appendix

A. OPTIMAL STEADY-STATE GROWTH OF DIVIDENDS DERIVED FROM OPTIMIZATION OF ALL OTHER POLICIES

In this appendix we illustrate the derivation of an optimal dividend policy from the simultaneous and continuous optimization of all other policies using explicit production, demand and advertising functions. Specifically, we will assume that all elasticity coefficients, depreciation rates, input prices and the interest rate are exogenously given and constant over time. In this simple case, we derive the explicit set of policies which at all points in time will satisfy the optimizing conditions given in equations (5a), (5b), (5c) in the text.

A.1. *The production function*

For our present purposes, it is both convenient and sufficient to assume that the production function is of a standard Cobb–Douglas form[1]

$$q_\tau = C_1 K_\tau^\gamma L_\tau^{1-\gamma}, \quad 0 < \gamma < 1 \tag{A.1}$$

where both the capital stock K_τ and labor inputs L_τ are measured in efficiency units. With the rate of interest κ and depreciation δ_κ constant, and the prices of capital goods in efficiency units fixed (i.e. $\dot{p}_K = 0$), K_τ is equal[2] to the integral of (depreciated) current dollar expenditures $I_K(t)$:

$$K_\tau = \int_{-\infty}^{\tau} \exp[-(\tau - t)\delta\kappa] I_K(t) dt. \tag{A.2}$$

[1] In keeping with usual practice, assume that all the materials and other 'non-value-added' inputs which are required to produce q_τ have fixed input–output coefficients, so that they only effect the magnitude of the proportionality c_1.

[2] If the rate of embodiment of technological change in capital equipment is h, and $I_K^0(t)$ is the deflated (constant dollar) outlay on capital equipment, then the Solow [32] expression for capital stock in efficiency units with continuous compounding is

$$K\tau = \int_{\infty}^{\tau} \exp(ht)\exp[-(\tau - t)\delta\kappa] I_K^0(t) d_t.$$

If h' is the rate of increase in market prices of units of capital equipment, we have $I_K^0(t) = I_K(t)\exp(-h't)$ with suitable normalization. But $\dot{p}_K = 0$ in efficiency units requires that $h = h'$, and substitution for $I_K^0(t)$ in the preceding equation gives the simpler form in the text.

It thus follows by differentiation that

$$\dot{K} = \partial K_t / \partial T = I_K(t) - \delta K_t. \tag{A.3}$$

Now equation (5b) shows that the optimal time path of investment outlays on capital stock is that which provides at each point in time a *stock* of capital K_τ for which the marginal profitability equals the sum of the short-term interest rate and depreciation rate (after setting $\dot{p}_K = 0$). The marginal product of capital is $\partial q_\tau / \partial K_\tau = c_1 \gamma q_\tau / K_\tau$, and marginal revenue is $p(\eta - 1)/\eta$ for any price where $\eta = -(p/q) \delta q / \delta p$ is the elasticity of demand. The optimal capital stock K_τ^* at any given point in time will consequently be given by

$$K_\tau^* / p_\tau q_\tau = (\eta - 1) c_1 \gamma / \eta (\kappa + \delta_K). \tag{A.4}$$

When elasticities and interest rates are constant, the optimal capital stock thus stands in constant ratio to current sales, whatever the optimal time path of sales may be.

With capital stock K_τ fixed, marginal costs of production $C'(q_\tau; K_\tau) = w'(\partial q_\tau / \partial L_\tau)^{-1} + v'$ where w' is the wage rate and v' all other marginal costs for materials and other 'non-value-added' inputs. The first term on the right will be inversely related to K_τ; total cost $C(q_\tau, K_\tau)$ will be minimized by the mix of capital stock and labor for which $(\kappa + \delta_K)(\partial q_\tau / \partial K_\tau)^{-1} = w'(\partial q_\tau / \partial L_\tau)^{-1}$ and this capital stock is also the one for which (5b) is satisfied. With $K_\tau = K_\tau^*$ at all times in accordance with equations (A.4), v' will be constant (along with κ and δ_K) by our assumption of constant input prices. Consequently, marginal costs $C'(q_\tau)$ are also constant and equal to

$$(\kappa + \delta_K)(\partial q_\tau / \partial K_\tau)^{-1} + v'.$$

A.2. *The demand function*

At any given point in time the quantity of a firm's output q_τ which will be bought by its customers depends on the price p_τ it charges and the elasticity of demand for its output $\eta = -(p/q)\partial q / \partial p$. The quantity which can be sold at a given price also depends on the level of general business activity, national income, population and other factors over which the firm has no control, all of which will be summarized in a general variable z_τ, and the composite effect of changes in z on q will be summarized in an 'income' elasticity ζ. It is also well understood that firms having market power ($\eta < \infty$) may shift their demand functions for a given p and z by advertising and promotional expenditures. But the advertising outlays of a given period affect the sales of future periods as well, though to a progressively diminishing degree as time goes on; and the total shift in sales at any time τ due to advertising is the summation as of that date of the then remaining effects of the entire history of the firm's previous promotional outlays. As Nerlove and Arrow [27] point out, it is analytically most convenient to define a stock of *goodwill* denoted by A_τ which will summarize the effects of current and all past advertising outlays on q_τ, given p_τ and z_τ. If we summarize the partial dependence of q_τ on A_τ by an elasticity coefficient v, and concentrate on the simple case where the demand function is linear in the logarithms, the full statement of our *demand generator* is thus

$$q_\tau = c_2 p^{-n} A^v z \xi \tag{A.5}$$

where c_2 is simply a constant and the other variables are as defined in the preceding paragraph. If we assume that a dollar of current outlay on advertising increases A by one dollar, and let $I_A(\tau)$ represent the amount of such expenditures at time τ and δ_A represent time rate of diminution in the effects of earlier outlays, we have by definition

$$A_\tau = \int_{-\infty}^{t} \exp[-(t-\tau)\delta] I_A(\tau) d\tau, \tag{A.6}$$

from which it follows by differentiation that

$$\dot{A}_\tau = \partial A_\tau / \partial \tau = I_A(\tau) - \delta_A A. \tag{A.7}$$

Now from (A.5) and (2), it is clear that the optimal time path of price to satisfy (5a) will be given by

$$p_\tau^* = \eta C'(q_\tau; K_\tau)/(\eta - 1). \tag{A.8}$$

Similarly, the optimal stock of goodwill A_τ at any time τ is the value A_τ^* for which (5c) is satisfied along with (5a) and (5b). We will assume that (5b) is always satisfied by holding capital stock K_τ at the optimal levels required by (A.5). These capital stock levels make $C'(q_\tau; K_\tau)$ determinate, and we assume prices everywhere satisfy (A.8) and thence (5a). It is now convenient to relate marginal production costs $C'(q_\tau; K_\tau)$ to the optimal price p^* by using (A.8), and we then find[1] that (5c) requires that

$$A_\tau^* = v p_\tau^* q_\tau / \eta (\kappa + \delta_A). \tag{A.9}$$

[1] From (2) we have $\partial R[p, A, z, K]/\partial A = [p - C'(q; K)]\partial q/\partial A$ so that (5c) becomes $p[1 - (\eta - 1)/\eta]v = A(\kappa + \delta_A)/q$, from which (A.9) follows directly.

The optimal stock of goodwill A_τ^* is thus proportional to current sales receipts $S_\tau = p_\tau q_\tau$, and the proportionality factor is constant over time under our assumptions that κ, δ_A, ν and η are constant.

From (A.4) we recall that optimal capital stock K^* also bears a constant ratio to sales under these assumptions, but the factors of proportionality are quite different for K_τ^* and A_τ^*. It also needs to be emphasized that – in spite of all the assumptions of constancy in elasticities and so on which we have made – these optimal advertising stocks in (A.9) differ fundamentally from the results of a traditional static analysis. In particular, under dynamic conditions the optimizing condition at each time point applies to the goodwill *stock* A_τ^*, and the optimal *rate or flow* of current outlay I_τ^* on advertising is that required at each τ to bring the stock up to but not beyond A_τ^*. In contrast, optimization in a one-period static model would derive the amount of optimal investment directly from the conditions of the given period alone. Although the general optimum in (A.9) covers the static one-period optimum as a special restricted case when the appropriate restrictions are imposed,[1] the *level* of optimal current 'investment in advertising' is much different in the case where dynamic effects are recognized than in the static case where they are ignored. This clearly brings out the importance of the distinction between 'one-period' optimization and optimization *along* a dynamic path which was emphasized in our introduction.

---

[1] As Nerlove and Arrow note ([27], p. 134), their equation (17) – our equation (A.9) – reduces to the formula for optimal advertising $u = \eta$ given by Steiner and Dorfman when the latters' static assumptions are imposed. Since Steiner–Dorfman derive their formula by an alternative route, it may be well to present here the static derivation of their formula which corresponds to the sequence of steps in the dynamic derivation summarized in the text from Nerlove and Arrow. The objective is to maximize profits $\Pi = pq(p, I_A) - C(q) - I_A$ which gives the two optimizing equations:

(i) $\qquad\qquad \partial\Pi/\partial p = (p - C'(q))\partial q/\partial p + q = 0$

(ii) $\qquad\qquad \partial\Pi/\partial I_A = (p - C'(q))\partial q/\partial I_A = 1.$

After dividing (i) by q, it is apparent that $-q^{-1}\partial q/\partial p = \partial q/\partial I_A$, so that in equilibrium $\eta = p\partial q/\partial I_A = u$ which is the static Steiner–Dorfman formula. If now we let $\nu = (I_A/q)(\partial q/\partial I_A)$, we have $\eta = pq\nu I_A^*$ so that the optimal *static* advertising $I_A^* = \nu pq/\eta$.

Under static assumptions, (A.9) in the text reduces to this formula, since in the static case $A_t = I_A(t)$ in each period because no carryover effect of advertising is recognized; consequently, $\delta\kappa = 1$, and since interest κ is charged on no carryover stock, it may be ignored.

A.3. *Optimal time paths of $I_K^*(\tau)$ and $I_A^*(\tau)$*

We are now in a position to derive the optimal time paths of current outlays on real investment $I_K^*(\tau)$ and advertising $I_A^*(\tau)$ from the optimal time paths of the stock of capital K_τ^* and goodwill A_τ^* given by equation (A.4) and (A.9). To have a dynamic steady state, we will use our previous assumptions of constancy over time in interest rates κ, input costs and all elasticity coefficients, and assume in addition that the primary 'driver' of the system, the exogenous variable z_τ, is growing at a rate $g_Z = (\partial z_\tau/\partial_\tau) z_\tau = \partial \log z_\tau/\partial z$ which is constant over time. We will also let g with appropriate subscripts denote the corresponding logarithmic time derivatives of other variables.

We have directly from (A.5) that[1]

$$g_S = g_q = \nu g_A + \zeta g_z. \tag{A.10}$$

We now invoke the optimality condition for advertising stock given by (A.9). Since A_τ^*/S_τ is constant, we have $g_A = g_S$ in equilibrium; and since optimal capital stock K_τ^* bears a constant ratio to sales, we find that *optimal* growth rates satisfy

$$g_K^* = g_S^* = g_A^* = [\zeta/(1-\nu)]g_z. \tag{A.11}$$

Equation (A.7) is definitional and so applies to the optimal time path of A_τ^* (as well as any other). The optimal rate of current outlay on product promotion must consequently be $I_A^*(\tau) = \delta_A A_\tau^* + \partial A_\tau^*/\partial \tau$, or

$$I_A^*(\tau) = [\delta_A + \zeta g_z/(1-\nu)]A_\tau^* \tag{A.12}$$

after using (A.11). Finally, since the optimal time path of advertising outlays produces the optimal time path of sales S_τ^*, we can substitute (A.9) into (A.12) to find that under our steady-state assumptions the optimal ratio $f_A^*(\tau)$ of advertising outlay to sales receipts is also constant over time with a value

$$f_A^*(\tau) = I_A^*(\tau)/S_\tau^* = [\nu/\eta(\kappa + \delta_A)] \cdot [\delta_A + \zeta g_z/(1-\nu)] = f_A^*. \tag{A.13}$$

---

[1] It should be emphasized that this equation makes no assumptions about the rationality or optimality of policy with respect to advertising. It merely assumes that product prices are constant (if one likes, because marginal costs are constant and prices are optimal).

Similarly, using (A.3) and (A.11) shows that optimal current (gross) investment on capital stock is

$$I_K^*(\tau) = [\delta_K + \zeta g_z/(1 - v)]K_\tau^*. \tag{A.14}$$

Combining this result with (A.4) in turn establishes the optimal fraction $f_K^*(\tau)$ of current sales receipts to be devoted to gross plant investment, which is

$$f_K^*(\tau) = I_K^*(\tau)/S_\tau^* = [(\eta - 1)c_1\gamma/\eta(\kappa + \delta_K)] \cdot [\delta_k + \zeta g_z/(1 - v)] = f_K^*, \tag{A.15}$$

also a constant over time.

Now with prices and marginal costs constant, it is apparent from (A.8) that all direct or marginal costs will absorb a constant fraction

$$f_d^* = (\eta - 1)/\eta \tag{A.16}$$

of sales receipts, and we will assume that 'overheads' (*other than* depreciation $\delta_K K_\tau$ on capital stock) are similarly optimized and constant at a level f_O^* as a percentage of sales receipts. But dividend payments are by equation (3) simply the excess of operating profits over outlays on advertising and plant investment. Substitution of the above leads directly to equations (6) and (7) in the text.

A.4 *Simple generalizations*

To this point for utmost simplicity we have assumed not only that interest and depreciation rates and elasticity coefficients were constant over time, but independent of levels chosen for ratios between either flow or stock variables. One simple but significant easing of these restrictions would allow steady growth trends in input prices; another would allow price elasticity η to depend on the fraction of sales receipts spent on advertising (or on the 'stock' ratio A_τ/S_τ); still another would allow the elasticity of demand v with respect to either of these ratios to be a (declining) function of their level;[1] and there are obviously many more which could be made subject to the

[1] As an illustration, suppose that the 'advertising goodwill elasticity' is made a declining function of the A_τ/S_τ ratio, say $= v_0 - b(A_\tau/S_\tau)$, where v_0 is some constant and $b > 0$. Then the optimal A_τ^*/S_τ^* in equation (A.9) simply becomes $v_0/[b + \eta(\kappa + \delta_A)]$, a perfectly determinate but lower value than before. Given the optimal A^*/S^* ratio, the value v^* at the optimum can be determined, and these lower values then enter into equations (A.13)–(A.15), reducing g_S and g_0^*. Some of the admissible changes suggested in the assumptions would require solutions of simultaneous nonlinear equations, but so long as convexity is retained, the solutions would be determinate.

underlying convexity required for determinate equilibrium positions or paths. As noted in the text, still other but more complex generalizations are available in terms of mutually consistent time paths of variation in the variables treated as time-invariant above.

B. EQUILIBRIUM STOCK PRICES IN A PURELY COMPETITIVE 'LOGNORMAL' MARKET

B.1. *Assumptions*

We assume a purely competitive market in which there are M investors $(l \ldots k \ldots M)$, each with an amount of wealth or investable funds[1] W_{0k} which is to be invested in savings accounts, government or corporate bonds, real estate or stocks. Future price levels of all goods (including those in the 'cost of living') are uncertain, so that *all of the available assets (N in number, indexed by $l \ldots i,j \ldots N$) have an uncertain real return.* With no transactions costs or taxes, we assume that each investor assesses a (*jointly*) *lognormal distribution* of the total real returns (including dividends as well as capital gains) of all N investments with respect to a common date in the future,[2] and that he also assesses the distribution of these portfolio outcomes to be lognormal.[3] We also assume that each investor is a risk-averter with a so-called constant elasticity or 'hyperbolic' utility function[4]

[1] Ideally, one would wish to base the analysis upon a preference ordering over alternative (stochastic) time-streams of consumption outlays and terminal wealth. But this is not necessary for present purposes, since Richard Meyer [25a] has shown that certain not unreasonable assumptions with respect to the stability of preferences as of different dates lead directly to the 'constant elasticity' form of utility function specified here, and that with this function over available consumption outlays, a derived function of the same form may be specified for investable funds themselves. For present purposes, the 'antecedents' of this utility function are not needed, and we start with the latter derived function itself in the indicated constant elasticity form.   [2] See n. 1, p. 192 above.

[3] Although a linear mixture of lognormal distributions is not strictly lognormal, it seems entirely reasonable to assume that the investor treats his portfolio return 'as if' it were lognormal – just as it is to assume that he treats the distribution of individual stocks 'as if' they were jointly lognormal. Any statistical distribution is to some degree an approximation, and indeed, the empirical work seems to indicate that the lognormal function fits the distributions of returns on mutual funds (i.e. large portfolios) and large diversified companies just as well as those of individual stocks. See [20].

[4] This utility function has the desirable properties that marginal utility $U'(W) > 0$ and diminishing $U''(W)$. Investors using it are 'risk-averse' in the sense

$U_k(W_k) = -W_k^{-\alpha_k}$ where $\alpha_k > 0$. We will assume that all investors (and 'the market') assess the same joint probability distribution[1] over the returns available on all individual securities (and hence over any stated mixture of securities). The *elasticities* of the utility function α_k *and* the amount of investable *wealth* W_{0k} *differ among investors.*

B.2. *Equilibrium prices in static context*

Each investor invests his available wealth W_{0k} in that portfolio or mix of investments which will maximize his expectation of the utility $E[U_k(\bar{W}_{1k})]$ of his random end-of-period wealth W_{1k}, given by his assessment, We index the different *portfolios* available to him by a subscript p, and let $\bar{g}_{pk}$ be the normally distributed relative rate of return available on the pth portfolio which might be held by the kth investor. Then $\bar{W}_{1k} = W_{0k}\exp(\bar{g}_{pk})$ over a unit period of time, and with our constant elasticity utility function we find that[2]

$$E[U_k(\bar{W}_{1k})] = E\{[-W_{0k}\exp(\bar{g}_{pk})] - \alpha_k\}$$
$$= -W_{0k}^{-\alpha}\exp[-\alpha_k(\bar{g}_{pk} - \alpha_k\sigma_{pk}^2/2)]. \qquad (B.1)$$

Out of all portfolio mixes available to any k'th investor, given his probability assessments and his wealth constraint, the portfolio which will maximize the expected utility of his ending wealth is consequently the one which will maximize the *certainty-equivalent* of his logarithmic portfolio return:

$$\theta_k = \bar{g}_{pk} - \alpha_k\sigma_{pk}^2/2. \qquad (B.2)$$

Now if we let $\bar{g}_i$ and σ_i^2 represent the mean and variance of the ith stock's relative rate of return (and σ_{ij} its covariance with the jth

---

that in choosing among portfolios they prefer greater returns with the same risk and lesser risk with the same return. The measure of the *degree* of risk-aversion is $r(W) = -U''(W)/U'(W) > 0$, which for our function $= (\alpha + 1)/W > 0$, i.e. a constant *proportional* risk-aversion. The function also satisfies the further desired requirement that $r'(W) < 0$ – the 'insurance premium' required on risks decreases with increasing wealth.

[1] In [20], I extend the model to allow for every investor to assess a *different* probability over all outcomes. All the conclusions drawn from the simple 'homogeneous' probability model in this paper carry through under the assumption of diverse assessments.

[2] First note that $E[-W_{0k}\exp(\bar{g}_p)]^{-\alpha_k} = -W_{0k}^{-\alpha_k}E[\exp(-\alpha_k\bar{g}_p)]$. But when α_k has a normal distribution, the expectation on the right may be evaluated as the '$(-\alpha_k)$th' moment in the usual moment-generating function for the normal distribution, with the result given in the text. See [1], p. 8.

stock) and if we let $f_{ik}W_{0k}$ represent the kth investor's dollar invest-ment in the ith stock with $\Sigma f_{ik} = 1$, it turns out that to a tight ap-proximation we can identify[1] $\bar{g}_{pk}$ with $\Sigma_i f_{ik}\bar{g}_i$ and σ_{pk}^2 with $\Sigma_{ij} f_{ik}f_{jk}\sigma_{ij}$.

For any given set of $\bar{g}$s and σ_{ij}'s, therefore, the investor's best portfolio is the set of f_{ik} which will maximize the Lagrangian function

$$\Sigma_i f_{ik}\bar{g}_{ik} - (\alpha_k/2)\Sigma_{ij}f_{ik}f_{jk}\sigma_{ij} - \omega_k[\Sigma_i f_{ik} - 1],$$

which gives the set of equations

$$\alpha_k(f_{ik}\sigma_i^2 + \Sigma_j \neq {}_i f_{jk}\sigma_{ij}) = \bar{g}_i - \omega_k; \; 1, \ldots, N \text{ securities} \qquad \text{(B.3)}$$

to determine the relative holdings f_i in his best portfolio, and ω_k is clearly the marginal riskless real valuation or shadow price on his wealth constraint, determined from the condition[2] $\Sigma_i f_{ik} = 1$. Let f_{ik}^* represent the value of f_{ik} obtained by solving the system of equations (B.3). These optimal values f_{ik}^* for any ith stock clearly depend upon the expected relative returns of all stocks, its own variance and covariance with all other stocks, and the investor's own[3] α_k and ω_k

---

[1] We need to evaluate $\bar{g}_p$ and σ_p^2 from

(i) $\qquad\qquad\qquad\qquad \exp(g_p) = \Sigma_i f_i \exp(g_i)$, subject to

(ii) $\qquad\qquad\qquad\qquad \Sigma_i f_i = 1.$

We expand (i) to obtain

(iii) $\qquad\qquad 1 + \bar{g}_p + 1/2\bar{g}_p^2 + \ldots = 1 + \Sigma_i f_i g_i + 1/2\Sigma_i f_i \bar{g}_i^2 + \ldots,$

and note that within the practically relevant ranges of g_i and g_p we have very strong inequalities between successive terms – in particular, $g_p^2/2 < < g_p$, and $\Sigma_i f_i \bar{g}_i^2/2 < < \Sigma_i f_i \bar{g}_i$. After cancelling 1's and taking expectations, we have

(iv) $\quad \bar{g}_p = \Sigma_i f_i \bar{g}_i +$ (the net difference between two positive second-order terms) + terms of higher order, and

(v) $\quad E(\bar{g}_p)^2 = \bar{g}_p^2 + \sigma_p^2 = E(\Sigma_i f_i g_i)^2 = \Sigma_{ij} f_i f_j \bar{g}_i \bar{g}_j + \Sigma_{ij} f_i f_j \sigma_{ij} +$ terms of *higher order*. Subtracting the square of (iv) from (v) gives

(vi) $\qquad\qquad\qquad \sigma_p^2 = \Sigma_{ij} f_i f_j \sigma_{ij} +$ terms of order 3 and higher.

[2] Technically, this form of the constraint ignores restriction on short selling (which would require absolute value notation in the constraint), but I show in [20] that (B.3) is still valid when probability assessments are homogeneous, as we are assuming here, and also more generally. In the same reference [20], the analysis of equilibrium market prices is extended to cover the combined effects of diverse probability assessments and constraints on short selling, and also the market equilibrium equations when investors assess lognormal distributions of ending prices, rather than treating the assessment of all $\bar{g}_i$s as independent of the current market price P_{0i} (as we have done here).

[3] It will be noted from equations (B.3) that even though all investors assess $\bar{g}_i$, σ_i^2 and σ_{ij} on the basis of the *same* probability distribution, the optimal portfolio mixes and values of all n_{ik}^* will differ among investors because of their different α_k^* and ω_k.

But his dollar investment in the ith stock will be $f_{ik}^* W_{0k} = n_{ik} P_{0i}$, where n_{ik} is the number of shares of the ith stock held by the kth investor, and P_{0i} is its current market price. If we let n_k be a diagonal matrix whose nonzero elements represent the *number of shares* of each security held by the kth investor, I be the identity matrix, $\underline{P}_0$ be the *diagonal* matrix $[P_{0i}]$ of market prices per share, and $\bar{g}$ be the diagonal matrix of expected relative returns on each security, and the (full) matrix Z represent the variance–covariance matrix $[\sigma_{ij}]$, then (B.3) may be written

$$\alpha_k \underline{P}_0 \underline{Z} n_k = W_{0k}[\bar{g} - \omega_k^I]. \tag{B.3a}$$

This equation may be solved to show explicitly the optimal number of shares of each security which the investor will hold *conditional upon any possible vector* of *market prices* P_0:

$$\underline{n}_k = \alpha_{k0}^{-1} W_{0k} (\underline{P}_0 \underline{Z})^{-1} [\underline{\bar{g}} - \omega_k^I]. \tag{B.3c}$$

But if n is the diagonal matrix of the total outstanding supply (number of shares) of each security, the market clearing conditions require that

$$n = \Sigma_k n_k = \Sigma_k \alpha_k^{-1} W_{0k} (P_0 Z)^{-1} [\bar{g} - \omega_k]. \tag{B.4}$$

The (unique) vector of *aggregate market values* for each security which is consistent with (B.4) is clearly[1]

$$\underline{P}_0 n = \Sigma_k \alpha_k^{-1} W_{0k} \underline{Z}^{-1} [\bar{g} - \omega_k]. \tag{B.5}$$

By derivation, the set of aggregate market values satisfying (B.5) are *equilibrium values*, because they simultaneously satisfy the market sharing conditions when, conditional upon these prices, all investors hold the security portfolios they prefer to any other consistent with their wealth constraints – i.e. the solution is also Pareto-optimal.

Now note that if we let the market's aggregate investable wealth be $W_{0m} = \Sigma_k W_{0k}$ and $h_{Wk} = W_{0k}/\Sigma_k W_{0k} = W_{0k}/W_{0m}$ be the fraction of the investors' investable funds to the total in the market, then (B.5) can be written

$$\underline{P}_0 \underline{n} = \underline{Z}^{-1} W_{0m} \Sigma_k \alpha_k^{-1} h_{Wk} \bar{\underline{g}} - \underline{Z}^{-1} W_{0m} \Sigma_k \alpha_k^{-1} h_{Wk} \omega_k \tag{B.6}$$

$$= \underline{Z}^{-1} (\alpha_m^{-1} W_{0m}) \bar{g} - \underline{Z}^{-1} \alpha_m^{-1} W_{0m} \omega_m \tag{B.6a}$$

---

[1] As intermediate steps, the right-hand side of (B.4) may be written

$$[\Sigma_k \alpha_k^{-1} W_{0k} Z_k^{-1} (\bar{g} - \omega_k)] \underline{P}_0^{-1},$$

since market prices $\underline{P}_0^{-1}$ are common to all investors; now post-multiply both sides of (B.4) by $\underline{P}_0$ and note that with both $\underline{P}_0$ and $\underline{n}_0$ diagonal, we have $\underline{n} \underline{P}_0 = \underline{P}_0 \underline{n}$.

where

$$\alpha_m = (\Sigma_k \alpha_k^{-1} h_{Wk})^{-1} \tag{B.7}$$

and

$$\omega_m = [\Sigma_k h_{Wk} \cdot \alpha_k^{-1} \cdot \omega_k]/\alpha_m. \tag{B.8}$$

Consequently, *the equilibrium market values of all securities are those which would be established by the entire market as a single decision-maker*, where the elasticity of the market's 'as if' utility function is proportional to a weighted harmonic average of the elasticities of the individual investors in the market (equation (B.7)), $h_{Wk} = W_{0k}/\Sigma_k W_{0k} = W_{0k}/W_{0m}$ and the shadow price ω_m of the market's investable wealth is a simple weighted average of the individual investor's ω_k, where the weights are the product of the fraction of the market's total funds in the hands of the individual investor and the reciprocal of the elasticity of his utility function (equation (B.8)). Equation (B.6) is the equivalent in matrix notation of (14) in the text on p. 192.

B.3. *Current stock prices as present values*

Our assumption that ω_m which serves as the riskless discount rate is constant over time, together with our assumption that all investors act in terms of constant elasticity utility functions with a constant market weighted average α_m over time, justify setting the certainty-equivalent of the total relative return (dividend and price increment) equal to ω_m for all time intervals, regardless of the autocorrelation of the prospective receipts.[1] But as we show just below, the fact that future stock-market prices, as well as future dividends, are uncertain requires that the market clearing differential equation for any stock at any time τ be written

$$\hat{D}_\tau/\hat{P}_\tau + d\log \hat{P}_\tau/d\tau = \omega_m \tag{B.9}$$

after reflecting the variance of the logarithms of market prices as well as those of the cash dividend receipt itself in the certainty-equivalent $\hat{D}_\tau$. With this convention, the ratio of the certainty-equivalent of the future dividend receipt $\hat{D}_\tau$ to the certainty-equivalent of the market price may be treated as if it were a certain dividend yield to be received at time τ, and the relative growth rate of the certainty-equivalent of market prices $\hat{P}_\tau$ may be treated as a sure

---

[1] See n. 1, p. 193 above.

capital gain to be realized at that time. The required general functional relation between the certainty equivalents of the dividend receipts and market prices over all *future* time, the solution of (B.9), is shown in equation (15) of the text.

We can most easily demonstrate that (B.9) is the appropriate form of the market clearing differential equation under our assumptions by considering two special cases. Consider for the moment that the rate of dividend which will be received at any time τ is pre-known with certainty to follow the steady-state growth path $D_\tau = D_0 \exp(g_D\tau)$, but that the stock price in the market is a lognormally distributed random multiple of this known dividend, i.e. $\hat{P}_\tau = \exp(\tilde{M}_\tau)D_\tau$. The random exponent $\tilde{M}$ for any short interval $\varDelta\tau$ beginning at τ is the normally distributed variable $\varDelta_\tau\tilde{M}_\tau = \varDelta_\tau\overline{M}_\tau + \epsilon_{M\tau}$. Let ϵ_M be independently distributed between *any* pairs of short time intervals $\varDelta\tau$, with the same variance $\sigma_M^2\varDelta\tau$ in any single short interval $\varDelta\tau$, and let the expectation $\varDelta_\tau\overline{M}_\tau$ be the same for all possible values of $\varDelta\tau$ and τ. We now recall that with constant elasticity utility functions, the logarithm of the certainty-equivalent of a lognormally random future receipt is equal to the expectation of the exponent less its variance (weighted by $\alpha_M/2$). From $\tilde{P}_\tau = D_0 \exp(g_D\tau) \exp(\tilde{M})\tau$ we thus have

$$\log \hat{P}_{\tau+\varDelta\tau} - \log \hat{P}_\tau = \varDelta \log \hat{P}_\tau = g_D\varDelta_\tau - \alpha_M\sigma_M^2\varDelta\tau/2$$

which in the limit as $\varDelta\tau \to 0$, gives

(a) $$d \log \tilde{P}_\tau/d\tau = g_D - \alpha_M\sigma_M^2/2 = \hat{g}_P.$$

In this simplified context, therefore, our differential requirement for the determination of the certainty-equivalents of future market prices would be

(b) $$D_\tau/P_\tau + \hat{g}_P = \omega_M$$

or

(c) $$D_\tau + d\hat{P}_\tau/d\tau = \omega_M\hat{P}_t.$$

The general solution of this equation is

(d) $$\hat{P}_t = \int_t^\infty D_t \exp[(g_D - \alpha_M\sigma_M^2/2) (\tau - t)] \exp[-\omega_M(\tau - t)]d\tau.$$

Note that even though the dividend receipt D_τ has been assumed to be certain, as a result of the uncertainty in market prices this value equation is *precisely* equivalent to

(e) $$\hat{P}_t = \int_t^\infty \hat{D}_\tau \exp[-\omega_M(\tau-t)] d\tau$$

if we set

(f) $$\hat{D}_\tau = D_t \exp[(g_D - \alpha\sigma_M^2/2)(\tau-t)],$$

which amounts to diminishing the certain dividend $D_\tau = D_t \exp[g_D(\omega_M - t)]$ to the indicated certainty-equivalent dividend receipt by changing it with the logarithmic variance of the random market price.

Now suppose in the alternative that M is a fixed nonrandom number (with $\sigma_M^2 = 0$), but that dividends are random and satisfy the assumptions made in section III.1. We now have $\tilde{D}_\tau$ for any future time τ a lognormal variable with $E(\log \tilde{D}_\tau) = \bar{g}_D\tau$ and var $(\log \tilde{D}_\tau)$ $= \tau\sigma_{g_D}^2$. Assessing the certainty equivalent of the dividend receipt in isolation using our constant elasticity utility function, we would have $\hat{D}_\tau = D_0 \exp(\bar{g}_D - \alpha_M\sigma_{g_D}^0)$. Moreover, since $\tilde{P}_\tau$ is now strictly and nonrandomly proportional to $\tilde{D}_\tau$, i.e. $\tilde{P}_\tau = \exp(M)\tilde{D}_\tau$, we would have the certainty-equivalent market price $\hat{P}_\tau = \exp(M)\hat{D}_\tau$, since var$(\log \tilde{P}_\tau) = var(\log \tilde{D}_\tau)$. We have thus established that *with lognormal distributions and constant elasticity utility functions, the certainty-equivalent of future market prices $\hat{P}_t$ when dividends are certain but price-dividend multiples are random is the same as the $\hat{p}_t$ when the P/D multiples are nonrandom and dividends are uncertain; in both cases, the certainty-equivalent of future prices $\hat{P}_t$ is the capitalization at the riskless rate of the certainty-equivalents of the future dividend stream when the dividend stream is changed with the uncertainty of the market prices.* Since the effects of either random multiples or randomness in the dividend receipt can be validly reflected in the definition of a certainty-equivalent dividend, their combined effects can be, as we have done.

Equations (B.4) and (15) consequently require that the certainty-equivalent log $\hat{D}_t$ must be charged with the variance of log $\tilde{P}_t$ as well as with the variance of log $\tilde{D}_t$, the random dividend itself. Now it is clear that under uncertainty with the expectationally steady-state growth conditions we are assuming, the *expected* growth rates of dividends and market values along their respective exponential trends will be equal (i.e. $\bar{g}_P = \bar{g}_D$ for any firm). It is also clear that (after netting out the 'systematic risk' due to covariance with prices of other stocks, which we reintroduced below) the deviations of log $\hat{P}_\tau$ from its trend values will be *positively* (but imperfectly) *correlated* with the deviations of log $\hat{P}_{D_\tau}$ from its trend, because investors (properly) believe changes in dividends convey information concerning (at least management's judgments regarding) the future prospects of a company. It follows that the variance of log $(\hat{P}_\tau + \hat{D}_\tau)$ will be often substantially larger than the logarithmic variances of the firm's dividends (and other operating results) about exponential trends. Since it is clear that the firm's policy choices with respect to company growth rates will directly deal with the latter variances, we will use σ_g^2 to represent the logarithmic variance of the company's operations and use a large multiple of this variance $C\sigma_g^2$ (with $C >> 1$) to represent the variance of the relative return on ith stock (including both dividend receipt and stock value) apart from covariance considerations.

Finally, we must also allow for the fact that their market equilibrium conditions given in equation (14) show that the current market value of any ith stock at any time, and the certainty equivalent $\hat{g}_i$ of its growth in value in the next unit period, will vary inversely with the weighted sum of its *covariances* with other securities, as well as with its 'own' variance which we have considered so far. The analysis is much simplified – and turns out to include all the major results needed for this paper – if we treat the summed covariance term as a constant, and we shall do so here.[1] To avoid misunderstanding, however, it must be emphasized that this does *not* involve setting *any* covariances to zero, nor ignoring their important role in determining stock values. It simply means that we will treat the summed covariances as a scalar parameter of the analysis and not also examine the effects of *changes* in covariances at this time.[2] This seems to be a reasonable simplification in the context of the principal

[1] The fuller analysis including the effects of changes in covariances will be published in [21].

[2] Actually the analysis is considerably more general. Consider a 'single (external) factor' model specified as $\tilde{g}_i = a_i + b_i z + u_i$ where the external index z and residual u_i are measured as deviations from their means. We have $E(z) = E(u) = 0$, and variances σ_z^2 and σ_u^2 but covariances $\sigma_{zu} = 0$. Then $\bar{g}_i = a_i$ and $\sigma_i^2 = b_i^2 \sigma_z^2 + \sigma_{u_i}$ and covariances between stock i and j are $\sigma_{ij} = b_i b_j \sigma_z^2$. Let the policy mix of the ith company be indexed by x. In terms of this popular model of stock prices, we have $d\tilde{g}_i/dx_i = da_i/dx_i$ regardless of db_i/dx_i. But $d\sigma_i/dx_i = 2b_i \sigma_z^2 db_i/dx_i + d\sigma_u^2$, and $d\sigma_{ij}/dx_i = b_j \sigma_z^2 db_u/dx_i$. The simplification in the text simply involves holding b_i constant and treating db_i/dx_i as zero, so that $d\sigma_i^2/dx_i = d\sigma_{u_i}^2/dx_i$ and $d\sigma_{ij}/dx_i = 0$. If the signs of db_i/dx_i and $d\sigma_{u_i}^2$ *are the same* (*either* positive *or* negative) and all $b_j > 0$, then the covariance effect will be a monotonic increasing function of the 'own variance' effect of changes in policies, and the analysis in the text would include the effects of *changes* in (as well as the *level* of) covariances with a simple adjustment of parameters.

issues raised in this paper, since a company's growth policy will usually be concerned primarily with changes in its policy mix which will raise its growth *relative* to other firms' and its uncertainties relative to those inherent in the general economy.

Since total differentiation of the equilibrium set (14) with covariance terms held constant shows that $df_{im}^*/d\bar{g}_i$ and $(-df_{im}^*/d\sigma_i^2)$ vary inversely with the (fixed) level of covariances, it is appropriate to represent the certainty equivalent $\exp(\hat{g}_i)$ by

$$\exp(\hat{g}_i) = \exp[\bar{g}_i - \alpha_m \sigma_i^2/2 - \alpha_m f(\sigma_{ij})], \qquad (B.10)$$

where $f(\sigma_{ij})$ represents the covariance terms held constant, and the subscript i refers to the ith group. But since $\bar{g}_p = \bar{g}_D$ for this stock, and the logarithmic variance of its ending value (including dividend receipt) is a multipe C of $\sigma_{g_D}^2$, we have finally for the certainty-equivalent over *any* short time period:

$$\exp(\hat{g}_i) = \exp(\hat{g}_D) = \exp[\bar{g}_D - \alpha_m C \sigma_{g_D}^2 - \alpha_m f(\sigma_{ij})] \qquad (B.11)$$

which directly gives (16) in the text.

C. MATHEMATICAL NOTES FOR SECTION IV

C.1. *Preliminaries*

When variances increase with futurity, the equations for stock prices (26') and duration (32) derived on pp. 207–8 involve the ordinate $f(w) = (2\pi)^{-1/2} \exp(-w^2/2)$ and right tail area $G(w) = \int_w^\infty f(\S)d\S$ of the standardized normal density function, as well as its right tail 'linear loss' function[1] $L(w) = f(w) - wG(w)$. By direct differentiation, we have

$$f'(w) = -wf(w), \quad G'(w) = -f(w), \quad L'(w) = -G(w). \qquad (C.1,2,3)$$

It will be convenient to make use of four newly defined variables. Lemmas proving their indicated sign for all finite values of w are established in section C.5 below.

$$\phi_1(w) = G(w) - wL(w) = G(w) - wf(w) + w^2 G(w) \qquad (C.4)$$
$$= (1 + w^2)G(w) - wf(w) > 0.$$
$$\phi_2(w) = G^2(w) - f(w)L(w) > 0. \qquad (C.5)$$

[1] See n. 3, p. 208 above.

$$\phi_3(w) = G^2(w) - L^2(w) - f(w)L(w) < 0. \tag{C.6}$$

$$\phi_4(w) = G(w)L(w) - w\phi_2(w) = 2G(w)L(w) - f(w)\phi_1(w) > 0, \tag{C.7}$$
$$= f(w)G(w) - 2wG^2(w) + wf(w)L(w) > 0.$$

C.2. *Properties of stock prices P_0 and duration T_3*

First note that the partial variation of both stock prices and duration with respect to our intermediate variable w (defined in equation (30)) is negative, since using (26′) (27′), (32) and (C.1–3) we have[1]

$$\partial A_3/\partial w = [-f^2(w) + wf(w)G(w)]/f^2(w)R \tag{C.8}$$
$$= -L(w)/f(w)R = -B_3 R,$$

and

$$\partial T_3/\partial w = [(-G^2(w) + f(w)L(w))/RG^2(w)] = -\phi_1(w)/RG^2(w) < 0 \tag{C.9}$$

by (C.5) and Lemma 2.

The statements in the text that both prices and duration vary directly with $\bar{g}$ and inversely with ω_m, $\sigma_{g_D}^2$ and covariances $f(\sigma_{ij})$, follow directly from the fact that R is independent of these four variables, and w varies directly with ω_m, $\sigma_{g_D}^2$ and $f(\sigma_{ij})$, but inversely with $\bar{g}$.

Now note that R varies directly with α_m, C and σ_w^2, while the numerator of w varies inversely with α_m and C. We have for α_m using (C.8) and $\partial w/\partial\alpha_m = R^{-1}(C\sigma_{g_D}^2 - w\partial R/\partial\alpha_m)$,

$$\partial P_0/\partial\alpha_m = D_0 \partial A_3/\partial\alpha_m = D_0\left[\frac{\partial A_3}{\partial w}\frac{\partial w}{\partial\alpha_m} + \frac{\partial A_w}{\partial R}\frac{\partial R}{\partial\alpha_m}\right] \tag{C.10}$$
$$= -D_0 B_3 C\sigma_{g_D}^2 + D_0[R^2 f(w)]^{-1}[wL(w) - G(w)]\partial R/\partial\alpha_3$$

which is everywhere negative since $G(w) > wL(w)$ by (C.4) and Lemma 1. For the duration T_3 with α_m, we have similarly, using (C.9),

$$\frac{\partial T_3}{\partial\alpha_3} = \frac{\partial T_3}{\partial w}\frac{\partial w}{\partial\alpha_w} + \frac{\partial T_3}{\partial R}\frac{\partial R}{\partial\alpha_m} \tag{C.11}$$
$$= \frac{-\phi_2(w)C\sigma_D^2 + [w\phi_2(w) - G(w)L(w)]\partial R/\partial\alpha_m}{R^2 G^2(w)}$$

which again is everywhere negative by (C.7) and Lemma 4. The signs of both derivatives on C are obviously the same as on α_3. Both

---

[1] Note that from (C.18) we have $\partial \log A_3/\partial w = -B_3 R/A_3 = -T_3 R$, using (32), and since $\partial w/\partial\bar{g}^0 = -R^{-1}$, we have $[(\partial A/\partial_3 w)/A_3](\partial w/\partial\bar{g}_D^0) = T_3$, which is used in moving from (33b) to (34b) in the text.

derivatives of σ_u^2 are also strictly negative by Lemmas 1 and 4, since the expressions are the same as (C.10) and (C.11) with the first terms on the right omitted, and the signs of $\partial R/\partial\alpha_m$ and $\partial R/\partial\sigma_u^2$ are both positive. This completes our proofs that both P_0 and T_3 also vary inversely with σ_m, C and σ_u^2 as asserted. For later references, however, we write out, using (C.9),

$$\partial T_3/\partial\sigma_u^2 = [\partial T_3/\partial R + (\partial T_3/\partial w)\,(\partial w/\partial R)]\,(\partial R/\partial\sigma_u^2) \tag{C.12}$$
$$= [-L(w)/R^2G(w) - \{\phi_2(w)/RG^2(w)\}\,(-w/R)]\,(\alpha_m C/R)$$
$$= [w\phi_1(w) - G(w)L(w)]\alpha_m C/R^3G^2(w)$$
$$= -\alpha_m C\phi_4(w)/R^3G^2(w) < 0.$$

C.3. Stability conditions on policy variations in section IV.4 of the text

With σ_u^2 exogenous, $R = \sqrt{(2\alpha_m C\sigma_u^2)}$ is not affected by the firm's decisions. In this section, consequently, R is treated as a *constant* in all equations. The simultaneous necessary conditions on v_0 and r for a maximum, (33a) and (33b) in the text using (35), become

$$P_1 = \partial P/\partial v_0 = P_0 T_3(\partial\hat{g}_D^0/\partial v_0) = 0 \tag{C.13}$$

and

$$P_2 = \partial P/\partial r = P_0[-(1-r)^{-1} + T_3(\partial\bar{g}_D/\partial r)] = 0. \tag{C.14}$$

The sufficient conditions require that $P_{11} < 0$, $P_{22} < 0$, and $P_{11}P_{22} > (P_{12})^2$, which are insured by the conditions imposed on our constraints in (11) and (11'). This is proved as follows.

$$P_{11} = P_0[(\partial T_3/\partial v_0)\,(\partial\hat{g}_D^0/\partial v_0) + T_3(\partial^2\hat{g}_D/\partial v_0^2)] \tag{C.15}$$
$$= P_0 T_3(\partial^2\bar{g}_D/\partial v_0^2) < 0,$$

since $P_1 = 0$ requires $\partial\hat{g}_D^0/\partial v_0 = 0$; $r = r^* < 1$; $T_3 > 0$ everywhere, and $\partial^2\hat{g}_D^0/\partial v_0^2$ and $\partial^2\hat{g}_D^0/\partial v_0^2 < 0$ by (11c) and equation (34a) in the text.

We also have

$$P_{22} = P_0[-(1-r)^{-2} + T_3(\partial^2\bar{g}_D/\partial r^2) + (\partial\bar{g}_D/\partial r)\,(\partial T_3/\partial r)], \tag{C.16}$$

and we can prove $P_{22} < 0$ by showing that the *sum* of the first and third terms is negative, since the second term is negative by (11a). Using (C.9) and $\partial w/\partial r = -(\partial\bar{g}/\partial r)/R$, we have

$$\partial T_3/\partial r = (\partial T_3/\partial w)\,(\partial w/\bar{g}_D)\,(\partial\bar{g}_D/\partial r) = [\phi_1(w)/R^2G^2(w)]\,(\partial\bar{g}_D/\partial r) > 0, \tag{C.17}$$

so that

$$-(1-r)^2 + (\partial \bar{g}_D/\partial r)\,(\partial T_3/\partial r) = -(1-r)^{-2} + [\phi_1(w)/R^2 G^2(w)]\,(\partial \bar{g}_D/\partial r)^2.$$

Finally, from (C.14), we have $(\partial \bar{g}_D/\partial r)^2 = [(1-r)T_3]^{-2}$, so that

$$-(1-r)^{-2} + (\partial \bar{g}_D/\partial r)\,(\partial T_3/\partial r) = (1-r)^{-2}\{-1 + \phi_1(w)/T_3^2 R^2 G^2(w)\} \quad \text{(C.18}$$
$$= \phi_3(w)/(1-r)^2 L^2(w) < 0,$$

where we have used $T_3^2 R^2 G^2(w) = L^2(w)$ from (32), and $\phi_1(w) - L^2(w) = \phi_3(w)$ from (C.4) and (C.6). The sign follows from the fact that $r^* < 1$ and $\phi_3(w) < 0$ for all $w < \infty$ by Lemma (3). Q.E.D.

For reference, substituting (C.18) in (C.16) makes

$$P_{22} = P_0[T_3(\partial^2 \bar{g}_D/\partial r^2) + \phi_3(w)/(1-r)^2 L^2(w)] < 0. \quad \text{(C.19)}$$

Now to prove that $P_{11}P_{22} > (P_{12})^2$, we note that from (C.13) we have,[1] at the point where $P_1 = P_2 = 0$,

$$P_{12} = \partial^2 P/\partial v_0 \partial r = P_0 T_3(\partial \hat{g}_D^0/\partial v \delta r) = P_0 T_3(\partial \bar{g}_D^0/\partial v \delta r). \quad \text{(C.20)}$$

Since $P_{11} < 0$ and $\phi_3(w) < 0$ in (C.19), we will have $P_{11}P_{22} > (P_{12})^2$ if from (C.15) and the balance of (C.19) we have

$$P_0 T_3(\partial^2 \hat{g}_D^0/\partial v_0^2) \cdot P_0 T_3(\partial^2 \bar{g}_D/\partial r^2) > [P_0 T_3(\partial \hat{g}_D^0/\partial v_0 \partial r)]^2$$

or

$$(\partial^2 \hat{g}_D^0/\partial v_0^2)\,(\partial^2 \bar{g}_D/\partial r^2) > (\partial \hat{g}_D^0/\partial v_0 \partial r)^2,$$

which is precisely the concavity assumed in the constraint function (11). Q.E.D.

We proved that stock price and the duration T_3 varies inversely with σ_u^2 in section C.2 above. In order to show that the optimal retention ratio also varies inversely with σ_u^2, we treat[2] P_2 as an implicit function of r^* and σ_u^2 in (C.14) which gives

$$dr^*/d\sigma_u^2 = -(\partial P_2/\partial_u^2)/\partial P_2/\partial r^*) \quad \text{(C.21)}$$
$$= -\frac{[(\partial \bar{g}_D/\partial r)\,(\partial T_3/\partial \sigma_u^2) + (T_3(\partial^2 \bar{g}_D/\partial r \partial(\sigma_u^2))]}{[-(1+r^*)^{-2} + (\partial \bar{g}_D/\partial r)\,(\partial T_3/\partial r) + T_3(\partial^2 \bar{g}_D/\partial r^{*2})]}$$

Using (11a), (C.12) and (11c), it is apparent that the numerator is negative, since the cross-derivative in its second term is zero.

---

[1] The last equation in (C.20) follows from differentiating (34a) in the text.

[2] Since the use of $\partial \bar{g}_D/\partial r$ in place of $\partial \hat{g}_D^0/\partial r$ in (C.14) insures the simultaneous satisfaction of (C.13), a proof that $\partial r^*/\partial \sigma^u$ when $P_2 = 0$ in (C.14) suffices to establish the inverse relation without further reference to the other condition $P_1 = 0$.

Consequently, the total differential is negative because the last term in the denominator is negative by (11a), and the first two terms taken together are negative, as was shown in (C.18). Q.E.D.

C.4. *Notes for section IV.5 in the text*: σ_u^2 *depends partially on* v_0

We now work with (36) $\sigma_u^2 = \sigma_{u0}^2 + f(v_0)$, with $f'(v) > 0$ and $f''(v_0) < 0$. The first term in equation (37) is strictly negative as asserted in the text if $\partial A_3/\partial R < 0$; using (C.4) and $\partial w/\partial R = -w/R$, we have

$$\frac{\partial A_3}{\partial R} = -\frac{G(w)}{R^2 f(w)} - \frac{L(w)}{R f(w)} \frac{\partial w}{\partial R} = -\frac{\phi_1(w)}{R^2 f(w)} < 0 \qquad (C.22)$$

by Lemma 1. Q.E.D.

Since $\partial \log A_3/\partial g_D = T_3$ as shown in fn. 1, p. 234, equation (37) can be written out in full as

$$P_1 = \partial P_0/\partial v_0 = P_0[-\alpha_m C\phi_1(w)f'(v_0)/R^2 G(w) + T_3(\partial \hat{g}_D/\partial v_0)] = 0 \quad (C.23)$$

after using (C.22) and (27'). This is our first necessary condition for a maximum. The second is given by

$$P_2 = \partial P_0/\partial r = P_0[-(1-r)^{-1} + T_3(\partial \hat{g}_D^0/\partial r)] = 0. \qquad (C.24)$$

It is obvious that $P_{22} < 0$, and we assume sufficient concavity in $v(r)$ and $f(v_0)$ and in equation (11c) to insure $P_{11} < 0$ and $P_{11}P_{22} > (P_{12})^2$ as well.

On p. 212 we described the strong and probably dominant channels by which a positive dependence of the rate of increase (σ_u^2) in variances with futurity upon the basic risk parameter v_0 would tend to reduce a firm's optimal retention ratios, but we recognized that these would be at least partially offset by a 'substitution' effect. To isolate the latter, we can solve within the bracket of (C.24) for $\partial \hat{g}_D^0/\partial v_0$ and substitute in (C.28) using (35). The latter bracket set to zero then gives the condition for optimal retentions when optimal policies $v_0 = v_0^*$ are continuously being followed. This requirement on retention ratios then reads

$$P_2 = -(1-r)^{-1} + T_3 \partial \bar{g}_D/\partial r + [\alpha_m Cf'(v_0)\phi_1(w)/R^2 G(w)]v'(r) = 0.$$
$$(C.24a)$$

For convenience, let $f'(v) = \zeta$, and consider the sign of the total derivative $dr^*/d\zeta$ in (C.24a). Since $P_{22} < 0$, the change in r^* will have the same sign as the partial derivative of $\partial P_2/\partial \zeta$. Since $\partial^2 \bar{g}/\partial r \partial \zeta$ is zero by assumption, we have[1]

$$\frac{\partial P_2}{\partial \zeta} = \left(\frac{\partial \bar{g}}{\partial r}\right)\left(\frac{\partial T_3}{\partial \sigma_u^2}\right)\left(\frac{\partial \sigma_u^2}{\partial \zeta}\right) + [\alpha_m C \phi_1(w)/R^2 G(w)]v'(r) \qquad (C.25)$$
$$- \alpha_m C \zeta v'(r)[\phi_1(w)G(w) + w\phi_4(w)](R^3 G^2(w))^{-1}(\partial R/\partial \zeta).$$

The second term is positive. The third term (including preceding sign) is negative when $w > 0$ (since $\phi_1(w)$ and $\phi_2(w)$ are both > 0 for *all* w by Lemmas 1 and 4 and equations (C.4) and (C.7)), but will turn positive when w is absolutely large and < 0. Within the first full term, the first element $\partial \bar{g}/\partial r$ is positive by constraint (11a); and the second element $\partial T_3/\partial \sigma_u^2$ is always negative by (C.12); while $\partial \sigma_u^2/\partial \zeta = v_0 + (\partial \sigma_u^2/\partial v_0)(dv_0/d\zeta)$. We have $v_0 > 0$, $\zeta > 0$, and $(\partial \sigma^2/\partial v_0) > 0$, but $dv_0/d\zeta$ is negative because of the requirement that $P_1 = 0$ for an optimum in (C.23). Although it seems reasonable to expect the negative product $(\partial T_3/\partial \sigma_u^2)v_0$ to dominate the entire expression in most cases, it is clear that at least partially offsetting interactions are always involved.

C.5. *Proofs of lemmas for equations (C.4)–(C.7)*

Lemma 1: $\phi_1(w) > 0$ for all $w < \infty$.
Proof: $\phi'_1 < 0$ for all $w < \infty$ since $\phi'_1(w) = wG(w) - f(w) - L(w)$ $= -2L(w) < 0$ for all $w < \infty$. But with $\phi'_1(w) < 0$ for all $w < \infty$ and $\phi_1(\infty) = 0$, it necessarily follows that $\phi_1(w) > 0$ for all $w < \infty$. Q.E.D.

Lemma 2: $\phi_2(w) = G^2(w) - f(w)L(w) > 0$ for all $w < \infty$.
Proof: $\phi'_2(w) = 2G(w)f(w) + f(w)G(w) + wL(w)f(w)$
$$= -f(w)G(w) + wf(w)L(w) = -f(w)\phi_1(w).$$
But by *Lemma* 1, $\phi_1(w) > 0$ for all $w < \infty$, so that $\phi'_2(w) < 0$ for all $w < \infty$. Since $\phi_2(\infty) = 0$, it then follows that $\phi_2(w) > 0$ for all $w < \infty$. Q.E.D.

Lemma 3: $\phi_3(w) = G^2(w) - L^2(w) - f(w)L(w) < 0$ for all $w < \infty$.
Proof: $\phi'_3(w) = 2L(w)G(w) - 2G(w)f(w) + f(w)G(w) + wf(w)L(w)$
$$= 2L(w)G(w) - f(w)\phi_1$$
$$\phi''_3(w) = -2G^2(w) - 2f(w)L(w) + wf(w)\phi_1 - f(w)\phi'_1$$
$$= -2G^2(w) + wf(w)\phi_1.$$

[1] As intermediate steps, we note that $\partial[\phi_1(w)/G(w)]/\partial w = [\phi_1(w)f(w) - 2G(w)L(w)]/G^2(w) = -\phi_4(w)/G^2(w)$ and $\partial w/\partial \zeta = (-w/R)(\partial R/\partial \zeta)$, and $\partial R/\partial \zeta > 0$.

CORPORATE GROWTH UNDER UNCERTAINTY 239

$$\phi'_3{}''(w) = 4G(w)f(w) + wf(w)\phi'_1 - w^2 f(w)\phi_1 + f(w)\phi_1$$
$$= 4G(w)f(w) - 2wf(w)L(w) - (w^2 - 1)f(w)\phi_1$$
$$= f(w)X(w)$$

where

$$X(w) = 2G(w) - (w^2 - 3)\ \phi_1,$$ and since $f(w) > 0$, $\phi'_3{}''(w)$ will have the same sign as $X(w)$. But $X'(w) = -2f(w) + 2(w^2 - 3)L(w) - 2w\phi_1 = 4[(w^2 - 1)L(w) - f(w)]$, and sgn $X''(w) =$ sgn $[2wL(w) - (w^2 - 1)G(w) + wf(w)] =$ sgn $[3wL(w) + G(w)] \geqslant 0$ for all $w \geqslant 0$. Since $X''(w) \geqslant 0$ for all $w \geqslant 0$ and $X'(\infty) = 0$, we have $X'(w) \leqslant 0$ for all $w \geqslant 0$; and since $X'(\infty) = 0$, we have proved that $X(w) > 0$, and therefore that $\phi'''(w) \geqslant 0$ for all $w \geqslant 0$.

Now since $\phi'''(\infty) = 0$, it follows that $\phi_3{}''(w) < 0$ for all $w \geqslant 0$. But since $f(w) \geqslant 0$ and $\phi_1(w) > 0$ for *all* $w < \infty$, using Lemma 1, it is obvious from $\phi''(w) = wf(w)\phi_1(w) - 2G^2(w)$ above that $\phi_3{}''(w) < 0$ for all $w \leqslant 0$. These two steps together show that $\phi''(w) < 0$ for *all* $w < \infty$. Using this result, and the fact that $\phi_3{}''(\infty) = 0$, we see that $\phi_3'(w) > 0$ for all $w < \infty$; and finally, since $\phi'_3(\infty) = 0$, we have $\phi_3(w) < 0$ for all $w < \infty$. Q.E.D.

Lemma 4: $\phi'_4(w) = G(w)L(w) - w\phi_2(w) > 0$ for all $w < \infty$.
Proof: $\phi'_4(w) = -G^2(w) - f(w)L(w) - \phi_2(w) - w\phi'_2(w)$
$$= -2G^2(w) - w\phi'_2(w)$$
$$= -2G^2(w) + wf(w)\phi_1(w) = \phi''_3(w)$$ above, which is < 0 for all $w < \infty$ by the proof in Lemma 3. Finally, since $\phi_4(\infty) = 0$, we have $\phi_4(w) > 0$ for all $w < \infty$. Q.E.D.

References

[1] Aitchison, J., and Brown, J. A. C., *The Lognormal Distribution* (Cambridge Univ. Press, 1963) (57).
[2] Arrow, Kenneth J., 'Optimal Capital Policy with Irreversible Investment', in *Value, Capital and Growth*, ed. J. N. Wolfe (Edinburgh University Press, 1968).
[3] Baumol, Wm J., *Business Behavior, Value and Growth* (Macmillan, New York, 1959).
[4] ———, 'On the Theory of the Expansion of the Firm', *American Economic Review* (Dec 1962).
[5] Brittain, John A., *Corporate Dividend Policy* (Brookings Institution, Washington, 1966).
[6] Brown, Donaldson, 'Pricing Policy in Relation to Fiancial Control', *Management and Administration* (Feb, Mar and Apr 1924).

[7] Dean, Joel, *Managerial Economics* (Prentice-Hall, New York, 1951).

[8] Dhrymes, Phoebus J., and Kurz, Mordecai, 'Investment, Dividend and External Financing Behavior of Firms', in *Determinants of Investment Behavior* (National Bureau of Economic Research, Columbia Univ. Press, 1967).

[9] Donaldson, Gordon, *Corporate Debt Capacity* Division of Research, Harvard Business School, Boston, 1961).

[10] Downie, J., *The Competitive Process* (Duckworth, London, 1958).

[11] Hakansson, N., 'Risk Disposition, the Chauchy Equations, and the Separation Theorem', forthcoming in *Econometrica*.

[12] Hicks, John R., *Value and Capital*, 2nd. (Clarendon Press, Oxford, 1946).

[13] ——, *Capital and Growth* (Oxford University Press, 1965).

[14] Kaplan, Donald M., 'The Corporate Capital, Structure and Marginal Financing Decisions', unpublished dissertation, University of California at Los Angeles, 1969.

[15] Leland, Hayne Ellis, 'Dynamic Portfolio Theory', unpublished Ph.D. dissertation, Harvard University, May 1968.

[16] Lintner, John, 'Distribution of Incomes of Corporations among dividends, Retained Earnings and Taxes', *American Economic Review* (May 1956).

[17] ——, 'The Cost of Capital and Optimal Financing of Corporate Growth', *Journal of Finance* (May 1963).

[18] ——, 'Optimal Dividends and Corporate Growth under Uncertainty', *Quarterly Journal of Economics* (Feb 1964).

[19] ——, 'Corporate Finance: Risk and Investment', in *Determinants of Investment Behavior* (N.B.E.R., Columbia Univ. Press, 1967).

[20] ——, 'Equilibrium in a Lognormal Securities Market', *Journal of Financial and Quantitative Analysis* (forthcoming).

[21] ——, *Contributions to the Theory of the Firm and Capital Markets* (Division of Research, Harvard Business School, forthcoming).

[22] ——, Lewellen, Wilbur G., 'Management and Ownership in the Large Firm', *Journal of Finance* (May 1969).

[23] ——, and Huntsman, Blaine, 'Managerial Pay and Corporate Performance', *American Economic Review* (June 1970).

[24] Macauley, Frederick R., *Some Theoretical Problems Suggested by the Movements of Interest Rates, Bond Yields and Stock Prices in the United States since 1856* (National Bureau of Economic Research, New York, 1938).

[25] Marris, Robin, *The Economic Theory of 'Managerial' Capitalism* (Free Press of Glencoe, 1964).

[25a] Meyer, Richard, 'On the Relationship among the Utility of Assets, the Utility of Consumption, and Investment Strategy in an Uncertain but Time-Invariant World', *Proceedings of the Fourth International IFORS Conference* (Venice, June 1969).

[26] Mossin, Jan, 'Optimal Multi-Period Portfolio Policies', *Journal of Business* (Apr 1968).

[27] Nerlove, Marc, and Arrow, Kenneth J., 'Optimal Advertising under Dynamic Conditions', *Economica* (May 1962).

[28] Penrose, Edith, *The Theory of the Growth of the Firm* (Blackwell, Oxford, 1959).

[29] Pratt, John W., 'Discounting Certainties, Stationary Preference, and the Value of Immediate Resolution' (mimeo, 7 Dec 1966), paper read at Seminar on Decisions under Uncertainty, Harvard Business School.

[30] Raiffa, Howard and Schlaifer, Robt, *Applied Statistical Decision Theory* (Division of Research, Harvard Business School, Boston, 1961).

[31] Solow, Robert M., 'Some Implications of Alternative Criteria for the Firm', Chapter 10 of this volume.

[32] ——, 'Technical Progress, Capital Formation, and Economic Growth', *American Economic Review* (May 1962).

[33] Steiner, Peter O., and Dorfman, Robert, 'Optimal Advertising and Optimal Quality', *American Economic Review* (Sep 1954).

[34] Turnovsky, Stephen J., 'The Allocation of Corporate Profits between Dividends and Retained Earnings', *Review of Economics and Statistics* (Nov 1967).

[35] Williamson, John, 'Profit, Growth and Sales Maximization', *Economica* (Feb 1966).

8 Modern Monopolies in Economic Development[1]

Siro Lombardini

I. DIFFERENT KINDS OF MONOPOLIES

In an economy which is substantially competitive, the main consequences of a few monopolistic situations are the price distortions
which have been analysed by the neo-classical economists. The
picture changes entirely if monopolistic situations are supposed to
be diffuse (we may then speak of a monopolistic economy). The
problem of price distortion is then superseded by the problem of the
interactions between the strategy of the firm and the dynamics of the
economy. We shall call 'monopolistic' that behaviour of the firm
which is capable of maintaining (in the long run) a profit margin
higher than 'normal' or of surviving for a long period in spite of
having costs higher than is technically and commercially necessary
(for instance because of higher wages or of special bonuses granted
to persons and bodies inside and outside the firms).

In fact the monopolistic firms can enjoy a higher rate of growth if
they can command a disproportionately large or productive share of
total national investment. This can occur if:

(a) There is a precapitalistic sector allowing an almost infinitely
    elastic supply of labour to be utilized in enlarging the capital-
    istic sector. When such a situation occurs, the monopolistic
    firms cause a break in the economic situation; we can then
    speak of *breaking monopolies*. Breaking monopolies have
    played an important role in the development of a few countries
    like Italy.[2] Their effect is the net result of the positive effects of

[1] I am indebted to Robin Marris and Terenzio Cozzi who have contributed
criticism and advice.
[2] S. Lombardini, 'Les oligopoles en Italie', *Revue Économique*, no. 6 (1965).
The interaction between the policy of the breaking monopolies and the economic
process may explain the emergence of transforming monopolies or the tendencies

the increased accumulation, of the negative effects of the price distortion and of some feedback effects which may be positive (as, for example, urbanization) or negative (as, for example, the curtailment of some free initiative).

(b) There are substantial possibilities of transforming the technology of the economy. To achieve such a transformation, large investments and a certain control of the market are required. We shall then speak of *transforming monopolies*.

Both the breaking and the transforming monopolies are of a transient type. Once the precapitalistic sectors are exhausted and the technological transformation completed, the maintenance of monopolistic power is jeopardized: a transformation of the system will occur.

When monopolies merely try to exploit barriers to entry to keep prices as high as possible, lacking either of the two above-mentioned conditions, we shall speak of *stagnant monopolies*. The higher profit may be devoted to unnecessary expenditures which may lead to:

1. An increase in demand. Then we may have a Keynesian tendency to full employment: price distortions become the main adverse consequence of monopoly.

2. An increase in rentiers' incomes which causes a more than proportionate increase in savings. Then monopolies may foster the rise of a stagnant economy in the Keynesian sense.

Two alternatives to classical exploitation of monopoly power, and to breaking and transforming monopolies, which are capable of avoiding the turning of monopolistic firms into stagnant monopolies, are provided by:

(c) international investment;

(d) demand creation by *commercial activity*, i.e. by policies of producing new commodities, or of differentiating the old ones and promoting their sale (mainly through advertising).

Although we shall hint at the first alternative, in this paper we shall pay attention mostly to the *modern* (demand-creating) *monopolies*, i.e. to those that succeed in exploiting barriers to entry (and thus in keeping their market power) though commercial activity.

---

towards stagnation which can develop in the economy. In both cases we have a transformation of the system. Different types of monopolies may operate at the same stage of development.

II. BARRIERS TO ENTRY AND MONOPOLISTIC PROFITS

The barriers to entry which contribute (together with the dynamics of the economy and the oligopolistic game played between rival firms) to the formation and the maintenance of the monopolistic power of the firm, are both the result of the process of technical and economic development and one of the objectives of the firm's policy. Technical barriers to entry are mainly due to the discontinuities created by certain kinds of technical progress which may be fostered by the enlargement of productive activities carried on by the firm in order to strengthen its market power.[1] In fact the increase of size may stimulate innovation which increases the optimum size of plant. Financial and institutional barriers are likely to be strengthened by the growth policy of the firm.[2]

Economies of scale in research and commercial activities and the financial advantages entailed by great size may supersede economies of scale in production. They will then lead to the formation of big conglomerate firms.[3] The oligopolistic game which is played between such big firms, capable of entering various markets, may affect the barriers to entry. Under certain conditions a cooperative game turns out to be advantageous to all, while under other conditions, the insider in a market may find it convenient to start a survival game. In the former case some of the objective factors contributing to the barriers to entry may become irrelevant, while in the latter case the strengthening of the barriers to entry may become a fundamental tool for carrying on the strategy of the firm.

To simplify our analysis, we shall disregard the implications of oligopolistic interactions among firms. But our results will help to clarify the problem of oligopoly since they will show how the process of development may at certain stages induce oligopolistic games.

We shall also disregard stagnant monopolies, in spite of the

[1] The effects of technical progress on the emergence of monopolies depend on the relation between its effects on the long-run cost curve and those on the dynamics of demand. The dynamics of demand depend on the intensity and on the effects of technical progress in the various sectors and on the income elasticity of demand for the products of the sector.

[2] I have dealt with this aspect of a monopolistic economy in *Il Monopolio nella Teoria Economica* (Milano, 1953) pp. 178–201.

[3] See the paper by O. E. Williamson, 'Managerial Discretion, Organization Form, and the Multi-Division Hypothesis', Chapter 11 in this volume.

importance they have had in some stages of economic development.[1] We can then say that barriers to entry enable the firms to earn profits higher than the normal rate of profit, assuring a level of external finance sufficient, together with the monopolistic profit retained by the firm,[2] to sustain accumulation. Let us assume that because of the exploitation of underutilized resources or of technical innovations or of commercial activity (mostly creation of new products), the monopolies succeed in obtaining sufficient development potential to make possible the full utilization of the finance that they can command. In this simplified picture of a monopolistic economy, monopolistic power implies an exploitation of consumers (if monopolies are in consumers' commodities sectors): this exploitation enables the firm to increase the share of total accumulation which is financed from retained profits. Either personal savings are then reduced or total accumulation is increased. The first alternative is more likely to occur in the case of modern monopolies because of the effects of commercial activities. To make our picture a bit more realistic, we must drop the assumption of a homogeneous system (intrinsically a monopolistic economy is not homogeneous). This is what we do in the following sections. One of the main results of our analysis will be to show that in a more general framework, structural changes occur for reasons different from those which have been considered by Pasinetti.[3]

III. THE ANALYSIS OF STRUCTURAL CHANGE

The implications of structural change cannot be adequately analysed with the mechanistic models usually adopted to study the

[1] The economic development of the United Kingdom in the 1920s and of the United States in the 1930s were characterized by the role played by stagnant monopolies. The fascist regimes made it easy for oligopolistic firms to play a nation-wide cooperative game, as I have shown in 'Italian Fascism and the Economy', in *The Nature of Fascism*, ed. S. J. Woolf (London 1968) pp. 152–64.

[2] We implicitly assume that all profits above normal are retained. In fact the retention ratio depends on several factors. See R. Marris, *Managerial Capitalism* esp. pp. 74 ff.

[3] L. L. Pasinetti, 'A New Theoretical Approach to the Problems of Economic Growth', in *Semaine d'étude sur le rôle de l'analyse économetrique dans la formulation de plans de dévelopment*, ed. Pontificia Academia Scientiarum (Città del Vaticano, 1965).

equilibrium of the firm and of the system. Such models assume a given structure: the performance of the economy is studied as if the preservation of its structure were the main goal of the system. The only feedback effects considered are those required by stabilization processes.

When we consider the interaction between the system and those firms which are capable of setting up rather autonomous strategies, cumulative processes may not be curbed by the stabilizing feedback effects: the outcome may be a structural change of the system which modifies its *modus operandi*, thus creating room, eventually, for cumulative processes different from the previous ones. We could of course logically conceive of a more general system which is preserved by such feedback effects.[1] But it is sometimes difficult to visualize *ex ante* a system general enough to make possible the consideration of all feedback effects as internal processes.

Any theoretical analysis of system structures requires institutional assumptions. Some economists seem to believe that the general assumption of free competition and of some equilibrating mechanism (justifying the assumption of a constant system) should enjoy a higher theoretical status than other alternative assumptions. I think this position must be rejected. Of course there may be some advantage, as a procedural device, in starting by analysing a very simple system (such as that based on the traditional assumptions): the results are not of a higher heuristic value than those which can be obtained by more complex analysis. In fact they could be misleading, as is the case when the dynamic properties of the system are reduced to the problem of its stability or of its convergence to a particular equilibrium path.

In this paper I do not intend to produce a model which can be tested statistically. I think theoretical reasoning can help to clarify preliminary problems, making it possible to exploit information unsuitable by its nature for statistical analysis.

Theoretical reasoning about structural change can also contribute to the clarification of the issues concerning the decision criteria of

---

[1] For the theory of the system we refer to, see L. von Bertalanffy, 'General System Theory: A Critical Review', in *General Systems*, ed. L. von Bertalanffy and A. Rapoport (Ann Arbor, Mich., 1962); Masanao Toda and Emir H. Shuford, Jr, 'Logic of Systems, Introduction to a Formal Theory of Structure', *General Systems*, X (1965); Jiří Klír, 'The General System as a Methodological Tool', ibid.; O. Lange, *Wholes and Parts: A General Theory of System Behaviour* (Oxford, 1965).

the firm. Some criticisms of the assumption that the firm maximizes profit are based on the analysis of the firm's internal organization. The analysis is normally developed with tools taken from other sciences, disregarding the interactions between the total economic system and its elements. In fact those interactions are an essential object of economic investigation. In my opinion the pattern (and even the criteria) of firm behaviour cannot be studied independently of the total system and prior to the analysis of its *modus operandi*. Yet some assumptions on the behaviour of the firm have to be made before starting the analysis of the system: the results of the analysis will then confirm the hypotheses or suggest a new, more fruitful approach.

IV. THE BEHAVIOURAL ASSUMPTIONS FOR A
GROWING MONOPOLY

The following assumptions about the behaviour of the firm will be made:

(i) The firm chooses between different strategies of development, each of which is characterized by particular values of given objective economic variables.

(ii) The firm's first objective will be to produce decisions which reduce uncertainty, i.e. decisions that do not worsen the relevant parameters of the probability distribution of each economic variable and improve at least one of these parameters: when indices of uncertainty (e.g. variances) are reduced, we can speak of uncertainty-reducing decisions. (Of course the decisions which we are considering are those which do not entail substantial additional costs.) To simplify the analysis, let us assume that the results of such decisions are simplified probability distributions: a *simplified* distribution can be compared with the distribution of alternative strategies on the basis of one parameter only for each period (let us say the mode), the variability of the other parameters being considered irrelevant.[1]

(iii) The capacity of each firm to reduce uncertainty is limited only by the profit of which it can dispose. The consequences of the

---

[1] By such simplifying assumptions we avoid the difficulties entailed by the consideration of uncertainty. Such difficulties are usually dealt with under other simplifying assumptions; see J. Lintner, Chapter 7 above.

reduction of uncertainty are increases in the upper limit of the gearing ratio and the retention ratio.[1]

We can then state that, for a growing monopoly (i.e. a monopoly that can find adequate outlets for its growth capacities), the higher the rate of profit, the more stable its expectation of growth, and the higher the level of external finance it can command, then the higher its rate of growth. In fact the greater the monopolistic power of the firm, the less interest does it have to pay in the financial market (which is intrinsically imperfect, both because of the stronger connections of monopolistic firms with financial institutions and because of the higher reputation that they enjoy).

If we consider oligopolistic interdependence, structural change could be brought about by differences in monopolistic power which may make it convenient for some firms to play survival games.[2] As we shall see, the different structural changes that can be visualized under our simplifying assumptions may make it possible for firms to keep and perhaps to increase their market power without embarking upon an oligopolistic war. Cooperative games are thus likely to be more appropriate. If the resulting collusion is sufficiently stable, then our disregard of oligopolistic interdependence, implied in assumption (i), can be justified.

A few more assumptions about the economy are required:

(iv) There are two sectors producing consumer goods, a monopolistic sector and a competitive sector. Some of the commodities produced by the competitive sector are completely different from those produced by the monopolistic firms (though they may be complementary); but most of the competitive commodities are to some extent substitutes for monopolistic products. To simplify the analysis, we might assume a more restrictive hypothesis: that the products of the competitive and of the monopolistic sectors are technically the same. Nevertheless they are considered as different commodities by the consumers because of their commercial attributes (trade marks, consumers' opinion generated by advertising, etc.).

(v) The monopolistic sector is characterized by barriers to entry due to:

1. technological discontinuities of production plants;

---

[1] I have tried to show how the reduction of uncertainty affects the gearing ratio and the retention ratio in *Monopolio, Concorrenza e Sviluppo* (Milano, 1970).

[2] M. Shubik, *Strategy and Market Structure* (New York, 1960) p. 203.

2. discontinuities in the costs of commercial activities at different scales;
3. the inability of possible new firms to acquire and organize the entrepreneurial structure needed to carry on complex technical, financial and commercial activities;
4. the financial barrier constituted by the monopolistic firm's ability to command a disproportionate amount of the external finance provided by household savings (which is higher the higher its rate of profit). The financial barrier may not be relevant if the threat of entry comes from an equally powerful firm operating in different markets or if there is a cooperative game solution.

The significance of the barriers to entry and their maintenance over time depends upon the strategies of firms, technical progress and the efficacy of commercial activity.

(vi) The competitive sector is characterized by free entry: the firms are all of relatively small size. At first, it may be convenient to assume that its firms are all alike (both actual firms and potential entrants): for all firms, price is therefore equal to average cost.

(vii) The sales promotion activities of the monopolistic sector cannot be carried on by the competitive sector both because of cost discontinuities and the lack of the necessary managerial facilities. At some stage of the analysis, the perfect homogeneity assumption for the competitive firms will be dropped: we can then assume that some commercial activities, of a different kind and of a different efficacy, can be carried on also in the competitive sector, in which some reorganization becomes possible.

(viii) There is one sector producing capital goods and intermediate commodities. We shall assume that this sector has a given degree of monopoly and that it can adapt its production to the demands of the other two sectors. For the sake of simplicity we assume that the third sector is fully integrated: it does not use capital goods but only labour.

(ix) Finance is provided by the firm's retained earnings, and by savings mobilized through the financial market: it is demanded only in order to carry on programmes for sales promotion and investment programmes which entail the purchase of new capital goods or, in some situations, the purchase of plant from competitive firms.

V. THE EFFECTS OF THE COMMERCIAL ACTIVITY OF THE MONOPOLISTIC SECTOR

The monopolistic firm endeavours to maintain and possibly to improve its profitability prospects by enlarging its commercial activities; we shall assume that:

(x) The amount devoted to this activity is proportionate to profits. Therefore, if the profits of the monopolistic sector grow at a rate higher than the national product, commercial activity is continuously expanded.

Sales promotion activities aim at making consumers willing to increase the consumption of monopolistic products at the expense of competitive consumer products: they usually also have an effect on the total propensity to consume, by causing upward shifts of the consumption function.[1] The demonstration effect is relevant because the prestige motive for consumption is spurred by commercial activities. The goods offered by the monopolistic sector are in general superior goods; sometimes their superiority is based on prestige grounds. For some commodities (such as automobiles), product changes, which are an essential ingredient of commercial policy, can be truly commercially effective only when the prestige motive supersedes other traditional motives for purchase. Sales promotion activities require the employment of single-use commodities as well as of capital goods.

(xi) We shall disregard the effects of the commercial activity carried on by firms in the capital-goods sector.[2] We are not concerned in this paper with the changes which can occur in its structure. It is sufficient to notice that the monopolistic power of the firms in this sector is due mainly to technological discontinuities, discontinuities

[1] The constancy of the average propensity to consume in the economic process (which contrasts with the falling propensity in cross-section) can be explained on the basis of the effects of sales promotion on the consumption function.

[2] In the capital-goods sector, sales promotion activities are mostly of the informative type: their effects on the growth of demand are rather small, at least above the level required to get the prospective buyers informed. There are a few interesting exceptions. The use of some capital goods (as for instance some office equipment) can be intensified through advertising. If the prospective buyers of such goods are very numerous, the difference between intermediate commodities and consumers' goods in the analysis of commercial activity is reduced.

in research activities, and financial obstacles to entry (which may be very important when the use of capital goods is acquired through a lease or when payment delays are granted to buyers).

Let us try to classify the effects of commercial activity. We can distinguish:

(a) *a substitution effect*: consumers are induced to substitute the commodities of the monopolistic sector for those of the competitive sector;

(b) *a consumption effect*: this is represented by the difference between the level of total consumption after commercial activity and that which would have occurred if the monopolistic firms had not carried out any commercial activity. Consumers are in fact stimulated to increase their total consumption. We can distinguish: (1) a *monopolistic consumption effect* which is that part of the increase in total consumption which materializes in additional purchases of monopolistic commodities, and (2) a *competitive consumption effect*. The former effect is usually larger than the latter. The competitive consumption effect may be relevant if there are complementarities between monopolistic and competitive commodities: in this case the substitution effect is likely to be weaker;

(c) *a barrier effect*: by carrying on commercial activities, monopolistic firms make if difficult for potential new firms to enter the monopolistic sector. Depending on the power of the barrier effect, the monopoly profit margin may be maintained, increased or decreased.

(xii) For the competitive sector we shall assume that freedom of entry keeps price equal to average cost. If wages and the rate of interest remain unchanged, and there are no increasing returns, the cost of production will not change with changes in the level of production.

(xiii) To simplify our analysis for all sectors, we shall assume that changes in wages and in the rate of interest will not bring about changes in the choice of technique of production.[1]

---

[1] A change in the rate of interest may change the techniques' capital intensity in either direction. See the contributions by L. L. Pasinetti, D. Levhari, P. A. Samuelson, M. Morishima, M. Bruno/E. Burmeister/E. Sheshinski, and P. Garegnani, in 'Paradoxes in Capital Theory: A Symposium, *Quarterly Journal of Economics* (Nov 1966). See also L. Spaventa, 'Realism without Parables in Capital Theory', in *Recherches récentes sur la fonction de production*, ed. Centre de Recherches Économiques et Sociales (Namur, 1968).

We can then summarize the relevant effects of commercial activity by evaluating:

the growth potential of the monopolistic sector, that is, the increase in the demand for its products resulting from the direct and indirect effects of commercial policy. The indirect effects are produced, via consumers' income increases, by the enlargement of the production of intermediate commodities and of capital goods (by the payment of the wage bill, of interest and of distributed monopolistic profit). In a similar way we can define:

the growth potential of the competitive sector.

Let us now turn to the financial effects of commercial activity. If the barrier effects are such that the profit margin is kept constant or increased, it is possible for the monopolistic sector to get a disproportionately large share of total savings. The personal savings which are available for the competitive sector depend upon:

the total level (and growth) of income;

the consumption effect of commercial activity in the monopolistic sector;

the quantity of personal savings absorbed by the monopolistic sector.

We can thus distinguish:

the financial expansion potential of the monopolistic sector, which is represented by the increase of production which would occur if the monopolistic firms were to utilize all the finance that they can command to increase their productive capacity (after implementing their commercial policy);

the financial expansion potential of the competitive sector: under our assumptions, competitive firms increase their capacity as required by the increase in the demand for their products, provided the finance available to them is adequate. If finance is inadequate the increase in production which *can* be financed represents the financial expansion potential of the competitive sector (we assume that the rate of interest remains unchanged: we shall mention later the effects on it of changes in financial expansion potential).

We now distinguish three alternative situations:

(a) The increase in demand for the monopolistic sector (i.e. its growth potential) is equal to its financial expansion potential. In this case we shall say that the monopolistic sector is *balanced*.

(b) The financial expansion potential is greater than the demand-growth potential in the monopolistic sector.

(c) The financial expansion potential of the monopolistic firms is less than their growth potential.

VI. THE PROCESS OF GROWTH OF MARKETS IN AN ECONOMY WITH A BALANCED MONOPOLISTIC SECTOR

We shall first consider the case in which the barrier effects are such as to make it possible (and convenient) for the firm to keep the profit margin constant (and hence under the assumptions of constant techniques and a constant price of capital goods, the *rate* of profit is constant).

(xiv) We shall then isolate a first set of phenomena by making the provisional assumption that there is some *deus ex machina* assuring full employment. Saving is therefore equal to investment. This assumption will be dropped in section XI.

In the case in which the monopolistic sector is balanced, a simple model can be of some help in determining the path of development. A few more sinplifying assumptions are required.

(xv) Sales promotion expenditures require the employment of commodities produced by the capital and intermediate sector. For the sake of simplicity we shall assume that the 'demand effect' of commercial activity is proportionate to the total amount of inputs used, the proportionality coefficient being λ.

(xvi) Total demand for monopolistic commodities is a non-homogeneous linear function of income and of commercial expenditure, the income coefficient being γ. The constant term in the demand function, q, is negative. That means that if no commercial activity is carried on, the demand for monopolistic commodities is zero unless income reaches a certain level. As mentioned, commercial activity changes the propensity to consume. In fact, because of the demand effect of commercial expenditure and of the constancy of the derivative of demand with respect to income, the ratio of consumption of monopolistic commodities to total consumption will increase provided that adequate finance is available to the monopolistic sector.

(xvii) The financial expansion potential depends on total profits: we shall assume that all monopolistic profits which are not used for commercial activities are invested and that they enable the firm to command external finance. For the sake of simplicity we shall assume that the external finance absorbed by monopolistic firms is proportional to their retained earnings. Let the proportionality coefficient, which we shall call the *financial attraction coefficient*, be ρ.

(xviii) We shall further assume that demand for capital goods is due to the increase in demand for consumers' goods (the acceleration principle), b_1 being the capital–output coefficient for the monopolistic sector, b_2 the same coefficient for the competitive sector (the capital and intermediate sectors having been assumed to be fully integrated).

(xix) Prices are normalized by taking the wage rate equal to 1. (In fact the model will determine only relative prices.) Income is thus expressed in wage units.

(xx) The constant (given) degree of monopoly of the capital and intermediate sector is expressed by the ratio between price and cost.

The model includes the following equations:

The price equation for the monopolistic sector:

$$p_1 = wa_1 + rp_3b_1 + \mu. \tag{1}$$

The price equation for the competitive sector:

$$p_2 = wa_2 + rp_3b_2. \tag{2}$$

The price equation for the third sector:

$$p_3 = \pi wa_3. \tag{3}$$

The equation defining the demand for monopolistic commodities:

$$x_1 = \gamma y + \lambda \frac{\sigma\mu}{p_3} x_1 - q. \tag{4}$$

Given the demand for monopolistic commodities (which is controlled to a certain extent by firms through their commercial activities), the demand for competitive commodities has to be adjusted in order to ensure balance between the financial expansion and the demand-growth potentials for both sectors.

The equation defining household disposable income. Household disposable income is given by the wages and interest paid (we shall here assume a retention ratio of one for monopolistic profits). For the second and third sectors the wages and interest paid are equal to the value of production; the monopolistic sector contributes to disposable income only a part of the value of its production (since monopolistic profits have to be subtracted):

$$y = (p_1 - \mu)x_1 + p_2x_2 + p_3x_3. \tag{5}$$

The equation expressing the demand for the products of the third sector:

$$x_3 = b_1 \dot{x}_1 + b_2 \dot{x}_2 + \frac{\sigma}{p_3} \mu x_1. \tag{6}$$

The equation expressing the balance between the value of investment by the monopolistic sector and the finance it can command:

$$(1 - \sigma)(1 + \rho)\mu x_1 = p_3 b_1 \dot{x}_1. \tag{7}$$

The financial balance for the competitive sector (stating that the value of the investment made by the sector is equal to the personal savings not absorbed by the monopolistic sector) can be derived from equations (5), (6) and (7).

The model includes seven equations to determine seven unknowns:

y: income

x_1: the production of the monopolistic sector

x_2: the production of the competitive sector

x_3: the production of the third sector

p_1: the price of monopolistic commodities

p_2: the price of competitive commodities

p_3: the price of intermediate commodities (third sector).

Let us recall the meanings of the parameters entering into the model:

w: the wage rate ($=1$)

r: the rate of interest

a_i: the labour input per unit of production of sector i ($i=1$, monopolistic sector; $i=2$, competitive sector; $i=3$, third sector)

b_i: the capital–output coefficient for sector i

μ: the monopolistic sector's profit margin

ρ: the financial attraction coefficient

π: the degree of monopoly of the third sector expressed as the ratio of price to average cost

γ: the disposable income coefficient in the demand function for monopolistic goods

σ: the share of monopolistic profit which is utilized to implement commercial activity

λ: the demand-effect coefficient of commercial activity.

The model has economically meaningful solutions only if the following two conditions are fulfilled:

$$\sigma < 1 \tag{8}$$

i.e. not all profit should be utilized in commercial activity;

$$\lambda \frac{\sigma}{p_3} \mu < 1 \qquad (9)$$

i.e. the demand effect of commercial activity financed out of the profit obtained from one unit of production must be less than one unit. (Not all the demand for the monopolistic commodities may be attributable to commercial activity.)

There is a causal relation between the first three equations and the other four.[1] Under our assumptions, prices are not affected by the distribution of demand between the sectors producing consumers' goods. Given the prices, we can easily solve the last four equations to obtain the quantity produced by each sector and income, as functions of time. The functions will retain economic meaning up to a certain point. When the production of one sector beomes negative (as we shall see, this may happen for the competitive sector), the system breaks down. We have then a chain of events which fall outside the framework of the model.

The solutions are:

$$x_1 = x_1^0 \exp(d\mu t) \qquad (10)$$

where

$$d = \frac{(1-\sigma)(1+\rho)}{p_3 b_1} \qquad d > 0. \qquad (11)$$

$$x_2 = K\exp(-lt) + \frac{m}{n} x_1^0 \exp(d\mu t) + \frac{1}{p_2 \gamma} q \qquad (12)$$

where

$$m = -\mu\left[\frac{1}{\gamma}\frac{\sigma\lambda}{p_3} + (1-\sigma)\rho + 1\right] + \left[\frac{1}{\gamma} - a_1 - rp_3 b_1\right] \qquad (13)$$

$$l = \frac{p_2}{p_3 b_2}, \quad n = \mu(1-\sigma)(1+\rho)\frac{b_2}{b_1} + p_2. \qquad (14), (15)$$

$$y = sx_1^0 \exp(d\mu t) + \frac{1}{\gamma}q. \qquad (16)$$

where

$$s = \frac{1}{\gamma}[1 - \frac{\lambda\sigma\mu}{p_3}] \qquad (17)$$

[1] In the sense specified by H. A. Simon in 'Casual Ordering and Identifiability', in *Studies in Econometric Methods*, ed. W. C. Hood and T. C. Koopmans (New York and London, 1953) pp. 49 ff.

$$x_3 = \zeta \exp(d\mu t) - b_2 lK \exp(-lt) \tag{81}$$

where

$$\zeta = x_{10}\mu \left[\frac{\sigma}{p_3} + \left(b_1 + b_2 \frac{m}{n} \right) d \right]. \tag{19}$$

The properties of the dynamic process given by the solution of the model are the following:

(a) The production of the monopolistic sector increases at a rate which is higher, the higher is the monopolistic profit margin, the higher is the attraction coefficient and the lower is the share of profit used to finance commercial activity. We must recall that the intensity of commercial activity helps to maintain barriers to entry: therefore the share of profits used in commercial activities is itself correlated with the profit margin. The growth of monopolistic production is higher, the lower is the capital–output coefficient and the prices of intermediate commodities.

(b) In the short run the rate of increase of household income is smaller than the rate of increase of monopolistic production; in the long run both tend to increase at the same rate.

(c) The dynamics of the competitive sector depend on the value of

$$\frac{m}{n}$$

The sign of this critical parameter is given by the sign of

$$m = -\mu \left[\frac{1}{\gamma} \frac{\sigma\lambda}{p_3} + (1-\sigma)\rho + 1 \right] + \left[\frac{1}{\gamma} - a_1 - \pi p_3 b_1 \right]$$

which is a linear function in μ. I shall write it as:

$$m = -h\mu + k.$$

$m = 0$ when $\mu = k/h$. We cannot state in general whether $k/h \gtrless 0$ but we can state that

$$\frac{k}{h} < \frac{p_3}{\lambda\sigma} = \mu.$$

We must remember that for condition (9) to be satisfied,

$$\mu < \frac{p_3}{\lambda\sigma}.$$

Therefore there is always an interval $[0 - \mu$ or $k/h - \mu]$ of values of μ which causes the competitive sector to shrink. It may be of some interest to note that the interval is larger, the larger is the value of γ, and the greater is the value of the financial attraction coefficient ρ.

The relation between the decision variables which contribute to the determination of the rate of growth of the monopolistic sector (mainly between the profit margin, and the share of profit which is used to finance commercial activity) makes optimizing behaviour quite an intricate problem. The question arises of whether monopolistic firms visualize the possibility of increasing their rate of growth by accelerating the shrinkage of the competitive sector and whether they will anticipate the transient character of their faster growth. In the early stages when the competitive sector is still large, we can get growth of the monopolistic sector at a steady rate for quite a long time. Only when the competitive sector is reduced to a negligible size are the monopolistic firms likely to visualize the impact of the structural changes which have occurred during the previous stage of development.

At this point it is perhaps convenient to make our picture more realistic, by assuming that the firms of the competitive sector are not all alike. The competitive sector has some features of Chamberlin's monopolistic competition (but the firms' commercial activity has only very limited efficacy). The strategy of the monopolistic sector may spur competition in the competitive sector. Some firms by their commercial activity are capable of causing the failure of other firms. Some reorganization may occur that makes the plants of the competitive sector (or at least of some firms in it) more like the plants of the monopolistic sector. (This may be the result of research activity which the firms of the competitive sector are induced to carry on by the strategy of the monopolistic firms.) Such an occurence contributes to changing the perspectives of the monopolistic firms. They may find it convenient to absorb some of the plants operated by competitive firms. Joan Robinson was the first to point out the gains that a large firm can obtain by organizing a market which was previously imperfect.[1] She emphasized mainly the possibilities which a large firm enjoys of utilizing existing plants better or of increasing their size and of implementing a discriminatory price policy. Still more relevant may be other advantages due to the superior organization

---

[1] J. Robinson, *The Economics of Imperfect Competition* (London, 1946; 1st ed. 1933) pp. 322–3.

of the big firm[1] and to the greater efficiency of its commercial activity. Thus the plants handed over to the big firm may become more profitable. The improved outlook may enable the monopolistic firms to increase their retention ratios; the banking system may also contribute to facilitating the acquisition of the plants. Let us assume that the effects of the changes occurring in income distribution on the propensity to consume monopolistic and competitive commodities are negligible. Then we can concentrate our attention on:

the financial expansion transfer effect, i.e. the increase in the financial expansion potential produced by the transfer of plants from the competitive sector to monopolistic firms;

the demand-growth transfer effect, i.e. the changes in the demand-growth potential caused by the reorganization of the plants acquired from the competitive firms. The reorganization is sometimes confined to the channels of distribution, the packing and labelling of products, and changes in some commercial activities.

VII. THE PROCESS OF GROWTH OF AN ECONOMY WITH AN UNBALANCED MONOPOLISTIC SECTOR

Let us now consider the case in which the financial expansion potential of the monopolistic sector is not equal to its growth potential. The commercial activity of the monopolistic firms causes a growth of demand for their products which is smaller or larger than the growth which can be sustained by the investment that the firms are able to finance at the current rate of interest, given the degree of imperfection of all markets. One way to make the two potentials equal is to change the retention ratio. But an increase in the retention ratio may not be feasible even when the growth potential is greater than the financial expansion potential, and a decrease may not be convenient in the opposite case.

(a) Let us assume that the financial expansion potential is greater than the growth potential. This may occur either because the effects of commercial activities are weak or because the financial attraction exerted by the monopolistic firm is very strong. In this case the firm may find it convenient to revive oligopolistic competition (it may

---

[1] See O. E. Williamson, below.

even deem it advisable to start a survival game) or it may reduce the financial potential by decreasing the retention ratio. The firm may be willing to use the finance which is available to it and may find other ways to do this. Then, under our assumption of full employment, the financial expansion potential of the competitive sector becomes less than its growth potential. Competition among the firms of the competitive sector may be spurred: the result may further reduce their prospects of growth. The transfer effect may be encouraged. We can thus single out a way in which monopolistic firms can exploit their excess financial expansion potential: it is by acquiring the plants of competitive firms in crisis. Another way is by intensifying their commercial and research activities. The monopolistic firm may thus be encouraged by the financial surplus to carry on a strategy of development which creates a more difficult life for the competitive firms.

If the monopolistic firms are not willing to use the finance that they could dispose of or they do not see concrete ways to implement expansion plans, different consequences may result:

1. Monopolistic firms may reduce their retention ratios; hence rentiers' incomes may increase. If the increase in rentiers' income is consumed, there may be non-negligible effects on the demand-growth potential of the monopolistic firms. An adjustment process thus occurs.

2. The monopolistic firm may simply not take advantage of as much finance as the financial market is willing to supply. If personal savings available to the competitive sector thus increase to a sufficient extent, the financial potential of the competitive sector may be made equal to its growth potential.

In both cases we can then speak of *limply growing monopolies* which would in the long run turn into stagnant monopolies.

(b) Let us now consider the case in which the financial expansion potential of the monopolistic sector is smaller than its demand-growth potential. This may occur because the monopolistic firm is much more successful in its commercial policy than in attracting finance. The finance available to the competitive firms is not fully utilized because of insufficient growth of demand for their products. Under our assumptions (of full-employment development), savers' attitudes may make it possible for the monopolistic sector to raise more finance, thus increasing its expansion potential. If the growth potential of the competitive sector is not affected, the shrinking of that sector may continue and sooner or later the monopolistic sector may increase its financial expansion potential and be able to exploit its demand-growth potential.

VIII. THE PROCESS OF GROWTH OF AN ECONOMY WITH A HETEROGENEOUS MONOPOLISTIC SECTOR

In the previous sections we have assumed that all firms in the monopolistic sector are alike and that for all of them the barrier effect makes it possible to maintain the current profit margin. To make the picture more realistic, we shall now assume that while for some firms the barriers effect is such as to maintain the rate of profit unchanged, for other firms it may be impossible to exploit the current barriers to entry. The former firms will either undertake more commercial activity or grant reductions in prices or increases in wages. Changes in prices are usually ruled out for several reasons:

(a) they may spur oligopolistic competition that the firms may not find it convenient to stimulate;

(b) the effects of price reduction on demand are uncertain;[1]

(c) price stability is a favourable condition for planning.[2]

Thus an increase in wages is the most likely outcome in such a case. An increase in wages has several effects on economic development:

1. It enhances commercial activity, since the increased workers' income is likely to be mostly or even entirely spent on the commodities produced by the monopolistic firms.

2. It causes an increase in the wages of the competitive sectors (and therefore an increase in the prices of their commodities). The increase is larger:

(i) the larger the rate of growth of the demand for labour of the the monopolistic sector relative to the rate of growth of population;

(ii) the more homogeneous the labour force employed in the monopolistic and competitive sectors;

---

[1] Price rigidities due to the uncertainty of the estimates of alternative strategies have been dealt with in my paper on 'Monopoly and Rigidities in the Economic System', in *Monopoly and Competition and Their Regulation*, ed. E. H. Chamberlin (London, 1954) pp. 398–420.

[2] J. K. Galbraith, *The New Industrial State* (Boston, 1967) chap. xvii, sect. 4. Price stability does not imply that the profit criterion has been abandoned.

   (iii) the more spatially close the competitive sectors are to the monopolistic sectors;

   (iv) the more open is the increase in wages in the monopolistic sector. (Sometimes increases are granted under disguised forms: better social services, bonuses, etc.);

   (v) the stronger the trade unions and the more unified their policy on a national basis.

Both effects of the increase in wages in the monopolistic sector tend to produce a shrinkage of the competitive sector. In the economy we are considering, increases in wages may start in a few monopolistic markets and then spread to others. Changes may be brought about in the efficacy of commercial activity in the various monopolistic markets and in the growth potential of the competitive sector. A chain of reactions starts which may cause changes in the structure of the system. With respect to the initial structure, the monopolistic economy looks intrinsically unstable.

IX. STRUCTURAL CHANGE IN THE ECONOMY:
THE TERTIARY SECTOR

Let us assume that the commodities of the monopolistic and of the competitive sectors are technically similar and let us have a look at the economy as a whole to appreciate better some of the effects we have outlined. Under the assumptions made, we can speak of real consumption measured by the number of technically equivalent commodities, no matter whether they are produced by the monopolistic or by the competitive sectors. As the latter shrinks, we have an increase in the money value of consumption higher than the increase in real consumption. The difference is a transfer of income from consumers to monopolistic firms, which makes it possible to increase commercial activities and to finance the investment required by the higher growth of demand for the monopolistic commodities. Changes in the efficacy of commercial activities and changes in the capital–output coefficient will play a fundamental role in determining the rate at which the monopolization of the economy is increased.

The propensity to save out of disposable household income may decrease while the propensity to save out of total income (including monopolistic profits) may rise or at least remain constant. Which of these outcomes is more likely also depends on capital- and labour-input coefficients.

We have so far considered monopolistic and competitive sectors producing consumers' commodities. To simplify the analysis, we have assumed that the capital-goods sector always adapts itself to the growth requirements of the other sectors. We must now turn our attention to the tertiary sector. The commercial activity of the monopolistic firms tends to produce substantial changes in the structure of this sector:

(a) it tends to eliminate the independent wholesale dealers and to change the nature of the retail dealers' activities;

(b) it tends to develop the service sectors: some services are produced to increase the efficacy of commercial activity. Some service activities are carried on within the monopolistic firms. Most of them are developed by independent firms: new branches of the tertiary sectors are thereby created. One effect of the change has to be mentioned. Since service activities are usually characterized by a low capital–output coefficient and a relatively high labour coefficient, any extension of the commercial and service activities of a monopolistic firm tends to lessen its capital–output coefficient. We can define a similar coefficient for the economy as a whole by assuming, for the sake of simplicity, that the monopolistic firms carry on only productive activities, the service activities being run by independent firms. Then a tendency for the capital–output coefficient to decrease may result from the development of the tertiary sectors. We shall mention a possible countervailing tendency.

X. TECHNICAL PROGRESS AND THE REALIZATION OF MONOPOLISTIC MARKET POWER. THE PSEUDO-NEUTRALITY OF TECHNICAL PROGRESS

So far we have assumed that monopolistic profits are utilized to promote commercial activities and to finance the investment required by the growth of demand. In fact part of the profits is used to develop research activities which are the main source of technical

CE K

progress. Since research tends to become more and more product-orientated, research activity is, to an increasing extent, connected with commercial activity. If its financial expansion potential is greater than its demand-growth potential, the firm will be more willing to intensify its research activity. Technical development is thus induced not only – and perhaps not so much – by the growth of markets,[1] but also – and perhaps mostly – by the relation between the expansion potential and the growth potential of the monopolistic sector.

Technical progress fostered by the dynamics of a monopolistic economy presents some peculiarities.

(a) First of all, monopolistic firms are particularly interested in product changes: product changes may be the most important prerequisite for successful commercial activity, which may be the most powerful means of preserving and even increasing monopolistic power.

(b) Product and process innovations may not be deemed convenient when they destroy capital values or cause the demand for old commodities to shrink (as happens with innovations which lengthen product life) unless they produce compensatory effects through increases in the efficacy of commercial activity and in barriers to entry. In the competitive sector, where there is free entry no destruction of capital values or of old demand can be a deterrent to innovation.

(c) Monopolistic firms are less preoccupied with the effects of innovation on the capital–output ratio than competitive firms because:

1. Capital costs are smaller for the monopolistic sector using retained earnings: also the procurement of external finance is usually cheaper for the monopolistic sector. Moreover, *wages* in the monopolistic sector tend to be higher than in the competitive sector.
2. The risk of being obliged, in the near future, to write off capital values because of innovation is reduced by the capacity of the monopolistic firms to control the orientation and the application of technical progress.[2]

Because of the predominance of the monopolistic sector, technical progress may not be neutral: the capital–output coefficient may tend to rise in the manufacturing sectors. As we have seen, other effects of the monopolization process, the enlargement of the service sectors

[1] See J. Schmookler, *Invention and Economic Growth* (London, 1966) pp. 104 ff.

[2] Apart from that, the monpolistic firm may find it convenient to introduce innovations which would be considered profitable by a competitive firm since it has investment opportunities elsewhere.

in particular, tend to lessen the same coefficient. If the two effects balance for the economy as a whole, we have a constant capital–output coefficient (we are not considering the effects of price changes, which are difficult to evaluate *ex ante*). Technical progress appears then to be neutral. In fact we have a pseudo-neutrality which has explanations and implications very different from those usually considered.

(d) We are interested in another feature of technical progress in a monopolistic economy. The monopolistic firms are capable of controlling an increasing portion of technical innovation because their financial strength enables them to intensify research, some of which cannot be carried on by firms below a certain size. That is not the only reason for the increasing concentration of the results of technical progress within the monopolistic sectors. The exploitation of most innovations requires some commercial activity that only large firms can carry on. The competitive firms which enjoy better financial conditions may try to react to the policy of the monopolistic sector by searching for useful innovations. The outcome may be an improvement in the condition in which plants of competitive firms (with the patented innovations) are handed over to the monopolistic firms. The concentration of innovation in the monopolistic sector may thus increase the barriers to entry. Let us call the increase in the margin of profit brought about by technical progress through a reduction in cost accompanied by an increase in the barriers to entry the *potential growth of monopoly power*, and let us ask whether such a potential increase in market power leads to a long-run increase in the degree of monopoly. The firm's financial expansion potential is increased. Since commercial activity has not increased its growth potential, there is not much room to enlarge productive capacity. The firm may be induced to intensify its commercial and research activities. To assess the final outcome, we must analyse how cost reductions, caused by technical progress, materialize. Considering both direct and indirect effects, for the economy as a whole we shall either have a substitution of intermediate commodities produced by the monopolistic sector for old commodities produced by the competitive sector, the former commodities being more productive than the latter, or a reduction in the labour employed, or both these outcomes. The increase in demand for capital goods induced by the intensified innovation activities of the monopolistic firms may not offset (through the multiplier mechanism) the direct negative impact on employment of technical progress: thus the demand for consumers goods will be curtailed. This process cannot continue for a long time. Increases in wages are likely to occur (reductions in price are ruled out by the considerations already pointed out.) The increase in wages and intensified commercial activity may increase the demand-growth potential of the monopolistic sector. Depending on this, the potential growth of monopoly power (which has been produced by technical progress) may or may not lead to an equivalent increase in the actual long-run degree of monopoly. The effects are anyhow adverse to the competitive sector. The impact on the competitive firms is even greater if technical progress produces the substitution of monopolistic goods for competitive ones.

The intensification of commercial activity may be facilitated by technical progress. In fact technical progress seldom leads to innovation in production processes which do not offer the possibility of changing the product and even of enlarging the number of commodities which can be produced. Interactions are thus established between technical progress and commercial activity. The monopolistic firms' strategy will be to try to achieve that kind of interaction which is most favourable for their growth.

XI. INFLATIONARY AND DEFLATIONARY TENDENCIES IN A MONOPOLISTIC ECONOMY

Let us drop the assumption of a full-employment path of development. In fact the dynamics of the economy may entail excess demand or insufficient demand for labour, depending on the growth of demand (as determined mainly by monopolistic commercial policy) and the rate of growth of the labour force. If pressure in the labour market develops, the tendency for wages to increase may be reinforced. Such an outcome has twofold effects: on one side it favours monopolistic commercial activity; on the other, it has adverse effects on exports (it may also reduce, via an increase in imports, the growth potential of the monopolistic sector). We must notice that wage increases due to inflationary tendencies are of a different kind from increases brought about by the process we considered in the previous sections: while the latter usually do not produce increases in the prices of monopolistic commodities, the former do raise prices. There is therefore a critical level of inflationary tension above which monopolistic firms will bitterly resist increases in wages. The monopolistic sector may then favour a deflationary monetary policy. Unfortunately such a policy has an adverse effect on the monopolistic sector because it reduces its growth potential, as well as on the competitive sector since it reduces its financial expansion potential (the effect on the financial expansion potential of the monopolistic sector is likely to be negligible).

What will happen in the opposite case, when the development of the monopolistic economy tends to produce an inadequate demand for labour? Such a case may occur when commercial activity is not very efficient and/or when the shrinking competitive sector is much more labour-intensive than the monopolistic sector. The increase in unemployment will have adverse effects on consumption which are likely to be mostly felt by the monopolistic sector. The unemployed labour will first cut the consumption of unnecessary commodities (or come back to inferior goods). The purchase of durable goods, which are to a large extent supplied by the monopolistic sector, can be easily postponed. Unfortunately a reduction in wages cannot help to restore the balance between the demand for and the supply of labour, not only for the reasons pointed out by Keynesian theory, but also because of the adverse effects that a reduction of wages has on the efficacy of the commercial activity. The monopolistic firms will then favour a Keynesian policy to achieve full employment. Such a policy meets other requirements of the monopolistic system.

XII. THE EFFECTS OF MONOPOLISTIC STRATEGY ON THE STRUCTURE OF PUBLIC EXPENDITURE. INTERNATIONAL RELATIONS. WELFARE EVALUATION

Monopolistic firms cannot assure a full-employment path of development. They will try to obtain their objectives through public expenditure policy. Monopolistic firms are interested not only in the level but also in the structure of public expenditure. Public expenditure may have similar effects to that produced by commercial activity (it may also promote technical progress in the interests of the more powerful monopolistic firms). For the process we are considering, the main effects of public expenditure are:

(a) a reduction in real investment or in real consumption if the economy has been developing along a full-employment path, and the main impact of public expenditure is represented by changes in the pattern of final demand;

(b) a substitution effect in favour of those monopolistic firms that succeed in exerting a stronger influence on the structure of public expenditure;

(c) an adverse effect for the competitive sector if public expenditure being financed through the issue of bonds, causes an increase in the rate of interest which is likely to affect its expansion potential more than that of the monopolistic sector.

When the barrier effects of their commercial policy are not adequate, monopolistic firms are likely to exert stronger pressure to get a favourable structure of the public expenditure. The 'congruence' between the structure of the public expenditure and that of the monopolistic economy is not only in the interest of the monopolistic sector but it also meets some of the requirements of economic policy. In fact in the short run a non-'congruent' public expenditure policy will produce inflationary tendencies.

In previous sections we have shown how the ability of the monopolistic sector to grow may undergo substantial changes when the competitive sector is reduced to a negligible size. As a reaction to this, the monopolistic sector may try to increase public expenditure, or revive the oligopolistic competition. The third way in which monopolies can keep their high rate of growth, in spite of the structural changes in the system, is by enlarging exports: this is facilitated by the spreading to other countries of new consumption standards created by commercial activity. A long-run excess of export over imports can be accomplished by a flow of investment abroad. Other weaker industrial countries may play the role of the domestic competitive sector, when the latter is no longer a reservoir for growth.

Cooperation by monopolistic firms may produce changes in economic policy. In a monopolistic economy there is no market mechanism ensuring that the dynamics of wages and of public expenditure are in harmony with the development of the growing monopolies and the changes brought about in the capital and labour coefficients by technical progress. Only if such a harmony is achieved can the profit plans of the firms be realized. Thus the need for indicative planning emerges. Such a need is felt less in those economies which can assure a high rate of growth for big firms, through the expansion of exports and investments abroad.

The results of our analysis can suggest reasons (in addition to those outlined by Kaldor[1] to explain the different rates of growth in various countries. The high rate of growth in countries like Italy can be explained by the reservoir of growth potential offered by the existence of a large 'competitive' sector. The study of the interaction between monopolistic firms' strategies and structural change in the economy can also contribute to understanding the new orientation of economic policy which is *induced* by the development of the system. In fact we shall get beyond neo-voluntarism in the approach to the problems of economic policy.

The development of the system has deprived traditional welfare economics of its foundations: consumers' preferences are no longer an independent rod by which one can evaluate the economy. Even social preferences are not independent of the strategy of monopolistic firms. A new approach to the problem of social welfare is required. We shall here make only one observation. In the short run, if the goal of the economic policy is to ensure full employment, we may be indulgent towards the strategy of the monopolies and towards the indicative planning that they foster.[2] If consumers' freedom and the freedom of society to produce its cultural values, rather than getting them as a by-product of the firms' decisions, are considered the main goal of social progress, then the score of the modern monopolistic economy is very low indeed. If, in addition, we take into account the world disruption which can be fostered, the welfare problems look still more intricate.

[1] N. Kaldor, *Causes of the Slow Rate of Economic Growth of the United Kingdom* (Cambridge, 1966).

[2] To maintain macroeconomic stability and the structure of the monopolistic economy are not the only goals of indicative planning. But the other goals (usually the only ones which are avowed) are hampered by the congruence between the structure of public expenditure and the distribution of monopolistic power, which both the monopolistic firms and the State administration want, for various reasons, to enforce. In indicative planning, wage policy has to help the monopolistic firms to obtain an adequate efficacy of commercial activity and to assure capital accumulation at the same time. Therefore 'incomes policy' is not an easy matter. The political power that some competitive sectors still have, defective understanding of the system among monopolistic firms and the persistence of a classical bias in the conception of the wage may explain the insufficient growth of wages for conspicuous periods, which causes a concentration of wage increases. A deflationary policy may then be required with all the negative consequences we have outlined.

9 The Modern Corporation and Economic Theory

Robin Marris

The original purpose of this paper was to attempt to survey and to consolidate the economic theory of the large, growing corporation as this has developed since the publication of *Managerial Capitalism*[1] and to relate the synthetic result to the various problems with which both phases of the present project are concerned. In the event, the relevant body of theory has in the author's opinion been so much further developed by the contributions of other participants to Phase I that a good deal of the original paper seemed redundant. It was therefore decided instead to provide a general discussion of the theory of the growth of the firm in a separate Introduction and to confine the present paper to related issues. The paper has been completely revised since the Long Island Conference (see Preface) and has been substantially influenced not only by the Conference discussions but also by all the other papers.

Managerial Capitalism was mainly concerned with the internal growth problems of the individual corporation in a generally 'modern institutional environment, described and interpreted from my personal viewpoint. The firm was seen as an administrative and financial organization, roaming the world economy seeking outlets for its services, growing mainly by diversification rather than by expansion of, or movement along, demand curves for a fixed catalog of products. But although the firm was highly 'creative', it was subject to a loosely defined set of dynamic restraints restricting the rate over time at which its creative activity could alter the immediate environment, for example the rate at which new markets could be found and developed.[2] I have since suggested we could describe these restraints as a 'super-environment'.[3] The whole

---

[1] See n. 5, p. 4 above. [2] See especially *Managerial Capitalism*, chap. 4.
[3] For a further discussion of this concept, see Introduction, p. 13.

analysis was concerned with a single firm in a 'constant' or 'given' super-environment, the data of which included, of course, the behaviour of all other relevant corporations. There were some hints of macro- and socio-economic implications, but these were not pursued very far.

The present paper by no means aspires to a more thoroughly 'general' analysis; rather it aims to explore certain specific aspects of the likely behaviour of a population of autonomous growth-seeking organizations. In particular, the paper is concerned with the relation between the 'static' theory of competition among giants, on the one hand, and theories of the growth of the firm on the other; and, in turn, with the relation between these two facets of the subject and the process by which the size-distribution of corporations, and hence, perhaps, a major element in 'static' market structure itself, is determined. Section I reconsiders the conceptual framework of this type of economic system as a whole, and also attempts to relate contemporary ideas about internal organization (such as discussed by Oliver Williamson in his paper below) to basic growth-model concepts, and more generally to set the stage for what follows. Section II is a venture into the field of 'static' oligopoly theory, essentially intended to help create a base for analysing a growing system. Section III outlines a 'simplified' growth model, whose coefficients are, hopefully, relatively easy to interpret and to employ in discussions of characteristics of an aggregation of growth models. Section IV attempts to bring the threads together and derive conclusions.

I. A CONCEPTUAL FRAMEWORK

Firms and products

How should we characterize the theoretical structure of an economic system in which large, autonomous, modern corporations play a dominant role? It is customary to see an economic system at a moment of time as a set of firms and a set of products. The firms are administrative and financial organizations which have come to exist as a result of a historical process of birth, growth and merger. The 'products' are defined from the demand side and by their technical

CE K 2

production requirements. The immediately perceived product set consists of a collection of consumer demand functions to tell us, *inter alia*, the quantity to be demanded for any specific constellation of prices and marketing expenditures of all products, but no separately identified product has a price cross-elasticity approaching infinity with any other product. There are also production functions to indicate the factor inputs required to produce any quantity of each product, on various assumptions concerning the number and identity of the contributing firms. The production functions therefore embody both technical and organizational information, including information concerning economies of scale.

If economies of scale are weak, relative to the sizes of markets, and if diseconomies set in whenever firms become 'large', we may have a 'competitive' system in which fairly large numbers of firms may produce individual products. In such a system, although it is technically and organizationally possible for firms to inherit special advantages in the production of individual products, competitive forces should cause the production functions of individual firms for particular products to tend to become similar. But in the system with which we are concerned, such conditions do not prevail. Returns to scale are generally constant or increasing, and markets in which more than one firm is trying to sell the same product are likely to be unstable. It is therefore convenient to define[1] the set of production functions explicitly in relation to the actual population of existing firms: each firm at a moment of time is associated with a characteristic subset of products, and each may produce a positive output of more than one product, but no product may be produced by more than one firm. Competition and rivalry occur through the production and marketing of close substitutes, rather than of identical products. The production functions are thus specific to firms and depend partly on specific skill and experience.

Clearly a firm must be allowed to choose not to produce some of its own characteristic products, and since no other firm is allowed to produce them by assumption, these products will not be produced at all.

It is sensible to include in the product set of the economy items for which there is no production? If so, how do we conceptualize the dynamic or long-term process by which the product set is expanded

---

[1] These definitions have been revised slightly from those of the original paper, in order to be consistent with those of Arrow's paper.

as technology, etc., advances? The answer is that we may include in the immediate product set items which are not produced but which could be produced on the basis of existing readily available knowledge, with the expenditure of only a modest amount of time and development resources. If the development of production would require substantial research (including marketing research to 'discover' or 'create' a demand curve), then this hypothetical product is not to be included in the immediate set. The long-run *growth* process of the system, achieved by a continuous version of the Schumpeterian activity of internal innovation,[1] consists of progressive expansion of the product set, as well, of course, as improvement in the production functions of existing members of the set.

The concept of a market

Our definitions imply the possibility of two modes of general competition among the population of firms. Given its production possibility subset, each firm might set prices and marketing expenditures on the basis of an appropriate optimizing criterion assuming that the corresponding choices of all other firms were fixed and would not be readjusted in the light of one's own choices. This is a general system of monopolistic competition, and is the basis of Arrow's paper and of the 'initial world' in Solow's paper. Alternatively, we may imagine a general system of oligopoly in which firms appreciate that their decisions will perceptibly affect the sales of other products and the profits of the respective firms so that, in turn, reactions must be expected.

Since the number of firms and products is quite large (i.e. there are at least fifty or a hundred firms), oligopolistic interdependence is unlikely to be completely general in the sense that any action by one firm will perceptibly affect all other firms; the reality is a chain of interconnecting oligopolistic markets. The case with no oligopolistic behaviour whatsoever, on the other hand, is a limiting one adopted essentially for convenience of anlysis. Our assumptions here will represent a system with potential oligopolistic behaviour spread in varying degree through the system, and will include the possibility of strictly monopolistic behaviour. Within the total product set we

[1] See Introduction, p. 7 above. I repeat here my debt on this point to Professor Archibald.

274   ROBIN MARRIS

define a set of *markets*, representing subsets of products each of which
has a sufficiently high cross-elasticity with every other member that a
group of firms actually or potentially producing these products is
likely to behave oligopolistically, i.e. to *recognize* their own mutual
interdependence. A market may therefore contain products for which
actual production is zero, but it is characteristic of the system that the
number of elements in a market subset is rather small, say less than
ten.[1] Market sets may intersect, but none may be a proper subset of
any other.

If the product set were immutable, and if births, deaths and
mergers among the firms were also ruled out, the general result would
be the outcome of oligopolistic decisions made by the firms in the
various markets for their characteristic products. This is further
tentatively explored in section II below. We do not know if there
could be a unique equilibrium. A 'static' analysis could still remain
appropriate in face of change, however, if change in the product set
occurred entirely exogenously, and was in no way directly related to
decisions and activity of the firms themselves. In reality, as already
mentioned, the process of change is by no means exogenous, and one
of our most important tasks is to accommodate our structural and
institutional concepts to the phenomenon of corporate growth and
innovation, with special reference, of course, to formal growth
models of the firm as they have recently developed.

From the firm to the corporation

So long as the concept of a 'firm' remained closely associated with
the concept of a product, or in the sense that the production possibility set of the individual firm was fixed and exogenous (as above),
it mattered little to economic theory whether in practice firms produced only one product or several. A firm's general behaviour would
be directly derived from data relating to the products which happened to lie in the production possibility set with which it happened

[1] In terms of our present definitions, the large-group model of the original
theories of monopolistic and imperfect competition related to markets in which
the number of products was fairly large. A group of firms would each select one
product from the group, and find a short-run equilibrium (resulting from each
firm's optimizing on its own demand function, assuming no reactions); if this
implied profits generally above normal, new firms would 'enter' by selecting and
producing some of the close substitutes which had not been selected by the
previous group, a process which continued until profits in general were normal.

to be endowed: a simple extension of the optimizing rules under single-product monopoly, oligopoly or for that matter competition, as the case might be, would determine the optimum output of each product and thus, by aggregation, the optimum scale of operations for the firm as a whole.[1] For example, provided all production costs, including managerial and supervisory costs, are truly decomposable among products, this kind of model implies that the general equilibrium allocation of output between all products would not change if, starting from a position of one-firm-one-product, some mergers were to occur. When the possibilities of managerial economies of scale, associated with diversification, are admitted, this prediction would be clearly invalid, but the required modification of the theory would not be very profound so long as the supposed mergers were assumed to have been accidental and exogenous. (The 'exogenous' mergers would be no more than an arbitrary modification of the basic data of the production possibility set, implying some arbitrary and accidental changes in predicted outputs.) But as soon as the diversified 'firm' is seen as an organic entity, whose production possibility set today is very much the result of its own ceaseless search for outlets for its own activities, everything changes. We have to consider very carefully the way in which the more transcendent role of the modern corporation interacts with its traditional role in economic theory of determining optimum outputs and inputs in relation to a highly specific list of products.

We see at once that the concept of the corporation cannot easily be decomposed; it is usually very much more than an arbitrary federation of one-product 'firms'. There are almost always common elements running through the skills of a corporate management, and this will influence the way the managers are likely, in fact, to choose to try and influence their own production set. The fusion of elements involved here can best be seen by considering the specifically organizational aspects of the problem. In another paper in this volume, Oliver Williamson characterizes two 'ideal-type' structures for the diversified corporation. In his 'unitary' form, the organization is strictly functional; the manufacture of each product lies in the hands of a general production division, and their sales promotion, etc., in

---

[1] For a discussion of these conditions under conditions of general monopolistic competition, see Introduction, p. 8 above; for a discussion of the corresponding conditions under oligopoly, see section II of the present paper, esp. pp. 299–300 below.

the hands of a general marketing division, while financial control of the whole system is maintained, in principle, by a general finance division. In this form, the organic unity is self-evident and, indeed, is associated with organizational disadvantages which form a main theme of Williamson's paper: the allocation of investment funds and marketing budgets is determined by high-level committees of senior executives (or in some cases actually at board meetings), representing the interests of functional divisions, rather than of products.[1] Williamson contrasts this form with the multi-divisional form, which becomes possible when the corporation becomes relatively large; in this form, an independent elite at headquarters, or 'staff', supervises a system of divisions organized around products, each such product or 'operating' division maintaining its own financial and marketing services and taking responsibility for a wide range of 'local' decisions concerning, e.g., outputs and prices. In principle, it might be thought, the M-form organization could behave precisely like a decomposable federation of 'quasi-firms' (Williamson's name for the operating divisions). In practice, to say this is to ignore the essential advantage of the M-form itself, namely the concentration of and specialization in strategic responsibilities at headquarters. What, then, are these responsibilities? They are, characteristically, (i) decisions relating to the rate and pattern of growth of the organization, and (ii) allocation of investment funds to production divisions (and the maintenance therefore, of procedures for evaluating the divisions' requests for funds). Decisions relating to growth in turn involve both financial and organizational decisions. 'Operating profits' must be allocated between research, development, new plant investment and dividends. Possible sources of external finance must be considered. The general price policy of the operating divisions must be influenced (high margins increase profits, provide finance for growth, but maybe depress sales.)

Some research and development activity may, of course, be organized on a divisional basis, perhaps on grounds of technical or organizational convenience, and perhaps as part of the general devolution of local responsibilities, but it is the essence of all 'development' activity that it is likely to lead to the establishment of

---

[1] How prices are determined in such systems remains a mystery which the behavioural school have only partly been able to resolve. See, for example, A. Kaplan, J. Dirlam and R. Lanzillotti, *Pricing in Big Business* (Menasha, Ill., 1958) chap. 3, the paper in this volume by Baumol and Stewart and the references quoted therein.

new operating divisions. We have previously conceded that in a general equilibrium model the production set of a 'firm' may theoretically include products for which the optimum output is zero, but in the more practical organizational world we now discuss, it is clear that these products will not be granted with operating divisions; if they 'exist' at all, they exist in the mind of headquarters only! Consequently, the strategic responsibilities of headquarters may be conceived to include both 'static' and dynamic (i.e. production-set expanding) activities, both types leading to potential increases in the number of quasi-firms of which the corporation is composed. In *Managerial Capitalism*,[1] I conceived of a diversification effort, consisting of repeated experiments with the marketing of new products, some of which 'succeeded', in the sense of finding a substantial market, and some of which did not. The combination of success rate and diversification effort, in that language, determines the rate of establishment of new quasi-firms in the present language: they are well named 'quasi-firms' because they are responsible for the Marshallian quasi-rents, i.e. short-run gross operating profits of the corporation to which they belong, but do not directly determine its longer-run activity (except to the important extent – see pp. 306-7 below – that the more successful they are in earning profits, the faster, other things being equal, the optimum growth rate in a well-defined growth model of the firm will turn out to be).

Apart from its strategic *responsibilities*, headquarters in the M-form firm also has the *function* of general supervision and control. For the full organizational advantages to be gained here, Williamson emphasizes, this control must be tight, rational and explicit. From this and the preceding arguments it follows that common elements of luck, skill and specialization must pervade the whole organization through the medium of headquarters. At least until recently, it was generally the case that the successful divisional manager was rather more likely to be promoted to another job in the same corporation than to a better job in another corporation, and also that a signficant proportion of headquarters staff will have been recruited by internal promotion. We expect to find significant co-variance therefore in the ups and downs of the profit-earning capacity and other skills of the operating divisions.[2] It is also worth noting that even in the absence of these human factors, a population of corporations each of whose

---

[1] *Op. cit.*, chap. 4.
[2] I owe this way of putting the point also to Professor Archibald.

existing quasi-firms at a moment of time could, in fact, be regarded as a randomly drawn small sample from the total population of quasi-firms (the list of all actual products with positive outputs) would display distinct variations in overall operating profitability. Operating profit rates[1] would converge to a general mean only if either the number of genuinely independent products manufactured by each corporation were large in terms of sampling theory, or if the regime of oligopoly in the markets for the outputs of quasi-firms were such that the profit rates of the quasi-firms were themselves converging.[2] The latter is particularly unlikely. However, it is precisely our case that the lists of the corporations' existing quasi-firms, and the skill with which they are managed, are far from random phenomena. Should they ever become so (which is not impossible), we could indeed face a different kind of corporate capitalism, a system of miniature planned economies, 'competing' in some sense to provide the service of resource allocation and long-term planning. Would it then matter much if the corporations were totally amalgamated into a form of centrally planned system? Oliver Williamson would argue that the excessive size would lead to 'control loss' (basically a failure of co-ordination due to the need to transmit information through too many nodes), from which one might argue that the basic case for a 'market technostructure' type of economic system (decentralization of planning among autonomous corporate giants)[3] – in other words the basic case for capitalism – lay mainly in reduction of control loss. But it seems to me that it is precisely those features of the well-organized corporation that reduce its control loss which create its homogeneity. In other words, either we have a decomposable system, or we do not.

The transcendent corporation

The foregoing discussion suggests an organizational scheme for the 'typical' M-form corporation, which I owe originally to Professor

[1] For a more precise definition, see below, p. 282.

[2] It has been observed, however, that the variation of the profitability of large corporations, pooled across industries, is smaller than that of smaller corporations. See Whittington and Singh, op. cit.

[3] See Oliver Williamson in the present volume, pp. 343–84 below, and of course, J. K. Galbraith, *The New Industrial State* (Boston, 1967).

Richard Rosenbloom of the Harvard Business School. In business-school terms, the picture is highly simplified, but it has been found rather convenient for describing the relevant interface between organizational and economic theory.

We can visualize the 'being' of the corporation as 'headquarters', the central resource-allocating unit, supported by operating divisions responsible for the production and marketing of the firm's established products. The latter's responsibilities are likely to include not only the routine production and marketing of their products, but also a certain amount of technical development and promotion of sales, together with the planning of investment for increases in output. The operating divisions can also be supposed to determine commercial policy at the tactical level, set prices, etc. – in other words they play oligopoly or monopoly games at their respective levels.

Operating profits are first identified in the divisions ('profit centers') and are then, as it were, appropriated by H.Q., which then has the task of reallocating them (together with receipts from external finance) between dividends, development and new plant investment.

'Development' expenditure may consist of both conventional 'R. & D.', and expenditure on any other growth-opportunity-creating activities such as investigation of the likely pay-off for entry into existing markets which the corporation has not previously considered, or also perhaps the investigation of merger possibilities (although regrettably in the present paper the important effects of mergers are not very explicitly considered). As already indicated, the extent to which development actively features explicitly in the formal organization will vary considerably from firm to firm, but the activity may nevertheless be represented formally by a box in an organization chart, as in Fig. 9.1. The first theorist explicitly to adopt this approach was John H. Williamson.[1]

In some firms the growth-creating box may not exist. Such a firm has finally decided on its entry strategies and makes no attempt to find new ones; it is content to accept its *existing* comparative advantages and does not perceive the possibility of obtaining information which might indicate comparative advantages in previously unknown territory. A firm which undertakes no development expenditure can grow at a rate no faster than the average autonomous growth, if any, in the markets it has been content to enter. This type

[1] See Introduction, p. 4, n. 5 above.

of firm will be called *immanent* and its growth rate is called the immanent growth-rate. This use of the concept of 'immanence' is taken from Existentialist jargon rather than from theology. The firm is described as immanent because it can influence neither the super-environment[1] (which by definition is beyond the influence of individual firms) nor its own immediate environment or actual set of investment opportunities.

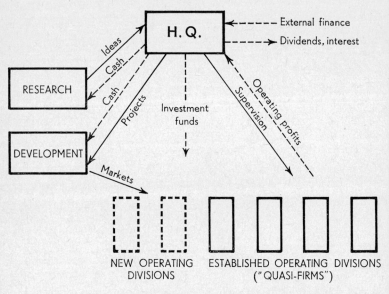

9.1. A transcendent M-form corporation

Firms which are not immanent are called *transcendent*. They perceive the possibility of changing their actual environment, subject to the constraints of the super-environment. Their development box exists. Although the lines between the two types of corporation may become blurred when we take account of expenditures designed to increase the strength of one's position in, and hence shares of, existing markets (such as cost-reducing research) or to stimulate the growth of demand of these markets, the distinction is one of kind rather than of degree. It is a distinction made for expositional, rather than empirical, purposes, since in the long run firms which

[1] For a further definition of super-environment, see Introduction, above.

persisted in truly immanent behaviour must be gradually replaced by the faster growth of the transcendent.

The H.Q. of the immanent corporation has in principle only a relatively simple range of tasks, such as supervising established production and commercial activities, encouragement of productive efficiency, labour relations, staff appointments, etc.! (In reality we know these operations can become at least sufficiently complex to provide the raw material for a behavioural model.) This firm does, however, have to take some decisions relating to the growth rate, because the immanent growth rate represents, in effect, only a maximum constraint; there is always the possibility of growing more slowly – acquiring new productive capacity at a slower rate than the immanent growth rate and so, deliberately, reducing one's share in individual markets. We can reconcile the concept of this kind of behaviour with the requirements of rational behaviour in the individual markets by noting that a relative decline in productive capacity would probably imply a reduction in commercial strength, undertaken voluntarily.

The H.Q. of a transcendent corporation faces a fundamental problem of allocation of financial and real resources arising from the fact that research and development activity requires time and resources, i.e. costs money, and that, whatever the effect on future profits and growth, the immediate effect on reported profits is adverse, since those expenditures must normally be deducted from operating profits in computing reported profits. As already indicated, the expenditures have many of the characteristics of investment, but they do not usually correspond directly to increased tangible assets in the balance sheet. Transcendent growth therefore requires two forms of finance, cash expenditures for development (i.e. creating opportunities) and the regular investment expenditures on tangible plant required to support the production of the goods whose sales are made possible by those results of development expenditure which prove successful. Investment is also required to support the 'immanent' element which must normally exist in the growth of the transcendent corporation – growth associated, that is, with the exogenous growth of demand in the existing markets. Once a new activity has been successfully developed and established, of course, it becomes an 'existing' activity, and responsibility for it must be transferred to an appropriately organized operating division. In effect, the number of operating divisions is increasing, and the flow of funds for regular investment is partly the result of immanent expansion among existing operating divisions, and partly the result of the increase in their numbers.

Conclusion: Distinguishing 'operating' from 'growing'

The upshot of the foregoing is that we can conveniently continue our investigation by turning aside to discuss the way prices, marketing expenditures and profits are determined in the operating divisions – in other words, the economic theory of quasi-firms – then take another look at long-run growth theory and finally discuss the relation between the two. For a separate discussion to be at all possible, we need to conceive of a theoretical 'static' world in which the quasi-firms behave as if they were either all independent, or all belonged to immanent corporations only. This is our subject in section II (and it is also, of course, the subject of Arrow's paper and the 'initial-size' discussion in Solow's paper).

We can thus characterize the concern of section II below, as the identification of the factors controlling the operating profit rate in a system of corporations, analysed as if immanent, which could in fact be transcendent. In section III we shall see how the operating profit rate so determined in turn affects the long-run growth rate, and how its distribution statistically among corporations greatly influences the long-run size-distribution of corporations. In the meantime we define the 'operating profit rate' of a corporation as the ratio of total reported profits, net of depreciation but not of interest, to the book-value of all tangible assets as it would be earned if the firm behaved as if immanent, i.e. as if the firm incurred no expenditure intended to expand the demand curve for its total services,[1] and as if its growth, if any, were entirely the result of autonomous demand growth (e.g. due to rising national income) in its markets for the products of its existing operating divisions only. Furthermore, the firm would be incurring no marketing expenditure designed to induce sustained growth in the demand for its existing products, although it might incur expenditures necessary to stabilize demand in face of competition.[2] It follows that the actual reported profit rate of an actually transcendent firm would represent the operating profit rate,

---

[1] For a definition of the total demand curve for a diversified corporation, see Introduction, p. 8 above.

[2] This would in fact mean that marketing expenditures incurred in the operating

less the ratio of development expenditures (i.e. all growth-creating expenditure wherever located) to total assets.[1,2]

II. TOWARDS A MORE GENERAL THEORY OF OLIGOPOLY

The following venture into the theory of oligopoly[3] (which, at 130 years, is now two-thirds as old as the theory of competition) is concerned essentially with the 'initial' conditions of a growing economic system. An individual firm, with given resources, may find that the outputs, prices and profits associated with its existing catalog of products are largely determined by static oligopolistic considerations which may be seen as exogenous: yet the resulting profits we know to be a major influence on the subsequent growth strategy, that is to say on the nature and intensity of the firm's efforts to change its environment and hence on its contribution to the forces affecting the development of economic structure. The corporations are playing a game in which the rules change (if slowly) partly as a result of the way they play. But here we are concerned with the starting-point, the game when the rules are given.

The 'rules' are an economic structure of markets, as described on

divisions, if allowed to grow at all, would grow no faster than autonomous demand, and they would have to be incurred in such a way that there was no cumulative effect. See Introduction, p. 10 above.

[1] We assume that static hierarchical expense at operating level as defined by Oliver Williamson in this volume would be 'optimal' in relation to whatever kind of oligopoly or monopoly was the game. For an analysis of this for the case of oligopoly, see section II, p. 301 below.

[2] To the extent that research and development activity makes use of capital assets which an accoutant would record in the books as tangible, there is an ambiguity, as they would strictly need to be deducted from total assets to define the denominator for the operating profit rate. As this leads to trivial complications of aggregation, we shall generally assume that all tangible assets are required for existing production, given optimum utilization rates.

[3] I am indebted to Francis Cripps, Claud Green, Adrian Wood and Herbert Scarf for help with this section. To Claud Green, then a first-year undergraduate at King's College, Cambridge, I owe the original idea behind the discussion of entry-deterrence, to Francis Cripps the stimulus of criticism and comment on my first attempts on the problem, and to Herbert Scarf, happily visiting Cambridge at the critical period, encouragement, constructive criticism and, above all, education in game theory. I also, of course, owe much to the discussion at the Long Island Conference, after which the section was completely rewritten. The relevance of Mancur Olson's brilliant book, *The Logic of Collective Action* (Harvard, 1965), will be apparent to all its readers.

pp. 273–4 above, plus some additional assumptions designed to remove any artificial or extra-economic restrictions of competition. No group of firms may make binding agreements in restraint of trade, either in the form of direct collusion against the consumer or in the form of coalitions against other actual or potential competitors, and they cannot make or accept side-payments or 'bribes'. A pair of duopolists, for example, may not bindingly agree to comply in a price-support scheme, nor may they bindingly agree that one leaves the market while the other charges monopoly price and transfers part of the profit to the leaver.

'Binding' agreements are enforced by legal or other 'extra-competitive' means such as collective boycott. We do not exclude tacit cooperative behaviour enforced by the well-understood threat of price war: indeed it is central to the argument that such threats may be sufficient to induce results little different from those of overt collusion. Thus the assumptions provide maximum 'competitiveness' in the system of rivalry between autonomous capitalist giants, and the more effective is 'anti-trust', the better they represent institutional reality. But it is also worth noting that at least in Anglo-Saxon countries, contracts in restraint of trade, although they have not always been criminal, have been generally difficult to enforce in the civil courts. Consequently, restrictive agreements, open or secret, written or oral, tacit or explicit, tend mainly to survive only as long as it is in the interests of all members to continue after taking account of the means and incentives for loyalists to punish defectors by legal economic sanctions. In other words monopolistic cooperative behaviour depends essentially on mutual interest and threat or bargaining strength.

The essence of oligopoly lies in situations where a change in commercial tactics (price, output, advertising) by one producer in a market has perceptible effects on the sales and profits of other producers and *may*, therefore, provoke reactions. It is accepted that the marginal calculus can be applied to such situations only on specific assumptions concerning the nature of the rivals' expectations concerning each others' reactions to their own actions. But it has also been noted that it may nevertheless be possible to identify specific upper and lower limits on the outcomes, given only some general assumptions of rational behaviour. These limits define the 'effective range' of the situation.

The concept of effective range may be illustrated by the example of two duopolists each producing a single partly-differentiated product, each of which has a fairly high price cross-elasticity of demand against the other product. Each knows how to produce only the one product and new entry is ruled out. Then the *lower limit* of the effective range is represented in a pair of prices such that neither producer would wish to lower his price (on the criterion of the relation between marginal cost and marginal revenue) even on the most optimistic assumption about his rival's reaction, namely the assumption that his rival's price remains constant.

The *upper limit* is where neither producer would expect an increase in profits from raising price even if he expected his opponent would follow with an equal proportionate increase. On some rather obvious assumptions (constant costs, similar demand curves, etc.) the point provides the same total profits as would be obtained by a single discriminating monopolist able to produce both products, and is sometimes therefore referred to as the 'monopoly' or 'joint-profit-maximizing' solution.[1]

If the duopolists make a succession of marginal decisions all based on the 'pessimistic' assumption that any price change will be followed they should reach the upper limit. Conversely, on a series of

---

[1] The lower limit for each producer is where his marginal cost equals his price times $(c-1)/c$, where c is the appropriate cross-elasticity. At the upper limit the condition is the same, except that for c we substitute the elasticity of demand for the one product on the assumption of an equal proportionate change in the price of the other, a feature of total demand conditions in the market. Because $(c-1)/c$ increases with c, a mutual lowering of price must lead the rivals towards the lower limit, and the higher the value of c the lower the level of prices in the lower limit. When c is infinite, the lower limit corresponds to the result of pure competition, with both prices equal to marginal cost. In pure competition between duopolists, however, it is not very realistic to define tactics in terms of prices, because it is difficult to conceive that the prices could differ more than momentarily; the duopolists should be constrained to behave as price-takers. Consequently Cournot worked in terms of the quantity each producer would choose to supply, and left the common price to find its own level at the point on the total demand curve for the product determined by the sum of the two quantities selected. Cournot's lower limit therefore represented the point where comparison of marginal cost and marginal revenue, on the assumption of one's opponent's quantity unchanged, would leave both unwilling to increase their quantities further. This result can be compared to the lower limit of the differentiated duopoly price game described above if both firms have identical cost curves, the prices are commensurable and all relevant elasticities are constant and greater than one. Then if both cross-elasticity and total elasticity are equal to one, the price in the lower limit of the price game is half the corresponding price in the quantity game; from this point the price-game price increases relatively to the quantity-game price if the total elasticity is high, relatively, to the cross-elasticity; and there does exist a range of possible values over which the former is greater than the latter.

'optimistic' assumptions they reach the lower limit.[1] The central problem, of course, is that since 'optimistic' behaviour tends to lead to unhappy results and vice versa, they should be expected to learn to change their assumptions as the sequence unfolds. Consequently, any attempt to apply the marginal calculus to predictions between the limits is bound to result in a theory lacking generality. Further progress has to depend on applications of game theory.

In game theory, decisions are not made marginally. The players are supposed to consider simultaneously all the various implications of their own possible policies in combination with possible policies of the opponent. The decision cannot be made by 'maximizing' in the sense that a monopolist maximizes profits on a known demand curve, because one does not know the result of an action until one knows the opponents' reaction, but the latter in turn may be designed precisely to prevent one achieving one's objective, because increased profits for you may mean reduced profits for him. But one may be able to find a policy to maximize one's minimum gain, assuming that the opponent's reaction to any choice you make is the most damaging possible. ('Minimaxing', meaning to minimize the maximum damage one can suffer, and 'maximining', meaning to maximize minimum gain, can be regarded as equivalent policies.) In 'one-shot' games with no possibility of prior knowledge of the opponent's strategy, it is difficult to think of any circumstances which could make a case for choosing other than this 'safety-first' policy (one would play differently if one knew one's opponent was trying to lose, but that would be prior knowledge). In the duopoly situation described above, if both players maximin they go straight to the lower limit.

If a game is 'constant-sum' (meaning that the sum of the pay-offs to all players is the same whatever strategies they adopt), all outcomes belong, in effect, to a Pareto-optimal set, since by definition no variation of strategies can make any player better off without making at least one worse off. In a two-person constant-sum game, the outcome of individualistic maximizing behaviour is therefore doubly secure; it is the unique outcome of the 'safety-first' policy and it

---

[1] The case of the kinked demand-curve, where one expects a price cut to be followed but an increase not, represents a form of 'super-pessimism' and stabilizes any price established between the limits. (The converse case would be super-optimism, and would lead to complete instability.) There is probably a stronger intuitive case for super-pessimism than for any other general attitude, but as we shall see below, the game-theoretic approach suggests that it is at heart irrational.

offers no incentive for a joint search for a more cooperative policy.

With more than two players, or in a non-constant-sum situation, the problem is profoundly changed by the likelihood that there may exist a solution in which a group of players (or all the players in the two-person non-constant-sum game) can all get more than each would get by safety first, thus creating a prima facie case for tacit collusion. The duopoly game can either be seen as a non-constant-sum game for two players, or as a game which includes the consumers on the assumption that they are too dispersed to form or join any kind of coalition, but in which the two producers, may although not necessarily will, form a tacit coalition to charge monopoly price.

At first, for the sake of argument, we arbitrarily restrict each player[1] to two strategies only: either to set persistently his upper-limit price, or to set persistently his lower-limit price, the former choice being labelled 'high', the latter 'low'. The result would appear as follows:

Table 9.1

A Game of Closed Duopoly: Pay-offs in Percentage Rates of Return
(Player 1's first)

Player 1	*Player* 2's Prices	
	'High' (H)	'Low' (L)
High	12,12	7,13
Low	13,7	10,10

If the choices are in fact restricted in the manner implied, and if once a policy is chosen it cannot be changed, and there is no pre-communication, the game is a 'Prisoner's Dilemma', after an example drawn from the plight of two criminals who are being separately interrogated concerning a murder they had in fact committed jointly. If both confess, both will be executed. If both refuse to confess, both may expect to be sentenced to life imprisonment (we are in the State of California, somewhere around 1950), and if one confesses, incriminating the other while the other says nothing, the 'rat' is pardoned and the victim of his double-cross is executed. In its pure form, there is no effective 'safety-first' policy in this game, i.e. there is no way of guaranteeing to stay alive at all costs. Even a prior agreement not to confess is unreliable, in view of the considerable

[1] For the effects of dropping the restriction, see p. 299 below.

reward to the one who breaks it. In such circumstances, 'honour among thieves' is difficult to sustain.

In the game described in the table, a unique safety-first solution does exist (at low, low), but as is also true of the pure Prisoner's Dilemma, there exists a still better solution for *both* players (at high, high), which cannot, however, be achieved without cooperation. As soon as the game becomes 'repeatable', with both producers expected to stay in business indefinitely, and able to change prices as often as they wish, the implications are notably different.

The case for presuming cooperation

It is widely accepted that there is then a very strong presumption that the upper-limit or 'cooperative' solution will be found, and sustained, without legal agreement or direct collusion. This conclusion can be reached by arguments at varying levels of sophistication. First one might envisage that the players initially consider the total implications of the situation and immediately appreciate that neither of the tactical pairs H, L or L, H can survive, because it will always pay the worse-off player to move away from the position even on the most pessimistic assumption about the opponent's further reaction (i.e. that he will not follow). Only the H, H or L, L situations, therefore, are viable, and the lower-limit situation represents the safety-first result.

Since both players are better off in the cooperative solution, any rational process of tacit 'bargaining' (which could be carried out through some trial moves) should inevitably lead to it. For example, suppose play begins at the lower limit, and one producer raises his price. The 'kinked demand curve' theory requires us to assume that the other cannot be expected to follow. But is this a rational belief? If my opponent raises his price and I do not follow, I must know we shall move to a situation which cannot last. If on the other hand, I do follow his price rise, I at least may hope he will not then revert and, indeed, I know it will be rational for him not to do so, because to do so would again mean instability and the danger of de-escalation. To accept price leadership is to play rationally.

Alternatively we can rewrite the game in terms of 'super-strategies'. These are rules for playing the game sequentially, e.g. super-strategy S_1, for a particular player, might read 'Whatever the other player does, always set the lower-limit price', and super-strategy S_2 might read 'At some early stage in the game, play high; if opponent also plays high, continue to play high yourself; if opponent plays low, follow him for a number of periods secretly chosen at random, then try again, and so on'. If both players choose S_2, they will eventually 'click' and settle at the upper limit. If they choose different super-strategies, the player using S_2 will do a little worse than the other, but his loss will only be slight and, significantly, the other player will fail to do better than in the cooperative solution. The game, when defined in terms of these super-strategies, has become 'stable', because once the S_2, S_2 solution is established, there is no incentive for either player to leave it. Thus the super-game has a stable solution which is also Pareto-optimal for the two players, in contrast with the one-shot game which had a Pareto-optimal solution which was unstable and a stable solution which was not Pareto-optimal. In a repeating game, it is the super-game solution which is relevant.

Finally, one can revert to thinking of the players as a potential coalition against the consumer. The coalition may, however, 'choose' any of the three outcomes (H, H) (H, L) L, H). Each such result is in effect an imputation of the spoils of exploitation among the coalition members. Each player can consider one of these imputations against the minimum he can guarantee by playing individualistically, i.e. the outcome of L, L or S_1, S_2. In a repeating game it stands to reason that no imputation can survive in which one member is worse off than he would be at worst when playing alone; therefore only the cooperative imputation is viable. (Or one could also include the non-cooperative lower limit as an imputation to the coalition but it is 'dominated' by the cooperative imputation.) The remaining imputations, none of which are dominated or dominate each other, can be seen as the 'core' of this particular game, and it can be proved at a high level of generality that in a repeating game only those elements in the core which have the equilibrium properties of the S_2,S_2-type solution in the super-game described above, can survive.[1]

It has in fact been found that in simulated oligopoly games played by humans with the aid of a computer, the longer the game is played

[1] Based on Aumann in *Essays in Mathematical Economics*, ed. Martin Shubik (Princeton, 1967). As I understand it, these elements represent Aumann's beta-core.

and/or the better the players already understand it, the closer the
average observed result approximates the computed value of the
cooperative solution.[1] Inevitably it is not easy to provide the participants in such experiments with financial incentive to rational
behaviour as is present in real-life situations when the sums at stake
are really large. Women players are said to be prone to non-cooperation; perhaps men players follow cooperative habits acquired from
their experience in the game of life. The direct evidence of actual
cooperative behaviour in the business world does not need to be
recited.

It has been usual in economics to base analysis on general pre-
sumptions of behaviour, such as the presumption of approximately
competitive behaviour or the presumption of a regime of monopolistic competition. With important exceptions in the work of
Joe Bain[2] and Paolo Sylos-Labini[3], the implications of a general
presumption of some form of oligopolistic behaviour have not,
however, been widely explored. But it seems that if we are to presume general rationality and *comprehension* (which is after all the
underlying presumption of all economic theories of this type), we
must presume that wherever oligopolistic interdependence exists, it
will be recognized, and that if a well-defined cooperative solution also
exists, that also will be recognized, *and* that where a cooperative
solution exists and is recognized, it will be adopted. Any other
presumption implies ignorance, irrationality or both. The theories of
Bain and of Sylos-Labini flow from a similar philosophy, but we
shall raise a question below as to whether their conclusions may not
in some cases in fact be inconsistent with a game-theoretic rationality.

The general analysis can of course be extended to markets containing more than two players. Clearly, however, provided the market
generally retains the feature that the cross-elasticities between all
pairs of products are fairly high, the 'learning' required to achieve
the cooperative outcome without direct negotiation is more difficult.
For example, if one small firm defects from the coalition involving
the cooperative imputation, and collective punishment is barred,
further defections may follow and it may be some time before the
market as a whole learns the lesson of experience. It is also more
difficult to be sure of the conditions for successful price-leadership, as

[1] See D. H. Stern in Shubik, op. cit.
[2] Joe S. Bain, *Barriers to New Competition* (Harvard U.P., 1956).
[3] Paolo Sylos-Labini, *Oligopoly and Technical Progress* (Milan, 1957).

required for re-escalation to a more generally profitable state of affairs. In the experiments referred to above, however,[1] it was found that although increasing the number of players from two to three did produce a noticeable reduction in the average observed price, further increases had less effect, and the average observed price even with as many as nine players did not fall very much more than half-way towards the theoretical non-cooperative price for that number of players.

The effects of unequal threat-strength

The arbitrary restriction on the tactical possibilities in the basic game, made above for expository purposes, ruled out consideration of a continuum of situations which must in practice, of course, be possible – where the players jointly choose pairs of prices yielding pay-offs such that both do better than at the lower limit, but one does better than he would at the upper limit, the other worse. All of these outcomes are possible results of tacit collusion;[2] even if a player finds himself relatively badly off in one of them, and is possibly rather annoyed, we cannot say that he will necessarily be able to do better, since from any retaliatory action not only his opponent but also himself will be damaged. His redress must if possible be obtained by threatening, in fact, just such a policy of attrition. The concept of a 'bargaining' solution is thus extended to take account of the use of threats; each of these intermediate outcomes can be seen as a possible division of 'joint-monopoly' profits, and one might expect that the tacit bargaining process would lead to divisions reflecting relative threat-strength. If, for example, the non-cooperative solution was much more damaging to one player than to the other, one might expect the former to accept a less favourable division. Early studies of the problem suggested that a 'fair' division should reflect relative strength quite precisely, and the most generally established method is to find the set of outcomes in which the ratio between the actual pay-offs is equal to the ratio between the gain which each represents over the players' respective pay-offs in the non-cooperative solution;

---

[1] Stern, op. cit. These were Cournot-type games with the moves defined in terms of choices of *outputs* (offers for sale in terms of quantity), but the comparison remains valid.

[2] They are all in the beta-core; see Aumann, op. cit.

this – the so-called Nash product[1] – maximizes the product of the gains in the pay-offs.

J. Harsanyi[2] and others have suggested that the players will necessarily reach the Nash solution if they 'bargain' rationally according to a set of defined principles. (For example, I must never reject a proposed outcome in preference to another so long as it represents at least a modest improvement for me, even though it may be a very much greater improvement for my opponent, and I must expect him to be as rational as me.)

The situation can be described more generally by means of a diagram in which the outcomes of joint strategies are represented in terms of the profits of each player measured along the two axes; a pair of coordinates defines a point which is the outcome of one joint strategy (pair of prices) giving the indicated profit pay-offs. The lower limit non-cooperative outcome is a single point. The range of outcomes we have been discussing belong to a class in which, as we move from one to another, we cannot improve the profits of one player without reducing those of the opponent. There is a Pareto-optimal frontier representing the joint strategies giving the highest profit outcome for one player, given the profits of the other, and vice versa. In conditions of strong increasing returns to scale, this frontier will be concave to the origin, and the non-cooperative lower limit will, of course, lie well inside it. The solutions we are discussing lie on the frontier, within the limits set by coordinates passing through the lower limit, which thus becomes, in effect, the origin for a subsidiary diagram. The Nash product is maximized by finding the point on the frontier which maximizes the area of a rectangle based on these coordinates.

The concept of a division based on threat-strength can of course be generalized to take account of other factors in the situation, especially when the actual outcomes are uncertain. In this connection, Martin Shubik[3] drew attention to the great importance of *financial* strength. Suppose the outcomes of the individual plays associated with a given pair of super-strategies in a repeating game are subject to a binary

---

[1] If the pay-offs are utilities, the individual scales do not have to be comparable; provided utility is measurable up to a linear transformation, the value of the non-cooperative solution provides the reference point for the measurement of units of gain.

[2] J. P. Harsanyi, 'A General Theory of Rational Behaviour in Game Situations' *Econometrica* (1966).

[3] *Strategy and Market Structure* (New York, 1960).

disturbance term with zero mean over the two players, and that, as a result, firms make unexpected profits and losses, the gains of one being the losses of the other. Assume that a firm which runs out of cash after a run of bad luck must leave the game – a game of economic survival. Then we can write the pay-off matrix for the super-strategies in terms of the probabilities of each player's winning before the end of a specified number of moves; other things being equal, the relative probabilities depend closely on relative initial financial resources and/or borrowing power. Since the winner takes all, this makes the game constant-sum. Alternatively, the pay-offs can be written in terms of the number of moves before the probability of one particular player's having won becomes greater than a specified value, and these figures in turn, if desired, can be converted into utilities for each player, thus allowing for possible differences in risk-aversion. But there may well exist strategies for which the probability of *either* player winning in the specified time is lower than in other cases; the former then dominate the latter and suggest the possibility of co-operative solutions. (Of course, to the extent that 'economic survival' is a one-shot game, cooperation without binding agreements may be more difficult.) If there is a cooperative solution, the player with the basically stronger position (e.g. larger initial cash resources) will be able to demand a greater share in it. An alternative interpretation is to regard the threat of a game of survival, i.e. of price war, as the basic sanction to cooperation generally.[1]

The effects of potential entry

Modern price theory has increasingly emphasized the effects of potential new competition,[2] in contrast to the intra-market situation, as the major influence on price policy. Oligopolists may well collude or otherwise cooperate to raise prices, it is argued, but their actions will be constrained by a common desire to deter new entrants into the market, whose appearance might otherwise be seriously damaging to all the incumbents. It may be fruitful to apply the methods of game theory to this problem also; to the best of the writer's knowledge all previous game-theoretic approaches to oligopoly have included as players only firms who in some sense are already 'in' the market.

[1] See also *Managerial Capitalism*, chap. 4.
[2] Especially in Bain and Sylos-Labini, op. cit.

Consider therefore a game in which the tactical choices are still artificially restricted but now, in addition to the 'high' and 'low' prices corresponding to the upper and lower limits of the game as previously defined, we provide a third possible choice, available to both players, which we call 'exit'. To play 'exit' means to attempt to produce nothing in this market – by implication one is demanding a price so high that nothing would be sold even if one were alone in the market – so 'exit' is 'non-entry' (consequently we do not need to designate a strategy for 'entry'; one enters by charging either high or low price.) Further, suppose that a player who 'exits' from this market has the opportunity to invest his capital elsewhere, at a constant rate of return which is e_1 for player 1 and e_2 for player 2. Because the players are not necessarily identical, their outside opportunities need not be the same: e_1 may differ from e_2, but these 'exit returns' are each independent of the policy of the other player; they are earned in industries (or perhaps the financial market) where the two firms are quite independent.

Apart from 'exit' (or a play within the industry) there is, as before, nothing else the firms can do with their capital, and for the time being we continue to assume a high degree of discontinuity; there are no permissible intermediate outcomes such as, for example, might let a player put part but not all of his capital in 'exit' and the rest (by implication from his tactics) in the industry; it is all in or nothing in. These assumptions might modify the previous game as follows:

Table 9.2
Duopoly Game with Entry and Exit

Player 1	Player 2		
	Exit	High	Low
Exit	e_1, e_2	$e_1, 15$	$e_1, 14$
High	$15, e_2$	12, 12	7, 13
Low	$14, e_2$	13, 7	10, 10

Note: 'Exit' means 'not enter' (see above); 'High' means 'enter and charge high price', etc. (see above).

The relative values of e_1 and e_2 can conveniently be employed as measures of the firms' respective comparative advantages between this market and other markets or investment, and are thus convenient tools for qualitative analysis. If they are equal, and less than 10, the cooperative solution is for both firms to stay in the market and charge a high price; the non-cooperative solution is the same with low price. If they are equal and lie between the L, L and H, H outcomes (i.e. between 10 and 12), the two firms can profitably stay in the industry if they can cooperate; if not, they are both better off to leave. This is the 'stop-loss' justification for floor-price agreements in distressed industries.

Bain's[1] type of approach can probably best be generalized by imagining that, for historical reasons, one firm has developed considerable comparative advantages in the industry. In Bain's picture, many of these 'barriers' are closely associated with factors we have previously identified as associated with bargaining strength (such as absolute size, cost of 'creating' adequate cross-elasticities, etc.), but for the time being let us express them collectively by differential values of e_1 and e_2. In order to define his measure of a 'barrier' to competition, Bain needs to assume the existence of a normal rate of profit in the general economy. Here, however, we can express the whole situation in terms of *comparative* advantage.[2]

Let the 'incumbent' be player 1, and let e_1 be so low (e.g. 5 per cent) that this player would be unlikely to wish to exit under any circumstances. Obviously if e_2 is less than 10 per cent (the non-cooperative solution when both firms are in the market), player 2 must enter the market, and one supposes that in time the cooperative solution (12, 12) will be found. The incumbent cannot deter him with any strategy. Intuitively, we can then see that since an additional entrant must inevitably depress profits considerably further, the process would stop even if we dropped the restriction on the number of players. This conclusion could perhaps be seen as a generalization of Sylos-Labini's[3] model, where in a concentrated oligopoly containing one or two giants, some 'small' firms might enter, but no more large ones (because the latter's output would so depress the price as to make entry unprofitable for *them*). In the present case, the 'smallness' of the potential entrant is defined by the relation between the effect of his entry on profits under the most unfavourable assumptions concerning cooperation (or rather lack of it), *relative* to the firm's best outside opportunity.

[1] Op cit.

[2] Although the more obvious way of expressing 'barriers' would be to endow the incumbent firm with higher pay-offs in the non-exit strategies, the analysis by means of varying exit strategies appears to be entirely equivalent, and is here more convenient.   [3] Op. cit.

The 'entry-deterrent' situation

In Bain's language, the foregoing case is one where the 'barriers to new competition', as measured by the comparison of the two relevant ratios – that of e_1 to player 1's pay-off from L, L and corresponding ratio for player 2 – are not high enough. We may conceptually raise the barriers by raising the assumed value of e_2 (i.e. increasing player 2's comparative advantage outside) until it lies between his pay-offs in L, L and H, H respectively. It then appears that player 1 may 'deter' entry by setting his price low. Provided the bluff succeeds, he is then better off than with any other outcome except H, E (which latter, of course , is clearly unviable). But here we face a paradox because player 2, on the principle of mutual rationality, should expect that if he calls the bluff a rational response would require player 1 to cooperate, i.e. to revert to a high price; otherwise both would suffer the painful experience of L, L.

It is quite possible that L, L is worse for both players than E, E. If so, the game as a whole has a maximin solution at E, E (if player 1 cannot deter entry and cannot achieve cooperation he should exit) and a cooperative solution at H, H. The E, E pay-offs may not, of course, be the same, but within the range of present assumptions they could be.[1] If so, H, H would maximize the Nash product. If the E, E pay-offs are slightly different, the Nash product will be maximized by an intermediate solution (see above) giving, for example, player 2 a smaller share of the market. The 'bluff' solution therefore corresponds to neither of the standard game-theory solutions.

Game theory does not regard the playing of low by the incumbent as an effective deterrent, because the opponent has a response which is highly painful to both. The latter can 'demand' his right to enter and share the fruits of cooperation by virtue of his threat-strength. But the entry-deterring hypothesis is supported by the argument that the L, E outcome leaves both players better off than the L, L out-

[1] The reader may find it convenient to follow the argument by assuming $e_1 = e_2 = 10$ per cent. This still leaves player 1 with a comparative advantage because his L, L (or H, H) pay-offs are higher than those of player 2 (e.g. he has an absolute cost advantage). The resulting game has no equilibrium point, because the joint minimax solution is E, E and at this point both players would wish to enter the industry if they could be sure that the other player would not, i.e. be sure the other player's tactics would remain unchanged. Indeed, the game has no strong equilibrium; at L, L both players would wish to exit unless they could expect that the other was going to exit, rather than to continue to play low.

come which is required for the potential entrant to exercise his threat. Game theory, by contrast, argues that the strength of the incumbent's 'deterrent' power must be measured not by the outcome if he is successful but by the minimum outcome he can guarantee from the use of the deterrent, namely the L, L outcome.

When a historically determined incumbent actually exists, the 'entry–exit' game may have a one-shot appearance, owing to the considerable non-recoverable costs of setting up production. Then it might appear as a one-shot game in which the incumbent's strategy is declared in advance, and he plays L. If really he never again could change his price (or if he could make a binding agreement to that effect), this would be the end of the matter. But the real-life entrant knows better, and he knows moreover that if he *does* enter, persistence of L, L (which is dominated in fact by E, E) must harm the incumbent more than himself, at least as compared with the cooperative solution, if not as compared with the non-cooperative solution. And so the argument goes on.[1]

The intuitive plausibility of the bluffing hypothesis suggests that it must be taken very seriously, but owing to its underlying instability we cannot accept it as a general solution; it is best regarded as a plausible deviation from the basic presumption of the cooperative solution, whose plausibility will vary with attendant circumstances.

---

[1] The problem arises from a significant difference between this game expressed in super-strategies, and the previous example. There, if one played S_2 (trying to induce the opponent to cooperate by periodic trials of high-price tactics), one was only slightly worse off than in the maximin (persistent L, L) solution, and the incentive to achieve cooperation was strong on both sides. Here, if the 'teaching' strategy fails, the result is worse for both players than in the maximin solution, and player 1 has an incentive to play S_2 only if he believes that he could not 'teach' player 2 to exit by persistent use of the low-price deterrent policy. It is true that if the game is re-written in terms of the original two super-strategies, S_1 and S_2, plus a third, S_3 representing the policy of persistently playing exit, it has a strong equilibrium at S_2 (implying eventual convergence to repeating H, H), but it also has *weak* equilibria at S_1, S_3 and S_3, S_1, because the player persistently exiting gets the same 10 per cent return whatever his opponent does, and this is an important economic feature of the game resulting from the assumption that in third markets the firms are not interdependent. One may of course add a further 'teaching' strategy, namely play high if opponent exits or plays high himself, otherwise play low, but it is less convincing, and although providing additional strong equilibria leading to H, H, it does not eliminate the weak equilibria at the points where one player insists on low and the other persistently exits. The question is, if a player has the 'teaching' policy available to him, which ought to lead to cooperation, is he or is he not likely to regard persistent exit as one of his rational alternatives? On the principle of mutual rationality, the answer is clearly negative, but perhaps this example stretches the principle too far.

For example, it is an advantage of the approach we are advocating above, that it can be applied to a new market which is being considered by several prospective exploiters, in which case, even if one firm has greater comparative advantage, the bluffing hypothesis is clearly more tenuous.

The cooperative presumption uniquely determines the number of firms in an industry; the bluffing hypothesis does so only on the additional assumption that the bluff succeeds. To the extent that its plausibility depends on the actual existence of an incumbent, there is a historical element in its determinism.

Predictions for prices, profits and efficiency

With 'low' barriers to entry (see above), we obtained a solution with *two* active producers, with *high* prices, high costs (due to weak exploitation of economies of scale) and moderate profits (12 per cent). With higher barriers, the cooperative or general solution produced exactly the same result, but the 'bluff' hypothesis predicts *one* firm, lower costs, lower prices, higher profits for the one firm and lower profits for the excluded firm. If we had then raised the barriers further (reducing player 2's comparative advantage by raising further his exit pay-off), we would eventually, of course, have reached a case where H, E dominated all other outcomes, so there would be one firm, high prices and very high profits. *Barriers to entry do, therefore, have a generally positive effect on profitability, but there is a substantial range of situations over which the effects may be neutral.*[1] *Except in the case of the bluff, however, there is no presumption that lower barriers means lower prices,* the reason for this paradox being that the cooperative solution in the case where the bluff is possible represents an analogy to the excess-capacity theorem of theories of imperfect competition. By contrast, it is an interesting feature of the bluff outcome that it better exploits economies of scale. We cannot, however, assert that this would be *socially* Pareto-optimal because we have no well-defined theory for determining whether two

[1] This may explain the modest, but significant, contribution of quantified entry-barriers to inter-industry explanation of profit rates. See Michael Mann, 'Seller Concentration and Barriers to Entry', *Review of Economics and Statistics* (1966); and Ken George, 'Concentration, Barriers to Entry', *Review of Economics and Statistics* (1968).

products manufactured inefficiently represents a socially superior situation to one product manufactured efficiently.[1]

Our analysis concludes that 'excess capacity' remains a significant general feature of oligopoly which will be more prevalent the lower the general level of entry barriers. If 'side-payments' are permitted, the problem can always be eliminated (e.g. in the above example the solution is H, E with the incumbent passing on enough of his profit for the other player to be at least as well off as in H, H, while he himself remains better off). Merger or 'rationalization' is an obvious way of achieving the effect of side-payments without bribes.

Towards greater generality and interdependence

The predictions of the duopoly with entry model are of a partial equilibrium strongly dependent on assumed discontinuities. We can (if we wish to) dispose of the discontinuities by the technique of a Pareto-optimal frontier described previously. (If some real-life discontinuities remain, it may well have missing sections.) Each point on the frontier represents an allocation of each firm's output (always with high prices) between the specified market on the one hand, and the external investment opportunity on the other. We can provide greater generality by adding another market containing two products of which each firm can produce one and both of which have low cross-elasticities against both the products in the first market. There will be a Pareto-optimal frontier representing a set of possible production allocations (statements of how much is produced by each firm in each market), and there will be a non-cooperative solution to provide the origins to indicate the Nash product for the total cooperative solution. We can add more markets, and if we wish we can eliminate any opportunity for investment in markets where the firms are not interdependent. In the two-person two-market case, with strong increasing returns in both markets, the case of total specialization will generally be a point on the Pareto frontier, but will by no means necessarily be the Nash solution. The latter may well involve partial de-specialization. Thus 'inefficient' diversification

---

[1] In a paper delivered as an undergraduate member of the Political Economy Club in Cambridge in 1947, the author attempted to solve this problem by the use of concepts of consumer-surplus. The assembled dons were so critical that the idea was not pursued.

is comfortably explained. Total de-specialization, where both firms produce in both markets, will not, however, in general lie on the frontier. In the market case, the corresponding proposition is that the frontier will not contain production allocations containing any pairs of markets in which both firms produce in both.

Finally we can try and extend the number of firms! We see at once that, having classified the products of the economy into markets, and having specified the firms by the products they may select,[1] we may classify the firms into interdependent groups, meaning groups of firms all of which are potential oligopolists in at least one market in which at least one other member of the group is also a potential oligopolist. No interdependent group, so defined, is to be a proper subset of another, but the groups may well intersect. If they did not intersect, and were generally fairly small in numbers, and if we retained the assumption that each firm had fixed capital resources and had no 'outside' investment opportunities, the 'general equilibrium' of the system would be the aggregate of the solutions we have now obtained for groups, *provided* each contained a unique beta-core. The problems of the n-person oligopolistic economy, therefore lie in the conditions surrounding the existence of such solutions, and in the problems created by intersections of the interdependent group of firms. If there *was* a solution for a finite set of firms of given size there would be a set of such solutions, each representing a utility outcome for each firm. There should be a Pareto-optimal frontier among these utility outcomes, so, in principle, we could maybe find a cooperative solution on this frontier to determine the optimum 'initial' size for all firms. The only thing left fixed in the analysis is then the specification of markets and the production possibilities of the firms.

Conversely, inasmuch as financial resources are a major element in threat-strength and cooperative solutions, and noting that this depends on the *total* size of a firm, we see how the dynamic forces which historically determine the sizes of firms have a major influence on the static solution. We also see an element of potential circularity in the static solution, because it appears both to influence and itself be influenced by the size-distribution of firms.

---

[1] This is the same system as that of Arrow in his paper above.

Oligopoly games with expense preference

William Baumol[1] and O. E. Williamson[2] have suggested 'static' theories of the firm in which the utility of the managers is associated partly with reported profits and partly with some other important variate, such as the value of sales or the level of expense (meaning the real volume of expenditure on such things as subordinate staff, advertising budgets, office furniture, or call-girls, which for any reason give pleasure to management). Expense is a deduction from profits, but may beneficially affect sales, so there is a transformation boundary between expense and reported profits which is not necessarily monotonic. This boundary will be shifted by price changes, both of one's own product and of one's opponent's, as well as, of course, by changes in one's opponent's expense. Once the boundary is specified, every point on it implies a level of profits, sales and expense for oneself and one's opponent. These in turn are translated into utilities. We thus have a more complex system of strategies and boundaries, but we expect that it would no doubt have a Pareto-optimal frontier and appropriate solutions.

It is not difficult to see, however, that these solutions may contain situations of some economic interest. For example, let us make enough assumptions that a duopoly game can be described in terms of only two strategies for each player, namely high expense and low expense (with appropriate demand conditions the associated price-strategy matrix could prove to be redundant). Let the outcome of each pair of such strategies be given initially in terms of rates of return for each player. The conditions are such that an increase in one's own expense, not matched by one's opponent, increases one's profits, but that high joint expense means low profits for both. Furthermore, unlike the case of the price games, not only are both players better off with joint low expense (corresponding to joint high price), but this solution offers a better result for *both* players than the outcome when one uses high expense and the other low: if profits were in fact the only criterion, the solution would be a settled point. But now add the assumption that the firms both have a utility function which combines profits and expense with appropriate weights. It is not difficult to see that as the assumed weight attached to expense is gradually

[1] *Business Behavior, Value and Growth* (New York, 1969).
[2] *The Economics of Discretionary Behavior* (Englewood Cliffs, N.J., 1964).

increased, the game eventually changes back to a Prisoner's Dilemma with a cooperative solution at high expense and a non-cooperative solution only at low. Thus, in an oligopolistic world, one does not predict that indulgence in expense will eventually be destroyed by the forces of competition. Where expense preference is general, by cooperation we may enjoy it. This conclusion is not necessarily vitiated if some firms do not have expense preference, for there can be cooperative solutions in which each firm is more or less permitted to indulge its own tastes. Oliver Williamson,[1] however, very reasonably supposed that there was a minimum tolerable level of profits, and it is clear that competition from a non-expense firm may then force an expense-orientated firm to give up its indulgence if the minimum profit level is endangered (as was the case in Williamson's empirical examples).

We can also envisage a game in which the taste for expense is represented, as in Baumol's original theory, in a taste for sales, and in which the dominant strategies are written in terms of advertising levels. Here again there may be a cooperative solution with both firms playing high advertising, and if the game is extended to include price strategies specifically, and if cross-elasticities with respect to price are relatively high, as compared to those for advertising, then we are likely to get a cooperative solution with high advertising and high prices.

Conclusions

Our basic conclusion is that a multi-divisional corporation, with a given but flexible endowment of capital, may perceive itself as playing a game with a number of other corporations with whom it is 'interdependent' in the sense that they all have the capacity to produce with reasonable efficiency in a common group of oligopolistic markets (using the concept of market structure described in section I). A cooperative solution to this game will uniquely determine the output of each player in each market, and hence the corporation's allocation of resources to its various divisions, its prices and its overall profits. We can see that if this particular corporation were endowed with more capital, the solutions would be different. We can arrange solutions for sets of possible sizes for each of the corporations arranged in a set of overall rates of return on each one's total capital

[1] Op. cit.

employed. Beyond certain boundaries of 'increasing returns' this set would be convex, in the sense that a higher size for the individual corporation, given the sizes of the others, would be tending to reduce its rate of return. By some appropriate criterion of motivation (e.g. maximization of welfare of stockholders, or of a managerial utility function), it may be possible to determine a general equilibrium for the size and production allocation of the whole interdependent group. A firm which, in partial equilibrium, has reached such a point can be said to be in static equilibrium. Its rate of return on capital is then uniquely determined in partial equilibrium.

The equilibrium stems from the limited, historically endowed technical knowledge of the firm. If the firm is out of equilibrium, it must somehow be able to move towards equilibrium, fairly rapidly, without affecting its historical endowment. Having reached equilibrium, it may then set about to search to change and improve its endowment of knowledge, including its information concerning markets it has previously ignored merely for lack of information (i.e. markets which lay outside its *perceived* game). The profits it earns from equilibrium we call its 'operating profits', and they provide, among other things, the finance for the expenditure required to support the search process. The search process, in effect, leads to changed comparative advantages, changed financial and other threat-strength, and so on. This, then, is a process of long-run growth, on which growth models of the firm are based. In long-run growth, it is possible for the static equilibrium size of the firm to expand *without* necessarily leading to any reduction in the overall operating profit rate. In other words the firm may grow in steady state.

Finally, our conclusions regarding static partial equilibrium price theory suggests that rational behaviour in a system of general oligopoly must lead to the cooperative solution in each oligopolistic market. This solution specifically determines the number of firms in an industry and indicates the effects of entry possibilities on price. If the cooperative hypothesis is strictly adhered to, we obtain results with small groups which are rather similar to the excess capacity theorems of large-group monopolistic competition: free entry leads to lower profits, but not lower prices. If the prospects for an entrant in the 'joint-monopoly' solution are inferior to his best outside opportunities, he will not enter; if his prospects outside are inferior to the most pessimistic outcome (low prices and 'non-cooperation' by the incumbent) inside, his entry is inevitable. Between these

CE L 2

situations, however, the entry-deterrent hypothesis may imply a bluff on the part of the incumbent which, if successful, leads to a solution which is not the cooperative solution of game theory. Although the result is not strictly stable, there are circumstances where one might plausibly expect it to survive for some while. If, and only if, this happens, prices will be lower, costs lower and profits *higher* than in the cooperative solution.

III. APPLICATIONS OF A 'LINEAR' GROWTH MODEL

A general introduction to steady-state growth models of the firm has been given above. The basic functions in these models, such as the dividend function and present-value function,[1] are usually assumed to be non-linear, partly because such assumptions seem intuitively plausible, and partly because they may seem necessary to avoid implausible extreme conclusions.[2] If, however, we are to make some progress in testing and identifying the growth models, and if we are to apply them more generally to economic problems at large (such as the problem of identifying the forces controlling the development of the size-distribution of corporations), we must attempt to simplify them. It would be convenient, at least, if important predicted variables, such as the growth rate, could be expressed as approximately linear functions of easily interpretable coefficients representing the 'structure' of the super-environment.

A possible linear model

Let us try a model in which both dividend function and present value function are, in fact, assumed to be linear. We could build up a linear dividend function by assuming that the normalized level of develop-

[1] For an explanation, see p. 17 above.

[2] For example, if we combine a linear dividend function with a present-value function which is not linear, but of the form $Y(g) = 1/(i - g)$ (see p. 22 above), it can be shown that the optimum growth rate with 'classical' motivation is either zero (or negative if permitted) or equal to the discount rate. But in the latter event, the valuation ratio is infinite, the so-called growth-stock paradox. Or, with a non-linear dividend function, e.g. incorporating 'dynamic diminishing returns', the paradox can be avoided but cannot be made impossible. See Lintner above, section III.

ment expenditure required to sustain a given growth rate was a fixed proportion of the excess of this growth rate over the immanent growth rate, the latter representing the autonomous growth rate of demand in the markets for the firm's existing products, i.e. the growth rate if the firm incurred no development expenditure. This function would be

$$f = a.(g - \bar{g}) \tag{1}$$

where $\bar{g}$ represents the immanent growth rate, g the desired growth rate and f development expenditure normalized by (i.e. divided by) assets.[1] The coefficient a is a constant measuring, in effect, the 'marginal cost of growth'. By assuming this marginal cost to be constant and independent not only of the passage of time, but also of the value of g, we make our basic linearizing assumption to be contrasted with the more usual assumption of dynamic diminishing returns implying that it increases with g. In other words we assume the super-environment to have 'constant malleability',[2] with the coefficient a providing an inverse measure of this malleability.

When development expenditure is normalized by assets, the operating profit rate,[3] which we will signify by $\bar{p}$, has a very simple relationship to the current dividend (per unit of assets) payable with a given growth rate, because the latter has to be the operating profit rate, less normalized development expenditure, less the required rate of new plant investment! if we assume, as usual,[4] that all growth is internally financed, the last-named is equal to the growth rate itself.[5] The dividend function becomes

$$D(g) = \bar{p} + a.\bar{g} - (1 + a).g. \tag{2}$$

As regards the present value function, we do not do great violence to Lintner's theory (when he introduces 'unstable' uncertainty – see p. 201 below) by assuming the form to be linear, although its precise form can in fact be ascertained by inspection of his equations. The essential proposition is that with uncertainty increasing with futurity, the number of years' purchase applied to a given current dividend will generally increase with the expected growth rate of the dividend,

---

[1] Cf. Solow, below, who normalizes by assets; the difference is mainly a matter of convenience.

[2] For definition, see p. 12 above.　　　[3] For definition, see p. 282 above.

[4] See p. 21 above for alternative assumptions.

[5] We assume (for convenience) that only a negligible quantity of tangible assets are employed by the development divisions.

but will always be finite. In a real-life stock market, which does not necessarily possess the rationality and understanding that the theory necessarily requires, a linear representation of this effect may be not unreasonable. It can be observed, in principle, by linear regressions (see Appendix B) of the reciprocal of the dividend yield on the various proxies (such as past growth rate, or normalized retained profits) which have been suggested for the expected growth rate. So we propose

$$Y(g) = y_1 + y_2 . g. \tag{3}$$

The coefficients arise from the degree of risk-aversion, the riskless discount rate and the rate at which uncertainty increases with futurity. The *ratio* y_1/y_2 expresses the market's preference for slow growth (of a *given* current dividend) over faster growth, and will tend to be higher, for example, the faster the rate of increase of uncertainty with futurity and the higher the degree of risk-aversion. The coefficient y_1, however, does not represent the valuation of a certain dividend; it represents the valuation of an uncertain dividend whose expected growth rate happens to be zero.

The resulting growth-valuation function is built up as follows:

$$\begin{aligned} v = v(g) &= D(g) . Y(g) \\ &= (\bar{p} + a . \bar{g} - g . (1 + a)) . (y_1 + y_2 g). \end{aligned} \tag{4}$$

This is evidently the equation of a parabola with a finite positive maximum. The growth rate at the maximum valuation ratio – the optimum growth rate for 'classical' motivation – is obtained very simply by differentiation:

$$g(\max v) = \tfrac{1}{2}(\bar{p} + a . \bar{g})/(1 + a) - \tfrac{1}{2} y_1/y_2. \tag{5}$$

Thus the optimum 'classical' growth rate becomes a linear function of the operating profit rate and the immanent growth rate, with a constant equal to half the stock market's 'growth-aversion' ratio, y_1/y_2, and a slope equal to one-half of one over one plus the cost of growth ($\tfrac{1}{2}/1 + a$). If we wanted to test this model on the assumption of universal classical motivation, it could be identified by regressions of growth rate on *reported* profit rate, making use of the fact that the latter is equal to the *operating* profit rate ($\bar{p}$, which we cannot easily observe) less $a(g - \bar{g})$.

Unfortunately a parabola, always convenient for a maximizing problem, is by the same token inconvenient when, as in the managerial case, we wish to maximize its independent variable subject to a constraint on the dependent variable. John H. Williamson has given a general statement[1] of the conditions at the optimum in the managerial case, on the assumption that the minimum permitted valuation ratio is a specific fraction of the maximum ratio, and it is also possible, on this assumption, to obtain a precise specific result with the present model. But the result cannot be even approximately linear: the predicted 'managerial' growth rate is found to be equal to the predicted 'classical' rate plus a number which is itself a complex function of the coefficients. All that can be said of this number with any simplicity is that so long as we take the relevant root of the equation of the solution, the number is always positive and that, of course, it is zero if the permitted proportionate reduction of the valuation ratio below the maximum is zero, and that it increases as the square root of the permitted reduction. It also increases (in a complex manner) with the operating profit rate. The effects of changes in the other coefficients are more difficult to generalize, although intuitively one would expect that a reduction in the cost of growth, for example, would increase the number, which represents, in effect, the degree of *effective* managerial growth preference expressed in the situation.[2] (The permitted reduction of the valuation ratio represents the general desire for growth, indicated by the extent to which the management is prepared to sacrifice stockholders' interests in favour of growth. The effective preference is the result in terms of actual extra predicted growth, and depends on the other coefficients of the model as well.)

An alternative linear model

An alternative approach is to assume a much more naïve type of stock-market behaviour, for example that the valuation of a share is based on the dividend only, or on the earnings only. Experiment suggests that the former is more likely to produce a reasonable approximation to the general behaviour of the parabolic managerial model, as described in the immediately preceding paragraph, which

[1] Op. cit.
[2] But see *Note*, p. 317.

is a desirable attribute owing to the former's evident theoretical superiority. The model we obtain is

$$v = v(g) = D(g) . Y(g)$$
$$= (\bar{p} - (1+a)g + a.\bar{g}).y_3 \tag{6}$$

Maximize v subject to $v = \bar{v}$.

The present value of the current dividend is now obtained from a constant, y_3, representing the number of years' purchase and entirely independent of the growth rate; the market is assumed to ignore completely the growth implied in the actual retentions.

The predicted managerial growth rate, with the above model, is

$$g = \frac{\bar{p} + a.\bar{g} - \bar{v}/y_3}{1 + a}. \tag{7}$$

(An earnings model has a similar result without the unit in the denominator.) It will be seen that this growth rate is twice as sensitive to changes in the operating profit rate as is the classical optimum in the parabolic model, a difference which will also be found in the same degree and in the same direction in the more complex results obtained from applying the parabolic model to the managerial case. The dividend model, however, has no sensible solution for the classical case, because it predicts that the classical optimum growth rate is always zero. We can, however, define a value of $\bar{v}$ which, while allowing the firm to behave *as if* managerial, would predict the same growth rate as in a more sophisticated model with classical behaviour (although to obtain full comparability we need to manipulate the coefficients to provide an optimum solution which is also a point on the parabolic valuation function). Then the extent to which the actual $\bar{v}$ lies below this value is a measure of growth preference.

A 'disturbed' steady-state and the size-distribution of corporations

A particular advantage of linear models is that, if the exogenous factors, such as the operating profit rate, are in fact uncertain, i.e. subject to probability distributions, we can determine optimum *expected* growth rates from the expected values of the exogenous factors and their *variances* in a fairly straightforward manner: in a linear model, the variance of the expected growth rate is in general a proportionate function of these variances. Inspection of equations (5) and (7) above, for example, shows that the standard deviation of a 'classical' growth rate (equation (5)) is $\frac{1}{2}/(1+a)$ times the standard deviation of the operating profit rate, and of a 'managerial' growth rate is precisely twice this figure, assuming in both cases that the operating profit rate is the only uncertain factor. If other factors are disturbed, independently of each other, equivalent results can be obtained by simple addition of variances. If disturbances are not independent, the necessary co-variances can be introduced without difficulty.

But what do we really mean by 'disturbance' in this context? In the case of an individual firm, required to determine its policy under conditions of uncertainty (and we have, of course, already implicitly assumed uncertainty in our treatment of valuation), we may say that the firm is subjectively uncertain about the characteristics of its own super-environment. These characteristics are apparently quantified by the coefficients and constants in the growth valuation function, such as operating profit rate, cost-of-growth coefficient and co-efficients of the present-value function. But the coefficients of the present-value function depend partly on the degree of uncertainty, so we appear to have encountered circularity. Strictly, we should look into the present-value function further, as is done by Lintner (p. 207 above), in order to separate underlying elements which are independent of the actual degree of uncertainty (such as riskless discount rate, degree of investor risk-aversion, etc.) and the elements expressing uncertainty itself, such as the variance of the expected dividends. In the present discussion, however, it is convenient to simplify the exposition by imagining that uncertainty is entirely concentrated in the dividend function and, as a further simplification, that as in the example above only the operating profit rate is in fact uncertain.

The present-value function depends on the uncertainty of expected future dividends, which depends in turn on the uncertainty of the growth rate. The growth rate, however, is a matter of choice for the firm, and we ask the question 'How do I determine my optimum growth rate, when I do not know my operating profit rate, but only its probability distribution, and I cannot make my decision until I know the resulting variance of my growth rate, because that determines my present-value coefficients?' Lintner deals with this problem by inserting uncertainty directly into the growth rate itself (rather than into the profit rate[1] and assuming that the long-run central value of the retention ratio is held constant, so that growth-rate deviations are directly reflected in dividend deviations. Here, however, I want to *derive* the variance of the growth rate from variances of exogenous factors in my model (in particular from the variance of the operating profit rate), so Lintner's otherwise reasonable line of attack is barred to me.

A convenient approach is to imagine that the firm expects its operating profit rate to be drawn out of a hat, the lottery being arranged to produce an expected value p, with normal variance σ_p^2. The draw will occur tomorrow and the value drawn will be treated as certain for the time being. I will determine my optimum growth rate according to that value, for the time being (but I do not yet know what the value is going to be). I do know, however, that after a certain moderate length of time another draw will be held, and I will repeat the procedure, and again at a later draw, and so on. I still cannot determine my growth rate, because I do not know my present-value function, but I do know that whatever my present-value function, the *variance* of the long-run average growth rate resulting from the process will be derived from the variance of the operating-profit-rate lottery in the way described above, and will be quite independent of the present-value function itself, on account of the linear character of our models (equations (5) and (7)), for both types of motivation. So I now know the variance of the expected future dividends, at each point in time, although I do not yet know the expected values themselves, but the latter are soon determined because we now have the present-value function and hence the missing element in the equations.

In order to produce Lintner's condition of 'unstable' uncertainty (meaning that uncertainty increases with futurity), which is required to produce a properly behaved present-value function, we must be more explicit about some of the relationships involved. By a heroic (or foolhardy) simplification, we may characterize the nature of the present-value function by saying that its value, for a given growth rate, depends on the path, through time, of the variance of the logarithms of the resulting dividend. In the series of lotteries described above, if the results of successive draws are independent of each other (there is no expected serial correlation between successive operating profit rates), we generate a process in which, looking for-

---

[1] But cf. Lintner, *QJE* (1964) op. cit.

ward to time t, the average growth rate realized over the intervening draws will of course be uncertain, normally distributed and with variance as predicted by the equations. Ten years later the corresponding variance will again be the same. With constant (normally distributed) variance in the long-run growth rate, the distribution of resulting dividends will be lognormal,[1] with logarithmic variance increasingly linearly over time at a rate equal to the constant normal variance of the growth rates. Lintner shows that in order to ensure convergence of the present-value series, given plausible assumptions about investors' attitudes to risk, it is necessary for the logarithmic variance of the outcome (dividend) to increase at an accelerating rate over time. This will occur, in our example, if there is positive serial correlation in the successive probability distributions of operating profit rates, i.e. if a firm which has good luck in the first draw is more likely than average to have good luck in the second, and vice versa, and so on. More precisely, we require a subjective belief in these conditional probabilities. The general explanation for this belief is that the amount of information available now to help evaluate the probability distributions diminishes into the future, but is expected to increase as the future unfolds; a firm which was actually successful, it is believed, will have revealed evidence concerning its own super-environment leading to a more optimistic evaluation of subsequent prospects.

The subjectively imagined process of drawing operating profit rates out of a hat could also be used to describe the generation of an objective distribution of the sizes of a population of firms behaving according to the model. But, in the objective process, we have no *a priori* reason for expecting serial correlation in the outcomes. The

---

[1] This statement is not strictly correct. The dividend declared immediately after one of the profit-rate 'draws' reflects both the profit-rate draw and the growth rate chosen. Per unit of assets this dividend is a *linear* function of the coefficients, because the dividend function is a linear function of the chosen growth rate, which is itself a linear function of the coefficients (substitute g as determined by equations (5) or (7) into the dividend function, equation (2)). To obtain the expected total dividend, t years hence, just after a draw, we must multiply this linear predicted value of dividends per unit of assets by the expected *level* of assets. The *distribution* of this dividend is therefore the product of a normal distribution with a lognormal distribution, the former resulting from the normally distributed variance of the operating profit rate in the dividend-per-unit-of-assets equation, and the latter from the process described in the main text. It appears, however, that as time passes, the lognormal effect will increasingly dominate the distribution of the logs of the total dividend, which is the distribution that mainly concerns us.

nature of the disturbance implied by the lottery is now, indeed, rather different. In place of uncertainty of knowledge concerning the super-environment of an individual firm, we are now perturbing successively the actual super-environments of a large number of firms. The perturbations are a cumulation of small factors affecting commercial success – in the case of the operating profit rate, the outcomes of the fortunes of war in the oligopoly game. We cannot draw on the proposition that success breeds success in the simple way that, e.g., increased size means larger profits and greater growth capacity, although we could perhaps use arguments such as that a successful firm gains psychological confidence and becomes more daring, these being favourable attributes for further success. But the same argument can also suggest recklessness or slack, both phenomena which have often been observed in real life.

With positive serial correlation in actual growth rates, the logarithmic variance of actual sizes increases at an accelerating rate over time in the same way as the variance in the subjective distribution described above. This implies an increase over time in the observed values of most generally accepted measures of industrial concentration, which is also at an accelerating rate. The effect, of course, can be damped by new births (for a more profound discussion of these matters, see Appendix A by John Eatwell). But we do not in fact require consistency in the objective and subjective probability distributions governing these processes. The subjective distribution governing the present-value function and the determination of optimum expected growth rates may remain permanently more 'explosive' with respect to time than the objective distribution governing actual growth rates, and the two types of distribution need not be reconciled in the light of experience, because the factor causing the divergence – the expectation that relevant information will become available in the future which is not available now – is itself permanent.[1]

It is worth noting that the linear model predicts that if, in fact, objective positive serial correlation in operating profit rates actually occurs, we expect to observe positive serial correlation in both observed growth rates and reported profit rates, but that the former correlation coefficient should be greater than the latter (because of the relations between the variances resulting from the nature of the model). We in fact usually observe the opposite state of affairs: profit

---

[1] I am especially indebted to discussions at the Long Island Conference for this passage.

rates are quite strongly serially correlated while growth rates are only modestly so. This is not necessarily a 'refutation', because in reality we would expect other disturbances in the super-environment, which could add to the variance of growth rates without adding to that of operating profit rates, and because there is a good deal of evidence that the type of data from which such observations arise tends to contain a deal of measurement disturbance of growth rates, not present to the same extent in the data on profit rates.[1]

Finally, we note that whatever the character of the process generating the objective size-distribution of firms (always accepting that our model at least predicts that it will take some form of proportionate effect, but may be damped or explosive as the case may be), there is a specific relationship between the development of the distributions of the various measures of size. We have already studied the development of the size-distribution of assets. If the objective distribution-generating process were, in fact, identical to that of the subjective distribution, and the latter were of the Lintner type with increasing uncertainty described above, we have already noted (p. 311, n. 1 above) the relation between the distribution of assets and that of dividends. On the same assumption, there is a further relationship between the development of the size-distribution of assets and that of market values, the latter, it will be remembered, relating to the former by the valuation ratio. After any draw in the lottery series, a lucky firm with classical motivation will choose an above-average growth rate and display an above-average valuation ratio, and conversely for the less fortunate firm. The distribution of market values will therefore develop a greater logarithmic variance than that of assets, and there is no obvious reason for expecting attrition of this difference. Interestingly, it does not occur in the case of 'managerial' motivation, because the managerially motivated firm is by implication attempting to stabilize the valuation ratio. If it is lucky, in the lottery it absorbs the advantage entirely in faster growth, rather than, as in the case of the classical firm, in a mixture of faster growth and higher valuation. By the same token (as we have already seen from equation (7), a given degree of general disturbance in the operating profit rates produces a greater variance of growth rates in a managerially motivated population, and the variances of profit rate

---

[1] For a discussion of data on serial correlation in profit rates, see John Eatwell's Appendix A, below; for a discussion of measurement bias, see my own Appendix B.

and of growth rate in such a population should be closer together. In the presence of serial correlation in operating profit rates, this population will also display, therefore, greater similarity between the serial correlation coefficients of observed growth rates and reported profit rates.

IV. SOME CONCLUSIONS

The three preceding sections of this paper contained discussions of aspects of the corporate system which were designed to represent some ingredients of a more integrated and more general theory, but it cannot be said that, even after discussion and revision, we are close to cooking the dish. It is possible to describe the kind of way the ingredients will blend, but not the precise end-product. In section I we tried to conceptualize the structure of an oligopolistic system populated by large diversified corporations. In section II we discussed the nature of general competition among them, assuming a chain of oligopolies, without taking account of the possibilities of long-run growth. In section III we studied the growth process which develops from a base of given results of playing the game described in section II on the board described in section I.

The growth process develops a size-distribution of *corporations*, which is by no means necessarily similar to the size-distribution of the quasi-firms (one-product operating divisions) of which they are composed; these could well result from a less dynamic process, although, to the extent that highly skewed size-distributions have been observed among populations which are specialized in quite narrowly defined industries, there is some evidence of similar forces at work to those which determine the general size-distribution. The size-distribution of the corporations, at a moment of time, was treated as a datum in the static oligopoly analysis of section II, and must clearly be a factor in the outcome of the general oligopoly game. Large corporations have larger threat-strength in any market, and can thus command more favourable shares in cooperative outcomes. Thus a corporation which has been fortunate in the growth process will tend to possess, of course, more and/or larger quasi-firms than the less fortunate firm, and will be able to ensure effective employment of these resources by obtaining, in the general cooperative solution, more and/or larger markets. This symmetry between the static and dynamic aspects of the problem is not inevitable; if it were not for the fact that size creates bargaining strength, there is no guarantee that the firms which had the capacity for fast long-run growth would be able to obtain adequate outlets for their resources, and they might therefore experience a falling rate of operating profit, over time, due to the pressure of the competitive environment. Because the symmetry exists, the system can expand with a persistent high level of concentration, which would probably be increasing if it were not for the existence of a modest rate of new entry into the population of large firms.[1]

The appearance of constant returns to scale as a phenomenon of industrial organization was clearly gradual, and we still see spectacular examples of rapid growth to large size of essentially owner-managed (or one-man-managed) concerns. It is also interesting to note that, at the time of writing, some of the best-known examples, on both sides of the Atlantic, are suffering set-backs, and that in the United Kingdom (December 1969) during one year the country's two best-known tycoons have been deprived of the management of the organizations they created and with whose success they were personally associated.[2] The *theoretical* effect of constant returns (i.e. removal of managerial economies), quite apart from the question of motivation, is a double one, and again displays a form of symmetry. In the static world, oligopoly becomes possible and likely. In the dynamic world, long-term growth becomes possible and likely, and carries with it the natural implication of concentration (because the growth rates, *pace* section III, are unlikely to be equal) and hence reinforces oligopoly.

Suppose a number of firms of moderate but equal size were suddenly presented with an already created static structure of markets as described in section I. Suppose they differed in comparative advantage in regard to different industries, but that in some sense they were equal in *general* ability; suppose these assumptions are sufficient to determine for each firm a unique share of specified markets (of course, we do not know that such an equilibrium exists), and thus an operating profit rate. Suppose we interpret the assumption of equal general ability to imply that the initial operating profit rates resulting from this game would be equal (i.e. each firm has

---

[1] See again Appendix A, esp. p. 407.
[2] Similar events have subsequently (1970) occurred in at least one large U.S. conglomerate and in a giant international company.

enough threat-strength to enforce a better solution if its operating profit rate is below average). From this initial drawing the corporations would grow at approximately equal rates, creating new outlets for new quasi-firms, stimulating expansion of demand for products of existing quasi-firms, and so on. They will gradually develop increasing comparative advantages in the fields in which they happened to specialize, and they will experience varying fortunes in the markets they discover. External economic events, and internal random disturbance of their general efficiency, will gradually cause the operating profit rates of the individual corporations to change and diverge. If we allow these disturbances to operate in the kinds of ways described at the end of section III, the growth rates will also diverge, distributed symmetrically if not precisely normally, and will generate skewed distributions of actual sizes which will be approximately symmetrically distributed logarithmically. The distribution of the observed population will then develop according to this effect, and to the effects of any new entry. Consequently, the reinforced, 'stable' regime of concentrated oligopoly, described above, seems to follow inevitably from the basic characteristics of the system, even if all firms start equal. In any economic-social system, it seems, where decentralization and individualism are manifested in considerable feedback of success on success – corporate success on corporate success, professional success on professional success, and private property breeding private property – the distribution of productive assets, of personal incomes and of private property will tend to become extremely skewed and, as is usually observed, often approximately lognormal: the large-scale concentrated corporate oligopoly capitalism we now inhabit is a natural consequence.

Whether these vague thoughts can be incorporated into more precise theories remains to be seen. We might take the simple economy of two corporations of equal size, with two markets, described in section II, and let it grow. Both firms begin with equal operating profit rates, but they will not (we saw) necessarily completely specialize one in each market. The solution does require, however, that at least one firm be completely specialized. Consequently, we only require chance divergences in the development of the factors governing the underlying profitability of each market for their operating profit rates to diverge, and hence for their growth rates to diverge. It is worth noting, however, that divergence is much more sure if we suppose it to arise basically from disturbance of the inherent qualities of the managements: without this assumption, it would seem that in our two-firm, two-economy model, the firm which experiences bad luck simply as a result of external factors (e.g. low growth in demand) should be able to use its threat-strength to redress the division of markets, much as would have been the case if the poor prospects in this market had been known at the outset. Being inherently as efficient as the other firm, but having experienced bad luck in the markets in which it has specialized, it will try to force its way into the other market. We often see this happening in real life. Of course, if sufficient time has passed, the recovery capacity of an unlucky firm will be affected by the development of comparative advantages; the lucky firm has learnt by doing in its own markets and thus erected some barriers to entry. Thus it remains the case that probably the most important single source of diverging growth rates is diverging quality of management, but the effect is most powerful when it develops in association with external factors as well. The conceptual organic unity of the corporation, albeit composed of diverse quasi-firms, remains an essential feature of the general character of the modern capitalist system. We have a system of competing planned economies, not a system of federations of competing quasi-entrepreneurs.

LATE NOTE

Since the manuscript was sent to press a suggestion has arisen which it is believed might lead to some progress in identifying growth models and discriminating between alternative behaviour hypotheses in statistical tests. Briefly the idea is to assume that the safe minimum valuation ratio in the 'managerial' model cannot be lower than the value which would be placed on the firm by a raider who intended to do no more than maintain its existing operating activities without further actual or attempted growth; he would thus be expecting to distribute the entire operating surplus to himself. With the parabolic valuation curve produced by the 'linear' growth model described above, this assumption makes the maximum possible managerial growth rate equal to precisely twice the corresponding 'classical' rate. Consequently the relationships between observed growth rates and observed (i.e. reported) profit rates predicted by the alternative hypotheses are greatly simplified (cf. pp. 306–7 above). It may then be possible to test the hypotheses by setting limits on the plausible values of the underlying coefficients (e.g. the coefficient a or 'cost of growth' should not be negative) and applying to regression studies of the type described in Appendixes A and B below. Some preliminary trials on the British data have proved rather interesting. It is hoped to publish an article shortly.

10 Some Implications of Alternative Criteria for the Firm

Robert M. Solow

To avoid elementary misunderstanding, I ought to begin by saying that there is unlikely ever to be a simple answer to the question: What does a firm maximize? In the first place, a firm, especially a large firm, may be unable to maximize anything. Different departments, different committees, different individuals may have different and even conflicting objectives which they pursue with a degree of success depending on a complicated balance of forces and personalities. In the second place, even if the firm does have a coherent objective or set of objectives – a utility function – it may be content with approximate solutions and rules of thumb. And in the third place, if the firm does actually maximize something, the thing that it maximizes in any concrete case is likely to be a very complicated quantity, depending on the relative strengths of many interests and persons – owners, managers, the government, public opinion – and on the character of the markets in which it operates. To understand the behaviour of a single complicated firm would be a combined operation in economics, sociology and psychiatry, and in the end the conclusions might not generalize very far, or at all.

Nevertheless, on a different level of abstraction it is useful to think of a 'typical' firm as maximizing something, and the question is: What thing? The orthodox answer to that question is, of course, profits or, more generally, the present value of the equity. Recently, mainly in response to the observed 'separation of ownership and control', alternative answers have been offered. In particular, it has been suggested (by Baumol) that large firms maximize total sales revenue subject to some constraint on the minimum tolerable profitability, or (by Marris) that they maximize their rate of growth, subject to some similar constraint (or perhaps maximize some utility function in which the rate of growth and profitability are arguments). My own inclination has been to prefer the orthodox answer; this paper has been stimulated mainly by the wish to know whether this inclination reflects mere middle age as much as it reflects any more respectable motive.

There is another possible view, according to which it may not matter very much exactly what firms try to maximize. It is perhaps more important to know how firms respond to changes in data, like tax rates, interest rates, wages, investment subsidies and the like. It is possible that the answer to this practical question is pretty much the same, regardless of what it is that firms are assumed to maximize. Firms with different objectives are unlikely to respond in exactly the same way to changes in data. But if their qualitative response is more or less insensitive, within limits, to the precise nature of their objectives, then it is at least possible to get on with research without first answering the much more difficult question about what they wish to accomplish.

That is the line I propose to follow here. To do so, I must formulate a model of the firm from the beginning, because the usual presentations (Marris, Williamson) suppress some important details. I do not hesitate to make very special assumptions about the demand and cost conditions facing the firm. They will simplify the analysis. It will probably not be hard to achieve greater generality, but that is hardly worth doing unless the preliminary results suggest that the analysis is worth pursuing.

STEADY STATE

The firm is assumed to be choosing now, once and for all, the constant rate at which it will grow forever. Call this rate g. Then the firm's output, capital assets, and employment will all grow perpetually at the proportional rate g. Changes in the general price level are assumed away, and the price of the firm's output, the price of capital goods, and the wage rate will all be constant. If technical progress is going on, it will have to be strictly labor-augmenting; then the wage rate is assumed to rise just fast enough to offset increasing productivity, so that the cost of an efficiency-unit of labor is constant. The whole economy is assumed to be growing at its natural rate, g_0. Obviously this creates a problem. If a firm should choose to grow forever at a rate g which is larger than g_0, eventually it (or whichever firm chooses the largest rate of growth) must dominate the whole economy, and the economy will be growing not at g_0, but at g. It is not hard to think of forces that might prevent this from happening. But it will be simpler just to interpret 'forever' to mean 'a long time, but not long enough for a single firm to become as large as the whole economy'.

COST CONDITIONS

The firm produces a single output. I will assume that it requires inputs in fixed proportions. This precludes any analysis of the influence of the firm's objective on the choice of technique, but that extension could easily be accomplished if it should turn out to be worth while. There are constant returns to scale. One unit of capital can be bought for m dollars, is subject to evaporative depreciation at the rate f per unit time, and provides capacity to produce b units of output. Since labor and other current inputs are required in fixed amounts per unit of output (and capital), and since the wage rate and the price of materials are assumed constant, we can summarize current costs by setting them equal to a constant, say a dollars per unit of capital or a/b dollars per unit of output.

DEMAND CONDITIONS

At any instant of time, the firm faces a falling market demand curve for its output. For simplicity, I shall assume the price-elasticity of demand to be constant. Since the economy is growing at the rate g_0 per unit time, one might plausibly assume that the demand curve is shifting upward at the same rate, g_0 per unit time, even if the firm makes no special effort to expand its market. But this sort of theory adds to its plausibility by assuming that firms can and do advertise, promote, and package in order to increase sales at a given price beyond the normal growth that occurs as the economy grows. Selling costs are costs, and one requires some assumption about their behaviour. I shall assume that if the firm maintains a constant price and makes no expenditure on selling costs, its sales will grow at some constant rate g_m which may be equal to or less than g_0. If it wishes to expand its sales (with price constant) at any faster rate, the firm will have to spend on promotion. I shall assume that to raise the rate of growth of its sales by one percentage point, the firm must spend on promotion a certain fraction of its sales revenue (price times quantity), and that each further increase of one percentage point in the rate of growth of sales requires a successively larger increase in the fraction of sales revenue devoted to promotion. That is, in order to achieve a steady growth of sales at the rate g, the firm must spend on selling costs the fraction $s(g)$ of its sales revenue; $s(g)$ is a non-negative, non-decreasing, convex function of g, with $s(g_m) = 0$.

This assumption has the peculiarity that spending a certain fraction of sales revenue on promotion generates a certain rate of growth of demand, while 'spending' a certain fraction of sales revenue on price reduction generates merely a once-for-all increase in quantity demanded. There is an analogy between this treatment of promotional expenditure and investment. Promotional expenditures are supposed to buy an increment to a stock of 'goodwill'. If the level of the demand curve depends on the stock, its rate of shift will depend on current promotional expenditure. It is merely convenient to normalize by the total sales revenue. I suppose one could argue that the level of price affects the rate of shift of demand, by controlling the rate of penetration of new markets. Something like that does happen temporarily when a price is suddenly lowered and new markets are tapped. But as a steady-state relation, it strikes me as absurd.

I have called the fraction $s(g)$ 'selling costs', but it can just as well include all costs – training and management costs, say – associated with expansion.

THE VALUE OF THE FIRM

The market value of the firm is the present value of the stream of dividends, discounted at whatever rate, i, is appropriate, given the pure rate of interest, the riskiness of the business, and whatever else matters. As always, in these circumstances, the value of the firm is independent of its financial structure, in the manner of Modigliani and Miller. Williamson's argument, that restriction to internal finance does not limit the rate of growth, applies here too. We might just as well suppose, therefore, that the growth of the firm is financed entirely out of retained earnings.

Suppose the firm chooses to fix a price once and for all and grow at a steady-state rate g. Its output will be $Q\exp(gt)$, where Q is the output at $t=0$, the current instant. According to the assumptions about demand, $Q\exp(gt) = p^{-n}\exp(gt)$, where n is the constant price elasticity of demand. Therefore $p = Q^{-1/n}$ and gross revenues will be $pQ\exp(gt) = Q^{\theta}\exp(gt)$, where $\theta = 1 - 1/n$. The firm's stock of capital goods is $K\exp(gt)$, so $Q = bK$ and $Q^{\theta} = b^{\theta}K^{\theta}$. After allowance for selling costs, net revenue is $T(g)b^{\theta}K^{\theta}\exp(gt)$, where $T(g) = 1 - s(g)$. Current production costs, including depreciation, amount to $(a + mf)K\exp(gt)$. Since the firm is growing at rate g, its net investment in new capital is $gK\exp(gt)$ at a cost of $mgK\exp(gt)$, and since the firm is financed entirely out of retained earnings this sum has to be deducted from net revenue along with operating costs to get the flow of dividends, namely $(T(g)b^{\theta}K^{\theta} - (a + m(f + g))K)\exp(gt)$. This quantity has to be discounted back to time zero (multiplied by $\exp(-it)$) and integrated over all future time to get the market value of the firm at the current instant

$$V = \frac{T(g)b^{\theta}K^{\theta} - (a + m(f + g))K}{i - g}.$$

This[1] makes sense, of course, only if i exceeds g; else the market value of the firm diverges, i.e. is infinite. One really has to bound the rate of growth well below the rate at which dividends are discounted (which presumably exceeds the pure rate of interest by some margin) because otherwise V will behave very violently as g approaches i. Marris avoids this problem by arguing that the rate of discount i is

---

[1] The firm need not choose a constant-price strategy. It could, for instance, generate a rate of growth of sales by a combination of advertising and perpetual price reduction (or even more advertising and perpetual price increase). Suppose, for example, it wishes sales to grow like Qe^{gt}, and prices to fall like $p_0\exp(-nt)$. Then it must induce its demand curve to shift upward at rate h so that

$$Qe^{gt} = [p_0\exp(-\pi t)]^{-n}\exp(ht) = p_0^{-n}\exp[(h + n\pi)t].$$

This is consistent provided that $g = h + n\pi$. Total sales revenue is then $b^{\theta}K^{\theta}\exp[(g - \pi)t]$ and net revenue after selling costs is $T(g - n\pi)b^{\theta}K^{\theta}\exp[(g - \pi)t]$. The value of the firm becomes

$$V = \frac{T(g - n\pi)b^{\theta}K^{\theta}}{i + \pi - g} - \frac{(a + m(f + g))K}{i - g},$$

which reduces to the constant-price formula when $\pi = 0$. The firm must then choose a best combination of g and π (or g and h), in view of its ultimate objective. I have not investigated this more complicated situation, but could do so if anyone thought the results likely to be interesting. The outcome probably depends very much on the exact shape of $T(.)$.

not independent of g, that somehow the dividend streams associated with higher rates of growth must be intrinsically more uncertain than those associated with lower rates of growth. He then takes i as a function of g bounded away from g above. I have no notion whether this is so; it doesn't seem to me to be a very compelling argument on its face. I shall accomplish the same purpose more simply by just assuming that $T(g)$ falls to zero for some g less than i. This requires that $s(i) > 1$. I would not argue that this is a compelling assumption either. Presumably if any firm could promise a dividend stream growing at a rate very near i, the market would soon revise i. The main thing is to restrict the analysis to rates of growth not too large.

The value of the firm is a function of K and g, its initial scale and its rate of growth. Both K and g are decision variables for the firm's management. Before I take up alternative criteria of choice, it is convenient to plot the behaviour of V as a function of K and g.

THE SHAPE OF THE VALUATION FUNCTION

In Fig. 10.1, the rate of growth g is plotted on the vertical axis and the initial stock of capital goods K is plotted horizontally. The locus of points where $V = 0$ includes, first of all, from the formula for V, the points $K = 0$. The elasticity of demand, n, has to be greater than one for the same reasons as always; therefore $\theta = 1 - 1/n$ is between zero and one. (It is only necessary that the elasticity of demand exceed one for price sufficiently high, but I am taking it to be constant for convenience.) The locus $V = 0$ also includes the points

$$K = (T(g)b^{\theta}/a + m(f + g))^{n}.$$

It leaves the vertical axis at $g = g_1$, where $T(g_1) = 0$, so $s(g_1) = 1$. From the restriction on s, g_1 is less than i. The locus falls, and cuts the horizontal axis at $K_v = (T(0)b^{\theta}/a + mf)^{n}$. V is positive everywhere inside the triangular region under the curve.

Next, one calculates that

$$\partial V/\partial K = \frac{T(g)b^{\theta}\theta K^{\theta-1} - a - m(f + g)}{i - g}$$

so that $\partial V/\partial K = 0$ where $K = (Tb^{\theta}\theta/a + m(f + g))^{n}$. This curve leaves the vertical axis where $T = 0$, therefore at $g = g_1$, and falls steadily, cutting the horizontal axis at $K_0 = (T(0))b^\theta \theta / a + mf)^n$. $K_0 < K_v$, because $0 < \theta < 1$. From the formula, $\partial V / \partial K$ is positive to the left of this curve and negative to its right.

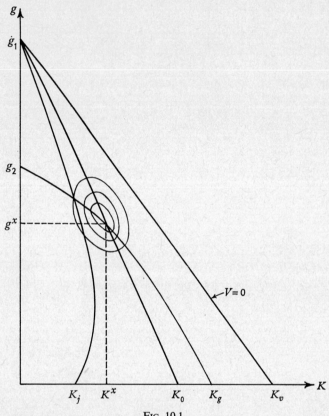

FIG 10.1

A similar calculation shows that

$$\frac{\partial V}{\partial g} = \frac{(T + (i - g)T')b^\theta K^\theta - (a + m(f + i))K}{(i - g)^2}$$

so that $\dfrac{\partial V}{\partial g} = 0$ when $K = 0$ and when

$$K = \left[\frac{(T + (i - g)T'b^\theta}{a + m(f + i)} \right]^n.$$

This curve leaves the vertical axis at $g = g_2$, where g_2 is the root of $T(g) + (i - g)T'(g) = 0$. Now $T(g_1) + (i - g_1)T'(g_1) = (i - g_1)T'(g_1) < 0$.

Moreover, $\frac{d}{dg}[T+(i-g)T']=(i-g)T''<0$, so $g_2<g_1$. The curve falls to the right, and reaches the horizontal axis at

$$K=K_g=\left[\frac{(T(0)+iT'(0)b^\theta}{a+m(f+i)}\right]^n.$$

It is algebraically possible that $T(g)+(i-g)T'(g)<0$ for all relevant growth rates. Then $\frac{\partial V}{\partial g}$ is always negative, and for any K, the maximum value occurs when $g=g_m$. It seems more plausible, however, to suppose that at $g=g_m$, where $s(g_m)=0$, also $s'(g_m)=0$. Then there is always a root g_2, strictly between g_m and g_1. (It is enough, of course, that $s'(g_m)$ be sufficiently small, i.e. less than $(i-g_m)^{-1}$.)

It is clear that $K_g<K_v$. $K_g\leqq K_0$ if $a+mf/(a+m(f+i))\leqq\dfrac{\theta T(0)}{T(0)+iT'(0)}$ and $K_g>K_0$ otherwise. The cleanest case is when $K_g>K_0$, and I have drawn Fig. 10.1 that way. The other possibilities are that the curve $\partial V/\partial g=0$ cuts the curve $\partial V/\partial K=0$ more than once or not at all. I will mention at the appropriate moment what these possibilities mean. It is clear from the formula for $\partial V/\partial g$ that for each fixed g it is positive for small K, then zero, then negative for large K.

The intersection at (K^*, g^*) is the point where V achieves its maximum value V^*. The largest market value a firm can have at $t=0$ is had by a firm which starts with capital goods K^* and grows forever at the rate g^*. (We are comparing only steady states, remember.) A firm which grows faster is worth less because the costs of expansion cancel the high sales. A firm which starts larger is worth less because its higher sales at each point of time drive down the price too much.

The locus of points along which V is constant at some value less than V^* is a closed contour surrounding (K^*, g^*). Each such contour passes through the horizontal when it crosses the curve along which $\partial V/\partial K=0$, and passes through the vertical when it crosses the curve along which $\partial V/\partial g=0$. The inner of any pair of contours corresponds to the higher value of V. If $\partial V/\partial K=0$ should cut $\partial V/\partial g=0$ again, this time from below, the intersection is a saddle-point, not a maximum. If there should be no intersection in the relevant range of rates of growth, the largest V occurs at the lowest relevant rate of growth, which may be negative.

ALTERNATIVE DECISION CRITERIA

(a) *Owner-oriented firms*

The usual shorthand is that the orthodox criterion is maximization of the present value of the firm. But that does not seem quite right in this context, when the initial stock of capital is also a decision variable; if two firms choose the same growth rate, it is not clear that the one choosing the higher (perpetual) V is doing the right thing if that choice requires it to acquire a more expensive initial stock of capital.

Marris avoids this difficulty by supposing that the orthodox criterion is maximization of the 'valuation ratio', V/mK in my notation. But this works only because he assumes that the valuation ratio is independent of the initial scale of the firm, and depends only on the rate of growth. He does this more or less by fiat, taking it for granted from the beginning that the rate of profit on capital is independent of the initial scale of the firm. This would be so, given the way I have set up the problem, only if $\theta = 1$, that is only if the firm's demand curve were infinitely elastic. (Just the exactly right degree of increasing returns to scale would do the trick, but that would be mere fluke.) Infinitely elastic demand is a peculiar starting-point for a theory that is supposed to be able to cope with the modern large corporation.

Williamson's procedure is not entirely clear to me. But I take it that in the end he treats the initial stock of capital as one of the exogenous givens of the problem. I shall be forced to do the same later in this paper, because the growth-oriented theories seem not to solve satisfactorily the problem of choice of initial scale.

For now, however, the more general formulation seems preferable. Somehow the firm must choose both K and g.

There seem to be (at least) two ways an 'orthodox' theory of the growing firm can be framed. One is to suppose that the management has, so to speak, just taken over a firm with a given size (stock of capital) and is stuck with it (except, of course, as it chooses a steady-state growth rate). This, as I have said, appears to be Williamson's world. The firm is confined to a historically given vertical in Fig. 10.1, and has only the steady-state rate of growth to choose. Presumably it chooses the rate of growth that maximizes the market value of the firm. That is, it sets $\partial V/\partial g = 0$; it chooses the rate of growth at which the given vertical crosses the locus where $\partial V/\partial g = 0$. At that point the vertical is just tangent to the highest attainable contour of constant V. This description assumes that the management inherits a $K \leqq K^*$. If $K > K^*$, the firm is already 'too big' and an orthodox management will presumably dispose of the excess capital and settle at (K^*, g^*).

The second alternative is more complicated. The scale of the firm is to be determined along with its rate of growth. The management recognizes that stockholders have the option of placing their funds either in this firm or in other firms, i.e. of composing a portfolio. The stockholders' interest is not so much in maximizing the value of any particular firm, nor in maximizing its valuation ratio; it is in distributing their available funds in such a way as to maximize the value of the whole portfolio. What is required is that $\partial V/\partial K$ should have a common value in all firms (except for modifications having to do with differential riskiness); and also that $\partial V/\partial g = 0$ in each firm. The common value of $\partial V/\partial K$ I shall call j; it is analogous in this sort of theory to the 'going rate of profit' or 'opportunity cost of capital'. Whether it is high or low in any given instance depends on general-equilibrium considerations, especially on the willingness of the public to hold and add to wealth and on the ability of firms to find and exploit profitable uses for capital. The latter depends in part on the reaction of the wage rate and the price of capital goods to changes in demand. They are jointly determined with other prices in general equilibrium, of course, and can be treated as parameters only from the point of view of the single firm.

The equation of the curve along which $\partial V/\partial K = j$ is

$$K = \left[\frac{T(g)b^{\theta}\theta}{a + mf + ji - (j-m)g} \right]^{n}.$$

It is natural to suppose that $j \geqq m$; why should stockholders want their firms to add the last m dollars worth of capital goods if doing so will add less than m dollars to the value of the equity? Nevertheless, the denominator in this last expression is always positive, because $i > g$.

To plot the curve in Fig. 10.1, observe first that $K = 0$ when $T(g) = 0$, therefore when $g = g_1$. Except at that point, the curve lies always to the left of the curve $\partial V/\partial K = 0$, and reaches the horizontal axis at

$$K = K_j = \left[\frac{T(0)b^{\theta}\theta}{a + mf + ji} \right]^{n} < K_0.$$

Along the curve, dK/dg has the same sign as $\dfrac{DT' + (j-m)T}{D^2}$ where D is the denominator $a + mf + ji - (j-m)g$. It follows that dK/dg is negative at $g = g_1$, because $D > 0$, $T' < 0$, and $T(g_1) = 0$. Moreover, d^2K/dg^2 has the sign of $D^2T'' + 2(j-m)(DT' + (j-m)T)$. It is therefore negative whenever $dK/dg = 0$. This means, in Fig. 10.1, that the curve $\partial V/\partial K = j$ either falls throughout or bends back at most once, before reaching the axis at K_j. In any case, the qualitative picture is as in Fig. 10.1.

The appropriate rule for the owner-oriented firm is: for any given stock of capital goods, choose the rate of growth that maximizes the value of the equity; if then $\partial V/\partial K > j$, add a little initial capital, find the new value-maximizing g, and repeat the process. In the diagram, the best choice is the point where the locus $\partial V/\partial K = j$ intersects the locus $\partial V/\partial g = 0$. This is a modification (and I think a correction) of Marris's version of the orthodox rule. He constrains the firm to achieve a certain average value per dollar of capital; I require it to achieve a certain marginal value per dollar of capital.

Notice that the solution I have suggested for the 'orthodox' firm is not the same thing as maximizing the market value subject to the constraint that $\partial V/\partial K \geqq j$. By moving a bit to the southeast, the firm could increase its market value while continuing to satisfy the constraint. The reason why this would not be a good thing for an owner-oriented firm to do is that the firm could acquire the necessary additional initial capital only by inducing its owners (or some other owners, it doesn't matter) to reduce their allocation of funds to some other firms. The other firms are pushed northwest. Since all firms have the same $\partial V/\partial K$, the shift of initial capital will not affect the total value of the composite portfolio (to first order); but the accompanying changes in growth rates, necessary to meet the constraint, will reduce the value of the whole portfolio. (The growth rates of different firms are assumed to be totally unrelated; that is part of the partial-equilibrium game.) Some of the artificiality of this discussion comes from the restriction to a once-and-for-all choice of a steady state. A more realistic framework would be less artificial but more complicated.

I have assumed, naturally, that $j \geqq m$, but otherwise unspecified. One can make a case that j should be equal to m: the marginal value of a unit of capital should be equal to its market price. The case is that if $j > m$, the firm would wish to borrow indefinitely at the rate i

to buy capital. Presumably m could be bid up to equality with j. I am not certain that this view takes sufficient account of the private economy's limited willingness to hold wealth. Nevertheless, the case $j=m$ yields an interesting enough result that it ought to be carried a bit further.

The curve along which $\frac{\partial V}{\partial K}=m$ is

$$K=\left[\frac{T(g)b^{\theta}\theta}{a+m(f+i)}\right]^{n};$$

we already know that $\frac{\partial V}{\partial g}=0$ when

$$K=\left[\frac{(T(g)+(i-g)T'(g)b^{\theta}}{a+m(f+i)}\right]^{n}.$$

These curves intersect when

$$(1-\theta)T(g)=\frac{1}{n}T(g)=-(i-g)T'(g).$$

The best rate of growth for an owner-oriented firm is the root of this equation. It depends on the elasticity of demand, on the shape of the selling-cost function, and on the interest rate, but not on any of the cost parameters, not even on m itself. (Note also that, if we ignore the restriction on $T(g)$, the optimal g tends to i as the demand elasticity approaches infinity.)

(b) Growth-orientated firms

Most theories of the 'managerial' firm emphasize growth as an independent objective. The search for growth must, however, be constrained by some minimal need for profit, because firms are obviously not willing to sacrifice everything for the last little bit of growth. The precise character of the constraint is not universally agreed, but it seems to be fairly widely accepted that the limit operates through the fear of takeover bids. A firm that grows too fast (or does too much of anything else) at the expense of profits will find its stock-market value falling so low relative to its assets that takeovers will become attractive.

Marris leans to the hypothesis that the firm seeks the largest rate of growth consistent with a safe minimum level of the valuation ratio (V/mK in my notation). This device simply won't work in the model I am using. It is easily seen, from the formula for V, that the firm can meet any constraint on the valuation ratio and grow at a rate very near g_1 by choosing its initial capital stock sufficiently near zero. That is hardly the name of the game. (Marris's device might be made to work if I had postulated a U-shaped cost curve, but then the optimal size of the firm would be determined primarily from the cost side.)[1]

The notion of a minimal safe valuation ratio comes from the idea that a firm with too low a value will be taken over and sold for scrap, so to speak. Williamson proposes instead that a takeover threatens when excessive lust for growth forces the value of the firm too far below the maximum value that it might have. I am not sure this makes sense within its own framework of ideas. Presumably the new management is tempted by the quick capital gain obtainable by reducing g and letting V rise; this suggests an odd mixture of motives. In any case, Williamson's criterion for the growth-oriented firm also runs into trouble in the model used here.

In Fig. 10.1, imagine a growth-orienated firm already committed to a stock of capital goods. The highest market value it can achieve occurs where $\partial V/\partial g = 0$ on that vertical. It can go for a higher rate of growth than that, and therefore a lower market value, so long as it does not let its market value drop below a given fraction of the maximum achievable value. The firm should, therefore, travel up the vertical until it intersects the lowest safe contour of constant market value.

But what vertical should the firm choose to be on? That is, what initial capital stock should it choose? The answer that seems to accord with the spirit of Williamson's criterion is that it should choose the initial capital stock that yields the highest safe rate of growth. But in the model used here, that stock of capital is infinitesimally small, as in the case of Marris's formulation. That is not obvious from the diagram, but it can be shown as follows. (I use subscripts for partial derivatives for typographical simplicity.)

---

[1] This point is further elaborated by Marris in his Postcript on p. 31 above. If there is a stage of rapidly-enough decreasing costs, the growth-oriented firm can find a positive optimal initial size and the model works. It does seem to me to retain a kind of bias towards initial smallness; for instance, the optimal initial size will presumably be on the falling part of the cost curve, so there will be (forever) some unexploited economies of scale.

Williamson's firm (in my reading) proceeds as follows. For any K, let h be the rate of growth that maximizes V; h is the root of $V_g(h, K) = 0$. Then for any K the firm chooses the rate of growth g defined by $V(g, K) = kV(h, K)$ where k is the smallest safe ratio of value to maximum value. This equation defines g as a function of K, since h is a function of K. What is dg/dK? By implicit differentiation,

$$dg/dK = \frac{kV_g(h, K)h'(K) + hkV_K(h, K) - V_K(g, K)}{V_g(g, K)}$$

$$= \frac{kV_K(h, K) - V_K(g, K)}{V_g(g, K)}$$

since $V_g(h, K) = 0$. Since $g > h$, the denominator is negative. So dg/dK has sign opposite to the sign of its numerator. From the formula for V_K, the numerator is

$$\frac{k(T(h)\theta b^\theta K^{\theta-1} - x)}{i - h} - \frac{T(g)\theta b^\theta K^{\theta-1} - y}{i - g}.$$

This has the sign of $q(T(h)\theta b^\theta K^{\theta-1} - x) - (T(g)\theta b^\theta K^{\theta-1} - y)$, where $q = k(i - g)/(i - h)$ and, for the moment, $x = a + m(f + h)$ and $y = a + m$ $(f + g)$. Note that $0 < q < 1$ because $k \leq 1$ and $i > g > h$. Adding and subtracting $q\theta x$ and θy we see that the numerator has the sign of

$$q[T(h)\theta b^\theta K^{\theta-1} - \theta x] + (\theta - 1)xq - [T(g)\theta b^\theta K^{\theta-1} - \theta y] - (\theta - 1)y$$
$$= (\theta - 1)(qx - y)$$

by virtue of the fact that $V(g, K) = kV(h, K)$. But $\theta - 1$ is negative and so is $qx - y$ ($0 < x < y$, because $h < g$, and $0 < q < 1$). The numerator is therefore positive for all $K < K^*$, and $dg/dK < 0$. So the firm can safely achieve a larger and larger g by taking smaller and smaller K. As in the case of Marris's formulation, this is not where the theory is supposed to lead us.

A WAY TO PROCEED

This inability to determine a sensible initial scale for the firm seems to me to be a weakness in the growth-oriented theories. Perhaps it is the very notion of a once-for-all steady-state choice of scale and rate of growth that lies at the root of the trouble. Even so, that notion seems to be forced on any theory that wants to make growth an independent objective for the firm, so the weakness may be endemic.

However that may be, I want to find some way to proceed with a comparison of the responses of different sorts of firms to changes in parameters. I can see only one simple way, and that is to assume that the initial scale of the firm is given by some historical accident. Then the only remaining decision for the management is the choice of a steady-state growth rate for the future. I don't find this a very satisfying resolution, because it seems to put much too much weight on the steady-state restriction; even if instantaneous choice of initial scale is ruled out in practice, the early stages of any plan for a growing firm might involve a movement into the 'right' steady-state path. But no equally simple alternative presents itself.[1]

On this view, the procedure is straightforward. $K(<K^*)$ is given. The 'orthodox' firm (Fisher Inc.) chooses its rate of growth to maximize its market value; it solves $V_g(g_F,K)=0$ for g_F. Marris Inc. chooses a larger rate of growth, constrained by a lower limit to the valuation ratio; it solves $V(g_M,K)=\bar{v}mK$, where $\bar{v}$ is a number equal to or a little less than one. Williamson Inc. also chooses a larger growth rate than the orthodox firm, constrained by a lower limit on the ratio of its value to the value of the orthodox firm; it solves $V(g_W,K)=kV(g_F,K)$ for g_W.

The position is shown in Fig. 10.2. $\bar{K}$ is the given initial capital stock. The equation of the curve $V_g=0$ has already been worked out. It is

$$A=b^{-\theta}K^{1/n}=\frac{T(g)+(i-g)T'(g)}{a+m(f+i)}$$

[1] A more general approach would pursue the analogy, pointed out earlier, between the 'stock' of goodwill' and the stock of anything else. Write the demand curve as Gp^{-n}, where G is the stock of goodwill. The rate of growth of G is an increasing concave function of the ratio of selling expense to total sales, but there is now no necessity to make any of these growth rates be constant by assumption. Correspondingly, it makes no sense to have 'the' rate of growth as the argument of a managerial utility function. Instead, one can imagine the management as maximizing $\int_0^\infty e^{-ht}S(t)dt$, where h is a subjective time-preference parameter and $S(t)$ is any measure of the size of the firm, such as sales or assets. This maximization is constrained by the differential equation for G, and by the need to maintain a safe minimum of profitability, perhaps expressed by the valuation ratio. In addition – this remark is due to Arrow – one can imagine the initial goodwill $G(0)$ as given, and any desired stock of capital goods as achievable instantly by purchase. Then the determination of initial size boils down to the value of $G(0)$. It certainly sounds more sensible to treat $G(0)$ as given, almost as part of the identity of the firm. On the other hand, even initial goodwill can be bought, by crash advertising, by buying up existing trade names, perhaps otherwise. It hardly matters: A model like this will, under most reasonable assumptions tend to a steady state and considerationsse like tho in the text will apply.

where the constant A is easily seen to be the ratio of initial capital stock to initial gross sales revenue (and therefore the perpetual steady-state ratio of capital stock to gross sales revenue). Fisher Inc.'s rate of growth, g_F, is found by solving that equation for the given value of K, as exhibited in the diagram.

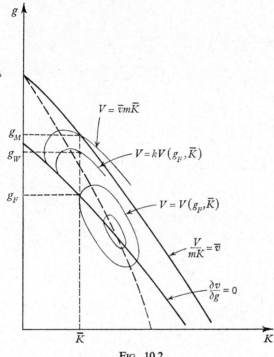

FIG. 10.2

The equation of the curve along which $V = \bar{v}m\bar{K}$ is

$$A = \frac{T(g)}{a + m(f + \bar{v}i + (1 - v)g)}.$$

This curve is drawn in the diagram. It lies always to the right of (i.e. above) the curve $V_g = 0$ (because $T' < 0$ and $i > g$). Marris Inc. finds its rate of growth by solving this equation, as shown in the diagram. Observe that if $\bar{v} = 1$, the equation for g_M becomes simply

$$A = \frac{T(g)}{a + m(f + i)}.$$

The equation of the curve $V(g,\overline{K}) = kV(g_F,\overline{K})$ is rather more complicated. But one can put it in the form

$$A = \frac{(i - g_F)T(g) - k(i - g)T(g_F)}{(i - g_F)(a + m(f + g)) - k(i - g)(a + m(f + g_F))}$$

where A is the same constant as before and g_F is the orthodox firm's rate of growth. The solution of this equation gives Williamson Inc. its rate of growth, g_W, as shown in the diagram. (In the diagram, g_W is less than g_M, but that is not necessary, and a smaller value of k could reverse the inequality. But of course $g_W > g_F$ as soon as $k < 1$.) I am going to ignore Williamson Inc. henceforward, and make comparisons between Fisher Inc. and Marris Inc. This is only because the Williamson criterion gives much more complicated answers. One can work them out, but since the Williamson criterion is not obviously more plausible than the Marris criterion, and since one has no close grip on the numbers involved, it hardly seems worth doing here.

A LIMITATION

As soon as I treat the initial K as a given, the initial output ($Q = bK$) is given. Therefore the initial price ($p = Q^{-1/n}$) is given. And since price is constant in steady-state growth, the price is given for all time. Moreover, this price is fixed independently of the firm's decision criterion. All three firms necessarily choose the same price. This limitation would disappear if the firms could choose their initial scale, for then the smaller scale would correspond to the higher price. One could ask how changes in data would affect price under each criterion. I cannot proceed that way for a reason already stated.

Alternatively, if the expenditure of selling costs affected the elasticity of demand for the product, different decision criteria would imply different prices. I have formulated the demand curve so that selling effort merely shifts the curve iso-elastically. That is primarily an assumption of convenience, but it seems appropriate in this context. There is no need to incorporate here the conventional static analysis of selling costs; it would not throw additional light on the consequences of growth maximization.

A CHANGE IN THE PRICE OF CAPITAL GOODS

The first exercise is to find out how Fisher Inc. and Marris Inc. react to a change in m, the price of investment goods. Such a change might occur either in the normal course of events or by way of an investment credit. By straightforward calculation,

$$dg_F/dm = \frac{(f+i)A}{(i-g_F)T''(g_F)}$$

$$dg_M/dm = \frac{(f+\bar{v}i+(1-v)g_M)A}{T'(g_M)-(1-v)mA}$$

$$= \frac{(f+i)A}{T'(g_M)} \quad \text{if } \bar{v}=1.$$

It is clear that the rate of growth, and the rate of investment ($=gK$), decrease when m increases, no matter which criterion the firm uses. To say more, I need to make specific assumptions about the function $T(g)$. For this purpose I shall take $T(g)=1-s(g-g_m)^2$, where g_m is a rate of growth so small that it is maintainable with zero selling costs. I shall take it that both firms choose larger rates of growth than that. I have already labelled g_1 the rate of growth at which T falls to zero; obviously, $s=(g_1-g_m)^{-2}$.

With this assumption, in the case $\bar{v}=1$,

$$\frac{dg_F/dm}{dg_M/dm} = \frac{g_M-g_m}{i-g_F}.$$

If Fisher Inc. would optimally choose to spend very little on promotion, so that g_F were near g_m, it would follow that this ratio is less than one, since $i>g_M$. One could say, then, that Marris Inc.'s investment would be more sensitive to control by investment credits than Fisher Inc.'s, but one could not easily say by how much.

A CHANGE IN THE RATE OF DISCOUNT

Imagine a change in i, the rate at which dividends are discounted by the market, such as might occur with a change in the rate of interest or in felt riskiness. One finds:

CE M 2

$$dg_F/di = \frac{Am - T'(g_F)}{(i - g_F)T''(g_F)}$$

$$dg_M/di = \frac{Amv}{T'(g_M) - Am(1 - \bar{v})}$$

$$= \frac{Am}{T'(g_M)} \quad \text{if } \bar{v} = 1.$$

In both cases, naturally enough, the rate of growth and the rate of investment fall if the rate of discount rises. I don't see any obvious further statement to make, except that when $T(g)$ has the special quadratic form,

$$dg_F/di = \frac{g_M - g_m}{i - g_F} dg_M/di - \frac{g_F - g_m}{i - g_F}.$$

Again, if g_F is rather near g_m, Marris Inc. responds more amply to changes in the interest rate than Fisher Inc.

AN EXCISE TAX

Suppose that an excise tax at rate z is levied on the sales of the firm. The formula for the value of the firm is modified only by multiplication of the revenues (but not the current or investment costs) by $1 - z$. Now, Fisher Inc. chooses its rate of growth so that

$$(1 - z) \frac{T(g) + (i - g)T'(g)}{a + m(f + i)} = A$$

and Marris Inc. chooses its rate of growth so that

$$(1 - z) \frac{T(g)}{a + m(f + \bar{v}i + (1 - \bar{v})g)} = A.$$

One calculates

$$dg_F/dz = \frac{T(g_F) + (i - g_F)T'(g_F)}{(1 - z)T''(g_F)(i - g_F)}$$

and

$$dg_M/dz = \frac{T(g_M)}{(1 - z)T'(g_M) - Am(1 - \bar{v})}$$

$$= \frac{T(g_M)}{(1-z)T'(g_M)} \quad \text{if } \bar{v} = 1.$$

Obviously, an increase in the rate of excise tax decreases the rate of growth and the rate of investment of both firms. By substitution, moreover,

$$dg_F/dz = \frac{A(a + m(f + i))}{(1-z)^2(i - g_F)T''(g_F)}$$

$$dg_M/dz = \frac{A(a + m(f + i))}{(1-z)^2 T''(g_M)} \quad \text{when } \bar{v} = 1.$$

Therefore

$$\frac{dg_F/dz}{dg_M/dz} = \frac{T'(g_M)}{(i - g_F)T''(g_F)}.$$

These results should be compared with those for a change in the price of capital goods. It emerges that the ratio of the two firm's responses to a change in the rate of excise tax is the same as the ratio of their responses to a change in the price of capital goods. If the rough judgment made earlier is correct, the two kinds of firms respond in qualitatively similar ways to changes in excise taxes, with the growth-maximizing firm possibly slightly more sensitive.

A TAX ON PROFITS

As a last exercise, imagine that there is a proportional tax on profit at the rate u. For this purpose, profits are defined as gross sales revenue, less selling costs, less current costs, less true depreciation. Outlay on net investment, which has to be deducted from the cash flow to give dividend payments for these internally financed firms, is of course not deductible for tax purposes. It is now a matter of some significance that the firm is assumed to finance its net investment from retained earnings, because in the normal course of events the interest on debt would be deductible for tax purposes. But I will hold to that assumption anyhow, because I am not much interested in the purely financial choices.

The market value of the firm is now

$$V = \frac{(1-u)(Tb^\theta K^\theta - (a + mf)K) - mgK}{i - g}.$$

The orthodox firm chooses its growth rate to satisfy

$$A = \frac{(1-u)((i-g)T'(g) + T(g))}{(1-u)(a+mf) + mi}$$

and the growth-maximizing firm chooses its rate of growth to satisfy

$$A = \frac{(1-u)T(g)}{(1-u)(a+mf) + m(\bar{v}i(1-\bar{v})g)}.$$

Now let the tax rate change. Then

$$dg_F/du = \frac{Ami}{(1-u)^2(i-g_F)T''(g_F)}$$

and

$$dg_M/du = \frac{m(\bar{v}i + (1-\bar{v})g_M)A}{(1-u)^2(T'(g_M) - Am(1-\bar{v})(1-u)^{-1})}$$

$$= \frac{Ami}{(1-u)^2 T'(g_M)} \quad \text{if } \bar{v} = 1.$$

In both cases an increase in the tax rate leads to a reduction in the rate of growth chosen. Moreover, the ratio of the two derivatives is exactly the same as it was in case of a change in an excise tax or in the price of capital goods.

This result is quite different from what happens in static theory. The incidence of a proportional tax on profits is wholly on profits if the firm is a static profit-maximizer; the profit-maximizing output is the same with and without the tax. In contrast, a firm that maximizes sales or revenue subject to a minimum-profit constraint will respond to a proportional tax on profits by reducing output. Before the tax is levied, the firm is 'spending' some possible profit to 'buy' an increase in sales; when the tax is levied, profit at the original output is reduced below the permissible minimum and the firm must give up some unprofitable output in order to build profits back up to the permissible minimum. In principle, then, response to a profits tax could distinguish one type of firm from the other.

In the growth situation, as we have just seen, this sharp distinction disappears. The value of a firm, unlike its static profit, is not reduced proportionately by a proportional tax on profits. This is because net investment is not deductible for tax purposes although it is a deduction from the cash flow whose present value is the value of the firm.

Therefore, imposition of the tax evokes a growth response from both Marris Inc. and Fisher Inc. The proper growth analogue of a proportional tax on profits is a proportional tax on the market value of a firm. Then whatever maximizes present value will maximize half of present value, and Fisher Inc. will make the same decisions with and without the tax. Marris Inc., however, will have to reduce its 'excessive' growth rate in order to get its market value up to the permissible minimum after tax.[1]

A NOTE ON TAXATION OF DIVIDEND INCOME AND CAPITAL GAINS

The existence of a stiff personal income tax with preferential treatment of capital gains – and realized capital gains at that – is bound to make it harder to distinguish between owner-oriented and growth-oriented firms. A management motivated only by the after-tax interests of its stockholders will find it advantageous to retain earnings so that its stockholders can, when they wish, get cash by selling off shares and paying the lower capital-gains rate on the appreciation. It would be a good idea to have a detailed analysis of the consequences for Fisher Inc. and Marris Inc. of changes in the tax rates on dividends and capital gains. I doubt, however, that the model I have been using can do justice to this problem. The trouble is not so much in the model of the firm as in the model of the stock market.

When capital gains have tax advantages, one observes corporations that pay no dividend, or a negligible dividend, but whose stock is held in the (correct) anticipation of appreciation. A model which makes the value of the equity be the discounted value of the dividend stream can cope with this phenomenon only by arbitrarily putting a heavy weight on the expectation of much higher dividends in the distant future. This is not very satisfactory, and not only because it fails to reveal the importance of preferential taxation of capital gains.

The proposition that the value of a firm is the present value of the dividend stream is usually deduced from the fundamental capital-market equilibrium condition that

$$iV = D + dV/dt.$$

[1] This is an example of the general point concerning qualitative effects in the two types of firm described by Marris on pp. 20–1 above.

This differential equation says that the sum of the dividend yield and the rate of appreciation must equal the rate of interest (or discount) at each moment of time – or else some opportunity for massive arbitrage would arise. The solution of this differential equation is

$$V(t) = \int_t^u D(z)\exp[-i(z-t)]dz + \exp[-i(u-t)]V(u).$$

This leads to the method of valuation I have been using if, and only if, $\exp[-i(u-t)]V(u)$ tends to zero as u tends to infinity. With preferential tax treatment of capital gains, one can imagine situations in which the best policy for a stockholder-oriented firm is to pay no dividends in any finite interval. All that I can do here is to develop briefly the implications of the valuation formula used earlier, with the warning that this may be far from the whole story.

Suppose there is a proportional tax on dividend income at rate x and a proportional tax on capital gains at rate y. Then the condition that an owner of the stock should be indifferent between holding and selling is

$$iV = (1-x)D + (1-y)dV/dt.$$

This differential equation generalizes the one given earlier. Notice that I am treating i as a purely subjective rate of discount. If it were a pure rate of interest, I would have to multiply the left-hand side by one minus the tax rate on interest income. If i is a mixed sort of concept, then some mixed sort of tax rate should be introduced; the reader ought perhaps to work out the case where interest income is taxed at the same rate as dividends.

If dividends grow exponentially at rate g and an end-condition like the one above is satisfied, the solution is

$$V(0) = \frac{(1-x)}{(1-y)}D_0\int_0^\infty \exp\{-[i/(1-y)-g]t\}dt = \frac{(1-x)D_0}{i-g(1-y)}.$$

The corresponding generalizations of the behaviour rules for Fisher Inc. and Marris Inc. are that g_F is the root of

$$A = \frac{T(g) + (j-g)T'(g)}{a + m(f+j)}$$

and g_M is the root of

$$A = \frac{T(g)}{a + m[f + wj + (1-w)g]}.$$

where A has the same meaning as before, $j = i/(1 - y)$ and $w = v(1 - y)/(1 - x)$. Notice that g_F does not depend on x (the tax rate on dividends). This is because maximizing the appropriately discounted stream of after-tax dividends is equivalent to maximizing the appropriately discounted stream of before-tax dividends. I imagine that this conclusion holds only because the simplifying end-condition is being assumed, probably improperly. Under this assumption, the effect of an increase in y (the tax rate on capital gains) is exactly like that of an increase in the rate of discount. The owner-oriented firm will reduce its rate of growth if y increases.

The case of the growth-oriented firm is more complicated in a different way. The discount rate becomes $j = i/(1 - y)$, as in the case of the owner-oriented firm. In addition, the required valuation ratio $\bar{v}$ is replaced by $w = \bar{v}(1 - y)/(1 - x)$, which is larger than $\bar{v}$, because typically y is less than x. On the other hand, one might expect a change in y to change $\bar{v}$ itself; if the threat of takeover prevents managements from letting $\bar{v}$ fall below some lower limit, then a tax on the profit from acquiring assets cheap may reduce the permissible lower limit (if capital gains were taxed away 100 per cent, then takeover would be no threat at all). Given the deficiency of the model I hesitate to make any qualitative comparison between the two sorts of firms, though common sense suggests that the differential between x and y should make more of a difference to Fisher Inc. than to Marris Inc.

CONCLUSION

It is only natural that I should have no clear idea about what this adds up to, since I began with a vague prejudice against the sort of theory I have been exploring. This prejudice was reinforced by the conclusion that, at least in the precise formulation I have used here, the growth-oriented theories seem to be unable to do one of the tasks they might be expected to do, namely to determine the initial scale as well as the rate of growth of the firm.

My second conclusion is that, in any case, growth-oriented and profit-oriented firms would respond in qualitatively similar ways to such stimuli as changes in factor prices, discount rate, and excise and profit taxes. On the evidence only of its behaviour in that kind of situation, an observer would find it hard to distinguish one kind of firm from the other. But he might also find it unnecessary if his main object were to predict or to control the firm's behavior.

It remains true, of course, that a growth-oriented firm will choose a higher rate of growth than a profit-oriented firm. One cannot know how much follows from that conclusion without some grip on the size of the difference. That seems to depend mainly on the character of selling costs, summed up in my formulation by the function $T(g)$. It may also depend on whether the model of steady-state choice can be taken as anything more than the crudest first approximation. These are not unrelated questions.

11 Managerial Discretion, Organization Form, and the Multi-division Hypothesis[1]

Oliver E. Williamson

Implicit in my previous research on the sources and consequences of managerial discretion [43], [46] has been the assumption that the firm is organized along the lines of what I will refer to here as the 'unitary form'. Although the possibility of divisionalization was recognized and some of the organizational effects of divisionalization were briefly discussed ([43], pp. 120, 124, 160–1), these were left mainly undeveloped.

I attempt here to remedy this by focusing explicitly on the 'multi-division structure'. What, in relation to the unitary form, are its structural and performance attributes? Although one might attempt instead to determine the properties of the multi-division form by evaluating it with respect to a hypothetical ideal, this comparative approach would appear to have two advantages. First, it exposes dimensions of the corporate control problem that may otherwise fail to be invoked. Second, much of what will prove testable in the theory of the firm is apt to relate not to some ideal standard but to the comparative performance of alternative organization forms.

Lest I be misunderstood, I should make it clear that the emphasis is on the central behavioral *tendencies* and the differential *capacities* for superior performance that these two organization forms possess. Individual comparisons are therefore hazardous, but on the average

[1] Research on this paper was supported in part by grants from the National Science Foundation and the Brookings Institution. The views expressed are my own. This paper is based on research that is developed more extensively in [49]. Helpful comments from David Conrath, Dale Henderson, Louis Pondy, Richard Posner, Sidney Winter, Jr, and Adrian Wood are gratefully acknowledged. More generally, the discussion of these issues by the participants at the September 1969 Glen Cove Conference, where the paper was first presented, is appreciated.

344 OLIVER E. WILLIAMSON

(assuming that the argument is correct) the differences indicated should obtain.

The paper begins with a brief examination of the structure and performance of the unitary-form organization, including a review of conventional competition in the capital market arguments. Section II introduces the multi-division form innovation. The unitary and multi-division structures are compared and the multi-division hypothesis is advanced in section III. The efficacy of competition in the capital market is re-examined in the light of this discussion in section IV; the implications of the argument for the conglomerate form of organization are also developed in this connection. Certain qualifications to the argument are given in section V. Some concluding remarks concerning organizational innovation and institutional failures are offered in section VI. For convenience in the exposition, unitary and multi-division enterprises will be referred to as U-form and M-form organizations respectively.

I. THE UNITARY-FORM ENTERPRISE

The discussion of the unitary or U-form enterprise is in two parts. First, the internal organization and resulting performance characteristics of the U-form firm are examined with respect to increases in firm size. Second, the extent to which the capital market serves as an effective constraint on discretionary behavior in an environment dominated by U-form firms is considered.

1. *Organization of the U-form enterprise*

The principal operating units in the U-form enterprise are the functional divisions – sales, finance, manufacturing, etc. Specialization by function has been the traditional way of organizing multifunctional activities and, in an enterprise of only moderate size, is the prevailing basis today. An organization chart displaying this structure is shown in Fig. 11.1.

The U-form organization can reasonably be represented as one which, in firms of moderate size, solves the division of labor question efficiently – including the provision for an effective strategic decision-making and control apparatus. Our interest here, however, is in firms of 'large' and particularly 'giant' size. Arbitrarily this large-firm universe will be taken to be the 500 largest industrials, 50 largest utilities, and 50 largest transportation companies as ranked in the *Fortune* 500 series in a recent year. The giant-firm subset will be taken to be the 25 largest industrials, the 10 largest utilities, and the 10 largest transportation companies. Of the roughly 40 per cent of national income and employment that is attributable to these three sectors in recent years, these so-called large firms account for somewhat over one-half and the giant-sized subset for almost one-fourth of the total ([49], chap. 1).

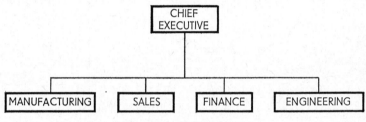

FIG. 11.1. Unitary form

The question to be addressed is what problems does the U-form enterprise experience when it expands if the U-form (functional) basis for decomposing the enterprise remains in effect throughout? An answer that is both compelling and compact is not easy to provide. (For a more extensive discussion than is given here, see [49], chaps 2, 3, 7.) The two effects of enterprise expansion that are of most interest to us here are that expansion under the U-form structure (1) is subject to cumulative control loss, which has internal efficiency consequences, and (2) eventually alters the character of the strategic decision-making process.

Finite spans of control naturally require that additional hierarchical levels be introduced as the U-form enterprise expands. Adding hierarchical levels can, if only for serial reproduction reasons, lead to an effective loss of control through incomplete or inaccurate transmittal of data moving up and instructions moving down the organizational hierarchy. Although various decoupling devices may be devised to reduce these transmission needs, these are costly and subject to diminishing returns. Decoupling merely alleviates but does not overcome the need for intrafunctional and peak coordination.

346 OLIVER E. WILLIAMSON

Information flows rarely take the form of simple serial reproduction, however. Rather, data are summarized and interpreted as they move forward and instructions are operationalized as they move down. Both processes provide additional opportunities for control losses to develop. These can occur in quite unintentional ways. If, however, the functional units of the firm view the hierarchical structure as affording opportunities to pursue local goals, deliberate distortions may be introduced into the hierarchical exchange process. Cumulative losses of these types stand eventually as an efficiency bar to the further expansion of the firm.

Expansion also eventually overcomes the capacity of the office of the chief executive to provide strategic planning and maintain effective control. The usual means for augmenting this capacity has been to bring the heads of the functional divisions into the peak coordination process. The natural posture for these functional executives to take is one of advocacy in representing the interests of their respective operating units.

This change in the composition of the strategic decision-making unit produces a shift away from preferences characteristic of the office of the chief executive, which tend to be enterprise-wide in scope, in favor of partisan interests more closely associated with the functional divisions. A persistent and collective pressure to provide more and better services is apt to develop; an expansionary bias in favor of staff expenditures easily obtains. A permissive attitude toward slack may also result.

The comparative static and dynamic-stochastic properties of a firm possessing these preferences have been presented elsewhere [43, 46, 49]. For our purposes here it is sufficient to note that, *ceteris paribus*, progressive expansion of the U-form firm (1) results in greater control-loss experience, and (2) the utility function of the firm is augmented to include the expense-preference inclinations of the functional divisions. Thus both internal efficiency and goal consequences are involved.

2. *Capital-market constraint*

Consider now whether, in an environment dominated by U-form enterprises, the capital market can effectively restore selection on profit (that is, extinguish non-profit pursuits) in firms that would otherwise display discretionary tendencies. What controls does the capital market have access to? What limitations does it experience?

In a general sense, the most severe limitation the capital market encounters is that it is an *external* control device. This constitutes a more serious impediment than is often appreciated. The possibility of monitoring firm performance through the direct metering of funds is impaired by the internal financing which most firms in the discretionary category have access to. The use of incentive devices of various sorts is impaired by the imprecision with which they apply and by the adaptive responses which they permit. The displacement threat which the capital market poses is subject to serious inference problems and experiences non-trivial displacement costs if the incumbent management is disposed to resist the takeover effort. (Again, for a more complete discussion, see [49], chaps 6, 7.)

Relevant in this connection is Shorey Peterson's observation that 'Far from being an ordinary election, a proxy battle is a *catastrophic* event whose mere possibility is a threat, and one not remote when affairs are in *conspicuous* disarray'. Indeed, even 'stockholder suits . . . may be provoked by evidence of *serious* self-dealing' ([33], p. 21); emphasis added). But as recent history has made abundantly clear, atomic weapons with their catastrophic consequences are ill suited to support military campaigns involving even half a million men. The principle is perfectly general: controls that have significant discreteness properties are appropriate only when an offense reaches egregious proportions. Otherwise, the remedy is too strong even to be invoked. Peterson concedes as much in his references to 'conspicuous' disarray and 'serious' self-dealing, and the evidence tends to bear him out [22, 46].

Discreteness is significant, of course, because it implies that either the original or secondary costs associated with the use of a change agent are substantial. Where takeover is concerned, non-trivial costs of both types are involved. Not only are the original costs of securing displacement apt to be significant, but once displacement is accomplished the successful takeover agency needs to face the transition costs which a displacement involves. As more than one successful raider has come to appreciate, these can be neglected only at some peril.

None of this is to suggest that the capital market in a U-form environment is wholly inefficacious in supplying incentives or enforcing lower-bound performance. Rather, the argument is that capital-market controls tend not to be delicately conceived.

II. THE MULTI-DIVISION INNOVATION

1. *Invention*

The historical development of the multi-division form has been traced by Alfred Chandler, Jr, in his superlative book titled *Strategy and Structure*. He reports that the M-form innovation was initially devised in the early 1920s, apparently quite independently, by Du Pont and General Motors; somewhat later, but still independently, it was adopted by Standard Oil of New Jersey and Sears [14]. It has been widely imitated and 'rediscovered' since.

The immediate cause for the innovation to be introduced was the onset of adversity. In Du Pont, the 'company's financial statement for the first half of 1921 provided the shock that finally precipitated a major reorganization. In those six months, as the postwar recession became increasingly severe, the company had lost money on every product except explosives' ([14], pp. 126–7). At General Motors, an inventory crisis together with the collapse of the auto market in 1920 produced the change ([14], pp. 156–7). Partial reorganization at Jersey was induced by excessive inventories, falling profits, and a declining market share ([14], p. 230), but it was not until earnings fell to the lowest level in 1927 of any year since 1912 (from \$117.7 million in 1926 to \$40.4 million in 1927) that major organization changes were induced ([14], p. 256). Although profit pressures at Sears were less dramatic, they also contributed to the change ([14], pp. 321–3).

The basic reason why the innovation became necessary, however, is traceable to more fundamental reasons than transitory market conditions. Chandler summarizes the defects of the unitary form, and consequently the needs for the multi-division structure, in the following way ([14], p. 369):

The inherent weakness in the centralized, functionally departmentalized operating company . . . became critical only when the administrative load on the senior executives increased to such an extent that they were unable to handle their entrepreneurial responsibilities efficiently. This situation arose when the operations of the enterprise became too complex and the the problems of coordination, appraisal, and policy formulation too intricate for a small number of top officers to handle both long-run, entrepreneurial, and short-run, operational administrative activities. To meet these new needs, the innovators built the multi-divisional structure with a general office whose executives would concentrate on entrepreneurial activities and with autonomous, fairly self-contained operating divisions whose managers would handle operational ones.

Illustrative of overloading conditions is the report of the troubles experienced by Du Pont following its diversification moves but prior to its adoption of the multi-division form ([14], p. 111):

> Broad goals and policies had to be determined for and resources allocated to functional activities, not in one industry but in several. Appraisal of departments performing in diverse fields became exceedingly complex. Interdepartmental coordination grew comparably more troublesome. The manufacturing personnel and marketers tended to lose contact with each other and so failed to work out product improvements and modifications to meet changing demands and competitive developments. . . . Each of the three major departments – Purchasing, Manufacturing, and Sales – made its own [forecasts] and set its own schedules.

Thus, as the complexity of its various yet intervolved activities progressively increased, its ability to supply the requisite coordination became strained and even collapsed. Unable meaningfully to identify with or contribute to the realization of global goals, managers in each of the functional parts attended to what they perceived as operational subgoals instead ([26], p. 156). The experience of Ford in operating the giant River Rouge plant as a U-form organization in the 1920s affords a similar example (although, it should be noted, others have interpreted the problems of Ford mainly in personality rather than structural terms ([32, chaps 8, 11).

The difficulties that the large, U-form enterprise became subject to (and which the M-form innovation was presumably designed to relieve) can be expressed in terms of indecomposability, incommensurability, non-operational goal specification, and the confounding of strategic and operating decisions. Incommensurability made it difficult to specify the goals of the functional divisions in ways which clearly contributed to higher-level enterprise objectives. Indecomposability made it necessary to attempt more comprehensive coordination among the parts; for a given span of control, this naturally resulted in a high degree of control loss between hierarchical levels. Moreover, to the extent that efforts at coordination broke down and the individual parts suboptimized, the intrinsic interconnectedness between them virtually assured that spillover costs would be substantial. The confounding of strategic and operating decisions served further to compromise organizational purpose. These, really, are the fundamental reasons why the U-form enterprise eventually encountered serious operating difficulties. Adversity merely made these structural conditions the more apparent.

Functional organization nevertheless was and is the natural way to decompose simple tasks. Preserving the functional form as the firm is gradually expanded is also to be expected. Eventually, however, the U-form structure defeats itself. This will obtain even if the U-form enterprise undergoes a simple radial amplification in size without concurrent diversification. If accomplished through diversification, coordination within the functional form can be expected to present even more severe problems.

The organizational innovation that was devised as a response to these conditions involved substituting quasi-autonomous operating divisions (organized mainly along product, brand, or geographic lines) for the functional divisions of the U-form structure as the principal basis for achieving compartmentalization. Inasmuch as each of these operating divisions is subsequently divided along functional lines (see Fig. 11.2), one might characterize these operating divisions as scaled-down, specialized U-form structures. Although this is a considerable oversimplification (for example, operating divisions may be further subdivided by product, geographic, or brand subdivisions before the final U-form structure appears), the observation has at least heuristic merit.

This simple change in the decomposition rules might not, by itself, appear to have other than superficial consequences. Indeed, for the reorganization to be fully effective really requires more. The peak coordinator's office (shown in Fig. 11.2 as the 'general office') also has to undergo transformation and an elite staff needs to be supplied to assist the general office in its strategic decision-making (including control) responsibilities. Chandler characterizes the reasons for the success of the multi-division form as ([14], pp. 382–3):

The basic reason for its success was simply that it clearly removed the executives responsible for the destiny of the entire enterprise from the more routine operational activities, and so gave them the time, information, and even psychological commitment for the long-term planning and appraisal. . . .

[The] new structure left the broad strategic decisions as to the allocation of existing resources and the acquisition of new ones in the hands of a top team of generalists. Relieved of operating duties and tactical decisions, a general executive was less likely to reflect the position of just one part of the whole.

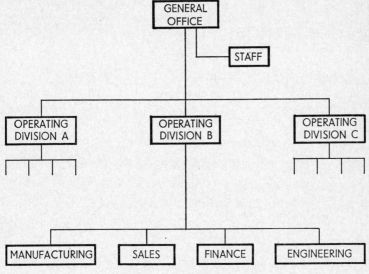

FIG. 11.2. Multi-division form

The nature of the transformation and the reasons for it were not unperceived by those who engineered the change. Among those who had been instrumental in bringing about the reorganization of General Motors was Donaldson Brown.[1] As the following statement (which was made in 1924, when he was a vice-president of General Motors) reveals, the change was undertaken self-consciously; the intended results were apparently clear ([12], pp. 195–6):

[1] Actually, General Motors had been organized more along the lines of a holding company than a U-form organization. Chandler observes that its 'diversity of activities proved almost impossible to manage effectively through the over decentralized holding company [that Durant had devised] . . . Sloan's transformation of Durant's tiny top office into a coordinating, appraising, and policy-making general office made possible the rational and profitable management of such an enterprise' ([14], p. 372).

Each division is equipped with a self-contained organization having complete jurisdiction over manufacture, sales, and finance, subject to control from the central authority. The ordinary, everyday questions of policy, embodying even such important matters as production schedules, inventory commitments, design of product, and methods of distribution, are left ordinarily within the consideration and decision of the divisions themselves, under certain general limitations, and in every way the men on the firing line are inspired with a sense of responsibility for results.

The central organization embraces talent in automotive engineering and research, and experts dealing with important problems of improved methods in manufacture and distribution, all of whom serve in a more or less advisory capacity. Apart from these important adjuncts, and certain necessary activities in finance and accounting, law, and related matters, the central organization deals almost exclusively with questions of policy. The president is general manager of the corporation in fact, but controls the operations by the establishment of principles and the interpretation of policies, and refrains from entering into questions of operating detail except in cases where the two are inseparable. The Executive and Finance Committees, as active bodies subject to the board of directors, have final jurisdiction over the entire business through the enunciation of policies and by direct action in matters involving essential points of policy.

2. *Imitation*

Imitation of the M-form innovation was at first rather slow. For one thing, however obvious its superior properties may have been to the innovators, others were naturally skeptical. In some industries (such as those engaged in metal processing) the divisionalized structure was not as easy to create as in others where distinct product or brand lines were readily established. In others, administrative inertia appears to have been substantial. Up through the 1930s, only a handful of other firms had accomplished the transformation ([14], chap. 7). A number of firms which by 1940 had reorganizational changes in the works postponed these with the onset of World War II.

Since 1945, however, large firms quite generally have undergone a reorganization along M-form lines.[1]

Among the imitators, a change in the chief executive was frequently essential to bring the reorganization off. Chandler observes this to have been the case at Goodyear ([14], p. 436), General Electric ([14], pp. 456–7), I.B.M. ([14], p. 458), International Harvester ([14], p. 460), and Ford and Chrysler ([14], pp. 462–3), among others. Occasionally firms were observed to make the change without the pressures of adversity or the retirement of key personnel, and no doubt this has become more common as the merits of the M-form structure have become more widely appreciated. But adversity appears to have been an essential goad for those who were first to innovate; and among those who were the early imitators, 'the essential reshaping of administrative structure nearly always had to wait for a change in the top command' ([14], p. 472).

III. PROPERTIES OF THE MULTI-DIVISION FORM

The preceding observations lead to the following summary statement regarding the characteristics and advantages of the multi-division form:

1. The responsibility for operating decisions is assigned to (essentially self-contained) operating divisions or 'quasi-firms'.
2. The elite staff attached to the general office performs both advisory and auditing functions. Both have the effect of securing greater control over operating-division behavior.

[1] Those who adopted the M-form structure later often expressed their reasons for going to this structure and explained its properties in terms strikingly similar to those given by Donaldson Brown in 1924. Consider the following 1956 statement of I.B.M. regarding its then recent organization changes (which it characterized as a 'new' pattern for progress):

> . . . the new alignment of the various areas is based on products. Each of the product divisions will, within the framework of policy established by the Board of Directors and general management, operate almost as an individual company with its own manufacturing, sales, and service functions. Each of these divisions is equipped with special skills and product knowledge to concentrate on developing the full potential of a specific market.
>
> Further strength is given the organization with the creation of the Corporate Staff, which, being separate from the operating organization responsible for developing, producing, selling and servicing goods, can closely examine the special areas of the business and assist the operating executives in solving problems in these areas.   (*I.B.M. Business Machines*, 28 Dec 1956)

3. The general office is principally concerned with strategic decisions involving planning, appraisal, and control, including the allocation of resources among the (competing) operating divisions.

4. The separation of the general office from operations provides general office executives with the psychological commitment to be concerned with the overall performance of the organization rather than become absorbed in the affairs of the functional parts.

5. The resulting structure displays both rationality and synergy: the whole is greater (more effective, more efficient) than the sum of the parts.

These are, by almost any standard, important observations concerning business behavior. That they have not had a noticeable impact on the modern theory of the firm is, probably, attributable to a failure to regard organization form seriously. This neglect of organization form is partly to be accounted for by a common tendency to invoke the standard behavioral assumption (profits maximization) without regard for circumstances.

The view taken here is that the behavior of the firm is jointly determined by market circumstances, internal efficiency, the strategic decision-making process, and internal compliance processes. Organization form has an immediate effect on the last three and an eventual effect on market circumstances. Attention will first be directed to its immediate effects. Thus we inquire in what respects does the M-form structure help to overcome the internal efficiency and strategic decision-making 'problems' that the large U-form enterprise is subject to? Also, and related, what internal compliance processes does the M-form management have access to that the U-form management is either unable or disinclined to employ and with what effects? To place the comparison between M-form and U-form structures on common grounds, it will be assumed that the two organizations in question are engaged in identical activities (same product lines and geographic spread) and are sizewise similar.

1. *Internal efficiency*

Assume here that the behavior of every member of the firm is functionally oriented to advance the goals of the peak coordinator.

Non-compliance and active subgoal pursuit are, for the purposes of this section, placed in abeyance. Also assume (this will be relaxed shortly) that each of the operating divisions in the M-form enterprise satisfies technical scale economies with respect to production and marketing and that there is an absence of market interdependencies and production externalities among these divisions. What, given these assumptions, are the simple control-loss consequences of the M-form organization in relation to an equivalent (in the sense described above) U-form structure?

It will be useful for the purposes of making this comparison to extend the concept of control loss introduced in section I. There, it will be recalled, only U-form organizations that differed with respect to size (and, hence, hierarchical level) were under examinaton. Cumulative control loss could thus be expressed as a function of the number of hierarchical levels. Here, however, size and the number of hierarchical levels are approximately constant; the comparison involves alternative organization forms with respect to internal efficiency. Thus it is inter-organizational differences in the value of the control-loss parameter rather than variations in the number of levels that is critical.

Assume, for purposes of standardizing the comparison, that the span of control in both U- and M-form organizations is identical. The value of the control-loss parameter can then be expressed as a function of the communication load and the ease of achieving coordination: *ceteris paribus*, control loss will vary inversely with the volume of communication and directly with the ease of arranging a coordinated response. Increasing the volume of communication leads to a decrease in control loss among operators by occupying (pre-empting) productive energies that would otherwise be available. It also reduces the value of control loss among members of the management hierarchy by crowding their capacity to summarize and interpret data flowing up and to operationalize instructions moving down. Increasing the ease of utilizing resources in a coordinated way is manifested as a decrease in the cost of accomplishing integration. Internal productivity is impaired to the extent that resources are incompletely utilized or intrinsic interdependencies, with respect either to marketing or production, go unrecognized or are given allowance for only with difficulty. Incomplete utilization of resources results in excess capacity relative to what could be accomplished with more efficient loading, while unadapted interdependencies have the parts of the organization pulling at cross-purposes.

The process of divisionalizing a U-form enterprise to create an M-form structure can be regarded as a decoupling operation of massive proportions. Ordinarily decoupling has communication-saving characteristics to commend it [20]; communication between the parts is reduced by isolating richly interacting from weakly interacting parts and/or by introducing relatively high thresholds to suppress sensitivity to connectedness. While the former is a pure gain (in that it eliminates redundant communications), the latter involves a tradeoff; a loss in the capacity to arrange an integrated response needs to be balanced against the realized reduction in information transfer costs that higher thresholds afford. The question to be addressed here is what are the net consequences of divisional-ization under the conditions described.

In substantial measure, the decomposition postulated above involves the definition of 'natural decision units' within an agglomer-ated structure and giving these independent standing. It thus permits a reduction in communication of the pure gain type. Not only does the firm have less cause to originate information, but its internal communication network is more compact.[1] Also, inasmuch as both market and production interdependencies are absent or minimal, integration losses are not experienced on this account. At most a sacrifice in the opportunity to pool resources efficiently against market fluctuations is involved. Assuming that the potential economise of such pooling are unimportant or can be realized for the most part at slight compromise to the divisionalized structure, integration losses in the M-form enterprise should be negligible. Altogether, therefore,

---

[1] The argument can be illustrated in an elementary way by considering a U- and an M-form firm, each with four hierarchical levels. In the U-form enter-prise the hierarchical levels are, from top to bottom, peak coordination, functional division chief, first-line supervisors, and operations. In the M-form firm the corresponding levels are peak coordination, product division chief, functional managers, and operations.

Intrafunctional coordination in the U-form firm involves two-way communi-cation across two hierarchical levels (operations to first-line supervisor to functional division chief), while interfunctional coordination requires that the peak coordinator also be included. In the M-form structure, by contrast, intra-functional coordination involves exchange across only one level (operations to functional division manager) while interfunctional issues can be resolved by adding only the product division chief. The M-form firm in this way achieves an apparent compression in communication needs in comparison with an equivalent U-form enterprise.

the M-form enterprise that meets the idealized conditions described should enjoy superior control-loss (internal efficiency) experience to that of its U-form counterpart. Put differently, the richly interconnected U-form firm can in these circumstances be regarded as one which fails to recognize essential decomposability and attempts excessive integration instead.[1]

If the operating divisions are not fully decomposable in this sense but experience some modest degree of technical or market interdependency, the decoupling described cannot be accomplished without cost. Certain of these costs can be attenuated by specification of appropriate interdivisional rules regarding internal pricing [4, 9, 15], non-interference in market test stipulations, and the like. If these interactions are extensive, however, the information exchange needs of the resulting M-form organization may be merely different from but not significantly less than its U-form equivalent. Its control-loss experience need not be better and could easily be worse. From a simple control-loss point of view, therefore, the M-form structure is to be preferred over its U-form counterpart in the degree to which decomposability (quasi-autonomy) into operating divisions is feasible or, at low cost, can be arranged. Even if, however, judged with respect to its simple control-loss properties, the M-form structure experiences net negative productivity effects, divisionalization of a large U-form firm may still be warranted on account of the advantages that the M-form firm offers in other respects.

[1] To illustrate what is meant by 'excessive' integration, consider Simon's parable of the two watch manufacturers, Hora and Tempus. Each is assembling an identical watch of 1000 parts. Tempus Co. has designed the work in such a way that all 1000 parts form a single, indecomposable whole. Hora Inc., however, has a design which provides for 10 major subassemblies of about 100 parts, each of which in turn is decomposable into 10 subassemblies of about 10 parts each. An interruption at any phase of the work means that the entire assembly stage at which the interruption occurs must be repeated, although all previously completed subassemblies are unaffected.

An interruption for Tempus means that the entire watch must be started anew, while Hora loses only the work at the most recent stage of subassembly operations. If the probability of interruption is ·01 per assembly operation (of which there are 1000 in Tempus Co. and 1111 in Hora Inc.), it can be shown that it will take Tempus about four thousand times as long to complete a watch as Hora.

Although the parable does not raise U-form versus M-form comparisons *per se*, the spirit is clearly similar.

2. *Strategic decision-making*

In substantial measure, enterprise objectives can be imputed from the goals associated with the locus of strategic decision-making in the firm.[1] It is therefore appropriate to inquire how different organization forms solve the capacity problem at the top and with what consequences.

2.1. *The capacity problem.* The M-form enterprise solves the problem of supplying requisite capacity at the top not by bringing operating executives into this activity but by creating a team of general executives and providing them with an elite staff. The general executives have no direct operating responsibilities. Indeed they have no direct access to the functional parts of the organization. Responsibility for achieving performance goals is fixed on the division managers: each division manager is expected to provide appropriate coordination among the functional parts within his respective operating division. Thus the general executives, having delegated this responsibility and lacking direct access to the functional parts, are able to become fully absorbed in enterprise-wide strategic considerations instead.

Attachment of an elite staff to the general office is a vital adjunct in supplying the peak coordinating function with requisite capacity. As already noted, this staff provides advisory functions to the operating divisions, acting in this respect as in-house management consultants, to help them set up procedures to execute their respective programs more effectively. It also serves an important planning and control function, undertaking *ex ante* studies of both general market conditions and new enterprise opportunities, and making *ex post* evaluations of the performance of the operating divisions. This provides the general office with important informational inputs for its own planning purposes, inputs that are less prone to the data

---

[1] Simon expresses it as follows: 'in view of the hierarchical structure that is typical in most formal organizations, it is a reasonable use of language to employ organizational goal to refer particularly to the constraint sets and criteria of search that *define roles* at the upper levels. . . . For high-level executives in these organizations will seek out and support actions that advance these goals, and subordinate employees will do the same or will at least tailor their choices to constraints established by the higher echelons with this end in view' ([38], p. 21); italics added).

distortion that occurs when information is processed up through the organizational hierarchy. It also permits the general office to audit divisional performance in a way which, left to its own resources, would be impracticable. Thus the strategic decision-making function can be said to have been solved in the M-form by (1) assigning this function to a team[1] of top executive generalists who are removed from operating responsibilities, and (2) supporting this group of general officers with an elite staff capable of performing the depth analyses necessary to discharge the strategic overseer task effectively.

2.2. *Goal pursuit*. The discussion of goal-pursuit consequences of the M-form organization will consider first the goal-pursuit character-istics of the general office, next those of the elite staff, and finally those of the operating divisions.

2.2.1. *General office*. As indicated, the general office is created as a means for overcoming the capacity problem at the top. The creation of such a general office does more, however, than relieve bounded capacity constraints. It also, as Chandler points out, alters the 'psychological commitment' of the strategic decision-makers. The subgoals associated with the separate functional divisions are no longer natural objects of pursuit.

Ths most important reason for this commitment shift is that the general executive position is defined in a way which not only frees it but removes it from narrow functional responsibilities. This is accomplished by reorganizing the firm so as to make the operating division rather than the functional division the principal operating unit. Strictly functional issues are therefore resolved intradivisionally, with the result that partisan functional input can be greatly reduced if not eliminated from the strategic decision-making process. Natural incentives to promote subgoals are in this way attenuated. The general executive is able to focus on genuine enterprise viability con-siderations and can consider the effect on the individual parts dis-passionately. The disposition to expand staff and tolerate slack is supplanted instead by a tendency to regard costs in a strictly instru-mental fashion. At the level of the general office, at least, the M-form innovation favors a shift away from the expense preferences charac-teristic of the U-form structure in favor of profits.

[1] The team will be treated 'as if' it were a group of equals, although in fact the differential formal rank and capabilities of these executives will be manifest on close issues.

CE N

2.2.2. *Elite staff*. Inasmuch as the staff attached to the general office has an important role in both formulating and executing strategic decisions, it is relevant to consider whether this group has own-preferences that run contrary to those of the general office, and if so whether these are apt to be important to an assessment of M-form performance. With respect to own-preferences, this group, like most professional staffs, may be anxious to extend the scope and quality of its services. Quantitatively, however, the elite staff is not apt to be sufficiently large, in relation to overall enterprise activity and employment, to have a substantial immediate effect on cost even if it is successful in realizing own-staff expansionary aspirations. More worrisome are its indirect cost consequences and its choice of evaluative criteria.

Since the relation of this staff to the operating divisions is mainly instrumental, identification with the operating divisions in a partisan sense is missing. Excellence is thus apt to be measured in terms of the criteria specified by the general office, which is principally revenues in relation to costs (profits), rather than by the size or prominence of the functional divisions. The elite staff serves to reinforce the preferences of the general office in this respect.

The indirect cost consequences of elite staff initiatives are more troublesome, however. Thus, although zealousness of the elite staff may have insubstantial own-cost effects, these may cumulatively become great when their operating-division consequences are assessed. Special precautions may therefore be needed lest the elite staff require the operating divisions to undertake planning and control activities (records, reports, etc.) the net benefits of which, while positive in terms of an elite staff calculus, are negative when expressed in terms of profits.

Note that no special moral superiority is assigned to either the general office or the elite staff. The reason why strategic decisions favor profitability is because this is the natural outcome of the way in which the M-form organization is structured. Organizational design thus involves more than technical efficiency considerations. It is also a means of eliciting self-regulatory behavior. The importance of this is too easily minimized. As Geoffrey Vickers has emphasized, however, 'the main control to which [strategic decision-makers] are subject is and is likely to remain control by role' ([42], p. 94). With a few exceptions, notably Chandler [14], the latter is a relatively neglected aspect of the organization-form literature.

2.2.3. Operating divisions. As indicated earlier, the operating divisions in the M-form organization have many of the attributes of independent firms. They might for this reason be described as 'quasi-firms'.[1] Each of these quasi-firms has a U-form structure. One might then reasonably expect them to display U-form preferences – which may or may not place these units in goal conflict with the general office. Whether it does depends jointly on organization form, size, and internal role expectations and incentive processes. If each of the operating divisions is individually small enough that the division manager's office possesses requisite capacity for peak (divisional) coordination, preferences, characteristic of the large U-form structure (and attributable to the extensive participation in the strategic decision-making process of partisan functional executives and to control-loss experience) need not obtain. Medium-sized, U-form operating divisions (just as independent, medium-sized, U-form firms) may display profits-maximizing preferences instead. Moreover, in consideration of the separable profit performance assignable to each of these divisions, deviant tendencies can presumably be checked, if not eliminated, through judicious use by the general office of incentive awards.

Although the argument has a certain *a priori* plausibility, it disposes too easily of the potential goal conflict between the operating divisions and the general office. For one thing, overcoming partisan functional representations does not necessarily dispose of partisanship altogether. An advocacy posture is still natural for division managers – only now, presumably, expense biases are supplanted by general size aspirations. Thus, whereas the heads of the functional divisions in the large U-form firm are observed to expend efforts to extend the size and prominence of their respective functional activities, the operating-division chiefs in the M-form firm are engaged instead in efforts to expand the size and prominence of their respective operating divisions. Although, for a given expansion of expenditures, the latter are apt to have a less pernicious profits impact, the potential for conflict needs be recognized. Moreover, if in addition either scale economies or design error has produced operating divisions of sufficient size that large, U-form goal consequences are induced at the divisional level, the conflict potential is compounded. Any claims, therefore, that the general office preference for profits will be prevailing requires that the efficacy of the internal compliance processes be

---

[1] The first use of this term, to my knowledge, is Richard Heflebower [23].

examined; merely to establish that a decisive preference for profits in relation to hierarchical expense prevails at the top of the M-form organization is not sufficient. We therefore turn to a consideration of whether and for what reasons the general office can be expected to be successful in constraining the operating divisions to perform 'appropriately'.

3. Internal control

3.1. *Internal resource allocation and auditing.* Internal resource allocation can be regarded both as a market substitute and an internal control technique. Here we examine resource allocation as an indirect control over personnel. The argument turns on the proposition that the renewal of resource commitments is vital to the continuation of each organizational subdivision. To the extent that performance and subsequent resource assignments can be connected in rational ways, the resource allocation process can be made responsive to differential performance. *Ceteris paribus*, those parts of the organization that are realizing superior performance will increase in relative size and importance, with all of the beneficial local gains associated with expansion. Moreover, recalcitrant parts of an organization might further be pressed to fall into line by using the resource allocation process to bring pressure from lower-level participants on otherwise unresponsive middle-range executives to comply with higher-level objectives: inasmuch as lower-level participants are among the first to feel the effects of a reduction in resources allocated to a particular task or function, and as lower-level support is usually essential to the effectiveness of a middle-range executive, the ability to manipulate resources in semi-punitive ways enhances the control of the higher-level group.

Auditing naturally plays an important role in any such efforts. Performance checks of three types should be distinguished. The first involves advance, the second contemporaneous, and the third *ex post* evaluation. An advance evaluation would entail reviewing proposed programs with respect to their intrinsic merits, balance between the parts, and general level of expense. Contemporaneous evaluation would entail checking current performance against projections, examining sources of variances and possibly comparing performance with that of the firm's principal rivals. Frequently more important than either of these, but an often neglected aspect of the control program, is the possibility of conducting *repeated ex post* evaluations.

Current variation may well be 'excused' in plausible ways, but where a persistent pattern of performance failures is identified, explaining variance becomes more difficult.

A distinction between the one-time and the persistent power of lower-level participants is relevant in this connection. It is invariably true that the one-time power of lower-level participants exceeds that which they can expect to exercise in a continuing way. Despite expertise in substantial amounts at the top, lower-level participants in the business firm can sometimes distort the data or execute directives in lackadaisical ways, either of which can effectively frustrate the objectives of the general office – on a one-time basis. But they cannot ordinarily expect to do this repeatedly. The cumulative evidence becomes too strong,[1] and their dismissal is too easily effected. Since indeed the usual employment relation is a continuing rather than one-time sort, the evident 'instantaneous' powers to which lower-level participants have access should not be uncritically generalized. Their persistent power is much less. Neglect of this possibility of developing a performance history has led some observers to overstate the power of lower-level participants.[2] By focusing on the short-run and the uncertainty associated with individual programs, they have failed to appreciate that inference techniques applied to a series of (individually) uncertain programs permit the surveillance agency to sharpen its evaluations significantly.

3.2. *U- and M-form comparisons.* The questions to be considered now are to what extent, if any, and for what reasons the M-form structure can be expected to exercise the compliance machinery with greater effectiveness than its U-form counterpart. Can the general office realistically expect that its preferences will prevail?

3.2.1. Direct intervention. Extensive intervention by the peak coordinator in the detailed affairs of the functional divisions is not feasible in the large U-form structure; the chief executive is apt

[1] The problem can be likened to that of estimating the mean of a populaton with varying sample size. The standard error of the sample varies inversely with the square root of the sample size. Thus, although any single observation may deviate substantially from the population mean if the variance is great, the sample mean for large sample size can be expected to converge to the true mean. I discuss this 'repeated-exposure' phenomenon elsewhere in connection with military procurement [45].

[2] Galbraith's technostructure theory of the firm [21] appears to rely on lower-level participant power that, for the reasons given, may often be only transitory.

neither to have the time not the expertise to engage in such activities. The greater capacity of the general office, together with the elite staff that it has access to, potentially permit more extensive intervention by the M-form organization. Yet this needs to be done with care lest the quasi-autonomous standing of the operating divisions be upset, which would violate the structural integrity of this organization form. The operating divisions could not really be held accountable if operating decisions were commonly prescribed.

To the extent, therefore, that the general office intervenes at the divisions, this is apt either to involve policy matters (planning and rule-making) or the provisions of 'consulting' services for special projects or problem situations. Albeit limited, these are relatively powerful control techniques and indeed distinguish the M-form from the U-form organization in this respect. It nevertheless bears repeating that, on a routine basis, neither the U- nor the M-form structure invites extensive intervention from the top in operating affairs.

3.2.2. Control over personnel. The screening–selection–promotion process is an important means of securing consensus within both the U- and M-form organizations. For all practical purposes, direct control over personnel rarely reaches down more than one level. Employment policies, however, can have pervasive consequences, and personnel changes at a high level are apt to have secondary effects across several successive hierarchical levels. Thus control over personnel at the top together with the disposition to exercise it is a potentially significant compliance measure.

For purposes of making U- and M-form comparisons, consider the problem of replacing the chief *operating* executives where mal-performance or non-compliance is detected. This should prove easier in the M-form than the U-form organization. The reason is related in an essential way to the manner in which the capacity problem is solved in each type of organization form. Recall that in the M-form organization, strategic and operating decisions are made by different personnel, while in the U-form organization the heads of each of the functional divisions (who are the principal operating executives) also share the strategic decision-making load. Thus for the senior executives responsible for strategic decision-making in the U-form organization to replace the head of a functional division requires that they reject one of their own kind. No such delicate choice is experienced in the M-form organization; here the relation between the heads of the operating divisions and the general office can be addressed on mainly professional grounds. One might therefore expect that, to the extent that operating executives attempt to deviate from strategic directives, their replacement can be effectuated more easily in the M-form organization.

3.2.3. Auditing and resource allocation. Probably the most important differences between the U- and M-form structures with respect to their compliance properties are those which are attributable to the auditing and resource allocation processes in each. Ths differences are both attitudinal and structural. The attitudinal argument follows that developed above in examining the problems of replacing the chief operating executives: the U-form executives who participate in the strategic decision-making process are simply disinclined to audit themselves. The structural reasons can be treated in three parts: commensurability, decomposability, and expertise.

Consider the commensurability aspect first. The essential difference to note between the U- and M-form organization structures in this respect is that comparative performance evaluations between the functional divisions in the U-form organization involved intrinsically different characteristics (the intractable apples and oranges comparison), while in the M-form organization, in which each operating division represents a 'profit center', a common denominator exists.

Decomposability makes resource allocation in response to *ex post* evaluations feasible in the M-form organization. In the U-form organization, however, implementing recommendations to shift resources around in a fully interconnected system in semi-punitive ways may be dysfunctional. Spillovers from intended rewards and punishments would, by reason of intrinsic interdependencies, almost certainly be extensive.

The differential expertise which these two organization forms are able to bring to bear in securing compliance is due to differences in the quality, commitment, and size of the staffs on which the senior executives can call. The staff attached to the general office is an elite one that is able to make depth evaluations of both the prospects and past performance of each of the operating divisions. A similar capability is missing (and indeed might threaten organization chaos) in the U-form organization: staff analyses of this sort here are made difficult by the lack of decomposability among the operating parts and may entail extensive second-guessing of the functional division heads – both in their capacities as operating officers and as strategic decision-makers. Such an undertaking, even if it were feasible, is not obviously functional. Altogether, the technical capability, incentives, and constitutional authority of the M-form staff must be regarded as superior to that of the staff attached to the chief executive's office in the U-form enterprise.

One concludes, therefore, that not only does the structure of the M-form organization yield internal efficiency and high-level goal-pursuit outcomes different from that which an equivalent U-form enterprise would display, but, in addition, the M-form structure facilitates the exercise of the internal compliance machinery in especially effective ways. That the preferences of an assertive general office in an M-form corporation should (up to a first approximation) prevail seems at least plausible.

4. *The multi-division form hypothesis*

To the extent that economists have been concerned with a rationale for the firm, it has mainly been in connection with such matters as scale economies, externalities, and uncertainty. The bureaucratic theory literature, by contrast, has been concerned with matters such as goal formation, subgoal pursuit, communication processes, and compliance machinery. Ths implications of the latter have sometimes been brought to bear on the former [17, 31], but this has been incomplete. That the argument has not been carried to completion is perhaps attributable to the failure to express it in organization-form terms. This provides the linkage that permits the theory of the firm and bureaucratic theory literatures to be more fully joined.

Ashby, with quite different interests in mind, has put the argument this way ([5], p. 53):

> That a whole machine should be built of parts of given behavior is not sufficient to determine its behavior as a whole: only when the details of coupling are added does the whole's behavior become determinate.

In part, at least, the M-form organization can be regarded as a different solution to the coupling problem than that provided by the U-form structure – one that takes advantage of essential decomposability. In the process it gives rise to, because of the natural incentives it sets up, different goal-pursuit tendencies.

The argument can be summarized in the following way: the transformation of a large business firm for which divisionalization is feasible from a unitary to a multi-division form organization contributes to (but does not assure) an attenuation of both the control-loss experience and subgoal pursuit (mainly staff-biased expansion) that are characteristic of the unitary form. Realization of these attenuation effects, however, requires that the general office be aggressively constituted to perform its strategic planning, resource allocation, and control functions. Both the form and substance of multi-division organization are required for this transformation to be effective. Expressed in conventional goal-pursuit and efficiency terms, the argument comes down to this: *the organization and operation of the large enterprise along the lines of the M-form favors goal-pursuit and least-cost behavior more nearly associated with the neo-classical profits-maximization hypothesis than does the U-form organizational alternative.*

It will be noted that the argument has been developed in comparative terms. It could, therefore, as easily be expressed instead as a U-form hypothesis; namely, the organization and operation of the large enterprise along the lines of the U-form favors goal-pursuit and cost behavior more nearly associated with the managerial discretion hypothesis than does the M-form organizational alternative. This equivalent statement makes evident an underlying symmetry that some may find disconcerting: if one accepts the affirmative argument on behalf of the M-form organization advanced above, a tacit acceptance of managerial discretion theory (in the context of large U-form organization) may also be implied. That is, if the M-form organization has, for the reasons given, the superior efficiency, motivational and control properties that have been imputed to it, then presumably the organization and operation of the large enterprpide along the lines of the traditional (U-form) structure contributes to control loss and utility-maximizing behavior of the sort described previously [43, 46]. To the extent therefore that the coincidence of large, unitary-form structures and non-trivial opportunity sets (mainly by reason of favorable product-market conditions) are observed in the economy, utility-maximizing behavior (and its attendant consequences) is to be expected.

It is important to note that the M-form enterprise does not

abandon the U-form structure; rather, it attempts to harness the U-form solution to the division of labor problems within a larger organizing framework. The technical benefits of the U-form organization are thereby preserved, while its undesirable control-loss and goal-pursuit properties are restrained. Expressed in opportunity set and utility function terms, the M-form enterprise is able, because of its superior efficiency properties, to operate on a larger opportunity set than a comparable U-form structure. Also, because of the separation of strategic from operating decision-making, the M-form enterprise favors goal pursuit more nearly characteristic of the firm of neo-classical theory. Finally, the decomposability and commensurability properties of this structure and the creation of an elite staff permit this organization form to secure a high order of compliance from its operating divisions. Altogether the M-form enterprise tends, through *internal* organization, to provide institutional underpinning for the prima facie standing ordinarily accorded to the profits-maximization assumption – support which, in large organizations that have access to product-market insulary, has hitherto been lacking.

This does not preclude the possibility that it may be more instructive, frequently, to employ managerial discretion models (such as those in [43]) to study the *short-run* behavior of individual operating divisions (quasi-firms). This appears to correspond with Armen Alchian's view that 'The wealth-maximizing postulate is usually appropriate (or least inappropriate) when applied to the [M-form] firm as a unit of analysis. But in seeking to explain individual behavior *within* the firm, utility-maximizing criteria are more general and powerful than wealth-maximizing criteria' ([2], p. 350).

IV. COMPETITION IN THE CAPITAL MARKET AGAIN

Although some may express misgivings, let us assume, *arguendo*, that a plausible *a priori* case had been made on behalf of the M-form hypothesis. Ths evidence now needs to be examined. Except for Chandler's study [14], this is mainly fragmentary. Ordinary prudence might, in these circumstances, favor a systematic development of the data prior to any effort to take the argument further. At the very least, efforts that are made to advance the argument might be regarded with cautious skepticism.

Bearing this admonition in mind, there are nevertheless three reasons for wishing to push ahead at this time. For one thing sharper tests of the basic hypothesis may be possible if certain applications of the argument are first developed. For another, lest inappropriate tests be performed, the hypothesis needs to be delimited. Finally, certain policy implications of the argument are too important to hold in abeyance until the evidence is wholly conclusive; the antitrust agencies [30] and the Congress [13] have been contemplating or are attempting to enforce limitations on conglomerate corporations based on theories and evidence that, at best, are incomplete. Presumably the potentially beneficial consequences of conglomeration deserve to be exposed.

A more extensive development of applications and qualifications is given in [49]. The discussion in this section is limited to an examination of the M-form impact on competition in the capital market, including effects that are attributable to conglomeration. Certain qualifications to the main argument are given in section V.

1. The separation of ownership from control

Although the emergence in the late 1800s of large, single-product, multi-function enterprises organized along U-form lines (in steel, meat-packing, tobacco, oil, etc. [14], chap. 1) presumably permitted the realization of scale economies (and perhaps monopoly power), it probably contributed to an eventual weakening of the ability of both product and capital markets to enforce selection on profits. Concern over this condition was expressed in the early 1930s by Berle and Means when they observed that the development of the large corporation had resulted in a separation of ownership from control with uncertain performance consequences [10].

The multi-function operations of the U-form organization represented a substitution of administrative integration for integration that had previously been accomplished through product-market exchange. If, ordinarily, an integrated firm is, both for size and complexity reasons, more difficult for an outside surveillance agency to monitor than a series of non-integrated firms, administrative integration of this sort may simultaneously impair the capital market's policing capabilities.[1] However favorable its operating efficiency consequences, the U-form innovation may have expanded the management's opportunity set in relation to that of the enterprise and in this way contributed to opportunities for discretionary behavior.

The concern over this condition expressed by Berle and Means has since been repeated by numerous other students of the modern corporation. A common finding is that the separation of ownership from control is extensive and that it is merely a matter of good fortune that the corporate sector performs as well as it does. In the background lurks the suspicion that one day these enclaves of private power will run amok ([29], pp. 7–9), and a search for substitute external controls has been set in motion on this account.

As indicated earlier, the M-form innovation was first 'discovered' in the 1920s. By the 1930s its effects on selected industries were beginning to be felt quite generally, foreshadowing its eventually pervasive transformation of the enterprise system. It is perhaps ironic that at the very time that the M-form innovation was beginning to take hold, widespread concern over the failure of the modern corporation to satisfy legitimacy tests was first expressed. It is the burden of the argument here that the perceived separation of ownership from control was mainly attributable to conditions observed in the large U-form firm and that, while the M-form innovation was designed mainly in response to the control-loss experience of the large, diversified U-form enterprise, this innovation has also had the effect of restoring integrity to the goal-specification and policing processes. Prior failure to distinguish clearly between internal and external control processes, including the relations between internal control and organization form, are responsible for the uncritical application of the early U-form argument to the later M-form condition.

Recall that the capital market was regarded as a less than wholly efficacious surveillance and correction mechanism for three reasons: its external relation to the firm places it at a serious information disadvantage; it is restricted to non-marginal adjustments; it experiences non-trivial displacement costs. The general office of the M-form

---

[1] This is almost certainly true when expressed in absolute terms, but may not be when regarded as a percentage. Thus, although surveillance and displacement costs will vary directly with the size and complexity of the corporation, the ratio of these costs to any of a variety of size measures (e.g. sales) may well decline.

organization has superior properties in each of these respects. First, it is an internal rather than external control mechanism with the constitutional authority and expertise to make detailed evaluations of the performance of each of its operating parts. Second, it can make fine-tuning as well as discrete adjustments. This permits it both to intervene early in a selective, preventative way (a capability which the capital market lacks altogether), as well as to perform *ex post* corrective adjustments, in response to evidence of performance failure, with a surgical precision that the capital market lacks (the scalpel versus the ax is not a wholly inappropriate analogy). Finally, the costs of intervention by the general office are relatively low. Altogether, therefore, a profit-oriented general office in an M-form enterprise might be expected easily to secure superior performance to that which the capital market can enforce. The M-form organization might thus be viewed as capitalism's creative response to the evident limits which the capital market experiences in its relations to the firm as well as a means for overcoming the organizational problems which develop in the large U-form enterprise when variety becomes great – although the conjunction of these two consequences in a single organizational innovation should probably be regarded as fortuitous.

The argument can be carried yet a step further by considering the effects of the M-form innovation on capital-market displacement efforts. *Ceteris paribus*, displacement is more likely the greater the unavailed profit opportunities in the target firm and the lower the costs of effecting displacement. In relation to the U-form enterprise, the M-form innovation enhances the attractiveness of making a displacement effort in both respects.

The realization of operating economies by reconstituting a large U-form enterprise along M-form lines represents a source of potential profit gain which, in the absence of reorganization, is unavailable. The resulting economies are due to more effective resource allocation (between divisions and in the aggregate), better internal organization (a reduction in technical control loss), and the attenuation of subgoal pursuit. Unitary-form organizations for which either divisionalization is difficult (the natural unit is the integrated form) or the management is otherwise disinclined to re-organize thus offer an opportunity to realize economies by a displacement agency which can effectively produce the change. *Ceteris paribus*, the potential profits are greater if the incumbent management is actively engaged in subgoal pursuit – although, it should be noted, the existence of subgoal pursuit is not essential for structural economies to be realized.

Existing M-form enterprises are probably the least-cost instruments for achieving displacement. For one thing they are apt to have superior inference capabilities; the elite staff of the M-form structure may even have as one of its principal assignments the discovery of potential takeover candidates. In addition, such firms are already experienced in the organizational advantages which this structure offers.[1]

Unitary-form enterprises that anticipate such takeover efforts may attempt to shrink the potential displacement gain by making appropriate internal changes: subgoal pursuit may be reduced or, possibly, self-reorganization along M-form lines may be initiated. Such forestalling efforts are not apt to be common, however, until the probability of a takeover attempt has reached a non-trivial value. Except in U-form enterprises which have been specifically targeted for takeover, this may require that there be a relatively large number of multi-division enterprises actively surveying takeover opportunities. With only a few multi-division firms performing this function, the probability that any one unitary-form enterprise will be the object of a takeover attempt is too small to warrant *ex ante* adaptation. Once the number of multi-division firms becomes sufficiently large, however, the effect on unitary-form enterprises that are otherwise shielded from product-market pressures is equivalent to an increase in competition in so far as subgoal pursuit is concerned. Selection on profits is thereby enhanced; the effects indeed may be pervasive. The argument thus reduces to the following proposition: internal organization and conventional capital-market forces are complements as well as substitutes; the two coexist in a symbiotic relationship to each other.

2. *'Conglomerate' organization*

2.1. *Conglomerate organization conventionally regarded.* The efficiency and market-power consequences of the so-called 'conglomer-

---

[1] Conceivably, however, this experience can be obtained by inducing M-form managers to join U-form firms which then take on the M-form structure by either self-divisionalization or themselves undertaking an acquisition effort.

ate' corporation have been a source of long-standing puzzlement. Mainly, the opinions of academics who have considered this phenomenon have been negative. Policy statements such as the following are common: 'Of all types of merger activity conglomerate acquisitions have the least claim to promoting efficiency in the economic sense' ([11], p. 679). 'Doubtless some conglomerate mergers are harmless; some may even be useful. But the merger of unrelated activities seldom offers much prospect of efficiency' ([19], p. 46). Perhaps the most explicit treatment of this argument is that offered by Igor Ansoff and Fred Weston [3]. They contrast vertical and horizontal mergers with conglomerate mergers. The complementarities (economies, market power) available from mergers of the first type give rise to what they regard as synergistic effects, while the conglomerate merger yields no such combinatorial gains ([3], pp. 51–2). They then go on to examine the appropriate control arrangements for each type of merger and indicate that while comprehensive controls are essential to realize the benefits of horizontal or vertical combination, 'financial targets' may be all that can usefully be employed in the conglomerate organization ([3], pp. 57–8).

Others who have viewed the conglomerate form have been somewhat more sanguine regarding its efficiency properties, but it has virtually no vigorous supporters among academics. Even in the business community there are numerous skeptics (as is evident in the 1 January 1969 issue of *Forbes*, for example).

The usual efficiency arguments on behalf of conglomerate organization rely either on risk pooling or operating economies. Morris Adelman has identified investment economies that are distinctively conglomerate in the portfolio diversification (risk) consequences which such a combination affords [1]. The typical static efficiency arguments in favor of conglomerate merger have been identified by Donald Turner as those which are attributable to commonalities in marketing, manufacturing, or administration ([40], pp. 1323–39). He goes on to observe that the possibility of such economies is naturally 'slight' in a 'pure' conglomerate merger ([40], p. 1330) If these exhaust the favorable arguments that can be marshalled on behalf of this organization form the beneficial effects of conglomeration might well be dismissed as *de minimis*.

2.2 *An alternative view.* One of the principal difficulties in dealing with the conglomerate phenomenon is that it is so ill specified. To say that the conglomerate corporation is a collection of dissimilar business activities is not very useful until degrees of dissimilarity are established and the relative importance of the parts is determined. Even this may not be sufficient, however; it is also essential that the control processes be considered. The free-form corporation needs to be distinguished from the M-form structure, even though they may be identical in terms of markets and technology. The argument here is restricted to the M-form version of the conglomerate; no special efficiency claims are either made or intended for conglomerate merger (or expansion) activity for which the M-form structure does not prevail.

Ths question to be addressed, therefore, is whether risk pooling and/or slight commonalities adequately reflect the investment advantages and operating efficiency properties of an M-form firm that is diversified in sufficient degree to warrant the conglomerate appellation. Consider the investment efficiency aspect first. It will be useful for this purpose to consider two alternative economies that differ only in the way that production is organized. Assume that the M-form structure prevails in both, but that in one economy the firms are specialized (divisionalized, say, according to brand or geographic lines) while in the other the firms are multi-market organizations. Will the latter (conglomerate) economy out-perform the former and why?

An answer to this turns in large measure on earnings retention proclivities. Assume that the retention of earnings by firms of both types is favored by either or both of the following two conditions: (1) the differential tax treatment of dividends together with non-trivial transaction costs associated with reinvestment; (2) positive ploughback preferences of the managements in conjunction with significant takeover frictions in the capital market.

If, for either of these reasons, an earnings retention bias exists, and since to assign cash flows to their sources constitutes what may often be a serious investment restraint, the economy organized along conglomerate lines might well enjoy an advantage over the specialized firm economy. The ear-marking of funds in the latter would result in what would frequently be delayed responses to market signals and otherwise arbitrary allocations of investment. In the conglomerate-firm economy, by contrast, cash flows, from whatever source, are not automatically retained by the sectors from which these funds originate but are (ideally) assigned on the basis of prospective yields instead.[1] The conglomerate acts in this respect as a miniature capital market; it internalizes the funds-metering function normally imputed to the capital market – a function which Baumol's analysis of the traditional mechanisms found to be defective ([8], p. 76).

It could of course be argued that these investments efficiencies are attributable to remediable system defects, and that these should be corrected. The position has merit, but it should be pointed out that the argument against conglomeration has been shifted. Until such time, therefore, as the necessary remedies have been proposed and put into effect, investment efficiency presumably warrants considera-tion in evaluating the consequences of M-form conglomeration for which resource shifts into high-yield activities can be expected.

The diversification argument is, however, subject to diminishing-returns qualifications. First, for a fixed-size firm (and assuming that all technical scale-economy conditions are satisfied), increasing the degree of diversification eventually encounters control-loss conditions. Prescribing the optimal degree of diversification thus requires sensi-tivity to the tradeoffs between static operating efficiencies and invest-ment alternatives. Second, as firm size increases for a fixed degree of diversification, the control-loss consequences of hierarchical organi-zation cumulatively become great. Lest proliferating variety become unmanageable, very large firms may need to maintain relatively high product specialization ratios or disperse some of the control which in the M-form structure is concentrated at the top and is fundamentally responsible for its special performance characteristics.

Whereas claims of investment efficiencies involve an extension of the M-form argument to include multi-market occupancy, operating economies obtain by a straightforward application of the standard M-form economies analysis given earlier. Multi-divisionalization without multi-market occupancy is sufficient for these to be realized. In consideration, however, of current anti-merger policies, which bear down hard on horizontal and vertical mergers, a vital route by which small U-form firms can quickly obtain the requisite size to

---

[1] Consider in this connection Robert Hansberger's explanation of Boise Cascade's acquisition of Ebasco:

> [Ebasco] didn't have the opportunity to invest their cash resources at the good rate of return we have. This is what provided the motivation for putting the two companies together. We have a large inventory of projects that involve the prospect of high return – and that require large amounts of cash. We can use that money . . . at returns well above what they can achieve.
>
> (*Fortune*, LXXX, Oct 1969, p. 136)

support the M-form structure and thereby realize the economies which it affords is by conglomerate merger.[1] If, therefore, the operating economies arguments of preceding chapters are correct, if M-form organization requires that large (but not necessarily giant) size be reached, and if alternative merger possibilities are barred, then, lacking countervailing considerations, operating economies grounds for conglomerate merger would appear to be more substantial than have previously been indicated.

A similar argument applies to the transfer process by which many technical innovations are brought efficiently to completion. If, often, efficient final supply (production, distribution) is facilitated by permitting large, multi-division enterprises to acquire the successful inventions of small firms, and if enforcement of the anti-merger statutes against horizontal and vertical mergers is to remain tough, conglomerate acquisition may be a vital means by which to maintain transfer-process viability.[2]

One possible countervailing consideration to these arguments is that, despite the prospect of immediate economies through merger, the time horizon employed is too short: if one is patient, the requisite size needed to support M-form organization, with its superior operating efficiency consequences, can be realized by internal expansion. The point is not contested, but it is relevant to note that the argument is now shifted: it is not whether managerial economies are available by merging unrelated firms (which otherwise lack requisite size to support the M-form structure), but rather rests on what adjustment path is to be preferred. To delay the realization of

[1] Consider in this connection the following observations of Tinkham Veale II (reported in the *New York Times*, 8 July 1969, Sec. F, p. 3):

> ... all too often owner-managers of small companies hit a plateau when sales reach the $5-million mark. At that point they can't seem to expand further.
> The company's head finds himself devoting too much time to legal, accounting, administrative and financial problems that he simply is not equipped to handle, and neglecting the production and engineering problems at which he is an expert in solving.

Veale accordingly regards conglomeration (albeit of a mixed M- and free-form variety) as a means of permitting these firms to move off this plateau.

[2] For a more extensive development of the transfer-process argument, see [41]. A somewhat different argument sometimes made is that the conglomerate form favors investment in R. & D. on account of its superior appropriability characteristics: unanticipated spillovers from R. & D. can be more easily utilized. In relation to smaller firms, however, the R. & D. commonalities enjoyed by large conglomerates may be more than offset by the disabilities common to large firms quite generally in the performance of early-stage innovative activity [41].

these economies by prohibiting such mergers presumably requires that offsetting eventual benefits be shown.

A further operating economies argument favorable to conglomeration that is not subject to this last qualification concerns the takeover issue. If the M-form firm is to perform the capital-market policing function (described in IV.1 above) while present anti-merger policies with respect to horizontal and vertical acquisitions are to remain in effect, preserving the conglomerate option may be essential. Otherwise the threat of takeover to firms operated by moribund managements will be rendered effete; bringing every form of market organization – including the conglomerate – under antitrust attack would have the unfortunate and presumably unintended consequence of impairing what Henry Manne refers to as the 'market for corporate control'.

2.3. *Social costs of conglomeration*. The above is an essentially affirmative statement on behalf of the conglomerate form of organization. Dealing, however, as it does mainly with potential rather than with actuality, neither the frequency nor extent of the indicated effects can be said to have been established. This awaits the development of the data. It is sufficient for our purposes here if the relevant dimensions of the issue have been more fully exposed and it is evident that the *a priori* case on conglomeration is not wholly negative.

That there may be social costs which the conglomerate generates in any particular case is, nevertheless, freely conceded. Among these are possible diseconomies due to ineffective or misdirected control activities, including internal subsidization of weakly performing operating divisions. Also, the conglomerate may be especially adept at exploiting tax or other legislative loopholes. In addition, the conglomerate process may, if carried to excess, result in the attenuation of either actual or, perhaps more commonly, potential competition among a compact group of super-giants – out of a condition of recognized mutual dependence, presumably. Finally, legitimate giant-size objections might in some cases be registered. These matters, while beyond the scope of the present paper, are addressed elsewhere ([49], chap. 9).

V. SOME QUALIFICATIONS

Only two qualifications will be offered here. The first is concerned with what might be characterized as the 'exempted' industries. The second deals with the specialization of the objective function suggested by the M-form hypothesis. This does not exhaust the possible qualifications, but these two are among the more important.

1. *Exempted industries*

The M-form structure may be created in a number of ways. The most common is to divisionalize the activities of the multi-product enterprise along product lines. A second would be to divisionalize on a geographical basis, where each plant, although producing a common product, was sufficiently autonomous to be evaluated separately. A third would be to set up parallel brand lines within a single product line, where the brands may (but need not) vary in quality. An industry for which the technology of the product makes divisionalization in any of these ways difficult or forced, especially if it were one for which large size is necessary to realize essential scale economies, would not be expected to be among those early to adopt the M-form structure. Integrated metal-processing industries come immediately to mind as one which, for purely technological reasons, could be expected to persist with the unitary form. It is perhaps not surprising, therefore, to find that the copper, aluminum, nickel, and steel industries have been among those which have been late to adopt the multi-division form ([14], pp. 404–23).

Public utilities and common carriers, for both technological and regulatory reasons, may also be slow to adopt the M-form structure. For one thing, the nature of the product may not lend itself easily to meaningful divisionalization along M-form lines. In addition, the regulatory authorities, so as to preserve 'clean' regulatory relations, may resist efforts at diversification into non-regulated areas. Finally, the regulatory process itself may impair the incentives to move away from the U-form structure even where this is feasible. Maximum rate of return regulation limits incentives to achieve least-cost results, particularly if the utility has access to an inelastic demand class upon which to lean for revenues.

Another product-market area for which an exception to the main argument might be expected is in the defense industries. Although divisionalization may be common among defense-related firms, the performance of those divisions specializing in defense work may not conform to that indicated by the M-form hypothesis. Thus although 'competition' at the contract proposal and award stage can indeed be vigorous, the structure of the task, the *ex post* flexibility of the contract, the unusual incentives which the parties on both sides of the contract experience, and the surveillance system provided, all combine to support contract execution that, frequently, exhibits many of the characteristics of the managerial discretion rather than the M-form hypothesis.[1]

2. *The objective function*

The question to be faced here is whether the utility function has been overspecialized by our statement of the M-form hypothesis. Thus, although the M-form organization may effectively concentrate discretionary choice at the top and produce a commitment shift in favor of profit objectives, conceivably the general office executives of the M-form organization also entertain other enterprise-wide objectives. Among these, growth and 'enterprise prestige' are probably the most conspicuous candidates.

Operational content is assigned to enterprise prestige only with difficulty. One suspects in any case that growth will often be an adequate proxy for it. Where this is not true, enterprise prestige objectives are apt to be of an *ad hoc* rather than systematic sort. This is hardly stuff from which to build models and will therefore be set aside.[2] Growth, however, is less easy to dismiss.

Growth (or enterprise expansion) might be regarded as the M-form counterpart of the hierarchical expense component that we have associated with the utility function of the U-form enterprise. Not only is this a natural generalization of the argument, but it follows along lines already suggested by William Baumol [6, 7] and Robin

[1] For an elaboration of this aspect of the argument, see [45].

[2] This is not to say that a good deal of public relations energies will not go into representing the activities of the enterprise favorably, but this should not be mistaken for goal-seeking. The folklore of enterprise is doubtlessly replete with 'examples' where enterprise prestige is alleged to have had a decisive effect on firm behavior. Even if occasionally this is true, its quantitative importance is hardly established.

Marris [27, 28] – although, it should be noted, neither of them make the organization-form distinctions suggested here. Expressing growth in asset or sales terms, as Baumol and Marris do, the favored growth path will display none of the staff-biased properties characteristic of the large U-form organization. Such growth aspirations as the firm entertains are apt to be manifested mainly in an aggressive acquisition policy and/or in the amounts of resources allocated to investment (interpreted broadly to include advertising, research and development, etc., as well as plant and equipment).

Although the Baumol–Marris argument is an attractive one, I am reluctant at this stage to complicate a reasonably clean hypothesis by including additional enterprise objectives before it is evident that profits will not do. I therefore merely note that (1) if the M-form hypothesis were to be extended to include multiple goals, a growth goal would be a most natural first extension; but (2) lacking a quantitative basis for assigning special significance to the growth goal, the simpler (profits-maximizing) version of the M-form hypothesis seems preferable; and (3) the case for generalizing the objective function to include other goals is less compelling when consideration is given to the systems consequences of the M-form innovation.

This last is an essential point. It can be illustrated by tracing the effects of the U- to M-form transformation across a series of four stages. The first stage corresponds with that which the separation of ownership from control literature typically (or at least implicitly) postulates: the large U-form enterprise prevails in an environment where the product market is imperfect and the capital market is subject to non-trivial inference and takeover frictions. As a result, characteristic U-form discretionary behavior obtains. The M-form innovation occurs at stage two. Although devised mainly as a means of overcoming control-loss problems of internal organization, it also, at least often, educes a profits preference at the top as well. The third stage involves the diffusion of the M-form innovation. Some firms imitate out of choice; for others M-form rivalry makes reorganization necessary as a survival measure. Stage four involves the opportunistic takeover of unadapted U-form (or permissive M-form) firms by aggressive M-form enterprises. The policing powers of the capital market are mobilized in this way, with the result that neo-classical profits maximization, except for transitory deviations, tends generally to be restored.

Conceivably this description oversimplifies too greatly; possibly system frictions remain that make it necessary to give greater weight to volitional considerations. A way of characterizing management styles[1] and evaluating more precisely the efficacy of alternative control procedures may be needed. These, however, are empirical matters that can only be resolved by examining the data. For our purposes here it is sufficient to indicate that an examination of the systems consequences of the M-form innovation provides greater *a priori* confidence in the profits-maximization hypothesis than would otherwise obtain.

VI. CONCLUDING REMARKS

Directly or indirectly the analysis throughout has been concerned with the relations between organization form, size, managerial discretion, and efficiency. Although the firm has been the immediate object of analysis, the systems implications of the argument are often as and sometimes more important than those that concern the firm itself. A capsule summary of the argument is that it is an attempt to consider 'organizationally interesting' properties of the modern corporation at what might be regarded as an intermediate level of analysis – where by intermediate is meant that the firm itself, rather than the parts (as is characteristic of behavioral theory) or the industry (neo-classical theory), is the primary unit of study.

It may be useful, by way of concluding, to draw attention to some of the implications of the argument for characterizing the competitive process. Organizational innovation in relation to dynamic capitalism is one of these. A second is the concept of 'organizational failure'.

1. *Dynamic capitalism*

The essence of capitalism, presumably, is its adaptive capacity to generate and select on viable alternatives. Given this emphasis on dynamics, it is suprising that more attention has not been given to the

---

[1] Relevant in this connection is Samuel Reid's recent study of conglomerate mergers in which he distinguishes between 'offensive' and 'defensive' styles [35].

full range of variety that innovation can take. As Schumpeter emphasized, the kind of competition that is decisive is that which comes from 'the new commodity, the new technology, the new source of supply, the new type of organization' ([36], p. 84). The interest of economists and others in product and process innovation in recent years has been considerable. Likewise the question of entry has received substantial attention. Innovation which takes the form of a new type of organization, however, has been relatively slighted. If, however, the multi-division form has the properties which we have imputed to it, it seems not inconceivable that this has been American capitalism's most important single innovation of the twentieth century. The conglomerate organization, regarded in these terms, becomes merely a modern variant on the original multi-divisionaliza-tion concept.

One of the reasons for this neglect may be that the benefits of organizational innovation are more difficult to appropriate than for most technical innovations: patents are unavailable and imitation is relatively easy. Also, it may not be evident initially which organiza-tional innovations will have more than transitory effects. Thus, whereas, 'reorganization' is a common response to crisis circum-stances, not all such changes have lasting consequences. Distinguish-ing the successful from the aberrant responses may not at first be easy. (Although the same may be claimed for technical developments, the degree of objectivity with which these can be established is probably greater.) But difficulties of these types do not render organizational innovation any the less important. As Arthur Cole has observed, 'If changes in business procedures and practices were patentable, the contributions of business change to the economic growth of the nation would be as widely recognized as the influence of mechanical inventions or the inflow of capital from abroad' ([16], pp. 61–2).[1]

Schumpeter himself may be partly responsible for this neglect. In his *Theory of Economic Development*, organizational innovation is discussed mainly in conventional monopoly terms (thus organiza-tional innovation is illustrated by reference to 'the creation of a monopoly position (for example through trustification) or the

---

[1] Jewkes expresses the same point in the following way: 'Whilst no one would wish to deny that technology and science (in that order) have contributed much to the raising of standards of living in the last two centuries, there is a disposition in these days to exaggerate the contribution they have made to and to underestimate that made by new social organizations and institutions' ([24], p. 12).

breaking up of a monopoly position' [37], p. 66). The treatment in *Capitalism, Socialism, and Democracy* uses as an illustration of organizational innovation 'the largest-scale unit of control' ([36], p. 84). Although this moves closer to organizational innovation in the structural sense employed here, it fails explicitly to call attention to the goal-pursuit and internal efficiency considerations that would appear to be at the essence of organization-form comparisons. Also, one might hope that institutional incentives might somehow be arranged that would induce now giant-sized firms to undergo mitosis – an innovation that could well have beneficial goal-pursuit and efficiency consequences but would run quite at variance with Schumpeter's second example.

If, more generally, organizational innovation often does or can be made to have self-renewal properties, the decay of capitalism anticipated by Schumpeter loses much of its inevitability. It is interesting to note in this regard that the M-form enterprise is, in relation to an equivalent U-form structure, much the less 'bureaucratic'. Mitosis of the M-form structure might likewise have anti-bureaucratic, enabling qualities. Although other organizational innovations even now in progress may (as did the U-form structure) work in the opposite direction, extrapolating the experience of the first two-thirds of the twentieth century does not seem to spell capitalism's early bureaucratic demise.

2. *Institutional failure*

Product-market failure is a thoroughly commonplace concept in economics, having found its place into intermediate and even elementary textbooks. Such was not always the case. The classification system and analytical apparatus that now prevails evolved only gradually.

Although this relatively advanced state of development of product-market failure analysis is to be counted as a distinct gain, it has sometimes had the unfortunate tendency to focus attention too exclusively on product-market conditions to the neglect of a variety of other types of institutional failures. But product-market failure is merely one of a family of institutional failures. Also included in the broader category are conditions that might be characterized as capital-market failure, organizational failure, regulatory failure, and judicial and political failure, among others. A treatment of institutional failures of these latter types has only recently emerged. At best, only a rudimentary beginning has been made on the concept of regulatory failure,[1] while judicial and political failures tend mainly to be regarded as beyond the purview of economics.[2] Capital-market failures, such as those discussed in earlier parts of this paper, are commonly assumed away, while failures of internal organization are rarely even raised.

If the main argument is correct, however, and internal organization does influence performance in important and predictable ways, then the sources of organizational failure (control loss, incentive defects, ineffective or dysfunctional compliance measures, and the like) presumably warrant further development. Indeed, the entire range of behavior which now, for lack of a more precise classification scheme, might be characterized as 'inexorable bureaucratic proclivities' (e.g. seniority practices) ought to be examined.[3] Out of this should emerge a better understanding of the limits of internal organization as well as proposals to remedy observed defects.

References

[1] Adelman, M. A., 'The Antimerger Act, 1950–60', *American Economic Review*, LI (May 1961) 236–44.

[2] Alchian, A. A., 'Corporate Management and Property Rights', in *Economic Policy and the Regulation of Corporate Securities*, ed. H. G. Manne, (Washington, D.C., 1969).

[3] Ansoff, H. I., and Weston, J. F., 'Merger Objectives and Organization Structure', *Quarterly Review of Economics and Business*, II (Aug 1962) 49–58.

[4] Arrow, K. J., 'Control in Large Organizations', *Management Science*, X (Sep 1963) 397–408.

[5] Ashby, W. Ross, *Design for a Brain* (New York, 1960).

[6] Baumol, W. J., *Business Behavior, Value and Growth* (New York, 1959).

[7] ——, 'The Theory of Expansion of the Firm', *American Economic Review*, LII (Dec 1962) 1078–87.

[8] ——, *The Stock Market and Economic Efficiency* (New York, 1965).

[9] ——, and Fabian, T., 'Decomposition, Pricing for Decentralization, and External Economies, *Management Science*, XI (Sep 1964) 1–32.

---

[1] For an attempt to examine the sources of regulatory failure, see [48]. See also the references cited therein, especially the work of Richard Posner [34], for a discussion of this condition.

[2] For a recent exception, see Gerald Sirkin ([39], chap. 4).

[3] Anthony Downs is concerned with this in his recent book on bureaucracy [18].

[10] Berle, A. A., and Means, G. C., *The Modern Corporation and Private Property* (New York, 1932).
[11] Blair, J. M., 'The Conglomerate Merger in Economics and Law', *Georgetown Law Review*, XLIII (summer 1958) 79–92.
[12] Brown, Donaldson, 'Pricing Policy in Relation to Financial Control', *Management and Administration*, I (Feb 1924) 195–8.
[13] Celler, Hon. Emanuel, 'A Study of Conglomerates: Where Are They Leading Us?', address before the American Management Association, 12 June 1969.
[14] Chandler, A. D., Jr, *Strategy and Structure*, (Anchor Books ed., New York, 1966).
[15] Charnes, A., Clower, R. W., and Kortanek, K. O., 'Effective Control through Coherent Decentralization with Preemptive Goals', *Econometrica*, XXXV (Apr 1967) 244–320.
[16] Cole, A. H., 'The Entrepreneur: Introductory Remarks', *American Economic Review*, LVIII (May 1968) 60–3.
[17] Cyert, R. M., and March, J. G., *A Behavioral Theory of the Firm* (Englewood Cliffs, N.J., 1963).
[18] Downs, A., *Inside Bureaucracy* (New York, 1967).
[19] Edwards, C. D., statement in *Economic Concentration, Part 1: Overall and Conglomerate Aspects*, Hearings Before the Subcommittee on Antitrust and Monopoly, 82nd Congress (Washington, D.C., 1964) 36–47.
[20] Emery, J. C., *Organizational Planning and Control Systems: Theory and Technology* (New York, 1969).
[21] Galbraith, J. K., *The New Industrial State* (New York, 1967).
[22] Hayes, S. L. III, and Taussig, R. A., 'Tactics of Cash Takeover Bids', *Harvard Business Review*, XLV (Mar-Apr 1967) 136–47.
[23] Heflebower, R. B., 'Observations on Decentralization in Large Enterprises', *Journal of Industrial Economics*, IX Nov 1960) 7–22.
[24] Jewkes, J., 'How Much Science', *Economic Journal*, LXX (Mar 1960) 1–13.
[25] Klaw, Spencer, 'The Soap Wars: A Strategic Analysis', *Fortune* (June 1963) pp. 123 ff.
[26] March, J. M., and Simon, H. A., *Organizations* (New York, 1958).
[27] Marris, R., 'A Model of the "Managerial" Enterprise', *Quarterly Journal of Economics*, LXXVII (May 1965) 185–209.
[28] ——, *The Economic Theory of "Managerial" Capitalism* (New York, 1964).
[29] Mason, E. S. (ed.), *The Corporation in Modern Society* (Cambridge, 1960).
[30] Mitchell, J. N., 'Antitrust Policies', *B.N.A. Antitrust and Trade Regulation Reporter*, 10 June 1969, x–9 to x–11.
[31] Monsen, R. J., Jr, and Downs, A., 'A Theory of Large Managerial Firms', *Journal of Political Economy*, LXXIII (June 1965) 221–36.
[32] Nevins, A., and Hill, F. E., *Ford: Expansion and Challenge, 1915–1933* (New York, 1957).
[33] Peterson, S., 'Corporate Control and Capitalism', *Quarterly Journal of Economics*, LXXIX (Feb 1965).
[34] Posner, R. A., 'Natural Monopoly and its Regulation', *Stanford Law Review*, XXI (Feb 1969) 548–643.
[35] Reid, S. R., *Mergers, Managers and the Economy* (New York, 1968).
[36] Schumpeter, J. A., *Capitalism, Socialism, and Democracy* (New York, 1947).
[37] ——, *The Theory of Economic Development* (New York, 1961).
[38] Simon, H. A., 'On the Concept of Organizational Goal', *Administrative Science Quarterly*, IX (June 1964) 1–22.

[39] Sirkin, G., *The Visible Hand: The Fundamentals of Economic Planning* (New York, 1968).

[40] Turner, D. F., 'Conglomerate Mergers and Section 7 of the Clayton Act', *Harvard Law Review*, LXXVIII (May 1965) 1313-95.

[41] ——, and Williamson, O. E., 'Market Structure in Relation to Technical and Organizational Innovation' (forthcoming).

[42] Vickers, Sir Geoffrey, *Towards a Sociology of Management* (New York, 1967).

[43] Williamson, O. E., *The Economics of Discretionary Behavior: Managerial Objectives in a Theory of the Firm* (Englewood Cliffs, N.J., 1964).

[44] ——, 'Hierarchical Control and Optimum Size Firm', *Journal of Political Economy*, LXXV (Apr 1967) 123-38.

[45] ——, 'The Economics of Defense Contracting: Incentives and Performance', in *Issues in Defense Economics* (New York, 1967) pp. 218-56.

[46] ——, 'A Dynamic Stochastic Theory of Managerial Behavior', in *Prices: Issues in Theory, Practice, and Public Policy*, ed. A. Phillips and O. E. Williamson (Philadelphia, 1968) pp. 11-31.

[47] ——, 'Corporate Control and the Theory of the Firm', in *Economic Policy and the Regulation of Corporate Securities*, ed. H. G. Manne (Washington, D.C., 1969).

[48] ——, 'Administrative Controls and Regulatory Behavior', (forthcoming).

[49] ——, *Corporate Control and Business Behavior* (Englewood Cliffs, N.J., 1970).

Appendices

Appendix A

Growth, Profitability and Size: The Empirical Evidence

John L. Eatwell

I. INTRODUCTION

The objective of this paper is to present as succinctly as possible the major empirical findings available in the economic literature which bear on the relationship between profitability, growth and size of the firm. I will comment only very briefly on the significance of the results, preferring that the reader should draw his own conclusions. The population from which I have drawn my sample has been strictly defined to cover only those studies dealing directly with the three variables with which I am chiefly concerned. I have excluded, therefore, for reasons of time and space, those papers dealing with important but tangential issues.

Surveys of empirical material are, by their very nature, somewhat unsatisfactory, for they involve the comparison of results obtained using different methodologies, samples and statistics, and the compression of necessary lengthy econometric argument into a few unsatisfactory sentences. I do not propose to punctuate the discussion that follows with elaborate critiques of particular authors' choice of statistic or technique, but a few introductory remarks may be appropriate.

1. The profit ratio

(*a*) *Numerator.* Rate of return is customarily defined as returns from trading profits and investment, and other income net of depreciation and charges for current liabilities. Investment income is excluded when the denominator of the profit ratio is net worth. The statistic should be calculated prior to taxation when considering an 'economies

of scale' argument, and net of taxation if discussing the firm's ability
to expand by self-financing. Among small firms, the problem of how
much officers' compensation should be included in profits [1, 3, 18,
78, 79] is very important. Alexander [3] devised a defensible method
for making suitable adjustment by assuming that small corporations
will adjust their officers' salaries to minimize taxes. Since deficit
corporations do not pay taxes they have no incentive to overpay
their officers: thus an adjustment is made based on the deficit
corporations' ratio of officers' salaries paid to the value of assets
used. This is not entirely satisfactory, particularly when one remem-
bers the positive correlation between executive compensation and
growth/size. Furthermore this problem is only really important in the
small firm, and becomes insignificant in absolute terms in the large
corporation.

(b) *Denominator*. The two most widely used denominators of the
profit ratio are book value of assets (total or net) and net worth
(book value of equity). Both measures introduce serious methodological problems in an inflationary period [60, 63, 67, 71]. The use of
net worth as a measure of corporate size, when firms resort to
external financing techniques other than the issue of equity, may
introduce systematic bias where different sizes of firms use differing
methods of finance.

Stekler [71] has shown that the shape of the size distribution of
profit rates is little altered when the profit ratio is calculated as a
percentage of net worth rather than of assets, and Table A.1 demonstrates the effect on the size distribution of profit rates of the addition
of an officers' compensation adjustment *à la* Alexander [3]. Clearly
the officers' compensation adjustment has the greatest effect on small
firms, but the shape of the distribution of profit rates is not fundamentally altered.

2. *The size of the firm*

A wide variety of measures may be utilized to measure the size of
firms, including book value of total assets [10, 15], book value of
net assets [34, 63, 67], sales [70], stock-market valuation [33, 36] and
employment [69]. Bates, in a discussion of alternative measures of
the size of firms (in Hart [34]) has illustrated the high degree of

correlation between various measures, and concluded that often the choice of measure can depend largely on convenience, availability and ease of calculation. Two major problems connected with the measurement of rate of change of size, however, are revaluations and the interdependence of net assets, growth and profitability.

(a) *Revaluation.* During inflationary periods firms may revalue the book value of equity [60, 67]. Such a revaluation will tend to bias

*Table A.*1

Comparison of Rate of Return after Taxes on Assets by Size Classes for all Manufacturing Corporations before and after Including Officers' Compensation Adjustment, 1947–51 Average

Asset size class ($ '000)	Rate of return without officers' compensation	Rate of return with officers' compensation
0–50	– 5·1	– 1·3
50–100	3·1	7·3
100–250	5·5	8·9
250–500	7·0	9·6
500–1000	8·2	10·0
1000–5000	9·3	10·1
5000–10,000	9·9	10·3
10,000–50,000	9·9	10·1
50,000–100,000	9·7	9·8
100,000 +	9·2	9·2

Source: Stekler [71] (20 U.S. two-digit industries).

profitability downward, and bias growth upward. Since there appears to be a tendency for the incidence of revaluation to vary positively with size [67], a systematic bias may be introduced into studies which utilize, for instance, the difference between opening size and closing size as a measure of growth.

(b) *Net assets, growth and profitability.* If growth is defined in terms of net assets [67, 74], we relate the growth of long-term finances of the business to its profitability in growth/profitability models. Since retained profits thus automatically lead to growth, there is likely to be a higher correlation between growth and profitability than if an alternative measure of size were used.

CE O

Ideally, the corporation should be a unique unit of study. Modern corporate structure is such that in many instances the classification of the corporation to a particular industry involves both loss of information and the introduction of systematic bias. *A priori*, it seems probable that the modern conglomerate will possess many similarities of organization and control across industries rather than within industries; and that in many cases the structure of functional relationships involving growth, profitability and size characterize the firm rather than an industry, trade, or some temporal distribution. Some of the results below corroborate this premise, but unfortunately most studies concentrate on a wide variety of sizes of firm classified by industry or selected at random. To illustrate the three-way interdependence of profitability, growth and size, this survey is divided into three sections which examine profitability and size, growth and size, and finally, profitability and growth.

II. SIZE AND PROFITABILITY

Examination of the relationship between profitability and size of corporations involves the study of the behavioural characteristics of a *static* phenomenon, size, and care should be taken not to confuse dynamic processes of change of the type discussed in 'managerial' theories of the firm[1] with comparisons of static states. None the less, the relationship between size and profitability is of importance in the process of corporate growth. For whether we consider the paramount role of profits to be the internal financing of expansion [55], or whether the part played by current profits in formulating expectations of future profitability and thus acting as an inducement to future expansion is held to be most pertinent [10], any systematic relation between profitability and size will determine to a significant degree the pattern of corporate growth [48, 49, 67, 71, 74]. Thus not only will the average profitability of different size groups of firms be important, but also the dispersion of profit rates within each size class may offer some clues about growth patterns through time. *A priori*, one might expect the variability of profit rates among large

[1] Cf. R. L. Marris, *Economic Theory of 'Managerial' Capitalism* (Macmillan, London, 1964); W. J. Baumol, *Business Behavior, Value and Growth* (Macmillan, New York, 1959).

firms to be less than the variability of profit rates among small firms, given the former's propensity toward greater diversification into product and geographic markets. This diversification will tend to reduce the variability of the firm's overall profit rate, and thus to endow the large corporation with greater certainty of profitability. If the average level of profitability declines with size, the expanding firm may find compensation for lower profitability in this greater certainty of income.

The majority of empirical studies have not, however, been directed toward the examination of the expansionary-possibility/inducements-inherent hypotheses for a given size, but have utilized the profit ratio as a measure of corporate efficiency [4, 12, 17, 18, 19, 22, 23, 24, 58, 59, 71, 78, 79]. It is difficult to develop any rationale for the utilization of the profit ratio as a measure of efficiency, other than its ready availability. The size distribution of the profit ratio would seem to have little relevance, in either a theoretical or a practical framework, to the problem of long-run costs associated with size of firms. The complex problem of empirical evidence on economies of scale and efficiency is reviewed pessimistically by Smith ([68], and note comment by Friedman). A promising solution to the problem of differentiating the proportion of the variance of costs attributable to factors unconnected with scale is provided by Pratten and Dean [62], who construct series of cost estimates for hypothetical plants of varying scale.

A further group of empirical studies of the size distribution of profitability centre around the problems of industrial concentration and the monopolistic barriers to efficient resource allocation revealed in the 'excess' profits earned in highly concentrated industries [7, 8, 52, 66, 69, 81]. These studies are not specifically concerned with the behavioural characteristics of the individual corporation; but the process of industrial concentration is a manifestation of the dynamic progress of corporations.

1. *The distribution of rate of return by size classes*

The size distribution of rates of return has been identified variously as embodying a negative correlation of profitability with size [19, 24, 78], a positive correlation [17, 18]; and [4, 69] (using data from [18]), to exhibit a parabolic relationship [48, 49, 71] and to exhibit

no significant relationship whatsoever [8, 11, 22, 23, 58, 75, 79]. The
negative relationships exhibited are not perfectly monotonic, and
are either connected directly with mergers [19] or associated with
the rapid expansionary phase in the United States economy of the
1920s.

The major study by Crum [18] in 1939 was to form the cornerstone
of much later work. He found that in almost all United States

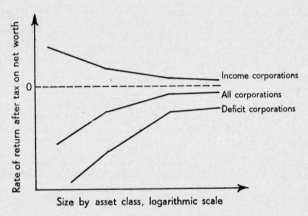

FIG. A.1. Distribution of post-tax profitability of U.S. manufacturing corporations, 1931-6.

Source: Crum (18)

industries in the period 1931–6 the form of the profitability relationship to size was of the general shape shown in Fig. A.1, with a
positive correlation between growth and size in almost all industries
examined, and a negative correlation between profitability and size
when only firms with positive income are included in the sample.
Crum's results are confirmed by Sherman's more recent study [66];
see Table A.2.

An attempt has been made to explain the relationship between
profitability and size displayed by income corporations by attributing
their declining profitability to the increasing capital-intensity of
production in large firms [69]. But the evidence cited indicates that
the assets/sales ratio reaches a peak in the $5 million to $10 million
size class, and thereafter remains fairly constant with increasing

Table A.2

Profit Rates (Profits before Taxes on Equity) in Income and Deficit Corporations (all U.S. corporations, 1949)

Asset class ($10,000)	All corporations	Income corporations	Deficit corporations
0–5	−3·4	19·4	−59·5
5–10	7·4	17·1	−24·8
10–25	10·5	17·2	−21·1
25–50	12·9	18·0	−17·8
50–100	13·5	18·2	−16·3
100–500	14·3	17·4	−13·4
500–1000	13·9	16·4	−11·9
1000–5000	14·6	16·2	−8·8
5000 +	13·9	14·3	−9·5

Source: Sherman [66].

size, indicating no further increase in capital-intensity. A more convincing explanation noted the greater variability of profit rates among small firms vis-à-vis large firms, and concluded that the positive correlation between profitability and size in the above diagram was a characteristic of the 1930s, when the mean profitability of all firms was low and small firms sustained heavy rates of loss [3].

The parabolic shape of the profits/size relationship, with peak profitability occurring in the median size class, or the next largest class, has been attributed to the process of aggregation of data across industries [11, 17, 72]. The computations in Table A.3 indicate that a major source of the variance of profitability in an aggregated sample is variation between industries, in addition to the variation between size groups.

This variance between industries is hardly surprising when the variability of economics of scale, monopoly power and the distribution of demand, and distribution of rate of growth of demand between industries, is taken into account. Given these factors and significant differences of average size between industries, 'across-the-board' studies should be viewed with a degree of scepticism.

When individual industry groups are analysed, any systematic relationship between mean class profitability and size disappears

Table A.3
Variation of Profitability and Size

Source of variation	Sum of squares	d.f.	Variance estimate	F.
1. Between industries	515·37	10	51·54	2·14
2. Between sales size groups	556·06	9	61·78	2·56
3. Residual	7063·36	293	24·11	
Total	8134·79			

Source: Barron [11] (U.K. quoted chemicals, textiles, footwear and non-electrical engineering).

(see Table A.4) [11, 67, 71, 72, 75]; and although the variance of intra-size-class profit rates clearly possesses some negative relationship with size, this series is not perfectly monotonic. Jones's study of the mechanical engineering industry [39] corroborates these results; in particular he confirms the non-homogeneity, and generally negative correlation with size, of the variance of profit rates in size classes.

The relationship between profitability and size might be tested further by regression analysis, though the frequency distributions above would not lead one to expect a significant linear relationship.

Table A.4
Rate of Return on Net Assets by Opening Size Class, 1948–60

Opening size (£)	Industry											
	Clothing and footwear			Food			Engineering			All		
	n	m	s	n	m	s	n	m	s	n	m	s
0–250,000	23	12·6	11·6	20	19·1	9·1	39	23·3	9·7	82	19·3	11·0
250,000–500,000	16	18·7	11·0	19	14·4	7·2	41	19·4	8·1	76	18·0	8·8
500,000–1,000,000	18	13·7	6·8	8	16·3	11·2	55	20·7	10·4	82	18·6	10·1
1,000,000–2,000,000	7	14·4	5·5	7	21·4	6·8	40	20·8	9·3	55	19·7	9·1
2,000,000+	6	15·5	4·1	19	18·5	5·8	39	17·3	6·0	69	17·2	5·8

n = number of companies.
m = arithmetic mean of rate of return on net assets (per cent per annum).
s = standard deviation, corrected for degrees of freedom.

Source: Singh and Whittington [67].

Three equation forms have been used to test the deterministic relation:

$$P = \alpha + \beta S + \epsilon \tag{1}$$
$$P = \alpha + \beta \log S + \log \epsilon \tag{2}$$
$$P = \alpha + \beta \log S + \gamma (\log S)^2 + \log \epsilon. \tag{3}$$

Table A.5

Regression Results

Equation	a	b	c	r^2	Source
(1)	20·15	−0·00012		0·01	67
	(0·56)				
(2)	−2·6	1·8		0·68	71
		(0·42)			
(2)	35·27	−1·9		0·05	67
		(0·41)			
(3)	−17·4	7·7	−0·54	0·99	71
		(0·40)	(0·04)		

Definitions: [71] S = geometric mean of asset size classes;
$\qquad\qquad$ P = returns after tax on net assets
$\qquad$ [67] S = opening size by net assets;
$\qquad\qquad$ P = returns on net assets.
Data:$\qquad$ [67]   U.K.: four quoted industries, 1948–60
$\qquad\qquad\qquad$ (profitable firms only).
$\qquad$ [71]   U.S.: 20 two-digit industries, 1947–51.

As expected, there is no significant simple linear relationship between size and profitability. In testing equation (2), the differences between the two studies are considerable, even when taking note of the fact that [67] used a restricted population (unprofitable and non-growing firms excluded) whilst [71] included total population data. A second difference in technique was in the use of grouped data figures in [71]. But for equation (2) the regression coefficients have opposite signs, and the difference in the level of explained variance is 63 per cent. The difference in sign may possibly be attributed to the difference in the range of population to which the equations are fitted. The parabolic equation (3) appears to fit the grouped data very well for *overall data*. Individual industry-explained variances were lower, but always in the high eighties. The importance of using individual industry data to exclude varying degrees of monopoly, growth rates and riskiness across industries is emphasized by Marcus

[53]. He tested equation (2) on 118 industry groups, and in only 35 of these was *b* significant at the 5 per cent level.

We may conclude that the empirical literature demonstrates that there is no consistent relationship between the mean rate of profitability by size classes when individual firms are considered, but the grouping of a large sample of firms may produce certain non-linear relationships. We also note that intra-class variability of profit rates decreases with increasing size, but that this is not a consistently monotonic phenomenon. Finally, if the sample consists solely of income corporations, there is a weak but significant negative relationship between profitability and size [67], and the small firms are those that make the largest losses most frequently [3]. Thus, given the *a priori* premises with which we began, the profitable, growing corporation may expect to encounter slightly lower profit rates as it moves into higher size classes; but the certainty of profitability will usually be increased and could reinforce the expansionary process.

2. *Profitability*

If profitability is in any way a causal phenomenon, derived from given combinations of economic resources and organization, then it should show a tendency to persist over time. The persistency of profitability may be examined by a simple intertemporal regression analysis, using the equation

$$P_{t+1} = \alpha + \beta P_t + \epsilon. \tag{4}$$

Singh and Whittington tested this equation, where

P_t = average rate of return on assets for 1948–54,
P_{t+1} = average rate of return on assets for 1954–60.

Their results are shown in Table A.6.

Table A.6
Regression Analysis

	a	b	r^2	Number of companies
Four U.K. industries	5·52	0·49	0·37	357
	(0·87)	(0·03)		

Source: Singh and Whittington [67].

To overcome the problem of distortion associated with extreme values, the problem was investigated further using Kendall's rank correlation coefficient. The results of this latter test confirmed the strong persistence in profitability of firms over time indicated in Table A.6. Although this conclusion may appear to conflict with the results obtained by Little and Rayner [44, 45], this is not in fact so. Little and Rayner examined the growth rate of earnings per share, which is an entirely different concept from the *level* of profitability. However, Little and Rayner's conclusion that the lack of persistence in growth of earnings per share indicates the irrelevance of differential standards of corporate management would appear to be unjustified. The persistence of the level of corporate profitability clearly indicates the non-random distribution of relevant forms of economic advantage among firms.

III. SIZE AND GROWTH

The size and growth rate of the firm are, respectively, the static and dynamic expression of the same economic phenomenon. Size is the historical expression of growth at one point in time, and the interrelations of state and process play a vital part in any theoretical framework dependent upon the concept of equilibrium. Economic analysis concerning the size of the firm has centered traditionally around the concept of optimum size, with growth part of a loosely defined adjustment mechanism which operates in a yet more loosely defined time dimension. In dynamic theories of the firm, interest centres around the rate of growth whilst the size of the firm defines the momentary scale against which growth and its ramifications are measured. Thus in both static and dynamic analysis the interrelationship of size and growth has direct relevance to the examination of the theoretical whole.

Frequency distributions of the mean growth rate of firms by size classes appear on casual observation to exhibit a remarkable heterogeneity in which no simple pattern may be discerned [39, 46, 76] (see Table A.7). The Welch–Aspin[1] test applied to distributions of mean growth rates in specific industries detected no significant

---

[1] B. L. Welch, 'The Generalization of "Student's" Problem when Several Different Population Variances are Involved', *Biometrika* (1947); A. A. Aspin, 'Tables for Use in Comparisons where Accuracy Involves Two Variances, Separately Estimated', *Biometrika* (1949).

*Table A.*7

Growth and Company Size, 1949–53,
by Net Assets

Size of company (£ '000)	Growth %
0–250	40
251–500	46·3
501–1000	48·1
1001–2000	45·6
2001–4000	42·8
4001–8000	50·4
8000 +	44·8

Source: Tew and Henderson [76] (2549 U.K. quoted companies).

differences between means; and Bartlett's χ^2 test[1] for homogeneity of variance indicated that there were significant differences between size group variances [39, 66]. Singh and Whittington also found no significant relationship when regressing growth on size. Using the equation

$$\log_e G = \alpha + \beta \log_e S + \log_e \epsilon \qquad (5)$$

r^2 and the parameter b were not significantly different from zero at the 5 per cent level [67].

The lack of any decisive relationship between growth and size, and the observation that, like many 'natural' phenomena, the size distribution of firms is positively skewed in number terms, but is symmetrical and approximately normal when numerical values are converted into logarithms, has stimulated attempts to analyse the relationship between growth and size as a stochastic phenomenon, the nature of the stochastic processes being defined by the mathematical characteristics of formal statistical distributions. The distribution most commonly compared to the size distribution of firms has been the lognormal distribution,[2] which is linked with the

[1] M. H. Quenouille, *Introductory Statistics* (Butterworth & Springer, London, 1950) p. 190.

[2] Consider a variate x ($0 < x < \infty$) such that $y = \log x$ is distributed normally with mean μ and variance σ^2; then x is lognormally distributed, i.e. a Λ variate. Distribution functions of x and y are

$$\Lambda(x \mid \mu, \sigma^2) = P[X \leqslant x] \qquad (x > 0)$$
$$= 0 \qquad [x \leqslant 0]$$
$$\Lambda(y \mid \mu, \sigma^2) = P[Y \leqslant y].$$

intuitively simple 'Law of Proportionate Effect' identified explicitly by Kapteyn[1] and introduced to economics by Gibrat[2] [25, 33, 34, 36, 37, 38, 40, 51, 57, 67, 70].

The general case of proportionate effect developed by Kapteyn states that at the nth time period the change in a variate (size) is a random proportion of some function of $x_{n-1}: \phi(x_{n-1})$; i.e.

$$x_n - x_{n-1} = \epsilon_n \phi(x_{n-1}). \tag{6}$$

The set $\{\epsilon_n\}$ consists of independent random variables having identical distributions. In the important case $\phi(x_i) = x_i$, the change in size is a random proportion of x_i. This case is that customarily referred to as the Law of Proportionate Effect:

When $\phi(x_i) = x_i$, (6) reduces to

$$x_n - x_{n-1} = \epsilon_n x_{n-1} \tag{7}$$
$$x_n = (1 + \epsilon_n)x_{n-1} = x_0(1 + \epsilon_1)(1 + \epsilon_2) \ldots (1 + \epsilon_n).$$

If the percentage increment ϵ_i is small, we have approximately

$$\log x_n = \log x_0 + \epsilon_1 + \epsilon_2 + \ldots + \epsilon_n. \tag{8}$$

Thus the logarithm of the firm's size results from the addition of many small random variable having identical distributions (with mean m and variance σ^2) to the logarithm of the original size. By the central limit theorem $\log x_n$ is asymptotically normally distributed with mean mn and variance $n\sigma^2$. Thus the size distribution of firms at time n will be approximately lognormal (cf. [2], p. 23 for a rigorous proof of this theorem).

The Law of Proportionate Effect thus asserts that the growth rate of a firm in any one time period is a stochastic phenomenon which results from the cumulative effect of the chance operation of a large

[1] J. C. Kapteyn, *Skew Frequency Curves in Biology and Statistics* (Noordhoff, Astronomical Laboratory, Groningen, 1903).

[2] R. Gibrat, *Les Inégalités Économiques* (Libraire du Recueil Sirey, Paris, 1931), chaps v-vii of which are reprinted in translation in *International Economic Papers*, No. 7 (Macmillan, London, 1957).

In his model Gibrat used a three-parameter lognormal distribution to characterize the distribution of income; the distribution function is given by

$$\Lambda(x \mid \zeta, \mu, \sigma^2) = 0 \qquad (x \leqslant \zeta)$$
and $$\Lambda(x \mid \zeta, \mu, \sigma^2) = (x - \zeta \mid \mu, \sigma^2) \qquad (x > \zeta).$$

ζ is used as a simple displacement parameter, and is adjusted to obtain the best fit. In economic literature the Law of Proportionate Effect is often referred to as 'Gibrat's Law'.

number of forces acting independently of each other [67], and that
the probability of a firm growing at a given rate in any one period of
time is independent of the initial size of the firm. A survey of studies
of the growth of the firm as a stochastic process may be found in
Hart [34], and an elegant discussion of stochastic processes in
Steindl [70].

The lognormal distribution is not the only distribution associated
with stochastic theories of the growth of firms. Under particular
assumptions it has been found a better fit may be obtained with a
Yule distribution [13], or, particularly in the larger size range, by the
upper tail of the Pareto distribution [70].[1]

If growth is a random process with respect to the size of the firm,
some interesting implications for the theoretical study of the corporate firm emerge. Firstly, if growth is a stochastic process, then this
implies that there is no optimum size of the firm; there is no causal
'adjustment mechanism' between size and growth. Furthermore the
implication is clear that there will be no continuity in the growth
pattern of firms; for no systematic bias in the distribution of growth
rates is consistent with the Law of Proportionate Effect. Finally, if
Gibrat's Law exists in the strong form outlined above, the concentration of any given industry will increase over time, for the larger firm
will possess the same probability of a given proportionate growth as
the small firm, and thus the logarithmic variance of the distribution
of firm sizes about the mean will tend to increase over time, and in
the limit become infinite![2]

Should the Law of Proportionate Effect fully describe the growth
process of a given size distribution of companies, the following
implications concerning the distribution may be made:

1. All size groups of firms have the same mean proportionate
   growth rate.
2. The dispersion of growth rates about this mean is the same for
   all size classes.[3]

[1] The Yule distribution is generated jointly by the Law of Proportionate
Effect and an assumed birth process, e.g. a constant birth rate of new firms in the
smallest size class [65]. The Pareto distribution is such that, say, the number of
firms with sales in excess of x, plotted against x on a logarithmic scale, yields a
straight line.

[2] The theoretical limiting characteristics of the lognormal distribution need not,
of course, inhibit its utilization for the analysis of phenomena occurring in
finite time.

[3] For complete generality, a size distribution should be tested for all moments
compatible with the Λ distribution, not just the first and second moments. It

Frequency distributions of average growth rates [21, 33, 34, 36, 51, 63, 67, 70] (see Table A.8) indicate that the first implication is indeed justified, as does rank correlation work by Ferguson [25]. The Welch–Aspin test applied to Table A.8 did not reveal a sufficient number of cases of significant differences between means to warrant the conclusion that the growth process for the period did not follow Gibrat's Law.

Table A.8
Growth of Firms,* 1962–67, by Opening Size Class

Size class ($ m.)	Number of observations	Mean	Estimated† standard deviation	Minimum	Maximum
0–2·5	28	11·48	11·45	−25·9	28·0
2·5–5·0	44	8·40	7·88	−3·5	37·4
5·0–10·0	50	10·69	8·27	−4·1	33·8
10·0–20·0	46	9·68	8·04	−0·4	35·4
20·0–40·0	38	9·18	7·85	−11·8	26·9
40·0–80·0	29	7·85	6·84	−6·4	26·3
80·0–160·0	22	7·14	5·96	−2·0	19·9
160·0–320·0	16	6·34	4·33	−4·3	12·9
320·0–640·0	13	9·51	6·89	1·6	21·8
640 +	4	9·67	7·18	3·1	17·8

* 290 U.S. manufacturing corporations, selected randomly from the 2,837 firms quoted in *Moody's Industrials*, which had continuous existence from 1961 to 1967.
† Corrected for degrees of freedom.

Source: Eatwell [21].

However, using Bartlett's χ^2 statistic for homogeneous variances it was evident that variances were not homogeneous between size classes and implication 2 was *not* fulfilled. Most studies indicate that the dispersion of growth rates is either negatively correlated with size [34, 37], or is heterogeneous between size classes with an overall tendency toward negative correlation [21, 34, 63, 67].

The implications of the operation of Gibrat's Law have been tested

should also be noted that Gibrat's Law may also be tested by observing the persistence, or lack of persistence, of company growth rates.

further by regression analysis, the first major study on stochastic theories of corporate growth being that by Hart and Prais [36]. Observing the symmetry of a series of Lorenz curves of corporate size for a sample of British quoted companies 1885–1950, they inferred that the frequency distribution from which the Lorenz curves were derived was lognormal, since the lognormal distribution is a prominent member of the family of distributions generating such curves [14, 41].[1] Assuming regression toward the mean,[2] Hart and Prais tested the equation

$$\text{Var } [x_{t+1}] = \beta^2 \text{ Var } [x_t] + \sigma_\epsilon^2, \tag{9}$$

where $x_{t+1} = $ log size at end of time period,
$\quad\quad\quad x_t = $ log size at beginning of time period,
and $\quad\quad \sigma_\epsilon^2 = $ variance of the distribution of the error term.

Equation (9) is a strong, two-parameter version of the Law of Proportionate Effect. A more general three-parameter version, including a general displacement term,[3] may be estimated by using the form

$$x_{t+1} = \alpha + \beta\, x_t + \epsilon. \tag{10}$$

Equations of form (9) have been tested by Hart and Prais [36], Hart [33, 34] and Samuels and of form (10) by Hart [34] and Singh and Whittington [67]; the results are shown in Table A.9. Clearly the relationship between β^2 and σ_ϵ^2 will determine the direction and extent of the size dispersion of firms over time.[4] If b (estimate of β) = 1 the process of growth is purely stochastic and Gibrat's Law is verified.

---

[1] Cf. J. Aitchison and J. A. C. Brown, 'On criteria for Descriptions of Income Distribution', *Metroeconomica* (1954).

[2] The simple lognormal distribution may be generated from the process:

$$x_{t+1} = x_t + \epsilon. \tag{a}$$

If there were regression toward the mean, perhaps because some optimum size is determined by, say, financial criteria, then (a) may be written

$$x_{t+1} - \bar{x}_{t+1} = (\bar{x}_t - \bar{x}_t) + \epsilon$$

and thus $\text{Var } [x_{t+1}] = \beta^2 \text{ Var } [x_t] + \sigma_\epsilon^2$.

If β is sufficiently below unity, the variance of the distribution about the mean may not increase over time [36].

[3] Cf. p. 401, n. 2 above.

[4] Defining the correlation coefficient r as

$$r^2 = 1 - \frac{\sigma_\epsilon^2}{\text{Var } [x_{t+1}]}$$

(9) can be reduced to $\dfrac{\text{Var } x_{t+1}}{\text{Var } x_t} = \dfrac{\beta^2}{r^2}$.

If $b < 1$ the smaller firms will grow proportionately faster and if σ_ϵ^2 is small the size distribution will regress toward the mean. If $b > 1$ large firms will grow proportionately faster and the dispersion of firm sizes will increase.

As Table A.9 illustrates, in recent years there has been a tendency

Table A.9

Regression Parameters of the Concentration Process

	Reference	Year	b	s(b)	r	Equation form
1.	[36]	1885–96	0·95	0·15	0·83	(9)
2.	[36]	1896–1907	0·91	0·05	0·89	(9)
3.	[36]	1907–24	1·09	0·03	0·92	(9)
4.	[36]	1924–39	0·92	0·03	0·88	(9)
5.	[36]	1939–50	0·75	0·02	0·85	(9)
6.	[33]	1950–5	0·99	0·02	n.a.	(9)
7.	[63]	1950–7 to 1959–60	1·07	0·02	0·92	(9)
8.	[67]	1948–54	1·025	0·016	0·94	(10)
9.	[67]	1954–60	1·033	0·015	0·95	(10)
10.	[67]	1948–60	1·043	0·025	0·91	(10)
11.	[34](a)	1958–60	0·97	0·0079	0·96	(10)
12.	[34](b)	1958–60	1·03	0·0052	0·97	(10)
13.	[67]	1948–54	0·987	0·012	0·97	(10)
14.	[67]	1954–60	1·000	0·014	0·96	(10)
15.	[67]	1948–60	1·015	0·023	0·92	(10)

Samples:

[36] Selected U.K. quoted companies. Size measured by stock-market value.

[33] Selected U.K. quoted companies. Size measured by stock-market value.

[34](a) U.K. manufacturing companies, £500,000 +.
    Size measured by net assets.

[34](b) U.K. manufacturing companies, all sizes.
    Size measured by net assets.

[63] 400 continuously quoted companies.
    Size measured by net assets.

[67] 4 selected industries, U.K. quoted companies (rows 8, 9, 10 all companies, rows 13, 14, 15 positive-growth companies only).

for *b* to be greater than 1, although this is not necessarily so when single-industry distributions are examined ([67], not shown in table). It is interesting to compare rows 8, 9 and 10 with rows 13, 14 and 15. Each group is calculated from the same data, except that the latter three include only companies with positive growth rates. In each instance *b* is significantly reduced, implying that small firms display a greater incidence of negative growth than do large firms, thus reinforcing our rejection of Gibrat's Law.[1]

Linear correlations of interperiod growth rates, and rank correlation studies, indicate that there is a tendency for growth to breed growth – for growth to persist between periods [67, 70]. This appears to be a direct contradiction of the Law of Proportionate Effect, but Ijiri and Simon have constructed a modified model of proportionate effect in which some serial correlation is incorporated. This model has only been tested in a simulation study and achieved good results when fitted to grouped size data. Further, the majority of studies of Gibrat's Law have been confined to the study of continuing firms with little analysis of the birth and death processes of firms concomitant with the growth process. Table A.10 clearly indicates that both birth and death are inversely correlated with size; thus even the use of the Yule distribution [13] will not overcome the problem of the skewed distribution of company death rates. It should be noted that in the application of the Yule distribution by Bonini and Simon [13] a company is 'born' by entering the top 500 United States firms, not as a new entrant to the business population.

The stochastic analysis of the growth rates of firms continues to yield interesting results, but recent studies [63, 67] indicate that the lognormal form of Gibrat's Law does not provide an adequate explanation of the size distribution of firm growth ratios. A weaker version which takes account of the serial correlation of growth may be able to rationalize the distribution in a fairly simple stochastic process, which, however, lacking the simplicity of Gibrat's Law, will be reduced in its generality and intuitive significance. Furthermore, although the size distribution of firms may be observed to 'look like', and possess certain characteristics of, the Pareto, Yule or lognormal distributions, there is no truly satisfactory method of objectively assessing the degree of semblance.

Under these circumstances our confidence in the proposed stochastic explanation of the size distributions may depend as much on how

[1] Mansfield [51] achieved similar results using transition matrices.

plausible we find the assumptions underlying the models as on our judgments of goodness of fit [38].

Table A.10

Births* and Deaths* in the Quoted Public Company Sector in the U.K., 1949–53

Size† (£ m.)	Births	Births as percentage of same-size companies	Deaths	Deaths as percentage of same-size companies
0–0·1	16	8·6	17	9·2
0·1–0·25	80	16·7	26	5·4
0·25–0·5	94	17·7	17	3·2
0·5–0·75	54	14·5	13	3·5
0·75–1·0	40	16·3	9	3·7
1·0–2·5	73	13·0	13	2·4
2·5–5·0	16	7·3	11	5·0
5·0–10·0	5	4·5	2	1·8
10·0–25·0	4	5·2	2	2·6
Over 25·0	1	—	—	—

* Births (deaths) by obtaining (losing) quotation on the Stock Exchange, 1949–53.
† Size by market valuation.

Source: Ma [47].

Some notes on optimum size

Whilst most relevant studies of growth and size are concerned with the stochastic analysis discussed above, some writers have attempted to search for the optimum size of the firm in the changing size distributions of firms [5, 6]. A technique of empirical analysis known as the 'survivor technique' has been applied to size distributions to attempt to elucidate the optimum size of the firm, utilizing the rationale that competition between different sizes of firm sifts out the more efficient enterprises [64, 73, 77, 82]. Firms are classified in an industry by size and the share of industry output coming from each size class over time is calculated. If the share of a given class falls it is deemed relatively inefficient, and in general is more in-efficient the more rapidly the share falls. At the scale of the firm it is not at all clear that this is a valid technique, for it is not obvious that efficiency of resource utilization and survival coincide. At the scale of the plant, however, the technique has some possibilities if the forces of competition may be assumed to be powerful and technological progress is very slow. Weiss [82] has demonstrated that by the use of this technique he finds a similar distribution of the minimum efficient scale of plant to that exhibited by Bain [8]. It appears that the firms in Weiss's sample do tend to adjust their plant size toward the technically optimal levels, but the adjustment is never complete. Saving [64] discovered that measures of optimum size of plants derived by the survivor technique were not significantly correlated with industry growth rates.

Utilizing the size distribution of profitability and growth of the kind we exhibit above, Singh and Whittington [67] have compiled Table A.11 which shows the 'best' size of firm for profitability (under two different definitions) and for growth during the two time periods of their study 1948–54 and 1954–60. It is interesting to note that whilst the highest pre-tax return on net assets is obtained generally in the smaller size classes, larger sizes tend to be optimal for post-tax profitability on equity. This is probably less an effect of the tax system than of the inverse correlation of the proportion of equity in net assets with size [71]. The best size for growth is almost invariably the largest.

*Table A.*11

The Best Size of Firm for Profitability and Growth

		Best size for rate of return/ net assets	Best size for post-tax rate of return/equity	Best size for growth
1948–54	Clothing	£$\frac{1}{4}$m.–$\frac{1}{2}$£m.	>£2m.	>£2m.
	Food	<£$\frac{1}{4}$m.	<£$\frac{1}{4}$m.	>£2m.
	Engineering	<£$\frac{1}{4}$m.	<£$\frac{1}{4}$m.	£1m. to £2m.
1954–60	Clothing	£$\frac{1}{4}$m. to £1m.	>£2m.	>£2m.
	Food	£1m.–£2m.	£$\frac{1}{2}$m.–£1m.	>£2m.
	Engineering	<£$\frac{1}{4}$m.	>£2m.	>£2m.

Source: Singh and Whittington [67].

This does not mean, however, that 'best size' has any relationship to the traditional definition of 'optimum size'.

IV. PROFITABILITY AND GROWTH

Empirical investigations of the relationship between growth and profitability cannot, unfortunately, tell us very much about the choice made by corporate management between these two variables, a choice which has figured prominently in recent theoretical work. Linear or log-linear single-equation estimates of the relationship are estimates of an underidentified reduced form and do not reveal the complete causal structure between the two variables.

A priori it might be expected that a significant relationship exists between growth and profitability, and that this relationship possesses elements of dual causation. Firstly, profitability is one of the vital contributions toward the ability of the firm to grow; not only will increased profitability provide greater possibilities of internally financed growth, but also the high level of profitability will serve as a superior attraction for external finance. Secondly, at any one time the rate of growth of the firm will determine the level of profitability attainable commensurate with that rate of expansion.[1] But this mutual relationship does not exist in a vacuum, but within an economic environment which imposes a variety of cross-sectorial, intertemporal and even psychological constraints upon it. The growth of the firm with respect to a given level of profitability will be influenced by the nature of management, the level of 'animal spirits',[2] the state and growth of aggregate and industrial demand, the competitive structure of industries and the technological parameters within the firm and the industry. Often these factors will explain a greater proportion of the variance of the growth rate than will profitability. Similarly with respect to the inverse relationship. The significance of all these factors may be expected to vary between industries, over time, and between different types of firms within an industry (small–large; long established–new entrant, highly diversified–uni-product).

None the less, the environmental parameters of the profitability–growth relationship are not expected to be distributed in such a heterogeneous manner that they obscure the relationship entirely.

---

[1] This argument is developed fully in E. Penrose, *The Theory of the Growth of the Firm* (Oxford, 1959).

[2] Cf. J. M. Keynes, *General Theory of Employment, Interest and Money* (Macmillan, London, 1936) p. 161.

We would expect to observe in a cross-section of firms a positive
association between growth and profitability, but would not necessarily expect this relationship to be a close one.

Thus, when we examine the contemporaneous long-run average
growth–profitability records of a cross-section of corporations, we
should expect to find a scatter engendered by the simultaneous
operation of the two relationships discussed above, which, in simple
linear form, may be formulated as

$$G = \alpha + \beta P + \epsilon \qquad (11)$$
and
$$P = \gamma + \delta G + u. \qquad (12)$$

Both (11) and (12) are subject to different sources and degrees of
error. However, when regressing long-term growth on long-term
profitability a convincing case has been made [67a] that (11), the
conventional, and intuitively more 'direct', profitability–growth
relationship, is likely to be identified, rather than (12).

A major justification for this assertion is that the variance of the
error term in (11) is likely to be *much smaller* than the variance of the
error term in (12). It follows from the economic specification of the
model that (12) is essentially specific to each individual firm and would,
therefore, vary a great deal between firms (given different capabilities of company managements, differing market conditions, and,
notably, given different expectations of future profitability and
growth). The effect of profitability on growth, on the other hand, will
tend to be relatively similar for quoted companies, since it is determined at least in part by the state of the capital market, which is
independent of the characteristics of the individual firm. Thus, in a
cross-section study, we would expect to identify the relatively
constant profitability–growth relationship (11), rather than the
volatile growth–profitability relationship (12). This is particularly so
since it must be remembered that the economic specification of the
model imposes at least two other restrictions. First, there are restrictions on the signs of the regression coefficients, e.g. if both (11) and
(12) are linear, the slope in (11) would be positive and in (12) it
would be negative. Secondly, the error terms in the two equations,
in a cross-section study, can be expected to be independent of each
other, since they are assumed to arise from entirely different economic
processes. Thus the bias of the least squares estimate of the identifiable regression equation (11) will be minimized (though not of course
eliminated, since covariance with dependent variable and with the

disturbance will in general be non-zero, for it contains the own-variance of the dependent variable).

1. *Growth, profitability and supply of finance*

The theoretical model of causality between profitability and growth has a long, and somewhat chequered, history, in the form of accelerator and liquidity theories of investment [55, 73]. Unfortunately many of the empirical studies of this relationship have concentrated upon the inter-industry, and even aggregate, pattern of reaction, and thus provide us with little information that is relevant to the growth process of individual firms. In this field of investigation, aggregation obscures a considerable amount of information, for the rate of growth appears to characterize the individual firm, rather than the industry or trade or even particular years [10]. Furthermore, annual studies of the profits–growth relationship yield no noticeable connection between year-to-year changes in the two variables [55]. Given that in any one year profitability is a fluctuating residual, whilst investment is customarily 'planned', this lack of consistent correlations sounds plausible. However, the relationship between average growth rate and average profit rate over a number of years *is* persistent, and clearly more relevant in causal terms [10]. The simple linear form with profitability as the independent variable has been tested by a number of authors [10, 21, 39, 60, 67], as

$$G = \alpha + \beta P + \epsilon. \tag{11}$$

Some results are exhibited in Table A.12.

All the regression coefficients were significant at the 5 per cent level. Other relationships tested have been of the form:

$$G = \alpha + \beta \log_e P + \epsilon \ [67] \tag{13}$$
$$\log G = \alpha + \beta \log_e P + \epsilon \ [60, 67] \tag{14}$$

and in almost all cases the simple linear relationship cited above gave the best explanation of the variance of growth rates. A series of models involving a variety of independent variables has been examined by Kuh [42] in search of a micro-economic theory of investment. The model most similar to (11) was

$$\frac{I_t}{K_t} = \alpha + \beta \frac{P_t}{K_t} + \gamma \frac{S_{t-1}}{cK_t} \tag{15}$$

where I_t = gross investment in equipment,
                                       K_t = gross capital stock,
                                       P_t = gross retained earnings,
                                       S_t = sales,

and c is an index of capital utilization.

Table A.12
Regression Results

Period of study	Author	b	r^2
1949–59	[10](a)	0·43	0·525 = r
,,	[10](b)	0·42	0·594 = r
1963–4 to 1967–8	[39]	0·24	0·064
1954–5 to 1960–1	[60](a)	0·69	0·712
,,	[60](b)	0·59	0·78
1948–54	[67](a)	0·57	0·55
,,	[67](b)	0·55	0·40
,,	[67](c)	0·84	0·61
1954–60	[67](d)	0·98	0·68
,,	[67](e)	0·35	0·09
,,	[67](f)	0·70	0·35
1948–60	[67](g)	0·27	0·19

Definitions:

[10](a)   47 quoted electrical engineering companies.
                Profits – gross rate of return on fixed assets.
   (b)   31 quoted food-processing companies.
                Growth – gross investment in fixed assets.
[39]   299 mechanical engineering companies.
                Profits – pre-tax return on assets.
[60](a)   87 public companies, recently revalued.
                Profits = gross rate of return from investment at
                1961 prices.
   (b)   87 public companies, recently revalued.
                Profits on gross assets.
[67](a), (d) Quoted clothing and footwear companies.
                Profits = post-tax rate of return on equity.
   (b), (e) Quoted food industries. Profits as (a), (d).
   (c), (f) Non-electrical engineering. Profits as (a), (d).
   (g)   All four industries. Profits as (a), (d).

Table A.13
Regression Results

Time period	*a*	*b*	*c*	*r*
1935–55	0·13	0·37	−0·11	0·62

Data: Small and medium-sized capital-goods producers.
Extreme values excluded.
Cross-sectional analysis of ten years' average values.

Source: Kuh [42].

It is remarkable that, given the variety of definitions and samples utilized in the calculations for Tables A.12 and A.13, the results possess a degree of homogeneity. Particularly extraordinary is the high percentage of the growth variance explained by Kuh's model of continuing firms over a twenty-year period. This contrasts with the results of fitting [67] (*g*) for a twelve-year period. It should be noted, however, that Kuh's sample involves a particular type of firm, extreme values are excluded from the distribution, and only retained earnings are considered.

It is interesting to note in Table A.12 that for the sample [67] the value of the regression coefficient for individual industries varied significantly with time period, as does the degree of variation in growth rates explained by changes in profitability. These results indicate that the relationship between profitability and growth can change substantially over time within individual industries [10, 67]. The *inter*-industry variability of the relationship was investigated by fitting to the data on three major United Kingdom industries [67] the equation

$$G = \alpha_0 + \beta_1 PD_1 + \beta_2 PD_2 + \alpha_1 D_1 + \alpha_2 D_2 + \epsilon \qquad (16)$$

where P = post-tax profitability,

$D_1 = 1$ for companies in engineering, 0 for others,
$D_2 = 1$ for companies in the food sector, 0 for others,

and the third (base) industry was clothing and footwear.
The parameters relating to the dummy variables, giving an indication of the relative significance of inter-industry differences, were all significant for the period 1954–60.
Equation (16) was also fitted to the population of large firms (firms

with assets greater than £2 million) only, and for the smaller (those with assets less than £2 million) only. Among the largest firms the relationship between profitability and growth did not seem to vary significantly between industries. It was apparent that the regression coefficients were considerably different between small and large firms, but the direction of the differences was not consistently the same. Analysis of covariance revealed that the difference between regression coefficients of large and small firms was not significant for the period 1940–54, but was significant for the periods 1954–60 and 1948–60.

These results suggest that for large firms one cannot reject the hypothesis that the growth–profitability relation across industries came from the same population. Thus, for the examination of large firms the industrial classification is less relevant than a classification based on some chosen characteristic of the firm as a corporate entity.

Jones has examined the intra-industry variation of the relation between profitability and growth [39]. Having divided his sample of 299 mechanical engineering companies into seven size groupings, upon testing (11) in each size grouping he found that in only two out of the seven was the regression coefficient significant at the 1 per cent level; in the remaining five groups it was not significant at the 5 per cent level – this even though the regression coefficient of the all-industry model was highly significant (Table A.12, [39]).

A further sidelight on the use of equation forms (11) and (16) has been the attempt to construct a model to describe the size of firms by the combination of a simple deterministic system and the Law of Proportionate Effect [21, 67]. The hypothesis was advanced that the residual growth rates were determined by the Law of Proportionate Effect, once the systematic influence of profitability on growth was removed. This model is not reasonable theoretically, for it ignores the interdependence of the distribution of profit rates and growth rates through the size distribution [21], and it was not surprising to find that although there were no significant differences between the mean of the size distribution of residual growth rates, there was significant heterogeneity of variances between size classes – thus denying the influence of Gibrat's Law.

The failure to fit the residual distribution to the predictions of Gibrat's Law suggested that perhaps the simple linear eqaution contains a specification error. By comparing the predictions of the dummy variables with actual frequency distribution of firms, and noting the weak homoscedasticity of the distribution of the error term, the inference is made that the relationship between growth and profitability of firms is complex and non-linear [67]. The curve shown in Fig. A.2 was then postulated from the data, and is very similar to that postulated by Parker [60], except that Parker's curvilinear relationship passed through the origin. Such a relationship contains the perfectly reasonable implication that growth responds in varying degrees to a given change in profitability, at different levels of profitability [39, 60, 67].[1]

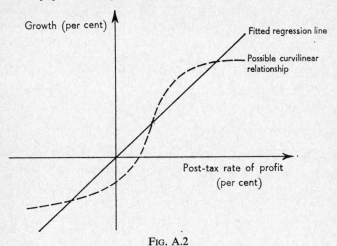

Fig. A.2
Source: Singh and Whittington [67].

2. Growth, profitability and expansion

There have been very few studies investigating the relationship between growth and profitability using growth as the independent variable. This is no doubt due to the obvious theoretical complexity of the inverse function and the difficulty of defining the causality underlying the reduced linear form. Recent theoretical discussion has, however, heightened interest in the inverse function, and Marris [54] has tested the equation

$$P = \gamma + \delta G + u. \tag{17}$$

[1] It should be noted, however, that although this relationship is reasonable economically, it may arise from the structural bias inherent in the simultaneity of the relationship tested.

Table A.14

Regression Results

Sample	c	d	r	t_d
[50]	6·9	0·53	0·78	7·0
[54](i)	8·1	0·39	0·73	3·7
[54](ii)	7·4	0·50	0·78	4·6
[54](iii)	8·1	0·38	0·63	3·0
[54](iv)	7·5	0·47	0·73	5·7

Data: [50] 36 medium-sized firms, 1948–54. Profit = rate of return on net assets. Growth = gross investment less depreciation.

[54] All companies in 131 manufacturing industries:
(i) = 1950–60; (ii) = 1950–5;
(iii) = 1955–60; (iv) = 1950–5 and 1955–60, pooled regression.
Growth = increase in net assets.

Source: Marris [54].

3. *Industry surveys*

Numerous inter-industry studies on profitability and growth are available in the literature, and the sample presented in the bibliography [29, 30, 74, 81] is by no means comprehensive. Because so many of the characteristics in which we are interested are unique to the firm, and show significant variations within and between industry groups, aggregated studies are of only limited usefulness in examining the modern corporation. Studies of the concentration process [29, 30, 81] often include industry growth as one of the variables regressed on income; for instance, Weiss tests the equation

$$Y_1 = \alpha + \beta X_1 + \gamma X_2 + \epsilon \qquad (17)$$

where Y_1 = average annual rate of return on equity,

X_1 = concentration ratio, 1954 (share of four largest firms),
X_2 = annual absolute growth rates of industries.

Data are for United States two-digit industries, 1949–58.

Table A.15
Regression Results

a	b	c	r
4·98	0·09	0·63	0·83
	(0·02)	(0·4)	

Source: Weiss [81].

George [30] has tested the more general form:

$$P = \alpha + \beta_1 G + \beta_2 C + \beta_3 R_4 + \beta_1 R_2 + \epsilon \tag{18}$$

where C = four firm concentration ratio,

$R_1 = 1$ for very high barriers to entry, 0 otherwise,
$R_2 = 1$ for 'substantial' barriers to entry, 0 otherwise,
data = 28 United Kingdom industries,

and found the result
$$P = 4·38 + 0·29G + 0·05C + 3·76R_1 + 0·57R_2. \quad r^2 = 0·73.$$
$$[0·07] \quad [0·02] \quad [1·30] \quad [1·13]$$

Less relevant are studies which regress the growth rate on the profit rate using inter-industry data and thus estimate inter-industry investment equations [74]. These results are intrinsically ambiguous except when the dubious assumption of identical industry investment behaviour equations is correct [43].

We have demonstrated that there exists a fairly strong, though somewhat erratic, relationship between growth and profitability of the firm. Significant differences in regression coefficients were identified between industries, small and large firms and inter-temporally; but the differences between large firms in different industries were not significant. Finally, a possible non-linear complex relationship between profit was identified by the analysis of residual growth rates.

V. CONCLUSION

In concluding this survey, we must note how very much, and yet, paradoxically, how very little is known about the dynamic behaviour of corporations. Ample corroborating evidence is now available on the characteristics of the relationship between profitability and size of firms. Yet we know little about the causality underlying these distributions. Similarly, the majority of the work on the size–growth relationship has concentrated, somewhat inconclusively, on the internal characteristics of the distributions of size and growth rates. Even if Gibrat's Law, or some variation thereof, had been found to be appropriate for the description of size distributions, the real-world causality underlying the generation of these distributions (as distinct from the mathematical causality) would not be known. Stochastic models are useful for studying the concentration process and as a 'check' on other models,[1] but they do not answer questions about the internal dynamics of corporate growth.

Little empirical evidence is available which clearly illuminates the behaviour of the corporation as such, and the large corporation in particular. We have seen that large firms enjoy greater certainty of profitability and growth, but at slightly lower rates than their somewhat smaller colleagues. It has also been evident that larger firms possess unifying characteristics across industry boundaries that small firms do not. But none of this gives a definite guide to the operational structure of the large corporation.

References

Abbreviations

AER	*American Economic Review*
BOUIS	*Bulletin of the Oxford University Institute of Statistics*
C.U.P.	Cambridge University Press
EJ	*Economic Journal*
Harv.Bus.Rev.	*Harvard Business Review*
H.U.P.	Harvard University Press
JASA	*Journal of the American Statistical Association*
JIE	*Journal of Industrial Economics*
J.Man.Stat.Soc.	*Journal of the Manchester Statistical Society*
JPE	*Journal of Political Economy*
JRSS	*Journal of the Royal Statistical Society*
MS	*Manchester School*
N.B.E.R.	National Bureau of Economic Research, New York

[1] i.e. any model which seeks to describe the pattern of corporate growth should yield a positively skewed, approximately lognormal size distribution of firms.

N.I.E.S.R.   National Institute of Economic and Social Research, London
O.U.P.   Oxford University Press
QJE   *Quarterly Journal of Economics*
R.E. Stat.   *Review of Economics and Statistics*
R.E. Stud.   *Review of Economic Studies*

[1] Adelman, I., 'A Stochastic Analysis of the Size Distribution of Firms', *JASA* (1958).
[2] Aitchison, J., and Brown, J. A. C., *The Lognormal Distribution* (C.U.P., Cambridge, 1954).
[3] Alexander, S. S., 'The Effect of Size of Manufacturing Corporations on the Distribution of the Rate of Return', *R.E. Stat.* (1949).
[4] Anthony, R. N., 'Effect of Size on Efficiency', *Harv.Bus.Rev.* (1942).
[5] Ashton, T. S., 'The Growth of Textile Business in the Oldham District, 1884–1924', *JRSS* (1926).
[6] ——, and Chapman, S. J., 'The Sizes of Business; Mainly in Textile Industries', *JRSS* (1914).
[7] Bain, J. S., 'Relation of Profit Rate to Industry Concentration, American Manufacturing 1936–40', *QJE* (1951).
[8] ——, *Barriers to New Competition* (H.U.P., Cambridge, Mass., 1956).
[9] Balderstone, F. E., 'Scale of Output and Internal Organization of the Firm', *QJE* (1955).
[10] Barna, T., *Investment and Growth Policies in British Industrial Firms* (C.U.P., Cambridge, 1962).
[11] Barron, M. J., 'The Effect of the Size of Firm on Profitability', *Business Ratios* (spring, 1967).
[12] Blair, J. M., 'The Relation between Size and Efficiency of Business', *R.E. Stat.* (1942).
[13] Bonini, C., and Simon, H., 'The Size Distribution of Business Firms', *AER* (1958).
[14] Champernowne, D. G., comment on Hart and Prais [36], *JRSS* (1956).
[15] Collins, N. R., and Preston, L. E., 'Size Structure of Industrial Firms', *AER* (1961).
[16] Corden, W. M., 'The Maximization of Profit by a Newspaper', *R.E. Stud.* (1952–3).
[17] Crum, W. L., 'The Effect of Size on Corporate Earnings and Condition', *Harvard University Division of Business Research Studies*, No. 8 (1934).
[18] ——, *Corporate Size and Earning Power*, H.U.P., Cambridge, Mass., 1939).
[19] Dewing, A. S., 'A Statistical Test of the Success of Consolidations', *QJE* (1921).
[20] Earley, J. S., 'Marginal Policies of "Excellently Managed" Companies', *AER* (1956).
[21] Eatwell, J. L., 'A Stochastic Theory of the Growth of Firms: Some Analytics, Some Tests', unpublished seminar paper (Harvard University, 1969).
[22] Epstein, R. C., 'Industrial Profits in 1917', *QJE* (1925).
[23] ——, 'Profits and Size of Firms in the Automobile Industry, 1919–1927', *AER* (1931).
[24] ——, *Industrial Profits in the U.S.* (N.B.E.R., New York, 1934).
[25] Ferguson, C., 'The Relationship of Business Size to Stability', *JIE* (1960).
[26] Florence, P. S., *The Logic of British and American Industry* (Routledge & Kegan Paul, London, 1953).
[27] ——, 'New Measures of the Growth of Firms', *EJ* (1954).

[28] Friedland, S., 'Turnover and Growth of the Largest Industrial Firms 1900–1950', *R.E. Stat.* (1957).

[29] Fuchs, V. R., 'Integration Concentration and Profits in Manufacturing Industries', *QJE* (1961).

[30] George, K. D., 'Concentration, Barriers to Entry and Rate of Return', *R.E. Stat.* (May 1968).

[31] Gordon, M. J., 'The Saving Investment and Valuation of a Corporation', *R.E. Stat.* (1962).

[32] Hall, M., and Weiss, L. W., 'Firm Size and Profitability', *R.E. Stat.* (1967).

[33] Hart, P. E., 'The Size and Growth of Firms', *Economica* (1962).

[34] ——, *Studies in Profit, Business Saving and Investment in the U.K.*, 1920–1962, vol. I (Allen & Unwin, London, 1965).

[35] ——, *Studies in Profit, Business Saving and Investment in the U.K.*, 1920–1962, vol. II (Allen & Unwin, London, 1968).

[36] ——, and Prais, S. J., 'The Analysis of Business Concentration: A Statistical Approach', *JRSS* (1956).

[37] Hymer, S., and Pashigian, P., 'Firm Size and Rate Growth', *JPE* (Dec 1962).

[38] Ijiri, Y., and Simon, H. A., 'Business Firm Growth and Size', *AER* (1964).

[39] Jones, W. T., 'Size, Growth and Profitability in the Mechanical Engineering Industry' (National Economic Development Office, London, 1969) unpublished.

[40] Kalecki, M., 'On the Gibrat Distribution', *Econometrica* (1945).

[41] Kendall, M. G., comment on Hart and Prais [36], *JRSS* (1956).

[42] Kuh, E., *Capital Stock Growth: A Micro-econometric Approach* (North-Holland, Amsterdam, 1963).

[43] ——, review of Stigler [74], *JPE* (1964).

[44] Little, I. M. D., 'Higgledy-Piggledy Growth', *BOUIS* (1962).

[45] ——, and Rayner, A. C., *Higgledy-Piggledy Growth Again* (O.U.P., Oxford, 1966).

[46] Lydall, H. F., 'The Growth of Manufacturing Firms', *BOUIS* (1959).

[47] Ma, R., 'Births and Deaths in the Quoted Public Company Sector in the U.K. 1949–1953', *Yorkshire Bulletin of Economic and Social Research* (1960).

[48] McConnell, J. L., 'Corporate Earnings by Size of Firm', *Survey of Current Business* (1945).

[49] ——, '1942 Corporate Profits by Size of Firm', *Survey of Current Business* (1946).

[50] Mackintosh, A. S., *The Development of Firms* (C.U.P., Cambridge, 1963).

[51] Mansfield, E., 'Entry, Gibrat's Law, Innovation and Growth of Firms', *AER* (1962).

[52] Mann, H. M., 'Seller Concentration, Barriers to Entry and Rates of Return in Thirty Industries 1950–1960', *R.E. Stat.* (1966).

[53] Marcus, M., 'Profitability and Size of Firm: Some Further Evidence', *R.E. Stat.* (1969).

[54] Marris, R. L., 'Incomes Policy and the Rate of Return', *J.Man.Stat.Soc.* (1966).

[55] Meyer, J., and Kuh, E., *The Investment Decision* (H.U.P., Cambridge, Mass., 1958).

[56] Mueller, D. C., 'The Firm Decision Process, an Econometric Investigation', *QJE* (1967).

[57] Newman, P. K., and Wolfe, J. N., 'An Essay on the Theory of Value', *Purdue Studies in the Social Sciences*, no. 6 (1962).

[58] Osborn, R. C., 'Efficiency and Profitability in Relation to Size', *Harv.Bus. Rev.* (1951).

[59] ——, 'Effects of Corporate Size on Efficiency and Profitability', *University of Illinois Bulletin*, no. 72 (1950).

[60] Parker, J. E. S., 'Profitability and Growth of British Industrial Firms', *MS* (1964).

[61] Prais, S. J., 'The Financial Experience of Giant Corporations', *EJ* (1957).

[62] Pratten, C., and Dean, R. M., *The Economics of Large-Scale Production in British Industry* (C.U.P., Cambridge, 1965).

[63] Samuels, J. M., 'Size and Growth of Firms', *R.E. Stud.* (1965).

[64] Saving, T. R., 'Estimation of Optimum Size of Plant by the Survivor Technique', *QJE* (1961).

[65] Simon, H., 'On a Class of Skew Distributions', *Biometrika* (1955).

[66] Sherman, H. J., *Profits in the United States* (Cornell University Press, Ithaca, N.Y., 1968).

[67] Singh, A., and Whittington, G., *Growth, Profitability and Valuation* (C.U.P., Cambridge, 1968).

[67(a)] Singh, A., and Whittington, G., *Growth, Profitability and Valuation: A Note* (Dept. of Applied Economics mimeo, Cambridge, 1970).

[68] Smith, Caleb A., 'Survey of Empirical Evidence on Economics of Scale', in N.B.E.R., *Business Concentration and Policy* (Princeton, 1955).

[69] Steindl, J., *Small and Big Business* (Blackwell, Oxford, 1945).

[70] ——, *Random Processes and the Growth of Firms* (Hafner, New York, 1965).

[71] Stekler, H. O., *Profitability and Size of Firm* (Univ. of California Press, Berkeley, 1963).

[72] ——, 'The Variability of Profitability with Size of Firms 1947–1958', *JASA* (1964).

[73] Stigler, G., 'The Economics of Scale', *Journal of Law and Economics* (1958).

[74] ——, *Capital and the Rate of Return in Manufacturing Industries* (Princeton U.P., Princeton, 1963).

[75] Summers, H. B., 'A Comparison of the Rates of Earnings of Large and Small Scale Industries', *QJE* (1932).

[76] Tew, B., and Henderson, R. (eds), *Studies in Company Finance* (N.I.E.S.R., Cambridge, 1959).

[77] Thorp, Willard J., *The Integration of Industrial Operation*, Census Monograph, No. 3 (U.S. Govt. Printing Office, Washington, 1924).

[78] U.S. Govt., *TNEC Monograph, No.* 13 (Washington, D.C., 1941).

[79] ——, *TNEC Monograph No.* 15 (Washington, D.C., 1941).

[80] ——, Federal Trade Commission, *Profit Rate of Manufacturing Corporations 1947–1962* (Washington, D.C., 1963).

[81] Weiss, L. W., 'Average Concentration Ratios and Industrial Performance', *JIE* (1963).

[82] ——, 'The Survival Technique and the Extent of Suboptimal Capacity', *JPE* (1964).

Appendix B

Some New Results on Growth and Profitability

Robin Marris

I. SOME NEW U.S. RESULTS

Professor Marc Nerlove has recently published[1] an important analysis of the factors explaining *ex post* total rates of return to share ownership in listed United States corporations. His basic sources of data were the published accounts of corporations which are available on the 'Compustat' magnetic tape, provided by a commercial service recording company results in computerized form. Professor Nerlove found that a considerable amount of time was required to edit this material, with the aid of his assistants, to bring it up to a reasonable minimum standard of accuracy and consistency for statistical analysis.[2] He eventually obtained a secondary tape containing series relating to a population of firms which had survived over a period of fifteen years and for which continuous series could be estimated. He then most kindly offered me a copy of this tape, from which I have computed the values of variables of special interest to the subject of this volume.[3, 4, 5]

[1] Marc Nerlove, 'Factors Affecting Differences among Rates of Return on Investments in Common Stocks', *Review of Economics and Statistics*, L 3 (1968).

[2] The data used by Whittington and Singh, op. cit., are based on a standardized system for recording company accounts by the Board of Trade and have been extensively checked for errors, gaps and inconsistencies. The 'Compustat' system records the accounts as published, and makes no attempt to fill in missing items.

[3] I am very grateful to the Harvard University Program on Technology and Society for financial support in this work, and to Paul Munyon, a Harvard graduate student in the year 1967, for help in programming and data processing.

[4] Professor Nerlove's procedure for dealing with missing observations was as follows: if a single observation was missing, it was estimated by interpolation provided both adjacent observations were available. If not, the whole series (for

United States results of special interest are as follows:

Table B.1

335 U.S. Listed Corporations Surviving through 1950–63: Means and Coefficients of Variation of Key Ratios

Variable	Mean, 1950–63	Coefficient of variation
	%	%
Annual growth-rate of Equity assets	9	73
Annual growth rate of sales	8	94
Return on equity assets after tax	12	40
Debt–assets ratio (leverage)	22	72
Retention ratio	50	35
Dividend yield[a]	4	33
Valuation ratio[b]	1·63[c]	33

(a) Average equity dividend during period as percentage of stock-market value at end of period.
(b) Last year of period.
(c) *Not* per cent.

---

the firm in question) was abandoned. In addition to Professor Nerlove's elimination of firms which did not meet these tests for any of the major variables with which I was concerned, I *further* eliminated all firms whose long-run growth rates or whose long-run profit rates were not strictly positive. Share prices, in my computations, were the average of the highest and lowest quotations for the indicated year (which are available on the 'Compustat' tape), following the recommendations of Singh and Marris (*Journal of the Royal Statistical Society*, 1966).

[5] It is important to understand that in both these data and in the Singh and Whittington data, the treatment of mergers may produce a significant number of artificially high apparent growth-rates. No problem arises when a relatively large firm buys a relatively small firm for cash made available from its regular flow of finance (e.g. retained profits): the cash paid for the shares is equivalent to cash paid for a collection of tangible assets. But where two giant firms merge by an exchange of shares, the firm whose name and identity survives is credited with a very large burst of growth while the other firm disappears and, according to the procedure, is eliminated from all the data; consequently, the discontinuous growth of the first firm is not offset by a corresponding discontinuous decline of the second. Inflation may also overstate growth rates because new assets are brought into the books at current prices, while old assets are only irregularly revalued (Singh and Whittington obtain comparability by adjusting, by estimation, the figures of firms known to have undertaken a discontinuous revaluation of their assets to show results as if they had not, i.e. they put the inflation back into the figures.)

These various sources of measurement bias must overstate the constant in the regression equation between growth and profitability, and may have significant but unknown effects on the coefficient. They must be part of the explanation for the fact that the average growth rate of the populations is notably faster than the

Table B.2

Cross-section Regression Results for 335 U.S. Corporations

Dependent variable	Independent variable	Intercept %	Regression coefficient	t-value for coefficient	R^2
g–EA	g–S	5	0·51	19	0·31
g–EA	ER	$3\frac{1}{2}$	0·45	14	0·20
L_c	L_o	5	0·70	21	0·51
DY	RP/EA	6	−0·25	9	0·64

Note: The data relate to the same population as Table 8.1, but the variables for each firm have been seperately computed and averaged for the subperiods 1950–6 and 1956–63, making 770 observations, which were then pooled, the relevant tests for legitimacy having proved satisfactory.

Abbreviations: g–EA, growth rate of equity assets.
g–S, growth rate of sales.
ER, return on equity assets.
L_c, L_o, closing and opening leverage.
DY, dividend yield.
RP/EA, retained profits/equity assets.

The following comments may be offered:

(i) The correlation between long-run growth rates of sales and of assets is quite good ($r = 0.55$), bearing in mind that these are industrially heterogenous cross-section results.

(ii) The behaviour of the leverage ratio seems to confirm my general arguments on this subject (see Introduction, p. 21 above). Although the coefficient of variation is quite high, the mean is low and we need a positive deviation of one and a half standard deviations to reach a ratio of 50 per cent. (With leverage at the mean value, i.e. about 20 per cent, and a ratio of the pre-tax, pre-interest return on net assets which typically is about three times the rate of interest ruling on corporate bonds during the period, the elasticity of earnings with respect to variations in profits works out at about 1·08; with a leverage ratio of 50 per cent, it is about 1·20; thus the amount of 'leverage' introduced into the dividend stream by the typical firm was quite trivial, and was small even among strongly deviant firms.) The figures in fact imply that the typical firm appeared to conform closely to a policy of long-run leverage stabilization (as required for the steady-state model); the regression equation in Table B.2 can be

---

aggregate growth rate of manufacturing assets, and why as many as 10 per cent of the firms display long-run average growth rates notably higher than their reported profit rate.

read as a difference equation with leverage converging to 18 per cent. Another way of looking at this result is by noting that, taken with other results, it implies a 'representative' policy of financing two thirds of asset expansion by retentions, with the rest divided about equally between 'steady' debt expansion (i.e. expansion proportionate to total assets expansion) and new stock issues.

(iii) In section III of my main paper I propose a 'linear' growth model in which the variance of the growth rates of firms is derived from the variance of 'operating' profit rates. Operating profit rates are in turn linked to reported profit rates (which we observe here), via the growth rate, through development expenditure. Consequently, the model also predicts a relationship between the variance of growth rates and the variance of reported profit rates. It is easy to see that on both the 'classical' and the 'managerial' criteria (although the effect is most marked with the former), the predicted profit-rate variance should be greater than the predicted growth-rate variance, whereas the figures in Table B.1 imply that the standard deviation of the rate of return was 5 percentage points (40 per cent of 12 per cent), while that of the growth rate was about $6\frac{1}{2}$ points. It is fair to note, however, that the factors leading to exaggerated growth rates, described in n. 5 above, are also likely to exaggerate their variance.

(iv) Almost any plausible growth model implies that there should be a negative constant in the regression of growth rates on observed profit rates, whereas Table B.2 shows this figure to be positive. Again, it is fair to point to the expectation that the treatment of mergers, and other factors in the data, will tend to impart upward measurement error into this constant.

(v) The final equation in Table B.2 represents an attempt to assess the present-value function, although the relationship is inverted to provide comparability with more familiar results. Because of the doubts discussed above concerning the validity of the observed growth rates of equity assets, we regressed the dividend yield (which would be $1/Y(g)$ in our previous notation, p. 17 above) on that part of the growth rate which was internally financed, in other words on the average level of undistributed profits normalized by assets. The significant negative regression coefficient is as predicted by theory and conforms with previous results (see Introduction, p. 4 above).

II. SOME NEW BRITISH RESULTS ON A RESTRICTED SAMPLE

In the hope of throwing some further light on the influence of the errors which are suspected to exist in the growth rates (see again n. 5 above), we carried out a special study on the original British data of Singh and Whittington[1] which has unfortunately not so far proved feasible on the United States data. From the Singh and Whittington data we first eliminated all firms without strictly positive growth rates and profit rates, as we had done with the United States data, and then further eliminated all firms which, over the relevant observation period, displayed a ratio between the total accumulated increase in net assets and total accumulated retained earnings which was other than 100 per cent. This effectively eliminates all firms which merged by exchange of shares and other 'artificial' means, but leaves in firms which bought other firms for cash from retained earnings. It also unfortunately eliminates firms which made any use of debt expansion (steady or otherwise) in their growth, and is generally a highly unrepresentative sample. Elimination of non-growing and unprofitable firms reduced the original population by about 10 per cent, leaving 690 pooled observations for the subperiods 1948–54 and 1954–60. The further elimination of firms with other other than 100 per cent internal-financing ratios reduced the figure to 265 observations. Interestingly, the restricted 265-group does not display markedly different mean characteristics from the 690-group, although, as we shall see, the regression results are very different. Mean growth rate of the 265 was 7·1 per cent compared with 9·2 per cent for the 690, and the mean post-tax return on equity assets[2] among the 265 was 11·5 per cent compared with 11·1 per cent among the 690.

The results are as follows:

[1] The data relate to all British companies quoted on the London Stock Exchange which survived through the indicated subperiod (thus the survival test is less stringent than for the U.S. data) in food, drink and tobacco, clothing, footwear, and non-electrical engineering manufacturing industries.

[2] The British data were processed in a way to provide growth-rate of total net assets but not of equity assets (meaning net assets less debt), but they do provide the rate of return on equity assets, net of tax. In the 265-group, however, the growth rates of net assets and of equity assets have to be virtually the same.

Table B.3

Results for Restricted Population of British Companies

Variables	Mean	Coefficient of variation
	%	%
g	7	57
ER	11·5	47

Regression Equations:

Dependent variable	Independent variable	Intercept (%)	Regression coefficient	t	R^2
g	ER	−1·0	0·71	30	0·78
DY	g	6·7	−3·0	14	0·41

Note: The data relate to 265 pooled observations relating to the periods 1948–54 and 1954–60. g signifies the growth-rate (which is the same for net assets and equity assets), ER is the equity rate of return and DY the dividend yield.

We do not give results for subperiods because the data are remarkably homogeneous.[1]

With all reservations appropriate to the unrepresentative character of these data, it has to be remarked that the 'improvement' in the results in relation to theoretical predictions is substantial. The value of R^2 in the growth–profitability relation is also worth noting.

[1] Singh and Whittington, op. cit., p. 159, interpret their results as displaying significant heterogeneity both between industries and subperiods. Alternative interpretations can be placed on their figures, but the big difference here is the effects of the restriction of the population. The main effect is the elimination of the non-growing and unprofitable firms, which provide a small proportion of the sample but a high proportion of extreme observations, and hence are a likely source of instability. I would argue that 'steady-state' growth theories cannot purport to relate to the circumstances of firms such as those, for example, displaying average negative profits over five-year periods (in some cases such firms display positive growth!).

Appendix C

Diversification, Merger and Research Expenditures: A Review of Empirical Studies[1]

Adrian Wood

I. INTRODUCTION

This paper attempts the limited and well-defined task of surveying empirical studies of diversification in American industry. As far as possible, merger is considered only as a subset of diversification. Similarly, the literature on research expenditures is related only to diversification. Although the review is restricted to the United States, important studies also exist for other countries (see [4], [26], [27]). Possible theoretical frameworks within which this empirical work may be placed are to be found in the analyses of Ansoff [1], Marris [14], Penrose [22] and Weston [36], as well as in my introductory survey in this volume.

Some problems of definition and a working convention

Diversification is a term that has been used to describe everything from the production of literally two different products (e.g. shoes and belts) to producing goods classified in five or six two-digit industries.[2] The problem is not helped by the character of the

---

[1] This piece was written in September 1968, and I have not attempted to update it to include material that has appeared more recently, except in two cases which bear upon work that is already reviewed here. I am very grateful to Robin Marris, George Eads and John Eatwell for their comments on earlier drafts.

[2] A brief review of the meaning of two adjectives commonly used in the literature on diversification: *Conglomerate*: sometimes used synonomously with 'diversification', but more usually used to mean diversification into products

Standard Industrial Classification (S.I.C.), which when applied uniformly at the two- or three- or four-digit levels (increasing order of specificity) generates anomalies in the definition of markets (some examples are given in [15]). The adaptation of the S.I.C. for studying diversification is made no easier by the nature of some of the theories. An attempt, for instance, to rank industries by some general index of 'marketing or technological concentricity' would raise more problems than it solved. A connected problem is that of classifying a highly diversified company by industry. For reasons of this nature, and for others that will become clearer subsequently, I shall adopt the following definitions as far as possible. Their main merit is that they tally to some extent with the S.I.C., although they are in many respects undoubtedly imperfect.

1. *Horizontal expansion* is defined as expansion within a four-digit industry.
2. *Vertical integration* is expansion outside a four-digit industry into a supplying or a customer industry. This is often difficult to identify in practice, but is of considerable theoretical importance.
3. *Narrow-spectrum diversification* is defined as expansion, other than vertical, outside a four-digit industry but within a two-digit industry *except* in the case of the five two-digit industries that I shall refer to as the 'engineering sector' (fabricated metal products, non-electrical machinery, electrical machinery, transportation equipment, and scientific instruments), when narrow-spectrum diversification is defined as expansion within this sector.
4. *Broad-spectrum diversification* is (other than vertical) expansion into a different two-digit industry, or between the engineering sector and another two-digit industry.

In general, I shall follow the convention of not attempting to classify firms by anything finer than two-digit industry.

---

unrelated to both the current technology and the current markets of the firm. *Concentric*: diversification into a product either sold to the current customers of the firm (marketing concentricity) or produced by a technology similar to that of the current product (technological concentricity).

II. DIVERSIFICATION: A CROSS-SECTION VIEW
OF ITS EXTENT

One would like to know the extent to which at the present time firms classified within one industry produce goods classified in others. This embodies the assumption that the classification of firms by industry remains viable: outside manufacturing, and perhaps also mining, this is empirically reasonable (see Table C.3). Using a less restrictive assumption for manufacturing, one can conceive of the ideal empirical framework as a firm/industry sales matrix for perhaps the 500 largest manufacturing firms, supplemented by more aggregated data for smaller manufacturing firms (not because they are necessarily less diversified, but because they are individually quantitatively less important) and non-manufacturing industries. To study the dynamics of diversification, one would like matrices of this kind over time (ignoring the complication of the changing composition of the 500 – see [11]), and also similarly structured information upon profits, capital stocks, investment and other variables.

In practice only the most meagre information is available. The primary sources for this data are the Bureau of the Census and the published accounts of corporations. The relevant data upon employment exist at the Census, but apparently cannot be published in anything but the most aggregated form without violating the 'no disclosures upon individual firms' constraint. Tables C.1 and C.3 are examples of Census publications. The alternative source is also barren, since corporations do not in general publish adequate breakdowns of either their sales or their profits by product lines, although pressure is increasingly being applied by investment analysts to encourage such disclosures (see [15]). It is also worth noting that firms' published figures for profits and fixed assets are often not comparable with one another because of differences in accounting procedures. This drives some analysts to use other proxies for profitability. A third source of relevant data is the lists of the products of large firms produced by *Fortune* and by the various investment manuals.

Table C.1 summarizes a recent set of Census figures on the extent of 'diversification' for the 200 largest manufacturing companies. One limitation of this type of data is that since one does not know in which industries the secondary employment is located, one cannot

*Table C.*1

The Extent of Employment outside the Primary two-digit Industry of the 200 Largest Manufacturing Companies, 1963 and 1958

*Firms classified by two-digit industry**	*Manufacturing Employment*			*Total Employment*	
	Total (1963)	*Percentage in different two-digit industry*		*Total* (1963)	*Percentage in non-manufacturing establishments*
		1963	1958		1963
Food and grocery stores	351,302	12·1	8·3	577,000	39·2
Tobacco	50,546	11·7	8·0	63,006	19·2
Chemicals	455,781	30·8	24·1	621,003	26·6
Petroleum	88,138	27·2	13·3	323,480	72·9
Rubber	132,576	23·8	33·0	172,936	23·3
Stone, clay, glass	110,844	29·2	25·1	144,042	23·6
Primary metals	563,777	15·2	18·9	699,070	19·4
Fabricated metal products	123,529	50·7	43·7	146,122	15·4
Machinery: non-electrical	298,031	34·5	29·1	425,010	30·0
Electrical machinery	758,665	29·2	36·7	1,050,474	27·8
Transportation equipment	1,486,988	23·9	25·2	1,684,940	11·7
All manufacturing	4,868,411	24·4	24·0	6,462,575	24·7

* Data given separately for only these 11 industries (food and grocery stores, however, is *not* a two-digit industry).

Source: 1963, computed from [35] Table 24, pp. 309–12. 1958, [33] p. 388.

make the important conceptual distinction between diversification and vertical integration. Gort [6] does make such a distinction upon the basis of unpublished data for 1954. He concludes that for his sample, only about 4 per cent of manufacturing employment outside the four-digit industry in which the firm is classified is vertical integration. However, 21 per cent of *total* employment outside the *two-digit* industry of the firm, and hence most non-manufacturing employment, is vertical integration. In addition, although one has figures for both 1958 and 1963, they do not in themselves reveal much about the change in diversification for the additional reasons that there may have been changes in the composition of the sample and the industry classification of individual firms within it. Also in both these Census tabulations and the results derived from the study of individual firms such as those of Gort, the information relates only to the very largest manufacturing firms and is an inadequate basis for generalization. This last problem will recur throughout the review.

The principal academic study in this area is that of Gort [6]. His work relates principally to 111 large manufacturing companies (named in an appendix). He had access to unpublished Census data for 1947 and 1954, and tabulated the 'product record' of each company from 1929 to 1954 on the basis of published sources. He presents a table similar to Table C.1 and also demonstrates that the ratio of non-primary to total employment declines sharply as the definition of industry is raised from four-, to three-, to two-digit levels

On the question of *direction* on non-primary employment, both manufacturing and non-manufacturing, he does not give employment statistics, but instead matrices of the *number* of products (and product additions and deletions 1929–54) in different two-digit industries, with firms also aggregated by two-digit industries. A slightly reduced version of his 1954 manufacturing product matrix is given as Table C.2. Although this evidence is highly suggestive as to the extent and directions of diversification, it is quantitatively very imprecise. Gort states that each of the 111 companies produced upon average in 15·6 manufacturing and 20·4 of all four-digit industries, but that 45·3 per cent of such activities accounted individually for less than 2 per cent of the total manufacturing employment of the company. Otherwise their size distribution is unspecified. This makes it very hard to judge the quantitative importance of broad-spectrum diversification, particularly since diversification cannot be distinguished from vertical integration.

Table C.2

Product Structure in Manufacturing for 111 Large Firms Grouped by Industry, 1954: Numbers of Products

Industry of product / Industry of firm	Food (12 firms)	Tobacco (5)	Textiles (4)	Paper (8)	Chemicals (14)	Petroleum (10)	Rubber (5)	Stone, clay, Glass (7)	Primary metals (10)	Fabricated metal products (5)	Machinery (13)	Electrical machinery (5)	Transport equipment (13)
Food	85				4						1		
Tobacco		18											
Textile products and apparel	2	2	22	3	8		26	2			1	2	
Wood, paper printing	9	3	1	56	12		7	14	4	12	14	10	4
Chemicals	47	1	6	22	161	57	29	19	9		1	14	8
Petroleum				1	10	17	1	1	7		1		1
Rubber			1	1	1		17	1		1			3
Stone, clay, glass	1		5	8	7		7	35	6	4	2	12	6
Primary metals					17	2	3		49	10	18	18	26
Fabricated metal products	3	2	1	1	9	2	10	5	42	20	7	21	26
Machinery: non-electrical	4		1	17	23	2	8	4	19	23	74	30	43
Electrical machinery				2	6		8	2	8	4	17	53	21
Transportation equipment	1				3		13		4	7	9	7	44
Instruments					3	2	1	3	4	3	8	6	6
Ordnance					7		8	1	1	1	3	2	15

Source: [6] Table 13, pp. 38–9.

A limitation of Gort's study is that it relates to data fifteen years old, which is especially unfortunate if there is truth in the often expressed (but empirically weakly supported) assertion that the last twenty years have seen more diversification activity than ever before. The study does, however, indicate that although diversification has been significant at least since 1929, it showed a tendency from 1947 to 1954 to increase in quantitative significance as measured by change in the proportion of employment in primary four-digit industries, and by changes in the number of products in secondary industries.

Another aggregated measure of the extent of diversification that is cited by Gort, and also by Narver [17] for 1958, is the proportion of multi- (four-digit) industry business enterprises both by number and employment. Numbers of such companies (in all sectors) increased from 0·3 per cent to 1·3 per cent of all companies, and from 38·4 per cent to 44·4 per cent of total employment over the period 1954 to 1958. Table C.3 summarizes part of Narver's Table 2. That

Table C.3

The Extent of Diversification in Broad Sectors of the United States Economy, 1958, as Measured by the Number and Employment of Companies with Plants in More than One Four-digit Industry

Industry	Number of multi-industry companies as a percentage of the total number of cos.	Employment of multi-industry companies as a percentage of total employment	Total employment
Mineral industries	2·8	46·9	575,000
Manufacturing	2·6	59·4	17,237,000
Wholesale trade	3·3	16·7	2,101,000
Retail trade	1·2	29·5	5,034,000
Selected services	0·7	16·0	2,869,000
Public warehousing	3·0	23·3	100,000
All industries	1·3	44·4	35,952,000

Source: [17] Table 2, pp. 12–13.

manufacturing is the most diversified sector is consoling in view of
the paucity of data for the other sectors.

This completes the survey of the current extent of diversification.
No very strong quantitative conclusions can be drawn upon the basis
of existing data; the deficiency is particularly great in the case of all
but the largest manufacturing firms.

III. THE INTER-INDUSTRY DIRECTIONS OF RECENT DIVERSIFICATION

Diversification can proceed by internal development or by acquisition. The primary sources of data for the record of internal diversification are those discussed in the preceding section: they offer even
less information on changes over time, in particular because the
degree of aggregation of Census data reduces both the comparability
of estimates at different points in time and the possibility of discover-
ing the exact nature of the incomparabilities. The evidence upon
mergers is more considerable. For this reason the discussion in this
section depends heavily upon evidence of diversification by merger.
Its relevance to internal diversification rests upon the presumption
that the direction and extent of diversification by merger are an
accurate reflection of internal expansion. But the relation between
the directions and means of expansion is itself one of the key points
at issue.

The primary source of merger data is the Federal Trade Commission. It has periodically published statistics upon the numbers and
'types' of mergers [31]. It is, however, debarred from making public
figures upon the *size* of individual mergers except where this information is derived from published sources. The F.T.C. data are supplemented by the various trade journals, especially by *Mergers and
Acquisitions*. For the pre-war period the record is less abundant, but
is adequate, and available in several secondary sources [13, 21, 24].

Two topics that have received a great deal of attention are neglected
here. These are the study of the numbers of mergers over time, and
the effects of mergers upon industrial concentration. As to the
directions of diversification and mergers, there are four principal
sources:

(a) Gort [6] on trends in inter-industry product additions of his

APPENDIX C

436

111 large firms 1939–55, which has data for number (but not size) of additions by internal development and merger.

(b) A list prepared by the F.T.C. of all the mergers made by *Fortune*'s 500 for 1960 between 1951 and 1961, without size information [30].

(c) The matrices prepared by the staff of the Senate Anti-Trust Committee of the principal acquisitions by number *and* size in assets of the 100 'most acquisitive' firms in the 113 most 'popular' four-digit industries (definitions discussed below) from 1950 to 1963 [2].

(d) The matrix prepared by the Census of all mergers within and between Census (approximately three-digit) industries by size measured by employment, 1959 to 1962, and certain summary tables drawn therefrom [29].

Item (c) is of immediate interest, and (d) provides material for an econometric study [37]. I shall consider (c) in detail: the '100 most acquisitive' firms are defined as those that (i) were among the 200 largest in terms of 1962 assets; (ii) made at least two acquisitions during 1950 to 1963 of firms which each had more than $1 million in assets; (iii) absorbed firms whose assets totalled at least $15 million. Industries were limited to those (i) with 1958 shipments in excess of $100 million and (ii) with at least two acquisitions of over $1 million by the above 100 firms. A reduced version of the matrix of *numbers* of acquisitions is given in Table C.4. A reduced version of the matrix by the size of the assets involved is given as Table C.5. It should be noted that this is not exact since the aggregation had to be performed upon size classes, not upon actual figures.

One may compare Table C.4 with Table C.6 which is Gort's (reduced) matrix of product additions (both by internal and external means) for 1950 to 1954 among his sample of 111 firms (which overlaps with the 100 'most acquisitive' firms by 45 firms). Although neither the samples nor the periods are strictly comparable, a strong resemblance would lend some support to the hypothesis that mergers and internal diversification take place in the same inter-industry directions, upon which Gort surprisingly does not offer any information. The general similarity of structure is considerable, and certain of the differences seem explicable in terms of the different compositions of the samples: e.g. (i) firms classified under fabricated metal products and rubber both show a wider spread of acquisitions in Gort's matrix, but both have larger samples of firms; (ii) the

Table C.4

'Product Acquisitions' of the 100 Most Acquisitive Manufacturing Firms, 1950–63: Number of Acquisitions

Industry of product \ Industry of firm	Food (10 firms)	Tobacco (1)	Textiles (3)	Paper, wood (14)	Chemicals (13)	Petroleum (11)	Rubber (3)	Stone, clay, glass (3)	Primary metals (8)	Fabricated metal products (3)	Machinery (8)	Electrical machinery (6)	Transport equipment (15)
Food, etc.	21			3									1
Tobacco													
Textile products and apparel	1		8			1							
Wood, paper and printing			1	51	5			3	1		8	1	
Chemicals	8	1		3	35	10	1	1		1	5	1	9
Petroleum					2	9							
Rubber							2						
Stone, clay and glass				2	5			10	1			1	5
Primary metals	2			4		1	1		11				3
Fabricated metal products	1								2		3	3	6
Machinery: non-electrical				2				2	1		18	8	17
Electrical machinery									3		9	12	12
Transportation equipment	1					1	2				2	1	20
Instruments	1			1	1				1		2	3	2

Note: To help comparability with the data in Tables C.2 and C.6, firms with more than one acquisition in a given four-digit industry are credited with only one acquisition in that industry.

Source: Computed from [32].

Table C.5

Mergers by the 100 Most Acquisitive Manufacturing Firms, 1950–63: Assets ($ million)

Industry of product	Food (10 firms)	Tobacco (1)	Textiles (3)	Paper, etc. (14)	Chemicals (13)	Petroleum (11)	Rubber (3)	Stone, clay, glass (3)	Primary metals (8)	Fabricated metal products (3)	Machinery (8)	Electrical machinery (6)	Transport equipment (15)
Food	735				75								
Tobacco													
Textile products and apparel	60	703					13						
Wood, paper, printing		13		2056	80				75	3	498	13	
Chemicals	108	3		28	1425	550	13	3		60	280	3	33
Petroleum					153	1280							
Rubber							63						
Stone, clay, glass				5	80			180	13			3	390
Primary metals	73				78		60	3	365				75
Fabricated metal products	3								15		75	75	45
Machinery: non-electrical					15		13		*		346	118	353
Electrical machinery									75		83	493	483
Transportation equipment	13					150	73				73	3	1026
Instruments	3				60	3				3	5	370	15
Totals	995	16	703	2164	1891	1983	235	161	471	561	875	1065	2420

Grand total: $13,540 million.

* The entry in this cell is inconsistent with that in Table C.4 (and in [32]).

Source: Computed from [32]

narrower spread of acquisitions of firms in the food industry in Gort's matrix is explicable in terms of the post-1954 acquisitions of two firms.

A further comparison is possible between Tables C.4 and C.6 and Table C.2 (the 1954 product structure of Gort's 111 firms). This would appear to suggest quite strongly that the directions of product acquisitions since 1950 have been more limited in scope than those of pre-1954 acquisitions in total, though how many of these can be classed as vertical integration and how many as diversification is an open question.

A detailed consideration of the disaggregated merger matrix (c) and Tables C.4 and C.5 reveals the following features (which are reinforced by the evidence for all firms in (d)):

1. There is a marked tendency for acquisitions to cluster along the diagonal of two-digit industries. This tendency is obscured in both the reduced matrices by the manner of reduction, but in the original only 258 out of 586 mergers or 44 per cent took place outside two-digit industries.

2. There has been very considerable vertical integration between wood products, paper and printing firms. Taking all four two-digit industries concerned as one industry for purposes of studying diversification reduces the *number* of mergers external to industries to 41 per cent of all mergers, and to 46 per cent of all *assets* involved (implying that such external mergers are on average marginally larger than those within two-digit industries).

3. The evidence of Tables C.2, C.4, C.5 and C.6 also indicates that many of the product additions undertaken by firms classified within machinery, electrical machinery and transportation equipment have been within the five two-digit industries that were defined as the engineering sector in section I (those three, plus fabricated metal products and instruments). For instance, counting this sector as one industry reduces the proportion of the *numbers* of extra-industry mergers to 25 per cent, and the proportion of *assets* to 23 per cent. Table C.2 shows that in 1954 only 172 out of 373 products in this sector were produced by firms within their two-digit industries, and Table C.6 shows that only 62 out of 129 product additions were made within two-digit industries during 1950 to 1954. This constitutes the evidence for the assumption embodied in the working convention above that the engineering sector as a whole exhibits a similar diversification pattern to most two-digit industries. Evidently, how

Table C.6
Manufacturing Product Additions of 111 Large Firms, by Industry, 1950–4: Numbers of Additions

Industry of product	Industry of firm												
	Food (12 firms)	Tobacco (5)	Textiles (4)	Paper (8)	Chemicals (14)	Petroleum (10)	Rubber (5)	Stone, clay, glass (7)	Primary metals (10)	Fabricated metal products (5)	Machinery (13)	Electrical Machinery (5)	Transport Equipment (13)
Food	11				2								
Tobacco													
Textile products and apparel		1		3	3	14	2						
Wood, paper, printing	1			17	5	2	1			2	1	2	1
Chemicals	17	1	11		40	15	4	2	1		1	3	2
Petroleum					2	4	1						
Rubber					1		6			1			
Stone, clay, glass					2	1		5	2			1	
Primary metals					4				5	1	1	3	4
Fabricated metal products					3		3		3	2		2	6
Machinery: non-electrical				3	11	2			5	1	18	11	24
Electrical machinery					1	3	1		2	2	3	12	7
Transportation equipment					2	1	8		1	4	5	2	22
Instruments					1	1	2	3			2	1	2
Ordnance					3	4	1	1					11

Source: Computed from [6] Table 16, pp. 46–7.

many of these acquisitions and mergers were vertical integration and how many diversification is impossible to deduce from the tables.

4. A fourth feature is the existence among the 100 firms of fifteen which we will label 'broad-spectrum conglomerate acquirers' (for reference they are Bordens, National Distillers, Philip Morris, Minnesota Mining and Manufacturing, W. R. Grace, Olin-Mathieson, Procter and Gamble, General Tire, Armco Steel, American Can, Continental Can, F.M.C., Litton, Martin-Marietta, and Textron). These firms are defined as having made more than two small ($1–5 million) acquisitions or one large (greater than $5 million) acquisition outside the industry (two-digit or wood and paper, or engineering, where appropriate) in which they are classified. They account for 69 per cent of the remaining 25 per cent of extra-industry mergers. With the possible exception of the can companies (both of which have diversified into paper and other packaging materials, which, together with cans, might be held to constitute a single industry for our purposes), these are all extremely prominent among the large companies to which the financial and business Press frequently refer as examples of extreme diversification [69, 87, 92, 120]. On average they each acquired 10·5 firms, as opposed to 5·0 firms for all other acquirers in this table. However, the average size of their acquisitions ($20·8 million) was only marginally smaller than that of all firms ($23·1 million). Some of their acquisitions, by industry, were engineering (49 acquisitions), wood and paper (34 acquisitions), chemicals (27 acquisitions), stone, clay and glass (23 acquisitions) and food products (13 acquisitions). Needless to say, attempts to classify these firms by industry may be misleading.

5. The final general characteristic of the remaining extra-industry mergers is that several of them represent moves paralleled by several firms within the same industry: e.g. (i) petroleum firms into certain chemicals; (ii) primary metal firms into insulated wire; (iii) gypsum product firms into paperboard packaging.

Given the various pieces of evidence above on the inter-industry directions of diversification, one may inquire about the economic characteristics of the industries into which and from which firms expand. Two studies are available: that of Gort ([6], chaps 7 and 8) covering the numbers of product additions down to the four-digit industry level both by internal development and merger over the period 1929 to 1954; and my own investigation [37] which analyses the employment involved in inter-three-digit industry mergers during

1959 to 1962. These two are evidently not strictly comparable; more importantly, in so far as they both relate to characteristics of industries rather than of firms, interpretation of their results in terms of firms' motives is not legitimate. For instance, the growth rates of a diversifying firm and its new division may be (possibly systematically) different from those of the industries in which they are located.

For four-digit industries entered 1929–54, Gort discovers by relative frequency analysis a strong positive correlation between the number of product additions in the industry and both the rate of growth of that industry and rapid technological change as measured by the proportion of technical personnel and the rate of increase of labour productivity. He finds that the number of additions is *un*related to cyclical stability of sales (as measured by the amplitude of fluctuations), to industry concentration ratios (proportion of shipments by the four largest producers), and to average plant and firm size (as measures of capital requirements as barriers to entry). These features held for the three subperiods 1929–39, 1939–50 and 1950–5. At the two-digit level, Gort's regression analysis yielded similar results, the correlation being strongest between the number of entries and the technical personnel ratio. He further found the magnitude of employment in an industry of firms classified in other industries to be significantly correlated with the technical personnel ratio in 1954. He also discovered that in a substantial proportion of the industries entered, the entrant rose over the period to be one of the top eight firms, but that the rate of growth of the industry entered was inversely related to this process.

My regression analysis of entry into three-digit industries within the two-digit industry of the acquiring firm yielded insignificant results. The results of the analysis of entry into three-digit industries in other two-digit industries were similar to those of Gort in that entry was strongly positively related to growth and research expenditures, and unrelated to concentration. An additional finding for which Gort did not test was a very strong negative partial correlation with average industry profit rate.

Gort also investigates the characteristics of industries from which firms diversify. He finds the extent of diversification in 1954 (as measured by the ratio of employment outside the industry of firms classified in it to total employment in the two-digit industry) to be significantly negatively related to the rate of growth of that industry, and significantly positively related to its technical personnel ratio and its degree of concentration. He discovers that more than twice as many four-digit product additions were made in industries growing faster than that in which the firm was classified, than were made in industries growing slower than the firm's classified industry, over the period 1929 to 1954.

My results also indicate that entry into other two-digit industries is positively related to research expenditure in the industry of origin, but *un*related to its rate of growth, concentration ratio and profit rate. A separate analysis of the engineering sector revealed merger into one three-digit industry from another to be associated with lower profitability and research expenditures of the industry being entered, and unrelated to differences of growth and concentration.

The evidence presented in this section seems to suggest the following conclusions:

(i) That at least in the 1950s among large firms in the United States, two distinct patterns of diversifying mergers are apparent, but that there is a marked preference for narrow-spectrum acquisitions among all but a few firms.

(ii) That being in an industry with high proportions of technical employees and research expenditures encourages and facilitates diversification into similar industries. This is particularly true of the engineering sector. Because of the difficulty of classifying broad-spectrum conglomerates by industry, it is not possible to draw such a clear conclusion for them, but ten out of fifteen are 'classified' within either the chemical or the engineering industries, which are both strongly 'technological'.

IV. DIVERSIFICATION, MERGER AND THE GROWTH AND PROFITABILITY OF THE FIRM

In developing a theory of diversification it is important to know what are the effects of different strategies of growth upon the firm itself. There is a heterogeneous set of empirical studies of the impact of diversification on the firm but a severe shortage of received theory. In particular the analysis of the contribution of merger as opposed to internal expansion to firm growth and profitability is confused by the differences in the time paths involved. As an example, take two identical firms α and β, which make single expansions at time t into a given market, by internal and external means respectively. It is clear that in general at time $t + 1$ year, β will have grown in size more than α. What will have happened to β's profitability will depend upon (i) the previous profitability of its acquisition, β^*; (ii) upon the extent of the 'premium' that β had to pay to acquire the assets of β^*; (iii) upon any changes that have occurred in the profitability of either β or β^* as a result of the merger. Meanwhile α will not have reached the break-even stage, nor will its growth have been noticeably affected.

What is less clear is the longer run, say $t + 10$. One does not know *a priori* what will be the relative situation of the two firms either as regards rates of growth (instantaneous or over the previous decade) or as regards profitability. The analysis of the long-run effects of merger contrasted with internal development is complex, and the possibility of making an empirical study of this subject in a world where firms are making frequent expansions using both external and internal means is remote. This is the principal weakness in Weston's book [36], which attempts to analyse the contribution of mergers to the growth of 74 large firms from around 1900 to 1948.

What he is in fact reduced to doing for lack of theory and data is to record the total of assets acquired as a proportion of total company growth over the whole period. His average figure of around 25 per cent is an understatement of the contribution of mergers to company growth at whose magnitude one can only guess. Most of the other empirical studies in this field deal with periods of ten years or less, which are difficult to evaluate in terms of long-term effects, especially if the period in question covers a merger boom in which the quantitative importance of diversification by merger swamps that of internal development.

Reid [24] makes an extensive analysis of 478 among *Fortune*'s 500 firms over the period 1951 to 1961. The 'dependent variables' that he uses are growth rates of sales, assets and employees, growth in stock price, and two measures of growth of earnings-per-opening-period-share. The 'independent variables' are various combinations of numbers of mergers undertaken, and their directions (horizontal, vertical, concentric, conglomerate) and industry classifications. The most consistently significant result that emerges from his F-tests of differences of means of the dependent variables classified by the various independent variables is that firms that undertake larger numbers of mergers grow in size faster than others. In terms of the remarks above, this is unsurprising given the shortness of the period;

only the fact that Reid uses data for numbers rather than size of mergers would seem to prevent this result being significant in every case. A less consistent result, especially when firms are broken down into two-digit industry groups, is that faster-merging firms perform worse than others in respect of stock price and earnings-per-share growth.

When firms are divided by the classification 'internal growth (which includes diversification as well as all other directions of growth), and horizontal, vertical, concentric and conglomerate mergers' (which involves considerable subjective judgment), the conglomerately merging firms are found to be growing in size significantly faster than all others. The significance of this result is reduced by subclassification by industry, which is itself rather questionable in the case of conglomerates. When this 'direction' classification is applied to earnings-per-share growth, conglomerate merging firms perform half as well as internal-growth firms and twice as well as horizontal, vertical and concentric merging firms. In the case of share-price growth, the relative gap between internal growth and conglomerate merging firms decreases, and the other types of merging firm remain relatively as far behind the conglomerates. (Subclassification by industry reduces the significance of these results also.) When conglomerates, are divided between 'offensive' and 'defensive' firms, the highest rates of size growth are found among offensive conglomerates followed by defensive conglomerates and aggressive internal-growth firms with similar rates. (This finding is difficult to interpret, since the criteria of 'offensiveness' were growth of assets and intensity of merger activity, and the criterion of 'aggressiveness' was growth of assets; [24], p. 202.) 'Stockholder welfare' as measured by the other dependent variables declines as one proceeds from aggressive internal-growth firms to offensive conglomerates to defensive conglomerates.

That the results depend crucially upon both the period studied and the criteria of classification chosen is demonstrated by a subsequent study which obtains substantially different results [28]. The interpretation of these results which Reid casts in terms of conflict of interests between stockholders and managers is affected by their limited empirical generality, as well as by the shortness of the period and the difficulty of proceeding from steady-state theoretical models to the analysis of the real world.[1]

[1] See, for example, my comments in the introductory survey in this volume.

There is a certain amount of further evidence in this area. Kelly [7] is anxious to avoid non-compatibility between firms other than in terms of merger behaviour. His approach is to select twenty-one pairs of firms with similar product structures which adopted different approaches (merger or internal) to growth during eight-year periods from 1946 to 1964, and to compare their records in terms of stock price, price–earnings ratio, capital turnover (sales per share of common stock) and profit margin on sales. By a series of non-parametric tests, of which capital turnover yielded the only significant result, he concludes that the two types of company do not exhibit differences in stock-price movements, but that merging companies raised their price–earnings ratios and capital turnovers, and at the same time suffered a cut in profit margins, relative to the experience of non-merging companies. The differences were particularly clear in the cases where the mergers were of a diversifying character. Reconciliation of these results with those of Reid is impaired by differences of sample, variables and methods.

Gort [6] investigated the relationship between size, growth and profitability of firms and the extent of their diversification. For a sample of 721 firms he discovered that the proportion of sales from secondary products did not increase with size, but that the *number* of secondary products did increase with size. For his 111-firm sample he found no clear relationships between the extent of any measure of diversification and growth and profit rates and retention ratios.

There have also been two industry case studies of diversification. Gilmore [5] examines twelve aerospace firms which are characterized mainly by the fact that they have *not* diversified extensively, in part because growth prospects in their primary markets seem good, and in part because they are unable to adapt from government contracting to successful commercial product marketing. He does discover, however, that they prefer internal development to acquisition as diversification strategies. Internal diversification is allegedly 'less risky' and 'more profitable', but the time lag to break-even tends to be five years or more, and also such internal developments constitute mainly insignificant proportions of total company sales and profits.

Miller [16], in his study of the extensive diversification in the automobile-parts manufacturing industry from 1950 to 1959, discovers a very strong preference for external expansion (22 of the 28 diversification moves studied). Of the thirteen companies studied, which in aggregate moved from 73 per cent of their sales from automotive parts in 1950 to 49 per cent in 1959, no company relied upon internal expansion alone, though one-third of the firms relied upon acquisitions alone. He also discerns a marked tendency for successive diversification moves to cluster either around a market or a technology, which may itself be unrelated to the primary activities of the company. Because he gives no company names and few relevant statistics, his results are difficult to generalize.

There are two more general business studies of anonymous samples of firms. Kitching [9] investigates 69 mergers in twenty-two large manufacturing companies, and classes them as successes or failures on the basis of interviews with company executives. As such, his basic information is not susceptible to generalization. Even his rating of the proportions of failures of mergers by type (vertical, conglomerate, etc.) is not instructive because the criterion of success is likely to have varied between companies. But he points out that companies reported achieving 'synergy' (roughly equivalent to economies of scale; see [1]) by function in the opposite order to that which is usually postulated by managerial text-books. (The companies ranked in descending order of importance synergy achieved in finance, organization, marketing, research and technology, and pooled production facilities.) Miller confirms this by accounts of the failures incurred when the firms in his study attempted to use spare capacity on their automotive-parts machinery for making other products. This discovery is ambiguous as to efficiency, strictly defined. To analyse this, one would need to isolate in 'synergy' those elements which represent genuine static economies of scale from looser dynamic economies and augmentations of 'market power'. In terms of profitability, however, the finding would suggest that broad-spectrum conglomerates will not necessarily be less profitable than narrow-spectrum conglomerates.

Young [38] offers the results of a study of 400 anonymous manufacturing companies. He ranks them by means of an equal-weighted average of sales growth, net profits growth, and growth in the price of common stock from 1950 to 1960, and adduces the following evidence to explain the differences between firms in the highest and lowest quartiles. Both groups have the same average size (which is consistent with other data). Many of his other independent variables are strongly correlated with each other. Fast-growing firms are based upon fast-growing primary industries, particularly defence markets and rapidly growing consumer markets. As one might imagine, they also produce a much higher proportion of 'highly technical' products. A majority of high-growth firms have diversified into 'basically different' fields; only one-third of the slow growers have done so. Of the diversifiers, the fastest-growing both diversified initially by acquisition and depend heavily upon sales from their new industries, to a significantly greater extent than the slowest-growing. This evidence would seem to contradict that of Gort.

The final contribution to this section is that of four articles from the financial and trade Press. First a *Fortune* survey of the record of their 500 in its first decade of growth [11]; all but one of the twenty companies on the list of leaders in sales growth from 1955 to 1965 grew primarily by merger (the exception was Xerox). But all twenty were too small to be included in the list of the 500 in 1955; most are still in the bottom half of the list. However, 'one large conclusion can be drawn from this list of twenty companies: massive growth in sales does not necessarily guarantee massive benefits to the stock-holders. Only six companies on this list were also among the 500's twenty leaders in earnings-per-share growth' ([11], p. 214).

Three articles upon diversified firms add some support to con-clusions drawn earlier. Kelly [8] analyses the pattern of diversifica-tion within 'overlapping fields of activity for eight major representa-tive companies', which are the activities of these firms within what I labelled the engineering sector. Both he and Carey [3] elaborate upon the very mixed results of diversification in terms of stockholder welfare. Carey rates only one of twenty-one selected diversified companies as best-grade investments, and five as speculative or unattractive. He attributes the failure of many diversified companies to improve their stockholders' lots largely to too rapid and too diverse expansions, particularly in the case of several of what I have labelled 'broad-spectrum' conglomerates. 'Less dramatic' diversifica-tion has proved more lucrative to stockholders. An article in *Printers' Ink* [23] documents the preference of companies for diversification by acquisition, particularly in the case of 'broad-spectrum' develop-ment.

It is difficult to summarize all this literature, since few of the samples and methods are comparable. The most solid conclusions are also the least surprising; in general it appears that over the last twenty years in the United States:

(i) The quantitatively most important part of broad-spectrum diversification has proceeded by merger, and in conspicuous cases has been associated with very high rates of sustained firm growth.

(ii) In terms of profit margin and possibly profit rate, merger is a less profitable form of expansion than internal development. But because of the character of the 'synergies' realized, broad-spectrum diversifying mergers are more profitable than other types of merger.

(iii) As far as stock price is concerned, the lower profitability of firms diversifying by merger is offset to a considerable extent by their higher rates of growth. The few very rapid cases of internal growth (I.B.M., Xerox, Polaroid) have combined the best of both worlds for their stockholders.

All this information relates only to the very largest companies. In terms of the financial economies of scale available to the smaller firm expanding by merger, there are reasons to believe that it may be more biased towards internal expansion.

V. RESEARCH EXPENDITURES AND DIVERSIFICATION

It is the purpose of this section to investigate further the connection between research and development activities and diversification. I shall neglect the many empirical studies of 'neo-Schumpeterian' hypotheses. Although the meaning of R. & D. statistics in terms of output of 'technical progress' has been questioned [10, 25], they measure one important aspect of the economic behaviour of capital- and intermediate-goods industries (the engineering sector plus basic metals; stone, clay and glass; petroleum; chemicals and rubber; and excluding the construction industry). The engineering sector in particular supplies the improved machinery and equipment that is responsible for much of the innovation in other industries; R. & D. is for it an important strategy to develop sale sof new products. Table C.7 shows the extent to which both privately and Federally financed R. & D. is concentrated in the engineering and process sectors.

Gort found that both the industries entered most often by diversifying firms and the industries in which the firms were most often based were characterized by high technical personnel ratios. He also found a positive relation between industries entered and productivity increases. My similar investigation [37] found that industries of

Table C.7

Distribution of Research and Development Expenditure by Industry
1964

Industry	Total R. & D. expenditure ($ m.)	Federally financed R. & D. expenditure ($ m.)	Percentages of total R. & D. expenditure	Percentages of privately financed R. & D. expenditure
Aircraft and missiles	5097	4607	39·4	8·8
Electrical machinery	2635	1628	20·0	18·0
Chemicals	1248	230	9·9	18·9
Machinery: non-electrical	1028	258	8·0	13·8
Other transportation equipment	1189	324	9·2	15·5
Instruments	483	208	3·7	4·9
Petroleum	337	27	2·6	5·6
Primary metals	191	8	1·5	3·3
Rubber	150	26	1·2	2·2
All other industries	533	34	4·1	8·9
Total	12,930	7346	100·0	100·0

Source: Computed from [12], Table 1.5.

frequent entry or origin were characterized by high proportions of
R. & D. expenditures to sales, controlling for growth, profitability
and other variables. Two further pieces of evidence of the connection
may be presented: Table C.8 compares the coefficients of specialization (which show how much of the R. & D. of firms classified in a
given industry is directed towards the products of that industry) and
the coefficients of coverage (which shows how much of an industry's
R. & D. is done by firms classified within that industry) with the
extent of diversification, for the capital- and intermediate-goods
industries.

Table C.8

Coefficients of Specialization and Coverage of R. & D. Expenditures in 1960 compared with Percentages of Manufacturing Employment within Primary Two-digit Industry in 1963

Industry	(1) *Specialization*	(2) *Coverage*	(3) '100 *minus diversification*'
Chemicals	80·3	77·0	69·2
Petroleum	52·6	93·4	72·8
Rubber	33·9	69·6	76·2
Primary metals	58·8	74·4	84·8
Fabricated metal products	32·4	23·5	49·3
Machinery: non-electrical	51·4	50·5	65·5
Electrical machinery	58·7	56·9	70·8
Aircraft and missiles	67·9	72·2 ⎫	
Other transportation equipment	58·1	87·3 ⎬	76·1
		⎭	
Instruments	32·0	56·5	n.a.

Source: [19] Table V, p. 1141 (cols 1 and 2); Table C.1 above (col. 3).

One further piece of evidence is the N.S.F. matrix of firm–product R. &. D. aggregated to about the two-digit industry level which shows in what industries R. &. D. is performed by firms classified within a particular industry. It has many cells for which information is not available, but the engineering submatrix is fairly complete, and is reproduced as Table C.9. This bears a strong similarity to the matrix of mergers in the engineering sector by asset size in Table C.5. The empirical relationship between diversification and research expenditures has been amply demonstrated: the direction or absence of causality remains to be investigated.

Table C.9
Firm–Product Matrix of Applied Research and Development: The Engineering Sector in 1963
(Sums in $ million)

Industry of product	Industry of firm Machinery	Electrical machinery	Transportation equipment
Fabricated metal products	15	16	30
Machinery: non-electrical	566	142	95
Electrical machinery	153	1376	648
Transportation equipment	130	348	4498†
Instruments	5	50	20
Total R. & D. of firms*	941	2347	5858

* This includes R. & D. expenditure outside the matrix.
† This includes $2848 million aircraft and missile research expenditures.

Source: [18] 1963, Table A-77.

References

[1] Ansoff, H. I., *Corporate Strategy* (New York 1965).
[2] Blair, J., in [32], pp. 84, 388.
[3] Carey, E., 'Diversification. When It Succeeded – When It Failed', *Magazine of Wall Street*, 26 Jan 1963.
[4] *Economic Trends* (Apr 1963 and Nov 1965), 'Acquisitions and Amalgamations of Quoted Companies'.
[5] Gilmore, J. S., *Defense Industry Diversification* (Arms Control and Disarmament Agency, 30 Jan 1966).
[6] Gort, M., *Diversification and Integration in American Industry* (Princeton, 1959).
[7] Kelly, E. M., *The Profitability of Growth through Mergers* (Pennsylvania State College of Business Administration, 1967).
[8] Kelly, R. E., 'The Galloping Trend toward Diversification', *Magazine of Wall Street*, 27 Nov 1965.
[9] Kitching, J., 'Why do Mergers Miscarry?', *Harvard Business Review* (Nov–Dec 1967).

[10] Kuznets, S., 'Problems of Definition and Measurement', in [20] pp. 19–43.

[11] Loomis, C. J., 'The 500: A Decade of Growth', *Fortune*, 15 July 1966, p. 213.

[12] Mansfield, E., *Industrial Research and Technological Innovation* (New York, 1968).

[13] Markham, J., 'Survey of the Evidence on Mergers', in *Business Concentration and Price Policy* (N.B.E.R., 1955).

[14] Marris, R. L., *Economic Theory of 'Managerial' Capitalism* (London, 1964).

[15] Mautz, R. K., *Financial Reporting by Diversified Companies* (New York, 1968).

[16] Miller, S. S., *Management Problems of Diversification* (New York, 1963).

[17] Narver, J. C., *Conglomerate Mergers and Market Competition* (University of California, 1967).

[18] National Science Foundation, *Basic Research, Applied Research and Development in Industry* (annually since 1962).

[19] Nelson, R. L., in [34], pp. 1138–42.

[20] Nelson, R. L. (ed.), *The Rate and Direction of Inventive Activities* (N.B.E.R., Princeton, 1962).

[21] Nelson, R. L., *Merger Movements in American Industry* (Princeton, 1959).

[22] Penrose, E. T., *The Theory of the Growth of the Firm* (Oxford, 1959).

[23] *Printer's Ink*, 18 Mar 1960, p. 22.

[24] Reid, S. R., *Mergers, Managers and the Economy* (New York, 1968).

[25] Sanders, B. S., 'Some Difficulties in Measuring Inventive Activity', in [20], pp. 53–77.

[26] Singh, A., *Take-overs, the Capital Market, and the Theory of the Firm* (Cambridge, forthcoming).

[27] Stacey, N. H., *Mergers in Modern Business* (London, 1966).

[28] Stone, J. M., 'Conglomerate Mergers: Their Implications for the Efficiency of Capital and the Theory of the Firm', unpublished senior thesis (Harvard University, 1969).

[29] U.S. Bureau of the Census, *Acquisitions and Disposals of Manufacturing Facilities*, 1959–1962, also as appendix to [33].

[30] U.S. Congress, House Select Committee on Small Business, 87th Congress, *Mergers and Super-Concentration* (1962).

[31] U.S. Federal Trade Commission, *Report on Corporate Mergers and Acquisitions* (1955).

[32] U.S. Senate Committee on the Judiciary, Subcommittee on Anti-Trust and Monopoly, *Hearings on Economic Concentration*, 88th Congress, 2nd Session, Part 1: *Overall and Conglomerate Aspects* (1964).

[33] U.S. Senate Committee on the Judiciary, Subcommittee on Anti-Trust and Monopoly, *Hearings on Economic Concentration*, 89th Congress, 1st Session, Part 2: *Mergers* (1965).

[34] U.S. Senate Committee on the Judiciary. Subcommittee on Anti-Trust and Monopoly, *Hearings on Economic Concentration*, 89th Congress, 1st Session, Part 3: *Innovation and Invention* (1965).

[35] U.S. Senate Committee on the Judiciary, Subcommittee on Anti-Trust and Monopoly, *Hearings on Economic Concentration*, 89th Congress, 2nd Session, Part 5A: *Concentration Ratios in Manufacturing* (1963).

[36] Weston, J. F., *The Role of Mergers in the Growth of Large Firms* (University of California, 1953).

[37] Wood, A., 'An Investigation of the Inter-Industry Pattern of Mergers', unpublished paper (May 1969).

[38] Young, R. B., 'Keys to Corporate Growth', *Harvard Business Review* (Nov–Dec 1961).

List of Contributors

G. C. ARCHIBALD, Professor of Economics, University of Essex, England

KENNETH J. ARROW, Professor of Economics, Harvard University, U.S.A.

WILLIAM J. BAUMOL, Professor of Economics, Princeton University, U.S.A.

JOHN L. EATWELL, Fellow of Trinity College, Cambridge, England

ENRICO FILIPPI, Professor of Business Economics, University of Turin, Italy

JOHN LINTNER, Professor of Economics and Business, Harvard University

SIRO LOMBARDINI, Professor of Economics, University of Turin

ROBIN MARRIS, Fellow of King's College, Cambridge

ROBERT M. SOLOW, Professor of Economics, Massachusetts Institute of Technology, U.S.A.

MACO STEWART, unaffiliated

OLIVER E. WILLIAMSON, Professor of Economics, University of Pennsylvania, U.S.A.

ADRIAN WOOD, Fellow of King's College, Cambridge

GIOVANNI ZANETTI, Professor of Business Economics, University of Turin